WE
WHO BUILT
AMERICA

WE
WHO BUILT
AMERICA

THE SAGA OF THE IMMIGRANT

BY

CARL WITTKE, Ph.D.

PROFESSOR OF HISTORY AND
DEAN OF THE COLLEGE OF ARTS AND SCIENCES
OBERLIN COLLEGE

NEW YORK: 1940
PRENTICE-HALL, INC.

Preface

IT IS A MOST important moment when an immigrant says farewell to his native land forever, and watches its coast line sink beneath the horizon for the last time. My father had this experience in 1889. Along with thousands of his generation, he undertook the journey across the Atlantic. In the United States, he established his home and his family, and lived for nearly half a century. Unpretentiously, simply, and harmoniously, his life blended into the American stream, and became a humble but honorable fragment of the record of forgotten thousands who have helped to build this nation. His plain virtues of perseverance, thrift, patience, and rugged honesty, and his remarkable gifts as a thoroughly trained mechanic, brought him a measure of success which enabled him to provide for those he loved the advantages of which his youth had been deprived. His deep-seated devotion to the basic ideals of our American life was born of a long and satisfying experience in the land of his choice.

Out of such experiences, I venture to believe, the real Epic of America must eventually be written. I have attempted here to do no more than to suggest some of the broader outlines of that epic story. No one realizes better than I how much work remains to be done.

It would have given me greater happiness to have my father read this book than anything else I have written. Now I can only dedicate it, with love and gratitude, to his memory.

CARL WITTKE

Contents

CONTENTS

PART III

THE NEW IMMIGRATION AND NATIVISM

CONTENTS

Introduction

"Keep, ancient lands, your storied pomp!" Cries she,
With silent lips. "Give me your tired, your poor,
Your huddled masses yearning to breathe free,
The wretched refuse of your teeming shore.
Send these, the homeless, the tempest-tost, to me!
I lift my lamp beside the golden door." [1]

FROM THE DAYS when the first courageous voyagers pushed their frail craft into unknown waters to hunt for riches and new lands across the western sea, millions of immigrants have made their way across the Atlantic to seek adventure, to escape poverty and unhappiness, and to find prosperity and opportunity in the new America. They came from all walks of life and for a great variety of reasons, but all hoped to find in the New World opportunities which the Old had denied them. Until the close of the World War, the gates to the United States stood open and almost unguarded, and although American politics have never been altogether free of nativism, the American people as a whole offered a generous welcome to those who wanted to throw in their lot with them. Indeed, as the late E. D. Adams once pointed out, it was the immigrants who "led America to expand the vision of her democracy into a haven of refuge, where all the races of the world might share in her peace and prosperity." Here was a "melting pot" for all the world, and for centuries one of the most compelling convictions of the American people was the thought that their country was destined to become the mother of a mighty race. The United States was divinely created, so many of our forefathers believed, to give freedom to the downtrodden of the earth:

A shelter for the hunted head,
For the starved laborer toil and bread.[2]

[1] Lines by Emma Lazarus, for the base of the Statue of Liberty.
[2] From W. C. Bryant, "Oh Mother of a Mighty Race."

INTRODUCTION

The American stock is so varied that one man may be descended from a half dozen immigrant groups and from as many religious sects. Historical societies have been founded by the score for the purpose of lauding the achievements of these groups and to see that each receives its "due place in history." The professional "joiner" often has to spread his membership over several groups if he wishes to show due respect for each of the immigrant strains represented in his family tree. The truth remains that it is difficult to define accurately any specific immigrant group, and family names are often the least reliable evidence of the racial origin of the individual. Many a Carpenter was originally a Zimmermann; a Frenchman named Blondpied settled in New England and had sons known as Blumpey and Whitefoot; and Israel Israel of Pennsylvania, despite the name, was a good Quaker.[3]

In spite of all the discouraging obstacles that beset the scholar who tries to thread his way through the complex history of immigrant contributions to America, the fact remains that the grand central motif of United States history has been the impact of successive immigrant tides upon a New World environment, or the inter-action of so-called "racial," or immigrant, characteristics with the forces of American geography. The evidence of the great signifi-cance of immigration in the development of American civilization is everywhere apparent, although not until comparatively recently have either scholars or the general public concerned themselves seriously with it.

In 1918, no less than 33 representatives of American immigrant groups joined in a pilgrimage to the tomb of Washington to pledge anew their allegiance to their adopted fatherland in a time of great international crisis. Sing Kee, a New York Chinaman, won the Distinguished Service Cross in the World War, and the famous "Lost Battalion," which Lieutenant Colonel Whittlesey led in the Argonne Forest, was largely recruited from Yiddish "push-cart men, sewing machine operators and buttonhole workers" from the Lower East Side of New York. Boston and New York have become the leading Irish cities in the world, and Massachusetts today has the second largest percentage of foreign-born population of any state in the Union. On Patriots' Day (April 19), the modern "Paul

[3] Edward Channing: *History of the United States* (New York, 1913), Vol. II, pp. 421-422.

[xii]

Revere" starts his ride from the Italian quarter of Boston; and Faneuil Hall, the cradle of American liberty, is a market place stranded on the shores of Boston's Italian district. One factory in Chicago, in 1909, employed representatives of 24 nationalities in its working force of 4,200, and there are at least 14 languages spoken in Chicago by groups of not less than 10,000. The immigrant theme has been an important one in American fiction, as the work of Rölvaag, Bojer, Willa Cather, and many others will testify.[4]

There are over twoscore languages and dialects spoken in the United States, and more foreign journals are published and read here in more languages per capita of population than in the whole of Europe! As late as 1937, 1,076 foreign-language publications, in 38 foreign languages, were issued in the United States; and there were 225 non-English periodicals in New York City alone. Indeed, only Vermont, Utah, and 6 Southern states were without foreign-language papers.[5]

Walt Whitman was half Dutch and Bret Harte half Jew, while Theodore Dreiser is of German stock and Hergesheimer stems from the "Pennsylvania Dutch." Nearly half of the painters listed in John C. Van Dyke's *American Painting and Its Tradition* are of mixed blood. A study of foreign settlements in Kansas, a state not always thought of in connection with immigration from abroad, revealed that 16 immigrant stocks were represented in the population and that church services in foreign tongues, involving several hundred congregations, were held in 58 counties.[6] Cleveland has had not only its "Shanty Town," "Whiskey Island," "Vinegar Hill," and "The Triangle" for its Irish, but a Bohemian "Cabbage Patch," a ghetto, a "Little Poland," a Chinese "Dopetown," and a German and Dutch "Dutch Hill." The city council of Cleveland, in 1929, contained four members of native stock, two Irish, six Germans, three Negroes, two Jews, two Jugoslavs, two Poles, one Hungarian, one Bohemian, and one Italian. Cleveland's municipal activities receive real color from its Hungarian picnics, its Italian street festi-

---

[4] See Percy H. Boynton: *The Rediscovery of the Frontier* (Chicago, 1931); also R. P. Boas and Katherine Burton: *Social Backgrounds of American Literature* (Boston, 1933).
[5] See Mark Villchur: "The Immigrant Press," in Francis J. Brown and J. S. Roucek: *Our Racial and National Minorities* (New York, 1937), pp. 573-594.
[6] See W. H. Carruth: "Foreign Settlements in Kansas," in *The Kansas University Quarterly*, Vol. I, pp. 71-84.

vals, its Norwegian "Sailor's Fest" at the opening of lake navigation, and from the exhibits maintained by each group in its regularly held "International Exposition." [7]

The late Professor Frederick J. Turner described the scenes of his youth at "The Portage," Wisconsin, as follows:

> The town was a mixture of raftsmen from the "pineries" —of Irish (in the "bloody first" ward), Pomeranian immigrants (we stoned each other), in old country garbs, driving their cows to their own "Common"; of Scotch, with "Caledonia" near by; of Welsh (with "Cambria" adjacent); with Germans, some of them university trained (the Bierhall of Carl Haertel was the town club house); of Yankees from Vermont and Maine and Connecticut chiefly; of New York Yankees; of Southerners (a few relatively); a few Negroes; many Norwegians and Swiss; some Englishmen; and one or two Italians.[8]

This was the America of the middle of the nineteenth century. It is still the America of our day, and although the various immigrant stocks have changed their relative positions, they are still building a new, composite American civilization. Rudolph Valentino was an Italian-American hero of the screen; Pola Negri is Poland's contribution;[9] Vilma Banky is Hungarian. Signor Antonio Lazerri was for years the famous infielder of the New York Yankees, and Al Simmons, of White Sox fame, is said to be an Americanized abbreviation of Aloysius H. Szymanski. The line-up of college football teams reads like the roll call of the League of Nations, and it was not many years ago that the final play in a World Series baseball game was made when a Serbian threw wild in an effort to deceive an Italian, thus permitting a native American from the Kentucky hill country to trot across the plate with the winning run.

Enough examples have been given to prove the point. As Horace M. Kallen has said, "America is a young country with old memories." Even the meanest and lowliest Old World peasant came from a land where the churches are centuries old, full of richly carved chancels, altarpieces, pulpits, sculpture, wood carvings,

---

[7] See W. G. Fordyce: "Immigrant Institutions in Cleveland," in *The Ohio State Archaeological and Historical Quarterly* (October, 1936).

[8] Letter to Constance L. Skinner, March 15, 1922, in *The Wisconsin Magazine of History* (September, 1935), Vol. XIX, pp. 101-102. See also Lawrence M. Larson: "The Changing West," in *Journal of the Illinois State Historical Society*, Vol. XVII, pp. 551-564.

[9] See *United America*, August 15 and 22, 1915; and January 21, 1928.

beautifully embroidered vestments, and walls hung with the paintings of old masters. In the songs and dances of their folk festivals, in their love of flowers and the beauties of the forest, in the elaborately embroidered bodice of a peasant girl, many centuries of Old World culture are revealed.

Statistics on immigration to the United States are available in great detail, although, for the earlier third of our national history— to say nothing of the colonial period—they are quite unreliable. Since 1790, something like 36,000,000 aliens arrived in the United States. The Census of 1930 showed that 11.6 per cent of the population of continental United States was foreign-born. If to this figure are added those born of foreign or mixed parentage, the total would reach 38,727,593. Millions rated as natives of the United States have grandparents of foreign birth. The largest portion of the immigrant population is massed in that section of the nation lying north of the Mason and Dixon line and east of a vertical line drawn through St. Louis.[10] In 1930, the largest foreign-born groups were, in order, the Germans, Irish, and immigrants from the British Isles. German stock has been declining since 1880, Irish stock since 1900; whereas Italian stock increased from 727,844 in 1900 to 3,336,941 in 1920. The United States Bureau of Census decided—somewhat arbitrarily, it must be admitted—for purposes of establishing "national origins," that 41 per cent of the white population of the United States in 1920 was of British and North Irish origin, 16 per cent German, and 11 per cent Irish Free State; these were followed in order by those who came from Canada, Poland, Italy, Sweden, the Netherlands, France, Czechoslovakia, Russia, Norway, Mexico, and Switzerland.[11] A study of immigration figures by decades shows that the greatest increase of foreign-born in the United States was from 1850 to 1860, when it was 84.4 per cent. The increase was 34.5 per cent from 1860 to 1870, 20 per cent from 1870 to 1880, 38.5 per cent from 1880 to 1890, 11.8 per cent from 1890 to 1900, and 30.6 per cent from 1900 to 1910.

[10] For statistical material besides the Census Reports, see Joseph A. Hill: "Compositions of the American Population by Race and Country of Origin," in *The Annals of the American Academy*, Vol. CLXXXVIII, pp. 177-184; H. G. Duncan: *Immigration and Assimilation* (New York, 1933); W. S. Thompson and P. K. Whelpton: "The Population of the Nation," in *Recent Social Trends* (New York, 1933), Vol. I, Ch. I; and T. J. Woofter, Jr.: "The Status of Racial and Ethnic Groups," in *ibid.*, Ch. XI.

[11] See also William Z. Ripley: "The European Population of the United States," in *The Smithsonian Report of 1909*, pp. 585-606; and E. A. Ross: *The Old World in the New* (New York, 1914), pp. 310-312.

The following table shows the European countries that have made the largest addition by immigration to the population of the United States from 1820 to 1929:[12]

Germany	5,881,032
Italy	4,628,868
Ireland	4,555,496
Austro-Hungary	4,129,342
Russia	3,340,858
England	2,606,551
Scotland	710,195
Wales	84,220
Not specified	793,741
Sweden (includes Norway from 1820-1860)	1,210,379
Total for Europe	32,128,908

The total immigration to the United States for the same period, by decades, was as follows:[13]

1820	8,385
1821-1830	143,439
1831-1840	599,125
1841-1850	1,713,251
1851-1860	2,598,214
1861-1870	2,314,824
1871-1880	2,812,191
1881-1890	5,246,613
1891-1900	3,687,564
1901-1910	8,795,386
1911-1920	5,735,811
1921-1929	3,865,509

Students of American history, since the days of Frederick Jackson Turner's famous essay, "The Significance of the Frontier in American History," have been emphasizing the statement that the year 1890, when the Census Bureau announced that it was no longer possible to draw a frontier line across the map of the United States, marked the end of an epoch in American history. It is

[12] See United States Department of Labor, *Annual Report of the Commissioner General of Immigration* (1929), Table 83, pp. 186-187.

[13] *Ibid.*, pp. 182-183. For fairly reliable estimates, especially for the period before 1856, see William J. Bromwell: *History of Immigration to the United States* (New York, 1856). For a good statement of the history of naturalization and the operation of present-day immigration laws, see, respectively, Frank G. Franklin: *The Legislative History of Naturalization in the United States* (New York, 1906); and Sidney Kansas: *United States Immigration, Exclusion and De- portation* (Washington, D. C., 1928). Also Brown and Roucek: *op. cit.*, pp. 661-680.

just as true to say that the enactment of drastic, restrictive legislation against immigrants, following the close of the World War, brought to a close an equally important epoch in American and, perhaps, in world history.

Since 1910, there has been almost no gain in the foreign-born population (white) of the United States. Since 1913, there have been only two years, 1920 and 1923, when the net immigration has been large enough to offset deaths among foreign-born whites and to leave a surplus. In 1930, 180,000 immigrants arrived and 53,000 departed; in 1931, 43,000 arrived and 89,000 departed. The number of immigrants to be admitted each year under the "national-origins" quota was fixed in 1929 at 153,541. Since November, 1930, more have been leaving than entering the United States.[14] So rapidly and drastically had the emigrant traffic to the United States declined that, in 1934, the Hamburg-Amerika Line closed its "Overseas Home" in Hamburg, which had served as a hotel for thousands of emigrants.[15] In 1937, the alien population of the United States was the smallest in years, and the number, of course, will grow less as aliens here become naturalized and new immigrants are debarred. The immigration quotas have for years remained unfilled.[16] Immigration, once welcomed as an economic boon, is today regarded as an eugenic menace. The processes of assimilation go on apace, and the second generation of immigrants, under a constant pressure to become "100 per cent Americans," are feverishly at work to suppress their individual characteristics and to conform to a standard behavior pattern.[17]

At the end of an epoch in American immigration history, it seems especially appropriate to review the whole history of immigration in its broadest political, economic, and cultural implications. The task is enormous, fascinating, and forbidding. Literally hundreds of historians of this and later generations must do further spadework before a definitive story can be told. Perhaps it can never be completely told, because some of its elements are elusive and constantly changing. Much of the work now completed has been done by descendants of some particular group who have sought to glorify that group, and therefore many of the accounts are unreliable and

[14] See also Louis I. Dublin: "A New Phase Opens in America's Evolution," in *The New York Times,* April 17, 1932.
[15] *Ibid.,* November 13, 1934.
[16] *Ibid.,* June 13, 1937.
[17] See Horace M. Kallen: *Culture and Democracy in the United States* (New York, 1924).

exaggerated. In this respect, moreover, there is little difference between descendants of the "old" and of the "new" migration. The history of hundreds of local communities will have to be written before the whole story can be told.[18] I am under no illusions as to the enormity of the task or as to what may be said about undertaking anything so difficult without waiting for all the evidence to come in. Nevertheless, if this treatment, imperfect and incomplete though it must be, stimulates others to enlist in this important and neglected field of historical research, and gives the reader at least some comprehension of the importance of the immigrant theme in the development of American life, I shall be satisfied.

I have tried to confine myself to an historical rather than to a sociological treatment of the subject, although I realize how difficult it is to draw a sharp dividing line between these fields of scholarship. I am assuming, moreover, that, at least as far as our present knowledge goes, we know nothing about a "pure race," and have no satisfactory, scientific method of accurately testing inherent racial qualities. I do not know, for example, what inherent racial differences may ultimately come to light between the "older" and the "newer" immigrants, but I assume that the task of hammering out a new civilization on the anvil of "Americanization" has been essentially the same before and after the Civil War. I am assuming also, of course, that our American civilization is basically Anglo-Saxon and that our population is, by a vast majority, English. I have therefore omitted all reference to English immigrants and have confined myself to non-English immigrant groups, excluding also the Negro, for whom an adequate and steadily expanding literature is already available.

Aside from the unreliability of much of the evidence, especially some of the publications of historical societies founded to exploit the achievements of particular immigrant groups, the problem of organization has been extremely troublesome. Both the chronological and the topical methods were tried, and, in the end, I found it necessary to combine the two, in some instances without very satisfactory results. Finally, I have tried in the footnotes to suggest how the subject may be followed beyond my incomplete and inadequate discussion. The footnotes are not intended to furnish a complete bibliography, but they do, I believe, refer to the more important accessible materials.

[18] See Carl Russell Fish: "The Pilgrim and the Melting Pot," in *The Mississippi Valley Historical Review*, Vol. VII, pp. 187-205.

WE
WHO BUILT
AMERICA

PART I

THE COLONIAL PERIOD

I hear the tread of pioneers,
  Of nations yet to be—
The first slow wash of waves where soon
  Shall roll a human sea.

The rudiments of empire here
  Are plastic yet and warm;
The chaos of a mighty world,
  Is rounding into form.

                    —John Greenleaf Whittier

The Immigrant Traffic

IT HAS BEEN ASSERTED that eight nationalities were represented on the initial voyage of Christopher Columbus to America. The new continent received its name from a German map maker, working in a French college, and in honor of a great Italian explorer sailing under the flag of Portugal. These were prophetic beginnings for the melting pot of the world. In a sense, of course, the whole colonial period is but the story of successive waves of immigration from the Old World to the New. It is the story of European expansion toward the first American frontier line along the Atlantic seaboard.

It is obvious that the colonial population was basically Anglo-Saxon, and early American cultures and institutions were basically English. Nevertheless, important non-English elements were present in the colonial population, and the "American blood of 1776" was already decidedly mixed. Even New England, where the Puritan fathers were never very hospitable to those "who walked another way," either religiously or otherwise, and which John Adams could describe as late as 1775 as 98 per cent pure English stock, had its Scotch-Irish on the frontier, its Huguenots in the larger cities, and an important Jewish colony at Newport, Rhode Island. In the colonial South, there were important colonies of Scotch-Irish and Germans, and South Carolina harbored so many French Huguenots that a section along the Santee River was known for years as the "French Santee," and travelers reported encountering Negroes who spoke a peculiar French dialect. In 1700, the little metropolis of New York was probably more cosmopolitan in its population than any European center of that time, and Philadelphia, still a small village, counted Dutch, French, Germans, Swedes, Danes, Scotch, Irish, and Finns among its population. To the more important of these groups in colonial society, attention must now be directed.[1]

Hector St. John de Crèvecoeur, in the well-known *Letters* in which he described conditions in the American colonies in the latter half of the eighteenth century, commented repeatedly on the urge for emigration to America, and in a significant and frequently quoted passage, wrote of the characteristics of immigrants as follows:

> The rich stay in Europe; it is only the middling and the poor that emigrate . . . . Everything tended to regenerate them; new laws, a new mode of living, a new social system; here they are become men: in Europe they were so many useless plants, wanting vegetable mould, and refreshing showers; they withered and were mowed down by want, hunger, and war: but now by the power of transplantation, like all other plants, they have taken root and flourished! Formerly they were not numbered in any civil list of their country, except in those of the poor; here they rank as citizens . . . his country is now that which gives him land, bread, protection and consequence: *Ubi panis ibi patria* is a motto of all emigrants.[2]

This one quotation epitomizes much of the history of the causes of immigration to the New World. *Ubi panis ibi patria!* The economic motive generally was uppermost in the immigrant's thinking, but political and religious unrest and persecution, the desire to experiment in a new environment with new plans for political and social salvation, wars, burdensome taxes, military service, the sheer quest of adventure, and the desire to escape the clutches of the law, especially in an age of barbarous civil and criminal codes, were other factors of major importance in driving population to America. Proprietors and promoters of colonies in the New World advertised the attractions of their holdings with the same shrewd appeals to the acquisitive instinct that have marked the peculiar technique of real-estate agents in every age.

William Penn broadcast the attractions of Pennsylvania—his "Quackerthal," as it was known in the German advertisements—with special zeal in the Netherlands and the Palatinate, areas which had been overrun and devastated in almost every Franco-German encounter in history. Penn's pamphlets were published in Dutch,

---

[1] For an analysis of colonial American population, see Stella H. Sutherland: *Population Distribution in Colonial America* (Columbia University Press, New York, 1936).

[2] Quoted in V. L. Parrington: *The Colonial Mind, 1620-1800* (New York, 1920) Vol. I, pp. 142-143, and 145.

German, and French, as well as in English, and their appeal was greatly strengthened by the inclusion of "America letters" from actual residents in the colony. South Carolina, in 1698, passed an act giving bounties for the importation of white servants, Irish and Catholics excepted. Profit-seeking ship companies found the immigrant trade a source of income, and land speculators circulated pamphlets and forged immigrant letters in order to depict a land flowing with milk and honey, where no taxes were paid and crops could be harvested without labor. "Newlanders" appeared in Old World villages as living specimens of New World prosperity, dressed in flashy clothes, wearing heavy watches, and their pockets jingling with coins.[3]

Throughout the eighteenth century, the colonies passed general and special naturalization acts for immigrants. *The Journals of the Virginia House of Burgesses* contain numerous acts of "denization" for non-English immigrants. An Act of Parliament of 1740 granted naturalization to foreign-born Protestants in the colonies after seven years' residence, and after certain oaths and the Sacrament, in the form prescribed by the Church of England, had been taken. While this Act remained the basic English statute for naturalization, the American colonies were often more liberal in their requirements for "denization," and naturalized immigrants after shorter intervals, either by a general law or by special acts. In Massachusetts, the residence requirement was at one time as low as one year. English authorities generally opposed the colonial naturalization acts and refused to give them the royal assent, but the colonies needed population and boldly championed a more liberal policy. Most Southern colonies granted land to newcomers on easy terms that involved political and social privileges. As a matter of fact, in many of the colonies, the main privilege connected with naturalization was the right to purchase and transmit land, and on this the owner's political and social privileges in turn revolved. In Pennsylvania, the policy was very liberal; in New England, it was much less so. Georgia, after the close of the French and Indian War, offered bounties to foreign Protestants and settlers from the British Isles, but the law was disallowed in England.

In spite of such interference from the home government, from the time of James II to the accession of George III, the British

---

[3] See Oscar Kuhns: *German and Swiss Settlements in Pennsylvania* (New York, 1901), pp. 27 and 79.

authorities generally were active in fostering foreign immigration, and on various occasions, to be discussed later, assisted Protestant refugees from France and Germany and the Low Countries to emigrate to America, often granting them letters of denization before they left England. After 1773, all naturalization was abruptly stopped, and in the next year, heavy financial burdens were imposed upon emigrants and shipmasters who violated the law—a change in policy that was not overlooked by the American Revolutionists when they compiled their grievances against George III in the Declaration of Independence.[4]

That the way to America was hard in the seventeenth and eighteenth centuries, and taxed the resources and the fortitude of even the most venturesome and courageous, calls for little proof. A voyage across the Atlantic in the seventeenth century might require anywhere from 5 weeks to 6 months. Franz Daniel Pastorius was on the way for 10 weeks in 1684; Penn's second trip (1699) required over 3 months. Sailing ships were frequently "wind-bound" for several weeks, or sprung leaks which delayed the voyage and brought all hands to the pumps. Moreover, the danger from pirates in the seventeenth and eighteenth centuries could not be entirely eliminated from a captain's reckoning. In 1748, a vessel landed in Philadelphia after encountering accidents and adverse winds for 6 months and 10 days, and 6 years earlier, Muhlenberg was on the ocean over 3 months before landing in Philadelphia.[5]

The principal ports of embarkation for those who came from the Continent were Rotterdam and Amsterdam. Emigrants from South Germany, for example, spent weary weeks in making their way down the Rhine, by boat or overland, to Holland, and were likely to be detained 5 or 6 weeks in Holland before sailing. Sometimes there were further delays in English ports, so that funds and provisions were exhausted before the ocean voyage proper really began. Immigrant chests were plundered in transit, loaded on the wrong ship, or sent to the wrong port.

---

[4] On this whole question of naturalization, see E. E. Proper: *Colonial Immigration Laws* (New York, 1900); Cora Stuart: "Naturalization in the English Colonies," in *American Historical Association Report* (1893), pp. 319-326; A. H. Carpenter: "Naturalization in England and in the American Colonies," in *The American Historical Review* (1903-1904), pp. 295-303; John R. Bartlett (editor): *Records of the Colony of Rhode Island and Providence Plantation, 1636-1792* (Providence, Rhode Island, 1856); and the *Archives* of the various colonies.

[5] See Karl F. Geiser: *Redemptioners and Indentured Servants in the Colony and Commonwealth of Pennsylvania* (New York, 1901), p. 48.

Conditions on shipboard seem unbelievably bad, in view of the modern standards of de luxe ocean travel, which the present generation finds essential to its comfort. A colonial forefather wrote: "Betwixt decks, there can hardlie a man fetch his breath by reason there ariseth such a funke in the night that it causeth putrifaction of the blood and breedeth disease much like the plague"; and the circular which William Penn issued for prospective immigrants advised them to stay on deck, "and to carry store of *Rue* and *Wormwood,* or often sprinkle *Vinegar* about the Cabbin." [6] Pastorius, who led the first German pilgrims to Pennsylvania, described the voyage as follows:

> Our treatment, as regards food and drink, was rather bad, for ten people received three pounds of butter a week, four jugs of beer and one jug of water a day, two dishes of pease every noontime, and four times in the week meat at noon, and three times, salt fish, which they must prepare for themselves with the butter which they have received, and there must always be enough saved from the noon meal to have something to eat at night . . . .[7]

Pastorius was inclined to complain of this meager and unsatisfactory bill of fare, but there were many instances where passengers fared far worse. There are cases on record of passengers on German immigrant ships in the eighteenth century who actually fought for the bodies of mice and rats, and one or two cases of actual cannibalism.[8] Lice, scurvy, dysentery, smallpox, various children's diseases, and the perils of childbirth were common experiences on the immigrant ships of colonial times. In 1711, of a total of 3,086 immigrants who embarked, 859 died en route or immediately after arrival. In 1743, of 400 redemptioners who set sail for Philadelphia, and who were packed in like herring, hardly more than 50 arrived. On one ship, which required 22 weeks to make the voyage from Ireland to New Castle, 75 passengers died en route, and their bodies were thrown overboard.

Under favorable conditions, the voyage across the Atlantic was seldom made in less than 8 or 10 weeks in the early years of the eighteenth century.[9] It was the rule that immigrants should fur-

[6] Quoted in E. A. Ross: *The Old World in the New* (New York, 1914) p. 17.
[7] Albert C. Myers: "Narratives of Early Pennsylvania, West New Jersey and Delaware, 1630-1707," *American Historical Association Report*, p. 389.
[8] See J. T. Adams: *Provincial Society* (New York, 1927), p. 176.
[9] Guy S. Klett: *Presbyterians in Colonial Pennsylvania* (Philadelphia, 1937).

nish all, or a large part, of their food supplies, and these were quickly exhausted or became spoiled in transit. Starvation, death from thirst, and shipwrecks were not uncommon.[10] Penn's prospectus of 1681 throws light on the charge made for such inadequate accommodations as were available to the immigrant:

> The Passage for Men and Women is Five Pounds a Head, for Children under Ten Years Fifty Shillings, Suckling Children Nothing. For Freight of Goods Forty Shillings per Tun; but one Chest to every Passenger Free.

In 1700, the colony of Pennsylvania passed an act that "no unhealthy or sickly vessel from any sickly place whatsoever shall come nearer than one mile to any of the towns or ports in this province." [11] In 1742, the colony purchased a 342-acre site for a pesthouse, the captain or owner of the vessel to pay the nursing charges for sick passengers and to be reimbursed from the passengers' effects. Massachusetts tried to prevent the landing of the lame and the sick in the ports of that province.[12] Perhaps the most convincing evidence of the frightful overcrowding of immigrant ships can be derived from such "reform" legislation as that of Pennsylvania in 1749, which stipulated a berth space 6 feet long and 1½ feet wide for every immigrant of 14 years or over. Unfortunately, the law said nothing about height. In 1766, the law was modified to require a height of 3 feet 9 inches for each passenger in the fore part, between ships, and 1 foot less for cabin and steerage. "No more than two whole freight passengers" were to sleep in one bedstead, unless parents desired to have their children with them. The law further provided that the shipmaster must carry a surgeon and a complete assortment of medicine, and that the vessel must be fumigated twice a week and washed twice during the voyage with vinegar.[13] This reform legislation was due in part to the agitation of the German Society of Pennsylvania, which had been formed in 1764 for the relief and aid of immigrants.

More need not be said of the conditions that prevailed in colonial

---

[10] See A. B. Faust: *The German Element in the United States* (New York, 1909), Vol. I, pp. 70-71. For a report on a shipload of German redemptioners arriving as late as 1805 on an American ship, see also Friedrich Kapp: *Immigration* (New York, 1870), pp. 183-186.

[11] Geiser: *op. cit.,* p. 60.

[12] See *Acts and Resolves of the Province of Massachusetts* (June 8, 1756), Vol. III, p. 982.

[13] See *Statutes at Large of Pennsylvania* (Harrisburg, Pennsylvania, 1908), Vol. VI, p. 433.

times in immigrant traffic. Specific illustrations of almost every imaginable nefarious and unsanitary practice by grasping ship companies and heartless shipmasters could easily be cited. And yet, the fact remains that thousands withstood the voyage, with all its suffering and disillusionments, and arrived sound in mind and body in the land of their dreams.

The problem of securing an adequate labor supply for the manifold activities to be carried on in a new land led to the introduction of white servitude in the colonies, and thousands of immigrants, too poor to make their way to America by other methods, came as "redemptioners," or indentured servants. Strictly speaking, indentured immigrants were those who had signed a contract before embarking binding them to service for a specified number of years to pay the cost of their transportation to and maintenance in the colonies, whereas redemptioners were transported without pay or indenture and might be "redeemed" by having relatives or friends pay for their voyage within a certain number of days. Otherwise, they too became indentured, and were sold into service by the captain of the ship to the highest bidder. The distinction between indentured servants and redemptioners was not rigidly observed, however, and needs no special emphasis here.

In 1683, about 12,000 persons, or one sixth of the population of Virginia, were indentured. The total for all the colonies was perhaps 250,000. An involuntary group of the indentured class was composed of paupers, vagrants, and convicts. As early as 1717, a Parliamentary statute had made the colonies a dumping ground for felons, and it has been estimated that the total number of felons sent to the colonies before the American Revolution was 50,000.[14] By no means all of the indentured servants were non-English immigrants, but so many foreigners were included in their number that a description of the indentured servant class properly belongs in a discussion of the conditions of colonial immigrant traffic. The Irish and the Germans bulked especially large in this phase of immigration history.

Indentured servants, or redemptioners, were generally bound out as servants for periods varying from three to seven years. They agreed to this service in repayment of the price of transporting them to the New World, which had been advanced, usually by the ship-

[14] See Marcus W. Jernegan: *Laboring and Dependent Classes in Colonial America, 1607-1783* (Chicago, 1931), pp. 46-48.

master. At the end of the period of servitude, they were to be released, given a suit of clothes and, in most cases, a stipulated amount of money or land, and invested with all the rights of citizenship. Although the redemptioners were victims of the worst features of immigrant traffic, from this stock came some of the best elements in the later American population. Some became successful farmers and planters. The majority probably became respectable and useful citizens, and a few attained positions of real leadership and distinction. Charles Thomson, secretary of the Continental Congress, and two signers of the Declaration of Independence (Mathew Thornton and George Taylor) began life in America as indentured servants. Daniel Dulany, one of Maryland's great lawyers, was an Irish indentured servant, and Mathew Lyon, "the Hampton of Congress," had been kidnaped and "spirited" into white servitude.

On arrival at the port, redemptioners usually were offered for sale to the highest bidder. Indeed, "soul-drivers" sometimes bought large lots of newly arrived immigrants, and then retailed them as servants among the colonial farmers and merchants, driving the new arrivals in lots of 50 or more through the countryside. Occasionally, a newly arrived immigrant would voluntarily sell himself into service, in order to gather experience in American methods before acquiring land or beginning to practice his trade.[15] That families were often disrupted by these auction sales of white labor, and that the immigrant was frequently a victim of the fraudulent practices of sharpers, was perhaps inevitable.

Colonial newspapers contain many advertisements that throw light on this traffic in indentured servants. "Just imported from Dublin . . . a parcel of Irish Servants both Men and Women, to be sold cheap" was a typical colonial advertisement.[16] *The American Weekly Mercury* for May 22, 1729, advertised the arrival from Scotland of "a parcel of choice *Scotch Servants;* Taylors, Weavers, Shoemakers and ploughmen, some for five and others for seven years; Imported by James Coults."[17] Schoolmasters were advertised as regularly as tailors and other artisans, and seem to have brought a lower price. During the early colonial period, a ship's captain might expect to get from 6 to 10 pounds for each adult whom he carried to America, and half as much for children between 4 and 14

[15] See Geiser: *op. cit.*, pp. 53-54.
[16] See Edward Channing: *History of the United States* (New York, 1913), Vol. II, p. 402.
[17] Quoted in Parrington: *op. cit.*, Vol. I, p. 134.

years of age. From 1760 to 1770, prices rose to 14 and 17 pounds. The price of indentured servants gradually rose in the eighteenth century from 10 pounds for 5 years' service to 14 pounds for 4 years' service. Advertisements for runaway indentured servants were fairly common, and laws for apprehending these servants were passed by several colonies. The names of Irish and English runaways seem to appear in the colonial papers most frequently, and the names of Germans very seldom. This is not necessarily a tribute to German steadiness or a comment on lack of initiative. The difference may be accounted for by the difficulty the Germans experienced with the English language.[18] Occasionally, advertisements were placed in Pennsylvania German papers to find out the whereabouts of children who had been sold without the consent or knowledge of their parents.

The indenture system, it is needless to add, brought in both desirable and undesirable immigrants, especially since the deportation of felons to the colonies and the kidnaping of prospective immigrants were common practices. Many colonial protests against the importation of English felons and exconvicts found their way to London, usually with little result. In 1751, a writer in the *Pennsylvania Gazette* sarcastically commented on British practice as follows:

[18] Professor Geiser (*op. cit.*, p. 80) quotes from the *Maryland Gazette* for March 16, 1769, as quoted in J. T. Scharf: *History of Maryland* (Baltimore, Maryland, 1857), Vol. II, p. 17 n., the following amusing advertisement in rhyme:

Last Wednesday noon at break of day,
From Philadelphia ran away,
An Irishman named John McKeohn,
To fraud and imposition prone;
About five feet, five inches high,
Can curse and swear as well as lie;
How old he is I can't engage
But forty-five is near his age . . . .

He oft in conversation chatters
Of scripture and religious matters,
And fain would to the world impart,
That virtue lodges in his heart;
But take the rogue from stem to stern,
The hypocrite you'll soon discern—
And find (tho' his deportment's civil)
A saint without, within a devil.
Whoe'er secures said John McKeohn
(Provided I can get my own),
Shall have from me, in cash paid down,
Five dollar bills, and half a crown.

Our Mother knows what is best for us. What is a little House-breaking, Shop-lifting, or Highway-robbing; what is a son now and then corrupted and hanged, a Daughter debauched, and Pox'd, a wife stabbed, a Husband's throat cut, or a child's brains beat out with an Axe, compared with this Improvement and Well peopling of the Colonies! [19]

Indentures varied within certain limits, but all provided for certain "freedom dues" at the expiration of the term of service. These generally included two complete suits of clothes, one new, and frequently other articles, such as corn, horses, an axe, or money, depending on the terms of the contract. In Pennsylvania, in addition to a new suit of clothes, the indentured servant got 10 bushels of wheat or 14 bushels of Indian corn, 1 axe, 2 hoes, a broad and a narrow one, and his formal discharge papers. The time of service for children usually extended to the time when they reached 21 years of age. Indentures could be sold or transferred to another master, and servants sometimes reindentured themselves for a second term.

Indentured service was not an unmixed blessing. Some immigrants received excellent treatment, and the practice at least assured them the necessities of life during the first years of residence in a strange, new land. No social stigma attached to indentured servants after they attained their freedom, and thousands of them succeeded in the New World. Many could read and write; some even knew Latin and French; and a Lutheran congregation in York, Pennsylvania, once purchased a pastor on indenture.[20] The following is a more or less typical form of indenture, concluded as late as 1821:

Eva Wagner with consent of her father to John M. Brown of Northern Libertyes, Philadelphia County, Riger, for five years, to have six months' schooling and at the end of the term two complete suits of clothes, one of which to be new, also one Straw bed, one bedstead, one Blanket, one pillow and one sheet. Con'n. 70 Dol's.[21]

Punishment for indentured servants generally involved an extension of the time of service or even a money fine. The master also had the right to inflict corporal punishment or to send the offender

[19] Quoted in Geiser: *op. cit.*, p. 105.
[20] See *ibid.*, pp. 71-76.
[21] Quoted in *ibid.*, p. 117.

to the public workhouse. Marriages by indentured servants required the master's consent, whether the other party to the marriage was a free person or another servant. Marriage sometimes involved a money fine or an extra period of service. In Virginia, ministers who married an indentured couple were subject to fine. Colonial laws, on the other hand, protected the servant against his master and at least theoretically guaranteed the right of appeal to a justice of the peace.

Indentured servants occasionally enlisted in the British Army, and during the Revolution, many served in the Continental Army. The number of indentured servants gradually declined as the eighteenth century advanced, partly owing to the rise of Negro slavery, but as late as 1817, vessels arrived in Philadelphia with hundreds aboard who were "bound out" to pay for their passage, and the practice of indenture in Pennsylvania did not actually end until 1831.[22]

[22] See *ibid.* See also Max J. Kohler: "An Important European Mission to Investigate American Immigration Conditions, and John Quincy Adams' Relation Thereto (1817-1818)," in *Deutsch-Amerikanische Geschichtsblätter* (Chicago, 1917), pp. 5-27; J. C. Ballagh: "White Servitude in the Colony of Virginia," in *Johns Hopkins University Studies* (Baltimore, Maryland, 1895); E. I. McCormac: "White Servitude in Maryland, 1634-1820," in *Johns Hopkins University Studies* (Baltimore, Maryland, 1904); and C. A. Herrick: *White Servitude in Pennsylvania* (Philadelphia, 1926). An interesting episode in the history of indentures was the pretentious scheme of Dr. Andrew Turnbull, who, in the summer of 1768, bought over 1,400 immigrants, including Greeks and South Italians, to colonize East Florida. The scheme collapsed in a few years. See W. H. Siebert: "Slavery and White Servitude in East Florida, 1726-1776," in *Florida Historical Society Quarterly*, Vol. X, pp. 1-23.

2

The Dutch

THE DUTCH OCCUPATION of New Netherland, where for 50 years the Dutch settlements divided the English colonies of New England from those of the South, is but a brief interval in American colonial history, but it left its stamp upon the Middle Atlantic region for long years after England had gained ascendancy there.

The story of Dutch settlements on Manhattan, and the expansion of Dutch influence from that point inland, is a familiar story that need not be repeated here in detail.[1] Henry Hudson, an Englishman, sailing in the service of Dutch merchants, introduced Europeans to the beautiful American stream which still bears his name. His ship, the *Half-Moon,* anchored inside Sandy Hook in 1609. His expedition went up the Hudson River beyond the site of present-day Albany. In 1621, the States-General of Holland chartered the Dutch West India Company, with extensive governing powers and a monopoly over trade. The first settlers came to Manhattan Island in 1623. In 1624, 30 families, mostly Walloons from the southern Netherlands, established Fort Orange. The next year, New Amsterdam, the first permanent settlement on Manhattan, was established. In 1628, it had a population of about 270, made up of traders, artisans, indentured workers, and others who seem to have chafed under company rule almost from the beginning. In 1629, the Charter of Privileges to Patroons was issued, granting patroonships as "perpetual fiefs of inheritance" to members of the Company who would found settlements of 50 people, thus instituting a kind of European feudalism, as a means of developing the colony. Dutch farms, known as "boweries," spread into Long Island and Staten Island from Manhattan, and prosperous farming communities devel-

[1] See Channing: *History of the United States* (New York, 1913), Vol. I, Chs. XVI and XVII; and Alexander Flick (editor), *History of New York* (New York, 1933), Vols. I and II, *passim.*

[14]

oped along Kinderhook Creek and at Wagen Dal and Bonte Koe.[2]

The stories of these early days furnished the substance for Washington Irving's *A History of New York*. The colony had a turbulent history from the outset. By 1664, all but two of the patroonships had been repurchased by the Company, and only Rensselaerswyck, on the Hudson near Fort Orange, stood out as a fair success. By that time the settlers were really tenants and not serfs, free from military service; and the patroons complained that the Company was more interested in trade than in helping them establish a colony of farms. The fur trade was the key to the prosperity of New Netherlands. By 1646, when the picturesque and irascible Peter Stuyvesant was commissioned as the new governor of the colony, 18 languages were being spoken in New Amsterdam; and the population included Dutch, Flemings, Walloons, French, Danes, Norwegians, Swedes, English, Scotch, Irish, Germans, Poles, Bohemians, Portuguese, and Italians.[3] The total population of New Netherlands at the time of the English conquest of the colony probably did not exceed 8,000. More important than chronicling the history of the Dutch colony, however, is a discussion of the Dutch characteristics and their continuance until well into the nineteenth century.

There are still churches in New York that trace their origin back to the beginnings of the Dutch Reformed Church in America, in 1628. Between 1700 and 1740, this Church had 65 congregations scattered throughout New York and New Jersey, served mostly by ministers from Europe. In 1771, there were 34 ministers for over 100 churches.[4] Until 1764, in at least three Dutch churches in New York City, all sermons were in Dutch; and even after the close of the American Revolution, prayers and occasional sermons were spoken in the Dutch language. Of some 50 books printed in Dutch from 1708 to 1794, 37 dealt with religious subjects. The dominie of the Dutch Reformed Church was an interesting figure as he mounted the high pulpit in his black gown, overhead a huge sounding board and beside him an hourglass to time the length of his discourse. Notices were passed up on the end of a long pole by the

[2] See T. J. Wertenbaker: *The Founding of American Civilization* (New York, 1938), Ch. II. For an analysis of the patroon system, see S. G. Nissenson: *The Patroon's Domain* (Columbia University Press, New York, 1937).

[3] See Flick: *op. cit.*, Vol. I, p. 285.

[4] See S. T. Corwin: *History of the Dutch Reformed Church in the United States* (New York, 1895).

clerk to the preacher, and velvet bags, also on poles and with bells, were used to collect money for the poor. Many of the Dutch churches were built in an octagonal shape.[5] In the old Dutch church at Albany, services were held until 1786 in the Dutch language, and for a long time after, the congregation remained bilingual. The congregation of the Reformed Nether Dutch Church of Schenectady dates from 1674.[6] The Dutch Church was unaffected by the British conquest and, for more than 100 years, remained in close connection with the classis of old Amsterdam.

Dutch housewives in America had the same reputation for cleanliness that their sisters enjoyed in the mother country. A Hessian who served in the American Revolution, describing the Dutch in the southern counties of New York, wrote: "The inhabited parts . . . are built up with the most beautiful houses, situated on the most agreeable sites. Their furniture would satisfy the finest tastes, and is of a quality that we cannot boast of at home. At the same time, everything is so clean and shining that I can hardly describe it." [7] The Dutch housewife, presiding at her huge oven, engaged in the ritual of soapmaking, or washing her great store of personal linens at quarterly clothes washings, was an institution of colonial New York.[8]

Schools and teachers in New Netherlands were few. They were expected to provide little more than a knowledge of the 3 R's and the Catechism. By a provision of 1629, patroons were expected to furnish schoolmasters for their holdings. Adam Roelantsen was probably the first schoolmaster in the Manhattan settlement (1638). The poor and the needy, "who ask to be taught for God's sake," were to receive instruction free.[9] Evert Pietersen, a schoolmaster in New Netherlands, agreed "to teach the children the Christian Prayers, commandments, baptism, Lord's Supper, the questions and answers of the Catechism, and before school opened to let the pupils sing some verse and a psalm." [10] Dutch almanacs were advertised

[5] See J. B. McMaster: *History of the People of the United States* (New York, 1914), Vol. I, pp. 55-56.

[6] See Nellie U. Wallington: *Historic Churches of America* (New York, 1907), pp. 79-81 and 101-105.

[7] Quoted in D. R. Fox: *Ideas in Motion* (New York, 1935), p. 69.

[8] See Helen E. Smith: *Colonial Days and Ways* (New York, 1900), pp. 117-119.

[9] See Flick: *op. cit.*, Vol. II, p. 25.

[10] W. H. Kilpatrick: "The Dutch Schools of New Netherlands and Colonial New York," in *United States Bureau of Education Bulletin* (1912), No. 12, pp. 73-76.

for sale in 1769, and perhaps later.[11] Among the heirlooms that have been handed down from colonial days are paintings and a number of Dutch clasped Bibles.

Public markets and fairs were introduced in New York by the Hollanders. In 1768, Peter Hasenclever, who learned iron smelting in Prussia, operated 4 furnaces and 12 forges in New York, and exported the best iron produced in America.[12] The Dutch beaver currency survived in New York for nearly 50 years. Sugar, from the refineries of the Van Cortlands and the Roosevelts, was marketed outside New York after 1730, and the De Peysters, Duyckincks, and Van Rousts were active in business for many years. The Roosevelt Sugar House, near Franklin Square, was worked until after the Revolution, and the Cuylers and Rhinelanders operated successful refineries and rum distilleries.[13] Dutch traders predominated in Albany throughout the eighteenth century. Ahasuerus Hendrickse and Carol Van Brugh were early silversmiths in New York, and by 1655, Jan Smeedes and Evert Duyckingk operated glass factories in the colony.[14] In 1764, of 72 names on a petition from Albany concerning the Indian trade, 60 were Dutch.[15] The Dutch in upstate New York were successful farmers, who sold their surplus to the city markets.

The influence of the Dutch, which persisted far into the eighteenth century in the region of New York City, and much longer in Albany and the Hudson River villages, was revealed perhaps most interestingly in the language, architecture, and customs of the people. The *uy* combination, in names like Schuyler and Spuyten Duyvil, was Dutch in origin, as were Bowery and Harlem. In time, original Dutch inflections were dropped; English words were taken into the language and curiously spelled in accordance with Dutch phonetics.[16] As late as 1841, the Reverend Thomas De Witt of New York preached a sermon in Dutch.[17] *Kill,* meaning creek, was common all over Delaware, New Jersey, New York, and parts of

---

[11] See *New Jersey Archives,* Vol. XXVI, p. 328.
[12] See Flick: *op. cit.,* Vol. II, p. 277.
[13] See *ibid.,* pp. 360 and 369.
[14] See W. C. Langdon: *Everyday Things in American Life, 1607-1776* (New York, 1937), Ch. III and p. 199.
[15] See Flick: *op. cit.,* p. 396. See also James Sullivan (editor): *Papers of Sir William Johnson* (Albany, New York, 1921), Vol. II, p. 781.
[16] See Wertenbaker: *op. cit.,* pp. 108-110.
[17] *Ibid.,* p. 115.

Pennsylvania. *Hook* was perpetuated in Sandy Hook. Gramercy Park was derived from *der krumme zee* (crooked lake). *Lope* was used for gallop, and *smere case* was a common article among the countryfolk of the Middle Atlantic region. Beets, endive, spinach, parsley, dill, and chervill were probably brought in by the Dutch. Place names and family names by the score attest their early Dutch origin. The Alrichs, a Dutch family of the seventeenth century, became the Delaware Aldriches. Many of the Conovers are descendants of the Van Coenhovens. The Catskills, Peekskill, and other place names of New York reveal their Dutch origin. Most of the folklore of the Hudson, America's most romantic stream, is Dutch in origin.[18]

Some old Dutch houses are still preserved in New York State, and early Dutch architecture has had a significant effect upon American building. The early Dutch houses were marked by half-doors and overhanging eaves. There was usually a hall running through the whole house, with a door at either end. The gable ends were often in stepped-up form. The word *stoop* is today in use in western New England, where Dutch influence penetrated, but is practically unknown in eastern New England. Some of the best examples of Dutch architecture in America are to be found in the Hudson Valley, in western Long Island, and in northern New Jersey.[19] "Dutch cellars" were common in New York as places to store food-stuffs in winter to keep them from freezing. These cellars consisted of holes about 18 feet long and 6 feet high, walled, roofed and covered with sod, and with a door facing south. The Dutch villages, with their curving streets, quaint houses, tiled roofs, and windmills, were characteristic of the New York landscape for many years. By the end of the seventeenth century, New Amsterdam was a town of brick. Sometimes colored bricks were used, with red or black tile laid in checkered patterns. The interiors were white-washed, with big mantels, tile hearths, and built-in beds. Old Dutch barns, with gable ends, low eaves, a large center door, and smaller side doors may still be seen in Dutchess and Albany Counties, with unique haystacks near by having roofs that rest on four or five poles.[20]

[18] See also *Addresses Made at the Annual Meetings of the Netherlands Society of Philadelphia, 1913-1930.*
[19] See Rosalie F. Bailey: *Pre-Revolutionary Dutch Houses and Families* (New York, 1936).
[20] See Wertenbaker: *op. cit.;* also Esther Singleton: *Dutch New York* (New York, 1909).

The "Santa Claus" tradition, a Dutch importation, was for decades unknown to the neighboring colonies around New York. The Dutch Santa was a sacred personage, who came over the roof tops and down the chimney with his reindeer and sleigh. Moreover, although there was no New Year's celebration in New England throughout the eighteenth century, among the Dutch of New York, the day was one for the exchange of gifts. It was "the great day of cake," when every gentleman called on every lady of his acquaintance, and every visitor received cake, wine, and punch. The custom has not died out altogether in New York even yet. An Englishman traveling in America in the early 1820's described the custom of New Year's day calls, which he correctly explained as being of Dutch origin.[21]

Other customs and practices imported by the Dutch continued for decades after Dutch rule in America had ended. There was, for example, the old Dutch custom of taking up a collection for the poor at weddings, which was observed for many years in New York. For years, cradles continued to be modeled after the Dutch cradles, which were deep-hooded, in order to keep the draft off babies. Dutch families brought over chests of linens, brass warming pans, and pewter, which were handed down as priceless heirlooms. Dutch funerals had their unique ritual. A funeral "inviter" made the rounds to announce the death, and to summon friends and relatives to the home. The deceased lay in a *doed-kammer,* a room practically never opened for any other purpose. Funerals, moreover, were expensive, for the family not only furnished the mourners with gloves, scarfs, and bottles of wine, but also served them *doed-koecks,* a special confection for the occasion. Dutch burials were usually made under the church floors.

The dress of the Dutch colonials was generally gay and bright-colored, as contrasted with the more somber patterns of New England. The patroon, or prosperous merchant prince, might wear a rich doublet, baggy breeches, a felt hat trimmed with long, colored plumes, and woolen stockings fastened at the knee either with silk scarfs or with metal sheaths, which were sometimes jeweled. A well-to-do lady's gown might be of crimson satin, with a pointed bodice and low-cut neck, full sleeves, starched and wired ruff and cuffs, and a "stomacher" held in place by jeweled brooches. Back-

[21] See Thomas Hamilton: *Men and Manners in America* (1834), Vol. I, pp. 273-274.

gammon, dice, and bowling were favorite sports of rich and poor alike, and drinking at an "excessive number of tippling houses" was one of the besetting sins of the New Netherlanders.[22]

The influence of the patroon families extended well into the nineteenth century. Stephen Van Rensselaer, who owned a vast estate on both sides of the Hudson, was the largest landholder in the country and the richest man in New York. Political leadership was in the hands of the landed aristocracy until well after the Revolution. Van Rensselaer, Abraham Van Vechten, Johan Jost Dietz, Dirck Ten Broeck, Hermanns Bleecker, James Van Schoonhoven, and others were all Federalists who joined with the New York merchants to battle the rising tide of Jeffersonianism. For 22 years of the first 40 years after 1789, the district including Albany was represented in the state legislature by a Van Rensselaer who was connected with the family of the great patroon.[23] Dutch contractual labor relations in the upper Hudson Valley, similar to the indentures of other colonies, continued long after the expiration of Dutch governmental control. Rents on the large estates were often paid in products, and in other respects as well, a quasi-feudal relationship prevailed.[24]

The persistence of Dutch traits in New York until well into the nineteenth century has often been overlooked by historians who regard the Dutch occupation of the Middle Atlantic seaboard as only a brief interlude in the more important story of English colonization. Yet a traveler described the Albany of 1801 as "indeed Dutch, in all its moods and tenses; thoroughly and inveterately Dutch."[25] The Hudson River towns were virtually Dutch village communities, and for years after the English conquest, it was difficult to find enough men who knew English sufficiently well for jury service.[26] In 1784, half the signs on William Street in New York City were still Dutch, and Dutch was spoken at the Hudson Market.[27] Huidekoper's memoirs describe his arrival in New York in 1796 and the home he visited, where he found the furniture in the house

[22] See A. M. Earle: *Colonial Days in Old New York* (New York, 1896).
[23] See D. R. Fox: *The Decline of Aristocracy in the Politics of New York* (New York, 1919), pp. 34-35 and 142.
[24] See Flick: *op. cit.*, Vol. II, p. 302; and *Reise Sr. Hohheit des Herzogs Bernhard zu Sachsen-Weimar-Eisenach durch Nord Amerika* (Weimar, Germany, 1828), Vol. I, pp. 114 and 118.
[25] Quoted in Fox: *The Decline of Aristocracy*, p. 31.
[26] See Irving Elting: "Dutch Village Communities on the Hudson River," in *Johns Hopkins University Studies*, fourth series (Baltimore), Vol. IV.
[27] McMaster: *op. cit.*, Vol. I, pp. 55-56.

to be Dutch, and his host and hostess dressed in Dutch fashion and speaking a provincial Dutch. He goes on to say that, "on Long Island, in New York, along the North river, at Albany, Schenectady, etc., the low dutch was yet in general the common language of most of the old people, and particularly of the Negroes . . . ." In upper New York, he found many of the inhabitants speaking Dutch "mingled with a few English words." This was especially true of the Mohawk Valley and towns along the Hudson, like Kinderhook, Fishkill, and Peekskill.[28] In 1788, during the struggle in New York to secure the ratification of the new United States Constitution, opposition of some of the older residents around Albany was overcome by issuing a Dutch translation of the new document.[29]

A visitor to America in 1794 referred to Albany as "an ancient Dutch settlement" whose inhabitants "retain all the manners of their European progenitors." He seemed to be especially impressed by the divided doors on most of the houses.[30] Wright Darusmont, writing as late as 1821, praised the sturdy Dutch farmers of the valley of the Mohawk, "a primitive race, who retain for generations the character, customs and often the language of their ancient country." He commented on their clannishness and their unwillingness to become Americanized.[31] When, in 1814, Holland was liberated from the rule of Napoleon, a meeting of Dutchmen was called in Albany to celebrate the occasion.[32] A commentator in 1857 observed that, in the Hackensack Valley, "the habits, manners and customs of the people were those of the good old Dutch . . . . They continue to use quite extensively the Dutch language." Until 1880, "Bergen County Dutch" was the common idiom in use in rural communities in northern New Jersey, and as late as 1897, old people could be found in Albany and Ulster County, New York, who could still speak Dutch.[33]

It is true that Dutch authority over the Middle Atlantic region,

[28] See Nina Moore Tiffany and Francis Tiffany: *Harm Jan Huidekoper* (Cambridge, Massachusetts, 1904), pp. 30, 37, 51, 76, and 77.
[29] See Wertenbaker: *op. cit.*, p. 116.
[30] See *Letters on Emigration by a Gentleman Lately Returned from America* (London, 1794).
[31] See Wright Darusmont: *Views of Society and Manners in America* (1821), pp. 128 and 308-309. He probably confused Dutch and Germans.
[32] See Fox: *The Decline of Aristocracy*, p. 182. For biographical sketches of prominent descendants of old Dutch settlers in New York, see *Holland-American Year Book for 1888* (New York 1888); also W. R. Shepherd: *The Story of New Amsterdam* (New York, 1926).
[33] See Wertenbaker: *op. cit.*, p. 117.

around the Hudson and the Delaware, ended in 1664. Nevertheless, vestiges of the Dutch occupation remained for nearly two centuries after the English conquest. Moreover, the meager Dutch immigration in the seventeenth century to what is now New York State produced sixty members of Congress and three occupants of the White House.[34]

[34] See also Ruth Putnam: "The Dutch Element in the United States," in *American Historical Association Report* (1909), p. 218; and H. T. Colenbrander: "The Dutch Element in American History," in *American Historical Association Report* (1909), pp. 193-201. These articles were written partly to counterbalance and correct the extravagant claims in Douglas Campbell: *The Puritans in Holland, England and America*, 2 vols. (New York, 1892), which created something of a sensation for a time but has now been thoroughly discredited.

3

The French

AFTER THE REVOCATION of the Edict of Nantes (1685), which ended toleration for French Protestants, the French Huguenot exodus was primarily responsible for whatever French influence existed in colonial days along that part of the Atlantic Coast destined to become the United States. There were Acadians (French Catholics) in some of the colonies, who had been deported from Nova Scotia in 1755 as dangerous neutrals, as the result of a military action which has received probably more than its proper share of notoriety because it became the theme of Longfellow's *Evangeline*. But the number of Acadians was small, and not comparable in importance with the French Protestant influx. Likewise, the sparse French population scattered around the fur-trading posts beyond the Alleghenies, although retaining their old French characteristics for decades, had little significance when compared with the Huguenot element which entered the seaboard colonies.

In spite of the fact that, in colonial times, New England was not noted as a section particularly hospitable or attractive to immigrants, there was a notable group of French Huguenots within its borders, particularly in the larger trading towns. Although it is impossible to trace any significant political influence to the Huguenots as a group in the colonial period, yet by the time of the Revolution this element produced a remarkable number of leaders of great power and influence.[1]

About 150 Huguenot families came to Massachusetts in the first two years after the revocation of the Edict of Nantes, and group settlements were established in Rhode Island and Maine as well. Many

[1] See E. H. Avery: *The Influence of French Immigration on the Political History of the United States* (University of Minnesota Thesis, Redfield, South Dakota, 1894). For an extended discussion of the European background and causes of the French Huguenot migration, consult Charles W. Baird: *History of Huguenot Emigration to America*, 2 vols. (New York, 1885).

of the immigrants came to America by way of England or Holland. In 1700, upon recommendation of the governor of Massachusetts Bay, the General Court voted 12 pounds from the public treasury to the French Church in Boston "for their encouragement as strangers and for the carrying on the public worship of God amongst them." [2] A French Protestant church seems to have been organized in Boston as early as 1685, and two years later the Council allowed it "to meete in the Latine Schoolhouse att Boston as desired." [3] It was not until a century later that the church was converted to use for Roman Catholic services. As a matter of fact, just because it was French, the church had always been suspected of Papist and Jesuit leanings. Pastor Ezechiel Carré of the Boston church, a former minister of the French colony in Narraganset, felt it necessary to write an exposition and repudiation of Jesuit doctrine. New England Puritans also looked askance at the French congregation because of its merry observance of Christmas, a festival that did not figure on the Puritan calendar. Pierre Daillé, most distinguished pastor of the Boston church, lies buried in the famous Granary burying ground on Tremont Street. Under his successor, André Lemercier, the church declined rapidly, owing to the rapid assimilation of its members and to numerous intermarriages with English stock.

One of the best-known Huguenot settlements in New England was the frontier community of Oxford, or New Oxford, located near Worcester, Massachusetts. Here, in 1687, some 30 Huguenot families obtained a grant of 2,500 acres, and managed to begin a settlement that was not finally abandoned until 1704. The history of the French frontiersmen was not a happy one. They were harassed by the Indians, and some of them were massacred. Others, in discouragement, returned to Boston. A monument, dedicated in 1884, at Oxford, Massachusetts, is all that is left to suggest that the site was once occupied by a French Huguenot community.

In Rhode Island, some 50 Huguenot families, under the leadership of their minister, Carré, and a doctor, Pierre Ayrault, settled Frenchtown in 1686. Here they made good wine and tried to introduce some of the amenities of French living, but their fate was much like that of the Oxford settlers. Their land title was challenged, their neighbors proved very inhospitable, and, in 1691, during the

[2] *Acts and Resolves of the Province of Massachusetts Bay* (1892), Vol. VII, pp. 640-641.
[3] Baird: *op. cit.*, Vol. II, p. 221.

first of the intercolonial wars, their settlement was attacked and scattered by a mob from neighboring Greenwich. Two families went to Boston; most of the others, to New York.[4] The leading French settlement in Maine was at Dresden. All in all, there were probably 4,000 French Huguenots in New England by 1700.[5]

From this New England Huguenot stock came some of the distinguished and influential leaders of eighteenth-century New England. Gabriel Bernon was a distinguished citizen of Newport, Rhode Island. Paul Revere, though born in Boston, was the descendant of the Huguenot Rivoires. The three Faneuil brothers, Jean, Benjamin, and André, hailing from La Rochelle, were successful merchants and colonial patriots in the early eighteenth century. When André died, in 1738, 1,100 persons attended his funeral, and the guns of many vessels in Boston harbor boomed a last salute.[6] He left his large fortune to his nephew Peter (Pierre), a *bon vivant*, who, next to John Hancock, was the most important merchant in Massachusetts. Much of Peter's wealth was derived from the slave trade and the liquor traffic. It was he who presented Boston with Faneuil Hall, destined to become "the cradle of liberty," as a public market house, where it still stands, after many vicissitudes and numerous remodelings, stranded on the shores of Boston's present-day Italian quarter. When Peter Faneuil died, in 1743, John Lowell, master of the Latin School, delivered his funeral oration. James Bowdoin, president of the Massachusetts Constitutional Convention during the American Revolution, confrère of Sam Adams in the revolutionary agitation, and later governor of Massachusetts, was the son of Pierre Baudouin, another immigrant from La Rochelle. Whittier's mother was descended from Huguenots who had changed their name from Feuillevert to Greenleaf.[7]

[4] See Gilbert Chinard: *Les Réfugiés Huguenots en Amérique* (Paris, 1925), pp. 110-111. Dr. Chinard's characterization of the attack on Frenchtown is interesting. He does not believe that it was directed against any individual settlers or even again the French as such. Rather, he regards the incident as "une des premières manifestations de cet état d'esprit qui à certains moments a fait se lever des groupements américains contre des éléments étrangers considérés comme inassimilables . . . . Nous pourrons constater l'existence des mêmes sentiments chez les habitants de Boston et expliquer ainsi leur hésitation prolongée à accorder certains privilèges aux Protestants français, malgré la sympathie très vive qu'ils manifestèrent pour ceux qu'ils accueillirent comme des frères persécutés."
[5] See L. H. Fosdick: *The French Blood in America* (Boston, 1919).
[6] See Chinard: *op. cit.*, p. 139.
[7] See *ibid.*, p. 221. For other changes in early French names, see *ibid.*, p. 216. Lestrange became Streing, Strange, or Strong. Similarly, Chamois was changed to Shanway, Fauconnier to Faulkener, Boutillier to Butler, Galopin to Galpin, Lepère to Lepper, Pettijean to Littlejohn, Marechal to Marshall, Roussel to

In proportion to their numbers, these French Huguenots probably represented a larger degree of capacity and culture than any other racial addition in colonial times. Perhaps they helped to temper the gloom of Puritanism by adding something of the lightness, joyousness, and refinement characteristic of the French temperament. They were also industrious, and made rapid progress toward economic independence. A considerable number became wealthy, and some became so much a part of the established order that, like some of the Faneuils, they took the King's side during the American Revolution and eventually, with thousands of other Loyalists, left the country. This is all the more significant, because the Huguenots, as a group, had a genuine passion for civil and religious liberty. Their assimilation proceeded so rapidly that they were soon completely lost in the English population.

In New York, the Huguenot stock was represented as early as the Dutch occupation, when a large number of French were to be found in the cosmopolitan population of New Netherlands. Peter Minuit, as well as his secretary, were Huguenots, and Peter Stuyvesant had a Huguenot wife, Judith Bayard. By 1688, 200 Huguenot families had arrived in New York. By 1696, a book was published in New York in the French language, and town proclamations were issued frequently in both Dutch and French during the period of the Dutch occupation. The French church of New York was founded in 1659, and still exists as "the French Church of the Holy Spirit." In 1704 a law was passed permitting the building of a larger church in New York City by the "French Protestant Church."[8] From 1683 to 1702, the church records of New Pfaltz were kept in French, and church services were conducted in that language for several decades. The language of general conversation was French, and the schoolmaster, Jean Tebenin, taught his pupils in French. In later years, however, when Dutch settlers moved in in increasing numbers, church services began to be held in Dutch, and presently the church records were also kept in Dutch. In the eighteenth century, Palatine Germans entered the community, and were eventually absorbed by the Dutch through intermarriage.[9]

Russell, and Mahieu to Mayo. Such a list again illustrates how dangerous it is to make pretentious claims for a particular immigrant group simply on the basis of family names.

[8] See *Colonial Laws of New York*, Vol. I, p. 526.

[9] See T. J. Wertenbaker: *The Founding of American Civilization* (New York, 1938), pp. 104-105.

New Rochelle, founded in 1689 under the leadership of the minister David Bourepos, was the most significant center of French Huguenot influence in New York. Its schools, both day and boarding schools, were widely known as excellent places to learn French and French manners. John Jay, Washington Irving, and Philip Schuyler were sent there as boys to learn French. Gouverneur Morris learned French and his aristocratic manners at the home of M. Testard, the New Rochelle minister. On weekdays, little comedies and tableaux were presented, and instruction was given in dancing. For the young ladies, there was instruction in the "ladylike accomplishments, music, singing, painting, embroidery, manners, etiquette, and the *jeux de société.*" The women of New Rochelle were famous for their invention of "rag carpets." The church of New Rochelle was completely assimilated to English worship by 1738. Strangely enough, New Pfaltz, or Nouveau-Palatinat, named in recognition of the aid accorded the Huguenots in Mannheim Germany, had a French communal existence until 1785. Many of the old family names and some of the old stone houses are still to be found in this community—a community with a German name, which remained French longer than any other in New York.[10]

In Pennsylvania, the Huguenot influence is hard to trace, because many came from the Alsace-Lorraine section or, by a period of residence in Germany or Holland, had already lost some of their French characteristics and even their French names. Some of the Kieffers of Pennsylvania, for example, were descended from the Tonnelliers, and the DeWittes from the LeBlancs. Marie Führe of Pennsylvania was really Marie Fereé, and her son appears as Fiere.[11] A careful student of the history of colonial Pennsylvania has concluded that, with the possible exception of South Carolina, no other colony received as large a number of French settlers, especially Huguenots.[12] Considerable advertising matter, beginning with the material prepared by William Penn, was sent out in French to attract immigrants.[13] As late as 1797, Pennsylvania passed a special act

---

[10] In addition to Chinard, see J. T. Adams: *Provincial Society* (New York, 1927); and especially, Howard Mumford Jones: *America and French Culture, 1750-1848* (Chapel Hill, North Carolina, 1927).
[11] See Chinard: *op. cit.*, p. 216.
[12] See W. F. Dunaway: "The French Racial Strain in Colonial Pennsylvania," in *The Pennsylvania Magazine of History and Biography*, Vol. LIII, p. 323.
[13] See Chinard: *op. cit.*, pp. 58-76.

affording relief to a group of distressed French immigrants.[14]   The Boudinots, DeLanceys, Jays, and Bayards of Pennsylvania, New York, and New Jersey were well-known and influential Huguenot families.   The Duponts, so closely identified with the history of Delaware from colonial times to the present, trace their ancestry to the Huguenots of Rouen.[15]

French Huguenots were brought into Virginia to superintend the planting of vineyards and the manufacture of wine, to introduce silk culture, and to make experiments with the soil to determine its suitability for rice culture.[16]   Like other Virginians, they almost immediately turned their energies to the planting of tobacco. Manakintown was the best-known settlement of French refugees in Virginia, and attained a reputation for the manufacture of excellent wine, although its other agricultural activities were not so successful.   The settlers received free land and were exempted from taxes for seven years.   Although the legislature refused to vote additional sums, many members of the House of Burgesses contributed from their private purse to the relief of the refugees.   The French Church continued to exist until well into the nineteenth century.   Three well-known ministers in early Virginia were the Frenchmen Phillippe de Richebourg, Louis Latané, and Benjamin de Joux.   The Fontaines and Maurys of present-day Virginia are descendants of Huguenot pioneers.

It was in South Carolina that the French were most numerous in colonial times.   Their story has been told in great detail by Professor Arthur H. Hirsch, and need only be summarized here.[17]   As early as 1679, Huguenots were being encouraged by Charles II and proprietors of the colony to come to South Carolina to raise olives, grapes, and silkworms.   In 1685, Huguenot exiles settled on the Santee River and, in spite of an inhospitable reception by residents already in the area, developed plantations along the river to such an extent that, for many years, the region was marked on early maps as "French Santee."[18]   When the question of granting representa-

[14] See *Laws of the Commonwealth of Pennsylvania* (Harrisburg, Pennsylvania, 1910), Vol. V, p. 210.
[15] In New Jersey, a bill was passed in 1695 requiring all deeds and conveyances made in German or French to be translated into English. *New Jersey Archives* (Paterson, New Jersey, 1894), Vol. XI, p. 222.
[16] See Philip A. Bruce: *Economic History of Virginia in the Seventeenth Century* (New York, 1896), p. 246.
[17] See Hirsch: *The Huguenots of Colonial South Carolina* (Durham, North Carolina, 1928).
[18] See H. L. Osgood: *The American Colonies in the Seventeenth Century* (New York, 1904-1907), Vol. II, pp. 327-328.

tion to the new counties of South Carolina with a large French population came up for discussion in the eighteenth century, there was considerable opposition from the older counties, although the non-English elements were practically completely assimilated by the middle of that century.

The largest and richest Huguenot settlement in South Carolina was Charleston. Next in importance, with its prosperity resting primarily on rice and indigo, was the Santee River district. Other Huguenot settlements in South Carolina were Goose Creek, St. Thomas, St. Denis, Orange Quarter, St. John's, Berkeley, St. Stevens, and Perrysburg, the last-named occupied by French-born in Switzerland.[19] The list of prominent present-day Charleston families of Huguenot stock is a long one, and would include such names as Bayard, Bonneau, Bacot, Chevalier, Dupre, Deslisles, Dubois, Gaillard, Guignard, Huger, Laurens, Legaré, Marion, Manigault, Neuville, Porcher, Ravenel, Saint Julien, Trevezant, and many others.

Six churches of the Reformed and Calvinistic faith were established by the French Protestants in South Carolina, all but one before 1706. For economic, social, and ecclesiastical reasons, the French churches were quickly absorbed into the Church of England. For one thing, it proved difficult to supply Huguenot ministers; then, there was no mother church in France to draw upon for support; and finally the children of South Carolina Huguenots were not only generally educated in English but also realized that their social and economic future was so bound up with the English that they readily became affiliated with the Established Church. Only the French Huguenot Church of Charleston remains, although its services have been held in English since 1828. By that time, there were hardly more than two or three people left in the congregation who could follow a sermon in French. French sermons are still delivered occasionally, but primarily to preserve the old historic tradition and not because many of the listeners understand them. In 1767, a new immigration of several hundred French Protestants came to New Bordeaux. The county is still known as d'Abbéville, but the congregation embraced Anglicanism more than a century ago.

Rice, indigo, and cotton were the main products of French Huguenot planters in South Carolina—not silk, wine, and oils, as the proprietors had wished. The inventions of Peter J. Guerrard

[19] For descriptions of each of these communities, see Hirsch: *op. cit.*

(1691) and Peter Villepontoux (1732) revolutionized the rice industry. Gideon Dupont discovered a water-culture method of tending rice, and Andrew Deveaux and Thomas Mellichamp made significant contributions to the culture of indigo and to the method of extracting its dyestuff. William Mellichamp was a pioneer salt manufacturer in the lower South. Colonel Gabriel Bernard, uncle of Rousseau, was the engineer who directed the building of the Charleston fortifications in 1736. The wealth of many of the French planters and merchants became proverbial. They became moneylenders to their English neighbors, they maintained private schools, and their homes gave evidence of a high degree of culture. From 1725 to 1765, the French had their own newspapers in South Carolina, and in the printing and bookbinding business had almost exclusive control during these years. Lewis Timotheé, son of a French Protestant refugee, issued what was to be the first securely established newspaper in South Carolina.[20]

The whole Huguenot immigration to the United States probably did not exceed 15,000, but a large proportion of these newcomers achieved distinction and prosperity before 1789. Hirsch estimated that, after 1700, the French blood constituted between one tenth and one fifth of the white population of South Carolina. By 1776, the French blood in South Carolina had been practically absorbed. "The French became English in language and religion, British in sentiment and policies. The fulcrum by which it was accomplished was economic necessity, the lever was political preferment."[21] Jacque Serrurier became Smith; Pasquereau was spelled Packerow; Lewis Janvier became Louis Jennings; Isaac Amyrand, a clerk in the South Carolina Assembly, changed his name to Amy.[22]

The Huguenots did not come to South Carolina, or elsewhere, as a class of destitute immigrants. They were not paupers, but a thrifty and progressive group. Their initial poverty "represented only a transition between a period of great prosperity and comforts in France and a period of prosperity in America."[23] As early as 1700, a visitor to the French Santee district discovered prosperous planters, with brick and stone houses. Their rapid assimilation is one of the most remarkable phenomena in the history of American foreign groups. When Lafayette landed at Georgetown, South

[20] See *ibid.*, p. 239.
[21] See *ibid.*, p. 90.
[22] See *ibid.*, p. 100.
[23] See *ibid.*, p. 253.

Carolina, in 1777, the Huguenot group had already lost its distinctive characteristics. When he came again in 1825, and visited Charleston, he was greeted by a military unit wearing uniforms like those of the Paris Guards during the French Revolution. In the parade marched members of a Huguenot benevolent society, founded in 1736 to help widows and orphans, but very few would have been able to discourse at length in French with their distinguished compatriot from beyond the seas.

French physicians were prominent in the colonial period, and some, like Drs. Porchier of Charleston, Jerauld of Medfield, Le Baron of Plymouth, Massachusetts, Pigneron of Newport, Rhode Island, and Gaudonnet of Newark, deserve to be remembered in the history of the profession in its early American beginnings. They not only practiced medicine but also taught apprentices.[24] It was during the American Revolution that Americans learned to know more of the French and their civilization. The number of teachers of French increased, American ladies began to adopt French styles, and bookstores began to display French books. French engineers—like Duportail, Launoy, Radière, Gouvion, Queneret, and L'Enfant—rendered valuable technical service during the war and exerted a great influence on the development of American engineering. L'Enfant, as is well known, made the plans for the new national capital. It is probably not so well known that he also designed the badge for the Society of the Cincinnati, and "thus fixed for good the eagle as the symbol of America." [25] Ninety chaplains came to the colonies on French ships during the Revolution, and thus Americans became better acquainted with Catholicism. One of these, Abbé Poterie, remained to found a church in Boston.[26]

During and after the Revolution, a swarm of French military men and nobility descended upon America, and with them came the French dancing master, the French hairdresser, French mirrors, French imported goods in the stores, French styles, and French balls. *Emigrés* driven out by the French Revolution gave additional stimulus to this imitation of French manners and customs in the upper circles of early American society. They brought in the French art of cooking, along with cotillions, waltzes and quadrilles, and French opera.

[24] See Adams: *op. cit.,* p. 61.
[25] D. R. Fox: "Culture in Knapsacks," in *Ideas in Motion* (New York, 1935), p. 44.
[26] *Ibid.,* p. 45.

New Orleans, always an Old World city and decidedly under French influence, had French opera before the end of the eighteenth century, and the children of the well-to-do had French dancing masters. French convent schools taught "gentle manners" and such subjects as were regarded as suitable for the female character. The French influence in New Orleans was a factor in the discontent that marked the transfer of Louisiana to the United States after the Louisiana Purchase, and charges of disloyalty on the part of the French population were repeated as late as the War of 1812. There was trouble over the language question, and the French were unfamiliar with trial by jury. In 1812, 22 of the 40 members of the Louisiana Constitutional Convention were of French origin. As a result, the Code Napoléon—and not English common law—became the basis of Louisiana legal practice; and even today the Louisiana system of jurisprudence differs significantly from that of other American states.[27]

The early non-Protestant French element within the borders of the present-day United States was largely a survival from the days of New France. As the number was small, this group need not be considered in detail. In 1755, about 6,000 Acadians were deported and scattered all along the coast of the English colonies. In New York, they could be "bound out" for service.[28] A large number of these Acadians found their way into Louisiana. By 1880, the Cajian population of Louisiana was 50,000. To this day, they have retained their customs, their folklore, and their folk music, as well as a peculiar French dialect showing the influence of a steady infiltration of English and Creole expressions.

Gallipolis, in Gallia County, Ohio, was settled in 1790 by some 500 French adventurers from Havre, Bordeaux, Nantes, and elsewhere. The venture had been promoted by Joel Barlow, a land agent of the Scioto Land Company, and his associate, William Playfair, an Englishman. The prospectus described Ohio as a land of neither frost nor taxes. Estates were sold in what turned out to be a tract that did not even belong to the promoting company. After many hardships, the United States Congress finally came to the relief of the disillusioned Frenchmen and gave them a grant of land farther down the Ohio River. The story of the Gallipolis settle-

---

[27] For interesting French survivals in New Orleans, see *New Orleans Guide*, Federal Writer's Project of the WPA (Boston, 1938).
[28] *Colonial Laws of New York* (Albany, New York, 1894), Vol. IV, p. 94.

ment is the usual one of suffering and struggle, and little save a few family names remains to suggest the French origin of this Ohio community. A satirical pamphlet published in Paris ridiculing the optimistic dreams of the colonists bore the title, "The Parlement of Paris on the Scioto." [29]

In the old Northwest and in the Mississippi Valley, there were little French Catholic settlements like Vincennes, Kaskaskia, Cahokia, Prairie du Rocher, Prairie du Pont, and others—each a cluster of settlers and traders around a fur trading post or stockade. They clung to their language and customs, showing little interest in politics, and were content with an easygoing, carefree existence. Gustav Koerner, making a foot tour through Missouri as late as 1833, described a visit he made to the old French settlements when the region was part of the Louisiana Territory:

> Indifferent farmers they were, fond of hunting and particularly fishing. Their social temperaments made them live in villages, where they could have music and dancing and could play at cards. They were a gay and harmless people, and indolent, though their young men would frequently hire themselves out to the fur companies for a year or two as hunters and trappers . . . . Of politics they knew little and cared less.[30]

As late as 1840, the traveler in Illinois could come upon French settlements a hundred years old, with long, narrow lanes, low-roofed, galleried houses, and garden plots shut in by stone walls or fences. The common field system was still in use, and the farming implements showed little progress from the days when the Mississippi Valley was a part of the French colonial empire. The church, with its iron cross, nunnery, and parochial school, remained the center of activity for the inhabitants, who were as light-hearted and as devoted to the fiddle and the dance in the nineteenth century as their forefathers had been in the seventeenth and eighteenth.[31]

[29] See Charles J. Herbermann: "A French Emigré Colony in the United States, 1789-1793," in *United States Catholic Historical Society Records and Studies* (New York, 1900), Vol. I, pp. 77-96. For other material on Gallipolis, see J. B. McMaster: *History of the People of the United States* (New York, 1914), Vol. II, pp. 146-151; H. Fouré Selter: *L'Odyseé Américaine d'une Famille Française* (Baltimore, Maryland, 1936), pp. 18-31; and W. G. Sibley: *The French Five Hundred* (Gallipolis, Ohio, 1933).

[30] Gustav Koerner: *Memoirs* (Cedar Rapids, Iowa, 1909), Vol. I, pp. 321 and 322.

[31] See McMaster: *op. cit.*, Vol. VII, p. 203.

4

The Welsh, Swedes, and Jews

THE WELSH

AMONG THE EARLIEST immigrants to Pennsylvania were a group of Welsh. Besides the usual economic urge, these pioneers were actuated by a desire to revive Welsh nationalism in America and to build a typically Welsh community, where the language and customs of Wales might be preserved and perpetuated. They acquired a tract of land in Pennsylvania of some 40,000 acres, lying west of Philadelphia, along what is now the main route of the Pennsylvania Railroad. The region was known for two generations as the "Welsh Barony." Apparently the settlers were men of some substance and education.[1] Between 1683 and 1699, several Welsh Quaker emigrations to Pennsylvania occurred. Most of the emigrants were farmers who carried on small-scale agriculture. Settlements like Gwynnyd, Bryn Mawr, Merion, Haverford, and Radnor testify to the early Welsh characteristics of the region around Philadelphia. George B. Roberts, a former president of the Pennsylvania Railroad and lineal descendant of a settler in the "Welsh Barony," helped to perpetuate these names as stations on the railroad.

Like other immigrant groups who dreamed of developing and preserving a state within a state, the Welsh were doomed to absorption in the English population. The process was practically completed in two generations. The settlements of Haverford and Merion were quickly Anglicized, but in Radnor Township and St. Davids, Welsh was used in church services and legal documents until the early eighteenth century. An old Welsh stone meeting house in Montgomery County, Pennsylvania, is still standing.[2] Two

[1] See Edith Abbott: *Historical Aspects of the Immigration Problem* (Chicago, 1926), p. 28, citing a letter written in 1800 from Cambria, Pennsylvania, to Wales referring to the prosperity of the writer and to a library of 1,000 volumes.
[2] See Charles H. Browning: *Welsh Settlement of Pennsylvania* (Philadelphia, 1912); and Nellie U. Wallington: *Historic Churches of America* (New York, 1907), pp. 73-78.

members of the first Pennsylvania Assembly were Welshmen. The group left some impression on colonial architecture in the middle colonies, especially through the Welsh *wynnestay*, a large, substantial home built for comfort and not artistic effect, and one of the precursors of the Pennsylvania colonial farmhouse. Thomas and David Lloyd were well-known figures in early Pennsylvania history. The latter became a leader of the popular antiproprietary party in colonial politics, and as chief justice did much to develop the crude legislation of early Pennsylvania into a system of jurisprudence.

The Welsh were regarded as desirable immigrants. As late as 1726, Maryland tried to attract Welsh farmers into that colony by granting special exemptions.[3] But the Welsh element was very quickly absorbed. Some distinguished families, like the Cadwaladers and the Merediths, are lineal descendants of the seventeenth-century pioneers, but Welsh immigration, which was never large during the colonial period, virtually stopped when Wales became more tolerant of the Welsh Friends. Quarrels with the Pennsylvania proprietor over quitrents led to the eventual division of the Welsh tract and to its opening to settlement by all nationalities.

THE SWEDES

Gustavus Adolphus of Sweden had ambitious plans for overseas expansion, but it was not until 1638, after the death of the great king, that two vessels of the Swedish West India Company landed some 50 colonists, under Peter Minuit, who built houses and a fort near the modern Wilmington, Delaware. They named their new settlement Christina, in honor of Sweden's youthful queen. Peter Hollender Ridder became the commander of Fort Christina in 1639, and shortly thereafter the colony was taken under royal protection.

The fur and tobacco trades were the leading occupations of the settlers, but both brought the Swedish colonists into immediate rivalry with the Dutch and English, who regarded the newcomers as interlopers. Only the exigencies of the Thirty Years' War and the exhausted condition of New Netherland following prolonged Indian troubles prevented the immediate expulsion of the Swedes by the Dutch. But in 1655, Peter Stuyvesant, with a formidable armada, descended upon the Swedish settlements, and, without bloodshed,

[3] See *Archives of Maryland*, Vol. XXXV, p. 597.

New Sweden passed under the control of the Dutch, only to be swallowed up by the English a decade later.

By 1642, New Sweden was a settlement of log cottages, with low doors and loopholes for windows. Their occupants raised vegetables, tobacco, and grain, and engaged in the lucrative fur trade. A chapel had been erected for religious services, and a windmill stood near Fort Christina. Johan Printz, famous for his portliness, became governor of the colony in 1642. Because emigrants were hard to get, deserters from the army, debtors, and Finns caught poaching or stealing wood in the royal forests were sent over to augment the population of New Sweden. Printz repeatedly asked for soldiers and colonists, but Sweden's troubles in Europe left little surplus energy for pushing the colonial venture.

In spite of many discouraging incidents, which need not be discussed here, the 300-pound governor built several small log forts, and concluded that his colony was "a remarkably beautiful country." His great regret was "that it was not occupied by true Christians." The soil was excellent, and new settlements were started, called Finland, Upland, Tequirassy, Tinicum, and Province Island. The clearings for agriculture were steadily enlarged, much rye was planted, and the livestock of the colonists increased. Printz Hall was a two-story log building which boasted a small library and several rooms that had glass windows with curtains. Steady progress was made under the greatest handicaps, but Governor Printz's chief source of worry was the steady encroachment of the Dutch and the intense rivalry over the Indian trade. For several years before the Dutch conquest of 1655, there was desultory fighting between the Swedes and the Dutch along the Delaware.

The territory of New Sweden once took in Delaware and parts of Pennsylvania, Maryland, and New Jersey. It bordered on two bays and had excellent shipping facilities. At the time of the conquest, the population was about 600, although one cannot be certain as to how many of these were Swedes and how many Finns. By 1663, the Swedes, Finns, and Dutch, plus a few Germans and Danes, had 110 "boweries" (farms) in the Delaware area, with 200 cows, 20 horses, 80 sheep, and several thousand swine.

William Penn described the Swedes on the Delaware as "a people proper and strong of body," with "fine children, and almost every house full . . . ." Swedish remained the dominant language after the Dutch conquest, and the Finns and Dutch acquired it as a second language. Swedish pastors and their churches had received support from the Swedish government, and the articles of surrender to the Dutch permitted the one remaining Swedish pastor to continue teaching the people their language and their religion. In 1693, nearly 1,000 individuals signed an appeal for Swedish pastors. In 1697, Charles XI of Sweden sent three ministers, with Swedish Bibles and hymn books. A church was built in Wilmington, the Old Swedes Church, and another in Philadelphia, the Gloria Dei Church. Altogether, from 1642 to 1779, 41 Swedish pastors were sent out to America.[4]

A Swedish Lutheran pastor wrote home in 1697 that there were 1,200 people in Delaware who spoke Swedish, and added: "The houses are built after the Swedish manner. The women brew excellent drink, as in Sweden." But assimilation with the English stock was proceeding rapidly. For many years, there were lingering evidences of Swedish influence on the Delaware, as in certain types of architecture, and the red cattle of eastern Pennsylvania were said to be descendants of those brought over by the Swedish colonists.[5] Nevertheless, the church records show how rapidly descendants of the Swedes were being Anglicized. By 1730, a preacher in one church felt obliged to hold three vesper services: one in German, one in Swedish, and one in English. By 1750, requests were coming from the old Swedish and Dutch settlements of Delaware and Pennsylvania for services conducted in English, "as otherwise their children would become unchristened heathens, or Quakers," and "their churches would be changed into stables alongside of Quaker meeting houses."[6] In 1752, the Reverend Acrelius wrote: "The youth were examined in Swedish so far as practicable . . . . Those who could not express themselves in Swedish had liberty to read in English." By 1770, they were catechized in English exclusively. In 1784, a disillusioned pastor lamented that "these descendants of the Swedes . . . have no more affection for anything from Sweden than if it were from Turkey." In 1787, the last Swedish minister

[4] See Amandus Johnson: *Swedish Contributions to American National Life, 1638-1921* (New York, 1921). See also Nellie W. Wallington: *op. cit.*, pp. 20-25 and 44-46; and "Extracts from the Journal of the Reverend Andreas Sandel, Pastor of Gloria Dei Swedish Lutheran Church, Philadelphia, 1702-1719," in *Pennsylvania Magazine of History and Biography*, Vol. XXX, pp. 287-299 and 445-452.
[5] See J. T. Adams: *Provincial Society, 1690-1763* (New York, 1927), p. 5.
[6] Israel Acrelius: *A History of New Sweden*, translated by W. A. Reynolds (Philadelphia, 1874), pp. 305 and 360-361.

returned to Sweden. Apparently, many of the descendants of the colonial Swedes were absorbed into the Episcopalian Church.[7] The services of the Swedish Church, in which the preacher sang the creed, were slowly modified. So were the Christmas customs, the Swedish games that had been imported, and the peculiar Swedish dishes prepared at Christmastime. Old World methods of agriculture and Old World tools gave way to English customs. Swedish and Finnish bathhouses crumbled into ruins; and the Swedish population intermarried with English, Welsh, and Germans. By the middle of the eighteenth century, disgruntled Swedes of the old generation were making the usual derogatory comments about the new. Acrelius, for example, writing in 1758, deplored the extravagance of the younger generation:

> Formerly, the church people could come some Swedish miles on foot to church; now the young, as well as the old, must be upon horseback. Then many a good and honest man rode upon a piece of bear-skin; now scarcely any saddle is valued unless it has a saddle-cloth with galloon and fringe. Then servants and girls were seen in church barefooted; now young people will be like persons of quality in their dress . . . .

Servants were beginning to wear wigs, and girls wore hooped skirts and other finery; log houses were giving way to "painted houses of stone and brick"; and where once the people drank ale and brandy, now they drank wine and punch. "Then they lived upon grits and mush, now upon tea, coffee and chocolate." In short, the inexorable forces of assimilation had done their work; "our Swedish people" were now "naturalized Englishmen."[8] John Morton, a member of the Continental Congress from Pennsylvania and one of the signers of the Declaration of Independence, was a lineal descendant of Morten Mortenson, one of the Swedish immigrants who had founded the short-lived New Sweden on the banks of the Delaware.[9]

[7] See Roy W. Swanson: "The Swedes and the New History," in Swedish American History Bulletin, Vol. III, No. 3, pp. 7-21.

[8] See Acrelius: op. cit., pp. 310 and 357.

[9] For other references on New Sweden, see Amandus Johnson: The Swedes on the Delaware, 1638-1664 (Philadelphia, 1915); Christopher Ward: The Dutch and Swedes on the Delaware, 1609-1664 (Philadelphia, 1930), which adds little, as far as New Sweden is concerned, to what Johnson has written; J. C. Clay: Annals of the Swedes on the Delaware (Chicago, 1914); Peter Lindeström: Geographia Americae, translated by Amandus Johnson (Philadelphia, 1925); and the excellent articles by Amandus Johnson and George H. Ryden in A. B. Benson and Naboth Hedin (editors), Swedes in America (New Haven, 1938), pp. 5-51.

THE JEWS

The total number of Jews in the United States at the end of the Revolution probably did not exceed 3,000, and some estimates put the figure as low as 2,000. Most of these Jewish immigrants were Spanish or Portuguese. Many were Marranos—that is, converts to Christianity—although in America, where there was no danger of the Inquisition, they frequently returned to their Jewish faith.

A number of these Sephardic Jews, from whom such distinguished Americans as David Belasco, Bernard Baruch, Justice Cardozo, and the Mendozas, Acostas, Pintos, and Cordobas trace their descent, settled in New York as early as the period of Dutch rule. In September, 1654, 23 Jews entered the harbor of New Amsterdam to establish themselves in the Dutch colony and, after an encounter with the irascible Peter Stuyvesant, succeeded in obtaining recognition for their right to trade, travel, and live in the colony, "providing the poor among them shall be supported by their own nation." [10] By 1664, the Jewish community had acquired a cemetery, but not a synagogue. The burial ground was near the present Chatham Square, and a few of the tombstones still remain. The inscriptions are in both Spanish and Hebrew. In 1682, the Jews of New York rented a house to be used as a synagogue, and, in 1728, the first regular synagogue in North America was erected on Mill Street. Though the old synagogue has disappeared, the congregation still exists. The official documents of the colony[11] contain frequent references to the Jews as a minority group. In 1748, Peter Kalm, the Swedish traveler who visited the colonies in the middle of the eighteenth century, wrote:

> There are many Jews settled in New York, who possess great privileges. They have a synagogue and houses, and great country seats of their own property, and are allowed to keep shops in town. They have likewise several ships, which they freight, and send out with their own goods.[12]

Rhode Island, with its liberal government and a tolerance for dissenting groups exceeding that of all other colonies, naturally

[10] Lee J. Levinger: *A History of the Jews in the United States* (Cincinnati, 1930), p. 61.

[11] See E. B. O'Callaghan (editor): *Documents Relative to the Colonial History of New York* (Albany, New York, 1856-1883), Vol. III, pp. 262 and 415; Vol. IV, p. 720; and Vol. VI, p. 56.

[12] Peter Kalm: *Travels Into North America (1748-1749)*, translated by J. R. Foster (Warmington and London, England, 1770-1771), Vol. I, p. 191. See also Burton J. Hendrick: *The Jews in America* (New York, 1923).

offered a sanctuary to the Jews. Newport, a thriving seaport in the days before the Revolution, combined the attractions of religious toleration with an opportunity to develop a profitable trade; hence the second Jewish settlement in what is now the United States was founded there. Longfellow, in one of his lesser poems, described the old Jewish cemetery at Newport, established in 1677. Near the old cemetery is the first synagogue, built in 1763, now the oldest in the United States.

There were some 60 Jewish families in Newport before the Revolution, many of whom became wealthy and influential because of their extensive trade with the West Indies and other foreign ports. The career of Aaron Lopez, a Portuguese Jew, was typical of many in this golden age of Newport Jewry. He arrived in Newport in 1752, with a younger brother, to join an older half-brother who had been in Rhode Island since the 1740's. In Portugal, the family had professed Christianity in order to escape the Inquisition. Aaron Lopez's first venture was in the candle business. With his father-in-law, Jacob Rodriques Rivera, a Spanish Jew, he engaged in various trading activities which took their ships to the African Coast, the West Indies, Central America, northern Europe, and the Mediterranean. Rivera introduced the sperm oil industry to America. By 1760, there were 17 factories in Newport alone for the manufacture of spermaceti candles, and for a time the Jewish merchants of Rhode Island, organized as the "United Company of Spermaceti Candlers," virtually controlled the industry in New England and the Middle Atlantic colonies. During the Revolution, when Newport was frequently harassed by British raids and the ships of Jewish traders were seized on both sides of the Atlantic, the Rivera and Lopez families, along with others, left Newport. Some went to New York and Philadelphia, some to Leicester, Massachusetts. The pre-Revolutionary prominence of Newport in the trade of the New World was never restored.[13]

[13] See Bruce M. Bigelow: "Aaron Lopez: Merchant of Newport," in *The New England Quarterly*, Vol. IV, pp. 757-776; Max J. Kohler: "Jews of Newport," in *Publications of the American Jewish Historical Society* (1897); and Morris A. Gutstein: *The Story of the Jews of Newport: Two and a Half Centuries of Judaism, 1658-1908* (New York, 1936). The diary of Ezra Stiles, President of Yale University, who was on friendly terms with many of the Rhode Island Jews, contains this interesting entry for August 10, 1769: "The Jews are wont in Thunder storms to set open all their Doors & Windows for the coming of Messias. Last Hail Storm 31 July, when Thunder, Rain & Hail were amazingly violent, the Jews in Newport threw open Doors, Windows, and employed themselves in Singing & repeating Prayers . . . ." [Quoted in Anita L. Lebeson: *Jewish Pioneers in America, 1492-1848* (New York, 1931).]

Among early Massachusetts Jews may be mentioned Abraham Touro, a merchant of Boston and Medford, whose vessels traded with the West Indies; Moses Michael Hays, whose portrait hangs in the Boston Masonic Temple as a past grand master of the ancient fraternity; and Judah Hays, his son, who was one of the founders of the Boston Athenaeum.[14]   There were isolated Jewish families in Pennsylvania and Virginia.   The best-known Jewish family of Philadelphia was the Franks.   There was a congregation of Sephardic Jews in Richmond, Virginia, shortly after the close of the American Revolution; and Washington, in 1790, was in communication with a Hebrew congregation in Savannah, founded by Portuguese Jews in 1734.[15]   Charleston, South Carolina, had a Jewish congregation by 1750, and the total Jewish population of that city was about 600 at the outbreak of the Revolution.[16]   Before the close of the colonial period, the Jewish peddler, with his pack or pack train, was already a familiar figure among the pioneers of the hinterland.

During the Revolution, as might have been expected, there were both Jewish "Tories" and Jewish "Patriots."   David Franks was a noted Tory; his relative, Lieutenant Colonel Isaac Franks, a patriot leader.   Solomon Pinto, who served in the Continental Army from 1777 to the close of the war, was one of the original members of the Society of the Cincinnati in Connecticut.[17]   Haym Salomon, born in Lissa, Poland, became a moneylender for the distressed Continental government.   He and other prominent Jews, such as Philip Minis, frequently advanced money to pay the bills of the Continental forces, much of which was never repaid.[18]   The number of Jews in the United States at the close of the Revolution was not significant, but there are Jews in the United States who are fully qualified for membership in the Sons and Daughters of the American Revolution.[19]   On Memorial Day, it has been the custom to hold services at the old Jewish cemetery in New York, in the little plot on the Bowery, between Oliver and James Streets, which is the

[14] See *The Jewish Advocate*, Boston, October 10, 1930.
[15] See Leon Hühner: "The Jews of Virginia from the Earliest Times to the Close of the Eighteenth Century," in *Publications of the American Jewish Historical Society* (1911), No. 20, pp. 85-105.
[16] See a series of pamphlets on the Jews of South Carolina by Barnett A. Elzas (Charleston, South Carolina, 1902 and 1903), reprinted from the *Charleston News and Courier*.
[17] See Lebeson: *op. cit.*, p. 214.
[18] See Charles E. Russell: *Haym Salomon and the Revolution* (New York, 1930).   See also Lebeson: *op. cit.*, Ch. XI.
[19] See *The American Hebrew* (New York), September 10, 1926.

second oldest Jewish cemetery in the United States. The ancient burial ground lies beneath the fire escapes of neighboring tenements and elevated trains rumbling overhead. It contains 75 graves, of which one fifth mark the resting places of Jews who served their country during the War for American Independence.[20]

[20] See *The New York Times*, May 31, 1933; also Leo M. Friedman: *Early American Jews* (Cambridge, Massachusetts, 1934).

5

The Colonial Emigration from Ireland: The Irish and Scotch-Irish

IN IRELAND, every grievance has been aggravated and every reform retarded by centuries of conflict over alien rule. It has been the peculiar destiny of the Irish race to be "forever separated from, yet circumscribed by its Anglo-Saxon neighbors in two continents." [1] In the nineteenth century, millions of Irish migrated to America. The migration from Ireland was also of great significance in the eighteenth century, although of somewhat different character. Strangely enough, in spite of the importance and the interest that attaches to this story of the Irish in two continents, little that is authoritative has been written about the Irish in America.[2]

The causes of emigration from Ireland in the eighteenth century are the familiar ones of religious persecution, economic oppression, and civil disability imposed by an alien government upon a conquered, unhappy people. Most of the emigrants from Ireland to America in the colonial period were the descendants of early Scotch Presbyterians who settled in Ulster in the seventeenth century and whose offspring departed for America in the eighteenth. The Ulster plantation was actually much smaller than is generally supposed, and a considerable part of the area was in fact allotted to "undertakers" who were native Irish. The settlers imported to northern Ireland came mostly from the Lowlands of Scotland, and many of them represented a rough, turbulent, lawless lot—elements

---

[1] W. F. Adams: *Ireland and Irish Emigration to the New World from 1815 to the Famine* (New Haven, Connecticut, 1932), preface.

[2] The most satisfactory treatments of the Scotch-Irish element are still those of Henry Jones Ford: *The Scotch-Irish in America* (Princeton, New Jersey, 1915); and C. A. Hanna: *Scotch-Irish, or the Scot in North Britain, North Ireland and North America*, 2 vols. (New York, 1902). The publications by the Scotch-Irish Society of America are as uncritically laudatory as those of other societies representing particular groups anxious for their rightful place in history. A disappointing treatment is that of Maude Glasgow: *The Scotch-Irish in Northern Ireland and in the American Colonies* (New York, 1936).

"that did not make for peace and order." Men proscribed on the Scotch borders frequently took refuge in Ireland. James I described them as "maisterles men and vagabondis wanting a lawfull trade, calling and industrie," and an Ulster minister concluded that "going to Ireland was looked upon as a miserable mark of a deplorable person . . . ." [3] In 1663, another divine, the Reverend Robert Blair, admitted that "Divine Providence sent over [to Ireland] some worthy persons of birth, education and parts, yet the most part were such as either poverty, scandalous lives, or, at the best, adventurous seeking of better accomodations, set forward that way . . . ." [4]

As a matter of fact, these Scotch immigrants to Ireland in the seventeenth century were probably little different in their turbulence, adventurous spirit, and occasional lawlessness from the pioneer on any recently opened frontier. Under the strict Calvinistic discipline of their preachers, and under the stimulus of a religious revivalism that left its mark upon their descendants in the highlands of Kentucky and Tennessee for nearly two centuries, the mass of Scotch immigrants were quickly reduced to a sense of order and conformity with the religious and moral codes of Ireland. The native Irishmen whom they encountered on the new plantation often became tenants and workmen on land they once had owned, and undoubtedly considerable intermarriage took place. As Professor Ford has pointed out, no gentleman denied the use of his name to a lady who claimed it for her child.

No Census figures are available, but it has been estimated that, by the middle of the seventeenth century, there were perhaps 100,000 Scotch and 20,000 English in the Ulster population of northern Ireland. Both the native and the recently imported stock seemed to multiply vigorously and rapidly. Presbyterianism, especially because of the experiences of its adherents during the civil wars of the seventeenth century, became not only a firm religious bond for the "Scotch-Irish" living in Ireland but also a force of real political significance.

In the late seventeenth and early eighteenth centuries, there was some persecution of the Scotch-Irish by the Episcopalian authorities, who were eager to impose uniformity in religious matters.

[3] Ford: *op. cit.*, pp. 101 and 102. The first 208 pages are devoted to a consideration of the background in Ireland for the Irish immigration.
[4] Quoted in *ibid.*, p. 103.

Religious restrictions, moreover, involved the curtailment of civil rights, such as the right to hold office in the army, navy, customs service, or law courts. There were restrictions on the right to maintain schools, and the Anglican establishment had to be supported by tithes imposed upon both Presbyterians and Roman Catholics. In spite of these irritating regulations, religious motives actually caused little organized emigration in the eighteenth century. The most important reason for the Scotch-Irish emigration was economic.

The economic motive for the Scotch-Irish emigration is to be found in the English commercial system, known as mercantilism, which England, like other nations in the seventeenth and eighteenth centuries, applied to her colonial dependencies. Irish produce of many kinds was gradually shut out from England; Irish ships were excluded from the colonial trade of the Empire; and, in order to prevent them from offering serious competition to their English rivals, prohibitive restrictions were placed on Irish woolen manufacturers, who had developed a prosperous industry in Ireland. The restrictions on woolen manufacture were so severe that the industry was virtually ruined in northern Ireland. A similar situation prevailed in other industries, such as the manufacture of glass and linen products, and shipbuilding. In 1666, tolls were imposed on Irish cattle imported into England; and, in 1670 and 1671, navigation acts were enacted forbidding the importation of products needed in the colonies, unless they had first passed through and been taxed in English ports. Irish vessels were excluded from American trade. Add to these grievances the discontent caused by an absentee landlord system, and the reasons are apparent for a heavy exodus of men who wished to try their fortune in the New World.

Heavy emigration from Ireland to the American colonies began in the second decade of the eighteenth century. The first shiploads went to New England, but the Scotch-Irish received a cool welcome among the Puritans, who manifested a decided national hatred for all who came from Ireland and resented the intrusion of religious dissenters in their colonies. A Scotch-Irish frontier settlement at Worcester, Massachusetts, was destroyed by a mob at night. Cotton Mather, in a sermon in 1700 referring to plans to send Irish to Massachusetts, denounced the proposals as "formidable attempts of Satan and his Sons to Unsettle us," and rejoiced

[45]

that "an overwhelming blast from Heaven" had brought the nefarious scheme to naught.[5] It is not surprising that the tide of
Scotch-Irish immigration quickly turned to Pennsylvania, where
land and citizenship could be acquired on easy terms, and where
religious differences were tolerated. Pennsylvania became the distributing center for the Scotch-Irish immigration of the colonial era.

Before tracing in detail the Scotch-Irish settlements in the American colonies and evaluating their influence, it is well to call attention to the difficulty in distinguishing accurately between the
Scotch-Irish and the so-called real Irish in this period. However
sharply the line may now be drawn and however insurmountable
the religious barriers between these groups today, there is much
evidence that no such clear differentiation was made in colonial
times. This has led to vigorous claims and counterclaims by exponents of the superior virtues of each group, and the historian finds
himself at sea in the welter of conflicting and often poorly substan-
tiated evidence.

It is true that, throughout the eighteenth century, colonial records repeatedly refer to the newcomers from Ireland simply as
"Irish." Edmund Burke spoke of these people as those "who in
America are generally called Scotch-Irish," but this was certainly
not always the case.[6] Irish and Irish-American historians have been
particularly active in rejecting the distinction. They argue that a
residence of more than a century in Ireland had made the emigrants
from that country really Irish, and that a great deal of intermarriage
had occurred with native Irish women, who imposed their faith
upon their offspring. Since Roman Catholicism was proscribed by
the laws of many of the English colonies in America, it is pointed
out that thousands of Irish Catholics became Protestants in America, either for the sake of economic and social advantage, for the
sake of their offspring, or because of intermarriage. Many Irish
Catholics may have abandoned their faith in the New World
because of this unfavorable legislation and because of the absence
of Catholic priests to keep it alive. Moreover, for 150 years, some
of the most beloved leaders of the Irish cause in Ireland were non-
Catholics. The unsuccessful rebellion of 1798, for example, was
led largely by "United Irishmen"—that is, Protestants like Wolfe

---

[5] Quoted in James B. Cullen: *The Story of The Irish in Boston* (Boston, 1890),
p. 67.
[6] Ford: *op. cit.*, p. 199.

Tone, who seemed to lay little stress on religious or racial differences.

Bishop England admitted that, previous to 1776, there were few Catholics in any colony except Maryland, Pennsylvania, and Virginia, to which a number of Irish servants had been transported.[7] John Carroll, in 1785, reported to the Papacy that there were over 18,000 Catholics in the United States, of whom nearly 16,000 were in Maryland, 1,500 in New York, 700 in Pennsylvania, and 200 in Virginia. At that time, there were 19 priests in Maryland.[8]

Michael J. O'Brien, historiographer of the American Irish Historical Society, has been perhaps the most ardent champion of the claims of the Irish during the colonial period and in the American Revolution.[9] By an examination of the muster rolls of the Continental Army, he finds that the Irish stock averaged 38 per cent of the American forces. Unfortunately, his conclusions on this point are based largely on a study of family names and the changes through which they passed—a plausible, but most unreliable approach to the problem.[10] O'Brien also contends that St. Patrick's Day was observed in the Army on General Washington's orders. This fact has been indisputably established. In fact, in 1780, the Commander in Chief hoped "that the celebration of the Day will not be attended with the least Rioting or Disorder." [11] Finally, a study of all vessels sailing from Ireland and registered at the New York and Philadelphia customs houses convinces O'Brien that only 43 per cent set sail from those northern ports from which the "Scotch-

---

[7] See Peter Guilday: *The Life and Times of John England* (New York, 1927), Vol. II, p. 366.

[8] See Edward F. Humphrey: *Nationalism and Religion in America, 1774-1789* (Boston, 1924), pp. 252-253.

[9] See Michael J. O'Brien: *A Hidden Phase of American History, Ireland's Part in America's Struggle for Liberty* (New York, 1919). See also contributions by the same author in the *Journal of the American Irish Historical Society,* especially: "Land Grants to Irish Settlers in the Colony and State of Virginia," Vol. XXIV, pp. 87-124; "Irish Settlers in Connecticut in the Seventeenth and Eighteenth Centuries," Vol. XXIV, pp. 125-141; and "The Scotch-Irish Myth," Vol. XVIII, *passim,* and Vol. XXIV, pp. 142-153.

[10] For example, the name Johnson is claimed to be derived from Irish Mac-Shane, Smith from MacGowan, Masterson from McTiernan, and Early from O'Muloghery. Other changes in Irish names, not all pointed out by O'Brien but illustrative of the process are: O'Bryan to Bryant, O'Toole to Tuthill, McNees to Nay, O'Shaughnessy to Chauncey, O'Meagh to Meade, MacNeill to Neilson, O'Hart to Hays, O'Heas to Hays, O'Knavin to Bowen, MacRory to Rogers, and so forth. While family names of undoubted Irish origin can be found in which these changes took place, it is most unreliable to reason that every such modern name must derive from an earlier Irish name. See also Thomas H. Maginnis, Jr.: *The Irish Contribution to America's Independence* (Philadelphia, 1913).

[11] O'Brien, *A Hidden Phase of American History,* p. 165.

Irish" would naturally embark, the rest setting out from seaports where the "Old Irish" predominated.

The champions of this point of view do not deny that many emigrants from northern Ireland were descended from the Scotch who were brought into the Ulster plantation. But they contend that long residence and intermarriage with the Old Irish stock had made them natives of Ireland. Their children grew up as Irish, although many clung to the Protestant religion of their fathers, and all their interests and possessions were inextricably bound up with the fate of Ireland. Religion alone cannot make a nationality. Donegal must be regarded as a very "Irish" county, and Derry and Tyrone were at least equally divided between descendants of the ancient race and the Scotch planters. Mere embarkation from Londonderry, the nearest port, it is maintained, could not be accepted as conclusive proof of Scotch nationality.

Without pursuing this fruitless controversy further, it may be pointed out that colonial records frequently refer simply to "the Irishmen," especially in advertisements for runaway servants. The total Roman Catholic population of Pennsylvania in 1754 was recorded at 1,365,[12] with 416 of this number classified as Irish and the rest as Germans. By 1789, there were many Irish Catholics in Philadelphia and Boston, and the Philadelphia Tammany Society was already under Irish Catholic control.[13] The Charitable Irish Society, formed in Boston in 1737 to help the poor and needy, had both Protestant and Catholic presidents, and the Hibernian Provident Society of New York, formed on St. Patrick's Day, 1801, admitted anyone to membership who had never helped Great Britain in her oppression of the Emerald Isle.[14] Bishop Carroll, on a visit to Boston in 1791, was invited to the annual dinner of the Ancient and Honorable Artillery Company,[15] and President Adams, in 1799, made a contribution to the building of a Catholic church in Boston. General Stephen Moylan, born in Cork in 1737, whose brother was a Catholic bishop, was the first president of the Friendly

---

[12] See *Pennsylvania Archives*, Vol. III, pp. 144-145.

[13] E. P. Kilroe: *Saint Tammany and the Origin of the Society of Tammany or Columbian Order in the City of New York* (New York, 1913), p. 144.

[14] See John D. Crimmins: *St. Patrick's Day* (New York, 1902), pp. 22 and 146. The Charitable Irish Society of Boston is not to be confused with a Scots' Charitable Society started in 1657, which was reorganized in 1684 and is still in existence. James B. Cullen: *The Story of the Irish in Boston* (Boston, 1890), p. 19.

[15] Maginnis: *op. cit.*, p. 88.

Sons of St. Patrick of Philadelphia, to which Washington himself was elected as an honorary member.[16] The second president was John M. Nesbitt, from northern Ireland.[17] Irish Catholics served in both armies during the American Revolution.[18] St. Patrick's Day celebrations were held before and shortly after 1800 in cities as widely scattered as Charleston, Savannah, Philadelphia, and Albany.[19]

That the Scotch-Irish were becoming sensitive about being confused with the Irish is evident from such stray bits of evidence as a protest in 1720 by the inhabitants of the Scotch-Irish settlement of Londonderry, New Hampshire, who solemnly resolved: "We were surprised to hear ourselves termed *Irish people*, when we so frequently ventured our all for the British Crown and Liberties against the Irish Papists." [20] This insistence upon a hard and fast distinction between the two groups increased steadily, and, in the nineteenth century, when hundreds of thousands of Irish Catholics migrated to America, there was ample reason to regard it as a perfectly valid differentiation. On the other hand, the proceedings and papers of the Scotch-Irish Congresses of the Scotch-Irish Society of America, founded in 1889 in Columbia, Tennessee, are as unbalanced and uncritically laudatory of Scotch-Irish achievement as any Irish publication has ever been. Indeed, one might almost conclude from such published proceedings that all of the United States are the result of the work of John Knox.

From 1714 to 1720, the years when the Scotch-Irish immigration to America reached significant proportions, 54 ships arrived in New England from Ireland. An even greater number proceeded to the ports on the Delaware, the eastern shore of Maryland, and South

[16] See Martin J. Griffin: *Catholics and the American Revolution*, 3 vols. (Ridley Park, Pennsylvania, 1907), Vol. II, pp. 227-365.
[17] See *A Brief Account of the Society of the Friendly Sons of St. Patrick* (Philadelphia, 1844), p. 215. One side of the medal of the Friendly Sons of St. Patrick represented Hibernia (with a harp) on the right, America (an Indian with quiver and bow) on the left, and Liberty joining the hands of both countries in the center. On the reverse side was St. Patrick, cross in hand, trampling upon a snake.
[18] See Griffin: *op. cit.*, Vol. I, pp. 325-352; and Vol. II, pp. 167-197. See also George Bancroft: *History of the United States* (Boston, 1875), Vol. X, p. 175; James Haltigan: *The Irish in the American Revolution and Their Early Influence in the Colonies* (Washington, D. C., 1908); Thomas A. Murray: *Irish Rhode Islanders in the American Revolution* (Providence, Rhode Island, 1903); and *Journal of the American-Irish Historical Society*, Vol. XXVII.
[19] See John D. Crimmins: *St. Patrick's Day: Its Celebration in New York and Other American Places, 1737-1845* (New York, 1902).
[20] *Provincial and Town Papers of New Hampshire*, Vol. III, pp. 770-771.

Carolina. The ebb and flow of Scotch-Irish immigration was closely responsive to the fortunes of the linen industry, thus illustrating again the importance of the economic motive in this migration to America. A generous estimate for the total Scotch-Irish addition to the American colonial population before 1776 would be between 150,000 and 200,000.

As already suggested, the Scotch-Irish were not particularly welcome in New England. Milton once referred to the Scotch-Irish Presbyterians as "the blockish Presbyterians" from a "barbarous nook of Ireland," and some of the New England colonial leaders were hardly more complimentary. The surveyor general of customs in Boston wrote in 1718: "These confounded Irish will eat us all up, provisions being most extravagantly dear, and scarce of all sorts." [21] The newcomers had the reputation of being a very pugnacious lot, and almost everywhere they settled developed friction with their neighbors over religious and other issues.[22] The Worcester, Massachusetts, settlement, to which the Scotch-Irish had been pushed as a sort of frontier guard, encountered so much difficulty with its neighbors that, in 1738, 34 families moved to Pelham, farther west. The Scotch-Irish migration in Massachusetts continued westward and northwestward from central Massachusetts along the west shore of the Connecticut River into Vermont, and along the east shore of the Connecticut River into New Hampshire. According to the Census of 1790, Massachusetts at that time had a "Scotch" population of 13,435 and an "Irish" element numbering 3,732. Families like the Morrisons, Pennells, Hendersons, Cochranes, Henrys, Clarks, McClellans, McCowens, Taggarts, and others were prominent in the Worcester settlement and its offshoot, Colerain. Other Massachusetts settlements like Pelham, Western (Warren), and Blandford, settled in 1741, still number many Scotch-Irish among their population. Their designation in the official records as "poor Irish people" apparently led to strong letters of protest to the governor.[23]

A small Scotch-Irish settlement begun in Maine in 1718 was later absorbed by Portland. By 1720, there were several hundred families on the Kennebec River and in eastern Maine. Samuel Waldo imported Scotch-Irish settlers to Maine, and one little settlement in

[21] Quoted in Ford: *op. cit.*, p. 224.
[22] See A. L. Perry: *Scotch-Irish in New England* (Boston, 1891); also C. K. Bolton: *Scotch-Irish Pioneers in Ulster and America* (Boston, 1910).
[23] See Perry: *op. cit.*, pp. 12-14.

[50]

the colony had the good old Irish name of Cork.[24] Londonderry, New Hampshire, was settled in 1719 by about 20 families. The site was selected by James McKeen, grandfather of the first president of Bowdoin College. By 1734, according to church records, there were 700 who attended the Lord's table for the sacrament. The culture of flax and potatoes was at once introduced, and the home manufacture of linen became an important factor in the growth and prosperity of the community. A record of the New Hampshire Council referred to the Londonderry pioneers as "sundry familys of Credit and reputation . . . most of them being farmers and disposed either to buy or rent lands . . . ." [25] Life in the new settlement seemed to be distinguished by all the rough amusements and contentiousness so typical of the frontier. In Rockingham, Hillsboro, and Merrimack Counties, at least 10 settlements were offshoots of the Londonderry community. Bedford, New Hampshire, was largely Scotch-Irish in colonial days, and the colony also had its Dublin. The McClellands, Campbells, McDonalds, McGregors, McNeils, Magills, and Fergusons were among the prominent families of this American Londonderry.[26]

The real Mecca for the Scotch-Irish in America, however, was Pennsylanvia, owing to its attractive climate and its liberal laws. By 1750, the Scotch-Irish element here constituted approximately one fourth of the total population of the colony; by the time of the Revolution, Benjamin Franklin estimated it at 350,000, or one third of the total. Forced by their own poverty to seek the area of free lands, and pushed along by the Quaker proprietary government, which wanted to get rid of a new, turbulent element by sending it out to the frontier, the Scotch-Irish of Pennsylvania became the typical western "Squatters," the frontier guard of the colony, and what the late Professor Turner aptly described as "the cutting-edge of the frontier."

The wave of Scotch-Irish immigration proceeded up the Delaware to Bucks County, and up the Susquehanna, following the streams and creeks, where the frontiersmen set up their cabins, their mills, and their Presbyterian churches. The Susquehanna and Cumberland Valleys became the strongholds of Scotch-Irish influence in Pennsylvania. Chester, Lancaster, and Dauphin Counties had a

[24] See *ibid.*, pp. 34-38.
[25] *Provincial and Town Papers of New Hampshire*, Vol. II, p. 718.
[26] See Thomas D'Arcy McGee: *A History of Irish Settlers in North America* (Boston, 1852).

large representation of Scotch-Irish; and such towns as Chambersburg, Gettysburg, Carlisle, and York still contain large numbers of the descendants of these early pioneers. Proceeding northwest of the Susquehanna River to its junction with the Cumberland Valley, the tide of Scotch-Irish immigration then flowed southwestward, usually around the Quaker settlements and into the back country of the colonies to the south, down the Shenandoah, and through the valleys lying between the Allegheny and the Blue Ridge Mountains, this area forming a natural trough for the spread of settlement into the southwest. Lord Adam Gordon described Winchester, Virginia, a typical settlement in the valley, as "inhabited by a spurious race of mortals known by the appelation of Scotch-Irish." The Scotch-Irish were the less permanent settlers, who frequently sold out their little clearings to the second wave of immigrants. Secretary Logan of Pennsylvania wrote in 1729 that "it looks as if Ireland is to send all her inhabitants hither," and contended that any five Scotch-Irish families make more trouble than fifty of any other nationality.[27] It is obvious that most of the trouble arose from the fact that the newcomers squatted on the proprietor's lands, for Logan went on to complain that both the Scotch-Irish and the Germans "frequently sit down on any spot of vacant land they can find, without asking question . . . ."

By 1730, Pennsylvania had its Derry, Donegal, Tyrone, and Coleraine townships. There was a Toboyne in Perry County, and a Fermanagh township in Juanita County, as well as an Ulster and a Chester County. By 1767, the Scotch-Irish frontier had reached the present Uniontown, Pennsylvania, and by the end of the century it had extended to the westernmost limits of the state.[28] Many frontiersmen in Pennsylvania were known as "Donegallians."[29] Pittsburgh became the most Scotch-Irish city in America, with its strict observance of the Sabbath and its Calvinist blessing on material prosperity. The Scotch-Irish moved westward with each stage of the frontier, and presently Ohio had its settlements of Aberdeen, Edinburgh, and Caledonia.

[27] See J. T. Adams, *Provincial Society* (New York, 1927), p. 187.
[28] For other Pennsylvania settlements, see *Proceedings of the Eighth Congress of Scotch-Irish* (Scotch-Irish Society, 1896), pp. 253-289.
[29] See John Walker Dinsmore: *The Scotch-Irish in America* (Chicago, 1906). Certain provincialisms in the speech of western Pennsylvania may be due to the Scotch-Irish, such as *lift* for *collect*, with reference to the church collection; *dousie* or *poorly* for *slightly ill;* and so on.

New Jersey had an important Scotch-Irish element in the eighteenth century; these people "settled in the back parts of the colony" [30] and were "presbyterians by education." Many were indentured servants, and there are references in the New Jersey newspapers to runaway servants "born in Ireland" who "speak with a brogue," [31] as well as to two persons sentenced to death for horse stealing, who were "natives of Ireland." Whether they were Irish Catholics or Protestants, the record, as usual, does not reveal. New York, too, had its Scotch-Irish settlements, especially in Washington County and Cherry Valley. In Virginia, largely because of the heavy Scotch-Irish influx, the Assembly, in 1738, created two new counties in the valley, Frederick and Augusta. The first county lieutenant (1745) of Augusta County was James Patton, a Scotch-Irishman.[32] In 1732, South Carolina granted twenty square miles to Ulster colonists, and four years later Scotch-Irish settled in Duplin County, North Carolina. There was also a colony of Scotch-Irish in South Carolina on the Santee tract, in Williamsburg township.

Mention should be made of several settlements by Scotch Highlanders and Irish Quakers. Sir William Johnson, famous Indian agent, settled a group of 400 Scotch Highlanders on his Crown grant of 100,000 acres along the Mohawk, near present-day Gloversville, New York. The settlement was somewhat on the order of a feudal estate. Many of this group became Tories in the Revolution and moved to Upper Canada. Shiploads of Highlanders came to the Carolinas after the suppression of the Jacobin rebellions of 1715 and 1745. In North Carolina, they settled along the Cape Fear River. Their town of Campbellton was renamed Fayetteville after the Revolution. Many of these settlers were prominent in the Regulator Movement, and fought on the Loyalist side during the Revolution. In Georgia, there was a Scotch settlement at New Inverness, a district known as Darien, and a McIntosh County.[33] Pennsylvania welcomed the emigration of Irish Quakers from Dublin. Actually, these people were the descendants of Englishmen

[30] See *New Jersey Archives*, Vol. XXVII, pp. 547-549.
[31] *Ibid.*, Vol. XI, p. 185; and Vol. XXV, p. 237.
[32] See Lyman Chalkley: *Chronicles of the Scotch-Irish Settlement in Virginia Extracted from the Original Court Records of Augusta County, 1745-1800*, 3 vols. (Rosslyn, Virginia, 1912). For interesting contracts for indentured servants, see Vol. I, pp. 80, 192 and 203.
[33] See J. P. MacLean: *A Historical Account of the Settlement of Scotch Highlanders in America Prior to the Peace of 1783* (Cleveland, Ohio, 1900).

who had come to Ireland in Cromwell's time, and they protested strongly that they were not Irish.[34]

The Scotch-Irishman was the typical frontiersman in early America. He was bold, courageous, democratic to a point of lawlessness, highly individualistic, querulous, a "squatter," an inveterate hater of Indians, and a chronic opponent and critic of the established order. The Scotch-Irish came from the Scottish border, where raids, feuds, and petty warfare had been the rule for centuries. In Ireland, they had found little peace, because here again they were expected to constitute a new cordon of Protestant influence and serve as border guard against the Irish. As Arthur Young had put it: "Men who emigrate are, from the nature of the circumstance, the most active, hardy, daring, bold, and resolute spirits, and probably the most mischievous." [35] In the American colonies, the Scotch-Irishman was the frontiersman *par excellence*, "the long-limbed pioneer with the long knife, the long gun, and the long memory." He carried the long rifle to the American frontier. He was pugnacious and had many prejudices. He believed in fighting the good fight, and his rigid Calvinism not only made him fiercely dogmatic and exclusive in church matters, but led him to emphasize Old rather than New Testament ethics.[36] He "squatted" on land whenever he found it available, and thus came into conflict not only with the proprietors but with the Indian owners as well. As far as the latter were concerned, the Scotch-Irish frontiersman followed the Scriptural injunction to smite and utterly destroy the heathen whenever the Lord delivered him into his hands.

It was generally conceded that the Scotch-Irish loved their whisky, and the vice of consuming too much of it occasionally extended upward in the social scale, even as far as the clergy.[37] The whisky barrel enlivened the house raisings on the frontier and added conviviality to an occasion which might otherwise have involved only hard work. Too much liquor was frequently consumed at weddings, wakes, and funerals, and it is well to recall that the same charges of intemperance and boisterous conduct made against the Irish immigrants in the nineteenth century were also directed

[34] See Albert Cook Myers: *Immigration of Irish Quakers Into Pennsylvania* (Swarthmore, Pennsylvania, 1902).
[35] Quoted in Ford: *op. cit.*, p. 208.
[36] See Perry: *op. cit.*, p. 47.
[37] See *Proceedings of the Eighth Congress of Scotch-Irish* (Scotch-Irish Society, 1896), pp. 336-337.

against the Scotch-Irish of an earlier day. Wedding processions followed the custom of "running for the bottle" to the bride's home, and heavy drinking and dancing followed the wedding ceremony. In Londonderry, New Hampshire, the wedding morn was always greeted by the fire of musketry, and shooting seems to have continued throughout the day, because of an irrepressible love for firearms. All amusements, especially wrestling, were likely to be rough, especially as judged by modern standards.

"Wakes" seem to have been as common among the Irish from the north of Ireland as among those from other parts of the island. They represented a mixture of seriousness, piety, and humor which seems utterly incompatible today. Prayers and Scripture readings were followed by a generous passing of the whisky bottle, "so that, before the dawn, the joke and the laugh, if not scenes more boisterous, would break in upon the slumbers of the dead." [38] The necessity of distributing food and ardent spirits both before and after funerals often became a heavy financial burden on the family of the bereaved.[39]

The semiannual fairs held among the Scotch-Irish settlements for a century always centered around the town tavern, with results that need no elucidation. In 1798, the town meeting of Londonderry voted to restrict the sale of liquor at fairs, because they had become something of a public nuisance.[40] It is apparent, from these and other incidents, that the life of the Scotch-Irish pioneer was in many respects no more attractive, composed, or dignified than that of other immigrant groups. Charles Lee once wrote to James Monroe denouncing the "Mac-ocracy" that was springing up in America, by which he meant "a banditti of low Scotch-Irish whose names usually begin with Mac— and who are either the sons of imported servants, or themselves imported servants," and now "Lords Paramount." [41] In such remarks, there must have been at least a measure of the innate hatred of the conservative for the leveling democracy of the Scotch-Irish frontiersman. Arthur Lee, writing in the same vein, described the inhabitants of Pittsburgh in 1784 as "Scots and Irish, who live in paltry log houses and are as dirty as in the north of Ireland, or even Scotland." [42] In the Valley of

[38] E. L. Parker's *History of Londonderry*, quoted in Ford: *op. cit.*, p. 242.
[39] See Perry: *op. cit.*, p. 45.
[40] See *ibid.*, p. 43.
[41] *New York Historical Society Publications* (1873), p. 431.
[42] Quoted in Burton J. Hendrick: *The Lees of Virginia* (Boston, 1935), p. 349.

Virginia, the Scotch-Irish, and to a lesser degree the Germans who followed them, arrested the westward expansion of the tide-water aristocracy and its institutions, and developed a new society entirely out of sympathy with the more conservative and older East.[43] A tombstone over the grave of a Scotch-Irish pioneer in the Shenandoah Valley presents a perfect epitome of the history of many a Scotch-Irish group:

> Here lies the remains of John Lewis, who slew the Irish lord, settled in Augusta County, located the town of Staunton, and furnished five sons to fight the battles of the American Revolution.[44]

In Pennsylvania, the frontier spirit of the Scotch-Irish element came into sharp conflict with the Quaker aristocracy who controlled the government of the colony. The Quakers were devoted to "quietism" in religion, and were followers of the "inward light"; the Scotch-Irish represented an aggressive, militant, dogmatic Presbyterianism. The Quakers were pacifists, opposed to war even with the Indians; the Scotch-Irishman, living on the exposed frontier, had a different conception of his duty toward the Indian, and believed in exterminating the heathen. The Scotch-Irish squatted on land which belonged to the proprietors, had not yet been opened to settlement, and whose occupation frequently involved trouble with the native owners. Finally, the democratic frontiersman resented the political monopoly of the eastern counties in the government of Pennsylvania. Again and again, petitions from Cumberland County for help and munitions to deal with the Indian menace were rejected by the Quaker government, which opposed the creation and expense of an effective frontier militia. The Scotch-Irish, and others on the frontier, complained bitterly that, while the Quakers used "soft words" and paid tribute to the Indians in the form of presents, "the Dutch and Irish are murder'd without Pity." [45]

For a generation after 1755, the frontier of Pennsylvania was in a state of almost continual excitement over the Indians. The best-known incident in a long series of controversies between the Scotch-Irish frontiersman and the Quaker government is known as the episode of the "Paxton Boys." After the French and Indian War,

[43] See Wesley M. Gewehr: *The Great Awakening in Virginia, 1740-1790* (Durham, North Carolina, 1930), p. 27.
[44] Quoted in J. T. Adams: *The Epic of America* (Boston, 1931), p. 78.
[45] See Ford: *op. cit.*, p. 323.

there had been acute border disturbances. In their rage against all Indians, and in some cases urged on by their pastors, Scotch-Irish frontiersmen attacked even the Christianized Indians near Bethlehem and Lancaster, and finally began a march on Philadelphia itself. The border was aflame with talk of insurrection, and the Quaker proprietary government was denounced at a number of meetings. An army, variously estimated at between 500 and 1,500, started the march for Philadelphia, threatening to kill the Moravian Indians sheltered there and to sack the town. The details of this uprising need not be described here. Suffice it to say that Philadelphia was thoroughly alarmed, and Benjamin Franklin was one of the commissioners sent out to negotiate with the discontented. They demanded the removal of the Indians from the colony, a return of prisoners held by the Indians, a reapportionment of representation in the Assembly for the benefit of the frontier counties, and a bounty on Indian scalps. In the end, the grandson of William Penn, in his proclamation as governor, granted only the last of these demands, including "for the scalp of a female Indian fifty pieces of eight." [46]

Needless to add the incident just described attained exceptional proportions. But the fact remains that the Scotch-Irish had many legitimate grievances, and also that they were the objects of much unfavorable criticism because of their turbulent, lawless spirit. The struggle between the frontier and the eastern counties of Pennsylvania continued well past the eighteenth century. It will be recalled that, during Washington's administration, the Scotch-Irish of Fayette and Westmoreland Counties played a leading role in the Whiskey Insurrection. Perhaps some of the same spirit has carried over into some of the feuds in the Kentucky and Tennessee mountains—a retarded frontier which harbors so many of the descendants of the Scotch-Irish pioneers, and where their customs and their folklore are still preserved. On the other hand, it must never be forgotten that these pioneers had legitimate reasons to protest against the conditions under which they were forced to live. They came late; because they were poor they were forced to go where land was cheap or free; and for years they had no voice in the politics of the colony. In the long struggle for recognition and greater democracy,

[46] For the Paxton Boys' Insurrection, see Ford: *op. cit.*, pp. 307-324 and Appendix D; also Sidney G. Fisher: "The Quaker Colonies," in *Chronicles of America* (Yale University Press, New Haven, Connecticut), Vol. VIII.

for religious and civil liberty, the disposition to become opponents of the established order—a trait brought from the old home across the seas—became greatly accentuated.

That the Scotch-Irish played a vigorous part in the American Revolution is well established, and in a colony like Pennsylvania, where the pacifist sentiments of Quakers and German sectarians were strong, their prompt alignment with the patriot cause was perhaps of decisive importance. Many of the Scotch-Irish entered the American Revolution with a deep, inherited hatred of England. Those who became Tories, especially in the Southern colonies, did so usually because of peculiar local conditions.

C. A. Hanna, in his notable two volumes on the Scotch-Irish, has made a striking compilation of Scotch-Irish services to the cause of American independence, especially in Pennsylvania, and thereby has brought upon himself the criticism of Irish writers like O'Brien and others who object to the use of the term "Scotch-Irish." It is true, nevertheless, that the Scotch-Irish helped to counteract the loyalist and pacifist sentiments of Quakers, Germans, and Episcopalians. Joseph Galloway blamed the Presbyterians primarily for the war. Curwen wrote: "Quakers and Dutchmen had too great regard for ease and property to sacrifice either on the altar of an unknown goddess of rather doubtful divinity." [47] The Bishop of Derry attributed a large part of the revolutionary sentiment to the migration from Ireland of "over 30,000 fanatical and hungry republicans." [48] General Henry Lee suggested that the line of Pennsylvania "might as well be called 'the line of Ireland.' " [49] John Stark, a native of Londonderry, New Hampshire, with volunteers from Derry, played an important role at the Battle of Bennington (1777), and it will be remembered that Patrick Henry spoke for the western counties of Virginia, in which the Scotch-Irish influence was paramount. Scotch-Irish Presbyterians had no monopoly on patriotism, but their synods quite early took a decisive stand on the merits of a revolution against English rule. A surprisingly large percentage of the leaders in the American Revolution were Presbyterians, and certainly the theory of Presbyterian republicanism, as

[47] *Journal and Letters of the Late Samuel Curwen* (London, 1842), quoted in C. H. Van Tyne: *The Loyalists in the American Revolution* (New York, 1902), p. 102.

[48] Quoted in D. S. Muzzey: *The United States of America* (Boston, 1922), Vol. I, p. 79. For other quotations, see Hanna: *op. cit.;* and O'Brien: *A Hidden Phase of American History*, Ch. VI.

[49] O'Brien: *A Hidden Phase of American History*, p. 176.

a matter of church polity, could easily be reconciled with the demands of the more radical democrats of 1776. The influence of Princeton was important also. John Adams called President Witherspoon the "animated Son of Liberty." [50] He was the only clergyman to sign the Declaration of Independence.

Among the permanent contributions of the Scotch-Irish to America, their introduction of Presbyterianism into the colonies perhaps deserves first consideration. By 1776, 500 Scotch-Irish communities were scattered throughout the colonies, of which nearly 70 were in New England, from 40 to 50 in New York, from 50 to 60 in New Jersey, over 130 in Pennsylvania and Delaware, over 100 in Virginia, Maryland, and Tennessee, 50 in North Carolina, and about 70 in South Carolina and Georgia. A zone of Scotch-Irish Presbyterian churches extended from the New England frontier to Georgia, for the advance of the Scotch-Irish pioneers was everywhere marked by the establishment of small Presbyterian churches. Many of these, especially in the Delaware and Susquehanna Valleys, are now over a century old. The Scotch-Irish Presbyterian preachers, according to Theodore Roosevelt, in his *Winning of the West,* "followed close behind the first settlers, and shared their rifles in hand, and fought the Indians valorously . . . . They exhorted no less earnestly in the bare meeting-house on Sunday, because their hands were roughened with guiding the plow and wielding the axe on week-days; for they did not believe that being called to preach the word of God absolved them from earning their living by the sweat of their brows." [51] The Presbyterian Church became a powerful force on the frontier, and played such a significant role in the life of frontier communities that, on numerous occasions, the civil authorities appealed to Presbyterian pastors to help them maintain law and order.[52]

Scotch Presbyterianism was the product of strong historical and theological forces. Because of the piety and enthusiasm of its adherents, it not only became a militant religion but also led occasionally to fanatical outbursts, such as marked the Great Revival of 1800 in eastern Kentucky. It made its greatest appeal to the Scotch-Irish, and was sponsored by James McGready and John McGee. Like the Puritans of New England, the Scotch-Irish had a

[50] Edward F. Humphrey: *Nationalism and Religion in America, 1774-1789* (Boston, 1924), pp. 66-104.
[51] Quoted in W. W. Sweet: *The Presbyterians, 1783-1840* (New York, 1936).
[52] See Klett: *op. cit.,* p. 68.

stern, unbending creed. It led them into formalism and a rigid insistence upon forms and outward observances.[53] The pulpit oratory of the Scotch-Irish preachers was fiery, hortatory, and extremely personal.[54] Hell opened before the preaching of these sturdy divines, and sinners saw themselves tumbling into its consuming flames. The high religious voltage of the Presbyterians was nowhere better exemplified than in that great evangelical quickening which swept the middle colonies in the 1740's known as "The Great Awakening." It became a powerful ferment in colonial society, gave a new impact to various movements for social betterment, and led to the founding of a number of colleges for the better training of the ministry. Even Benjamin Franklin could not entirely resist the pleadings of the revivalists and, on at least one occasion, emptied the contents of his pockets into the collection plate.[55]

By 1700, there were about a dozen Presbyterian churches in the colonies. The first Presbyterian Church of Philadelphia was organized in 1698, and, in 1706, the first American presbytery was organized in that city, largely through the efforts of Francis Makemie. The first American synod met in 1717, and the first General Assembly of the Presbyterian Church convened in Philadelphia in 1789. In New England, the conflict with the Congregationalists was so fierce that the only Presbyterian center to really thrive was Londonderry. Ford has called the Philadelphia presbytery the real "tap root" for American Presbyterianism. Because church organization was democratic and the separation of Church and State rigidly adhered to, Presbyterianism spread rapidly westward, battling primarily with the Baptists and Methodists for the religious conquest of the New West. Among the valiant champions of early Presbyterianism in New England, the Reverends William Homes and Thomas Craighead deserve to be remembered. Though born in Massachusetts, Jonathan Dickinson was probably the most distinguished Presbyterian leader in colonial New York, while among the pioneer preachers of western Pennsylvania, Joseph Smith, Mathew Henderson, John McMillan, and Thaddeus Dodd were outstanding.[56]

In one respect, the Presbyterian ministers of colonial days were

---

[53] See J. T. Adams: *Provincial Society*, p. 281.
[54] See Ford: *op. cit.*, Chs. XI-XVI.
[55] See Charles H. Maxson: *The Great Awakening in the Middle Colonies* (Chicago, 1920).
[56] See Dinsmore: *op. cit.*

unique. Almost all had a reputation for vivid pulpit oratory and for an erudition which set them apart from their fellows of other faiths. The schoolhouse and the kirk went together wherever the Scotch-Irish frontier moved. The extraordinary zeal of this group for education is revealed in its emphasis on a learned ministry, in its founding of schools and colleges, and in its printing of catechisms and other books. Catechizing was a feature of Presbyterianism. It spread knowledge of religious principles and kept believers orthodox. The *Shorter Catechism* of 1744 proclaimed: "It is found by Experience, that there is more Knowledge diffused among the Ignorant and younger Sort by one Hour's Catechising, than by many Hours of Preaching." [57] At intervals, young and old gathered in barns or log homes to study the catechism, so that "the seed sown in the sanctuary was harrowed in by the catechizing." [58] Presbyterians emphasized a theology intended to combine head and heart. The founders of American Presbyterianism were men of good training and "sound learning," and candidates for the ministry had to pass rigid trials of their ability. In one instance, for example, when a candidate was being examined for religious work among the Germans, the examining committee found that "tho he appeared well skilled in The Learned Languages yet inasmuch as they found him altogether ignorant in College Learning, and but poorly read in Divinity, his ordination to the ministry must at present be deferred." [59]

Ministers gathered their sons and other youths about them to instruct them in theology, and out of such efforts grew the Presbyterian academies of colonial Pennsylvania. William Tennent established his "Log College" at Little Neshaminy Creek, Pennsylvania, about 25 miles from Philadelphia, and trained his four sons and a number of distinguished American pastors here. To the vivid imagination of George Whitefield, this 20-foot square log house resembled the schools of the old prophets. Tennent's son, Gilbert, became an itinerant evangelist. Samuel Blair, who studied at the "Log College," established a similar school at Flagg's Manor, in Chester County, Pennsylvania. Francis Allison directed a school at New London, which Charles Thomson and other distinguished early Americans attended. Dr. John McMillan founded Washing-

[57] Quoted in Klett: *op. cit.*, p. 198.
[58] Quoted in *ibid.*, p. 199.
[59] Quoted in *ibid.*, p. 201.

ton Academy, one of the predecessors of Washington and Jefferson College. Presbyterians have always been prominent as members of the board of trustees of this institution and of the University of Pittsburgh.[60] Samuel Finley's school at Nottingham, Pennsylvania, had Benjamin Rush as one of its graduates. David Caldwell, a Scotch-Irish minister, started a classical school in 1767 near Greensboro, North Carolina, and ambitiously called it "the Eton of the South." Other institutions in which the Scotch-Irish Presbyterians have been influential are Allegheny College, Waynesburg College, Westminster College, and Geneva College—all in Pennsylvania.[61] Various academies were organized by ministers on their way westward, such as Greensville College and Blount College in Tennessee, Transylvania Seminary and Centre College in Kentucky, and Wooster College in Ohio. The educational history of Kentucky and Tennessee really begins with the schools conducted by Presbyterian ministers. Throughout, the main emphasis was on finding "pious youth of promising genius" who "might be serviceable in preaching the gospel." Latin and Greek were basic to the curriculum. Subscriptions to these wilderness academies were often paid in wheat, linen, whisky, or other products of the community. Scotch-Irish schoolmasters were numerous in the colonies, especially in Pennsylvania.[62] A company chartered in 1759 for the relief of ministers' widows and children was probably the first insurance company in the United States.[63]

Princeton, the College of New Jersey, was, of course, Scotch-Irish Presbyterianism's most significant contribution to higher education in colonial America. When the synods of New York and Philadelphia united in 1758, the College of New Jersey became their authorized training school. It attracted students from almost every colony, and was far more than a college for New Jersey, as its original name implied. Started in 1746, its first president was Jonathan Dickinson and its second the Reverend Aaron Burr. Dr. John Witherspoon, who came over from Scotland in 1768 to direct the destinies of the little college, gave Princeton its national reputation and became a national figure in American politics during the Rev-

[60] See Robert Garland: "The Scotch-Irish in Western Pennsylvania," in Western Pennsylvania Historical Magazine (April, 1923), Vol. VI, No. 2, pp. 65-105.
[61] See Mary Hiner: The Scotch-Irish and Academies in the Transallegheny Frontier (M. A. Thesis at the University of West Virginia, 1933).
[62] See also Ohio State Journal, August 10 and September 11, 1889.
[63] See Klett: op. cit., p. 186.

olutionary era. Analyzing the career of the 230 students graduated from Princeton between 1766 and 1773, Hanna has found among them 12 members of the Continental Congress, 24 members of the United States Congress, 3 Justices of the Supreme Court, 5 men who held Cabinet positions or their equivalent, 1 Vice-President, and 1 President. Nine members of the Constitutional Convention of 1787 were Princeton men, the highest number from any college. Thirty-six sat in state constitutional conventions. The list is long and notable, and reflects the national scope of Princeton's influence at a time when Yale and Harvard were purely provincial institutions.

One need not accept the extravagant conclusions of John Fiske, Henry Cabot Lodge,[64] Theodore Roosevelt, in his *Winning of the West,* or even the late Professor Ford as to the importance of the Scotch-Irish group in the development of the United States. But the conclusion is inescapable that this element has made a notable and lasting contribution, and that it represents one of the most desirable immigrant groups.

The Scotch and the Scotch-Irish have for generations maintained their various societies and organizations in the United States. In 1859, for example, the St. Andrews Society of Charleston, South Carolina, celebrated its 129th anniversay.[65] New York, in the 1850's, had its Highland Guards, Scottish Guards, and Caledonian Fusileers, typical of the military companies to be found among other immigrant groups during the period.[66] In many places Caledonian clubs regularly celebrated St. Andrews Day.[67] Scottish athletic clubs staged annual games and exhibitions.[68] A big Scottish festival, with bagpipes, reels, kilts, and quoits, was held in New York in 1861 for the benefit of the 79th regiment, "the Highland Regiment" that went off to the Civil War with uniforms patterned after those of the Black Watch.[69] The men proved to be good fighters, but they were intractable and undisciplined, and 37 of them were arrested for mutiny and desertion.[70]

Scottish-American Societies of note were the Order of Scottish

[64] See Henry Cabot Lodge: "The Distribution of Ability in the United States," in *Century Magazine,* 1891, Vol. XXXXII, pp. 687-694.

[65] See *The Charleston Mercury,* December 1, 1859.

[66] *The New York Tribune,* June 6 and 10, 1850.

[67] See *The Cincinnati Commercial,* December 1, 1881; and *The Albany Argus,* December 10, 1849.

[68] See *The New York Times,* October 17 and August 21, 1877.

[69] See *The New York Tribune,* August 16, 1861.

[70] *Ibid.,* August 19 and 20, 1861. Also Fred A. Shannon: *The Organization and Administration of the Union Army* (Cleveland, 1928), Vol. I, pp. 180-181.

[63]

Clans, the Order of the Sons of Scotland, Robert Burns clubs, curling clubs, and others with more or less charitable and philanthropic objectives, all holding regular meetings and celebrations intended to perpetuate and cultivate Scotch games, literature, poetry, or music.[71]   In Boston, an Irish Protestant Mutual Relief Society held regular meetings, and the local Catholic paper commented: "It is singular how they retain all the old bitterness against Catholicity.   They were always a problem to us." [72]   Scotch-Irish congresses, arranged by the Scotch-Irish Society of America, were held for a number of years, and have resulted in a vigorous effort to promote a feeling of group solidarity among the descendants of Scotch and Scotch-Irish American pioneers.   Their publications ceased, however, after 10 volumes had been issued.   The Pennsylvania Scotch-Irish Society remains active.   Its published proceedings begin in 1890.[73]

The number of distinguished Americans who trace their descent from this immigrant stock is remarkably large, even after all necessary allowances have been made for the great intermixture of many strains which has occurred in a nation so heterogeneous as the United States.   William Maclure is often referred to as the "father of American geology."   Alexander Wilson was a distinguished ornithologist.   Alexander Graham Bell, James Laurie, and James Pugh Kirkwood have distinguished themselves as engineers and inventors.[74]   Peter Campbell, born in Carnock, Scotland, became the "dean of the linoleum industry," and was as well known in his field as was Andrew Carnegie in the iron and steel business.   Robert Clarke, who had been brought to Cincinnati by his parents in 1841, became a pioneer in American printing and publishing.   James Gordon Bennett was a pioneer in journalism.   Robert Dollar developed his famous steamship line.[75]   Hundreds of Scotch and Scotch-Irish mechanics, whose names have been forgotten, have made notable contributions to the development of American industry, and Scotch florists and botanists are still a familiar sight in parks, botanical gardens, and floral establishments.

[71] See Peter Ross: *The Scot in America* (New York, 1896), pp. 411-441.
[72] *The Boston Pilot*, April 29, 1854.
[73] See Frederick D. Stone: "First Congress of the Scotch-Irish in America," in *Pennsylvania Magazine of History and Biography*, Vol. XIV, pp. 68-71. The Census of 1930 lists 354,323 foreign-born Scotchmen in the United States.
[74] Ross: *op. cit.*, pp. 214-219.
[75] For other names, see *Immigrant Contributions to American Life: Scotland*, Pt. II (W. P. A. Project, Los Angeles, 1937).

The Scotch-Irishman's tenacity, firmness, and determination, his courage and his self-reliance, have helped him to make a notable record in political leadership, for which the group as a whole seems to have a remarkable capacity. A list of distinguished Scotch-Irish leaders would begin with James Wilson and John Witherspoon and include such men as Henry Knox, James Monroe, Andrew Jackson, James K. Polk, James Buchanan, William McKinley, and Woodrow Wilson, as well as many celebrities only slightly less important, such as Thomas H. Benton, John C. Calhoun, Marc Hanna, and Horace Greeley. A large number of Scotch-Irish have attained distinction in the ministry, on the bench, and in journalism.

Despite the remarkable number of famous names which this group has produced, nevertheless, there is no more occasion for it than for any other group to develop a theory of racial superiority. Even the Ulsterman or the Scotsman from the Lowlands of Scotland already represented a considerable admixture of other blood strains, and in America the processes of racial intermixture went on apace. The Scotch-Irish in America have had vigorous champions. They have seen to it that their contributions to the United States have not been forgotten. As Professor Paxson pointed out in a recent review:

> The Scotch-Irishman has shown as much ability to survive in the world of historiography as he showed in the eighteenth century while pushing the farmer's frontier up the interior valleys, through the gaps to the West, and down the river courses toward the Mississippi.[76]

[76] Frederick L. Paxson, in *The American Historical Review*, Vol. XLII, p. 792.

6

The Colonial Germans

ALTHOUGH THERE WERE individual German settlers and isolated German settlements in America before the eighteenth century, there was no sizable and important wave of German immigration until the beginning of that century, when Germany was seething with distress and discontent, and conditions were such as to make the perils of emigration preferable to remaining at home.

At the close of the Thirty Years' War, many of the German states were on the verge of political, social, and economic collapse. Devastation, misery, and want were the natural consequences of prolonged warfare. The economic bankruptcy following in the wake of war was aggravated by crop failures and famine, especially in the Rhine Valley. Germany was still only a geographical expression; it remained divided and disunited among scores of petty autocracies and principalities. The tyranny of autocratic rulers, their religious intolerance, and the burdens of taxation which they imposed upon their unhappy subjects were often in inverse proportion to the extent of their domains.

In an age of political, social, and economic disturbance and suffering, the mind of man has often turned to religion for comfort and salvation, and so in Germany, during and after the Thirty Years' War, there was a notable rise in pietism and mysticism. Scores of sects, as well as some who remained true to the established Reformed or Lutheran Churches, began to experiment with new ways of salvation, which often involved, not only changes in ritual and religious beliefs, but also a desire for an opportunity to experiment in some new environment with a new social and economic order. The German mind was at the height of its emotional unrestraint, and to church people and sectarians, America beckoned as the promised land, where their dreams might be realized. Needless to add, religious experimentation of this kind frequently brought on waves of intolerance and persecution, and controversies with the state authorities over military service or over the education of the young. Again, immigration to the New World seemed to offer the most immediate relief.

To these factors must be added the propaganda of profit-seeking ship companies who sought cargo for the immigrant trade, and the seductive techniques of advertising agents who came into the German Palatinate and other parts of western and southern Germany to advance the interests of promoters and speculators like William Penn and of others of lesser integrity. Pamphlets issued in the German language were distributed by the hundreds. They described New World conditions that never existed. Many of these prospectuses and many of the letters from immigrants circulated in the peasant villages of the Rhineland were misleading and exaggerated accounts, or even forgeries. "Newlanders" and "soul snatchers," appearing in fine clothes and costly jewelry, told fabulous tales of the new land, and vouched for the truth of their stories from their own experience and observations. Thousands, too poor to finance the trip to America, came as "redemptioners," sold themselves into service for a number of years to pay their passage, and suffered all the hardships generally connected with the colonial immigrant traffic, which has already been described in an earlier chapter.[1]

The only major German colonization experiment in colonial New England was a settlement at Waldoboro, Maine, but it was of such minor importance that it need not be considered here.[2] The "Palatine emigration" to New York, on the other hand, was a movement of major significance. Indeed, the name "Palatine" became so familiar in colonial America that it was often indiscriminately applied to any body of German Protestant immigrants. In this case, the immigrants actually came from the Palatine area, a region on both sides of the Rhine and its tributaries, the Neckar and the Main.

As in many instances of German immigration in colonial times, religious causes were important in this migration to America, but economic factors provided the dominant motive for leaving the old fatherland for the new. The devastation of war, heavy taxes, the

[1] See A. B. Faust: *The German Element in the United States* (New York, 1909), Vol. I, pp. 63-68 and 70-71; also Oscar Kuhns: *German and Swiss Settlements in Pennsylvania* (New York, 1901), pp. 27 and 79.
[2] See Faust: *op. cit.*, Vol. I, p. 269 *et seq.;* and H. L. Osgood, *The American Colonies in the Seventeenth Century,* (New York, 1904-1907), Vol. II, pp. 510-511.

desire for better land, and a succession of hard winters combined with religious quarrels to start the trek to America. To these causes must be added the coöperation of the British government, which, in Queen Anne's time, promoted the settlement of German immigrants in New York as a kind of government redemptioner scheme to produce naval stores for the British Navy. The English government paid the expenses of transportation and settlement, with the result that the Palatine migration to New York turned out to be the largest single immigration to America in the colonial period. The settlers were to be virtually indentured servants of the British government, and were to remain in that status until the profits from naval stores had paid all the expenses of their transportation.

In 1708, Pastor Joshua Kocherthal led the first contingent down the Rhine to Holland. By 1709, German Palatines were arriving in Rotterdam at the rate of 1,000 a week. The journey took anywhere from a month to 6 weeks, and could never have been negotiated save for the aid received from kindly people along the way. They were housed in shacks and then shipped to England, where the government soon discovered that it was getting more than it had bargained for and tried desperately to stop the flow of emigration from the upper Rhine country. About 13,500 reached England. Of these, 2,257 Roman Catholics were turned back. London's facilities for housing the "poor German Protestants" were strained to the utmost. The immigrants were sheltered in taverns and tents, churches raised collections for them, and the British workers complained because of the expense to the government and because the newcomers were depressing their scale of wages. Riots broke out and disease ravaged the immigrant tent colonies. Some died; some went to Ireland. Others went to Virginia to work as miners in Governor Spotswood's venture to develop the iron resources of that colony; still others went to North and South Carolina.

It took nearly 6 months to transport the immigrants to America. The ships were overcrowded, the food was poor, and the supply of fresh water was quickly exhausted. Typhus fever became synonymous with "Palatine fever." The experience of the Palatines was typical of that of many colonial immigrants. Of 2,814 who started for America in 1710, 446 died on the way. Children became orphans on the voyage and were apprenticed into service. John Peter

Zenger, destined to become famous in the battle for freedom of the press in America, was one of these.

By 1711, seven villages had been established in New York on the Robert Livingston manor, and the British government had spent over £100,000 on the settlement project. It is not necessary to discuss in detail the long controversy between the German immigrants in New York and their landlord or Governor Hunter. Presently, however, some 50 families moved to the Schoharie Valley. Others followed, and, by 1713, villages had sprung up in this new region. One of them, later renamed Herkimer, remains one of the best-known of the German settlements in a region which for years was described as the "German Flats," and was known far and wide as excellent farming country. Other groups went from New York to Pennsylvania as indentured servants. Pennsylvania soon became the mecca for German immigrants, as it was for the Scotch-Irish group; but this was due, not so much to the discouraging effect of the misfortunes of the Germans in New York, as to the superior attractiveness and more vigorous advertising campaign conducted by the Pennsylvania colony.

By 1750, the Germans in New York occupied a strip some 12 miles long along the left bank of the Mohawk. The soil was excellent; some 500 houses had been built, mostly of stone; and the region prospered in spite of Indian raids, to which there are frequent references in the *Papers of Sir William Johnson*. Modern New York towns in this region—such as Mannheim, Oppenheim, Herkimer, and others—are evidences of the German influence in this "German Flats" section.[3] By 1784, a *Deutsche Gesellschaft* was organized in New York City to help German immigrants on their arrival in America. German revolutionary officers like Heinrich Emmanuel Lutterloh and General von Steuben served as its presidents, and years later, John Jacob Astor, himself a German immigrant from Baden, willed $20,000 to the society.[4]

In 1683, under the leadership of Francis Daniel Pastorius, the good ship *Concord*, "the Mayflower of the German immigration,"

[3] For the Palatine migration, I have followed the most recent account, which supersedes all others, in W. A. Knittle: *Early Eighteenth Century Palatine Emigration* (Philadelphia, 1937). See also Osgood: *op. cit.*, Vol. II, p. 495; and Faust: *op. cit.*, Vol. I, Ch. IV.

[4] Gustav Koerner: *Das deutsche Element in den Vereinigten Staaten von Nordamerika, 1818-1848* (Cincinnati, 1880), p. 96; and Kenneth W. Porter: *John Jacob Astor, Business Man* (Cambridge, Massachusetts, 1931), Vol. II, pp. 1091-1094.

brought 13 German families to Philadelphia. Germantown, the first permanent settlement of German immigrants in the United States, was established, and the stream of German immigration began to run into Pennsylvania with such force and volume that its influence is still apparent in the life of that state. Pastorius himself was certainly one of the most learned men in the America of his day, "not forgetting Cotton Mather." He had traveled in five countries, had been a student at five German universities, and had some knowledge of eight different languages.[5] His followers came from Crefeld, near Holland. Attracted by the advertising matter circulated by Penn in the Netherlands and in the Rhine Valley, Pastorius came as agent for a Frankfurt land company which had purchased 25,000 acres for speculative purposes. The settlers immediately set to work to clear the forest. Their town was incorporated in 1689, with Pastorius as its first burgomaster, and by 1701 it was ready to hold its first annual fair (*Jahrmarkt*).[6]

Germantown became the center for the distribution of the German immigrants into the neighboring counties of southeastern Pennsylvania. After the areas in southern and eastern Pennsylvania, particularly along the Susquehanna, had been filled in, the tide of German immigration, like that of the Scotch-Irish, overflowed down the Valley of Virginia and into the back country. German pioneers usually followed the Scotch-Irish, frequently buying up their little clearings as this restless element moved farther westward in search of more elbowroom. The Germans thus constituted a second and more permanent farming frontier. Lancaster County soon was known as "the farmers' paradise," [7] and travelers

[5] See M. D. Learned: *The Life of Francis Daniel Pastorius*, 2 vols. (Philadelphia, 1908).

[6] See Jesse L. Rosenberger: *The Pennsylvania Germans* (Chicago, 1923); Edward W. Hocker: *Germantown, 1683-1933* (Philadelphia, 1933); S. W. Pennypacker: "The Settlement of Germantown and the Causes Which Led To It," in *Pennsylvania Magazine of History and Biography*, Vol. IV, pp. 1-41; and A. D. Mellick, Jr.: "German Emigration to the American Colonies," in *Pennsylvania Magazine of History and Biography*, Vol. X, pp. 241-50 and 375-391. This publication is a storehouse of information for the Pennsylvania Germans and contains scores of articles of great value. Indispensable sources of information on the subject are the *Publications and Proceedings of the Pennsylvania German Society*, which, by 1930, had reached a total of more than 40 volumes; and the *Lancaster County Historical Society Papers*, which also total some 40 volumes. See also F. R. Diffenderfer: *The German Immigration Into Pennsylvania Through the Port of Philadelphia, 1700-1775* (Lancaster, Pennsylvania. 1900).

[7] See, for example, Nina Moore Tiffany and Francis Tiffany: *Harm Jan Huidekoper* (Cambridge, Massachusetts, 1904), p. 63. Huidekoper commented on conditions in Carlisle, Pennsylvania, in 1802.

often commented on the greater stability and prosperity of the German farming communities as compared with their more adventuresome "Irish" neighbors.

Figures for all immigrant groups in the colonial period are most unreliable but, by 1727, the German population of Pennsylvania probably reached 20,000, and by 1745 another 25,000 had settled in the colony. Benjamin Franklin, in 1766, told a committee of the House of Commons that he estimated the German immigrants at one third of the Pennsylvania population.[8] By the outbreak of the American Revolution, the proportion was still roughly the same, and the total has been variously estimated at between 110,000 and 125,000.[9] In general, the Germans settled the limestone areas of Pennsylvania, which they correctly assumed would prove to be great wheat-producing sections. Here they introduced small-scale farming and diversified products. A half-circle drawn from Easton, on the Delaware River, as center would include the most important Pennsylvania-German settlements as they extended up the Lehigh Valley into Lancaster County, across the Susquehanna, down the Cumberland Valley, and overflowed into Maryland.

The Shenandoah Valley became the main avenue for the advance of the German element into Virginia and North Carolina. By 1750, an almost continuous zone of German settlements had been established along the frontier from the head of the Mohawk, in New York, to Savannah, Georgia. Shortly after the Revolution, men and women of German stock joined the march through the mountain gaps and down the river valleys into Kentucky, Tennessee, and the New West.

The movement of Germans into Maryland did not begin until after the first quarter of the eighteenth century. Maryland then acquired an important German element in and around Baltimore, and another in the western counties, where it got the overflow from Pennsylvania as it moved through the valley and into the Southwest. Germans have been active in the life of Baltimore since its founding and incorporation as a town. Zion's German church, established in Baltimore in 1755,[10] is still thriving in the very center

[8] *German-American Annals* (New York and Philadelphia, 1897-1919), Vol. VI, p. 256.

[9] See Koerner: *op. cit.*, p. 21; and Faust: *op. cit.*

[10] See Fritz O. Evers: *Zion in Baltimore* (Baltimore, Maryland, 1930); and the Zion church program in honor of the 200th anniversary of the founding of Baltimore: *Deutsche Feier des zweihundert jaehrigen Bestehens der Stadt Baltimore* (September 15, 1929).

of Baltimore's business section. The German Society of Maryland has been in existence since 1783. Frederick was founded in 1745 by a group of German Palatines; and Hagerstown was laid out by Jonathan Hagar, a Pennsylvania German. In 1727, Germans from Pennsylvania crossed the Potomac above Harper's Ferry and founded New Mecklenburg, later renamed Shepardstown. German artisans, butchers, wagon and harness makers, tanners, and iron and coppersmiths have been important in the economic life of Maryland communities since colonial times. George A. Shryock, son of a German immigrant to Pennsylvania, was one of the first to make paper out of straw, if not actually the discoverer of this process.[11]

In Virginia, the first German settlement was made in 1714 under the auspices of Governor Spotswood, who undertook to promote the working of the mines and the smelting of iron ore at Germanna, about 10 miles northwest of present-day Fredericksburg. In spite of the governor's ardent support, the community failed by the middle of the century. Most of the Germans in the Shenandoah Valley came across the Potomac, above Harper's Ferry, from Pennsylvania and Maryland. The Valley of Virginia was untouched by the nineteenth-century German immigration, and practically all of its present German stock is descended from immigrants who came into the valley before 1800 as an overflow from Pennsylvania and because of a desire for greater economic opportunities.

In this natural avenue between North and South, a valley from 20 to 30 miles wide between two ranges of mountains, the Germans intermingled with the Scotch-Irish pioneers, though not always harmoniously; and towns like Staunton, Woodstock, Winchester, and Shepardstown still give evidence of the presence of these two streams of settlement. There are still many village names and post offices in the Valley of Virginia which testify to their German origin. The greatest German influence was exerted in the region between Winchester and Staunton. Until the middle of the nineteenth century, Pennsylvania German could be heard on the streets of these communities, and German papers from Pennsylvania had a considerable circulation in this region. The Germans of the valley established forges for iron and nail manufacturing, and developed

[11] For an account of Maryland Germans, see *Publications of the Society for the History of Germans in Maryland* (Baltimore, Maryland); J. T. Scharf: *History of Western Maryland*, 2 vols. (Philadelphia, 1882); and D. W. Nead: *The Pennsylvania-German in the Settlement of Maryland* (Lancaster, Pennsylvania, 1914).

charcoal burning as an industry. This region, with its "Pennsylvania Dutch" bake ovens, folklore, huge barns, and other characteristics of the Pennsylvania Germans, was as well known as the parent communities themselves. Many descendants of the Germans in the valley served in the Confederate regiments of Stonewall Jackson.[12]

The German settlements in the Carolinas were of less importance, although Pennsylvania German was occasionally heard in some of the back counties of North Carolina until the end of the first third of the nineteenth century. The Moravian settlement at Winston-Salem is still a point of interest because of its famous Easter customs and Easter music. The settlement of New Bern was the work of Palatine Germans and Swiss, under the leadership of a Swiss nobleman, Christopher de Graffenried.[13] Graffenried's venture had much of the get-rich-quick feature about it and, after many hardships, ended in failure, although the town of New Bern survived and, for a short period, was actually the capitol of North Carolina. About 12,000 Swiss, most of them from the German cantons of Switzerland, came to America by 1750. A Swiss colony at Purysburg, South Carolina, founded in 1732 to raise silk and cultivate vineyards, lasted to the time of the American Revolution. The first organized Lutheran church in the Carolinas was the German and Swiss Church in Orangeburg, South Carolina, established in 1735. By 1770, over 3,000 German Protestants had settled in North Carolina, mostly of Pennsylvania German stock, and Lutheran churches flourished in these German sections of the Carolinas for many years. Dr. H. M. Muhlenberg, the patriarch of American Lutheranism, made several visits of inspection to the Carolinas.[14] Saxe-Gotha, in South Carolina, was settled in 1764 by some 600 Germans, but by 1850 it had lost all evidences of its German origin, save for the

[12] See Hermann Schuricht: *History of the German Element in Virginia* (Baltimore, Maryland, 1898), Vol. I; James W. Wayland: *The German Element of the Shenandoah Valley of Virginia* (Charlottesville, Virginia, 1907) and "The Germans of the Valley," in *Virginia Magazine of History*, Vols. IX, X, XI, and XIV, *passim*.

[13] For an account of this interesting colony, see G. D. Bernheim: *History of the German Settlements and of the Lutheran Church in North and South Carolina* (Philadelphia, 1872) and *Christoph von Graffenried's Account of the Founding of New Bern* (North Carolina Historical Commission, Raleigh, North Carolina, 1920); W. L. Saunders (editor), *The Colonial Records of North Carolina*, Vol. IV, p. 18; A. B. Faust: "Swiss Emigration to the American Colonies in the Eighteenth Century," in *American Historical Review* (1916-1917), pp. 21-43; and V. H. Todd: "Baron Christoph von Graffenried's New Bern Adventures," in *University of Illinois Studies* (Urbana, Illinois, 1912).

[14] See Bernheim: *op. cit.* See also *The Colonial Records of North Carolina*, Vol. VIII, p. 630; and Osgood, *op. cit.*: Vol. II, p. 232.

popularity of its German sausage and Christmas cakes.[15]   In 1766, the German Friendly Society of Charleston was founded, with Michael Kalteisen as its first president.   It was devoted to charitable and social purposes.

Georgia had few non-English immigrants, but one group, the Salzburgers, who will be mentioned again later, founded Ebenezer in 1734, some 25 miles from Savannah.   By 1741, over 1,200 of these pious, German-Austrian Protestant exiles had settled in Georgia, and were receiving aid from German church groups in Halle and Augsburg, as well as some initial support from the British government.

A discussion of the customs and institutions of the Germans in colonial times may be centered, for practical purposes, on the Pennsylvania Germans, or the "Pennsylvania Dutch," as they are known to this day.   It may well begin with a brief discussion of their religion, for German Protestantism, in its various forms, was more responsible than any other force for the preservation of the German element of colonial times as a separate cultural group in America. There is much truth in the statement of the late Heinrich Maurer: "The essence of the Pennsylvania German personality is German Lutheranism." [16]   With the mental equipment of the typical seventeenth- and eighteenth-century German burgher and peasant, these people were simple souls, devoted to the accumulation of material goods, and conservative farmers.   They hoarded their hard-won money more as an heirloom than for the sake of its productive power; they opposed speculation and the introduction of newfangled ideas; and, though they naturally favored a democratic system, they had none of the explosive radicalism of the frontiersmen.

The Pennsylvania Germans may be divided roughly into two groups: the "church people," comprising the adherents of the regularly established Lutheran or Reformed Churches; and the "sectarians," adherents of dozens of minor groups, some lasting but a short time, others surviving to the present time.   The number of German Catholics in the colonies was small.[17]

[15] See *Der deutsche Pionier, Erinnerung aus dem Pionierleben der Deutschen in Amerika* (Cincinnati, 1869-1887), Vol. III, pp. 6-7.
[16] For a series of articles on the Pennsylvania Dutch, see Heinrich H. Maurer: "Studies in the Sociology of Religion," in *The American Journal of Sociology*, Vols. XXX, especially p. 412, and XXXI.
[17] For a letter from Governor Dinwiddie of Virginia to Governor Morris of Pennsylvania, in 1755, referring to "the dangers we are in from the German Roman Catholics," see *Pennsylvania Archives* (Philadelphia, 1852), Vol. II, p.

The great patriarch of the German Lutherans in America was Heinrich Melchior Muhlenberg, born in Hanover in 1711 and educated at Göttingen and Halle. In 1742, he went to Georgia and then to Pennsylvania, where he founded a Lutheran church in Philadelphia. In 1748, he took the lead in promoting the formation of a Lutheran synod, not only to further the work of the Lord in America, but to combat the irregularities and help overcome the difficulties which arose in churches widely scattered over the Pennsylvania German farming country. Lutheran churches complained to the colonial governor that they were being exploited by vagabond preachers who were corrupting the morals of the people,[18] and friction between Lutherans and members of the Reformed Church sometimes reached such extremes as to involve the defacing of each other's property.[19] Like a modern St. Paul, Muhlenberg spread the gospel of Lutheranism through even the remotest settlements. He tried to keep it pure and in complete conformity with the accepted practices of the mother church in Germany, and he visited other colonies and recorded his experiences faithfully in his diary. In 1754, a synod of the Lutheran Church was held, including Dutch, German, and Swedish pastors; and, by 1765, at least 40 Lutheran congregations in Pennsylvania, New York, New Jersey, Maryland, and Virginia were regularly connected with and responsible to the synod.[20] Muhlenberg remained in constant contact with Halle, and the Lutheran Church in colonial America was greatly influenced from that center of German Protestantism. All three of Muhlenberg's sons received their theological training in Halle.[21]

No less competent a judge than John Wesley paid tribute to the founders of the German Lutheran churches in Pennsylvania, not only as men of wisdom, good sense, and piety, but also as men of "good breeding and address." [22] Much of the credit for the establishment of German Lutheranism on sound and lasting foundations must go to Muhlenburg, who proved to be a man of great piety, de-

---

423. See also the Reverend Lambert Schrott: *Pioneer German Catholics in the American Colonies, 1734-1784* (New York, 1933).

[18] See *Pennsylvania Archives*, Vol. II, pp. 183-184.

[19] See *Maryland Historical Magazine*, Vol. X, pp. 59-61.

[20] See Ernest L. Hazelius: *History of the American Lutheran Church, 1685-1842* (Zanesville, Ohio, 1846).

[21] See *Berühmte deutsche Vorkämpfer für Fortschritt, Freiheit und Friede in Nord-Amerika* (Cleveland, 1888); and Johann L. Schulze: *Nachrichten von den vereinigten deutschen Evangelisch-Lutherischen Gemeinden in Nord-Amerika* 2 vols. (Halle, Germany, 1787).

[22] Quoted in Maurer: *loc. cit.*, Vol. XXX, p. 412.

votion, intelligence, and organizing ability. Muhlenberg established the Lutheran parochial school system, to go hand in hand with the Church and to help preserve the Germans as a separate religious and cultural unit in a strange land. Although he met with great success, nevertheless, toward the close of his career, he lamented the fact that, as "God is my witness, I worked against the English as long as I could, but I cannot longer resist." [23]

As Muhlenberg was the patriarch of the Lutherans, so the Reverend Michael Schlatter was the great leader of the German Reformed Church. Schlatter made his first mission to America in 1746, when he estimated that there were 46 German Reformed congregations in the colonies. These had, for the most part, been under the wing of the Church of Holland, but in 1747 Schlatter organized a German Reformed Church in America. At Germantown, on one occasion, he administered the Lord's Supper to 58 persons, and reported that among them were "some that had not been at the table of the Lord for ten or twelve years." [24] Schlatter spoke most disparagingly of the German Protestants in Pennsylvania as "the dregs of the people, poor, rude, ignorant of divine things, and so occupied with their rustic labors and domestic affairs" that they had no time to instruct their children in religion. Schlatter was especially hostile to the "sects and erring spirits" from Germany who had deserted the regular, established denominations.[25] He waged unrelenting war against the sectarians, and tried to buttress the position of the German Reformed Church by encouraging, even with British aid, the establishment of schools, for which he served as superintendent until 1757. Something of the instability of the Germans in religious matters, and the difficulties encountered by men like Muhlenberg and Schlatter, may be gathered from the experience of the famous Indian agent and trader, Conrad Weiser. Although born a Lutheran, Weiser joined the German Reformed Church; later he became converted to one of the sectarian groups,

[23] Quoted in *ibid.*, p. 417. Another wrote: "The German who becomes English is like a silk-worm that leaves its safe cocoon; as a *Buttervogel* he takes a sad end." [Quoted in *ibid.*, p. 427.] For further information on the Lutheran Church in Pennsylvania from 1638 to 1820, see Theodore Emanuel Schmauk: "A History of the Lutheran Church in Pennsylvania (1638-1820) from the Original Sources," in *Proceedings of the Pennsylvania German Society,* Vol. XI, pp. 1-355; and Vol. XII, pp. 357-588.

[24] H. Harbaugh: *The Life of the Reverend Michael Schlatter* (Philadelphia, 1857), p. 141.

[25] See *ibid.*, pp. 144 and 260.

Beisel's cloister at Ephrata, and finally returned to his allegiance to the Reformed Church.

The sectarians constituted the other group of Germans in Pennsylvania, as distinguished from the "church people." These sects ran the whole gamut of religious experience and experimentation. The Mennonites, of which there were several varieties who differed on minor matters of doctrine and procedure, the Dunkards, and the Schwenkfelders represented the more important of these sects. But there were many others, such as the New Born, the New Mooners, the Mountain Men, the River Brethren, the Brinser Brethren, the Society of the Woman in the Wilderness, the Separatists, the Inspired, the Gichtellians, the Zion's Brueder, and the Quietists. Lancaster County alone had between 20 and 30 different groups of German sectarians.

While they differed violently with each other on many points, most sects had much in common. A common strain of mysticism and a desire to withdraw from the world in order to practice their own mode of salvation pervaded them all. Generally they were conscientious objectors and pacifists, as a matter of religious conviction, and refused to take part in military affairs. Indeed, they were often officially exempted because of their "tender conscience." [26] They also refused, as a rule, to have anything to do with the worldly, political affairs of their colony, or to hold office. Sometimes they refused to participate in judicial procedures, or even to pay taxes. Some, like the followers of Conrad Beisel at the Cloister of Ephrata, believed in a monastic form of life; others became hermits; while still others remained in their communities, but observed meticulously the requirements of their particular faith. Groups like the Moravians or Herrnhuter at Bethlehem were organized as communistic societies based upon religious principles.[27] That groups of this kind frequently caused special problems for the government of the colony may easily be imagined.

It is impossible to discuss in detail the principles or experiences of all these German sects, but brief attention may be accorded to two or three of the important ones. The Mennonites, unlike the

[26] For the difficulties of the Schwenkfelder during the Indian Wars, see *Americana-Germanica* (Philadelphia), Vol. II, No. 1, pp. 47-59.
[27] See Dr. Hellmuth Erbe: *Bethlehem, Pennsylvania—eine kommunistische Herrnhuter Kolonie des 18. Jahrhunderts* (Stuttgart, Germany, 1929). Also Heinz Kloss: *Um die Einigung des Deutschamerikanertums* (Berlin, 1937), pp. 93-116.

Dunkards, were not immersionists, but had their own form of adult baptism, by pouring. They refused to take oaths of any kind and would not participate in any of the affairs of a temporal government. They rejected all arms, except the sword of the Spirit.[28] Among their peculiar ceremonies and customs were the washing of feet; the salute with a kiss, carefully confined to members of the same sex; and the complete and rigid rejection of all worldly diversions and pleasures. At church, the men sat on one side, the women on the other; there was congregational singing, but no instrumental music and no choir. To this day, the Mennonites reject secret societies and all organizations other than their Church, and observe the strictest rules in matters of dress and amusements. The "Old Order Amish" Mennonites have no churches, but meet in houses, and are therefore also known as "House Amish," to distinguish them from the "Church Amish," or "Progressive Amish." The "Old Order" dress very plainly, use no carpets or curtains in their homes, use hooks and eyes instead of buttons, and shave the upper lip while allowing the beard to grow.[29]

Count Zinzendorf was the outstanding leader of the sectarians, and more particularly of the Moravians, who, in spite of their geographical home, were essentially German. The group traced its religious ancestry back to John Hus. It was firmly established in Bohemia and Moravia, and counted the great Comenius as one of its leaders. In 1722, a group of the brethren left Moravia and took refuge at Herrnhut, Saxony, on the estate of Count Zinzendorf, who became a convert. Thereafter, the sect was often referred to as "the Herrnhuter." The Moravians were particularly interested in missions, and to this day they maintain missionaries in many parts of the world. The first Moravian settlement in America was made in Georgia in 1734 or 1735. After building a schoolhouse for the Indians and refusing to give military service, the group moved in 1740 to Pennsylvania, where they founded Nazareth and Bethlehem. From here, their influence spread rapidly. They sent preaching missionaries into the outlying frontier areas and established missions among the Indians. In 1755, these missions extended as far west as Gnadenhütten, in the Ohio country.[30] Gnadenhütten and

[28] For exemption from militia service in Pennsylvania, see *Pennsylvania Archives*, first series, Vol. III, pp. 121 and 128-129.
[29] See C. Henry Smith: *The Mennonite Immigration to Pennsylvania* (Norristown, Pennsylvania, 1929).
[30] For accounts of the missions, see "Extracts from Moravian Missionaries

Schönbrunn, which has now been completely restored, were founded in 1772. John Heckewelder, David Zeisberger, and Christian Friedrich Post are the names of Moravian missionaries who were intimately connected with the early history of white settlement in the Ohio country. Zeisberger translated religious books and hymns into the Delaware Indian language, and he and his confreres promoted churches and mission schools wherever they went.

Bethlehem remained the center of Moravian influence in America, although the missionaries of this sect went as far south as Georgia and established settlements in the Carolinas.[31] In the fall of 1752, Bishop August Gottlieb Spangenberg visited the North Carolina settlements. President Washington made a similar visit later, and was greeted by "several melodies . . . partly by trumpets and french horns, partly by trombones." To this day, the Moravians of Winston-Salem and Bethlehem observe their traditional Easter rites—a sunrise service, with elaborate music, and bands playing old Moravian chorals. These services attract thousands of visitors. The courage, endurance, self-sacrifice, and humanity of the Moravians in colonial times constitutes one of the finest chapters in the history of colonial beginnings in America. In spite of the open hostility of the Lutherans and members of the German Reformed Church, and frequent difficulties with "the Irish settlements," the work of preaching to frontiersmen who had seen no ministers for years and the effort to Christianize the Indians went on without serious interruption.[32]

The Salzburgers, who settled in Georgia and began silk culture, would probably have been forgotten by the historians of the colonial period save for their influence on the founders of Methodism, who

Diaries for 1749," in *Virginia Magazine of History*, Vols. XI and XII; and W. E. Connelley: *Heckewelder's Narrative and Journal, 1797* (Cleveland, 1907), pp. 34-57.

[31] See Adelaide L. Fries: *Records of the Moravians in North Carolina*, 4 vols. (Raleigh, North Carolina, 1922-1930).

[32] See Marie J. Kohnova: "The Moravians and their Missionaries, a Problem in Americanization," in *The Mississippi Valley Historical Review*, Vol. XIX, pp. 348-361. See also "Extracts from the Brethren's House and Congregation Diaries of the Moravian Church at Lititz, Pennsylvania, Relating to the Revolutionary War," in *The Pennsylvania German*, new series (1912), Vol. I, pp. 849-862; J. F. Sachse: *The German Sectarians of Pennsylvania, 1708-1800*, 2 vols. (Philadelphia, 1900); and many articles in the *Pennsylvania Magazine of History and Biography* and *Publications of the Pennsylvania German Society*. Also Joseph M. Levering: *A History of Bethlehem, Pennsylvania, 1741-1892* (Bethlehem, Pennsylvania, 1903). For a select bibliography of the Pennsylvania Germans, see *The Pennsylvania German*, Vol. XI, pp. 460-472.

happened to cross the Atlantic with one of their groups.[33] Early Methodism owed much to the religious ideas of the German sectarians, particularly with reference to their protest against ecclesiastical formalism and their emphasis on good works, an inner regeneration, and the "priesthood of all believers." It was on a voyage to Georgia that the Wesleys were "taught the way of the Lord more perfectly." Charles Wesley attended Moravian services in London, where he came under the influence of Count Zinzendorf. His brother John attributed his own "religious experience" in 1738 to the influence of Peter Böhler, and actually spent three months at Herrnhut. He had been deeply impressed by the piety of the Salzburgers. Both of the Wesleys were also greatly influenced by the singing of the German sectarians and learned to appreciate the value of hymns as a way to further the purposes of a religious service. They found the originals for many of the early Methodist hymns in the *Herrnhuter Gesangbuch,* from which they borrowed both themes and melodies.[34]

The Pennsylvania German farmer, like every other pioneer, went to work with his axe as soon as he arrived in America. He usually selected a wooded area for his future homestead, for he knew this to be the best farming land. Like other pioneers, many a Pennsylvania German farmer began life in a sod house or "cave," and then passed rapidly through the succeeding stages of the log cabin to the large stone houses which still mark the "Pennsylvania Dutch" sections. They were often erected on the slope of a hill, with one side only one story high, and many of them had a date stone near the gable indicating the name of the owner and the date of construction. Near by or underneath the house was the spring, which served as refrigerator, and near by was also an outside bakehouse. Roofs were generally of tile. Even more important than the houses

---

[33] See P. A. Strobel: *The Salzburgers and Their Descendants* (Baltimore, Maryland, 1855); Samuel Urlsperger: *Amerikanisches Ackerwerk Gottes* (Augsburg, Germany, 1754); Adelaide L. Fries: *The Moravians in Georgia, 1735-1740* (Raleigh, North Carolina, 1905); and John Preston Haskins: "German Influence on Religious Life and Thought in America During the Colonial Period," in *The Princeton Theological Review*, Vol. V, pp. 49-79 and 210-241.

[34] See James T. Hatfield: "John Wesley's Translation of German Hymns," in *Publications of the Modern Language Association* (1896), Vol. XI, pp. 171-200. A stray item in the *Cincinnati Enquirer*, July 21, 1883, refers to the descendants of the Salzburgers in Effingham County, Georgia, calling "a county prayer-meeting, attended by the whole population, to pray for rain" to end a prolonged drought which threatened their crops.

were the huge barns. Frequently they were made of stone at the bottom and of frame higher up, and painted yellow or red. The Pennsylvania German barn is recognizable in all localities in which the German farmers settled. To the materialistic farmer, who had little interest in the refinements of living but much in the comfort and care of his livestock and crops, the barn frequently overshadowed the house in importance and received major attention. These barns were two stories high, with pitched roofs, suggestive of the type used in Europe. They were sufficiently large and so well built that heavy teams could be driven into the upper story to load and unload grain. A normal size was 100 feet long, 40 feet wide, and 40 or 50 feet high. The lower story contained the stables, with feeding passages opening on the front. The front of the upper story projected 8 or 10 feet over the lower to provide a shelter for wagons and implements. It contained the hay mows and grain lofts, and served as the threshing floor. A complete, modern Pennsylvania German barn also includes a cellar under the driveway, a corncrib, and a shed attached.[35] The ancestor of the Pennsylvania German barn was the barn of Upper Bavaria in the southern Black Forest country.

The German farmer took great pride in his sleek and well-fed cattle, housed them well instead of letting them roam wild over the countryside, and was frequently accused of taking better care of his livestock than of his family. A Frenchman, recording his observations in 1795, wrote: "The houses are small, and kept in very bad order; the barns are large, and in very good repair."[36] This characteristic also found expression in such bits of folklore as the proverb: "Eine gute Kuh deckt viel Armut zu," and the couplet:

Weibersterbe isch ka Verderbe!—
Aber Gaulverrecke, des isch e Schrecke!

In contrast to his more wasteful Scotch-Irish neighbors, the Pennsylvania German farmer had a reputation for hard work and intensive cultivation. He cut down the trees in making his clearing and gradually removed the stumps, instead of merely girdling them and leaving them to rot in the ground. He knew how to feed and care for his livestock, and he constructed high fences to keep out

[35] See Faust: *The German Element in the United States*, Vol. I, pp. 131-138.
[36] Quoted in W. F. Worner: *Old Lancaster, Tales and Traditions* (Lancaster, Pennsylvania, 1927). pp. 88-89.

neighbors' animals. He was economical with his wood supply as with everything else. He lived frugally, being almost miserly in matters of household furnishings and dress. A garden, an orchard, and a beehive were necessary appendages to Pennsylvania German farms. The German farmers raised much of their simple vegetable diet in their own kitchen gardens, concentrating especially on cabbage and turnips. They were probably the first to cultivate asparagus and cauliflower in America. Their Conestoga wagons, drawn by four or eight horses, were "ships of inland commerce." The bottom of the wagon box was concave, long and slightly curved, and often painted blue. Canvas, of linen or hemp, covered the arches made of projecting poles and hoops of wood, giving the effect of a hugh bonnet. The running gears were generally painted a bright red.

The Pennsylvania Germans had large families, because children were an economic asset. They worked extremely hard, had the instinct for owning property, and were desirous of having each generation add something to their patrimony. That little was left for the niceties and refinements of life in such a rigid regime of grubbing for a living need hardly be stressed. The greed for property, extending to the point of avarice and to the exclusion of most of the finer things of life, is an ever-recurring theme in practically all the stories of Pennsylvania German life, even to this day.[37] It must be remembered, however, that many a German farmer began life in America as a redemptioner, with little in the way of intellectual and cultural activity behind him and little time to acquire an interest in things of the mind during his first years in this country.

The Pennsylvania Germans brought with them a mass of folklore and superstitions pertaining, not only to agriculture and livestock, but also to marriage, omens, dreams, disease, medical treatment, and folk medicine. Many clung so tenaciously to these curious beliefs that they still play an important part in Pennsylvania German communities. In recent years, there have been interesting and tragic cases arising from the persistence of the old belief in powwowing, "hexing," measuring, and other remedies for "the evil eye." [38] The Pennsylvania German farmer of colonial times, as well as some of his

---

[37] See, for example, such stories as those of Elsie Singmaster; and Helen R. Martin: *Tillie, the Mennonite Maid; The Schoolmaster of Hessville;* and many others.

[38] For an interesting account, see Edwin M. Fogel: *Beliefs and Superstitions of the Pennsylvania Germans* (Philadelphia, 1915).

present-day descendants, read and believed in almanacs, watched the skies for signs, and patronized witch doctors.[39]

Whatever else was said about the Germans of colonial Pennsylvania—and not all their neighbors by any means were happy over their arrival—the testimony as to their thrift and industry seems to be universal. Benjamin Franklin, whose comments on the Germans were not always laudatory and who once called them the "boors of the Palatinate," wrote in 1753 that the industry of the English seemed to diminish in the New World, "but it is not so with the German laborers; they retain their habitual industry and frugality they bring with them, and, receiving higher wages, an accumulation arises that makes them all rich." [40] Governor Thomas believed that "their Industry and Frugality have been the principal Instruments of raising [Pennsylvania] to its present flourishing condition beyond any of his Majesty's Colonys in North America." [41] A French traveler, visiting the neighborhood of Bethlehem in 1794, commented on how the Irish became poor and how "their places have gradually been filled by Germans who are thriving there . . . ." [42] Another traveler, visiting Bedford in 1802, observed that "the superior cultivation of the land, and preservation of the inclosures, indicate this to be a German settlement, or canton, everything has the appearance of ease, the result of assiduity and labour . . . . They live much better than the Americans, descendants of the English, Scotch and Irish. They are less addicted to the use of spirituous liquors, and possess not . . . that unsettled disposition, which frequently, from the slightest motives, induces them [English, Scotch and Irish] to wander hundreds of miles in the hope of meeting with a more fertile soil." [43] As a final illustration, a quotation from the diary of an English observer may be cited, for it describes conditions as he saw them among the

[39] See also August C. Mahr: "A Pennsylvania Dutch Hexzettel," in *Monatshefte für deutschen Unterricht*, Vol. XXVII, No. 6, pp. 1-11. It is well to recall that, in his *Book of Phisick*, William Penn prescribed for bruises butter, black snails, and "new cow-dung as much as will go into a great oyster shell and half as much new hen dung." Quoted in J. T. Adams: *Provincial Society* (New York, 1927), p. 126.
[40] Quoted in S. E. Weber: *The Charity School Movement in Colonial Pennsylvania, 1754-1763* (Philadelphia, 1905), p. 11.
[41] Quoted in *ibid.*, pp. 12-13.
[42] Cazenove's *Journal*, quoted in R. W. Kelsey (editor and translator): "A Record of the Journey of Theophile Cazenove Through New Jersey and Pennsylvania," in *Haverford College Studies* (Haverford, Pennsylvania, 1922), p. 23.
[43] F. D. M. D. Michaux: *Travels to the Westward of the Allegheny Mountains* (1802), p. 27.

Pennsylvania Germans in 1816. After commenting on their clannishness, he added:

> They are a persevering, industrious people, they cultivate
> the earth with care, their fields have an air of neatness
> about them rarely to be discovered in America. The most
> respectable of them go on, adding dollar to dollar, and
> pack them up securely in an Iron chest. Tho' used to the
> habit of hiding their hard earnings they know not what to
> do with their money after they got it. The utmost indeav-
> ors are used to get the money, and then to keep it secret that
> they have got it. The men, in their leisure hours smoke,
> drink whiskey and water, and ride on fat horses. The
> women raw boned, brown skinned, and barelegged, have
> neither grace nor beauty. They share with their husbands
> the labours of the field, and tend about their house as
> menial servants.[44]

Manasseh Cutler, in 1788, called Lancaster "the best built inland town in America." [45]

The Pennsylvania German father exercised a patriarchal juris-diction over his family, and frowned upon all innovations that seemed to challenge the old homely virtues of thrift and hard work. But in spite of the utmost frugality in other respects, the Pennsylvania German ate like a trencherman, and his housewife made a lasting contribution to American culinary art.[46] *Sauerkraut und Speck* and *Schnitz und Knöpf* were well-established delicacies among the Pennsylvania Germans and were consumed in large amounts. On Shrove Tuesday, the Pennsylvania German housewife baked *Fastnachtskuchen,* as her European ancestors for generations before her had done. Baptisms and funerals were occasions for great feasting. At Christmastime, in early colonial days, the special dishes were fresh sausage and roasted pig, the maws stuffed with a mixture of potatoes, bread, onions, and spareribs. Apples, nuts, cider, cakes, beer, and molasses candy completed the Christmas meal. The Pennsylvania German was proud of his capacity for food, and the women were proud of their reputations as cooks and housewives. In Pennsylvania German hotels, the menu frequently

---

[44] From the diary of George Fowler, quoted in Otto L. Schmidt: "The Missis-sippi Valley in 1816," in *The Mississippi Valley Historical Review* (September, 1927), pp. 142-143.
[45] Quoted in Worner: *op. cit.,* p. 78.
[46] See J. George Frederick: *The Pennsylvania Dutch and Their Cookery* (New York, 1935); and W. K. Dorman and Leonard Davidow: *Pennsylvania Dutch Cook Book* (Reading, Pennsylvania, 1935).

included the traditional "seven sours and seven sweets." Dried cut apples, potato soup, filled pig stomach, souse, liver pudding, funnel cakes, and vinegar punch were other delicacies. Lancaster, Reading, and Allentown had their regular fairs; and, at the curb markets, all kinds of delicacies were readily obtainable, from fowls, butter, eggs, cider, apple butter, and smearcase to pigs' feet and *Apfelschnitz*. Harvest festivals, hog killings, and apple-butter boilings provided social interludes in which gastronomic pleasures were among the major concerns of those who attended. Stone and mortar ovens for baking were generally at the back of the house. Apple mills and cider presses were operated by horses going round and round, and special springhouses were built on Pennsylvania German farms to preserve the milk, butter, and cream. Apple butter was a favorite delicacy, and *Apfelschnitz* were frequently made at bees, attended by neighbors who met to cut and pare the apples into pieces, called *Schnitz*.[47]

Although the farming activities of the Pennsylvania Germans have been emphasized, it should not be forgotten that there were many skilled artisans among them. A Pennsylvania German farmhouse in colonial times was generally a small manufacturing concern, an economic unit, in which implements, furniture, kitchen utensils, clothing, and bedding were made. The women wove a coarse cloth of linen and wool, and did the spinning and knitting. A girl was valued for marriage purposes by her ability to keep house, and a Pennsylvania German doggerell emphasized the desirability of learning to spin:

> All die Mädche misse lerne
> Gut zu schpinne un zu zwerne;
> Die wu scheene Kleeder welle
> Misse sich ans Schpinnrad schtelle.[48]

German millwrights, wagonmakers, gardners, and forgemen were often preferred to workmen of other nationalities.[49] William Rittinghouse erected the first paper mill in Pennsylvania; Christopher Saur and his family are famous in the early history of printing; John

[47] For further details, see H. K. Landis: "Pennsylvania German Foods," in *The American-German Review* (September, 1938), pp. 38-41 and 53.
[48] Quoted in Wertenbaker: *The Founding of American Civilization* (New York, 1938), p. 278.
[49] See the advertisement in *New Jersey Gazette,* July 12, 1773, quoted in *New Jersey Archives,* Vol. XXVIII, p. 560; and J. Fitzpatrick (editor), *Diaries of George Washington* (Boston, 1925), Vol. III, pp. 444, 140, and 141.

Huber started a furnace in Lancaster County and later sold it to the famous "Baron" Heinrich Wilhelm Stiegel of Mannheim, who became better known for his glassworks than for his iron furnaces, in which he made stoves: "Baron Stiegel ist der Mann, der die Ofen machen kann." [50] Germantown was well known for its thread stockings; in 1775, 60,000 dozen pair were reported to have been manufactured in this town alone.[51] The "Kentucky rifle" was really turned out by the German gunsmiths of Lancaster.[52]

In spite of their concern with religious matters, the colonial Germans apparently were "rough children of nature," as Silas Deane once described them,[53] with the morality of a rather rough, simple peasant folk. Numerous advertisements appeared in Pennsylvania German papers from inland counties near the close of the eighteenth century in which bridegrooms denied that they were the fathers of infants on whose account the law had forced them to marry their mothers.[54] "Bundling" was common not only among the Germans in the middle colonies but also among New England Puritans, and it must be remembered that "benefit of clergy" was often unavailable in the outlying frontier counties for years at a time. The manners and tastes of the inhabitants of the colonial Pennsylvania German countryside were not refined by either education or intercourse with strangers, and taverns were the only places for public entertainment.[55]

[50] *The Pennsylvania German,* Vol. VII, pp. 155 and 156. The feast of roses, when a rose is given to pay for the Baron's gift of a church many years ago, is still observed in Mannheim.

[51] *Ibid.,* Vol. VII, p. 155.

[52] Wertenbaker: *op. cit.,* p. 284.

[53] *Collections of the Connecticut Historical Society,* Vol. II, p. 283.

[54] See James O. Knauss: *Social Conditions Among the Pennsylvania-Germans in the Eighteenth Century, as Revealed in German Newspapers Published in America* (Lancaster, Pennsylvania, 1922), p. 125.

[55] See the comments of an English traveler on Lancaster, in 1807, quoted in Worner: *op. cit.,* pp. 148-149. The quaint will of Daniel Rosenberger, probated in Philadelphia in 1771, throws further light on the emphasis upon creature comforts: "I give to my loving wife Fronica for her own, our bedding and bedstead, with what is belonging to it, her chest with all linen cloth, our pewter ware, two pots, and one cow. Likewise I give to my loving wife for her yearly maintenance, the new stove room, kitchen and cellar, what she has use for, firewood to the house, 8 bushels of rye, 5 bushels of wheat, 3 bushels of buckwheat, a fat hog of one hundred weight, apples as much as she useth, all which to be yearly during the time she remains my widow. . . ." [Quoted in Rosenberger: *op. cit.,* p. 142.] For further discussions of the Pennsylvania Germans, see also J. L. Rosenberger: *Through Three Centuries; Colver and Rosenberger Lives and Times, 1620-1922* (Chicago, 1922); Oswald Seidensticker: *Bilder aus der deutsch-pennsylvanischen Geschichte* (New York, 1886); and Cornelius Weygant: *The Red Hills* (Philadelphia, 1929).

Contemporary comments on the education of the Pennsylvania Germans and their general intellectual and cultural level are misleading and contradictory. Many, like Franklin, William Penn's Secretary, and Governor Gordon had serious misgivings about the clannishness and isolation of the German settlers.[56] William Smith, first provost of the University of Pennsylvania, considered them "utterly ignorant," and favored a scheme of charitable schools to Anglicize them—a plan which was bitterly and successfully opposed by the German sectarians, who at once recognized it as an attempt to interfere with their language and their religion.[57] The rate of illiteracy among the German immigrants undoubtedly was high; it may have been as much as twenty-five per cent. The sectarians, as a rule, were opposed to much education, believing the old German proverb: "Wie gelehrter, wie verkehrter." Moreover, to Lutherans and sectarians alike, education was essentially a Church affair; Church and school must go together and all learning must have a decided religious emphasis. Many of the Germans in Pennsylvania opposed the introduction of public schools in the nineteenth century in favor of parochial schools, on the theory that a child belonged first to God and the Church, then to his parents, and finally to the State. In colonial days, settlements were often so far apart that it was impossible to support preachers or teachers, churches or schools. Theophile Cazenove commented on the "total lack of education" of the Pennsylvania Germans whom he encountered, and referred to their poorly equipped houses, their "slovenliness and lack of comfort." [58]

Although Franklin on one occasion denounced the newcomers "as the most stupid of their own nation" and accused them of knavery as well as ignorance, he admitted that, in the elections, "they come in droves and carry all before them." Then, perhaps to make another honest penny and to control their thoughts on public affairs, he began publishing a German newspaper, the *Philadelphische Zeitung*. It was admitted that the Germans imported "many foreign books" and that they had their own printing houses in Pennsylvania.[59] Christopher Saur printed the first German

[56] See E. E. Proper: "Colonial Immigration Laws," in *Columbia University Studies* (New York, 1900), Vol. XII, No. 2, p. 48.
[57] See also *Collections of the New York Historical Society* (1920), pp. 459 and 463.
[58] Quoted in Kelsey: *op. cit.*, pp. 34, 83, and 84. See also Kuhns: *op. cit.*, p. 149.
[59] Weber: *op. cit.*, p. 14.

Bible in America, issued the first German almanac in 1739, which was widely read in all the colonies for nearly fifty years, published a hymnal for Conrad Beisel's Ephrata community, and issued the first wholly German newspaper in America. He printed hymn books and catechisms for most of the German sects. It has been estimated that, prior to 1754, over 200 different publications were issued from the various German presses in the colonies; and, beginning in 1786, the Pennsylvania legislature ordered its *Journal* and other official papers to be printed in German translations.[60] The number of German publications in the eighteenth century is astonishingly large, and goes far to refute the idea that the Pennsylvania Germans were ignorant and illiterate.

Saur's *Der Hoch-Deutsche Pennsylvanische Geschicht-Schreiber* had 4,000 readers, from Pennsylvania to Georgia. Henry Miller published *Der Wöchentliche Philadelphische Staatsbote* between 1762 and 1779. From 1732 to 1800, a total of 38 German newspapers existed in the American colonies at various times. Other early newspapers that deserve mention were the *Neue Unpartheyische Lancäster Zeitung,* the *Germantauner Zeitung,* and the *Reading Adler.* Franklin's *Philadelphische Zeitung,* founded in 1732, was badly edited in poor German by his protégé, Louis Thimothee. Franklin also had a financial interest in other German papers.[61] Liebert and Billmeyer were selected to print the German translation of the proceedings of the Pennsylvania legislature. Hundreds of religious books appeared from the various German presses, including hymnals, catechisms, and bibles. From 1747 to 1791, seven editions were printed of Teerstegen's *Geistiges Blumengärtlein inniger Seelen.*

The German schoolmaster functioned under as great hardships in colonial times as his colleagues in some of the other immigrant groups, for, as has been said, many of the sectarians saw no need for education anyway, other than that provided for in the religious tenets of their own group. But there were exceptions even here, such as Beisel's school at Ephrata, which attracted pupils from outside the community. Teaching in most of the schools in the eight-

[60] See *German-American Annals,* Vol. I, pp. 48 and 49; also Oswald Seidensticker and H. A. Rattermann: "Geschichte der deutsch-amerikanischen Zeitungspresse von ihrem Anfang bis zum Jahre 1850," in *Deutsch-Amerikanisches Magazin,* Vol. I, pp. 269-289, 405-433, and 568-587.
[61] See Knauss: *op. cit.;* also Worner: *op. cit.*

eenth century was of course done in German. Although missionary attempts from the outside to establish charity schools among the
Pennsylvania Germans were bitterly opposed, such efforts did stimulate some of the denominations to pay more attention to the education of their children.[62] Pastors like Muhlenberg and Schlatter
were greatly interested in education, and themselves conducted
church schools. Other German schoolmasters in colonial Pennsylvania were Boehm, Weiss, Stiefel, and Hoecker. Christoph Dock,
who taught in Pennsylvania from 1714 to 1744, probably deserves
credit for having published the first pedagogical book in America,
his *Schul-Ordnung* of 1750.[63] By the end of the eighteenth century,
there were German bookstores in Lebanon, Easton, Reading, York,
Lancaster, Harrisburg, Germantown, Philadelphia, Baltimore, and
elsewhere; and there was a German evening school in Philadelphia
in 1754. The Lutherans established the present-day Franklin and
Marshall College, with a son of Heinrich M. Muhlenberg as its first
president. While Lutherans and members of the Reformed Church
both insisted on educated, trained ministers, the sectarians did not.
The latter had a fundamental distrust for most professional men,
especially for doctors and lawyers. They expressed the familiar
fear that no one would be left to farm if all were to be educated.
The Moravians, who differed with their fellow sectarians in their
attitude toward education, started little missionary schools and also
a girls' academy in Bethlehem.

In 1772, one bookseller had 700 German books for sale, and hundreds of books were imported. But the fact remains that the most
widely read publications among the Pennsylvania Germans were
the German almanacs, with their curious mixture of genuine information, superstition, and folklore. The task of establishing a
public-school system in Pennsylvania was seriously complicated until
well into the nineteenth century by the presence of the German element and its rather retarded attitude toward modern education by
the State. As late as 1836, the Honorable H. A. Muhlenberg wrote,
in explanation of this attitude: "The Germans of our state are not
opposed to education as such, but only to any system that to them

[62] See C. F. Hausmann: *Kunze's Seminarium and the Society for the Propagation
of Christianity and Useful Knowledge Among the Germans in America* (Philadelphia, 1917).
[63] See A. B. Faust: "Der deutsche Schulmeister in der amerikanischen Geschichte," in *Deutsch-Amerikanische Geschichtsblätter* (Chicago, October, 1910).

seems to trench on their parental and natural rights." [64]   The desire
for parochial schools remained strong and was constantly reinforced by a strong attachment to the Pennsylvania German dialect,
which, in turn, received the full support of the Church; for it was
clear that the future of the German churches was intimately associated with the preservation of the language and the clannishness of
the Pennsylvania German communities.

"Pennsylvania Dutch" may properly be described as the oldest
immigrant language still in daily use in the United States.   Basically, it is the language of the Upper Rhine dialects, to which have
been added many common English words and inflections.   The result is an almost incredible mixture of German and English in
spelling, words, and sentence structure.   The language has survived
largely because of the clannishness of the Pennsylvania Germans,
based on their religious separatism.   In recent years, because the
language has shown signs of gradually dying out, a concerted effort
has been made to perpetuate it.   A number of writers both of lyrics
and prose are today using this curious patois as the vehicle for their
literary expression.   In 1883, E. H. Rauch produced a dramatic
version of *Rip Van Winkle* in Pennsylvania Dutch, and shortly
thereafter, Alfred Moss and E. L. Newhard issued a Pennsylvania
Dutch edition of Gilbert and Sullivan's *H. M. S. Pinafore*.   Newspapers like the *Lancaster Sunday News* and those of Allentown and
other "Pennsylvania Dutch" cities began in the 1930's to publish a
series of letters and other material in this language, "as part of the
general survival at this time of the old dialect."   A European student, on a visit to the United States in 1931 to study this curious
survival, was able to hear sermons delivered in Pennsylvania
Dutch.

It is impossible to give any clear notion of what "Pennsylvania
Dutch" is like without going into greater detail than space permits,
but a few typical sentences may be reproduced in order to give some
understanding of the language.   Thus, "Ich habe geketcht einen
Kold," can be easily deciphered by anyone.   In a discussion of the
superiority of the good old days, before corrupting innovations crept
in, one finds: "Do waren Wir net getruwelt mit Lichter, Schaukel-
stuhle, un carpets; net gebattert von Hupps, oder 17 Unterrock,
Teitlacking, un seidens Dresses."   To illustrate the wholesale adoption of English words and their German phonetic spelling, one may

---

[64] Quoted in Kuhns: *op. cit.*, p. 149.

point out that office becomes *affis,* porch *bortsch,* Jack *Dschack,* turnpike *tornpeik,* old-fashioned *altfaschen,* and so forth.[65]

In spite of the rather drab, materialistic civilization that marked the life of Pennsylvania German communities, there is much in the history of the German colonial stock that is of interest and importance to the student of the fine arts. Many of the Germans, whether sectarians or "church people," had a great interest in music, and emphasized singing and instrumental music as a vital part of their religious services. The Germans and Swedes around Philadelphia and the Moravians at Bethlehem tried to develop, not only singing, but also instrumental accompaniments in their religious services, and the same was true of some other sectarian groups. Bethlehem was a musical center in the eighteenth century and has remained the center of the Bach cult in America. Haydn's *Creation* and the *Seasons* had their American *premières* here.[66] In addition to the organ, concerts at Bethlehem in the eighteenth century used the violin, viola, flute, and French horn. Washington attended concerts in the Lutheran church in Philadelphia and in the Moravian settlement of Salem, North Carolina, in 1791.[67] The Moravians of Georgia used trombones and French horns to announce the death of one of their brethren, and Zinzendorf himself wrote some of their funeral chorals. Organs were fairly common in German churches in the larger Pennsylvania communities, although their introduction ran counter to the Quaker tradition of doing without music in the service. Philip Fyring and David Tanneberger of Lancaster County were early Pennsylvania organ builders, the latter having built no less than 27 church organs before his death in 1804.[68] Zithers, spinets, and hand organs were not unknown in Pennsylvania German farmhouses.

[65] For further details, see H. L. Mencken: *The American Language* (New York, 1936), p. 447 *et seq.;* and the scholarly work done by Heinz Kloss: "Die pennsylvaniadeutsche Literatur," in *Mitteilungen der Deutschen Akademie* (Munich, Germany, 1931), Vol. IV, pp. 230-272. See also Heinz Kloss: *Lewendiche Schtimme aus Pennsilveni* (New York and Stuttgart, Germany, 1929). Also Daniel Miller: *A Collection of Pennsylvania German Productions in Poetry and Prose* (Reading, Pennsylvania, 1903); *Proceedings of the Pennsylvania German Society,* Vol. XII, pp. 57-99 and 108-139; and William S. Troxell (editor), *Aus Pennsylfannia* (Philadelphia, 1938).

[66] See John T. Howard: *Our American Music: Three Hundred Years of It* (New York, 1931), pp. 19-26 *passim.*

[67] See O. Sonneck: *Early Concert Life in America, 1731-1800* (Leipzig, Germany, 1907) and J. C. Parsons (editor), *Extracts from the Diary of Jacob Hiltzheimer* (Philadelphia, 1893), p. 166. See also W. A. Hausmann: "German-American Hymnology," in *Americana-Germanica,* Vol. II, No. 3.

[68] See Knauss: *op. cit.,* p. 136; Worner: *op. cit.,* pp. 46-47; and *Choral Music*

The Ephrata Community of Conrad Beisel, to be referred to again in another connection, was famous, among other things, for its music. Beisel himself wrote a crude treatise on harmony, which antedates Billings' *New England Psalm Singer* by a quarter of a century. In 1739, Saur printed Beisel's *Zionistischer Weyrauch-Hügel* of 692 songs, perhaps the first hymn book issued in America; and, in 1766, there appeared *Das paradiesische Wunderspiel,* in which 441 of the songs were by Beisel. Beisel had his own system of harmony and a unique system of notation. His music was entirely unlike ancient church music and had none of the rhythm of the Reformation music. Beisel wrote a dissertation on harmony as a preface to the *Turtel Taube* (1747). Sometimes he wrote all four parts consecutively on one staff, shifting the clef to suit the voice; and he also wrote five-, six-, and seven-part music. His music contained strange progressions, violating all the rules of harmony hitherto recognized, and most of it was to be sung in falsetto, with the lips half open.[69]

Pennsylvania German red earthenware is well known to the student of American pottery. Milk pans, plates, jugs, and apple-butter crocks were made by hand. They are of an old-rose, brick color, of various shapes, glazed or unglazed, and often have wavy thumbnail lines on them. Plenty of good clay was available, and "Pennsylvania Dutch" pottery did not die out until 1840. In the olden days, many farmers had peacocks; and the image of this bird appears not only on the pottery, trays, and glassware of the Pennsylvania Germans but on their bedquilts, towels, and chinaware, and in their books as well. The tulip motif also appears on almost all "Pennsylvania Dutch" products, such as chests, tables, birth and marriage certificates, hymn books, boxes, bottles, ironware, barns, and tombstones.[70] The birth and marriage and baptismal certificates (*Geburtschein, Trauschein,* and *Taufschein*) always hung on the wall, and revealed these same symbols of folk art. The finest examples of *fractur* painting, colored illuminations accompanying Gothic lettering, usually in dove and tulip designs, did not die out in Pennsylvania until the middle of the nineteenth century.

and Musical Life in Pennsylvania in the Eighteenth Century, 2 vols. (Philadelphia, 1926 and 1927) (a publication of the Pennsylvania Society of the Colonial Dames of America); and *German American Annals,* Vol. VI, No. 3, pp. 161-166.
[69] For an excellent article on and reproductions of this music, see Julius F. Sachse: "The Music of the Ephrata Cloister," in *Proceedings of the Pennsylvania German Society,* Vol. XII.
[70] See the collections in the Museum of Fine Art in Chicago and Philadelphia.

Some of the finest examples of the household furniture of the Pennsylvania Germans are on exhibit in the Pennsylvania Museum of Art. They include bun-footed, many-paneled chests, gate-leg tables with balusterlike legs, painted dower chests (*Truhen*), spoon racks, dressers, cupboards, and so forth. Pennsylvania German furniture usually had a colored background and bright decorations, as on their pottery and in their *fractur* painting.[71] Stove plates, too, were decorated with fantastic figures, some of them from the *Bible;* and even the "German stoves," made of tile or iron and backed up against the chimney, aroused the interest and admiration of connoisseurs like Franklin. The houses themselves were ornamented with gables and painted date panels, with the popular tulip decoration;[72] and wrought-iron weather vanes, hinges, and foot-scrapers on houses and churches suggested the *Volkskunst* of medieval Germany.[73] Stiegel glassware has become a special attraction for antique collectors.[74]

During the American Revolution, the German population was sharply divided between the Church people, who had no conscientious scruples about fighting, and the sectarians, who would have no part "in setting up and pulling down kings and governments" by force and violence. Even during the intercolonial wars, the sectarians had refused to render military service and had been excused as conscientious objectors.[75] During the Revolutionary War, they were generally given the option in most colonies to pay a commutation

---

[71] For a good account of these subjects, see Edwin A. Barber: *Tulip Ware of the Pennsylvania German Potters* (1903); Harold D. Eberlein and C. V. Hubbard, "Household Furniture of the Pennsylvania-Germans," and "Fraktur Painting in Pennsylvania," in *The American-German Review* (June, 1937), pp. 4-9 and 11-16, respectively. See also Guy F. Reinert: "Slip Decorated Pottery of the Pennsylvania Germans," in *The American-German Review* (March, 1936), pp. 12-14 and 49.

[72] Interiors of Pennsylvania German houses have been reconstructed in the Pennsylvania Museum of Art in Philadelphia.

[73] For a beautifully illustrated article on the subject, see G. Edwin Brumbaugh: "Colonial Architecture of the Pennsylvania Germans," in *Proceedings of the Pennsylvania German Society*, Vol. XLI. Also B. A. Uhlendorf: "German-American Poetry. A Contribution to Colonial Literature," in *Jahrbuch der deutschamerikanischen historischen Gesellschaft von Illinois*, Vols. XXII and XXIII.

[74] See C. F. Huch: "Baron Heinrich Wilhelm Stiegel," in *Mitteilungen des deutschen Pionier-Vereins von Philadelphia* (1907), No. 5, pp. 1-16; and F. W. Hunter: *Stiegel Glass* (Boston, 1914). For additional references to the Pennsylvania Germans, see Wertenbaker: *op. cit.*, pp. 256-345; and Langdon: *Everyday Things in American Life, 1607-1776* (New York, 1937), pp. 63-109. For the best bibliography on the subject, see Emil Meynen: *Bibliographie des Deutschtums der kolonialzeitlichen Einwanderung in Nordamerika* (Leipzig, Germany, 1937).

[75] See Harbaugh: *op. cit.*, pp. 323-327; and *Statutes at Large of Pennsylvania* (Harrisburg, Pennsylvania, 1908), Vol. V, p. 200; and Vol. IV, p. 393.

fee, furnish a substitute, or pay special taxes. In North Carolina, the Moravians were exempted from military duty on payment of a triple tax. In general, the Moravians and Schwenkfelders paid their military fines and suffered little from their patriotic neighbors. Other sectarians were often seriously misunderstood, however, because they refused to take a "test oath" of allegiance to the Revolutionary government. Some were banished; others lost their estates. Many took care of soldiers quartered in their homes, furnished supplies, and rendered noncombatant services or, like the Moravians at Bethlehem, did hospital work as the Good Samaritans for Washington's sorely tried army during the terrible winter at Valley Forge. The Moravians were undoubtedly the most friendly to the Revolution, but they, too, stoutly refused to take an oath abjuring King George. The schoolhouse at Ephrata was turned into a hospital after the Battle of Brandywine.[76] Christopher Saur's press maintained its pacifist convictions; Saur's sons became Tories, eventually leaving the United States for Nova Scotia; and, in 1778, the family's property was confiscated and sold. Probably no other German family in America had become as wealthy as this old family of printers and publishers, who now paid a heavy penalty for their loyalty to the English king. In 1780, Christopher Saur III issued a pamphlet in German appealing to the Germans to return to the allegiance of their king, which was revised and approved by General Knyphausen before publication.[77] Some German Tories fought with the Hessians during the New Jersey campaign, and two Germans were hanged in 1778 as spies in Lancaster County, Pennsylvania.[78]

The German Church people had no conscientious scruples about war, and many distinguished themselves in the course of the Revolution. Four companies of infantry were raised in Reading, Pennsylvania, before June, 1775.[79] Charleston, South Carolina, created a volunteer company after the Battle of Lexington known as the German Fusileers. In May, 1776, Congress authorized a German regiment, to be recruited in Pennsylvania and Maryland, which saw service in a number of campaigns in New Jersey under the command of Nikolas Haussegger and Ludwig Weltner. Pulaski's corps was

[76] McMaster: *op. cit.,* Vol. II, p. 83.
[77] See James O. Knauss: "Christopher Saur the Third," in *Proceedings of the American Antiquarian Society* (April, 1931).
[78] See Knauss: *Social Conditions Among the Pennsylvania-Germans in the Eighteenth Century,* p. 157.
[79] See *ibid.,* p. 155.

largely recruited in the neighborhood of Bethlehem. In the Mohawk Valley, the four batallions recruited in the "German Flats"—largely German and commanded by Nikolas Herkimer—helped at the Battle of Oriskany to turn back St. Leger's forces, prevent their junction with Burgoyne's army, and thus save the rich farmlands of the valley from the foraging parties of Burgoyne's hard-pressed army.

Among the distinguished colonial Germans who served in the war are Peter Muhlenberg, who dramatically relinquished his Lutheran pastorate in Virginia to become commander of a regiment, and Christopher Ludwig, the honest baker who became director of baking for the Continental Army. From abroad came John Kalb, a Franconian peasant, who became a "baron" in America and laid down his life at the Battle of Camden; Heinrich Emmanuel Lutterloh, who became quartermaster general of the Continental Army; and Baron Friedrich Wilhelm von Steuben, who became army drillmaster, and whose services as organizer and administrator Washington never ceased to value. Von Steuben's book on military regulations became a textbook for the American army.[80]

Of the Hessians, German mercenaries who fought for the British during the Revolution, it has been estimated that some 12,000 remained in the United States after the war, although as yet no one has tried to follow their later history. As early as August, 1776, the Continental Congress had begun to lure the Hessians from their British allegiance by promising them all the rights of native Americans, in addition to 50 acres of land apiece for the common soldiers and much larger quotas for the officers. Thousands of copies of this propaganda literature were printed, to be circulated among the "foreign troops," and the backs of tobacco wrappers were used to scatter this information. Congress, at one time, even toyed with the idea of raising a corps of German volunteers consisting entirely of Hessian deserters.[81] At the close of the war, pamphlets were printed in German in South Carolina and New Jersey inviting the Hessians

[80] For material on von Steuben, see *Jahrbuch der deutsch-amerikanischen historischen Gesellschaft von Illinois*, Vol. XXX; Carl Wittke: "Washington and Steuben," in *The Open Court* (Chicago), Vol. XLVI, pp. 93-107; and John M. Palmer: *General von Steuben* (New Haven), 1937. See also J. G. Rosengarten: *The German Allied Troops in the North American War of Independence* (Albany, New York, 1893); Benjamin Rush: *An Account of the Life and Character of Christopher Ludwick* (Philadelphia, 1831); H. M. M. Richards: "The Pennsylvania-German in the Revolutionary War, 1775-1783," in *Proceedings of the Pennsylvania-German Society*, Vol. XVII, p. 542; and *Der deutsche Pionier*, Vol. VIII, pp. 450-456.

[81] See *Journal of Congress*, Vol. V, pp. 640, 653, and 708.

to stay and take up land at bargain prices. Hessian prisoners in Virginia and Pennsylvania, where they could easily fraternize with their countrymen and hear their own tongue spoken, were helped by German settlers to escape to the West and become farmers. Some of these were among the first pioneers to cross the Alleghenies. As prisoners of war, they had been permitted to keep their own gardens in Virginia, raise poultry for their own use and for sale, and attend performances at a country theater built by themselves, which gave two performances a week at "parquette tickets $4.00 (paper) and parterre $2.00." Many worked on neighboring farms or at their own trades.[82] Of the 1,100 Hessian prisoners brought to Reading, Pennsylvania, only about 300 returned to Germany. A large group settled in Baltimore, to work at gardening or handicrafts. Many were absorbed in the Pennsylvania German counties as farmers, and some found employment as schoolmasters.[83] In the mountains of the Carolinas, there are still some descendants of German prisoners taken with Burgoyne at Saratoga, and they are still called "the Hessians." [84]

SUMMARY

From this brief summary of colonial immigration, it is clear that non-English immigrants contributed little to the political institutions of the colonial period except, perhaps, to their democratization. These institutions were basically Anglo-Saxon and remained so. But the influence of non-English immigrants on the social, economic, and cultural development of colonial America was significant. The diversity of religions in colonial America—to take just one more example—made religious toleration an absolute necessity, and the final separation of Church and State was not so much a matter of democratic theory as an inescapable and practical necessity.

"The blood of 1776" was a mixture of many immigrant stocks. A passage from Crevecoeur's well-known *Letters from an American*

[82] See G. S. Ford: "Two Eighteenth-Century German Publicists on the American Revolution," in Ford: *On and Off the Campus* (Minneapolis, 1938), pp. 281-283.

[83] See D. R. Fox, *Ideas in Motion*, the chapter on "Culture in Knapsacks"; E. J. Lowell: *The Hessians in the Revolution* (New York, 1884); and Carl Wittke, *George Washington und seine Zeit* (Bremen, Germany, 1933), Ch. III.

[84] Edward Channing: *History of the United States* (New York, 1913), Vol. VI, p. 7.

Farmer, which appeared in 1782, may furnish an appropriate close for this discussion of the colonial era:

> What then is the American, this new man? He is either an European, or the descendant of an European; hence that strange mixture of blood, which you will find in no other country. I could point out to you a family whose grandfather was an Englishman, whose wife was Dutch, whose son married a French woman, and whose present four sons have now four wives of different nations . . . . Here individuals of all nations are melted into a new race of men, whose labours and posterity will one day cause great changes in the world. Americans are the western pilgrims, who are carrying along with them that great mass of arts, sciences, vigour, and industry which began long since in the east; they will finish the great circle . . . . The American ought . . . to love this country much better than that wherein either he or his forefathers were born. Here the rewards of his industry follow with equal steps the progress of his labour . . . . Wives and children, who before in vain demanded of him a morsel of bread, now, fat and frolicksome, gladly help their father to clear those fields whence exuberant crops are to arise to feed and to clothe them all, without any part being claimed, either by despotic prince, a rich abbot, or a mighty lord. Here religion demands but little of him; a small voluntary salary to the minister, and gratitude to God; can he refuse these? The American is a new man, who acts upon new principles; he must therefore entertain new ideas, and form new opinions . . . .[85]

[85] J. Hector St. John de Crèvecoeur: *Letters from an American Farmer* (London, 1782), p. 42.

PART II

THE OLD IMMIGRATION

7

The Immigrant Traffic

FROM 1790 TO 1820, only about 250,000 immigrants entered the United States. The "American stock" of 1790, already a mixture of many groups, thus was left fairly free to multiply, without any appreciable additional admixture from without. It fully lived up to expectations, and demonstrated its vigor by bringing about a tremendous increase in population from somewhat over 3,000,000 at the time of the Revolution to over 10,000,000 by 1830. This was due almost wholly to "native" reproduction. Marriages were contracted early in those early days, and many a woman was a grandmother by forty. During the era of free lands, large families were an asset to a frontier community. From the point of view of immigration and population study, the colonial period was more or less of a unit and has been treated as such.

In the nineteenth century, and with increasing volume after 1830, the tide of emigration set in again from Europe. Wave after wave rolled over the cities and prairies of the New America. The Irish, the Germans, and the Scandinavians, in more or less sharply defined but overlapping streams, poured into the United States; and these major groups, together with several minor ones, constitute the "old emigration" from western and northern Europe, in contradistinction to the newer groups that came in the last quarter of the century from the south and east. Each deserves detailed treatment. In each case, specific causes, to be treated later, operated to start the emigrant tide on its way across the Atlantic and to keep it flowing steadily for decades. Aside from the universal desire for adventure and greater opportunity, there were certain causes for emigration common to all these groups; and it must be remembered that much of the European emigration was artificially stimulated and encouraged by interests in America desirous, for one reason or another, of bringing in a larger population.

First of all, as already suggested, the earlier population movements were influenced by the "America letters" written home by those who had ventured out first and whose accounts of the New Canaan were eagerly awaited and devoured by those who had remained behind. Christopher Saur's "America letters" praising "the goodness I have heard and seen" were printed and reprinted many times in Germany during the latter half of the eighteenth century, in order to induce people to come to Pennsylvania.[1] What the United States after 1776 symbolized to the liberty-loving, thwarted, and exploited Irishman can readily be imagined, especially when the glowing accounts that reached the Irish countryside assured the readers that "there is a great many ill conveniences here, but no empty bellies." In 1818, an enthusiastic reporter described the region around Wheeling in extravagant terms that must have been irresistible. He wrote:

> I believe I saw more peaches and apples rotting on the ground than would sink the British fleet. I was at many plantations in Ohio where they no more knew the number of their hogs than myself . . . . The poorest family has a cow or two and some sheep . . . good rye whiskey; apple and peach brandy, at forty cents a gallon . . . . The poorest families adorn the table three times a day like a wedding dinner—tea, coffee, beef, fowls, pies, eggs, pickles, good bread; and their favorite beverage is whiskey or peach brandy. Say, is it so in England? [2]

Gottfried Duden's rosy picture of Missouri, which he painted as a budding center for German culture in the American West, had a tremendous effect on a young Germany just passing through its period of *Sturm und Drang*.[3] The "America fever" was a highly communicable disease, spread by thousands of letters that reached the little cottages of peasant and burgher in Ireland, Germany, and Scandinavia.

Ole Rynning's *America Book*, first published in 1838, describing an America where wages were high, prices low, land excellent, religion and government free, and servant girls without outside work

[1] See Oscar Kuhns: *German and Swiss Settlements in Pennsylvania* (New York, 1901), p. 27.
[2] Letter of Samuel Crabtree, quoted in Edith Abbott: *Historical Aspects of the Immigration Problem* (Chicago, 1926), pp. 40-41.
[3] See Gottfried Duden: *Bericht über eine Reise nach den westlichen Staaten Nord-Amerika's* (Elberfeld, Germany, 1829); and Dorothy A. Dondore: *The Prairie and the Making of Middle America: Four Centuries of Description* (Cedar Rapids, Iowa, 1926), pp. 172-174.

to do save milking the cows had a large circulation in Norway and went through several editions.[4] "America letters" to Sweden depicted a land where "the hogs eat their fill of raisins and dates" and, "when they are thirsty, they drink from ditches flowing with wine." Sober Scandinavians would hardly be swept off their feet by such extravagant inventions; but they were duly impressed by reports of Iowa's supply of corn, hogs, and pumpkins, and by the report that all doors could be left unlocked because there were no beggars in America, that the climate there was healthier and more invigorating than in their native Sweden, and that there were no artificial class distinctions, ceremonies, or "title-sickness" in the new land across the sea. "There are no large estates," wrote one Swedish-American, "whose owners can take the last sheaf from their dependents and then turn them out to beg." Ministers and churches were said to be less worldly in America, and "there is ceaseless striving to spread the healing salvation of the Gospel." Hired men and maids ate at the same table with their employers and wore clothes of the same style. "Neither is my cap worn out," added another, "from lifting it in the presence of gentlemen." Small wonder that enthusiastic newcomers wrote: "We see things here that we could never describe, and you would never believe them if we did. I would not go back to Sweden if the whole country were presented to me."[5] "It is no disgrace to work here," wrote a Swede in 1841. "Both the gentleman and the day laborer work. No epithets of degradation are applied to men of humble toil . . . . I do not agree . . . that in order to appreciate the blessings of monarchy, one must live in a democracy."[6]

Not all of the letters that came from immigrants in America were, of course, as optimistic and laudatory as those just cited. The Swedish pastor, Gustaf Unonius, cynically observed that "the American competes with the mosquitoes to bleed the emigrant."[7] Some "America letters" expressed bitter regret for having yielded

[4] See T. C. Blegen: *Norwegian Immigration to America, 1825-1860* (Northfield, Minnesota, 1931), Ch. IV.

[5] Professor George M. Stephenson has collected and published many Swedish "American Letters"; the above selections are quoted in his: "When America was the Land of Canaan," in *Minnesota History* (September, 1929), Vol. X, No. 3, pp. 237-260. See also "A Typical 'America Letter'," in *Mississippi Valley Historical Review*, Vol. IX, No. 1, pp. 71-74.

[6] Quoted in George M. Stephenson (editor and translator): "Letters Relating to Gustaf Unonius and the Early Swedish Settlers in Wisconsin," in *Augustana Historical Society Publications*, Vol. VII, p. 51.

[7] Quoted in *ibid.*, p. 48.

to the lure of the New World. But the great majority were enthusiastic descriptions of a land of unlimited opportunity, in contrast with what was available to the poor at home. They were first read and reread by the simple, credulous people to whom they were originally addressed, then widely circulated among relatives and friends, and often read by the entire village. They were discussed in the home, at the market place, in church, and at the county fair; and were often printed for wider circulation in the newspapers. One or two such "America letters" were sufficient stimulus to spread the "America fever" through an entire parish.

Ship companies and organizations interested in land speculation did their part to keep the America fever burning at the proper temperature. Advertisements in American newspapers reveal a veritable flock of emigration agents; immigrant bankers dealing in remittances, steamship, and railroad tickets; and dealers in foreign exchange, each of whom had his special reasons for keeping the immigrant tide flowing in a steady, unbroken stream to the United States. Land agencies, with acreage for sale in Texas, Missouri, Wisconsin, and other parts of the West, advertised their bargains in newspapers published at the Eastern ports of arrival.[8] A New England Land Company, incorporated under Iowa law, offered to assist emigrants to reach the western Eldorado it had for sale and to arrange for an easy payment plan. Such offers frequently received editorial endorsement from the papers in which the advertisements appeared.[9] An "Irish Pioneer Emigration Fund" brought in Irish servant girls.[10] There was a Foreign Emigration Association in Maine in the 1860's to bring over servant girls under the Contract Labor Law of 1864. The American Emigrant Company, the Columbia Emigrant Agency, and the American Emigrant Aid and Homestead Company were other organizations interested in bringing immigrants to Chicago and the West.

Scores of *Emigrant Guides,* more or less reliable, were issued during the nineteenth century in various European languages, as well as in English. Reverend J. O'Hanlon's *The Emigrant Guide for the United States,* published in Boston, was recommended as especially good for the Irish.[11] For Germans, Traugott Bromme's *Missouri und Illinois—Taschenbuch für Einwanderer und Freunde*

---

[8] See, for example, *The Boston Pilot,* August 28, 1852.
[9] See *ibid.,* August 7, 1852.
[10] See *The Toledo Blade,* June 16, 1857.
[11] See *The Boston Pilot,* September 4, 1852.

der Länder und Völkerkunde (Baltimore, Maryland, 1835) and Francis J. Grund's *Handbuch und Wegweiser für Auswanderer nach den Vereinigten Staaten von Nord-Amerika* (Augsburg, Germany, 1854) are illustrations of what was available to the prospective immigrant on both sides of the Atlantic.[12] Hugo Risbeth's *Emigrantens Vän* was issued in Stockholm in 1881. Another guide in the Swedish language was Bojeson's *Till Amerika*. James S. Foster published a booklet of detailed instructions for immigrants who contemplated settling in the Dakotas.[13] These guides were usually strange mixtures of sound advice and optimistic overstatement. Their significance as a factor in promoting and directing immigration is clear, however, from the fact that scores of them were issued under various auspices.[14]

In the middle of the last century, the Middle West needed population above everything else. To attract desirable immigrants was the overpowering ambition of practically every new state in this region. State after state began to enact legislation to encourage and stimulate migration to its borders artificially. The attractions offered by favorable legislation and the persuasiveness of the agents of state immigration commissions were important factors in explaining the immigrant tide into the Mississippi Valley.

By its constitution of 1850, Michigan gave the franchise to all newcomers who had declared their intention to become naturalized and who had resided in the state for two and a half years. Its immigration agency, established in 1848 and not abolished until 1885,

---

[12] Grund wrote (p. 31):

> Bedenkt, dass die Flasche guten Weins in Amerika zwei Dollars kostet, und dass Ihr für Einen und Einen Vierteldollar baar Geld im Westen einen Acker Landes bekommt . . . . Die Amerikaner haben nicht viel Achtung für Leute, welche Stundenlang in Wein und Bierhäusern herumliegen (in ihren eigenen, Schenken sind nicht einmal Stühle zum Niedersetzen da); denn "die Zeit ist Geld" sagte Franklin . . . .

[13] "Outlines of History of the Territory of Dakota and Emigrants' Guide," in *South Dakota Historical Collections*, Vol. XIV, pp. 71-178.

[14] For other examples, see Calvin Colton: *Manual for Emigrants to America* (London, 1832); S. H. Collins: *The Emigrants' Guide to and Description of the United States of America*, fourth edition (Hull, England, 1830), containing some "America Letters"; John F. Carr: *Guide to the United States of America for the Immigrant Italian* (New York, 1911), prepared for the Connecticut D. A. R.; K. F. W. Wander: *Auswanderungs-Katechismus* (Glogau, Germany, 1852), showing the supply and demand for the various trades and professions in the United States; H. F. Wellinghoff: *Fingerzeige für Auswanderer nach den Vereinigten Staaten von Nordamerika* (Bremen, Germany, 1855), by the agent for the Baltimore German Society; and the Reverend D. R. Thomason: *Hints to Emigrants* (London, 1849), by the secretary of the Emigrants' Friend Society of Philadelphia.

issued attractive pamphlets in German, and its first immigration commissioner was instructed to spend half his time in New York and half in Stuttgart, Germany. Wisconsin had a special commissioner as early as 1851, and its board of immigration, created by legislative act in 1867, published pamphlets in seven different languages. From 1871 to 1875, 35,000 copies were printed for distribution in Europe. Other material was distributed in New York, in taverns and at the docks; and advertisements lauding Wisconsin's attractions were published in eight foreign newspapers, such as the London *Times,* the Tipperary *Free Press,* the *Baseler Zeitung,* and the *Leipziger Allgemeine Zeitung.* In 1880, Wisconsin issued 10,000 pocket maps of that state, with legends in English, Norwegian, and German.[15] The Wisconsin Constitutional Convention of 1846 gave the franchise to immigrants after a declaration of their intention to become naturalized and one year's residence in the state.

Minnesota followed a similar policy of encouraging immigrants to enter its borders. In 1855, in the person of Eugene Burnand, the state had a commissioner of immigration who could speak English, French, and German. Burnand was especially eager to attract Belgians, Swiss, French, and Germans, but made little effort to bring in Scandinavians.[16] In 1864, the legislature offered a cash prize of $200 for the best essay advertising the state to immigrants. The Swede Hans Mattson and the Norwegian newspaper man Hjelm-Jensen did valiant service in turning the Scandinavian tide into Minnesota.

From 1860 to 1862, Iowa had a state commissioner of immigration, the German-born lieutenant governor, Nicholas J. Rusch, who maintained offices at 10 Battery Place, New York City. Later, an

[15] See T. C. Blegen: "The Competition of the Northwestern States for Immigrants," in *The Wisconsin Magazine of History,* Vol. III, pp. 3-29. Blegen (p. 23) reprints the following interesting advertisement from *Der Volkfreund aus Schwaben:*

Auswanderer! Die fünfte gemeinschaftliche Reise nach dem Staate *Wisconsin* (Nordamerika) findet von Bremen aus, am 4. April, mit dem neuen Express-dampfer *Elbe,* statt. Überfahrt von Bremen nach New York nur neun Tage . . . . Wertvolle Karten und Broschuren über Wiskonsin sendet auf Verlangen gratis und portofrei der Commissar der Einwanderungsbehörde gennanten Staates: K. K. Kennan, in Basel, Schweiz."

See also *Annual Reports of the Commission of Immigration of the State of Wisconsin* (Madison, Wisconsin, 1871-1873).
[16] See Livia Appel and T. C. Blegen: "Official Encouragement of Immigration to Minnesota During the Territorial Period," in *Minnesota History Bulletin,* Vol. V, pp. 167-203.

[106]

immigration board, similar to those in other states, was created. A handbook, *Iowa: The Home for Immigrants,* was prepared in English, German, Dutch, Danish, and Swedish; and agents were sent to Holland, England, and Germany to make propaganda for the state. Governor Merrill of Iowa called a convention in Indianapolis in 1870, which was attended by representatives from 22 states and two territories, railroad and steamship lines, boards of trade, and German immigrant societies, to urge Federal legislation to prevent frauds and abuses in the handling of immigrants, to establish a Federal Bureau of Immigration to coöperate with the various state bureaus, and to bring about better shipping conditions. In a sense, the convention was the answer of the growing West, eager for population, to the restrictions on immigration favored by some of the Eastern states.[17] The Iowa board, in 1870, was composed of Mathias Rholfs for the Germans, Edward Munn and C. Rhymsburger for the Dutch, and Claus Clausen for the Scandinavians. In Iowa, as in other states, the commissioners worked in close coöperation with the railroads; but unlike many other states, Iowa required full citizenship before granting the right to vote.

Indiana, in 1868, required only six months' residence in the state, one year in the United States, and a declaration of his intention to become a citizen for a foreigner to vote.[18] Kansas, in 1872, royally entertained the Grand Duke Alexis and, immediately following his visit, sent special agents to Russia to seek settlers. This action, together with a law of the legislature exempting Mennonites from military service, were largely responsible for the large Mennonite settlements of Kansas.

A promoter for the Dakotas particularly urged women to come to this virgin region, where its 160 acres and "other attractions will soon find you a nest and a mate." Lapsing into verse, he pointed out that out in the Dakotas:

> There is no goose so gray, but, soon or late,
> Will find some honest gander for a mate.[19]

[17] See *House Executive Document,* 43 C. 1 S., No. 187; Marcus L. Hansen: "Official Encouragement of Immigration to Iowa," in *The Iowa Journal of History and Politics,* Vol. XIX, pp. 159-195; and O. B. Clark: "Advertising Propaganda of Early Iowa," in the *Mississippi Valley Historical Review,* Vol. VIII, p. 9 *et seq.*
[18] See *The Cincinnati Enquirer,* September 8, 1868.
[19] Quoted in George A. Batchelder: "A Sketch of the History and Resources of Dakota Territory (1870)," in *South Dakota Historical Collections,* Vol. XIV, pp. 181-251.

In connection with this brief summary of state encouragement to immigration in the nineteenth century, reference to the special effort made by the South after the Civil War to attract immigrants may be included here. Although some of the larger cities of the South had a sizable immigrant population, as will be shown later, immigrants in general had avoided a section which was devoted to but one crop, and that cultivated by slave labor. The old South had few attractions for the European who wished to stake out a farm or who sought an opportunity to ply his trade and to prosper in the growing industrial centers of the United States. After the close of the Civil War, some of the Southern leaders conceived the plan of attracting immigrants from Europe to their states, thereby supplanting what they regarded as the troublesome Negro labor population and aiding in the reconstruction of the South and in the diversification of its economic life.

State bureaus of immigration and immigration commissioners were created in the Carolinas, Florida, Virginia, Texas, Alabama, Georgia, and Louisiana. Texas worked in close coöperation with railroad and steamship companies. John A. Wagner, an influential German of Charleston who had been an officer in the Confederate Army, became commissioner of immigration for South Carolina, and sent his agents and his publications into Germany and Scandinavia.[20] Maryland sent an agent to Germany in 1865 and printed a pamphlet describing its advantages for German colonists.[21] Newspapers, local groups, realtors, and railroads joined forces with the states to attract immigrants to a section which they had hitherto generally avoided. The task was not easy and met with comparatively little success, but the propaganda for more immigrants continued. Many Southerners were convinced that immigration meant prosperity, that it would lessen the South's dependence on the colored race, and that it would help the Southern whites to overthrow the radical Negro carpetbag control of post-bellum days.

To solve their labor difficulties, some Southerners entertained the plan of importing Chinese laborers.[22] Southern immigration associations were formed and immigration conventions organized.[23]

---

[20] See Francis B. Simkin and Robert H. Woody: *South Carolina During Reconstruction* (Chapel Hill, North Carolina, 1932), pp. 244-246.

[21] See *New York Tribune*, October 9, 1865.

[22] See *Boston Transcript*, March 9, 1870; and January 24, 1870. See also *The Cleveland Leader*, May 6 and 12, 1870.

[23] See *Cincinnati Enquirer*, November 8, 1883.

Reports on industrial and agricultural resources and on climate were issued along with much other publicity, and a special committee of the Convention of 1870 resolved "that the introduction of Chinese labor would be of great benefit," since the Chinese were "industrious, frugal, obedient, and attentive to the interest" of their employers.[24] The South Carolina Railroad offered free land to immigrants, and plans were made for a direct line of steamships from Charleston to Europe.[25] Local communities raised their own funds to attract immigrants to their locality.[26]

Northern promotion companies were quickly organized to take advantage of this reversal of opinion in the South. "The true method of reconstruction," announced a pamphlet for the American Emigrant Company (New York, 1865), "is the infusion into the exhausted system of the South of the fresh blood of vigorous free emigrants from the Northern States and Europe." Incorporated with an authorized capital of one million dollars, the company was ready to furnish labor to employers, maintain agents abroad to import workers, and guarantee delivery on contract for a proper fee. The company's pamphlet gave as references Chief Justice Chase, Gideon Welles, Henry Ward Beecher, Charles Sumner, and a host of lesser lights. How it secured these sponsors is not apparent. Similar companies were formed in Boston.[27]

Virginia, in 1866, passed an act to encourage immigration, appointing General G. Tochmann, a Polish rebel of 1830, as one of its agents. Kentucky began taking steps to attract immigrants in the early 1870's.[28] In 1864, West Virginia appointed a Frenchman, born in Alsace, as its state commissioner of immigration and, in 1870, published the *West Virginia Handbook*.[29] A Chinese Labor Convention was held in Memphis in 1869 [30] to bring in cheap labor. In 1858, the notorious Parson Brownlow had said of Tennessee: "Leave us in the peaceful possession of our slaves, and our Northern

[24] See *Proceedings of the Immigration Convention* (Charleston, South Carolina), 1870, 84 pp.
[25] See *The Boston Transcript*, May 5, 1870. See also *The Cleveland Leader*, November 1, 1867, November 30, 1867.
[26] See Friedrich Kapp: *Immigration, and the Commissioners of Emigration of New York* (New York, 1870), p. 119.
[27] See *The American Emigrant Aid and Homestead Company* (Boston, 1867).
[28] See *The Toledo Blade*, February 13, 1873; and *Cleveland Leader*, January 11, 1870.
[29] See *First Biennial Report*, Department of Archives and History of West Virginia (1905), Vol. I, pp. 80-87.
[30] See *The Ohio State Journal*, July 15, 1869.

Neighbors may have all the paupers and convicts that pour in upon us from European prisons!" By the close of the Civil War, however, he, like other Tennesseans, approved the incorporation by the legislature of an American Emigration Society, capitalized at $5,000,000, designed to sell land to immigrants recruited from the North and from abroad, and to bring in Irish, Norwegians, and Germans. Hermann Bokum, "a ripe German scholar," became Tennessee's commissioner of immigration and issued *The Tennessee Handbook and Immigrants' Guide* (1868).[31] In his eagerness to promote a direct steamship line from Hamburg to New Orleans, in order to make the latter the chief port of entry for all immigrants into the Mississippi Valley, the president of the Louisiana Emigration Company made a personal study of European conditions in 1869. Two agents of the Turkish government were actually reported in Richmond, Virginia, for the purpose of purchasing land on which to colonize 200 Armenians.[32] Once more, in the 1880's, when the South was rapidly becoming industrialized and the "New South" had its latchstring out for industries, cheap labor, and capital, immigration conventions were held in several states "to swell the tide of returning prosperity." [33] It was even rumored that all the Waldenses were thinking of leaving Europe and settling in North Carolina.[34]

In spite of these sporadic efforts, the immigration propaganda of the South after the Civil War fell far short of expectations. Some immigrant colonies were settled in the Southern states, like the Swedish town of Stockholm near Richmond, Virginia, in 1865; a Danish dairying colony in Mississippi;[35] and scattered German and Italian settlements in Texas, Louisiana, and Virginia.[36] Actually, however, the foreign population of South Carolina declined from 9,986 in 1860 to 7,686 in 1880. It was far easier and more attrac-

[31] See W. B. Hesseltine: "Tennessee's Invitation to Carpet-Baggers," in *The East Tennessee Historical Society Publications*, No. 4; and *Cleveland Leader*, August 20, 1867.
[32] *Cincinnati Enquirer*, September 19, 1868.
[33] See E. P. Oberholtzer: *A History of the United States Since the Civil War* (New York, 1931), Vol. IV, pp. 521-522. See also *Proceedings of the Immigration Convention of Texas of 1887* (Dallas, Texas, 1888), 48 pp.; and *The Richmond Dispatch*, April 14, 1893.
[34] See *The Cleveland Plain Dealer*, February 28, 1893.
[35] *Cincinnati Enquirer*, January 15, 1870.
[36] See *Cleveland Leader*, November 12, 1867; and Hermann Schuricht: "History of the German Element in Virginia," in *The Thirteenth and Fourteenth Annual Reports of the Society for the History of the Germans in Maryland*, pp. 127-128.

tive for European immigrants to go West to their kinsmen than to settle below the Mason and Dixon's line. For many years the South remained a backward section as regards schools, roads, housing, and economic development. Germans and Italians alike were "not willing to settle down and live on bacon and corn bread," and the European prejudice against the South could not be removed in a single generation.[37]

Steamship and railway companies had a special interest in stimulating the immigrant traffic, for obvious reasons, but the latter had an additional objective in promoting the disposal of their railroad lands to actual settlers. In 1870, Jay Cooke, as the financial promoter of the Northern Pacific Railroad, employed Hans Mattson, who resigned his position as secretary of state of Minnesota to undertake the assignment, to go to Sweden to advertise the resources of the road and to draw up a plan for the disposal of its lands. J. J. Hill may have saved his road from financial disaster by promoting the settlement of Minnesota by Norwegian and Swedish farmers, whose bumper crops quickly tripled the earnings of the railroad.[38] Hill, in order to make the Red River Valley district more attractive to settlers, described it as an area "where the depth of the humus was equal to the height of a man." [39] The Northern Pacific at St. Paul gave special passes to ministers of the Gospel, so that they might more frequently visit outlying immigrant settlements where no church had as yet been organized. When a trainload of Dunkards moved from Indiana to North Dakota, they went by special train, with streamers on the railroad cars advertising "the bread basket of America." The Atchison, Topeka, and Santa Fe Railroad, through its foreign immigration department, extended its activities to the Ural Mountains, bringing over 15,000 Russian-German Mennonites to Kansas. By 1883, they had settled along the route of the railroad in Kansas, with branch settlements in Oklahoma and Colorado.[40]

[37] See R. H. Woody: "The Labor and Immigration Problem of South Carolina During Reconstruction," in *The Mississippi Valley Historical Review*, Vol. XVIII, pp. 195-212; W. C. Hunt: "Immigration to the Southern States, 1783-1865," in *The South in the Building of the Nation*, Vol. V, pp. 595-606; and *Cincinnati Enquirer*, July 1, 1868; and Bert J. Loewenberg: "Efforts of the South to Encourage Immigration, 1865-1900," in *The South Atlantic Quarterly*, Vol. XXXIII, pp. 363-385.
[38] See Matthew Josephson: *The Robber Barons* (New York, 1934), p. 235.
[39] Quoted in Lawrence M. Larson: "The Norwegian Element in the Northwest," in *The American Historical Review*, Vol. XL, pp. 69-81.
[40] See C. B. Schmidt: "Reminiscences of Foreign Immigration Work for Kansas," in *Kansas Historical Collections*, Vol. IX, pp. 485-496; and Richard Sallet: *Russland-deutsche Siedlungen in den Vereinigten Staaten* (Chicago, 1931).

The Burlingame and Missouri Railroad also was active in attracting Mennonite settlers to the American West.[41]

The Illinois Central Railroad carried on one of the most vigorous colonization programs of any road in the United States. It sent a Norwegian clergyman to Quebec to work among the immigrants; it made a special effort to attract Germans, enlisting the support of Lieutenant Governor Francis Hoffman of Illinois for this task, who was to receive a commission as land agent for every German he brought in; it maintained an "intelligence office" and immigrant "runners" in New York; and it supported a land department, which issued great quantities of advertising in several languages. After 1870, it employed General John Basil Zurchin, a Russian engineer who had been an officer in the Civil War, to organize the Agencyja Polskiej Kolonizacyi to bring Poles into Illinois. Zurchin was successful to an unexpected degree in developing both Polish agricultural and mining colonies.[42]

A similar intensive program was maintained by the railroads in order to attract immigrants into the Pacific Northwest. The Northern Pacific had a "Land Committee" which published maps and descriptive matter in several languages, and maintained agents in all the leading countries of western and northern Europe. By an arrangement with steamship companies, immigrants could buy through tickets to Duluth or St. Paul. Temporary immigrant houses, with stoves and beds, were prepared to receive the immigrant when he arrived in the West. Farms were sold on easy terms. The advertising program for immigrants was especially extensive after Henry Villard acquired control of the road in the 1880's.[43] It supported two immigration bureaus, one in Boston and one in Portland, Oregon; issued special immigrant half-fare certificates; and waged extensive advertising campaigns in the foreign press.[44] Needless to add, many a customs and immigration officer at Castle Garden, New York, was in the pay of some railroad company and was expected to use his persuasive powers, supported by his official status, to direct

[41] See *The New York Times*, February 19, 1879.
[42] See Paul W. Gates: "The Campaign of the Illinois Central Railroad for Norwegian and Swedish Immigrants," in *Norwegian-American Studies and Records*, Vol. VI; and *The Illinois Central Railroad and Its Colonization Work* (Cambridge, Massachusetts, 1934). See also *Toledo Blade*, January 12, 1857.
[43] See James B. Hedges: "The Colonization Work of the Northern Pacific Railroad," in *The Mississippi Valley Historical Review*, Vol. XIII, pp. 311-342.
[44] See James B. Hedges: "Promotion of Immigration to the Pacific Northwest by the Railroads," in *The Mississippi Valley Historical Review*, Vol. XV, pp. 183-203.

the immigrant to some particular spot in the Western prairie country.

The New York Times for June 23, 1853, contained a vivid and inspiring description of the arrival of a German emigrant ship in the North River:

> Moustached peasants in Tyrolese hats are arguing in unintelligible English with truck-drivers; runners from the German hotels are pulling the confused women hither and thither; peasant girls with bare heads, and the rich-flushed, nut brown faces you never see here, are carrying huge bundles to the heaps of baggage; children in doublets and hose, and queer little caps, are mounted on the trunks, or swung off amid the laughter of the crowd with ropes from the ship's sides. Some are just welcoming an old face, so dear in the strange land, some are letting down huge trunks, some swearing in very genuine low Dutch, at the endless noise and distractions. They bear the plain marks of the Old World. Healthy, stout frames, and low, degraded faces with many; stamps of inferiority, dependence, servitude on them; little graces of costume, too—a colored head-dress or a fringed coat—which could never have originated here; and now and then a sweet face, with the rich bloom and the dancing blue eye, that seem to reflect the very glow and beauty of the vine hills of the Rhine.
>
> It is a new world to them—oppression, bitter poverty behind—here, hope, freedom, and a chance for work, and food to the laboring man . . . to the dullest some thoughts come of the New Free World.

Stout hearts as well as "healthy, stout frames" were needed to survive the immigrant traffic which brought so many of our ancestors to the promised land. Many did not survive the ordeal; others survived it only to fall victims in American ports to disease or to some of the worst exploiters of helpless humanity that any generation has ever seen; and many no doubt cursed the day they left their native firesides. As far as handling their human cargo was concerned, immigrant ships of the middle nineteenth century showed little improvement over those of a century earlier. The horrors and perils of the sea voyage may have been exaggerated or multiplied in many of the accounts left by immigrants who survived the ordeal and lived to relate their experiences to their grandchildren, but after due allowance is made for overstatement and the desire to tell a dramatic, heroic tale, enough is left to make the horrors of some of the immigrant ships comparable to the suffering of the middle passage during the African slave traffic.

Shipowners usually chartered the lower decks to agents at a fixed rate per ton of cargo, and neither the owner nor the agent therefore manifested great concern about overloading the boat with human freight. Immigrants were packed into the steerage. The usual height of the steerage deck was from four to six feet, and the lower deck was hardly more than a black hole. Departure for America was frequently delayed because the captain had to wait for a load of freight before sailing. In the meantime, immigrants were either robbed and exploited in the ports of embarkation or their supply of provisions became exhausted. The first law of the United States Congress dealing with steerage conditions, in 1819, provided that there should be no more than two passengers for every five tons' capacity. A ship of 1,000 tons but with steerage of only 500 tons could take on passengers for the whole tonnage, and the captain and owners could be relied upon to take 400 instead of half as many. No provisions were made for ventilation; nor was the space used for freight and for officers' and first-class passengers' quarters to be deducted in computing the room allotted to steerage passengers.

Steerage quarters five feet high often had two tiers of beds, and below was the "orlop-deck," a hole to which no regulations whatsoever applied. The only fresh air available came through the hatches, and these had to be closed when air was most needed—namely, during a storm. Emigrants in steerage were for many years expected to furnish and cook their own food, and two rooms on the upper deck, perhaps five by four feet each, were set aside as the steerage galley. Passengers literally fought with each other for use of the grate and hooks on which to hang their kettles, and frequently had to consider themselves fortunate if they succeeded in getting their food half cooked. Bread became mouldy, fish and meat spoiled, and soup was finally made from grease or mutton tallow.[45]

Diseases like "ship fever" (typhus), cholera, smallpox, and dysentery broke out frequently on shipboard and flourished in the almost indescribable filth that followed a heavy storm. Hundreds, when they landed, were ready for the hospital, or for such inadequate care as the overburdened port facilities could offer. The vessel's inner walls were generally without paint or plaster, and ships frequently

[45] See also a letter in 1833 describing the food in steerage in *The Missouri Historical Review*, Vol. XIV, pp. 46-55.

began the return voyage without disinfection. Although Congress passed various regulatory acts in 1819, 1824, 1847, and 1855, it was not until well after the middle of the century, when steamships began to crowd out the old sailing vessels, that much improvement was possible.[46]

Conditions on Irish immigrant ships from Liverpool were especially bad. Steerage passage from Ireland to the United States in 1830 cost about $12. The cost of provisions for the trip was perhaps $15. As the wages offered by American canal companies were from $10 to $15 a month, hundreds of Irishmen took the risk. The ships on which they came were generally overcrowded and undermanned, and there were not enough ships in the 1840's and 1850's to carry all those who were eager to come. The steerage passengers suffered from lack of food and water and from disease; there were charges of gross immorality, for the sexes were not properly segregated and the crews sometimes took advantage of female passengers.[47] In 1847, the *Lark* arrived with Irish immigrants in Quebec. She had started with 440 passengers, of whom 158 had died en route and 186 became sick.[48] In 1847, a ship arrived in Philadelphia with 230 Irish immigrants. During the passage, there had been 22 births on board.[49] In the same year, the average mortality rates at sea and in quarantine among immigrants destined for Canada was 7.21 per cent for adults and 8.84 per cent for all passengers, including children. For those coming from Liverpool, the death rate was 15.39 per cent; for those coming from Ireland, it was 7.86 per cent.

A medical man, describing the disease-stricken Irish from Cork and Liverpool, wrote: "I never saw people so indifferent to life; they would continue in the same berth with a dead person until the seamen or captain dragged out the corpse with boat-hooks . . . ."[50] An emigrant, describing a trip in steerage from Liverpool to New York on the ship *India* in the winter of 1847-1848, has left us a nauseating account of the Irish passengers, whose food supplies had already been half exhausted by an eleven-day wait in the port of embarkation. Heavy storms were encountered, during which boxes of food were pitched about between decks and all hatches closed.

---

[46] See Kapp: *op. cit.*
[47] See John F. Maguire: *The Irish in America* (London, 1868).
[48] See Kapp: *op. cit.*, p. 23.
[49] See *Cincinnati Enquirer*, September 29, 1847.
[50] Quoted in Gilbert Tucker: "The Famine Immigration to Canada, 1847," in *The American Historical Review*, Vol. XXXVI, pp. 533-549.

Three hundred passengers had to remain below, in spite of intolerable heat, vomiting, and filth. When, after four days, the storm subsided and the hatches were again opened, the rush to the ladders was so great that several were injured. By the fifth week out, 15 had died of ship fever and had been buried at sea; 42 were sick in bed, many so delirious that they had to be tied down, and, to cap the climax, an epidemic of diarrhoea broke out, probably from the drinking of impure water. The voyage lasted eight weeks. Upon arrival in Staten Island, the stricken were hauled off to the hospital in carts, with straw for beds. If this recital seems too nauseating to the reader, it can only be added that some of the most lurid details have been omitted.[51]

The newspapers of the 1850's and 1860's were full of statistics as to the mortality rate on immigrant ships, and Horace Greeley, in a series of editorials in his *New York Tribune,* sought to expose the evils of the whole immigration system.[52] From November 15 to November 17, 1853, of 4,344 passengers leaving Europe for the United States on ten vessels, 469 died en route. Statistics collected in a Senate document which refers to steerage passengers as "the lowest order of humanity, . . . filthy in their habits, coarse in manner, and often low in their instincts," show that, in 1853, 312 vessels arrived in New York in four months with 96,950 passengers. Of these, 1,933 died at sea and 457 were taken to a New York hospital.[53] A ship arrived in Boston from Sweden in 1853 with 58 dead of cholera.[54] In 1851, after a passage of 36 days, the packet ship *Washington* arrived from Liverpool in New York with 5 cabin passengers and 956 in steerage—the largest number of passengers carried by one ship up to that time.[55] In September, 1850, the *New York Tribune* reported the experiences of a German immigrant family of five members. After 60 days at sea, a five-year old girl was the only member left.[56] In 1858, it took the Hamburg immigrant ship *Howard* 96 days to reach New York. During the

[51] See William Smith: *An Emigrant's Narrative; or a Voice from the Steerage* (New York, 1850), 34 pp. For an even worse picture, see the report of the New York Commissioners of Emigration, in 1868, on the ship *Leibnitz,* arriving from Hamburg after 70 days out, in Kapp: *op. cit.,* pp. 188-195.

[52] See *New York Tribune,* November 19, 22, and 26; and December 3, 1853.

[53] See "Steerage Passengers on Immigrant Vessels," in *Senate Executive Document,* No. 23, 43 C. 1 S. (Washington, D. C., 1873).

[54] See *Ohio State Journal,* October 20, 1853. See also *Cincinnati Enquirer,* June 8, 1847.

[55] See *New York Tribune,* March 31, 1851.

[56] See *ibid.,* September 23, 1850.

last 42 days, there had been no drinking water, a food shortage, and 37 deaths from cholera.[57] Perhaps even worse are the tales of the brutality, drunkenness, and lack of discipline of some of the crews; stories of criminal attacks on girls, sometimes even by officers, and the screwing off of planks in order to reach the quarters of the women passengers.[58] Many ships had no doctors on board and were little more than "swimming coffins." [59]

Some companies, like Train and Company, had a much better record, and boasted of their performance in newspaper advertisements.[60] Others advertised "roomy steerage quarters" and provided medicine for the sick and free board, consisting of salt beef, bacon, beans, peas, rice, potatoes, perhaps coffee or tea, and, "for the men, a drink of brandy . . . in the morning." [61] The American Emigrant Company, in its pamphlet issued in New York in 1865, carried an advertisement of a steamboat company requiring steerage passengers to provide mattress, bedding, and "mess tins" (plate, mug, knife, fork, spoon, and water can) but furnishing coffee, sugar, bread, butter, and oatmeal for breakfast; beef, pork, or fish, soup, potatoes, and bread, with plum pudding on Sunday, for one o'clock dinner; and tea, sugar, biscuits, and butter for supper. The American Steamship Company, in 1873, charged $32 for steerage passage and $40 for "first steerage." [62]

Bremen was the chief port of departure in the nineteenth century for Germany, and here conditions seem to have been much better than in Liverpool, in Irish ports, or even in Hamburg. The Bremen city government passed regulations to make the port a safer

[57] See Hermann Wätjen: *Aus der Frühzeit des Nordatlantikverkehrs* (Leipzig, Germany, 1932), p. 154.
[58] See *ibid.*, p. 162.
[59] For other examples of the horrors and sufferings of the immigrant traffic, see *Cincinnati Enquirer*, December 30, 1846; *The New York Times*, February 21, 1853; and Edith Abbott: *Immigration: Select Documents and Case Records* (Chicago, 1924). The report of the Commissioners of Emigration to the New York Legislature for 1852, reprinted in *The New York Times* for February 17, 1853, shows 2,190 vessels arriving with 300,992 aliens, of whom 118,611 were Germans and 118,131 Irish. Of this number, 24,315 went to hospitals, 335 had to be cared for as lunatics, 20,339 were supplied with board and lodging, 763 were buried in New York, 433 were sent back to Europe, and 117,600 were given temporary relief in the way of food and shelter. Aliens in the hospital at Ward's Island numbered 10,966, of whom 1,201 died. See also *Congressional Record*, 36 C 1 S, Pt. II, pp. 955, 1013, 1146-1147, 1265-1266, and 1368.
[60] See *The Boston Pilot*, November 13, 1852; and *The Boston Transcript*, November 14, 1853.
[61] For an emigrant's contract with a Bremen company, see *Missouri Historical Review*, Vol. XIV, pp. 42-46.
[62] See *Ohio State Journal*, August 6, 1873.

place for emigrants as early as 1832. Nevertheless, many an unsuspecting emigrant was greeted upon his arrival in Bremen by stage coach, and later by train, by porters and hotel men (*Bauernfänger*), who soon had him at their mercy. In 1851, Bremen created a bureau of information to end this exploitation, and emigrant hotels (*Auswandererhäuser*) were made available at a modest charge. Hamburg, through private resources, established a *Verein zum Schutze von Auswanderern*, and the Hamburg *Senat* created an emigration commission to protect the emigrant. Many Germans sailed to the United States on American three-deckers, boats of from 350 to 1,000 tons, which had brought cotton to Europe. Inspection of immigrant ships in the Elbe and the Weser Rivers, before their departure, was later provided, although the requirements for comfort and sanitation remained modest enough, and a fixed routine was established for those on board. In 1837, steerage passage from Bremen to the United States cost $16.[63]

From 1855 to 1875, conditions gradually improved, partly because of legislation in the United States and European countries to protect the immigrant—Germany leading the way—and partly because of the transition from sailing vessels to steam, thus providing greater speed and reducing the average time for the voyage from 44 to 13 days. Competition for the immigrant trade, together with the progress of inventions, brought the use of mechanical ventilation, running water, separate berths, washrooms, ships' hospitals and doctors, and more rigid inspection upon arrival. Nevertheless, in the 1880's and 1890's, two thirds of the passenger list of many a trans-Atlantic liner still traveled steerage and had about one fifth of the ships' deck space.[64]

In spite of this depressing recital of the sufferings and miseries of emigrant voyages, it must not be forgotten that thousands upon thousands survived and that these counted the cost lightly, in view of the new opportunities open to them in America. There were also clear days and nights on shipboard, with the stars, the moon, and the glimmering waves; and on such days and nights there was dancing, singing to the accompaniment of the accordion, and games

---

[63] For interesting details on the trade from Hamburg and Bremen, see Wätjen: *op. cit.*; and Joseph Pachmayr: *Leben und Treiben der Stadt New York* (Hamburg, Germany, 1874).

[64] See E. J. Anderson: "Voyage of the Immigrant," in *Swedish-American Historical Bulletin*, Vol. XI, No. 3, pp. 70-103; and Rudolf Brandenburg: *Imported Americans* (New York, 1904).

on deck. It was not all a voyage of darkness and storms and rolling, pitching seas. Lasting friendships were formed on the voyage that ripened with the years in America. Occasionally, immigrants praised the captain of their vessel for the discipline he maintained and because "he was like a father to us all." A Norwegian, writing in 1854, described the voyage as follows:

> When the weather was pleasant, we often had a good time, for all kinds of games and amusement were allowed. We frequently danced. Even the Captain, himself, was often with us, entertaining us with adventure and hunting stories and the like. On the evening of the day after Pentecost we had a ball. We each gave twelve cents and the captain contributed the rest. We had three musicians, and then we danced and drank till late in the night. We each contributed a little money and bought a gold watch chain for our captain. It cost fifteen dollars.[65]

The sea voyage safely passed, the immigrant was likely to run afoul of the beasts of prey in human form who waited to pounce upon him on his arrival in New York, to exploit his ignorance of the English language, and his "greenness" about American conditions generally. New York was infested with "runners," who were paid by trucking firms, railroad ticket offices, and immigrant hotels and boarding houses for no other purpose than to compete with other runners and lead the unsuspecting immigrant into the clutches of the hotelkeeper or baggage agent. Runners were paid from $10 to $30 a week, or a certain percentage of the business they secured. Competition became extremely keen and, on many occasions, violent; for, in order to hold his job, a runner had to be a good "shoulder hitter" as well as a persuasive talker.

When a ship arrived, runners rushed to the gangplank and began fighting with other bullies over the immigrant's luggage, in order to get him to stop at a particular boarding house. These immigrant hotels and boarding houses were generally operated, not by native Americans, but by foreigners who congregated like vultures in the seaport towns to prey upon their own countrymen. In the worst of these houses, the immigrant was overcharged for everything, particularly for the storage of his baggage, which was then held as security until all bills had been paid. Occasionally, but not often, an immigrant runner's license was revoked for fraud. Usually, the

---

[65] Quoted in *Norwegian American Historical Association Studies and Records*, Vol. III, p. 63.

law was indifferent to the plight of the stranger in a strange land.[66] Occasionally, too, charges were lodged against runners and steamship, baggage, or railroad agents who had cheated unsuspecting immigrants out of hundreds of dollars or had collected sums of money as commissions for securing jobs that never materialized. The newspapers then usually recorded that the culprit had "left for parts unknown," and that ended the case.[67] An article in *The New York Times* for June 23, 1853, accurately described the arrival of an emigrant ship as follows:

> Every one in the great City, who can make a living from the freshly arrived immigrants, is here. Runners, sharpers, pedlars, agents of boarding-houses, of forwarding offices, and worst of all, of the houses where many a simple emigrant girl, far from friends and home, comes to a sad end . . . .

Some immigrants hung around the German boarding houses in Greenwich Street, each day losing more of their savings. Others, Irish and Germans, settled down in the Eleventh Ward, to become peddlers and ragpickers and to succumb to the vice of intemperance. Horace Greeley maintained that 90 per cent of the "rum holes" in some wards of New York were kept by foreigners. Immigrants were delivered into the tender clutches of keepers of places that were half brothels, half combination grog shops and boarding houses. The editor of the *Tribune* urged benevolent societies of the foreign-born to erect model boarding houses to cope with these evils.[68] A pamphlet delivered to passengers on an American line running from England to New York in 1838 warned against "the infernal gambling hells, dens of infamy, houses of ill fame" set up by "delinquents, great and small, from all nations, which you will find as thick as blackberries, at the port to which you are bound, and at landing will swarm and buzz about you like so many bees." Immigrants were urged to get out of New York as quickly as possible and to start for the West.[69] Thousands were so badly fleeced in New York, however, that they had to stay in the city and seek immediate employment. By 1850, there were 16,000 tenement houses in New

---

[66] See *New York Tribune*, July 12, 1850.

[67] See *Cincinnati Enquirer*, September 22, 1883; and *New York Tribune*, November 28, 1883.

[68] See *The New York Tribune*, November 10, 1853.

[69] See *Goodwin's Advice to Emigrants* (New Haven, Connecticut, 1841), 21 pp. See also Thomas Butler Gunn, *The Physiology of New York Boarding Houses* (New York, 1847), pp. 255-262.

York housing over half a million people, many of them immigrants who were stranded in the city.

Finally, in 1855, Castle Garden was established in New York as a compulsory landing place for immigrants, from which runners and sharks were debarred and in which official agencies were set up to give the immigrant sound information, exchange his money at an honest rate, and sell him tickets for his destination inland at a fair price. The runners protested violently against this interference by the state with their private "vested interest." An "Emigrant Runners' Indignation Meeting" was held at the Battery in New York; violent speeches were made against the government's interference with legitimate private business and flaming rockets were shot into the air over Castle Garden. A week later, another meeting was held, and a large force of police had to be mobilized to prevent serious consequences.[70] On the more favorable side of the picture, however, it should be pointed out that an effort was made to take care of all immigrant arrivals who were sick by sending them to the New York hospitals. Here they were cared for in wards until recovery. Sometimes they went out to work in the spring and returned to the hospital in winter, their wives and children being fed and cared for in the meantime.[71]

The immigrant frequently resorted to a "booking office" to buy his ticket Westward. Here he could easily be overcharged both for fare and freight, and often he bought a through ticket only to find, when it was too late, that it would carry him only halfway. There was false weighing of baggage, overcharging, and bullying and brutal treatment by agents and runners when the immigrant tried to protest. Often the journey inland was purposely delayed in order to help the boarding house or saloonkeeper, who was the booking agents' confederate. Two tallies of the baggage were frequently kept, one for the company and one for the emigrant. "Stools" among the immigrants themselves were promised free passage by runners if they induced their entire party to patronize a certain railroad or canal company, and when they demanded their pay, were threatened with exposure to their friends. Here again, it must be emphasized that much of the exploitation came from the victim's own countrymen rather than from native Americans.[72]

[70] See *The Boston Transcript*, August 14, 1855; and *Boston Herald*, August 8 and 15, 1855.
[71] See *The New York Times*, May 20, 1853.
[72] See Baron A. von der Straten Ponthoz: *Forschungen über die Lage der*

The ordinary prices by steamer and canal from New York to Albany and thence inland were reasonable enough, and the railroads tried to stop the selling of bogus tickets by swindlers in New York,[73] but forwarding houses were hard to regulate and generally charged the immigrants higher rates, on one pretext or another, in order to divide the profits with their agents and runners. In the 1840's, the "official" table of prices was as follows:

New York to Albany . . . . $ .75
New York to Buffalo 4.50
New York to Cleveland 7.00
New York to Detroit 8.00
New York to Milwaukee 14.50
New York to Chicago 14.50

Baggage up to 50 pounds was supposed to be transported free. Children under twelve paid half fare; those under two were carried free.[74] A Norwegian immigrant, in 1847, was able to go from New York to Albany, up the Hudson, for $.50. To go by rail from Albany to Buffalo cost $12, but by way of the Erie Canal the rate was only $7.50, including meals, with a special price of $2 if immigrants brought their own food.[75]

Immigrant travel over this route, across New York and then into the West by way of the Great Lakes, was heavy. Immigrant trains were not distinguished for their accommodations and comforts. Often the cars used were springless boxcars, with hard benches and no drinking water, and the immigrant passenger was of course expected to bring or buy his own food. Sometimes the coaches had absolutely no conveniences, not even seats, except for long boards running lengthwise along both sides of the cars, so that many had to sit or lie on the floor.[76] Newspapers recorded the passage of long immigrant trains through Albany and Buffalo, trains with extra locomotives and long lines of cars, filled with Germans, Dutch, Swiss, or Scandinavians.[77] In Chicago and other terminal points,

Auswanderer in den Vereinigten Staaten von Nord Amerika (Augsburg, Germany, 1846); and Kapp: *op. cit.*, pp. 61-84.

[73] See *The Cleveland Plain Dealer*, March 8, 1854.

[74] See *Ueber Auswanderung von einem Kaufmanne in Bremen* (Bremen, Germany, 1842), pp. 30-32.

[75] See G. J. Malmin (editor and translator): *America in the Forties: The Letters of Ole Munch Raeder* (Minneapolis, 1929).

[76] See Emeroy Johnson (editor), *Early Life of Eric Norelius* (Rock Island, Illinois, 1934), p. 107.

[77] See *Ohio State Journal*, July 15, 1854; and *Toledo Blade*, March 26, 1873.

runners for land companies, railroads, and state immigration commissioners met the incoming trains.[78]   In 1853, a resident of Chicago wrote: "One fourth of the persons you meet in Chicago cannot
speak a word of English, and a good part of the remainder cannot
speak it well.   Germans, Irish and Norwegians seem to be as plenty
as natives." [79]   The immigrants were so numerous in Milwaukee in
1842 that they were forced to lodge in the streets, while in Racine
and Southport all tavern facilities were exhausted.[80]   In the 1850's,
emigrant trains passed over the New York and Erie road at regular
intervals, attracting much attention with their car windows trimmed
with green vegetation and their passengers smoking long German
pipes and singing German songs.[81]

Traffic on the Erie Canal boats passed through beautiful country
at what would now be regarded as a snail's pace.   Canal boats were
greatly overcrowded.   In 1842, Gustaf Unonius wrote:

> In Albany, we boarded a canal boat from Buffalo . . . .
> With justice this part of the journey may be called a tor-
> ture, because the crowding of the boat is simply unbear-
> able, and the passage through the locks, especially at night,
> is anything but pleasant.[82]

The writer had to admit, however, that he "sought in vain for
human bones protruding from the soggy ground and disclosing the
graves of starved Europeans." [83]

The immigrant traffic from New Orleans upstream to St. Louis,
Cincinnati, and other river ports was considerable.   Apparently the
congestion of passengers and the inadequate accommodations on
river steamers were such as to duplicate on a somewhat reduced scale
many of the objectionable features of the immigrant traffic overseas.
An item in *The Memphis Eagle* referring to the overcrowding of
river boats with immigrants pointed out that "every boat which had
them at all, had them in droves of hundreds, crowded and penned
up like cattle; and nearly every boat buried from 15 to 20 between
this place and New Orleans." [84]   Passengers were packed in a space
of some 30 by 40 feet behind the engines of the boat, where the heat

[78] Gates: *The Illinois Central Railroad,* p. 198.
[79] Quoted in *The New York Times,* June 21, 1853.
[80] *Baltimore Patriot,* August 3, 1842.
[81] See *Atlantische Studien,* Vol. II, p. 73.
[82] Quoted in George M. Stephenson: "Letters Relating to Unonius," in *Augustana Historical Society Publications,* Vol. VII, p. 81.
[83] Quoted in *ibid.,* p. 117.
[84] Quoted in *Albany Argus,* May 28, 1849.

from the ship's boilers was terrific. In 1849, the steamer *Winfield Scott* from New Orleans reached Louisville with over 400 German immigrants aboard, "having buried upwards of thirty while on the way up, who died of cholera, ship fever, and other diseases." The deck and hurricane roof of the boat swarmed with immigrants, "many of whom," according to *The Louisville Democrat,* "looked as though they were in a dying state." [85] The cholera broke out all over the Middle West in 1849, and numerous deaths were reported, not only on river and lake boats, but on canal boats destined for Buffalo as well.[86] In January, 1854, *The Louisville Journal* reported fourteen ships tied up at Cairo, as a result of the suspension of navigation. Two thousand immigrant passengers were set ashore. Suffering from want of food, cholera, and yellow fever, they tried to make life in the adjoining woods bearable by keeping up huge fires.[87]

In spite of all the romance that surrounds the river boats in song and film today, immigrant travel up the Mississippi, along its tributaries, and on the Great Lakes seems to have been quite perilous. Thousands of immigrants entered the Mississippi Valley by these routes. The newspapers of the period before the Civil War contain a surprisingly large number of accounts of boiler explosions on river and lake steamers, in which passengers were killed, frightfully scalded, or even blown overboard by the force of the explosion.[88] In 1850, the steamer *G. P. Griffith* burned on Lake Erie with 300 aboard, 256 of whom were immigrants. Only 35 were saved.[89] In 1842, German immigrants were severely injured when the flue of a Mississippi River boat collapsed. The year before, the steamboat *Erie* was lost by fire at Buffalo. Of its 200 passengers, 95 of whom were Swiss immigrants traveling in steerage, only 30 were saved. Apparently the accident had been caused by bottled spirits of turpentine placed too near the fire in the boiler room.[90] As late as 1870, a boat burned at LaCrosse, Wisconsin, resulting in the deaths of an undetermined number of immigrants.[91] The mortality rate

[85] Quoted in *ibid.,* May 24, 1849.
[86] See *ibid.,* July 3, 1849.
[87] Cited in *The Boston Pilot,* January 28, 1854.
[88] See *Albany Argus,* June 14, 1849.
[89] See *The Ohio Statesman,* June 21, 1850.
[90] See *Baltimore Patriot,* July 12 and 13, 1842. For another description of the same accident, see Stephenson: *loc. cit.,* p. 62. According to this account, 200 of the 250 passengers died. Apparently there were 200 life preservers, but no one had time to make use of them.
[91] See *Boston Transcript,* May 23, 1870.

of the river traffic was high, partly because many immigrants arrived at New Orleans or some Eastern port half starved and greatly debilitated from the ocean voyage. The change in climate and water produced many cases of typhus and diarrhoea.[92] Finally, the boats were infested with cardsharpers and other professional sharpers, from whom immigrants could protect themselves on occasion only by appointing regular watches from among their number, who stood guard at night equipped with firearms to prevent robbery.[93]

In spite of risks and suffering, immigrants generally counted the cost low, for in the Mississippi Valley land was available at ridiculously low prices. Newcomers were known to have bought as many as 40 acres of "improved land," with farm buildings and part of the land cleared, at a cost of $2 or less an acre. A house cost $30, fencing perhaps $15, a brood sow with a litter of pigs $3, a fresh cow and calf $10, and enough fowl could be secured for a few additional dollars. Small wonder that enterprising immigrants were willing to run the risks of mental and physical suffering, when $150 was all that was needed to begin farming effectively!

The plight of the immigrant did not leave Americans entirely unconcerned. Organizations were formed among immigrants already here to help newcomers from the fatherland and to do philanthropic work of many kinds among the new arrivals. The German Society of New York was started before the end of the eighteenth century and never lost its interest in benevolent activities for German immigrants. Irish Emigrant Societies were formed in Philadelphia, New York, Boston, Savannah, Charleston, and elsewhere to do relief work and to combat the frauds and outrages perpetrated on newcomers. In 1851, an Irish Emigrant Industrial Savings Bank was created to protect the immigrant from exploitation, through which $30,000,000 were sent to Ireland within the next 36 years.[94] In New York, a society organized for immigrant relief had the Mayor as its president in 1843 and Horace Greeley as its secretary.[95] In 1841, the German Society of Maryland took care of

[92] See *Albany Argus*, May 26, 1849.
[93] See James D. Burn: *Three Years Among the Working-Class in the United States During the War* (London, 1865), p. 133.
[94] See *The Boston Pilot*, October 16, 1852; and *Old Countryman*, May 3, 1843. See also Peter Guilday: *The Life and Times of John England* (New York, 1927), Vol. II, p. 5; and Sister Mary Evangela Henthorne: *The Career of the Right Reverend John Lancaster Spalding, Bishop of Peoria, as President of the Irish Catholic Colonization Association of the United States, 1879-1892* (Urbana Illinois, 1932), pp. 20-21.
[95] See *Old Countryman*, April 12, 1843.

the German passengers stricken with typhus on the ship *Virginia* and in this one case alone paid bills amounting to $400.[96]   At mass meetings of Scandinavians, special societies were advocated to protect Scandinavian immigrants landing in New York.[97]   The superintendent of one of the German emigrant houses in New York reported in 1883 that, in the ten years of its existence, that house had furnished food and lodging to 69,989 people.[98]   The work of some of these houses was generously supported by the churches of the city.[99]

In 1847, New York created a Board of Commissioners of Emigration.   Thurlow Weed and Archbishop Hughes had been active in advocating such a board.   Among its membership, two names should be remembered for special devotion and outstanding service —namely, that of Andrew Carrigan, an Irishman and president of the Irish Emigrant Society, and that of Friedrich Kapp, a distinguished leader of the German element.   The Board of Commissioners of Emigration gave advice and aid to immigrants, found employment for them, and inspected the ships that brought them in. The captain of each vessel was compelled to file complete data for each voyage at the mayor's office, subject to a fine of $75 for each omission.   The owner of the ship, or consignee, had to give bond for each passenger named in the report to cover possible costs of relief and hospitalization, or he could commute this obligation by paying $1—later $2.50—per person to the New York City Health Commissioner.   In 1855, the board was authorized to buy the old fort at the foot of Manhattan Island and convert it into an emigrant landing station.   From that time to 1890, when immigration control was transferred from state to Federal authorities and Ellis Island came into use, every immigrant landing in New York entered the United States through the gates of the famous Castle Garden.[100]

All had to land here, and no one was allowed on the pier except by permission.   This was the first effective means of combatting runners, and the latter sought injunctions in the courts, held protest meetings, and tried in every way to prevent this interference with their business profits.   The first superintendent of Castle Garden was John A. Kennedy, who, in 1860, became superintendent of the

[96] See *Baltimore Patriot and Commercial Gazette*, September 7, 1841.
[97] See *The Toledo Blade*, May 27, 1873.
[98] See *The New York Tribune*, November 1, 1883.
[99] See *Der deutsche Pionier*, Vol. XVII, p. 201.
[100] See *The New York World*, April 6, 1890.

New York Police Department. Various departments and services were maintained at Castle Garden, such as a bureau of registration, ticket offices for legitimate railroad agents, exchange brokers, a city baggage delivery service, a labor exchange, a letter-writing department, and a general information desk. By 1868 and 1869, the labor exchange at Castle Garden could not fill one tenth of the requests for railroad laborers, and only a small portion of the requests for Irish and German farm laborers.[101]

Prior to 1847, all passengers landing in New York who were ill were taken care of in the Marine Hospital, at quarantine. In 1849, this hospital was restricted to use for contagious diseases only. Owing to the Irish famine and the hordes of Irishmen swarming into the United States in the late 1840's, the New York Board of Commissioners of Emigration selected Ward's Island for the care of all immigrants having noninfectious diseases. After 1863, all diseases were treated there with the exception of smallpox, which was the special concern of a hospital on Blackwell's Island.[102] Occasionally, the commissioners of emigration rented churches and other buildings to house destitute immigrants.[103] The extent of their activity in this respect may be judged from an early report in 1851 which revealed that, in four months, the commissioners had furnished lodgings on Canal Street to 39,000 destitute immigrants, who remained an average of four days each. In one night, 196 Sullivans and 95 Shays registered in the Canal Street lodging house. In the four months under consideration, employment had been found for nearly 8,000.[104]

Simultaneous with the efforts of private charities and the New York board described above, a series of laws dealing with immigration was passed, beginning with the Act of 1819. These laws dealt with attempts, still feeble and inadequate but becoming increasingly rigid and effective, to prevent overcrowding by stipulating a certain amount of deck space for each passenger, which varied depending on whether the vessel passed through the tropics or not. Further legislation dealt with berths and sleeping quarters, ventilation, provisions and supplies, storage space, toilets, and sanitation. Fines

[101] See Kapp: *op. cit.*, p. 117. For a brief biography of Kapp, see Edith Lenel: *Friedrich Kapp, 1824-1884* (Leipzig, Germany, 1935).
[102] For some comments on Ward's Island and its "Emigrant Asylum," see Frederika Bremer: *The Homes of the New World*, 3 vols., translated by Mary Howitt (London, 1853), Vol. I, pp. 70-71.
[103] See *New York Tribune*, January 24, 1852.
[104] See *ibid.*, June 6, 1851.

were prescribed, including, by the Act of March 3, 1855, which superseded all other acts, a payment of $10 by the captain for every passenger (not counting cabin passengers) over eight years of age who died at sea "by natural disease." Penalties became a lien on the vessel. Needless to add, these laws were defective and their enforcement was still more so, since there was as yet no coördinated American immigration policy, but they do indicate a tardy recognition of the eventual responsibility of the Federal Congress for the immigrant traffic.[105]

[105] For United States laws dealing with immigration, up to 1855, see W. J. Bromwell: *History of Immigration to the United States* (New York, 1856), pp. 206-217.

8

The Irish

FROM 1820 TO 1920, over four and a quarter million Irish immi-✓ grants came to the United States. One cause for this extraordinarily heavy emigration was the constant pressure of population on the resources of the Emerald Isle, for in Ireland the density of population was greater than in any other country of western Europe. The dominant industry of Ireland was agriculture. It was under the control of an aristocracy, many of whom were absentee landlords who rented their land to scores of small farmers or cotters, who in turn farmed with the most antiquated implements and backward methods.

Economists are agreed that Ireland witnessed a progressive deterioration of its farming class from 1815 to well past the middle of the century. Taxation, finance, and the courts were under the control of the landed aristocracy. The normal wage in Ireland was sixpence a day including one meal and eightpence a day without food. The food of the peasant, in his happiest and most prosperous times, consisted of nothing more than potatoes, a little milk, and occasionally fish. Meat was so scarce that many families never saw it from one year to the next. The peasant's hut, in which he usually reared a large brood of children, was filthy, damp, cold, and smoky. It had but one room to house the whole family, which, at least in some cases, included the family pig. Education, even of the most rudimentary sort, was impossible for hundreds of families. Drinking and its natural accompaniment, rioting, constituted the prevailing curse of the Irish people. The slums of Dublin were notorious for poverty, disease, and filth in the early decades of the nineteenth century. If one adds to these distressing conditions exploitation by a foreign power (England) and the denial of political privileges to the native Irish, and the burden of paying tithes for the support of a Church establishment which Irish Roman Catholics hated, it is obvious why Ireland was a fertile recruiting ground for immigrants in the nineteenth century and why the immigrant tide to the United States could not be stopped once it had begun to flow. Between 1815 and 1830, the more substantial farmers constituted the bulk of the Irish immigration to America; after that date, the flood gates were open to all.[1]

Ireland, in the nineteenth century, was conquered territory. Every rebellion against English authority had been ruthlessly suppressed. Repressive measures did not make the Irish less bellicose. A foreign Church weighed on a population that was intensely Catholic, and that suffered under discrimination and repressive legislation directed against the adherents of that faith. The British commercial system was repressive also, and continued to be applied in the old spirit of eighteenth-century mercantilism. Absentee landlords milked the country of its wealth, robbed their tenantry of every incentive to make permanent improvements, and often brutally evicted renters who failed to meet their obligations promptly. The British government usually favored Irish emigration as good riddance to a troublesome population. A part of the London press heaped reproaches on the departing Irish and described them as "departing marauders whose lives were profitably occupied in shooting Protestants from behind a hedge," "demons of assassination," "vermin," "snakes," and the "scum" that flows across the Atlantic.

The Irish emigrant trade really began in the years 1816 and 1817. From 6,000 to 9,000 Irish sailed for America in each of these years. In 1818, the number more than doubled. Vessels began to be chartered for the specific purpose of transporting emigrants, although, as a general practice, vessels that had brought American cargoes of cotton or timber to Ireland departed with human cargoes for the return voyage. As the emigrant trade grew, the evils of the emigrant traffic described in the previous chapter made their appearance. Although these abuses may have been exaggerated during the years when traffic was fairly normal, there can be no question of what occurred when, for special reasons, it was extraordinarily heavy.

In 1827, the Irish immigration to America reached 20,000. By 1831 and 1832, it exceeded 65,000. After 1835, with the exception

[1] See W. F. Adams: *Ireland and Irish Emigration to the New World from 1815 to the Famine* (New Haven, Connecticut, 1932), Ch. I. This is by all odds the best book written to date on Irish immigration, and I am heavily indebted to it.

of 1838, there were never less than 30,000 Irish crossing the Atlantic in any one year. In 1842, the total reached 92,000.

This movement across the sea was aided and abetted by the desire of contractors for cheap labor to build the internal improvement projects that were sweeping the United States like a mania in the decades before the Civil War. As early as 1818, 3,000 Irish were employed on the Erie Canal alone. There was hardly a canal built anywhere in the United States before the Civil War without Irish labor. By 1826, 5,000 were at work on four canal projects. Road work was equally alluring, as was railroad building. Many employers sent money to Ireland to pay for the passage of the cheap labor they desired; others found employment for the Irish in the mill towns springing up in New England. Thus was begun that "Roman Conquest" of New England which has essentially modified its English and Protestant characteristics, and which has made a state like Massachusetts—next to one or two of the mountain states —the strongest Catholic state in the nation in proportion to its population. Thus, "solid groups of Irish of the lowest class were thrown as cohesive masses into the melting pot." [2] The majority were illiterate, and thousands knew no English.

Potato famines had always meant disaster for a population such as Ireland's, which constantly bordered so close on starvation. There had been famines before 1845, but that year marked the beginning of a succession of cold, damp summers, with the resultant potato rot, a plant disease which destroyed practically the whole crop. Pestilence, fever, starvation, and death descended upon the Irish countryside, and nearly one fourth of the population succumbed. Relief ships from America provided little aid. Fortunate was the man or woman whose friends in the United States could send the passage money promptly!

The figures for the period of the Irish famine immigration mounted to startling totals: 92,484 in 1846, 196,224 in 1847, 173,744 in 1848, 204,771 in 1849, and 206,041 in 1850. [3] The Census of 1850 reported 961,719 Irish in the United States; by 1860, the total had reached 1,611,304. These were to be found in greatest numbers in New York, Pennsylvania, Massachusetts, Illinois, Ohio, and New Jersey. The character of Irish immigration changed under the pressure of intolerable suffering and famine. The poor, small far-

[2] Adams: op. cit., p. 195.
[3] See American Historical Review, Vol. XXXIII, p. 591.

mer, who had constituted the bulk of the migration up to 1835, who knew English, had sufficient energy to be proud of his independence, and was determined to rise, gave way to a new type—namely, the laborer, with little background aside from his potato patch, who was ignorant of the English language, of a mercurial temperament, and likely to find life and progress in the United States very difficult.

Early in 1847, the roads to Irish ports were literally thronged with immigrant families. Sometimes strong men actually battled with each other at the ports of embarkation to secure passage on ships entirely inadequate to provide transportation for all who wished to go to America. The description of the ravages of the Irish famine tax the reader's imagination. Children and women were described as too weak to stand; the livestock had perished, people were eating carrion, and "the weekly returns of the dead were like the bulletin of a fierce campaign." [4] Beggars crowded the roads and the city streets. People huddled half-naked in fireless and foodless hovels. Thousands crossed to Liverpool and demanded transportation to the United States on crowded and filthy emigrant ships whose resources were taxed to the utmost. In 1847, a young English Quaker reported the town of Westport as "itself a strange and fearful sight, like what we read of in beleagured cities; its streets crowded with gaunt wanderers, sauntering to and fro with hopeless air and hunger-struck look—a mob of starved, almost naked, women around the poor-house clamouring for soup tickets . . . ." [5] An organization in Philadelphia, in six months, collected $48,000 in cash and $20,000 worth of articles, and sent seven relief ships to Ireland. [6] American Protestant churches appealed for aid for the stricken Irish. At the same time, those interested in promoting immigration circulated handbills and maintained agents in the principal towns of Ireland. The Irish needed little encouragement, for they remembered the letters written home by Irishmen as early as 1830 emphasizing that in America meat, flour, and gin are cheap, that "there is no complaining on our streets," and that, "if a man like work, he need not want for victuals." [7]

The Irish temperament is noted for its buoyancy and optimism,

---

[4] Sir Charles G. Duffy: "The Distressed Condition of Ireland, 1847: An Irish View," quoted in Edith Abbott: *Historical Aspects of the Immigration Problem* (Chicago, 1926), pp. 116-120.
[5] Quoted in Abbott: *op. cit.*, pp. 116-121.
[6] See Thomas D'Arcy McGee: *A History of Irish Settlers in North America* (Boston, 1852), p. 139.
[7] Quoted in Abbott: *op. cit.*, p. 77.

for its ability to extract the maximum satisfaction from whatever joys life has to offer.   A poet of the 1850's wrote:

> But though her sons in exile roam,
> They sleep on Freedom's pillow,
> And Erin's daughters find a home,
> Beyond the Western billow.[8]

Hope sustained the voyagers across the Atlantic, but for many it vanished like the rainbow when the actual conditions of life in America had to be faced.   Almost all Irish immigrants had to begin in the United States as unskilled laborers, and many got no farther. Year after year, the Irish Emigrant Society of New York advised immigrants to shun the cities of the Atlantic seaboard and to scatter throughout the United States, particularly into the West.   "Thousands continually land entirely penniless and are at once in a state of destitution," the warning continued, "whereas such person should have at least five pounds on his arrival to enable him to prosecute his journey to the interior." [9]   The advice was sound, but thousands found it impossible to follow, for all their earthly possessions had been used up during the voyage.   They arrived in the New Canaan with their pockets empty.   The almshouses and hospitals were filled to overflowing, and beggars wandered aimlessly through the streets. Men and women accustomed to no other existence than eking out a living from the soil were suddenly left stranded in congested cities. They had no trade and no particular skills; many did not even know the language.   They were destined to become the unskilled, marginal workers of the America of the middle nineteenth century, with all that that implies.   Many lurid accounts of Irish "shanty towns" are available to the historian of the Irish immigration.   Some are descriptions obviously colored by a deep hatred for the newcomer, but there is enough in the comments of friendly critics to indicate that conditions were deplorable, to say the least.   Indeed, one who is familiar only with the Irish-Americans of the twentieth century may find it hard to credit the tales told about their ancestors of several generations ago.

The Irish, as a class, came to America with less means than many other immigrant groups.   The majority were poverty-stricken. Having no money to proceed Westward on their own account, they

---

[8] *New York Tribune,* October 4, 1851.
[9] Quoted in Adams: *op. cit.,* p. 235.

usually got out of the cities only when contractors for internal improvement projects recruited them in the labor markets of the East and transported them to the West and South. On their arrival in the port towns and larger cities, the Irish crowded the tenements, sometimes twenty or more families living in one house. These Irish tenements were hardly more than "human rookeries." What a difference it might have made, and what an excellent investment it might have turned out to be, had the government used its funds to transport the Irish into the West and helped them to become established as farmers on the public lands! There are many unnamed graves of Irishmen along the canal and railroad routes which they helped to build.[10] In South Boston in 1850, the Irish slums were buildings from three to six stories high, with whole families living in one room, without light or ventilation, and even the cellars crowded with families. Saloons were the curse of the neighborhood, and police records abundantly reflected this unhealthy condition.[11] The death rate among the children of the Irish poor was alarmingly high. Disease, particularly during cholera epidemics, always ravaged the immigrants living in hovels in the western and eastern sections of New York City worse than in other communities. Secret societies arose in the Irish shantytowns among Irish laborers with such names as "the Corkonians," "the Connaughtmen," and "the Far Downs," who engaged in bloody brawls and riots, which even the repeated denunciations of the Church authorities seemed powerless to stop.[12] In some of the "better-class" tenement houses in New York, Negroes were preferred as tenants to the poor Irish and Germans.[13]

Misery loves company, especially among the Irish, and the Irish are a congenial people. Unfortunately, the drink evil, already acute in Ireland, became a positive menace in America. Large numbers of Irish rushed into the saloon business. Whiskey often was a part of the contract by which Irish laborers were employed in construction gangs. The saloon influence quickly led to a connection with machine politics. Laborers on canals and railroads in the

[10] See Stephen Byrne: *Irish Emigration to the United States* (New York, 1874), p. 12.

[11] See Abbott: *op. cit.,* pp. 596-600.

[12] See Henry A. Brann: *John Hughes* (New York, 1892), p. 89.

[13] For a report on immigrant tenement houses in New York (1857), see Abbott: *op. cit.,* pp. 633-638. There was a row of tenements in New York, called "Ragpicker's Paradise," inhabited entirely by Germans with their dogs, who collected and sold rags, paper, and bones.

West, as well as workers in the cities, were organized into clubs under the leadership of saloonkeepers, in order to exploit them politically and to provide greater profits for the liquor business.[14] Here may be found at least one answer to the query raised by the *Chicago Tribune,* in its issue of December 23, 1853:

> Why do our police reports always average two representatives from 'Erin, the soft, green isle of the ocean,' to one from almost any other inhabitable land of the earth? . . . Why are the instigators and ringleaders of our riots and tumults, in nine cases out of ten, Irishmen?

The Irish immigrant boarding house was particularly notorious, and worse by far than the German *Gasthaus* that developed in the port towns. It has frequently been described as little better than a "sty." Usually, it was a brick building with a grog shop on the first floor, full of runners and loafers of all kinds. A saucer full of free tobacco stood on the counter to satisfy the taste for nicotine of the runners and "shoulder-hitters," who got through life largely on their brawn and muscle. The baggage room for immigrants was in the cellar. The upstairs rooms were overcrowded and distinguished by their lack of cleanliness. It was to such a place that a Paddy, just arrived in New York, in his caped and high-waisted coat, brimless *caubeens,* knee breeches, woolen stockings, and rusty brogues, was likely to be taken. And it was here that he was likely to be exploited by his own countrymen, through fraud and exorbitant charges enforced by ruffianism.[15] Sympathetic critics like Thomas D'Arcy McGee, one of the most distinguished Irishmen in the history of the United States and Canada, deplored the effect of this overcrowding of the larger cities on the Irish character. Family ties were being weakened and broken in the United States, and McGee saw the second generation of Irishmen becoming less faithful in their allegiance to the Church. "That abstract Irish reverence for old age," which had always been one of the finest traits of the Irish, was being lost. "We meet every day," wrote McGee, "the apostate children of Irish parents, sons of emigrants, and themselves the worst enemies of emigrants, . . . afraid to profess their religion, . . . ashamed of their origin."[16] Orestes A. Brownson, who

[14] See Peter Guilday: *The Life and Times of John England* (New York, 1927), Vol. II, p. 515.
[15] See Thomas B. Gunn: *The Physiology of New York Boarding Houses* (New York, 1857), pp. 263-269.
[16] McGee: *op. cit.*, p. 237.

had been a Calvinist, transcendentalist, universalist, socialist, and skeptic, but concluded his career as a devout member of the Roman Catholic Church, believed that the Irish held fast to their orthodox faith but could by no stretch of the imagination be called an "advance guard of humanity," as far as their level of civilization was concerned.[17]   Year in, year out *The Boston Pilot,* a leading paper among the Irish, which was under the direct influence of the Catholic hierarchy, pleaded with the Irish to regard America as their home and to recognize the responsibilities and obligations of their new citizenship.[18]   Jeremiah O'Donovan, in 1864, put his description of the Irish in Albany into verse, and was satisfied that they were on the high road to successful Americanization:

> The Irish there, are worthy of applause,
> They help to make and regulate the laws;
> To what I say, exceptions may be few,
> That all are moral, honest, faithful, true.
> They love the Isle had given them their birth,
> The greenest Isle that can be found on earth;
> Though hard it be to split true love in two,
> They love the land of their adoption too.[19]

The Irish laborer in the middle nineteenth century frequently found himself in difficulties because of shameless exploitation and bad working conditions, and because of the resentment harbored against him by native Americans who feared his competition, although apparently few Americans had any wish to do the heavy, dirty, unskilled labor that fell to the lot of the Irishman with his pick and shovel. Newspapers friendly to the Irish immigrant warned him to stay away from the canal and railroad construction projects, for "these railroads have been the ruin of thousands of our poor people" and their workers are treated "like slaves" by the railroad contractors.[20]   Wages were low, usually $1 a day but often less; they were not clearly fixed and were paid partly in whiskey and "store pay," or merchandise, sold at high prices. Friends of the Irish urged them to form protective associations, with objectives

[17] See E. D. Branch: *The Sentimental Years, 1836-1860* (New York, 1934), p. 384.
[18] See *The Boston Pilot,* June 24, 1854.
[19] Jeremiah O'Donovan: *A Brief Account of the Author's Interview with His Countrymen* (Pittsburgh, 1864), p. 283.
[20] See *The Boston Pilot,* July 31, 1852.

somewhat like the trade unions, in order to stop competition, rivalries, and fights between warring gangs that drove wages down in their competition for the available jobs. Above all, the Irish were advised to go to the country to work on farms or squat upon government land in the West, to "do anything, in fact, in preference to railroading." [21]

Irish longshoremen were employed at the docks in all the leading sea- and lake ports. They bitterly resented the invasion of Negroes, who were often brought in expressly to depress the wage scale. Riots between Irish and Negro dock workers were not infrequent. It is this economic competition that helps to explain the strong hostility of the Irish toward the abolitionist movement, and the New York draft riots during the Civil War.[22] Workers on the Chesapeake Railroad and Ohio Canal were known as the Longfords and Corkonians. On some of the Ohio canals, Irish and German pick-and-shovel workers received only $.30 a day, with board, lodging, and a "jigger-full" of whiskey. Everywhere the Irish were doing the hard work, even in the South, where they were so badly treated at one time that Bishop England found it necessary to publish a warning in Irish newspapers advising Irish workers to avoid the South.[23] Accidents, deaths, and injuries were numerous in road building and canal digging, and cave-ins occurred frequently in excavations for tunnels. Little tumble-down markers in tiny Catholic burying grounds along the route of these internal improvements still bear mute testimony to the hazards of pick-and-shovel work.

In the 1840's and 1850's, little "Dublins" sprang up in the factory towns of New England and in the Middle Atlantic states, for the Irish were invading the mill centers. The Irish population of Boston trebled in a decade. Often the mill population was the residue from the labor supply that had dug the canals or constructed the mill race. In Rhode Island, for example, the first Irish millworkers were recruited from those who had built the railroad between Providence and Boston, and the Woonsocket Irish Catholic settlement was due entirely to the construction of the Blackstone

[21] See *ibid.*, July 31 and September 25, 1852.
[22] See E. D. Fite: *Social and Industrial Conditions in the North During the Civil War* (New York, 1910).
[23] See *The Charleston Mercury*, May 12, 1859; and Guilday: *op. cit.*, Vol. II, p. 501. See also *Cincinnati Gazette*, October 4, 1880.

Canal.   Irishmen went into the mill towns of Pawtucket and the "coal pits" between Fall River and Newport.[24]   At first, the competition of Irish labor was resented by other workers.   Towns tried to restrict the sale of lots so as to keep out Catholic purchasers, and the sign "No Irish Need Apply" was posted in some of the factories. The children of the Irish were twitted and abused on the playground and in the schoolyards much as some Irish children today join in making life uncomfortable for "dagos," "wops," and "kikes." But the economic urge was irresistible; and the Irish captured the mill towns, only to be in turn dispossessed in a later generation by Poles, Italians, French-Canadians, and the products of the "new" immigration.

Irish workers had a bad reputation for rioting and brawling, and the newspapers of the middle of the last century are full of graphic accounts of their bloody battles.   In 1853, for example, the eviction of an Irishman from a circus performance at Somerset, Ohio, for smoking a pipe started a battle in which Irish railroad workers fought all night and into the next day.   A company of militia had to be called from Zanesville to restore order.[25]   Feuds between groups of Irishmen hailing from different counties in Ireland led to frequent riots.   On one occasion, in Indiana, 400 militia had to be called out to stop an impending assault by several hundred belligerent Irishmen from County Cork.[26]   A riot that broke out along the line of a projected Pacific railroad, in 1853, over the election of a foreman of a labor gang, would have had serious consequences but for the timely intervention of a Roman Catholic priest, who served as peacemaker.[27]

After reading the many accounts of brawling and fighting among Irish workingmen that appear in the American newspapers, one becomes aware of the fact that not all the trouble was due to the Irishman's belligerent temperament, his love of the bottle, or his belief that contentiousness is the spice of life.   Much of this rioting was the result of intolerable labor conditions.   The brawls were often efforts, however misguided and unwise, to achieve an improve-

[24] See William Byrne *et al.*: *History of the Catholic Church in the New England States* (Boston, 1899), Vol. I, p. 356.
[25] See *Ohio State Journal*, September 19, 1853.
[26] See Logan Esarey: *A History of Indiana* (Indianapolis, 1915), Vol. I, pp. 95-96.
[27] See *St. Louis Republican*, quoted in *The New York Times*, January 19, 1853.

ment in labor standards at a time when the labor movement had hardly begun. There were strikes for higher wages on internal improvement projects, many of which led to a display of force, particularly when contractors refused later to respect the agreements they had been forced to accept.[28] In 1840, a serious riot broke out when the wages of Irish laborers on an aqueduct in New York City were cut from $1 to $.75 a day.[29] There were similar disturbances, caused by wage reductions, on the Illinois Central, the Buffalo and State Railroad, the Steubenville and Indiana, and other lines.[30]

The reign of terror instituted by the "Molly Maguires" in the anthracite coal regions of Pennsylvania is well known to students of American history, and is usually described as one of the worst examples of mob rule and blackmail in the whole history of labor relations, for which Irish coal miners are held primarily responsible. Viewed from a longer perspective, the incident is but another illustration of the battle for better working conditions in the coal-producing areas, although the movement fell under the control of criminals and ended in a number of executions. The anthracite coal regions of Pennsylvania had a mushroom growth in the 1830's, with immigrant labor, poor housing facilities, and all the evils of company towns and company stores as natural concomitants of this rapid expansion. The region suffered from the evils of overdevelopment and frequent business slumps, which weighed especially heavily upon the Irish coal miners. Working conditions in the mines were terrible, with no safety requirements, inspection, or proper ventilation. From 1839 to 1848, wages were $1 or $1.25 a day for miners and $.82 for ordinary laborers. In 1869, a peak of $18.20 a week was reached, but by 1877 the wage had declined again to $9.80. "Breaker boys," aged 7 to 16, worked like slaves in the mines under mine bosses whose character left much to be desired. An editorial in *The Boston Pilot* exposed conditions in the coal mines—the inadequate pay, the "murderous neglect" of ventilation, the "rancid provisions" available at high prices in company stores, the explosions in the firedamp caverns in which Irish and Welsh miners were blown to pieces, and the "scandalous ungenerosity"

[28] For the account of a strike of tunnel workers on the Hocking Valley Railroad, see *Ohio State Journal*, August 1, 1854.

[29] See Allen Nevins (editor), *The Diary of Philip Hone* (New York, 1927), Vol. I, p. 472.

[30] See *The Boston Pilot*, January 7, 1854.

subsequently shown by the operators toward their mutilated work-men—and concluded by denouncing some of the owners as men with "the conscience neither of Christian nor of Pagan." [31]

Irish benevolent societies were formed to deal with some of these problems. The Ancient Order of Hibernians, a semisecret organization, became the backbone of the miners' unions. In a very long story of real class war, the responsibility for violence in the Pennsylvania coal fields seems to be pretty well divided. By 1860, the Molly Maguires terrorized the whole anthracite region, elected sheriffs and constables, and resorted to arson, blackmail, and murder. The organization was not finally broken up until 1875, when, because of the detective work of James McParlan, 19 were hanged after trials held in an atmosphere of great excitement and prejudice. The incident for a long time blackened the record of Irish-Americans, and many refused to see the industrial conditions which had provoked such criminal action. Furthermore, it must be added that the better elements among the Irish population denounced the Molly Maguires, particularly the Church, which threatened the leaders of this organization with excommunication.[32]

That temperance was a virtue which many Irish immigrants found it hard to cultivate is abundantly evident from the comments of friendly and sympathetic critics. In 1830, an Irish immigrant wrote home:

> Give my very kind love to Father, and tell him if he was here he could soon kill himself by drinking if he thought proper .... I can go into a store, and have as much brandy as I like to drink for three half-pence, and all other spirits in proportion.[33]

A part of Charleston, where there were many "low groggeries," was known in the Boston neighborhood as "Dublin Row." [34] In editorials on "the corner grocery," where rum was available at three cents a glass, The New York Times thundered against the prevalence of drunkenness in the 1850's, but without special ref-

[31] See ibid., May 24, 1862.
[32] See George E. McNeill: The Labor Movement: The Problem of To-Day (New York, 1887), pp. 264-267; F. P. Dewees: The Molly Maguires (Philadelphia, 1877); Anthony Bimba: The Molly Maguires (New York, 1923); and J. F. Rhodes: History of the United States (New York, 1920), Vol. VIII, Ch. II. These accounts are quite different in their appraisal of the organization.
[33] Quoted in Marcus L. Hansen: "Immigration and Puritanism," in Norwegian-American Studies and Records, Vol. IX, p. 11.
[34] See The Boston Traveller, January 12, 1857.

erence to the Irish, who were not the only victims of the unregu-
lated American saloon. It described the "grocery" as

> . . . a school for murder, . . . a rotten, crazy-looking
> wooden tenement with leaking casks and damaged fruit
> strewn about it, and filled with five or six half-drunken,
> wholly-brutal men, and youths, on whose lowering brows
> vice has set its mark, that it may know them again.[35]

During the height of the nativist disturbances of 1855, an Irish
weekly in New York counseled the Irish to abandon "their intemperate habits, their rows, their faction fights." [36] Circulars were
issued to immigrants to keep them out of grog shops until the
"friends of temperance and good order" could get hold of them.[37]
Clergymen, both Catholic and Protestant, agreed that effective temperance work was the most urgent demand of the times. Many
riots of Irish laborers, especially on pay day, when drinking began,
lasting well into the next day, were attributed to too easy access to
bountiful supplies of cheap whiskey.[38] Railway passenger cars
sometimes were stoned because inebriated Irishmen refused to pay
their fares.[39] A Catholic historian denounced the rioting as the
manifestations of a "semi-civilized race." [40] Bishop Ireland, decades later, still opposed the American saloon, believing that the
Catholic Church should speak out against it and that liquor dealers
and saloonkeepers should be excluded from membership in Catholic societies.[41] Another American leader in 1841 deplored the fact
that "an Irishman and a drunkard had become synonymous terms,"
and that, "whenever he was to be introduced in character, either on
the theatre, or the pages of the novelist, he should be represented
habited in rags, bleeding at the nose, and waving a shillelah." [42]
The W. C. T. U., established a generation later under the leadership of Frances Willard, had a special department for work among

[35] *The New York Times*, April 23 and 26, 1853.
[36] Quoted in Abbott: *op. cit.*, p. 818.
[37] See the circular in the Library of the Ohio State Archaeological and Historical Society, Columbus, Ohio.
[38] See *The Boston Traveller*. January 19 and February 17, 1857. For other
incidents of rioting and mob rule, see *The New York Times*, January 3, 1853; and
Albany Argus, September 11, October 3, and November 6, 1849.
[39] See *Boston Traveller*, May 11, 14, and 19, 1857.
[40] Byrne: *The Catholic Church in New England*, Vol. I, p. 362.
[41] John Ireland, Archbishop of St. Paul: "The Catholic Church and the
Saloon," in *The North American Review* (October, 1894), pp. 498-505.
[42] P. H. Morris (editor), *A Memoir of the Very Reverend Theobald Mathew*
(New York, 1841), pp. XIII and XIV.

the foreign-born. As late as 1881, it maintained that "compulsory education and prohibition of the grog shop will prove the strong hands to lift Patrick from the gutter and help steady his legs for all time." [43]

The Boston Pilot, a paper under strong Church influence and a genuine friend of the Irish, denounced the uncleanliness of Irish homes and the prevalence of the drink evil, which seemed to affect wives and husbands alike. The editor was particularly incensed over the "Paddy funerals," which brought the Irish in Boston and elsewhere into disrepute. Irish "wakes" brought together "a crowd of people drinking and smoking as they would in a common bar room." At funerals, the "boys" frequently remained outside the church smoking and drinking while the services were going on. Then began the procession to the churchyard—"a long train of tumble-down vehicles" driven by "brutes." Driving pell-mell, even racing with each other, the procession ran over toll bridges, "the drivers apparently well 'corned,' and the insiders ditto, and singing or screaming at the top of their lungs." Sometimes there was a race to the grave and a bloody fight before the body was buried. "We have seen as disgusting a set of savages gathered together to bury a corpse as could scarcely be matched in any part of the world," complained the enraged editor. He blamed these scenes, to be sure, on Irish "radicals," and called on the priesthood and Irish-American societies to put a stop to such ruffianism and vulgar display, but there is evidence that occasionally Irish Catholic funerals and wakes in the middle of the last century that had no connection with "radicals" ended in the same disgraceful scenes.[44] Yet, as Brownson predicted in his *Quarterly Review:*

> Out from these narrow lanes, blind courts, dirty streets, damp cellars, and suffocating garrets, will come forth some of the noblest sons of our country, whom she will delight to own and honor.[45]

It is well to remember that American cities were not models of cleanliness, order, and decency before the Irish came, and that the 1840's and 1850's were particularly distinguished for ruffianism and

[43] *Report of the Annual Convention of the National W. C. T. U.* (Evanston, Illinois, 1881).
[44] See *The Boston Pilot,* May 6, July 1, and August 26, 1854; and *The Boston Traveller,* May 11, 1857.
[45] *The Boston Pilot,* July 1, 1854.

rowdyism. America had not yet learned the peaceful, orderly processes of the democratic way of life. In Boston, the actor Kean had been mobbed in 1825, and so was the office of the *Liberator* a decade later. There were numerous affrays between whites and Negros, even in New England, and Boston's reputation for orderliness had not been too good in revolutionary and prerevolutionary days. In New York City, King Mob settled many an issue, as, for example, when a street car ran over an eleven-year-old girl, and the mob pelted the cars with brickbats and tried to tear up the rails.[46] New York had its antirent, antiactor, anti-Negro, and anti-Catholic riots; and the lower region of the city, known as "Five Points," was a cesspool of iniquity. Some riots were started by native Americans; some were due simply to an exhuberance of animal spirits plus a plentiful supply of hard liquor. The Irish were perhaps more excitable, more impulsive, less cautious, and less industrious than some other groups, quicker to start a quarrel, and more reluctant to stop a fight. But the United States of the 1850's had plenty of ruffianism, by no means all inspired by immigrants, and numerous gangs of "plug-uglies." The police force of the time was utterly incompetent to deal with the problem, especially as long as they were not in uniform. *The New York Times,* in 1853, pleaded for a uniformed force:

> We must know the *man;* not on minute inspection, but from afar . . . we must have an ocular token whereby we may discern whether he be coward, or courageous; whether he comes to our assistance, or avoids the *melee.*[47]

To combat the drink evil, especially among the Irish, Father Mathew, "the Apostle of Temperance," visited the United States at the middle of the last century. Others had already begun the work for temperance, such as Father Bernard O'Reilly of Rochester, who became president of the Hibernian Temperance Society in the 1830's. In 1840, the Rochester Hibernian Total Abstinence Society was organized, and over 50 took the pledge at one Sunday service in Father O'Reilly's church.[48] According to McGee, who was constantly concerned about "the slum congestion, the groggeries,

---

[46] See Nevins: *op. cit.,* Vol. II, pp. 656-657.
[47] *The New York Times,* April 6, 1853. See also *ibid.,* January 5, 1853; and J. T. Headley: *The Great Riots of New York, 1712-1873* (New York, 1873).
[48] See Frederick J. Zwierlein: *The Life and Letters of Bishop McQuaid,* 2 vols. (Louvain, Belgium, 1925), Vol. I, p. 82.

and the scheming demagogic Irish leaders" that were leading his countrymen astray, over 300,000 took the pledge of temperance within two years as a result of Father Mathew's visit.[49] Great meetings were conducted all over the country, and the celebration of Mass was followed by a temperance lecture. The "Apostle of Temperance" also spoke occasionally under Protestant auspices. His work in Ireland was so successful that *The Boston Journal* reported the arrival of a whole shipload of Irish "teetotalers." [50] Speaking in Fanueil Hall in 1849, Father Mathew was reported to have administered the pledge to 1,300 journeymen tailors who had marched to the meeting in a body.[51] Every male Catholic in Hartford, Connecticut, joined his Catholic Temperance Society.[52] In 1842, Milwaukee had its Catholic Total Abstinence Society.[53] Father Mathew Temperance Societies and the Mathewite Sons were established in 25 states, as far west as California.[54] Apparently the temperance movement among the Irish-Americans had considerable lasting success,[55] extending even to the point of conducting St. Patrick's Day celebrations on temperance principles. In some parts of the United States, the Father Mathew Temperance Societies were later merged into the Catholic Total Abstinence Union, an organization which had the support of many leading clergymen.[56]

The United States has been known and ridiculed as a nation of "joiners." One reason may be the large immigrant element, which has had its special incentives in a new land to form benevolent, patriotic, and social organizations to keep alive the memories of a common origin. The Irish were no exception, and Irish societies of many kinds—such as the Hibernians, athletic clubs, and sodalities—exist in large numbers, generally closely connected with the Church and the Catholic hierarchy.

In the years of the heavy Irish migration, just before the Civil War, military companies were extremely popular in the United

[49] See Isabel Skelton: *The Life of Thomas D'Arcy McGee* (Gardenvale, New York, 1925), pp. 169 and 190.
[50] See *Baltimore Patriot and Commercial Gazette*, May 3, 1841.
[51] See *Albany Argus*, July 30 and August 2, 1849.
[52] See Byrne: *The Catholic Church in New England*, Vol. II, p. 191.
[53] See Humphrey J. Desmond, "Early Irish Settlers in Milwaukee," in *Journal of the American Irish Historical Society*, Vol. XXIX, pp. 103-111.
[54] See Branch: *op. cit.*, pp. 236-239; and Hugh Quigley: *The Irish Race in California and on the Pacific Coast* (San Francisco, 1878), p. 291.
[55] See *Baltimore Patriot and Commercial Gazette*, February 20 and April 3, 1841; and *The Boston Pilot*, August 28, 1852.
[56] See W. W. Folwell: *A History of Minnesota* (St. Paul, 1921), Vol. III, pp. 176-177.

States, and every important immigrant group had them. They satisfied a love for military drill, gaudy uniforms, and display; but, above all, they provided the excuse for arranging many a convivial occasion that gratified the social instincts of a good-natured, friendly, hospitable, and patriotic people.[57] Irish militia companies under various names—such as "the Jasper Greens," "the Hibernia Greens," "the Napper Tandy Light Artillery," "the Emmett Guards," "the Irish Rifles," and "the Jackson Guards"—sprang up even in the smaller towns and attracted much newspaper comment by their frequent parading. Some served valiantly in the Mexican War, although most of them were organized in the following decade.[58]

In New York, in 1852, the 9th regiment with 350 members, the 69th with 280, the Emmett Guards with 68, the Shields Guard of Brooklyn, the Irish-American Guard, and the Mitchel Light Guard of New York paraded at the Battery and were reviewed by the Irish exile Thomas Francis Meagher.[59] In 1853, the Irish militia of New York City numbered 2,600 and the German companies 1,700. There was also a "Garde Lafayette," in which commands were given in French.[60] These companies usually wore uniforms of gaudy colors, trimmed in red and gold. Some had bearskin caps, with plumes of red and green. The 4th of July was an especially popular day for parades. It was then that visits were exchanged between companies in different cities, accompanied with much conviviality and banqueting.[61] Parades and balls seemed to be especially appropriate, too, on St. Patrick's Day.[62] On these occasions, the parades were generally reviewed by mayors and city councils, and at the banquets, the toasts were eloquent and the punch bowls full.[63] Although Irish leaders urged Irish immigrants to get

[57] See Jeremiah O'Donovan: *Immigration in the United States, 1840-1860—Immigrant Interviews* (Pittsburgh, 1864).
[58] See, for example, *The New York Times*, January 20 and 28, 1853; *The Boston Pilot*, September 4, 1852; and September 8, 1860; and *The Albany Argus*, May 9, 1849.
[59] See *The Boston Pilot*, August 7, 1852.
[60] McMaster: *A History of the People of the United States* (New York, 1914), Vol. VIII, p. 75.
[61] See *Albany Argus*, May 9, 1849.
[62] See *Cincinnati Enquirer*, March 18, 1859.
[63] See, for example, *The New York Times*, March 18, 1853; John D. Crimmins: *Irish-American Historical Miscellany* (New York, 1905), p. 227; *The Charleston Mercury*, March 19, 1859; and *The Boston Transcript*, March 17, 1870. At a ball given at Niblo's Garden, in New York, in honor of the Irish patriot Meagher, a United States Army officer toasted "the Eagle of America, perched upon the Harp of Erin—Her broad pinions sweep its strings, and every chord is responsive to the song of Liberty." (*The New York Times*, January 12, 1853.)

military training and discipline, occasionally a voice was raised in criticism of the formation of separate companies and regiments based on racial origins on the ground that this would contribute to the perpetuation of immigrant stocks as separate nationalities.[64]

For many years, fire fighting in the United States was in the hands of volunteer companies. The opportunity to become a "fire laddy" was irresistible for many Irishmen. These companies performed superhuman feats of strength and heroism. Each firehouse, especially in large cities like New York, also attracted a group that ran along to every fire, so that "running with the machine" eventually degenerated into a sport which attracted the hoodlums and gangs of the Bowery districts. The volunteer firemen of the 1840's and later decades appeared in brilliant uniforms and ponderous equipment of the comic opera variety. Much feasting and drinking seemed to be part of the routine of these organizations, and until the temperance movement made its inroads upon the profession, companies frequently had a steward, whose business it was to ladle out liquor to exhausted firemen from a barrel hauled along with the engine to each fire.

When an alarm sounded, the rivalry between the companies was likely to be so keen that a race was started for the only fireplug available in the neighborhood of the conflagration. Specially competent fighters raced ahead to capture the hydrant or cistern and to hold it at all costs until their colleagues arrived with the machine. Feuds and brawls were frequent, and occasionally a building burned to the ground while the heroic fire laddies were settling their long-standing rivalries. In 1845, the Philadelphia commissioners reduced the annual appropriations for fire companies because of their turbulent and riotous conduct. But nine years later, a lively battle was fought in the "City of Brotherly Love" between Irish Catholic and Irish Protestant fire companies.[65] In 1860, there was another battle royal of firemen in New York, involving several companies, "with stones, trumpets and pistols. A dozen were carried off to the hospital . . . . The end will be," predicted the editor of *The Boston Pilot*, "a paid department, acting as a branch of the police." [66] After the close of the Civil War, the volunteer system of

[64] See *Providence Journal*, quoted in *New York Tribune*, April 22, 1850.
[65] See *Cleveland Plain Dealer*, June 14, 1854; *New York Weekly News*, August 9, 1845; *Albany Argus*, November 16, 1849; and *Cincinnati Gazette*, April 24, 1849.
[66] *The Boston Pilot*, July 14, 1860.

fire fighting was gradually abandoned in the larger cities.[67]

How the Irish established themselves on the police force of the larger American cities needs no discussion. As late as 1933, a study of the New York force revealed that, out of a total of approximately 20,000 policemen, 2,309 were themselves foreign-born and 11,014 were of foreign-born parentage, representing 42 countries in all. Ireland led the list of foreign-born policemen with 1,533, and also the list of those of foreign-born parentage with 5,671.[68]

Nearly all that has been said hitherto has concerned the Irish immigrant as a city dweller. It has been shown that most Irishmen began as unskilled laborers, working in construction gangs on the docks, in the streets, or, with the rise of industrial towns like Lowell and Paterson, in the mills—wherever brawn and not skill was the chief requirement. Many ended their days as unskilled workers in the cities and towns. But although it is true that the Irish immigrant is primarily a phenomenon of urban civilization in the United States, some did go into agriculture. Students of immigration have speculated on the reasons why a predominantly rural people should have shunned the land in their new home. Poverty, of course, made it impossible for large numbers to leave the port towns in which the immigrant ships happened to land them. Ignorance of improved American methods of farming was another reason, along with memories of bitter experiences on the land in Ireland. Irish gregariousness and the incentive of cash wages in the city were other factors. In some cases, the demoralizing effects of the saloon and political clubs in the cities operated to keep Irishmen from moving West.

Wherever he went, the Irishman was likely to remain wasteful and generous, helping his neighbor, whoever he was, when in distress, sighing in his soul for the Emerald Isle across the sea, and always willing to help those whom he had left behind. Along with these qualities went another—namely, the desire to be with people. This could not be satisfied on a farm. A successful Irish farmer in Missouri expressed the feelings of many of his countrymen when he wrote home in 1821 that, in spite of all the advantages America had to offer, in Ireland, after a day's work, he could attend a fair, a

[67] See Herbert Asbury: *Ye Olde Fire Laddies* (New York, 1930). The author seems to have drawn very heavily on George W. Sheldon: *The Story of the Volunteer Fire Department of the City of New York* (New York, 1882).

[68] See *The New York Times*, December 21, 1933.

wake, or a dance, or he could sit with a neighbor by a cheering turf fire. "If I had there but a sore head," he continued, "I would have a neighbour within every hundred yards of me that would run to see me. But here everyone can get so much land, and generally has so much, that they calls them neighbours that lives two or three miles off . . . ." [69] Adams has estimated that, before 1845, when the heaviest Irish migration began, about 10 per cent of the immigrants went into agriculture.[70] No reliable figures can be cited for the later period, but there is no dearth of evidence to show that Irish farming communities were not an unknown quantity in the American West of the last century.

As early as 1818, several Irish societies in the Eastern cities petitioned Congress for a land grant in Illinois, where land should be sold to Irish only, on fourteen years' credit, in order to build on the prairies "a new and happy Erin in the bosom of the West." Congress refused.[71] In 1845, at the fourth annual meeting of the Irish Emigrant Society, speculators who had New York real estate to unload put up placards advising immigrants to stay out of "the sickly West." [72] McGee, on the other hand, wrote editorials in great profusion in his paper, *The Celt,* advocating that his countrymen leave the city for the farm. He wrote a poem celebrating the attractions of Illinois and, in 1856, was instrumental in bringing about an Irish Emigrant Aid Convention, composed of 80 lay and clerical delegates, in Buffalo. Its purpose was to found an Irish state under the surveillance of the Church, somewhere in the West or in Canada. Irish-Americans of means were to form stock companies to buy land, which they were then to resell on the installment plan to poor immigrants. The program collapsed mainly because no one was available to push it through and partly because the Eastern clergy were lukewarm, even hostile, to the proposal. It was often charged, and with some justification, that some of the priests were promoting the clannishness of the Irish and keeping them from going West so as to be the better able to hold their parishes together, to maintain parochial schools for the children of their parishioners, and to protect them against the "insidious advances of heresy." It was argued that the spiritual wants of Cath-

[69] Quoted in Adams: *op. cit.*, p. 342.
[70] See *ibid.*, p. 341.
[71] See McMaster: *op. cit.*, Vol. IV, pp. 393-395.
[72] See *New York Weekly News*, May 3, 1845.

olic communities could best be satisfied when large groups lived in compact settlements in the larger towns.[73]

McGee's *Celt* and *The Boston Pilot* waged a long journalistic battle over this issue before McGee finally gave up his residence in the United States in disgust and went to Canada. The *Celt* maintained that the Irish were losing their religion in the United States because, in the public schools, they came in contact with "infidel companions" who ridiculed "Paddy-boys," "Paddy-churches," and "Paddy religion." *The Pilot,* as a rule, opposed a Westward movement of the Irish, and believed the Roman Catholic faith could best be nurtured in the cities.[74] As for the proposed Irish migration to Canada, that immediately encountered the hostility of militant Canadian Protestants like George Brown of the *Toronto Globe,* who denounced the whole plan as "a deep scheme of Romish Priestcraft to colonize Upper Canada with papists . . . with no schools, no roads, and no progress." For decades after the Civil War, clerical leaders like Bishop Spalding and Archbishop Ireland worked on plans to settle the Irish in Western farming communities; and, in 1874, Thomas Ambrose Butler wrote *The Irish on the Prairie,* in which he forecast a New Ireland which will "plant all the joys of the old Land amidst the bright scenes of the New." [75]

Thousands of Irish workers on canals and railroads did eventually settle down as farmers along the routes they had helped to develop. This was particularly true in Illinois, where Irish farmers settled along the canal from Peoria northward, although Chicago remained an irresistible attraction for many who found the farm too lonely and dull. In 1860, there were over 87,000 Irish in Illinois, and 32,000 more settled in this prairie state within the next decade. Although thousands drifted to the cities, there was not a rural county in the state that did not have Irish among its farming population. In McHenry County, for example, there was an Irish farming settlement that supported three good-sized Catholic churches.[76] An item in *The Boston Transcript,* in 1855, reported the departure of ten Irish families from Newburyport for Illinois with capital re-

[73] See Skelton: *op. cit.,* pp. 259 and 230.
[74] See *The Boston Pilot,* July 28 and September 22, 1855.
[75] See Dorothy A. Dondore: *The Prairie and the Making of Middle America: Four Centuries of Description* (Cedar Rapids, Iowa, 1926), p. 248.
[76] See John F. Maguire: *The Irish in America* (London, 1868), p. 246; and A. C. Cole: *The Era of the Civil War, 1848-1870* (Springfield, Illinois, 1919).

sources of from $300 to $1,500 per family, with which they proposed to buy land.[77] The trustees of the Wabash and Erie Canal offered immigrants and laborers farms of 40, 80, and 160 acres on easy terms, in partial payment for work done on the canal.[78] The Illinois Central Railroad was built largely by German and Irish immigrant labor. The workers were frequently paid in scrip, which they exchanged for farmland. The Irish bought thousands of acres of Illinois Central land, although a statement in the *Illinois State Register,* in 1853, to the effect that three fourths of the Irish who were employed on public works in Illinois from 1833 to 1853 took up homesteads is probably an exaggeration.[79] Many Irish railroad workers settled down as farmers in Will County and in La Salle, Illinois.[80]

A letter in *The Boston Pilot* for August 4, 1860 described the beginning of an Irish agricultural settlement in Allegaw County, Michigan. Kentucky had been proposed as a "New Ireland" as early as 1795.[81] In Iowa, there were Irish Catholic farming communities near Council Bluffs and an Irish settlement, called "Garryowen," in Jackson County. *The Boston Pilot* had many subscribers among Irish farmers in this state and occasionally printed requests from Catholic settlers asking that a priest be sent out to care for their religious needs. In 1860, there was a *Corpus Christi* procession in Dubuque, Iowa, attended largely by German and Irish settlers, and the Trappist Monastery near Dubuque was a center of Catholic worship for Irish farmers, who came in from the neighborhood to attend Mass.[82]

In Wisconsin, the Irish, unlike the Germans, did not consciously form farm colonies but turned to the land usually after their internal improvement jobs had been completed. There were 21,000 Irish in Wisconsin in 1850 and 50,000 in 1860. In Kenosha County, for example, there were 1,209 Irish in 1850, of whom 656 were in the rural communities. A decade later, the number had risen to

[77] See *Boston Transcript,* April 13, 1855.
[78] See *Cincinnati Gazette,* March 22, 1848.
[79] See Paul W. Gates: *The Illinois Central Railroad and Its Colonization Work* (Cambridge, Massachusetts, 1934), pp. 89, 95-97, 234, and 252.
[80] See also W. J. Onahan: "Irish Settlements in Illinois," in *The Catholic World* (May, 1881), Vol. XXXIII, pp. 157-162.
[81] See Frank Monaghan: "The Proposed Settlement of New Ireland in Kentucky," in *Mississippi Valley Historical Review,* Vol. XX, pp. 399-402.
[82] See *The Boston Pilot,* November 3, 1855; November 20, 1852; August 26, 1854; July 14 and October 13, 1860; and June 28, 1862.

718. In the rural county of Racine, Wisconsin, there were 609 Irish in 1850. After a painstaking study of four Wisconsin counties, Dr. Joseph Schafer came to the conclusion that the Irish represented a relatively fluid element between farm and city, and generally withdrew from communities where the Germans predominated. Where the Irish did settle down, they proved to be just as good farmers as anybody else, although they were likely to move and develop several farms and homes within a lifetime, in contrast to the Germans, who usually settled but once. In Ozankee County, where Irish farmers settled among the Germans, many of them spoke German.[83]

In South Dakota, an eccentric Sioux City newspaper man planned an Irish settlement in Brule County around 1869. He proposed to bring Irish-Americans to homesteads in the Dakotas, so that they might be ready to strike at England through Canada whenever "England's embarrassment and Ireland's opportunity" should come.[84] In Holt County, Nebraska, the Irish settlers of O'Neill City, named after the Irish Fenian General John O'Neill, had a similar purpose in inviting their fellow countrymen to join them in Nebraska. O'Neill offered lots for sale, and denounced the clergy, politicians, and saloonkeepers for trying to keep the Irish in the cities.[85] There were Irish agricultural colonies in at least six Nebraska counties by the 1880's. Other successful colonies were established in Kansas, Arkansas, Virginia, and Georgia.

Bishops Joseph Cretin of St. Paul, Mathias Loras of Dubuque, and Fenwick and Byrne were all interested in promoting the settlement of Irish upon farms, but no leaders of the Church could be compared in enthusiasm for such projects with Bishop Spalding of Peoria and Archbishop Ireland of St. Paul.[86] Besides wishing to raise the moral and economic level of Irish communities, these

[83] See Joseph Schafer: "Four Wisconsin Counties," in *Wisconsin Domesday Book, General Studies* (Madison, Wisconsin, 1927), Vol. II, pp. 83-106.

[84] See *South Dakota Historical Collections,* Vol. VI, pp. 117-130.

[85] See *O'Neill's Irish American Colonies in Nebraska* (Chicago, 1876); and *Nebraska History,* Vol. VII, p. 11; and *Nebraska Historical Society Proceedings,* Vol. XV, p. 28. At a meeting held in the New York Tabernacle in 1857, addressed by a priest and organized to promote the establishment of Roman Catholic immigrant settlements in Nebraska, Archbishop Hughes arose in the gallery to denounce the whole scheme. (See *The Boston Traveller,* March 28, 1857.)

[86] Archbishop Ireland helped establish a Catholic Colony of Ghent, composed of Belgians, in Lyon County, Minnesota. See Thorstina Jackson: "Icelandic Communities in America: Cultural Backgrounds and Early Settlements," in *Journal of Social Forces,* Vol. III, p. 684.

leaders of the Church felt that their faith could best be maintained by taking the Irish out of the cities. Certain publications in the Eastern cities were held responsible for leading some Irish Catholics into "the school of socialism" and getting them to join labor unions, which might lead to "communistic infidelity." [87] Considerable friction and rivalry developed between Western and Eastern bishops because of these colonization projects, for they involved a fundamental conflict of interest between West and East. Clergymen in well-established Eastern parishes, with large churches and schools—some of them still in debt—naturally opposed any movement which would deprive them of their membership. Archbishop Hughes of New York was always a vigorous opponent of colonization projects.[88]

Bishop Ireland planted his first colony in Swift County, Minnesota, in 1876. He himself selected the tract, and the railroad company which owned it gave him the exclusive right of disposal for three years. He sent in a priest and built a church in the settlement before the settlers arrived. The railroad company furnished the lumber for houses. The settlement was widely advertised to attract Irish to the new region. No saloon was permitted in the community and a temperance society was promptly organized. Organizations like the St. Paul Catholic Colonization Bureau, the Irish Catholic Colonization Association, and the Irish-American Colonization Company combined their energies to find recruits. In 1879, a convention was called in Chicago under the stimulus of Bishop Ireland and other clergy, and notices were sent to Irish Catholic societies and Irish Catholic papers like the *St. Paul Northwestern Chronicle,* the Notre Dame *Ave Maria, The Boston Pilot,* the Brooklyn *Catholic Review,* and the New York *Irish-American.*

The Irish Catholic Colonization Association of the United States was incorporated under Illinois law, with a capital stock of $100,000 and a board of directors composed of three bishops, two priests, and four Catholic laymen. As president, Bishop Spalding made a tour of the East to sell stock, but subscriptions totaled only $83,000, coming largely from the relatively poor, who could take but one or two shares apiece. Colonies were established in Nobles County, Minnesota, on land of the Northern Pacific Railroad, and in Greeley County, Nebraska, on land of the Burlington and Missouri road.

[87] See J. L. Spalding, Bishop of Peoria: *The Religious Mission of the Irish People and Catholic Colonization* (New York, 1880), pp. 127 and 205.
[88] See Spalding: *op. cit.,* pp. 127-153.

In each case, settlers were to pay for their holdings in easy payments. In its first five years, the society paid 17 per cent dividends, and in 1884 it paid for a resident priest assigned to Castle Garden. The colonies were successful, and the company was dissolved in 1891.

In 1881, Bishop Ireland's colony in Swift County, Minnesota, had 800 families in four villages. Eventually, Irish agricultural settlements in this vicinity spread over 300,000 acres. The land for Adrian, in Nobles County, was secured by the Archbishop from the railroad and was then sold at a profit. The total cost to an Adrian colonist for a 160-acre farm, a house, and the breaking of 30 acres was $1,174, which the settler paid back in installments over a number of years. The railroads and land agents worked in close cooperation with representatives of Archbishop Ireland, Bishop Spalding, and the Irish Catholic Colonization Association. Minnesota had its Shieldsville, an Irish colony named after General James Shield, the Irish hero of the Mexican War; as well as its Kilkenny, Erin, and Montgomery townships, little islands of Irish agricultural settlements which successfully withstood the Scandinavian inundation of the Northwest. In Arkansas, along the line of the Little Rock and Fort Smith Railroad, there were Irish farming colonies in Perry and Yell Counties, and Bishop Fitzgerald predicted that "St. Patrick's Colony" would succeed, provided "the same thrift, enterprise, energy, and intelligence" were applied "as shown by the Germans." [89]

The importance of the Irish in the history of the Roman Catholic Church in the United States and the role of the Church in the life of Irish-Americans are so generally recognized that the statement that the Catholic Church in America became essentially an immigrant church in the 1840's, and continued for decades to receive its strongest additions from abroad, will hardly be challenged by anyone familiar with the facts. There were Roman Catholics in America at the time of the Revolution, but they were under special disabilities in a number of the American colonies. The first great accession of Roman Catholics came from the purchase of Louisiana,

[89] For these colonization ventures, see Spalding: *op. cit.*; Philip H. Bagenal: *The American Irish and Their Influence on Irish Politics* (Boston, 1882); Sister Mary Evangela Henthorne: *The Career of the Right Reverend John Lancaster Spalding, Bishop of Peoria, as President of the Irish Catholic Colonization Association of the United States, 1879-1892* (Urbana, Illinois, 1932); and *The Boston Pilot*, July 20, 1861.

which brought into the American Church about 100,000 communicants. Others came in with the annexations following the Mexican War, but none of these additions can be remotely compared in importance with the great flood of Irish who came across the Atlantic in the 1840's and later decades.

Lay and clerical leaders have testified to the special mission of the Irish to preserve and spread Roman Catholicism in the United States. "What Ireland has done for the American Church, every Bishop, every priest can tell," wrote Maguire in 1867, in his book on *The Irish in America*.[90] "There is scarcely an ecclesiastical seminary for English-speaking students," he added, "in which the great majority of those now preparing for the service of the sanctuary do not belong, if not by birth, at least by blood, to that historic land to which the grateful Church of past ages accorded the proud title—Insula Sanctorum." "We must at once admit," said Bishop Spalding, "that the Irish race is the providential instrument through which God has wrought this marvelous revival," by which Catholicism in the United States was given "vigor and cohesiveness." [91] And Bishop McQuaid of Rochester contended that, of all Europeans, the Irish

> . . . are best fitted to open the way for religion in a new
> country . . . . They were not appalled by the wretched-
> ness of religious equipments and surroundings in their
> new homes on this side of the Atlantic . . . . They had
> lived among the bitterest foes and had never quailed or
> flinched . . . . In such a school of discipline, they have
> been trained to do missionary work . . . .[92]

Moreover, the belief that large numbers of Irish left the Roman Church after coming to America is now discredited. The Irish remained faithful sons and daughters of Mother Church.

It has been estimated that there were 30,000 adherents of the Roman Catholic faith in the United States in 1790. By 1830, the Church claimed 600,000 and, by 1860, 4,500,000 members. Both figures are probably too large. The Metropolitan Catholic Almanac of 1852 listed 1,980,000 Catholics in the United States. By that time, there were Catholic newspapers in nine of the leading cities

---

[90] Maguire: *op. cit.*, p. 540.
[91] Bishop Spalding, quoted in Bagenal: *op. cit.*, p. 63.
[92] Zwierlein: *op. cit.*, Vol. I, p. 116.

and Catholic publishing houses in Baltimore, Philadelphia, New York, and Boston.[93]

In New York State, in 1829, there were 13 Roman Catholic churches, 5 of them in New York City and Brooklyn. The number of communicants more than doubled in the next decade, and, by 1830, Protestant clergymen of New York were inveighing against the menace of the Pope in America.[94] In 1836, the diocese of New York and half of New Jersey contained about 200,000 Catholics, and of the 38 priests, 35 were Irish and 3 German.[95] The Society for the Propagation of the Faith in Paris, the Leopoldine Foundation of Vienna, and the Bavarian *Ludwig Verein* sent money and vestments to the United States in order to help establish Catholic parishes. Baltimore was still referred to as "the Rome of the United States," although there were now 4 new dioceses in the West: Cincinnati (1823), St. Louis (1827), Mobile (1825), and Michigan (1823). In 1835, the Boston diocese embraced 26 churches and the New York 19, and Catholic religious orders showed a steady growth. In 1852, there were 6 archbishops, 26 bishops, and 1,385 priests in the United States. The rapid expansion of the Church was due almost entirely to Irish, and, to a lesser extent, to German Catholic immigration.[96]

The creation of new Roman Catholic parishes paralleled closely the spread of Irish laborers along canal routes and other internal improvements projects. John Power, an Irish priest, preached to Irish laborers along the canals of New York and Connecticut in the 1840's. Churches like the one in Utica, New York, were started to serve Irish workers on the Erie Canal. The first St. Patrick's Day banquet was held in Utica in 1821. The Erie Canal was described as "a capital road from Cork to Utica." [97] In Ohio, the establishment of new parishes followed the building of the Ohio canals, turnpikes, and railroads. By 1846, President Polk was appointing Roman Catholic chaplains to accompany the Irish volunteers who had enlisted for the Mexican War.[98] In 1846, according to *The*

[93] McGee: *op. cit.*, p. 230.
[94] Fox, *The Decline of Aristocracy in the Politics of New York* (New York, 1919), p. 372.
[95] See the Reverend Theodore Roemer: *The Leopoldine Foundation and the Church in the United States, 1829-1839* (New York, 1933), p. 178.
[96] See Maguire: *op. cit.*, pp. 378 and 443.
[97] M. M. Bagg: *The Pioneers of Utica* (Utica, New York, 1877), pp. 474, 516, and 633.
[98] See *New York Weekly News*, August 1, 1846.

Boston Pilot, there were 740 churches and 737 priests in the United States; by 1854, there were 1,712 churches, 7 archbishops, 32 bishops, and 1,574 priests.[99]   Already there was considerable maneuvering within the Church with regard to the filling of vacant bishoprics, "to prevent the growing power of the Irish clergy in the United States." [100]   But the Irish control of the Catholic hierarchy in America remained unchecked.

The rapid transformation of New England into a Roman Catholic stronghold was especially striking.   Early Boston had been no paradise for Catholics.   The first Catholic church in Boston was dedicated in 1803, and the first bishop of Boston, the Reverend John de Cheverus, appointed in 1810.   Bishop Fenwick, sent to Boston in 1825, proved to be a vigorous, broad-gauged leader.   He started a parochial school in 1827.   By 1835, there were 40,082 Catholics in the New England diocese.[101]   In New England, as in the West, the rise of Roman Catholic parishes can easily be traced by following a map for internal improvements projects and the establishment of mill towns.   Thus the church at Windsor Locks, near Hartford, Connecticut, was founded because of the excavation of a canal by Irish workmen.   The organization of the Norwich church followed the construction and opening of the Worcester and Norwich road.   Woonsocket, Rhode Island, got its Catholic population by drawing workers from the Irish immigrants.   The Westfield Canal and railroad building in that region developed Catholic congregations west of the Connecticut River.[102]   These Irish Catholic settlements and churches encountered violent prejudices at the outset, and Irish laborers frequently were excluded from New England boarding houses.

In Lowell, Massachusetts, the first Irish workmen arrived in 1822 to build a canal.   They were followed by hundreds, who at first lived only in tents in a district known as "Paddy Camp Lands."   By 1831, there was a settlement of 500 Irish in 100 cabins on a strip of land near Lowell, known as New Dublin.   There were the usual complaints of heavy drinking and much brawling, and a priest was brought in to steady the workers.   The first church was built

[99] See *The Boston Pilot,* January 21, 1854.
[100] Guilday: *op. cit.,* Vol. II, pp. 256 and 257.
[101] See James Fitton: *Sketches of the Establishment of the Church in New England* (Boston, 1872).   For statistics on every state and territory, see Byrne: *Irish Emigration to the United States.*
[102] See Fitton: *op. cit.,* pp. 189, 201, 203, 220, and 326.

on land donated by the mill owners. Apparently, the company had no scruples about contributing from its treasury for the support of Catholic schools and churches, and justified the donations because of the steadying influence which priests and churches were believed to have on the turbulent, undisciplined community. In 1833, a Hibernian Moralizing and Relief Society was organized in Lowell, which developed into the Lowell Irish Benevolent Society. In 1849, Father Mathew visited the community to give new life to its Catholic Temperance Society. The history of the Lowell community, as far as the rise and influence of the Catholic Church is concerned, is typical of many New England mill towns.[103] After 1845, Irish immigrants rapidly drove the daughters of New England farmers out of the factories. The Irish bandmaster, Patrick S. Gilmore, is said to have composed "Seeing Nellie Home" as a result of his romance with Nellie O'Neill, who sang in the choir of Lowell's St. Patrick's Church, which was dedicated in 1831.[104]

As the Irish element grew in numbers, and its churches and parochial schools multiplied, it was perhaps unavoidable that friction should develop between militant Protestants and militant Catholics, between the champions of a public-school system and those who favored Church schools. This controversy reached its most violent stage in the bigotry and barbarity of the Native American and Know-Nothing agitations, to be discussed later as part of the nativist reaction to immigration. In New York, Bishop Hughes fought for a division of school funds for the support of Roman Catholic schools. Governor Seward supported him and was politically embarrassed forever after by his stand on that occasion. He was denounced by Whigs and Democrats alike for preparing the way in America "for the whore of Babylon." [105]

Controversies arose over the reading of the *Bible* in schools and over textbooks to which Roman Catholics objected as being unfriendly and unfair to Catholicism. Such controversies led to an

[103] See George F. O'Dwyer: *The Irish Catholic Genesis of Lowell* (Lowell, Massachusetts, 1920).
[104] See also William Byrne: *History of the Catholic Church in the New England States*, 2 vols. (Boston, 1899); John Rothensteiner: *History of the Archdiocese of St. Louis*, 2 vols. (St. Louis, 1928); and the Reverend Joseph A. Griffin: *The Contributions of Belgium to the Catholic Church in America, 1523-1857* (Washington, D. C., 1932).
[105] Nevins: *op. cit.*, Vol. II, p. 569. See also Edward Channing: *History of the United States* (New York, 1921), Vol. V, pp. 216-217; Bagenal: *op. cit.*, p. 51; and *The Life of Archbishop Hughes* (New York, 1864).

acute fear in some quarters of the growing influence of the Roman Catholic Church in the United States.[106] In the meantime, Catholic papers like *The Boston Pilot* unwisely printed questionable stories reflecting on the conduct of Protestant ministers, calling them "Simoniacs to a man" and "the most venal people in the land," and denouncing "mixed marriages" and "foreign anarchists," all in one breath. In the latter category were included all German, French, Italian, Polish, Hungarian, and Irish radicals in the United States.[107] In violent editorials, this journal lashed out against the "common schools," opposed compulsory school laws as invasions of the rights of the Church and the family, and referred to "Ignorance, Atheism, and Disobedience" as the "three apples of Sodom, plucked from this tree of State education."[108] To provide higher education for Catholics, the Church sponsored St. Louis University, Xavier University, the University of Notre Dame, Fordham University, the College of the Holy Cross, Villanova College, Loyola University, Georgetown University, and numerous female seminaries. Catholic books, dealing largely with matters of faith, were extensively advertised in Catholic papers.[109] When Brownson's *Quarterly Review* criticized the standards and the curricula of Catholic colleges, *The Pilot* heatedly denied the charges, adding that "there would be fewer Garibaldians, fewer Mazzinians, fewer scoundrels in Italy, if there were in that devoted country less colleges and more plain common schools . . . ."[110]

Devout Irishmen, of course, followed their clerical leaders in matters of religion and religious education. In politics, they learned to follow the orders of the ward boss. The latter's affiliations generally were more intimate with the saloon than with the Church. To an Irishman, politics proved to be the salt and breath of life, and Irishmen in America found it hard to resist the temptation to plunge at once, and deeply, into the American political stream. They learned the tricks of the political game from native American leaders, and then rapidly improved on their instruction. From the first, Irish allegiance was to the Democrats. The name itself had its allure. "Federalist" and "Whig" were names that had little

---

[106] See also *The New York Times,* April 12 and 14 and March 21, 1853.
[107] See *The Boston Pilot,* June 24, 1854; April 28, 1855; July 21, 1860; and April 19, 1862.
[108] See *ibid.,* April 24, 1852.
[109] See, for example, advertisements in *ibid.* for 1854.
[110] *Ibid.,* August 4, 1860.

significance for an immigrant who had come to the United States to enjoy freedom and democracy. Moreover, both Federalists and Whigs were suspected, with much truth, of a nativism that frowned upon the newcomer, seeking to protect American institutions from the inundations from abroad and opposed to the easy and quick naturalization of foreigners. Irishmen had little in common with the "Anglomen and monocrats" who supported Federalists and Whigs. Posing as friends of the poor, the Democrats, in the tradition of Jefferson and Jackson, opened their hearts to the immigrants, and sought to win and hold their support by admitting them at once to the inner sanctuary and to the minor spoils of the American political system. Irishmen generally had an ingrained hatred for aristocracy and long-standing reasons to be "agin the government." By the year 1820, Tammany Hall was Irish. Tammany celebrations toasted Ireland's sons and their patron saint, St. Patrick, and Tammany used its charities to win and to hold the immigrant vote.[111]

A regiment of well-drilled Irish voters, once organized in any of the larger port towns, was able to enlist new arrivals among the immigrants as soon as they landed. The Irish usually were more interested in local political issues than in national questions, but thorough organization in the local communities led to party solidarity on any issue that might arise. Needless to add, immigrants favored universal manhood suffrage, and the Democratic leaders championed what their supporters wanted. A deliberately cultivated Anglophobia helped to preserve Irish unity. Irish wit and adaptibility, a gift for oratory, a certain vivacity, and a warm, human quality that made them the best of good fellows at all times— especially in election campaigns—enabled the Irish to rise rapidly from ward heelers to city bosses, and to municipal and state officers of high distinction.

The Irish added turbulence and excitement to political cam-

---

[111] As early as 1805, the *Freeman's Journal* commented on the Irish in Tammany as follows:

> We now find the order assuming quite new features and the descendants of Kilbuck conversing in a transatlantic tongue. A learned stranger would not have been esteemed ridiculous, if, upon invitation, in this body, he had pronounced, that the ancient language of Ireland was that of the aborigines of America.

[Quoted in E. P. Kilroe: *Saint Tammany and the Origin of the Society of Tammany or Columbian Order in the City of New York* (New York, 1913).]

paigns. They also contributed a new picturesqueness and dramatic quality to the methods of political campaigning and canvassing the vote of large masses of people. By building up strong political machines in the cities, they became, along with the Solid South, the one stable element that kept the Democratic party—then a minority group—alive after the Civil War and gave it its occasional chance for victory. Reformers have often overlooked the fact that the same political boss who bought votes, stuffed ballot boxes, and brazenly perpetrated naturalization frauds was also the warm-hearted leader who got the immigrant his pushcart license, "fixed" arrests for petty violations of the law with the police and the judge, and sent the poor their Christmas turkeys and coal in winter, paid their rent when the landlord threatened eviction, and sent flowers to their funerals. Indeed, some political bosses contended that they were public benefactors, for they took money out of the public till to help bring about a fairer distribution of this world's pleasures among the underprivileged.

In 1852, a poem addressed to the Irishmen of the United States, began with the admonition:

> Fellow exiles! claim your station
> In the councils of the nation;
> Be not aliens in the soil
> Which exacts your sweat and toil
> For this land your fathers fought,
> With their blood was freedom bought.
> We can boast as brave a stock
> As that which sprung from Plymouth rock . . . .[112]

The admonition seems to have been utterly unnecessary, if one may judge from the turmoil raised in native American quarters when the Irishman plunged into the game of American self-government. No other immigrant group has ever taken so quickly and completely to the American political system, especially as it functioned through the machine politics of the larger American cities. By nature, the Irishman seems to have possessed many of the qualities that make for a successful politician. To be sure, he began on a low level in the United States, but there was no other level on which he could begin. His flair for oratory and good fellowship was an invaluable asset as he began the slow ascent on the American political escalator from ward heeler to United States Senator and Cabinet member.

[112] *The Boston Pilot*, September 11, 1852.

Hostile critics of the Irish-Americans voters, who huddled like cattle in the early shantytowns, believed they knew the reason why "Paddy" would not leave the city for the farm. "They would then lose the glory of having a Paddy O'Bluster in one office," bitterly commented one observer in 1839, "a Rory McWhackem in another, a Tearaway Batterscull in a third . . . . They might then bid fare- well to the sublime delights of a shillelah row at election times"— and brandy! [113]

The Irish worker was described in doggerel verse that reflected his importance to the machine that sought his vote,

> He slowly moves his rake, and swings
> His pick with easy sweep
> Seeming to be not quite awake,
> And yet not sound asleep.
>
> We gazed upon the dreamy scene
> And of its beauties wrote
> And could not help but realize
> The power of a vote.[114]

Another selection in this early anthology of Irish vote-selling, graft, and rioting described the landing of Barney O'Toole, "a broth of a boy," in the New Canaan. He got a job immediately in one of the city parks, only to conclude, after swinging his pick for a day, that he was meant to be a judge.

> Then he lit up his pipe and he put on his coat,
> And he ran for an office; they counted the vote,
> And they figured it out by the Tammany rule,
> And who was elected, but Barney O'Toole.
> Then he bought a new coat and a diamond so fine,
> And a lad for five cents give his boots a nice shine;
> Then he talked about court, legislation and school,
> For he now was a statesman, bold Barney O'Toole.[115]

References to the plug-ugly methods of the 1850's were frequent, and the Irishman, though by no means solely responsible for the shoulder-hitting methods of American city politics, came in for more

[113] See Blarney O'Democrat: *The Irish Office-Hunter-Oniad* (New York, 1839), pp. III and IV.

[114] Quoted in George Watertown: *Hibernia: or, Ireland the World Over, Show-ing How Pat Rules America. Historical, Poetical and Statistical. A Repository of Original Songs, Odes and Poems, with Legends, Superstitions, and Facts, Re-lating to the Irish, and Illustrative of Their Wonderful Capacity to Govern* (New York, 1871), p. 49.

[115] Quoted in *ibid.*, p. 98.

than his share of criticism. Witness the following stanza, printed in 1871, when apparently the good old days were passing:

> Where are now the Roughs I cherished,
> Where the voters once called mine?
> Some for too much rum have perished,
> Some the prison walls confine.
> Voting early, voting often,
> Voting morning, noon and night,
> And ready, always ready,
> For a riot or a fight.[116]

At the risk of painting the lily, reference may be made in concluding this part of the discussion to probably the most stinging satire in rhyme ever written about the Irish immigrant who voted immediately upon arrival and was charged with polluting the pure stream of American political life. This immigrant epic was the work of one "Blarney O'Democrat." It was written in 1839, telling in 71 pages of indignant, scurrilous verse the story of the Irish-Office-Hunter-Oniad. The scene is the sixth ward of old New York, the home of dirty, illiterate, vulgar, swearing, whiskey-drinking Irish democrats,

> Who thinks that freedom most consists
> In proving points, with sticks and fists.

It is here that "clubs have softened many a head." At a political rally, the first speaker, who regrets that he has not been christened Patrick, proves to his Irish hearers that all good things in America came from Ireland and that Christopher Columbus himself was an Irishman.

> And hence America, ye ken,
> Of right belongs to Irishmen!
> And Washington, I've understood,
> Was somewhat touch'd with Irish blood.

The third speaker is a German,

> . . . gaunt and grim, with bushel head, and lamp post limb.

who regrets that he has not been born in Ireland. Nevertheless, like a good Jacksonian Democrat, he hates all things aristocratic with sufficient violence to make him acceptable. Another Irishman,

---

[116] Quoted in *ibid.*, p. 94.

who is ashamed of the whole performance, arises at the meeting to urge his fellow countrymen to leave the city for the farm. He is listened to respectfully until he uses the fatal words:

> Seek for public posts no more.

At that point, his exhortation is rudely ended by the application of a shillelah to his muddled Irish head. Perhaps the climax of political oratory is reached when the greatest classical orator of New York's bloody sixth ward arises to contrast the weakling leaders of antiquity with the bosses of the "bloody sixth":

> There's Homer, boys, who lived in Spain,
> And wrote of Shakespeare, and Tom Paine;
> There's Joan of Arc, the queen of might,
> Whom Caesar poisoned out of spite;
> There's Hellespont, so mighty fine,
> Who lived in Ovid, near the Rhine,
> And swam across the pyramid,
> To seek Leander, who was hid;
> There's Brutus who would never yield,
> But beat the French at Flodden field;
> There's Hector, who was dipt in Styx
> (A wood the ancients used to mix)
> Which left him so, he could not feel,
> Till Hotspur shot him in the heel;
> And there are fifty more, no doubt,
> All scholars famed, and heroes stout,
> But what are they, with all their riches,
> Their ancient deeds, and foreign speeches,
> Merely a pack of sons of bitches,
> Compared to one, we all should study,
> The *leader* of the Sixth, so bloody!

The epic comes to a dramatic close when a disappointed Irish office seeker breaks the calm and harmony of the political rally by threatening to eat meat again and to join the Whigs. Immediately, fists began to fly. The rally ends in a terrific fight,

> For every man in that grim ring
> Fought like a true Milisian King.

The description of this fight is a classic, but cannot be reproduced here. The epic ends on a significant note—all appear to be better friends than ever, once Irish inhibitions have been completely released:

Three Hodmen, with their grimy faces,
Were in three Lawyers' fond embraces;
Three Magistrates, in corner handy,
With Paupers three, were drinking brandy;
And all the various rest—Inspectors—
Custom-house Officers—Tax Collectors—
Constables—Editors—Tavern-Keepers—
Loafers—and Nightmen—and Street Sweepers,
Sat in a ring, like brother and brother,
All making love to one another!
And meeter companions were never together—
All peats of one turf-bog, and birds of one feather.

There was a sufficient measure of truth in these exaggerated effusions in rhyme to indicate how many Americans reacted to the role played by the Irish immigrant in American politics. On the other hand, it may be said that American cities were not any too well governed before the foreigners came. Philadelphia, for example, with fewer foreigners by far than New York or Boston, has never been a model of civic virtue; and many native American bosses have been of fine Anglo-Saxon lineage. There can be no doubt that American city government became more complicated and difficult to administer because of the immigrant vote. But, as the late James Bryce—who certainly was not under any misapprehension about the evils of city government in the United States—once wrote:

> New York was not an Eden before the Irish came; and would not become an Eden were they all to move on to San Francisco . . . . There is a disposition in the United States to use the immigrants, and especially the Irish, much as the cat is used in the kitchen to account for broken plates and food which disappears.[117]

In 1809, Tammany Hall, which claimed to be thoroughly "native," put up an Irish Catholic for office. Nevertheless, in the first third of the nineteenth century, the Wigwam of the Tammany Society was regarded by the Irish as the home of bigotry and 100 per cent Americanism. By the late 1830's, however, Tammany was effectively wooing the immigrants. For one thing, it opened a bureau to aid them in becoming naturalized. In 1834, the Whigs of New York complained that Irishmen, armed with stones and bludgeons, had driven their voters from the polls.[118] The New

[117] See M. R. Werner: *Tammany Hall* (New York, 1928), p. 62.
[118] See McMaster: *op. cit.*, Vol. VI, p. 227.

York *Truth Teller,* an Irish paper, was subsidized by the Democratic party.[119]   In the 1840's, thousands of Irishmen were naturalized, at reduced court fees, by Tammany judges who signed their citizenship papers without question, provided applicants were sponsored by the right party bosses.   It was charged that prisoners were released from jail on Election Day to march to the polls under the banner of Tammany.   Petty jobs on public works provided the immigrant with the necessary incentive to remain loyal to the "ward heeler."   The saloon, an ally of the machine politician, became the rendezvous for loafers and bruisers, who were prepared, at a moment's notice, to stuff a ballot box or seize control of the polling place.   Meetings were generally held by ward politicians in the saloons,[120] which were the only clubs where the poor immigrant was welcome.   Francis Lieber, in 1835, deplored as dangerous to the American system the many special appeals at electiontime addressed solely to the "true-born sons of Ireland," who thus were encouraged to maintain a kind of dual political allegiance, to the old as well as to the new fatherland.[121]

Although there were earlier instances when political observers credited the immigrant vote with special importance, as in the national election of 1844, when the Whig press attributed the success of Polk in New York State to the votes of 10,000 Irishmen employed on internal improvement works,[122] the national election campaign of 1852 was really the first in American political history in which both parties made a systematic effort to win the German and Irish vote which recent immigration had made a prize well worth seek-

[119] See Nevins: *op. cit.,* Vol. I, pp. 190 and 327.
[120] See Gustavus Myers: *The History of Tammany Hall* (New York, 1901). As late as the 1890's, Archbishop Ireland, writing about the Irish in the United States, commented:

> Saloon-keepers made themselves the centers of groups of their countrymen, whom they guided in the novel road of American politics, and whom they sought to guide, also, in religious affairs. They were officials in church societies, marshals in church processions, chairmen in church meetings. They contributed liberally—as a matter of business —to church works, and paid rent for prominent pews . . . .

Catholic papers carried liquor advertisements, liquor was sold at church fairs and picnics, and clergymen were often afraid to offend the powerful saloonkeepers in their congregations. [John Ireland, Archbishop of St. Paul: "The Catholic Church and the Saloon," in *The North American Review* (October, 1894), pp. 504-505.]
[121] See Francis Lieber, *The Stranger in America* (London, 1835), quoted in Abbott: *op. cit.,* pp. 436-440.
[122] See McMaster: *op. cit.,* Vol. VII, p. 839.

ing. General Winfield Scott, "Old Fuss and Feathers," the Whig candidate for President, found it especially necessary to court the immigrant vote because of a letter he had written more than ten years earlier to the American party of Philadelphia, in which he had expressed sympathy for nativist principles. In his campaign speeches, the General referred feelingly to the "rich brogue of the Irish and the foreign accent of the German," which reminded him of the battlefields of the Mexican War, where these people had so loyally fought the battles of their adopted fatherland. To make doubly sure of his strategy, Scott attended Mass on a Sunday morning and Protestant services in the evening.[123] Because the Democrats, with Pierce as their standard-bearer, were suspected of low-tariff leanings, the Whig *New York Tribune* tried to shake the traditional allegiance of the Irish by the query: "Will Irishmen support a British policy"? [124] *The Boston Pilot,* however, remained neutral in the campaign, contending that neither Scott nor Pierce could do anything especially significant for Catholics. The editor resented appeals for the "Catholic vote," and deplored "the alarming increase of small Irish politicians," job seekers, and "Customs House Catholics." *The Irishman,* a Scott paper published by the Whigs of New York, was denounced as "an insult to both native and adopted citizens." [125] Horace Greeley's "excessive tenderness" for Catholics in general and for those of Franklin Pierce's home state of New Hampshire, whose constitution still retained anti-Catholic features, in particular was dismissed as "a stale trick." [126] Above all, Catholic editors of papers like *The Pilot* saw in Whiggism of 1852 a certain radical "Free-Soilism," which they believed was analogous to the anticlerical radicalism of Europe. Radicalism, whether by native Americans or immigrants, was regarded as the greatest menace to republican institutions, and its exponents were advised to make "an early visit to the confessional." [127]

There is little evidence to show that the immigrant vote in 1852 had decisive effects. Indeed, there is little evidence that the appeal to the immigrant vote was ever decisive in the long annals of American party battles, with the possible exception of one or two

[123] Rhodes: *op. cit.,* Vol. I, p. 276.
[124] *New York Tribune,* September 9, 1852.
[125] See *The Boston Pilot,* September 11 and October 16, 1852.
[126] See *ibid.,* August 28, 1852.
[127] See *ibid.,* November 13, 1852. See also Martin J. Spalding, *Miscellanea,* quoted in Abbott: *op. cit.,* p. 474.

campaigns. Nevertheless, there has not been a national campaign since 1852 in which the political parties have not made a conscious bid for the immigrant vote by playing especially upon either the pride or the prejudices of immigrant groups. The election of 1852, especially in New York, was spirited. Fists and paving block seem to have been as effective as ballots in a battle in which electors were "hurled into the street without vestige of clothing," hundreds received broken bones, and the police collected a "cart-load of bludgeons" in one ward alone. After the shouting and the tumult were over, however, *The Times* quoted with approval the editorial comment of a Western newspaper publisher who wrote:

> Once more a Protestant is just as good as a Catholic, and a native-born citizen as a foreigner. Not having any imported blood in our veins, we have not felt upon an equality with mankind for a few months past. Now, till the commencement of another Presidential campaign, "all men are free and equal." [128]

The decade of the 1850's was a period of significant change in American political parties. It witnessed the death of the Whigs, the Know-Nothing interlude, a division in the old Democratic party, and the rise to success of the Republicans. In a decade of such sweeping party realignment, thousands of voters, including the more important immigrant groups, exchanged their old allegiances for new political affiliations. In some states, particularly in the election of 1860, this realignment of foreign-born voters may have been decisive, as will be shown in a later chapter. The Irish alone remained faithful to the Democratic party. There were some Irish Republicans by 1860, to be sure, but not many. In that year, the bulk of the Irish vote was cast for Stephen A. Douglas, and Irish-Americans remained true to their Democratic leaders.

The Irishman's hatred for the Negro was undoubtedly a decisive factor in any explanation of the reasons for Irish opposition to the newly formed Republican party. As early as 1850, an editorial in the *New York Tribune* commented on the strange phenomenon of the Irish, "themselves just escaped from a galling, degrading bondage," voting down every proposal to give equal rights to the colored race and coming to the polls shouting: "Down with the Nagurs!

[128] *The New York Times*, January 4, 1853. See also *The Boston Pilot*, September 11, 1852.

Let them go back to Africa, *where they belong!*" [129] The Irishman opposed the emancipation of the Negro in large part because he feared his competition in the labor market. During the Civil War, Irish longshoremen of New York bitterly resented the invasion of Negroes in the field of pick-and-shovel work, in which the Irish had long had a monopoly. There were frequent riots when Negro workers were used in the larger sea and lake ports to break strikes of longshoremen during the Civil War. These events go far to explain the fundamental reaction of Irish immigrants during the 1850's to abolitionism and Free-Soilism of any kind.[130]

In addition, influential Irish leaders, especially among the clergy, associated the abolitionist agitation with radicalism in general—a radicalism which, in the United States as in Europe, might ultimately be directed against the Roman Catholic Church. They argued therefore for strict obedience to the law and faithful observance of all parts of the United States Constitution, including its guarantee of slavery.[131] *The Boston Pilot* favored strict enforcement of the fugitive slave law of 1850,[132] declaring: "Abolitionism is no longer Christian. Its prime leaders are prime infidels. They think they can do in a day what it took the Church centuries to accomplish." [133] As late as the fall of 1861, Archbishop Hughes of New York urged support of a war for the Union, but added: "We despise, in the name of all Catholics, the 'Idea' of making this war subservient to the philanthropic nonsense of abolitionism." [134] Brownson, the noted convert to Catholicism, wrote of the Free-Soil reform movement in Massachusetts that, "with the cant of religion and morality on their lips, its leaders are . . . infidels, blasphemers, as well as traitors and disorganizers." Little wonder that Theodore Parker replied: "Not an Irish newspaper is on the side of humanity, freedom, education, progress." Moreover, to many Irishmen the triumph of abolitionist Republicans seemed to imply a revival of Puritanism, foreign to the Irish background and temperament. In Massachusetts, at least, Republicanism was essentially Know-Noth-

[129] *New York Tribune,* May 11, 1850.
[130] See Fite: *op. cit.,* p. 189.
[131] See editorials in *The Boston Pilot* for the 1850's.
[132] See *ibid.,* June 17, 1854.
[133] *Ibid.,* October 20, 1860.
[134] Quoted in *New York Herald,* October 8, 1861. Apparently Hughes had supported Buchanan vigorously in 1856. See *Steubenville Herald,* November 19, 1856. For Irish who were exceptions to the rule, see F. L. Herriott: "Iowa and the First Nomination of Lincoln," in *Annals of Iowa,* Vol. VIII, p. 196.

ing in character. Massachusetts Republicans believed they saw a connection between "Roman hierarchy and Southern oligarchy" whereby "the foreign vote constitutes the cornerstone of American slavery." [135]

The Irish, in 1860, were as dubious about Lincoln's qualities for leadership as millions of other Americans. "Very good men have made their marks," commented *The Pilot*, "Lincoln has made his —with an axe." [136] The same paper, however, praised Lincoln's first inaugural address for its candor, though "no brilliant model in composition," and urged every citizen to support the President.[137] By August, 1861, the editor deplored that Irishmen were being neglected by the Lincoln administration with regard to appointments and promotions in the Army and the civil service, and, in 1862, he advised the election of a Democratic Congress.[138]

The Irishmen of the Northern states, for the most part, shifted to a prowar position after the firing on Fort Sumter. They had not voted for Lincoln, but they were ready to support the Constitution. Irish bishops and Irish editors called on their followers to respond as patriots to the call to preserve the Union; in spite of the nefarious alliance of Know-Nothings and abolitionist Republicans, "the flag of our Union is not to be abandoned." [139] When the emancipation proclamation was announced, many Irish opposed it. Their criticism of the President became more outspoken. They could not believe that white and black could live together, equally free, and they rejected amalgamation as abominable and disgusting.[140] In the fall of 1862, *The Boston Pilot* was urging an armistice, although its pages continued to point with pride to the heroic

---

[135] For these quotations, see W. G. Bean: "Puritan Versus Celt, 1850-1860," in *The New England Quarterly* (March, 1934), pp. 70-89. Theodore Parker, though an enemy of nativism, joined in the attack on the Irish by saying:

> The Catholic clergy are on the side of slavery. They find it the dominant power and pay court thereto, that they may rise by its help. They like slavery itself; it is an institution thoroughly congenial to them, consistent to the first principles of their church . . . .

(Quoted in *ibid.*, p. 82.) Harriet Beecher Stowe approved of a plan of the Dublin Ladies' Anti-Slavery Society to circulate antislavery material at Irish ports of embarkation. [See Annie H. Abel and F. J. Klingberg. *A Side-Light on Anglo-American Relations, 1839-1858* (Lancaster, Pennsylvania, 1927), pp. 30-31.]

[136] *The Boston Pilot*, October 13, 1860.

[137] See *ibid.*, March 16, 1861.

[138] See *ibid.*, August 24, 1861; and August 9, 1862.

[139] *Ibid.*, April 27, 1861.

[140] See *ibid.*, December 13, 1862.

response of Irishmen to the call to arms. Apparently the paper was too Republican to suit its Southern readers, and many subscriptions were lost below Mason and Dixon's line.[141] The New Orleans *Catholic Standard,* as might have been expected, was an out-and-out Confederate paper, while the South Carolina Charleston *Catholic Miscellany* and the Baltimore *Catholic Mirror* denounced "Irishmen who had not the pluck to raise a regiment some years ago, to save themselves from church burners and assassins North and West," and who "are now raising regiments to march on the South, where the foul spirit of Know-nothingism received its quietus . . . ." [142]

The most widely publicized internal disturbance in the North during the Civil War was the rioting precipitated by the draft law in the summer of 1863. Draft riots occurred in Boston, Portsmouth, New Hampshire; Troy, New York; Newport, Rhode Island; and Lancaster, Pennsylvania; as well as in Maine, Ohio, New Jersey, Vermont, Pennsylvania, and Illinois. None, however, reached the proportions of those in New York City.[143] For these latter outbreaks the Irish were severely attacked throughout the country, and all rioters were promptly and unfairly classed as Irish. At least two of the Irish wards in New York City remained perfectly quiet, and their colored residents were not disturbed.[144] In the first ward, Irish porters and laborers formed a guard to fight off the rioters.[145]

The fact remains, however, that the Irish were the worst offenders in the riots that held New York in the grip of a terror so widespread that Federal troops had to be summoned into the city to restore order. The reputation of the entire Irish group was damaged by the incident throughout the nation.[146] More than opposition to the draft was involved. There was a feeling held in some quarters,

---

[141] See *ibid.,* June 8, 1861; and October 4 and 11, 1862.

[142] *Ibid.,* June 1 and 8, 1861.

[143] See *The Boston Traveller,* July 17, 1863; and *The Boston Pilot,* August 16, 1863. See also Fred A. Shannon; *The Organization and Administration of the Union Army, 1861-1865* (Cleveland, Ohio, 1928), Vol. II, pp. 219, 221-223, and 234. As a matter of fact, the incident has been greatly magnified. Stewart Mitchell, in his *Horatio Seymour* (Cambridge, Massachusetts, 1938), p. 335, concludes:

> The net result of the "great draft riots" was three days' disorder, possibly seventy-four deaths at most, and probably eighteen, the burning of a colored orphan asylum, an orgy of journalism, and a scramble for fictitious damages . . . .

[144] See *The New York Tribune,* July 20, 1863.

[145] See *The New York Evening Post,* quoted in *New York Herald,* July 18, 1863.

[146] See *The New York Times,* July 14, 15, 16, 17, 18, and 22, 1863.

and not without justification, that draft officials had drawn especially heavily upon the Democratic wards in New York. Above all, the riot took the form of a huge anti-Negro demonstration, and politicians seized the opportunity to stir up their followers against going to war for "niggers," while the rich remained at home. Why, according to the New York *Daily News*, should a worker leave his family destitute while he goes out to war to free a Negro who will then compete with him for a job? [147]

Apparently, in his efforts to quell the disturbance, the Governor of New York also appealed to Archbishop Hughes to use his influence to stop the rioting, pillaging, and bloodletting that was going on, it was alleged in the excited press, in the Negro districts of the city. At any rate, a bulletin was prominently displayed throughout the city containing an appeal by the Archbishop "to the Men of New York who are now called in many of the papers Rioters." They were summoned to the Bishop's residence to hear an address. The announcement carried the interesting advice not "to be disturbed by any exhibition of municipal or military presence." "You who are Catholics, or as many of you as are," the call continued, "have a right to visit your bishop without molestation." Needless to add, the bulletin of the Archbishop stirred up a veritable newspaper war in New York. But the crowd came and heard the Archbishop, who appeared in purple robes and with the insignia of office. According to one reporter, the crowd was "of one nationality." The Archbishop made no mention of the Negroes who had been the special victims of the disorder. His address, moreover, contained some curious passages, but, in the main, it was a plea to the faithful to return to their homes. Peace was restored.[148] The *Tribune* described the crowd as decent and well-behaved workingmen, not "identified with the unreasoning and merciless rioters." [149] Apparently, as Bryant wrote in *The New York Evening Post*, the shepherd had "summoned the wolves" and "the sheep attended also." [150] The *New York Herald* blamed the "niggerhead and copperhead press" for starting the riot [151] among the workingmen, who were then joined by ruffians, thieves, jail-

---

[147] See *The New York Tribune*, July 15, 1863; and *The New York Herald*, August 2, 1863.
[148] See *The New York Times*, July 18, 1863.
[149] *New York Tribune*, July 18, 1863.
[150] Quoted in *New York Herald*, July 18, 1863. See also Brann: *op. cit.*, p. 170.
[151] See *New York Herald*, July 21, 1863.

birds, and "grog-shop rowdies."[152] "Irish they all were," wrote
N. P. Willis in his *Home Journal,* "every soul of them—but they
were the dirty, half-drunken, brutal rowdies, who are the leprosy of
that fair-skinned race . . . ," and not the respectable Irishmen of
New York.[153]

Other clergymen in the city and elsewhere joined Archbishop
Hughes in denouncing the rioting and in issuing a plea for peace.
All the churches were filled on the Sunday following the incident.
One Irishman wrote to *The New York Times* proposing that his
countrymen raise $50,000 to rebuild the colored orphan asylum
which had been destroyed.[154] The newspapers seemed to agree on
the high praise due the New York police force for its method of handling the riot. Certainly many of those on the force were Irishmen.
Nevertheless, the reputation of all Irish-Americans suffered for
years as a result of the wide notoriety given to these riots.[155]

The Union Army, during the Civil War, was "an amalgam of
nations."[156] Over 400,000 foreign-born helped to save the Union.
Many fought in the ranks of the Confederacy. Within 20 yards of
Castle Garden were two large recruiting tents, with banners, offering large bounties for recruits, and recruiting agents tried to per-
suade the newcomers in their own tongue to join the colors.[157] Both
Irishman and German, as William H. Russell put it, were "fighting
con amore and *pro dolore* ($)."[158] Marching songs from many

---

[152] See *ibid.,* July 24, 1863. See also *New York Tribune,* July 20, 1863.
[153] See *Home Journal,* quoted in *New York Tribune,* July 20, 1863.
[154] See *The New York Times,* July 22 and 29, 1863. See also *New York Herald,*
July 20, 1863.
[155] The *New York Tribune* especially commended the Germans of the Seventeenth Ward. Although the draft fell heavily on them also, they set "a bright
example of good order to the whole of the Empire City." (See *ibid.,* July 18,
1863.)
[156] *The New York Herald,* July 11, 1861, wrote:

> It is no uncommon thing to find men of a score of nations at one mili-
> tary post—Americans (North and South), English, Irish, Scotch, Cana-
> dians (both French and English), French, German, Portuguese, Spanish,
> Greek, Hebrew, Italian, Russian, Polish, Hungarian, Swedes, Danish—
> men of all complexions, save the irrepressible one, and of every shade
> of character.

[157] See Fite: *op. cit.,* p. 194.
[158] See A. C. Cole: *The Irrepressible Conflict 1850-1865* (New York, 1934), p.
309. For an account of recruiting technique, including advertisements containing Irish poetry, see *Boston Transcript,* August 31, and October 7, 18, and 24,
1861. "You have fought nobly for the Harp and Shamrock—fight now for
the Stars and Stripes . . . . Your adopted Country wants you!" (*Ibid.,* October 3, 1861.) A Catholic priest was promised for each regiment (see *ibid.,* October 1, 1861). See also Channing: *op. cit.,* Vol. VI, pp. 425-426.

nations and in many languages could be heard during the Civil War. The Irish did their full share in the war between the States, in spite of their devotion to the Democratic party and their hatred of abolitionism. Many enlisted in the hope of striking in some way at England, and were grievously disappointed when none of the crises in Anglo-American affairs during the Civil War led to hostilities with the British. In Irish regiments, green flags were carried alongside the American colors.[159]

There were many foreigners of Irish and German birth in the Confederate Army also. Irish companies, such as the "Emerald Guards," as well as German companies came from Charleston and western Tennessee to fight under the Stars and Bars of the Confederacy. The South maintained recruiting agents in Europe, and sent an agent to Ireland to counteract the recruiting efforts of the Union government among the Irish people.[160] A correspondent for *The London Times*, describing his visits to Confederate camps between Vicksburg and Cairo in 1861, was surprised to find so many Irishmen, "sometimes entire companies." [161] He attributed the phenomenon to the suspension of work on the levees and railroads of the Mississippi Valley, and to the necessity for Irishmen to find work so that they might eat. Some immigrants, both Irish and German, were forcibly enrolled upon landing in New Orleans and were given the alternative to fight or starve.[162] Germans and Irish were conscripted by the Confederacy. Consequently, some deserted.[163] A thousand Irish Catholic soldiers, captured in battle, swore allegiance to the South and were equipped to fight against their former comrades. When they were sent to stop a raid in Mississippi, they ran up the white flag and deserted in a body again to the boys in blue.[164] Some accounts fix the number of Irish in the Confederate Army at 40,000. Generals "Pat" Cleburne and Joseph Finnegan were two Irish-born Confederates, and John H. Reagan, the able Postmaster General of the Confederacy, was born in Tennessee of Irish parents.

The number of Irish in the Union Army has been estimated at

---

[159] See F. A. Shannon: *op. cit.*, Vol. I, p. 40. For a comment on the *Trent* affair, see *Boston Pilot*, February 15, 1862.
[160] See Channing: *op. cit.*, Vol. VI, p. 426.
[161] See *The London Times*, quoted in *The New York Times*, July 27, 1861.
[162] See *The New York Times*, June 26, 1861.
[163] See *The Boston Pilot*, May 17, 1862.
[164] See Ella Lonn: *Desertion During the Civil War* (New York, 1928), p. 187.

170,000. Newspapers issued after the firing on Fort Sumter contain numerous references to the forming of Irish companies, regiments, and brigades. From Massachusetts came two Irish regiments carrying the Irish flag, the 28th and the 9th Massachusetts Volunteers, the latter commanded by Colonel Thomas Cass.[165] The Emmett Guards of Worcester, Massachusetts, were in New York by the end of April, 1861.[166] Irish contingents were raised in Iowa, Indiana, Ohio, and Illinois, especially Chicago.[167] The 15th Michigan Infantry was known as the "Mulligan Regiment" and had a Catholic chaplain.[168] The "Irish Western Rifles" came from New York State,[169] and three Irish companies recruited in Rochester were attached to the 105th New York Regiment.[170] The 75th of New York was called the "Irish Rifles." The 69th New York regiment was commanded by Michael Corcoran. To the call for 1,000 men, 7,000 responded.[171] The 20th New York, known as the "Ulster Guards" came from the coal and iron regions of Ulster County.[172] Four Irish regiments were recruited in New York in May, 1861, to be known as Colonel Meagher's Irish Zouaves, Colonel Barry's regiment, the Saint Patrick's Brigade, and the Irish Volunteers. "Rally round the Green Flag" was a call that brought thousands into regiments in which the flag of Erin was as conspicuously displayed as were the Stars and Stripes.[173] The Irish regiment from Iowa was under the command of Colonel G. M. O'Brien; the Irish legion from Illinois was commanded by Colonel Timothy O'Meara.[174] Companies or regiments of Irish came also from Buffalo, Cleveland, Detroit, Philadelphia, and elsewhere.[175] *The New York Times* praised the loyalty of the Irish element in its editorial columns;[176] *The New York Herald* advocated a revival of Irish

[165] See W. H. MacNamara: *The Irish Ninth in Bivouac and Battle* (Boston, 1867) and *History of the Ninth Regiment Massachusetts Volunteers* (Boston, 1899). See also *The Boston Pilot*, July 27 and September 28, 1861; and January 18, 1862.
[166] See *The Boston Pilot*, April 27, 1861.
[167] See *ibid.*, July 6 and October 5, 1861; and January 25, 1862.
[168] See *ibid.*, March 8, 1862.
[169] See *ibid.*
[170] See Zwierlein: *op. cit.*, Vol. I, pp. 278-279.
[171] See *The Boston Pilot*, May 4, 1861.
[172] See *ibid.*, May 11, 1861.
[173] See *ibid.*, May 11, 1861; and September 20, 1862.
[174] See *ibid.*, October 4, 1862.
[175] See Cole: *op. cit.*, p. 311; *New York Herald*, November 8, 1861; and *The Boston Pilot*, August 30, 1862.
[176] See *The New York Times*, April 16, 17, and 28, 1861.

immigration;[177] *The Boston Pilot* ran serial articles expounding the record of Irish-American patriotism; and Horace Greeley's *Tribune* rejoiced that "The Irish spirit of the North is thoroughly aroused." [178] Here was the Irish answer to the nativists of the 1850's! The military record of the Irish-Americans, like that of other foreign-born groups, effectively silenced Know-Nothingism for several decades.[179]

The record of Irish regiments on the battlefield is a record not essentially different from other groups who rallied to the defence of the Union. At the outset of the war, there were some disciplinary problems among Irish volunteers. For a time, these threatened seriously to disturb the newly won harmony among the many American groups. *The New York Times* and the *Brooklyn Eagle* accused the Fire Zouaves of New York of cowardice at the first Battle of Bull Run—an engagement in which very few seem to have distinguished themselves for bravery in the face of the enemy. The Zouaves had marched to the front 850 strong, attired in fez caps, red fireman's shirts, and blue pants. They left 200 dead, wounded, and prisoners on the battlefield of Bull Run, and received a rousing welcome from the firemen on their return to New York City.

Unfortunately, they refused to submit to discipline in their quarters at the Battery, and at night, almost to a man, they climbed the gates, evaded the sentries, and disappeared into the city. They testified that, "while they are ready at any moment to return to active service, they cannot brook confinement in any quarters near the city, which has been so long the scene of their labors in the Fire Department." [180] Some of the Fire Zouaves got drunk in the city and, in the end, 75 had to be dismissed from the service.[181] There were Irishmen at Bull Run who fought with courage; there were others who moved to the rear as soon as they heard the boom of the enemy's cannon. In this respect, their record is identical with that of others who participated in this first great debacle of the Civil War. On other occasions, Irish soldiers became unruly when furloughs were denied them; but, here again, the record of other groups in the Union Army is not essentially different. General

[177] See *New York Herald,* December 9, 1861.
[178] *New York Tribune,* August 23, 1861.
[179] See *The Boston Pilot,* October 19, 1861; and July 5, 1862.
[180] *The New York Tribune,* August 23, 1861.
[181] See *The New York Tribune,* August 15, 21, and 29, 1861; *The New York Herald,* September 19, 1861; and *The New York Times,* November 4, 1861; and August 11, 1861.

T. F. Meagher distinguished himself by unusual valor at Fredericksburg, and Colonel Mulligan's men, besieged by a greatly superior force at Lexington, fought for two and a half days without water.[182] Regiments like the 69th New York won their laurels in several major campaigns, where the green flag waved in glory beside the Stars and Stripes. Finally, it should be pointed out that Catholic Sisters of Charity were assigned to military hospitals. Sister Anthony, of the Cincinnati Sisters of Charity, was gratefully remembered by many a stricken soldier, whether Catholic or Protestant, as "the Angel of the Battlefield."

The Civil War left Anglo-American relations in a state of severe strain, because of incidents which had arisen during the war involving British neutrality and because of irritating events along the Canadian border.[183] To Irishmen living in America, this was not a matter for regret. Indeed, many Irish-Americans had enlisted for the war at the instigation of leaders who wished them to get military training and with the vague hope that somehow or other they might find an opportunity to turn their guns against England, their traditional enemy. The war was followed by the Fenian invasion of Canada, one of the most amazing examples of group activity by an immigrant element in all the annals of American history. The incident had international complications; it was used by Secretary of State Seward to bring pressure to bear on England to settle post-Civil War issues and it was handled with unusual caution by American politicians, who did not wish to antagonize the large bloc of Irish voters at a time when American party lines were being redrawn after the war.

Not all Irish leaders were agreed on how Irish-Americans could best serve their beloved fatherland, but none ever forgot the sorrows of the Emerald Isle. Patrick Ford of *The Irish World,* for example, favored revolution and separation from England, whereas John Boyle O'Reilly, editor of *The Boston Pilot,* favored home rule for Ireland, to be won by constitutional methods. Some advocated support of the Fenian Brotherhood and its extreme program; others, like McGee, denounced the Fenians and their theories of divided allegiance as a "racket" to rob poor Irish workers and servant girls of their hard-earned wages.[184] The Fenian organization itself

[182] See *New York Tribune,* September 25, 1861.
[183] See Carl Wittke: *History of Canada* (New York, 1933), Ch. XVI.
[184] See T. D. McGee: *The Irish Position in British and in Republican North America* (Montreal, Canada, 1866), p. 6.

was divided in leadership and program. Some Church leaders favored the movement; others opposed it as vigorously.[185]

Nevertheless, thousands of Irish-Americans in the United States organized as a Fenian Brotherhood, with "circles" in the Army and Navy, as well as among the civilian population, and resolved at the close of the war to take advantage of strained relations between the United States and England in order to launch a movement which would bring freedom to Ireland,

> the lonely and the lovely Bride
> Whom [the English] have wedded, but have never won.

The plan eventually adopted was to do something for Ireland by twisting the tail of the British lion in Canada. Irish veterans of the Civil War were eager to put their military training to further use. A convention of Fenians at Cincinnati created, on paper, an Irish Republic, with a full complement of officials, and began to sell bonds and prepare for a Canadian invasion. It was confidently expected that the Canadians would join the movement and that the United States government would quickly recognize the new republican government to be set up in Canada.

On June 1, 1866, the hosts of Fenianism crossed the Niagara border, 1,500 strong, seized Fort Erie, and threw up entrenchments. The American authorities proved extremely lax in preventing the mobilization of Fenians along the border, and the American Secretary of State, probably with an eye on the Irish voters, waited five days before issuing a neutrality proclamation. Several minor engagements were fought, and then the foolhardy venture collapsed. Hundreds of Fenians were arrested on their return to the United States, but were eventually paroled and returned to their homes at the expense of the United States government. A similar raid across the Vermont border also ended in failure, and Colonel W. R. Roberts, president of the "Irish Republic," was eventually arrested. Another attempted invasion, in 1870, was thwarted by the coöperation of United States and Canadian authorities. The incident became an issue in American politics in the uncertain party situation following the war, and many Americans asked themselves with McGee what the eventual results might be of having an "alien population, camped but not settled in America, with foreign hopes and

[185] See *Boston Transcript*, March 5, 1866.

aspirations unshared by the people among whom they live?" [186]

Until after the World War, the Irish question remained an issue in American politics, to be revived for political purposes on almost every occasion when Irish votes were needed. The hatred of England was almost universal among Irish-Americans, and one suspects that the feelings of Irishmen were often stirred to fever heat for the politician's ulterior purposes. Irish repeal meetings have been addressed by leading politicians since the 1840's.[187] New York mayors have continued to review St. Patrick's Day parades to the present time, although they are not always decked out in a green suit, green tie, and green kid gloves, as on the occasion, in 1870, when Mayor Hall reviewed the hosts of Irishmen marshaled by Tammany Hall under bosses Kelly, Croker, and Murphy.[188] Politicians still contribute to Irish causes, as when Greeley, in 1872, reminded the voters of his $1,500 gift for Irish relief during the potato famine; and they are still subject to criticism if they are too respectful to England, as on the occasion when Mayor Hewitt seemed to glorify Queen Victoria on her Golden Jubilee, in 1887,[189] or when President Arthur, three years earlier, happened to choose the Queen's birthday to dedicate the Brooklyn Bridge.[190] And to this day, political oratory always reaches unusual heights of eloquence at St. Patrick's Day celebrations.[191]

Space does not permit a discussion of the many campaigns in which the Irish vote seemed to be especially significant. Several—

[186] For a detailed account of the Fenian movement, see any of the leading papers, such as *The Boston Transcript* for 1866; John A. Macdonald: *Troublous Times in Canada* (Toronto, Canada, 1910); and Clyde L. King: "The Fenian Movement," in *University of Colorado Studies*, Vol. VI, No. 3.

[187] For early examples, see Nevins: *op. cit.*, Vol. II, pp. 662, 671, and 676.

[188] See Werner: *op. cit.*, pp. 121-122.

[189] See *New York World*, October 20 and 23, 1888.

[190] See A. M. Schlesinger: *The Rise of the City, 1878-1898* (New York, 1933), p. 90.

[191] However, Irish St. Patrick's Day oratory probably never reached higher flights than in the address, in 1855, by the Irish patriot exile Thomas Francis Meagher, when he said:

> On the girdle of faded gold there is in ancient letters the name of her —the forsaken, but not forgotten one—whose sons and daughters we this night, with love and pride, confess ourselves to be . . . . It is a festival of memory . . . on whatever spot the stars come forth and keep guard this night, the children of a little island—meet together in loving sympathy and remembrance. . . . I drink to her whose son I am proud to be, though she be poor, indeed, though we miss her crest and shield from the bright heraldry of other nations, though like her eldest sister of Zion, she has become as a widow, she that was a princess among the provinces.

(Quoted in Crimmins: *op. cit.*, pp. 230-236.)

like the campaigns of 1868 and 1872, and the battle between Blaine and Cleveland for the Presidency in 1884—must suffice as further illustrations.[192]

From the political turmoil that followed Lincoln's assassination, Johnson's accession to the Presidency, and his subsequent controversies with the radical Republicans over reconstruction arose a necessity to rebuild party lines. No group of voters was too insignificant to woo at the ballot box. The issues raised by Fenianism and the raids on Canada provided a ready-made occasion to fish for Irish votes. President Johnson had maintained strict neutrality, for which his radical opponents, eager to catch Irish votes, lost no time in condemning him. The eccentric George Francis Train, campaigning for Johnson during the Congressional elections of 1866, denounced the radical Republicans, who now courted the Irish-American "Finnigan vote," as erstwhile Know-Nothings and convent burners. Johnson's speech in defense of Catholics Train concluded "should be in every Catholic home. Johnson is an older Fenian than the eldest of you." [193]

All this was but preliminary skirmishing for the Presidential campaign of 1868. Now the Democrats accused Schuyler Colfax, Republican Vice-Presidential candidate, of being deliberately anti-Catholic. *The Chicago Republican* promptly denied the charge, insisting that the party organization could not be held responsible "for sermons which divines may preach from the pulpit." A special campaign sheet was published for the Irish by the Republican party organization, and prominent Irish leaders were induced to take the stump for Grant and Colfax and urge Irish veterans to "rally 'round the flag." *The Irish People,* a Democratic paper edited by D. O'Sullivan, received a check for $1,000 from prominent

[192] For other examples, see *Toledo Commercial,* May 13, 1876; *Cleveland Leader,* April 1, 1870; and *Ohio State Journal,* November 1, 1889.
[193] *National Intelligencer,* July 25, 1866. The *Cincinnati Enquirer* for September 24, 1866, printed a poem, "The Finnigan Vote," dedicated to "all those Finnigans who have taken such a sudden liking for the wily Rads." The fourth stanza read as follows:

When Rads take the chair in your Finnigan halls,
And dance at your picnics and waltz at your balls,
It is not for the love of poor Bridget and Pat,
The haughty old Rads, consent to do that.
Faith, they have the same raison more potent to move
Those kindly attentions to Patrick than love
For merry or sad, by their looks you can note
That they have their eye on the Finnigan vote.

Republicans and promptly changed its politics. In exasperation over these tactics of the campaign, *The Chicago Post* for September 9, 1868, paid its respects to these adopted citizens in language seldom exceeded in violence even at electiontime. The editor exploded:

> Teddy O'Flaherty votes. He has not been in the country six months . . . . He has hair on his teeth. He never knew an hour in civilized society . . . . He is a born savage—as brutal a ruffian as an untamed Indian . . . . Breaking heads for opinion's sake is his practice. The born criminal and pauper of the civilized world . . . a wronged, abused, and pitiful spectacle of a man . . . pushed straight to hell by that abomination against common sense called the Catholic religion . . . . To compare him with an intelligent freedman would be an insult to the latter . . . . The Irish fill our prisons, our poor houses . . . . Scratch a convict or a pauper, and the chances are that you tickle the skin of an Irish Catholic.[194]

In 1872, Horace Greeley, as candidate of both the Democrats and the Liberal Republicans, had difficulty in holding the Irish vote, in spite of his excellent record as an opponent of Know-Nothingism and his contribution of $1,500 in 1849 to the suffering Irish. Needless to add, this act of philanthropy was given wide publicity during the campaign. The fact that Horace Greeley was a teetotaler and had been associated with some curious reform movements during his career did not help his chances among the Irish, however. Grant was extremely popular, and his popularity was sufficient to carry along his Vice-Presidential running mate, Henry Wilson of Massachusetts, whose record as a Know-Nothing was well known and who was described by the *Tribune* as "one of the most rampant and bigoted of the political proscribers of the German and Irish-Americans." [195] Grant's military record proved a tremendous asset with his Irish comrades in arms. Meetings were held in New York, St. Louis, and elsewhere by "Irish-American Republican Clubs" to remind the voters that Grant had succeeded in his diplomacy with England; that, by bringing about the abolition of slavery, he had "elevated the foreign laborer to a position heretofore denied him by Southern pro-slavery Democrats"; and that he had done more

[194] Quoted in Charles H. Coleman: *The Election of 1868* (Columbia University Press, New York, 1933), pp. 302-304.
[195] *New York Tribune*, August 26, 1872.

for Irishmen "than any of the party demagogues who had boasted that they always held Irish votes in their pockets." [196]

In the Blaine-Cleveland campaign of 1884, both parties bid for the half-million Irish votes. The campaign was distinguished by its mudslinging features, by the closeness of the result, and by the effort of the Republicans to wean the Irish from their traditional Democratic allegiance—a process which was successful at least to the extent that, for the next decade, there was a considerable group of so-called Blaine Irish Republicans that the party recognized in distributing spoils of office. The friends of Blaine made a studied effort in 1884 to win Irish votes. Blaine's mother was a Catholic, and so were some of his relatives. His sister, it was reported, was a mother superior in a convent, though the reference was probably to a cousin, Sister Angela. Moreover, Blaine's "spirited foreign policy" had been directed against the British, whereas the free trade policy of the Democrats was denounced as a pro-British device.

The Irish World and *The Irish Nation* gave Blaine their support, and their editors, John Devoy and Patrick Ford, were enthusiastic Blaine men. Irish-American organizations appeared in Republican parades. The Republicans emphasized Blaine's "Donegal and Londonderry blood," and the Democrats countered by pointing out that Cleveland had a maternal Irish ancestry also. A great Irish-American rally for Blaine was held in Chickering Hall, in New York; and in Boston, a convention of the Irish Land League announced that, if Blaine were elected, "Ireland would be free in thirty days." The Democrats tried to frighten the Irish by quoting articles Blaine had written 30 years earlier in *The Kennebec Journal* to prove that he was a prohibitionist. A special pamphlet issued by the Democratic party represented Blaine as a Know-Nothing and as a persecutor of Catholics and the foreign-born. When the famous slip about "Rum, Romanism, and Rebellion" occurred at a Blaine rally, at the close of the campaign, handbills by the thousands were left the next day at the doors of Roman Catholics quoting the remark as a deliberate insult to Irishmen. The incident may have been decisive in turning the election in New York, on which the national outcome depended.[197]

[196] *The New York Times,* September 20 and 25, and November 2, 1872. See also *New York Tribune,* September 6, 1872.
[197] See E. P. Oberholtzer: *A History of the United States Since the Civil War* (New York, 1931), Vol. V, p. 204; and D. S. Muzzey: *James G. Blaine, a Political Idol of Other Days* (New York, 1934), pp. 203, 308-317, and 415.

When Cleveland ran again in 1888, he was described as "the British candidate," because of his advocacy of tariff reform; and both Cleveland and Harrison were quoted as having insulted the Irish group.[198] In the incident of the Murchinson letter, when the British Ambassador advised voting for Cleveland, the Republicans had a rallying cry against Cleveland of special force among the Irish. Lord Sackville-West was promptly labeled the "British Election Agent," and the battle cry became, "No English Free Trade!" [199] In 1888, Blaine addressed a great rally in Madison Square Garden. Over the platform hung an Irish flag inscribed "Home Rule for Ireland." The decorations were of emerald green, and the keynote of the meeting was: "Every Irishman who votes for free trade is a practical ally of England."

The anti-British motif in Irish-American politics reappeared in numerous campaigns until after the close of the World War. During the Venezuela boundary controversy of 1895 and the Boer War, some Irish-American leaders welcomed the opportunity to revive anti-British propaganda. In the election of 1916, many Irish voters opposed President Wilson on the ground that he had been too lenient during the World War with England, their traditional enemy, and too severe with Germany, their friend. The chief spokesmen for Irish self-determination at the Peace Conference of Versailles in 1919 were two Irish-American leaders whose relations with President Wilson proved to be anything but harmonious. In 1920, both the United States Senate and the House of Representatives adopted resolutions on the Irish question, virtually suggesting to the British Prime Minister how the issue should be settled.[200]

The Americanization of the Irish proceeded so rapidly, in spite of the alarmists of the 1850's and 1860's, that no detailed discussion

[198] See *The New York Tribune*, November 4, 1888; and *Cleveland Plain Dealer*, October 30, 1888.

[199] *The New York Tribune*, October 26, 1888. See also *The Ohio State Journal*, October 24 and November 5, 1892.

[200] For these and similar incidents, see W. R. Thayer: *The Life of John Hay* (Boston, 1915), Vol. II, pp. 234 and 220; R. M. McElroy: *Grover Cleveland, the Man and the Statesman* (New York, 1923), Vol. II, p. 197; Joseph P. Tumulty: *Woodrow Wilson as I Know Him* (New York, 1921), p. 214; Edward F. McSweeney: *Ireland Is an American Question* (New York, 1919); *Mississippi Valley Historical Review*, extra number (February, 1923), pp. 468-480; and *The London Spectator*, Vol. LXI, pp. 1496-1497. To the end of his career, Archbishop Ireland cautioned Catholics of Irish descent not to hurt the Church by dragging in Irish national quarrels. He deplored the political segregation of citizens along lines of their birth, saying: "It is wrong to have a so-called Irish-American vote . . . . The Church has suffered from a lack of Americanism."

of this process is necessary here. The Irish have become so much a part of present-day Americanism that it seems curious indeed to review the characteristics they brought with them two generations ago and to describe the reception they received from their American contemporaries. The Irishman is now so thoroughly Americanized that he is not averse to joining in denunciations of later immigrants whose ideas he considers dangerous to American institutions, apparently completely forgetful of the treatment his ancestors received 75 or 100 years ago. Indeed, a few Irish politicians have joined in the hue and cry to deprive other groups of their civil rights.

The Americanization process was already under way at the very time when the Irish element seemed most alarming to the nativists. Irish conventions in the 1850's to provide emigrant aid or to advocate the repeal of the union with England revealed an interest in things other than saloons and city politics. A crop of Irish journals published in the United States before the Civil War showed a healthy interest in public, church, and Irish affairs. Financial contributions to the Irish cause and for the relief of relatives and friends in Ireland ran into the millions, proving, not only an abiding interest in filial and patriotic obligations, but a measure of prosperity for immigrants whose main income came from pick-and-shovel work and domestic service. In the 1850's, the Irish sent at least $1,000,000 a year and many prepaid tickets to their friends and relatives in Ireland.[201] In less than 20 years, Alexander T. Stewart, "the lucky Irishman," became the owner of the finest store in the world and one of the largest real-estate owners in New York.[202]

Charitable institutions were established in several cities in the 1850's,[203] and clubs were organized for literary and social activities.[204] In 1855, the Young Catholic Friends' Society of Boston began its twentieth series of lectures.[205] There was an Emmett Monument Association in Boston, which sponsored lectures on Irish freedom in the 1850's; and, in 1855, the four Irish societies of Salem held a levee for charity, with Gilmore's Band as the main attraction.[206] Irish reading rooms, Erina assemblies, and Tom Moore

[201] See Cole: *The Irrepressible Conflict, 1850-1865*, p. 121; and *Cincinnati Enquirer*, September 21, 1859.
[202] See *ibid.*, p. 132.
[203] See *Boston Transcript*, July 12, 1853.
[204] See *ibid.*, December 1, 1853.
[205] See *Boston Herald*, December 4, 1855.
[206] See *ibid.*, December 19 and 31, 1855. See also *Albany Argus*, March 10, 1849.

Clubs were established in several cities.[207]   In 1860, New York had an Ossianic Society, which published Gaelic manuscripts and documents dealing with Irish history.[208]   The American Irish Historical Society was founded in Boston in 1897.

The transformation of the Irishman in America was rapid and attracted the attention of many commentators. Perhaps the evidence of English travelers may be used as the most reliable, for certainly few of them began with any bias in favor of Irish-Americans. William Chambers, in his *Things as They Are in America,* admitted that Irishmen in the United States "soon acquire the sentiments of self-respect common to the American character." He found the transformation remarkably rapid, and testified to the ability of Irish workers to save money and to become "more Americanized than the Americans." The same observer wrote:

> In the second generation . . . the Irishman has disappeared. Associating in and out of school with the shrewd native youth, laughed, if not instructed, out of prejudices, the children of Irish descent have generally lost the distinctive marks of their origin. . . . It is wonderful to notice how soon an Irishman in a long-tailed coat and patched knee-corduroys is transferred into a hotel garçon, dressed neatly in a white jacket and pants, combed, brushed, and rendered as amenable to discipline as if under the orders of a drill-sergeant. Thus smartened up, the Irish have become a most important people in the United States. Irish girls . . . are here received with a sigh of delight, and what American housewives and hotelkeepers would now do without them, is painful to reflect upon. . . .[209]

Another English observer, who spent three years among the working classes in the United States during the Civil War, was even more complimentary, and his comments deserve extended quotation. In 1865, he wrote of the Irishman in the United States in the following words:

> Instead of the indolent deportment, careless manner, and slouching gait, which characterized him at home, the young Hibernian receives the genteel inspiration of fashion, and speedily has himself tailored into external respectability; he learns to walk with his head erect, and assumes an air in keeping with his altered condition. That crouching servility and fawning sycophancy to people above his grade,

[207] See *The Boston Pilot,* May 1, 1852; and March 11 and January 28, 1854.
[208] See *ibid.,* September 8, 1860.
[209] William Chambers, *Things as They Are in America* (London, 1854), p. 189. See also Charles Mackay: *Life and Liberty in America* (1857-1858), p. 243.

which made him a slave in all but the fetters, is cast aside, and he dons the character of a free citizen of the United States.[210]

The writer was especially impressed with the Irish-American's shrewdness, common sense, and fund of ready wit; and with the records of the money-order offices, which constituted "a lasting memorial of the industry, prudence, filial duty, and affection of thousands of the sons and daughters of the Green Isle . . . ." He concluded that the Irish "are often more American than the natives, who trace their genealogies back to the pioneers." [211]

By the time of the Civil War, Irishmen themselves were sensitive about their complete acceptance as genuine Americans. They especially resented the Irish plays that were so much in vogue on the American stage during this period. They criticized these plays as un-Irish in tone and sentiment; and they denounced the stage Irishman, who was invariably dressed in old-fashioned, battered garments, with a pipe in his hatband and a shillelah in his hand, from whose lips issued language that was both inelegant and blasphemous.[212]

The Irishman has long since given up his monopoly of the pick and the shovel. Today French-Canadians, Italians, Poles, and others of the newer immigration do the heavy construction work which was once the special province of the Irish immigrant laborer. The Irishman has moved up in the scale, both economically and socially, to become a factory worker, a boss, or an employer; and thousands have successfully invaded the professions. Paddy has taken up clerking, bookkeeping, and business or has become a traveling salesman. In law, politics, and the Church, he has been especially successful, perhaps because these professions require that warm human touch, mixed with a certain dash and quickwittedness so characteristic of many Irishmen. In the Church, the Irish have had almost a monopoly of the positions in the Catholic hierarchy in America, although their domination in this field is now being challenged by representatives of other groups. American journalism has enlisted many distinguished men and women of Irish blood, and the field of politics remains peculiarly the Irishman's own. Bridget, once the answer to an American housewife's prayer for adequate domestic help, has hung up her kitchen apron, except perhaps

[210] James D. Burn: *Three Years Among the Working Classes in the United States During the War* (London, 1865), pp. 15-16.

[211] *Ibid.*, pp. 17 and 46.

[212] See *The Boston Pilot*, October 6, 1860; and *The New York Times*, April 27, 1853.

[185]

in some parts of New England, to become a seamstress, a factory worker, a saleslady, a stenographer, or a schoolteacher. She dresses well and is often more American than her American coworkers, though some of the rosy complexion of her ancestors may have been lost in the process of adjustment to her new environment.

The Irish, for the most part, retain that devotion to family which has always marked this warm-blooded and warmhearted people. They are convivial and generous, sometimes to a fault, frequently improvident, and do not often come in conflict with the law except for intemperance, minor offenses, and occasional difficulties arising from the political graft of some of our larger cities. They know how to handle men, which accounts for much of their success in business, the Church, labor unions, and politics, where so much depends on friendship, human sympathy, and understanding. The Irishman's extravagance of speech has affected the American language,[213] and a number of Irish words and phrases have been absorbed into our daily speech. The Irishman's contributions to drama, music, and the productive arts will be considered in a later chapter. What the Irishman has done for American literature, the vaudeville stage, and the wit and humor of the parlor and smoking room must remain largely undescribed, for these things belong to the intangibles that color a civilization but refuse to submit to statistical proof and appraisal.

There are Irish who have remained in the slums, while others have risen to places of distinction and influence in many walks of life. Perhaps the great majority, as has been said, have attained "that state of respectable mediocrity which is the foundation of American society." [214] But in whatever station he may now find himself, the Irishman has helped to modify the Puritan heritage of America. He has tempered its somber colors and more gloomy outlook with the joys of life. In spite of his mercurial temperament, it may still be said of the Irishman, as it was when Irishmen first began coming to America in large numbers:

> How gallantly, indeed, do Irish wit, and cheerfulness, and hospitality, and patriotism, ride on the wreck of individual hopes, and sparkle through the very waves of adversity! [215]

[213] See H. L. Mencken: *The American Language* (New York, 1921).
[214] W. F. Adams: *op. cit.*, p. 350.
[215] Samuel G. Goodrich: *Ireland and the Irish* (Boston, 1841), quoted in Abbott: *op. cit.*, p. 741. For biographical sketches of prominent figures among the Irish of Boston in 1890, see Cullen: *The Irish in Boston*, pp. 167-429. The 1930 Census reports 923,642 persons in the United States who were born in Ireland and 3,791,522 one or both of whose parents were natives of Ireland, born here.

9

The Germans

THE TIDE OF German immigration rose in the middle nineteenth century as the Irish began slowly to recede. Throughout the century, the two overlapped. The city-dwelling, land-shunning, unskilled, mercurial Irishman presented a vivid contrast to the patient, home-loving, philosophic, phlegmatic, plodding German peasant and artisan, who settled in the city to ply his trade and, by thrift and industry, acquired a home, or who went into the West to become a farmer in the prairie country. The German represented the plain, homely virtues of perseverance, patience, thrift, and respect for authority, with just enough idealism to save and build homes in the New World. Like the Scandinavian, he lent a certain conservative, stabilizing force to nineteenth-century immigration. It must not be assumed, however, that Germans were always welcome or that their virtues were immediately recognized. Moreover, so sharp was the contrast between the Irish and German temperaments that, for two generations, the American vaudeville and variety stage exaggerated these characteristics for comic effect, and the success of many a vaudeville team depended on playing off the contrasting qualities of the stage Irishman with those of the "Dutch" comedian.

In the century before the World War, over 5,300,000 Germans came to the United States. If to this number be added other groups who represented a fundamentally German culture but came from Switzerland, Russia, and Austria, the total exceeds 7,000,000. The Census of 1910 reported 8,282,618 in the United States who gave Germany as the country of their origin—that is, who were either native Germans or one or both of whose parents were born in Germany. In 1850, the German element constituted nearly 26 per cent of the foreign-born population; in 1860, the percentage was over 31 per cent. Friedrich Kapp calculated the German immigration from 1819 to 1871 at 2,358,709, and estimated that this represented an actual importation of money to the amount of half a billion dollars and a potential productive capacity of over one and three quarter billion dollars.

Shiploads of German immigrants arrived at all the leading American ports, including New Orleans, throughout the nineteenth century. Many remained in the Eastern states and cities, but thousands moved inland into the Mississippi Valley. Immigrant trains, "stretched to the length of a monstrous serpent," rolled in daily to Buffalo in the 1840's and 1850's over the Buffalo and Niagara Railroad. Immigrants were compelled to camp in the streets or to occupy empty buildings until they could find lake or rail transportation to carry them farther westward. Thousands came up the river from New Orleans and distributed themselves throughout the Mississippi Valley. By 1832, German immigration to the United States exceeded 10,000; by 1834, 17,000; by 1837, 24,000; and from 1845 to the outbreak of the Civil War, 1,250,000.[1]

The primary cause of German immigration was undoubtedly economic. America was the promised land of cheap and good soil. Agents of steamship companies, real-estate promoters, and employees of Western states eager for population worked hard to convince the average German artisan and peasant that America was a land of unrestricted opportunity. "America letters" from successful immigrants were also exploited to their maximum advantage. Attracted by cheap public and railroad lands, and later by free homesteads, the German became a pioneer farmer, and he became an important factor in opening the New West to farming and in winning the Mississippi Valley for agriculture. German artisans, trained in the thorough discipline of the old guild apprentice system, found a ready demand for their mechanical skills, and the German tradesman became a factor in the industrial expansion of a new country that was just beginning to experience the first effects of a tremendous economic revolution.

The disturbed political conditions of western Europe, particularly in the German states, provided another motive for the emigration of many Germans before the Civil War and was especially responsible for the emigration of men of substance and excellent

---

[1] The newspapers of the period are full of notices of arrivals and of immigrant trains passing through the country. See, for example, *Cleveland Leader*, December 2, 1844; and *Cincinnati Enquirer*, October 15, 21, 23, 26, and 30, and November 3, 1868.

training, who provided the leadership for many years to come for the German element in the United States. The downfall of Napoleon had been followed all over Europe by a period of reaction against the liberalizing, reforming, and democratizing forces which the French Revolution had released and which Napoleon's imperial system had by no means extinguished. The period of European history after 1815 is familiar to students as the age of Metternich, when Europe, under the dominance of the Austrian reactionary, experienced a return to censorship, suppression, and espionage. Every effort was made to stamp out the last sparks of liberalism and democracy; and censorship of the press, of public meetings, and of schools and universities was relied upon to prevent the recurrence of the unsettling democratic tendencies of the late eighteenth century. When rebellion against authority nevertheless broke out, it was ruthlessly suppressed.

In Germany, which was still divided among scores of petty princes, reaction was in full sway. But the liberal movement, fed by the Wars of Liberation against Napoleon, a foreign oppressor, could not be completely suppressed. It lived on in the universities, among the intellectuals, and among youthful patriots who dreamed of the eventual unification of Germany under a republican system that would establish freedom and political equality for all. The essentials of this liberal movement, which was destined to break out in the abortive revolutions of 1830 and 1848 and eventually to be swallowed up by the unification of Germany under Bismarck and Prussia, are well known to students of nineteenth-century history. Space does not permit a detailed treatment here. Suffice it to say that, as a result of these abortive revolutions and of the persecution and unrest that characterized the Germany of most of the last century, the United States received a group of German immigrants who represented men of property and education, men of substance and social standing. Many became distinguished German-Americans, providing an intellectual and political leadership for the German-American farming and working classes which, on occasion, gave to that element an influence transcending its actual numerical strength. Many a German farmer in the West was a "Latin farmer," who was more familiar with Virgil than with guiding a plow through a furrow in prairie soil; and there were German workers on the railroads and in the shops who knew Homer in the original.

The centers of the German liberal movement in the first half of the nineteenth century were the *Burschenschaften* of the universities, where the student corps not only drank and dueled but also pondered the sufferings of the fatherland and dreamed of a unified German republic, and the *Turnvereine,* which were later introduced in the United States and remained a flourishing part of the organizational life of many German-American communities. Some comment on the spirit and purposes of the *Turnvereine* will illustrate the idealism that actuated much of the leadership of the German immigration.

German turner organizations trace their origins to the dark days of Napoleonic domination of Prussia, when the German Empire lay hopelessly disrupted and prostrate under the heel of the French conqueror. In this hour of German humiliation, a few dauntless spirits planned a war of liberation, from which it was hoped Germany would emerge united and free. In 1811, Friedrich Ludwig Jahn —"Vater Jahn," as he was affectionately known to his followers in later years—established his first *Turnplatz* on the Hasenheide, in Berlin. His plan was to emphasize the importance of physical exercise and strength as factors in national development, and to create a new organization that would stress physical training as a means of fostering patriotic ideals. The ancient plea of Juvenal for *mens sana in sano corpore* was the motto of the turner movement, and the turner sought to develop, not only a sound body which would be prepared for service in the coming struggle for a unified, republican Germany, but also a mind sensitive to liberty and freedom. Patriotism, hatred of all oppression—political, ecclesiastical, and intellectual—and a passionate devotion to liberty were and have remained, even in America, the fundamental principles of the turner movement.

The promises to democratize the German states made by quavering rulers after the expulsion of Napoleon were forgotten in the age of reaction that dawned upon a war-weary Europe after 1815. The turner movement was suppressed, and Jahn himself spent five years in a Prussian jail. The fervent liberalism of the movement could not be entirely suppressed, however, and, in 1848, it burst forth anew in glorious but ill-fated revolution and in the Frankfurt Parliament. Many of the German immigrants to the United States were intellectuals and political refugees who had been members of the *Turnvereine* and who now transplanted the German *Turnge-*

meinde, along with their other organizations, to their adopted fatherland.

It would be misleading, however, to leave the impression that the bulk of German immigrants in the nineteenth century were intellectuals, university graduates, or men of high social standing. They were not. The great majority of them were enterprising peasants and artisans, who came to America primarily for economic reasons. Nevertheless, some further comment on the type of German leadership in the United States is desirable, for it was this leadership that gave the cultural tone to German immigrant communities.

Among the victims of the so-called *Demagogenverfolgung* started by Metternich in 1817 were Karl Follen, Francis Lieber, Karl Beck, E. A. Rivinus, Robert Wilhelm Wesselhöft, Franz Joseph Grund, a Bohemian German, and Franz W. Gräter. Follen, Beck, Gräter, and Grund were teachers at Harvard; the Wesselhöfts were distinguished physicians in Philadelphia. Grund, besides teaching mathematics, wrote campaign biographies for the Democrats and Whigs in 1836 and 1840, respectively, and received a consul's post from both as his reward. Karl Follen, who had written revolutionary poetry and had sponsored the festival of the *Burschenschaften* at the Wartburg, introduced physical training at Harvard and became a Unitarian minister and an abolitionist leader.[2] Lieber has been called the "first academic political philosopher." He taught swimming and physical education in Boston, and political economy and history at South Carolina College and at Columbia University. In his *Political Ethics* (1838-1839) and *Civil Liberty and Self-Government* (1853), he gave a new turn to political speculation about the origin and nature of the State, and helped to explode the compact theory and the natural rights philosophy.[3]

Among the *Dreissiger,* the group that emigrated after the political disturbances of 1830 and before the "Forty-Eighters," names like those of Gustav Körner, Judge J. Bernhard Stallo, Dr. Konstantin Hering, Dr. Oswald Seidensticker, Friedrich Münch, Friedrich

---

[2] See G. W. Spindler: "Karl Follen," in *Jahrbuch der Deutsch-Amerikanischen Historischen Gesellschaft von Illinois* (1916), Vol. XVI, pp. 7-247.

[3] See Parrington: *The Romantic Revolution in America (1800-1860),* Vol. II, pp. 93-98. See also Ernest Bruncken: "Francis Lieber: A Study of a Man and an Ideal," in *Jahrbuch der Deutsch-Amerikanischen Historischen Gesellschaft von Illinois* (1915), Vol. XV, pp. 7-61.

Theodor Engelmann, whose German-born son was an officer in both the Mexican and Civil Wars, George Bunsen, and Wilhelm Weber stand out. Körner spent four months in jail in Munich because of student street disorders for which his *Burschenschaft* was responsible. After participating in an unsuccessful uprising in Frankfurt in 1833, he fled to the United States, making his way up the Hudson, thence by canal to Buffalo, by steamer to Cleveland, through the Ohio Canal to Portsmouth, and finally by river boat to St. Louis. He settled, along with many Germans of his kind, in Belleville, St. Clair County, Illinois—a typical "Latin farmers" settlement. Körner was first active in Democratic politics and became a judge on the Illinois Supreme Court in 1845. Later he joined the new Republican party, during the early years of which he was very influential. He served as Lieutenant Governor of Illinois and, in 1862, as Minister to Spain, and was still active in the Liberal Republican movement of 1872.[4]

Friedrich Münch exchanged his philosophical studies in Germany for the axe and the plow in Missouri, but finally managed to do newspaper work and to write novels and philosophical essays.[5] Another pioneer in Missouri reported that "the songs of liberation of the years 1817 and 1818 made the primeval forests of Missouri ring." He cut his first corn with a sword his brother had used in 1813 against France.[6] George Bunsen, who came to Belleville, Illinois, in the early thirties, became superintendent of schools in his community and introduced features of the Pestalozzi method of instruction. Wilhelm Weber became editor and owner of the St. Louis *Anzeiger des Westens.*[7] Men like L. A. Wollenweber and Carl Dominique, German university products, handled picks and shovels in the 1830's in building the Schuylkill Canal.[8] Many "Latin Farmers" went to ruin, losing their farms to their day laborers; some saved themselves by moving in time to the cities to practice the professions for which they were really trained. It is

---

[4] See H. A. Rattermann: *Gustav Körner,* reprinted by *Deutsch-Amerikanische Geschichtsblätter* (Chicago, 1903).
[5] See *Missouri Historical Review,* Vol. XIX, p. 114.
[6] See W. G. Bek: "The Followers of Duden," in *Missouri Historical Review,* Vol. XVIII, pp. 428 and 431.
[7] See also Gert Göbel: *Länger als ein Menschenleben in Missouri* (St. Louis, 1877). This is a charming story of a German professor of mathematics who settled with his family in Missouri in the 1830's.
[8] *Mitteilungen des deutschen Pionier Vereins von Philadelphia* (1909), No. 13, pp. 16-17.

evident that all intellectual activity among the Germans did not begin with the better-known Forty-Eighters.

As a matter of fact, the Forty-Eighters did not really come in significant numbers until 1850 and 1851, and many who actually came in 1848 returned shortly to Germany. For a time, German-American affairs were seriously disturbed by considerable friction and bad blood between the "Grays," as those Germans who came before 1848 were called, and the "Greens," those who came after 1848. Among the latter were many radical reformers and revolutionists who wanted to make the world over, beginning with the United States, which was to become the center of a world of republics.[9] The Greens chided the older German element for their poor journalism, their ineffectiveness in American politics, and their failure to end slavery and clericalism in the United States immediately upon their arrival. Körner, leader of the Grays, was derisively referred to as "der graue Gustav." The Greens refused to recognize the cultural achievements of their predecessors, and a fierce journalistic war broke out between the two groups. The Greens were impatient for the millenium and were radical reformers. Some were merely waiting impatiently in America "bis es drüben wieder los geht"; others were planning a separate German state in America, where their Utopian plans might be speedily realized. It must be admitted that they were neither modest nor slow about announcing their program, which involved, among other things, attacks on American Puritanism, Sabbath observance, and the "Methodists," a rather all-inclusive word of opprobrium. Leaders of the Grays, on the other hand, had become absorbed in the activities of their new home; they had no interest in such fantasies as a separate German state in the American Union, and they were not concerned with a program of sweeping reforms which included attacks on the Church, the Presidency, the Constitution, slavery, and other items in a program designed to upset the American republic for a utopia.[10]

Among the Forty-Eighters were men of distinction, such as Karl Heinzen, Friedrich Hecker, Friedrich Hassaurek, Bernhard Dom-

[9] See, for example, Pösche: *The New Rome: or the United States of the World*, referred to in Hildegard Meyer: *Nord-Amerika im Urteile des deutschen Schriftums bis zur Mitte des 19. Jahrhunderts* (Hamburg, Germany, 1929), pp. 60-61.

[10] See Ernest Bruncken: "German Political Refugees in the United States During the Period from 1815 to 1860," in *Deutsch-Amerikanische Geschichtsblätter von Illinois*, 1903 and 1904.

schke, Heinrich Börnstein, George Schneider, Lorenz Brentano, Hermann Raster, Wilhelm Rapp, Casper Butz, Reinhold Solger, Emil Pretorius, Louis Prang, Dr. Ferdinand V. Löhr, Gottlieb Theodor Kellner, George Hillgärtner, Oswald Ottendörfer, Gustav Struve, the Goldmark family of Vienna, and the greatest German-American of them all, Carl Schurz. Solger became a leader of the Republican party in the East; Schurz and Körner built up the party among the Germans of the West. Pretorious, Prang, Brentano, Börnstein, Schneider, and Kellner were prominent publicists and German newspaper editors. Hassaurek, a Viennese, was editor of the influential Cincinnati *Volksblatt.* Struve was one of those who, like Friedrich Kapp, eventually returned to Germany. Ottendörfer became owner of the *New Yorker Staats Zeitung,* and Raster was editor of the *Buffalo Demokrat.* Dr. Löhr, who had been a leader in the German modernist Catholic movement, practiced medicine and published a German paper in California. Karl Heinzen was probably the most radical thinker of them all and deserves a place in the history of American political theory.[11] Hecker, who had proclaimed the revolution in Baden in 1848, settled on a farm in Illinois.[12]

These men were the true heirs of Kant, Fichte, and Hegel in their devotion to freedom of thought and belief, and their gradual extinction has meant the end of the cultural flowering time of German communities in the United States. That they were often disappointed on their arrival in the new land was perhaps to be expected. Indeed, the period from 1849 to 1854 was the period of homesickness, when many who later became distinguished and enthusiastic Americans sighed for an opportunity to return to their native land. They raised money for Gottfried Kinkel, a hero of the revolution who toured America in 1851, with the foolhardy expectation that Germany was ripe for revolution and that they would soon be able

[11] See Paul O. Schinnerer: "Karl Heinzen, Reformer, Poet and Literary Critic," in *Jahrbuch der deutsch-amerikanischen historischen Gesellschaft von Illinois,* Vol. XV, pp. 84-144.
[12] For further details on the Forty-Eighters, see Joseph Schafer: "Carl Schurz, Immigrant Statesman," in *Wisconsin Magazine of History,* Vol. XI, p. 374; and *Carl Schurz, Militant Liberal* (Evansville, Wisconsin, 1930); Claude M. Fuess: *Carl Schurz, Reformer, 1829-1906* (New York, 1932); Chester V. Easum: *The Americanization of Carl Schurz* (Chicago, 1929); *Mitteilungen des deutschen Pionier Vereins von Philadelphia* (1909), No. 10, pp. 26-31; *Der deutsche Pionier,* Vol. VIII, pp. 514-515; Bruncken: "German Political Refugees in the United States," in *Deutsch-Amerikanische Geschichtsblätter von Illinois,* Ch. II, bibliography; A. J. Townsend: "The Germans of Chicago," in *Jahrbuch der Deutsch-Amerikanischen Historischen Gesellschaft von Illinois,* Vol. XXXII, pp. 1-153; and Josephine Goldmark: *Pilgrims of '48* (New Haven, Connecticut, 1930).

to return to the fatherland to help give the death blow to tyranny and oppression. They formed German revolutionary societies and military companies in the United States, and their newspapers thundered against the tyranny of the Metternich system.[13] For a time, the rationalists, freethinkers, and atheists among the Forty-Eighters controlled half the German newspapers in the United States.[14] They were disappointed to find slavery firmly established and nativism rampant in a free republic. There were too many churches, they believed, and Puritanism they regarded as an invasion of their personal liberty. They found little dignity in American politics—only shirt sleeves and tobacco cuds. There was little art in America. Some of the Forty-Eighters made little effort to understand America's good qualities, but denounced the whole American scene as half-barbarian.

By 1854, however, the majority of them had decided to remain in the United States. Their money had run out and the hopes for a German revolution been dashed to pieces. Many had found employment as bartenders, artisans, piano teachers, "Latin farmers," and professional men. The rising antislavery agitation provided ample relief for all who still sighed for opportunities to rebuild the world.[15]

During this period of hypercritical tension and homesickness for the fatherland, considerable literature appeared criticizing the newly adopted country and urging Germans to remain at home. Germany had its comfortable beer gardens, its theater, music, and even freethinking societies and *Turnvereine,* and the highest praise that could be given to anything in America was to describe it as "gerade wie in Deutschland." A series of articles entitled *Atlantische Studien—von Deutschen in Amerika* and published in Göttingen in 1853 pictured the United States as the land of Barnum and humbug. They featured the American fad for spiritualism and, as in later years, the crime and murder sensations. They stressed the rowdyism of American politics, and pointed out how "respectable Germans" before election became "damned Dutchmen" in the eyes of American leaders as soon as the polls were closed.

Karl Büchele, writing in 1855, admitted that there was freedom

[13] See, for example, files of *Der Westbote* (Columbus, Ohio) and *Ohio Statesman,* November 17, 1851; and *Cincinnati Commercial,* October 22, 1851.
[14] See *North American Review,* (1856), Vol. LXXXII, pp. 266-267.
[15] For an excellent article on the subject, see E. Schlaeger: *Die sociale und politische Stellung der Deutschen in der Vereinigten Staaten* (Berlin, 1874).

from police surveillance in the United States, but criticized the prying, fanatical concern that people had in their neighbors' business. "Nowhere," he wrote, "are idealistic dreams and fancies dispelled as fully and completely as under the disintegrating influence of the rudely materialistic Philistinism existing in America." [16] Ferdinand Kürnberger wrote *Der Amerikamüde,* and Friedrich Gerstäcker's *Nach Amerika* described the sufferings of the immigrant traffic.[17] Kürnberger described the prairie "near Pittsburgh" (!) as an "endless grassy plain," with absolutely nothing on it. "The air burned as in a blast furnace." There was not a bird or butterfly visible and no sound of an animal, not even the hum of an insect. "Everything that was not a salamander seemed to be dead." Nikolas Lenau once referred to "die verschweinte Staaten," and Heine distrusted a country

> Wo die Menschen Tabak käuen,
> Wo sie ohne König kegeln,
> Wo sie ohne Spucknapf speien.[18]

In spite of abundant evidence of outstanding intellectual and

[16] Karl Büchele: *Land und Volk der Vereinigten Staaten von Nord Amerika. Zur Belehrung für Jedermann, vorzüglich für Answanderer,* quoted in Edith Abbott: *Historical Aspects of the Immigration Problem* (Chicago, 1926), pp. 142-146.

[17] See Dorothy A. Dondore: *The Prairie and the Making of Middle America: Four Centuries of Description* (Cedar Rapids, Iowa, 1926), pp. 300-303.

[18] Quoted in Gerhard Desczyk: "Amerika in der Phantasie deutscher Dichter," in *Jahrbuch der Deutsch-Amerikanischen Historischen Gesellschaft von Illinois,* Vol. XXIV-XXV, pp. 9-142. For an excellent and indispensible account, see Meyer: *op. cit.* The spirit of the disillusioned Forty-Eighters is revealed in a poem by Niklas Müller, who came to New York in 1853, which follows in part:

> "Nach Westen flieht die Weltgeschichte!"
> So lautet des Sehers Wort;
> nach Westen zog ich mit dem Lichte
> der Sonne wandernd zog ich fort.
> So kam ich auch mit manchen Braven
> ins Land des edlen Washington—
> den Fuss im Nacken seines Sklaven,
> sprach dir der freie Bürger Hohn.
> Die Freistatt hab ich zwar gefunden,
> vor den Bedrängern fand ich Ruh,
> doch schmerzen noch die alten Wunden—
> O Statt der Freiheit, wo bist du?

(Quoted in Meyer: *op. cit.,* p. 59.) See also a novel by a Roman Catholic advising Germans against leaving Germany, J. A. Stelzig: *Der Gränzbauer und der Kohlen-Toni in Amerika* (Regensburg, Germany, 1867.) The same Lenau who referred to "die verschweinte Staaten" also wrote:

> Du neue Welt, du freie Welt,
> an deren blüthenreichen Strand
> die Fluth der Tyrannei zerschellt,
> ich grüsse dich, mein Vaterland.

liberal leadership among the German immigration of the period before the Civil War, it must be emphasized again that the bulk of the immigration was not for political but for economic reasons. The reaction to the political disturbances of 1830 and 1848 is not enough to explain so complex a movement as the immigration of hundreds of thousands to a new land. Even the so-called Forty-Eighter emigration came largely from southwestern Germany, especially from districts where small agricultural holdings were the rule. In this region, survivals of the agrarian system of the Middle Ages were effectively challenged for the first time in the early nineteenth century. The common lands were being divided up and modern methods of agriculture were gradually introduced. Peasants mortgaged their holdings in order to participate in this modernizing process, and when crop failures occurred in the 1840's and 1850's, they were forced to emigrate. In such a period of severe readjustment, agricultural areas are fertile fields for the propagandists of emigration.[19]

It is impossible, within the limits of this discussion, to consider in detail the spread of German immigrants throughout the United States in the nineteenth century. Several states have been selected for brief consideration because they are typical of what went on in other states. Most of the German immigration was a matter of individuals seeking new opportunities; but there were also a number of colonization companies to promote the settlement of particular areas. In some cases, the purpose of these companies was to establish compact German communities or a German state, where the German language and customs might be forever preserved. Many of these colonization projects were launched primarily as money-making ventures. Others combined with economic objectives certain charitable, religious, or patriotic purposes. As far as realizing the ambition of forming a solid German area in America is concerned, all were failures. The very conditions of frontier settlement made failure inevitable.

Among the better-known societies formed after 1830 to colonize the United States with Germans may be mentioned the Giessener Auswanderungs Gesellschaft, which contained a number of university men and planned to settle a German state in Arkansas; the Rhein-Bayerische Gesellschaft; and the Mainzer Adelsverein, which

---

[19] See Marcus L. Hansen: "The Revolutions of 1848 and German Emigration," in *Journal of Economic and Business History*, Vol. II, pp. 630-658.

was interested in the development of Texas.[20]   In addition, there were numerous colonization societies originated in the United States to promote German settlements, such as the Pittsburgh Homestead Association, the Cincinnati German Association, and the Chicago Land Verein, which helped to establish New Ulm, in Minnesota. As far as the immigrant's dream of a "German state" in the United States or his plans to make the United States bilingual are concerned, it should be pointed out that these were the ideas of some of the educated minority only.   They had little support either from the rank and file of immigrants or from the German government. Men like Schurz looked forward to a rapid assimilation of the German group, especially politically.   It was Schurz who said: "Es gibt in dieser Republik keine deutsche Politik." [21]

Many German immigrants remained in New York State. By the close of the 1850's, the German population of New York City was estimated at 100,000, with 20 churches, 50 schools, 10 bookstores, 5 printing establishments, and a German theater.[22] By 1860, the German section of New York extended from Chatham Square to Astor Place, as far as St. Mark's—an area of the old Bowery which was marked in these years by German beer gardens, bowling alleys, and numerous German societies, and to which the German element clung until the 1890's.[23] By 1836, New York had two German dailies, and the first political demonstration of the Germans against nativism occurred here in 1834. From New York City, the German tide spread inland, generally along the Erie Canal. Germans began to come to Buffalo in large numbers in 1831, and by the end of the decade and the early 1840's, an influential German element had been added to the original New England strain in that city. The Buffalo Germans built stores, foundries, flour mills, tanneries, breweries, and bakeshops. Mechanics representing many trades settled in the city and, besides making a living, established musical societies and introduced a type of Continental leisure quite in contrast with the habits of the New England Yankee.[24] A residue of less enter-

[20] For a list of such companies, see Oscar Canstatt: *Die deutsche Auswanderung* (Berlin, 1904), pp. 70-73.
[21] Quoted in Heinz Kloss: *Um die Einigung des Deutschamerikanertums* (Berlin, 1937), p. 221.
[22] See *The Boston Traveller*, May 23, 1857.
[23] See Alvin F. Harlow: *Old Bowery Days* (New York, 1931).
[24] See Gustav Körner: *Das deutsche Element in den Vereinigten Staaten von Nordamerika, 1818-1848* (Cincinnati, 1880), pp. 139-144; and Friedrich Kapp: *Geschichte der deutschen Einwanderung in Amerika* (New York, 1867).

prising or less fortunate Germans remained behind in the larger cities like New York and lived in quarters as poor as any of the slums in which the poorest Irish were to be found. American missionaries and charitable workers were greatly concerned about the future of this group, particularly their children, who ran idle through the streets instead of going to school, or who helped their parents eke out an existence by picking up rags and coal or selling matches in the city streets. It is well to remember that every group left its human backwash in the larger cities.[25]

In Pennsylvania, the newer German immigrant element was added to the old Pennsylvania Germans, with whom they had little in common except origin and language, and who lived on the farms, in contrast with the newer group, which converged upon the cities. By 1837, the Pennsylvania legislature was publishing its laws and the governor's messages in German translation, and a law was passed permitting German instruction in the schools. By 1840, the German vote of Pennsylvania was regarded as important, and campaign biographies of Van Buren and Harrison appeared in the German language. By 1846, a German *Sängerfest* (competitive singing by German singing societies) was held in Philadelphia. Nearly a decade earlier, a call had been issued for a convention of all Germans in the United States to discuss plans for preserving the German language in America; to promote a German press, normal schools for training German teachers, and a German university; to urge Congress to shorten the time required for naturalization; to reduce the price of public lands; and to combat nativism. Conventions were actually held in 1837, 1838, and 1839. Although most of the delegates came from the Eastern states, Ohio sent ten representatives in 1837. A teacher's seminary was actually opened in 1841, but soon collapsed, because of lack of funds and also because it was dominated by German liberals, whose unorthodox views offended German Lutherans and Catholics. In spite of its failure, the whole movement gave a great impetus to the German press in America and to the founding of German literary and musical societies.[26]

Much of the German immigration went West, along the Erie

[25] See F. W. Bogen: *Report of the Reverend F. W. Bogen to His Subscribers, 1853-1854*, 8 pp. Bogen was a Protestant missionary pastor, who collected money for work among the German immigrants in New York and, among other things, distributed copies of Washington's *Farewell Address* in English and German to all newcomers.

[26] See Körner: *op. cit.*, Ch. II.

Canal to the Great Lakes and thence to the prairies.[27]   Cincinnati has included prominent Germans in its population since the beginning of the nineteenth century, and became one of the leading German-American cities in the United States.   Martin Baum, a successful businessman, was Mayor of Cincinnati in 1807.   The first German paper in Cincinnati was a weekly, *Die Ohio Chronik,* started in 1826.   After 1805, the Pennsylvania synods of the Lutheran and Reformed Churches sent itinerant ministers into Ohio. The first German singing society was organized in Cincinnati in 1823, and the *Cincinnati Volksblatt,* one of the best German papers in the Mississippi Valley, made its appearance in 1836.   By 1840, the Germans were well established in the Ohio River town.   Many owned vineyards or were engaged in trade and industry, such as the jewelry business and the manufacture of stoves and musical instruments.   The German penetration of Cincinnati, which led to the development of the famous "Over-the-Rhine" district, as the area across the canal where the Germans settled was known, was well under way by the middle of the century.[28]

By the middle of the 1840's, life among the German element in Ohio was in full bloom.[29]   Columbus, Cleveland, Dayton, and other cities had sizable and important German colonies before 1850. Cleveland had German societies and churches by 1836.[30]   Toledo had attracted both a strong German Lutheran and a German Catholic element, which was organized into many societies.   Its leading paper, the *Toledo Express,* published by the Marx brothers, Emil, Guido, and Joseph, was established in 1856.[31]   Union County, one of the best agricultural sections in Ohio, attracted a large German Lutheran farming population from Bavaria and Hesse-Darmstadt beginning in 1830.[32]   South of the Western Reserve, German farmers from Pennsylvania settled a 50-mile-wide strip along the water-

[27] See Jacob W. Myers: "The Beginnings of German Immigration in the Middle West," in *Journal of the Illinois Historical Society,* Vol. XV, pp. 592-599.

[28] The old Miami Canal entered Cincinnati from the north, bending eastward at Canal Street toward the Ohio River. North and east of the Canal was "Over the Rhine," a section where beer gardens, concert halls, and breweries flourished, and where backyards were surrounded by latticework.

[29] See Helmut Trepte: "Deutschtum in Ohio bis zum Jahre 1820," in *Jahrbuch der Deutsch-Amerikanischen Historischen Gesellschaft von Illinois,* Vol. XXXII, pp. 154-409.

[30] See E. M. Avery: *A History of Cleveland and Its Environs,* 3 vols. (1918).

[31] See Clark Waggoner: *History of the City of Toledo and Lucas County, Ohio* (Toledo, Ohio, 1888).

[32] See W. L. Curry: *History of Union County, Ohio* (Indianapolis, 1915); and *History of Union County, Ohio* (Chicago, 1883).

shed, as many place names and family names in Stark, Tuscarawas, Wayne, and Holmes Counties indicate. Canton, Massillon, Alliance, and Steubenville have large German elements, and many of the inhabitants are descendants of Pennsylvania Germans who moved westward. Some places in Ohio that have a strong Pennsylvania German element were hardly touched by the nineteenth-century immigrants.[33] Germantown, in Montgomery County, had five German churches in 1845 and was once a close rival of Dayton. Auglaize and Henry Counties still have vigorous German communities and rural centers, some of them strongholds of German Catholicism.

Indiana has a specially strong German section around Fort Wayne, and Concordia College was established by German Lutherans in 1840. In Illinois, the German element exceeded 130,000 by 1860, and was distributed through Chicago, Belleville and St. Clair County, Galena, Quincy, Alton, Peoria, and Peru. The first German paper in Illinois, Theodor Engelmann's *Belleviller Beobachter*, made its appearance in 1844. The colony at Belleville contained many professional men and "Latin farmers," many of whom later drifted to St. Louis.[34] Chicago was a German cultural center, with a theater, bands, orchestras, lodges, and singing societies before 1860. In 1850, Schiller Festivals were being held in Belleville and Chicago, and, in 1851, the first *Turnvereine* in the State of Illinois appeared in Chicago and Peoria.[35]

Germans felt particularly at home in Wisconsin, because the soil, climate, and products were similar to those in their old homes, because the laws of the state were hospitable to immigrants, and because the state authorities were eager to attract settlers. The heaviest German immigration into Wisconsin occurred from 1840 to 1860, and again from 1880 to 1890. Milwaukee became the distributing center for German settlers, and with its music, drama, and other cultural activities, reached its flowering time in the 1850's. Travelers commented on literary and musical Milwaukee, "the German Athens," as they contrasted its cultural level with the crudities

[33] See J. B. Mansfield: *The History of Tuscarawas County, Ohio* (Chicago, 1884).

[34] See Körner: *op. cit.*, pp. 244-281.

[35] See also T. C. Pease: *The Frontier State, 1818-1848* (Springfield, Illinois, 1918). For names of prominent German families in Illinois and their activities, see *Deutsch-Amerikanische Geschichtsblätter*, published by the German American Historical Society of Illinois.

and dullness of other American frontier towns. In general, the Germans selected the heavily wooded areas in the eastern and north-central counties of Wisconsin for their settlements. Many were able to buy from Irish and American pioneers farms that were already partly cleared. The German farmer introduced a more intensified type of agriculture. He used fertilizer and diversified his crops; he turned to dairying and livestock; and, whereas the Yankee farmer frequently farmed around the stumps, he removed the stumps. Germans were active both politically and culturally in the early history of Wisconsin, and the state has never quite lost some of the characteristics implanted by the heavy nineteenth-century immigration.[36]

By the 1830's, the German advance up the Missouri was well under way. Some of the settlers came across the country from the East; others came up the river from New Orleans. The region along the Missouri, from its mouth 125 miles inland, has not lost its German character to this day. Part of the early German immigration to Missouri was due to Gottfried Duden's famous report on that region, and to the Deutsche Ansiedlungs Gesellschaft of Philadelphia. The town of Hermann, Missouri, was laid out in the midst of the panic of 1837, and managed to survive. By 1839, it had a population of 450, a German military company, a band, and a singing society. Its settlers turned mainly to the cultivation of grapes. The town is still famous for its wine, and has streets named after Schiller, Gutenberg, Goethe, and Mozart. The Continental Sunday flourished in Hermann, and Germans from St. Louis occasionally made excursions to the "Little Germany" up the river. A theater guild presented German plays there on Sundays from 1848 to 1866 without interruption, and a German rationalist society existed there from 1852 to 1902. The first newspaper published by these German intellectuals was Der Licht Freund; this was followed by the Hermann Volksblatt.[37] St. Louis has always had a large German element, which still centers largely in the southern part of the city. The St. Louis Anzeiger des Westens was started as a weekly in 1835. By 1845, the city had two German

<hr />

[36] See Körner: op. cit., pp. 281-291. See also Joseph Schafer: "The Yankee and the Teuton in Wisconsin," in Wisconsin Magazine of History, Vol. VI, pp. 125-145, 261-279, and 386-402; and Vol. VII, pp. 3-20 and 148-171.

[37] See William G. Bek: The German Settlement Society of Philadelphia and Its Colony, Hermann, Missouri (Philadelphia, 1907); and "Gottfried Duden's Report, 1824-1827," in Missouri Historical Review, Vol. XIII, pp. 44-56, 157-181, and 251-281; and Vols. XIV, XV, XVI, and XVII, passim.

dailies. The arrival of the Germans made a distinct change in St. Louis society, and the old French music, dances, and customs soon capitulated before the German invasion.[38] By 1870, the little settlement sponsored by the eccentric Gottfried Duden, who had come to the United States because he believed overpopulation to be the cause of Germany's crime and misery, had spread until German farmers and artisans occupied half a dozen Missouri counties.

The story of the German immigrant was much the same wherever he settled in the Middle West. Space permits only brief mention of German settlements in other states. Michigan had its German element largely in and around Wayne County.[39] Iowa had few Germans until the 1850's, although the Cincinnati Deutscher Westlich Ansiedlungs Verein settled Gettysburg, Iowa, in 1842. Later, strong communities developed, especially in and around Davenport.[40] In Minnesota, the Germans ranked second in number to the Scandinavians as late as 1900.[41] A German colonization company was active in Colorado in the decade after the Civil War,[42] and there were small artisan and farming groups in California by 1860.[43]

The number of German communities in the Southern states is surprising, in view of the general assumption that all immigrants avoided the South because of slavery. As a matter of fact, there were Scandinavians at Thorsby, Arkansas, Danes engaged in dairying in Mississippi, Swedes in Louisiana, Italians in Tennessee and Louisiana, Irish and French in several cities, and so many Germans that they deserve special comment.[44]

The Germans of Richmond, Virginia, had their first *Volksfest* in 1840, in honor of Gutenberg. The celebration in 1857 in honor of the revolutionary hero Baron von Steuben was in part arranged to impress the nativists of the South with the strength and respecta-

[38] See E. D. Kargan: "Missouri's German Immigration," in *Missouri Historical Society Collections*, Vol. II, pp. 23-34; and *St. Louis in früherem Jahren: ein Gedenkbuch für das Deutschtum* (St. Louis, 1893).

[39] See John A. Russell: *The Germanic Influence in the Making of Michigan* (Detroit, 1927).

[40] Körner: *op. cit.*, p. 294. See also Joseph Eiboeck: *Die Deutschen von Iowa und deren Errungenschaften* (Des Moines, Iowa, 1900).

[41] See also William F. Folwell: *History of Minnesota* (St. Paul, Minnesota, 1921-1930).

[42] J. F. Willard and C. B. Goodykoontz: *Experiments in Colorado Colonization, 1860-1872* (Boulder, Colorado, 1926).

[43] *Der deutsche Pionier*, Vol. IV, pp. 370-373; and Vol. VIII, pp. 287-288.

[44] See W. L. Fleming: "Immigration to the Southern States," in *Political Science Quarterly*, Vol. XX, pp. 276-297.

bility of the German element of Virginia. The German Rifle Company, a singing society, a *Turnverein,* a Schiller Society, a German benevolent organization, and a dramatic club assembled in full force in Capitol Square and marched to a park to unveil a bust of Steuben. In 1850, a German freethinkers' congregation was established in Richmond. Wheeling, then still a part of the Old Dominion, had a strong German element; and *Die Virginische Staatszeitung* was published there prior to the creation of the State of West Virginia. The *Richmond Anzeiger* was started in 1853, and after 1860, for over a year, the *Richmond Enquirer* printed several pages of German in each issue. Out of a population of nearly 38,000 in Richmond in 1860, 7,000 were Germans. The city had a German Lutheran, a Catholic, and a Reformed church; two German breweries; and a number of prominent German doctors, musicians, and horticulturists. In 1863, because there were so many Germans within the limits of the Confederacy, a *Deutsches A-B-C und erstes Lesebuch* was published for their benefit in Richmond. Such evidence suggests that the population of the South was not quite as "homogeneous" as generally supposed.[45]

In Louisville, Kentucky, a semiweekly German paper was established in 1840. Two years earlier, a German Catholic congregation was founded. In 1849, the well-known *Louisville Anzeiger,* which had a long history extending into the present century, was established as a daily newspaper. By the 1850's, the river city had the usual quota of German societies, and at one time supported three German papers. The German population was sufficiently numerous and active in the life of the city that some of the fiercest Know-Nothing riots in the country occurred in Louisville in 1856.[46]

Nashville, Tennessee, too had an influential German community. Wartburg, a German settlement promoted by a colonization company in eastern Tennessee in 1845, had attracted 800 settlers by 1848.[47] The *Tennessee Staatszeitung,* published in Nashville, was

---

[45] See Edward Channing: *History of the United States* (New York, 1913), Vol. VI, p. 126. See also Hermann Schuricht: "History of the German Element in Virginia," in *Thirteenth and Fourteenth Annual Reports of the Society for the History of the Germans in Maryland* (1900), Vol. II, pp. 30-53.
[46] See *Der deutsche Pionier,* Vol. I, pp. 15-18, 46-50, and 108-112.
[47] See *ibid.;* Vol. X, pp. 12-19; and Baron A. von der Straten Ponthoz: *Forschungen über die Lage der Auswanderer in den Vereinigten Staaten von Nord, Amerika* (Augsburg, Germany, 1846), p. 185; and Hildegard Rosenthal: *Die Auswanderung aus Sachsen im 19. Jahrhundert, 1815-1871.* (Stuttgart, Germany, 1931), pp. 71-74.

a Unionist paper during the Civil War.[48]   After the war, Tennessee attracted numerous German immigrants to the neighborhood of Memphis, and 400 Swiss Germans were induced to settle near Knoxville.[49]   In 1839, there was a German reading circle in Natchez. Cullman, Alabama, had a German paper known as *Der Alabama Pionier*.   In 1841, Mobile, Alabama, had a *Freundschaftsbund* to promote literary and benevolent activities,[50] and, in 1872, a German mass meeting was held there to support Greeley for President.[51] There was a Stuttgart in Arkansas settled by Germans under the leadership of Pastor Bürkel [52] and, in 1866, it was reported that the 107th Ohio Volunteers, a German regiment in the Civil War, had acquired a tract of 5,000 acres in Florida and had gone there in a body to raise cotton.[53]

Charleston, South Carolina, had a large German-American colony before the Civil War.   The first arrivals, before 1830, were keepers of small stores and saloons.   Some employed black concubines to attract the colored trade, and it was generally agreed that their moral and business standards were low.   The group could hardly have been regarded as a desirable addition to the city's population.[54] After a yellow fever epidemic and the great fire of 1838, however, there seems to have been a genuine revival in the moral tone of Charleston; at any rate, the later German immigrants were of distinctly higher caliber.   By 1842, Charleston had a German population of 1,200, with two military companies, a German fire company, and a literary society.   In 1844, the first German paper, *Der Teutone*, was established, and by 1846 a *Turnverein* and a German Masonic lodge had been organized.   German artisans and workmen contributed greatly to the life of the city and were highly respected. The town of Walhalla was founded by a group that came after 1848, and by 1870 it had a population of 1,500.   Unquestionably, the most distinguished leader of the Germans in Charleston was Johann Andreas Wagener, who was born in Hanover in 1816 and came to the United States at the age of fifteen.   He was prominent in every activity of the German group, as well as in all civic affairs.   He

---

[48] See *Boston Transcript*, March 26, 1866.
[49] See *Cleveland Leader*, March 25 and 30, and May 26, 1870.
[50] See Körner: *op. cit.*, pp. 358-359.
[51] See *Der deutsche Pionier*, Vol. IX, p. 451.
[52] See *ibid.*, Vol. XVIII, pp. 318-320.
[53] See *Boston Transcript*, January 20, 1866.
[54] See J. A. Wagener: "Die Deutschen in Süd-Caroline," in *Der deutsche Pionier*, Vol. III, pp. 152-155.

served as an officer in the Confederate Army and two terms as Mayor of Charleston. In 1859, Charleston celebrated a Schiller anniversary, with fireworks, a concert, and a torchlight procession. Twelve German societies marched in the parade.[55] Similar festivals were held in New Orleans, Augusta, and Savannah, Georgia.

In the early eighteenth century, Louisiana had a "German Coast," *Côte des Allemands,* extending on both sides of the Mississippi above New Orleans and occupied by a few Germans, some Swiss soldiers who stayed in Louisiana after 1768, when their term of service expired, a few settlers from Lorraine, and several German families who had come in 1774 from Frederick County, Maryland. In the nineteenth century, thousands of Germans arrived in New Orleans. Many did not proceed to the interior but remained in the city. New Orleans soon had a German quarter, as well as Irish, French, and American quarters.[56] In 1837, a German sharpshooting company was organized in New Orleans; in 1838, a Deutscher Liederkranz began to sing German *Lieder* there; and in 1842, a German newspaper, *Der deutsche Courier,* made its first appearance.[57] The owners were Alfred Schücking and Joseph Cohn, a German Jew. New Orleans attracted its quota of German liberals in the 1850's, and a society was formed in Louisiana to further the democratization of Germany. The *Deutsche Zeitung* of New Orleans was published without serious interruption until 1915. Probably the most distinguished German in Louisiana was Christian Rosellius, who became one of the greatest legal authorities on the Civil Code.[58] After the Civil War, a few German laborers were imported to Louisiana to work on the plantations.[59]

Three excellent monographs are available for a study of the German element in Texas, and there is no need to discuss the German-American sections of that state in detail.[60] The German section of

[55] For an account of the German element in South Carolina, see *Charleston Mercury,* January 22, April 21, and November 15, 1859; Carl Süsser: "Der unbekannte Deutschamerikaner," in *Deutsche Rundschau* (June, 1934), pp. 173-178; *Der deutsche Pionier,* Vol. III, pp. 165-169, 212-214, 234-239, 268-272, 295-298, and 342-344; and Vol. VIII, pp. 323-333, 369-376, and 408-416; and George J. Gongaware: *The History of the German Friendly Society of Charleston, South Carolina, 1766-1916* (Richmond, Virginia, 1935).

[56] See Thomas L. Nichols: *Forty Years of American Life* (London, 1864), p. 69.

[57] See Körner: *op. cit.,* pp. 371-379.

[58] See Robert T. Clark, Jr.: "The German Liberals in New Orleans, 1840-1860," in *The Louisiana Historical Quarterly,* Vol. XX, pp. 1-17; and Emil Lehmann: *Die deutsche Auswanderung* (Berlin, 1861), p. 13.

[59] See *Boston Transcript,* January 30, 1866.

[60] See R. L. Biesele: *The History of the German Settlements in Texas, 1831-*

Texas covers a triangle between Seguin, New Braunfels, and San
Antonio. In 1900, about one third of the population of Texas was
of German blood. New Braunfels was established in 1845 because
of the activities of a colonization society known as the Mainzer
Adelsverein. Friedrichsburg was founded in 1846, and other German communities in Texas date back to the period before the Civil
War. In general, the German settlements of western Texas were
distinguished by a more intensive agriculture and by a large diversification of crops and occupations. The region west of the Colorado River maintained its German characteristics at least until the
World War. The first Texas *Sängerfest* was held in New Braunfels
in 1853, and the next year a German convention was held in San
Antonio. Many of the leaders of the German communities in
Texas were liberals or radicals, who denounced slavery and attacked
clericalism and the Puritan Sabbath, thereby arousing considerable
opposition among their American neighbors. The *San Antonio
Zeitung*, edited by Dr. Adolf Douai, was outspokenly antislavery.
The Sisterdale settlement was largely a colony of "Latin farmers,"
where the classics were as evident in the log cabins of these Texas
Germans as the tools of the pioneer. In 1904, there were still nearly
30 German papers in the state and dozens of German societies.[61]

Frederick Law Olmsted stumbled upon the German farming
settlements in West Texas and described them in his much-quoted
Journey Through Texas. He found the Germans living on little
ten-acre enclosures, cultivating a diversity of crops, and raising cotton with free labor. He was impressed with the wide main street
of New Braunfels, lined with cottages, stores, and workshops stuc-
coed or painted, many with verandas and gardens. He found an
excellent inn, with stenciled panels and prints on the walls. Above
all, he encountered educated and cultivated people in the "Latin
farming" districts of Texas:

> You are welcomed by a figure in blue flannel shirt and
> pendant beard, quoting Tacitus, having in one hand a long
> pipe, in the other a butcher's knife; Madonnas upon log

1861 (Austin, Texas, 1930); G. G. Benjamin: "The Germans in Texas," in *The
German-American Annals,* new series, Vol. VII, pp. 3-33, 103-120, 164-176, 208-
256, and 283-305; and Moritz Tiling: *History of the German Element in Texas,
1820-1850* (Houston, Texas, 1913). See also R. L. Biesele: "The San Saba Colonization Company," in *Southwestern Historical Quarterly,* Vol. XXXIII, pp. 169-
183.
[61] See also *Deutsch-Texanische Monatshefte* (San Antonio, Texas); and *The
New York World,* October 21, 1868.

walls; coffee in tin cups upon Dresden saucers; barrels for
seats, to hear a Beethoven's symphony on the grand piano;
. . . a book-case half filled with classics, half with sweet
potatoes.[62]

At one house, after supper, the neighbors came in to dance to the
tones of a fine piano and, after the ladies had retired, "the men had
over the whole stock of student songs, until all were young again." [63]
Scenes of this kind occurred in settlements where pioneers still had
to shoot panthers that came out of the hills to kill their stock.   But
Olmsted found faults as well as virtues among his German hosts.
Worst of all, he thought, was their:

> . . . free-thinking and a devotion to reason, carried . . .
> to the verge of bigotry, and expanded to a certain rude
> license of manners and habits, consonant with their wild
> prairies, . . . and an insane mutual jealousy, and petty
> personal bickering, that prevents all prolonged and effec-
> tive cooperation—an old German ail, which the Atlantic
> has not sufficed to cleanse.[64]

The German farmer enjoyed an excellent reputation for industry,
thrift, and dependability wherever he settled; and most states, in
their eagerness to find settlers for their vacant lands, were willing
to offer special concessions to attract German immigrants.   The
German farmer usually was shrewd in selecting the best farming
country available and, as a rule, preferred wooded areas, a sign of
superior soil.   He also was interested in accessibility to the markets
and usually did not gamble on the chance development of a railroad
or canal, which might suddenly drive up the value of his land.   One
student of the German-American farmer has concluded that the
German element in the United States developed over 672,000 farms
with a total area of 100,000,000 acres.[65]   The German farmer was
essentially conservative, a hard worker, a careful investor, and anything but a speculator.   In the words of Professor Ross: "Taking
fewer chances in the lottery of life than his enterprising Scotch-Irish
or limber-minded Yankee neighbor, he has drawn from it fewer big
prizes, but also fewer blanks." [66]

[62] Frederick Law Olmsted: *A Journey Through Texas; or A Saddle-Trip on the
Southwestern Frontier* (New York, 1857), p. 430.
[63] *Ibid.*, p. 198.
[64] *Ibid.*, p. 430.
[65] See Joseph Och: *Der deutschamerikanische Farmer* (University of Freiburg
dissertation).
[66] E. A. Ross: *The Old World in the New* (New York, 1914), p. 53.

German settlers were regarded as valuable acquisitions in any state where there were waste places to be brought under cultivation. German farmers seldom ended in the poorhouse or became a burden upon the neighborhood.[67] Sometimes they paid more attention to their farms than to the dwelling in which they lived. The dwelling, in the pioneer state at least, was likely to be a very humble and unpretentious structure, in contrast to a granary and stables of much larger dimensions. The improvement of the farm, rather than individual comfort, was of immediate concern. Members of the family usually joined in the labor necessary to develop a homestead out of an unbroken prairie.[68] In 1833, one German farmer bought a 150-acre farm in Missouri, with 30 acres cleared; a crop of corn, wheat, oats, potatoes, cotton, and pumpkins standing in the field; and one horse, 10 cattle, 11 sheep, about 50 hogs, chickens, bees, plows, harness, and implements—all for $1,000. He added: "I have just finished a house which cost me $45.00." [69]

The wasteful methods of the American pioneer irritated the German farmer. Moreover, he was offended by the temporary nature of American pioneer farms, for the German looked upon his holding as something permanent, not to be sold but to be handed down from generation to generation, as in Europe. "There is scarcely a farm," wrote a German farmer in Missouri to his family in Germany in 1835, "that is not for sale, for the American farmer has no love for home, such as the German has. I am building a smokehouse, a kitchen, a milk-house over one of the excellent springs near our house, a stable for the horses and one for the cows. My American neighbors say that I am building a town . . . ." [70] The German farmer frowned upon his lazy neighbor, who sat all day around the hearth "spitting into the fire," whittling a piece of wood in utter silence, or going hunting or visiting while his fences were decaying and the livestock played havoc with his crops. Whittling seemed to be "the national custom of the North American," even to the

[67] See *Illinois Journal*, July 25, 1855, quoted in *Journal of the Illinois State Historical Society*, Vol. VII, p. 12. See also *Niles Weekly Register*, February 10, 1821.
[68] See Francis J. Grund, quoted in Abbott: *op. cit.*, pp. 271-275.
[69] *Missouri Historical Review*, Vol. XV, p. 534. For a fine description of the actual beginnings of pioneer life among the German farmers of Missouri, see Friedrich Münch: "Sonst und jetzt," in *Der deutsche Pionier*, Vol. IV, pp. 226-233. See also Adelbert Baudissin: *Der Ansiedler im Missouri-Staate* (Iserlohn, Germany, 1854).
[70] *Missouri Historical Review*, Vol. XV, pp. 663-664.

extent of mutilating tables and chairs. The American pioneer seemed inexcusably wasteful with all he possessed, never laying aside a sufficient reserve for emergencies. The German farmer, on the other hand, seemed to his American neighbors to be inexcusably frugal, materialistic, and penurious. He was especially interested in livestock and often exceptionally competent in vine culture, forestry, gardening, and developing nurseries. In states like Wisconsin, he turned to dairying, raised Holstein cattle and bees, fattened geese for the markets, and developed horticulture—all in conjunction with his regular farming activities.

After 1870, although the German immigration remained large, its character changed rather markedly. Fewer peasants and more industrial workers and artisans came in this later period. Moreover, the type of intellectual and cultural leadership provided by groups like the Forty-Eighters was no longer apparent. Immigration figures rose after the Franco-Prussian War, reaching their highest point in 1882, because of financial troubles and the economic disarrangement in Germany resulting from the change to an industrial society, high taxes, and the increasing burden of compulsory military training. In the 1890's, however, German immigration declined again, thus reflecting Germany's phenomenal progress as an industrial nation, her growing prosperity, and the extraordinary success of Bismarck's "state socialism"—that progressive social legislation which provided for the protection, welfare, and insurance of the German working classes. Moreover, it must be recalled that, by the end of the century, the frontier had ceased to be the important force it once was in the development of the United States. The era of free lands was drawing to a close, and the drift into the cities and factory centers was already in progress.

In another respect also German immigration of these later years differed from the influx of earlier times. There was much less criticism of the German government and less political liberalism on the part of the new arrivals. The early German-American press had followed the stirring events of 1848 with the greatest interest and had been sharply critical of the German political regime. By 1870, however, the German-American press was much less concerned with the defense of liberalism and more concerned with the unification of Germany by any conceivable method. Consequently, it reported with pride and praise the events of the Franco-Prussian War. For the most part, it hailed Bismarck's policy of unification by blood and iron as a great, statesmanlike achievement. That the political liberalism for which the Forty-Eighters had fought had no place in Bismarck's Prussian-dominated German Empire was apparent but aroused little concern. Liberalism was sacrificed for the more important achievement of unification.

In the period after 1871, Germany made phenomenal progress. It was natural for Germans in America to glorify the achievements of the new German Empire and its ruling family, and to bask in the reflected glory of German success. Many editors of German papers in the United States in this later period were imported from Germany, not as part of a German propaganda to win America, as was foolishly asserted during the World War, but rather in answer to a natural demand for newspaper talent which the American-born group could no longer supply. The whole tone of the German-American press changed as a result of these developments to one of glorification and praise for German progress and of pride in the German nation. A concerted effort was launched on the part of many German-American leaders to preserve the German language and German culture as long as possible in the United States. They fought a losing battle against the steady progress of the natural forces of Americanization, but this did not diminish their efforts to preserve *das Deutschtum* in America.

Germans did not readily shed the customs of their fatherland when they came to America. Hence, for a time, their Continental viewpoint conflicted so sharply with the prevailing Puritanism of early America that it became a source of friction with native Americans and led to violent attacks against the German element during the nativist agitation before the Civil War. It must be admitted at the outset that many Germans, especially the intellectual leaders, took delight in flaunting their Continental tastes in the face of Americans, whom they regarded as little better than barbarians, without culture or refinement, art or music, and with little of the joy of life. Americans seemed bound by the narrow Puritanism of their forefathers, and needed to be enlightened and emancipated. The struggle between the champions of the Continental Sunday and the Puritan Sabbath was particularly acute and prolonged in the Middle West. Neither party to the conflict revealed much tact or tolerance. To some of the leaders of the German immigration, a compromise between the two culture patterns seemed impossible. One could remain a German or one could become thoroughly Americanized, but to become a "German-American" seemed to imply sinking to a lower cultural level.[71]

The German immigrant loved his beer and his beer gardens, his Sunday picnics and dances and theatrical performances. His many organizations devoted to music, art, drama, sharpshooting, bowling, cards, and *turnen* sought to cultivate the joys of life along with other more immediate objectives. Good beer and good food and good music went together, and Sundays were especially popular for *Ausflüge,* picnics, and entertainments of every sort.

Frederika Bremer has left us some charming and penetrating observations about the Cincinnati and Milwaukee of the 1850's. Her comments about these typically German cities strikingly reveal the fundamental differences between the *Weltanschauung* of German and native American communities of the Middle West in antebellum days. Cincinnati, "the Queen of the West," had "her throne upon the banks of the beautiful river, with a background of encircling hills," and was a thoroughly cosmopolitan city by 1850. "The Germans live here," Miss Bremer commented, "as in their old Germany. They are *gemüthlich,* drink beer, practise music, and still ponder here "über die Weltgeschichte . . . ." [72] They cultivated the vine along the heights bordering the Ohio River, and made American sherry and champagne for Nicholas Longworth. On Sunday evenings, they would congregate, with their pipes and their beer, *unter den Lauben,* to talk and argue and to sing the songs of the fatherland.[73] An Italian count who had visited Cincinnati nearly 20 years earlier was startled by the "Ja, mein Herr" he heard in the streets of Cincinnati, and he was surprised at the number of cafés and breweries with German signs and at the many inhabitants of the city in German peasant costume, of black velvet, with red vests and big silver buttons.[74]

[71] See a poem by Karl Heinzen:

> Sich amerikanisieren
> Heisst ganz sich verlieren;
> Als Teutscher sich treu geblieben
> Heisst Ehre und Bildung lieben;
> Doch lieber indianisch
> Als teutsch-amerikanisch.

[72] Frederika Bremer: *The Homes of the New World* (London, 1853), Vol. II, p. 359.
[73] See Charles Mackay: *Life and Liberty in America* (London, 1859), p. 317.
[74] See Lynn M. Case (editor), "Translations from the Notes of an Italian Count, Francesco Arese," in *Mississippi Valley Historical Review,* Vol. XX, pp. 381-399.

In Milwaukee, Miss Bremer found the Germans occupying a portion of the city known as "German Town." Here were German houses, German inscriptions on doors and signs, German newspapers, German music, dancing, and the other pleasures which "distinguish them from the Anglo-American people, who, particularly in the West, have no other pleasure than 'business'."[75] St. Louis Miss Bremer found to be an interesting mixture of French, Spanish, Irish, and German characteristics.[76] Its bookstalls contained many foreign books and magazines. By the 1860's, the German immigration seemed to have swallowed up the other groups. German was spoken on the street; and bock beer, lager beer, and *Maiwein* were extensively advertised. Liquor was consumed in large quantities under the Southern sun of Missouri, and, in some of the theaters, the audiences smoked and drank beer served by German waitresses. In the public *Lustgarten* scattered about the town, German bands played nightly; and German families, including the children, sat for hours, in Continental fashion, drinking beer and listening to the music.[77] As beer gardens arose on the outskirts of many American cities, they immediately came into conflict with Sunday closing laws.[78] It was generally admitted, however, that German beer gardens and wine parlors were orderly places, where a drunken customer would have been promptly ejected either by the proprietor or by his fellow guests.[79]

On the least provocation, German-Americans, then and now, arranged picnics, celebrations, and festive occasions which could be enjoyed outdoors or amid the conviviality of the lodge rooms or the *Weinstube*. Concerts were not enough to satisfy their love of song, and so German singing societies frequently serenaded their friends throughout the city with *Ständchen*. Grover Cleveland spent many an evening in the German beer halls of Buffalo, especially at Schenkelberger's, where he enjoyed the sausage and the sauerkraut[80] and played pinochle and 66, games especially popular

[75] Bremer: *op. cit.*, Vol. II, p. 223. See also *ibid.*, pp. 236-237.
[76] See *ibid.*, Vol. II, p. 350.
[77] See Allan Nevins (editor): *American Social History, as Recorded by British Travellers* (New York, 1931), p. 400. This is the diary of Edward Dicey, an English newspaperman who visited the United States in 1862.
[78] See *Atlantische Studien* (Göttingen, Germany, 1853), Vol. III, pp. 141-157.
[79] See *Cincinnati Gazette*, July 3, 1880; *New York Sun*, January 7, 1894; and *Der Westbote*, July 15, 1858.
[80] See Allan Nevins: *Grover Cleveland* (New York, 1932), pp. 42, 57, and 73.

among the German element. German bakeries and cafés had a reputation for good food, cleanliness, and an air of domesticity.[81]

The W. C. T. U. had the temerity to set up a department to work among the Germans. It distributed temperance leaflets, including a paper, *Der Bahnbrecher*, in German communities. The effort was an utter failure. Nothing better illustrates the incompatibility of German and American tastes and temperament than these futile attempts by high-minded American reformers to change the social habits of a Continental people whom they never were able to quite understand or appraise.

Whitsuntide, or the German *Pfingstfest*, was a popular German festival in the late spring. It was zealously observed by German societies, with picnics, outdoor amusements, singing and dancing, general merrymaking, and the quaffing of lager beer.[82] Tables were set with beer, wine, cheese, rye bread, and sausages. "The beer foamed and the brown loaves disappeared with double velocity," and Horace Greeley, total abstainer though he was, was broad-minded enough to suggest that "our native citizens would find pleasure in participating in the festivities." [83]

Masquerade balls were popular among the Germans, and each group, depending on the part of Germany from which it came, observed its special local traditions, like the Kirchwei festivities of the Swabians and the Duerkheimer Wurstmarkt of the Rhenish-Bavarians.[84] "German Day" celebrations have been annual occasions to the present time, and are primarily efforts to mobilize all the Germans of the community once a year for an outing, singing, and speechmaking. Anniversaries of historic events in German-American history, such as the bicentennial and the 250th anniversary of the settlement of Germantown, have been carefully observed.[85]

American holidays, such as the Fourth of July, were sometimes more enthusiastically celebrated by the early Germans than by their American neighbors. In 1844, for example, the Germans of Columbus, Ohio, began the day by wakening the city with cannon fire discharged by two German artillery companies, who kept up a

[81] See *The New York Sun*, January 7, 1894.
[82] See *The New York World*, May 27, 1890; and *The New York Times*, June 1, 1879.
[83] See *The New York Tribune*, April 27 and May 21, 1850.
[84] See *Cincinnati Enquirer*, November 13, 1883; *Cleveland Plain Dealer*, September 26, 1887; and *Columbus Dispatch*, January 15, 1883.
[85] See *Cincinnati Enquirer*, September 24 and October 8, 12, and 19, 1883.

steady cannonade until noon. At noon, a procession formed at the market place and, after listening to patriotic songs by the *Lieder-kranz,* the parade started for a grove, which was gaily decorated with flags and bunting, and where a long table laden with food awaited the hungry and thirsty marchers. Over the table hung a huge portrait of Washington. The day was spent in eating, drinking, singing, and speechmaking, with toasts to Independence Day, to the signers of the immortal Declaration, to Washington, Jefferson, Jackson, the soldiers of the Revolution, the President of the United States, the Governor of Ohio, the old fatherland, German women, girls, education, and the city of Columbus! Games and contests completed the day's observances, and the crowd paraded back to the State House, where, after more songs, it finally disbanded. Later, the German *Turnverein,* fire companies, and singing societies had their separate celebrations; and the local German paper severely chided the native Americans for not properly observing the birthday of the Republic.[86]

German housewives and German cooks have added much to the culinary varieties of the present-day United States, as evidenced by the many articles of food which have not only been adopted as delicacies by the American stomach but have also found their way into American dictionaries, frequently with their original German spelling unchanged. Wieners, frankfurters, sauerkraut, *Braun-schweiger Leberwurst, Lebkuchen,* zwieback, *Hasenpfeffer,* and delicatessen are examples of the influence of German immigration on American eating habits. Other German culinary achievements that are fairly well known in parts of the United States include German coffee cake, cottage cheese pie, cole slaw, potato salad, dill pickles, rye bread with caraway seeds, pumpernickel, and German pancakes. Stein, rathskeller, and lager beer indicate the influence of the German immigration upon American drinking habits.

The American observation of Christmas has gained much by the incorporation of German Christmas customs. New England Puritans did not celebrate Christmas, and Christmas festivities in the West and South before 1840 were altogether different from our present practice. Traveling through the South before the Civil

[86] See *Der Westbote,* July 12, 1844. One toast was drunk to:
> Was wir lieben fern und nah;
> Jetzt an des Sciotos Strande,
> In dem neuen Vaterlande,
> Dir dies Glas, Amerika!

War, Olmsted found Christmas celebrated by "mischief and drunken uproariousness." Signs were removed, plows placed on housetops, and effigies erected in the streets, much after the manner of Hallowe'en rowdyism. Balls were popular. "Christmas serenades" were given, with the band blowing into tin horns and beating on tin pans. Visits were made from house to house. The doors were kicked, as a special form of greeting, summoning those within to join the march to the public square.[87] In Missouri, before the Civil War, Christmas was celebrated in American households, not with a Christmas tree or church service, but with promiscuous firing of guns; and the crowd roamed about from house to house and farm to farm to be regaled by the owners with whiskey and baked goods.[88] The exchange of presents did not seem to be a part of these boisterous Christmas festivities. In some Northern cities, as late as 1860, places of business were closed on Christmas Day in the German sections only.[89]

The Germans brought the German Christmas celebration with them to America, including the observance of the day as a church festival. They introduced the German Christmas tree. German Christmas cakes were baked by German housewives with the ceremony amounting almost to a special ritual. The inimitable German Christmas songs have become part of the musical heritage of all Americans. The German New Year's celebration, or *Sylvesterfeier,* included singing, dancing, theatrical performances, plenty of good food and drink, kissing all around, and a "Prosit Neujahr!" on the stroke of twelve.[90]

The number and variety of German organizations in which the German element found expression for its gregarious and convivial instincts is literally legion. Some of these German societies are rapidly approaching the century mark of their existence in the United States or have already passed it. Besides the innumerable singing societies and musical organizations which marked the life of every community where there was an appreciable German element, the Germans had their *Kriegervereine,* composed of veterans

[87] See Olmsted: *op. cit.,* pp. 68-69, 77, and 497.
[88] See Göbel: *op. cit.,* pp. 80-81.
[89] See *Der Westbote,* December 3, 1853; December 19, 1856; and December 27, 1860. See also W. G. Bek: "The Followers of Duden," in *Missouri Historical Review,* Vol. XVI, pp. 350-351; and Gustav Körner: *Memoirs* (Cedar Rapids, Iowa, 1909), Vol. I, p. 330.
[90] See *The New York Times,* January 3, 1863. The editor concluded: "Taken all-in-all, the Germans had the best of the New Year's Festival."

of the German army; their fraternal and benevolent organizations; societies to unite the Bavarians, the Low Germans (*Plattdeutsche*), and other German groups; literary and study clubs; Humboldt societies devoted to lectures and discussions of the arts and sciences; church societies and charitable enterprises; German lodges of Odd Fellows, Masons, Knights of Pythias, Maccabees, Druids, and so on, showing the influence of American fraternal orders on the German element; and other societies still to be discussed in some detail.

At the great annual picnics, *Volksfeste,* or celebrations commemorating German heroes like von Steuben or literary figures like Goethe and Schiller, these organizations usually combined to produce a great assembly recruited from the entire German community. In 1894, a parade of German singers in New York included 10,000 marchers, who had come to the city to inaugurate a singing competition that lasted three days and cost $50,000.[91] In Cincinnati, in 1881, when the Hecker monument was dedicated by the Germans of the city, the parade included the Schimmelpfennig Encampment; the Germania, Harugari, Druid and Herwegh Männerchöre; the Cincinnati Turngemeinde and its singing society; the Badischer Unterstützungsverein; the Deutsch-Oestreichischer Unterstützungsverein; the Deutscher Krieger Verein; the Schwäbischer Verein; two German-Swiss societies; two benevolent societies, composed of Rhenish Palatines and Germans from Hesse-Darmstadt; a Gambrinus Society; an organization of German butchers; a military company; and several other organizations.[92] Twenty years earlier, when the New York Germans celebrated their third annual Steuben festival, 11 military companies, 35 German singing societies, several turner and dramatic societies, and numerous other German organizations participated in the festivities in a wooded grove outside the city.[93] It should be added that there has always been a certain contentiousness and querrulousness among the Germans in their many societies. *Deutsche Haderei* and *Vereinsmeierei* have become proverbial among the Germans, and have led to many schisms and much unnecessary duplication in the organizational life of German-American communities.

German sharpshooting clubs, *Schützenvereine,* and competitive shooting matches for prizes and honors, *Schützenfeste,* were unique

---

[91] See *New York Sun,* June 23, 1894.
[92] See *Cincinnati Commercial,* September 4, 1881.
[93] See *New York Express,* quoted in *Charleston Mercury,* July 2, 1859.

German activities introduced into the United States; and the German ceremonial of crowning the champion sharpshooter as *Schützenkönig* was studiously imitated, with all the banqueting, speaking, and parading called for by such occasions in Germany. The Philadelphia Schützenverein was founded in 1846, and the first *Schützenfest* held in Philadelphia, in 1854, was attended by visiting sharpshooting clubs from New York and New Jersey. Although earlier attempts had been made, a national *Schützenbund* was not successfully launched until 1893. Many of these competitive matches lasted three days or even a week, and a number of clubs maintained their own shooting grounds and a park for outings, dances, and banquets. In 1898, the national organization consisted of 65 affiliated clubs.[94] Frequently representatives were sent to Germany to compete in an international *Schützenfest*.[95]

To a lesser degree than the Irish, the Germans also figured in the history of volunteer fire fighting in the pre-Civil War days, but they seem to have been less zealous for this kind of public service than their Irish fellow citizens. Nevertheless, there were many volunteer German fire companies in the larger cities. The Franklin Spritzen Compagnie of St. Louis was organized in 1845.[96] The German Fire Company of Charleston, South Carolina, was formed in 1838 and, in 1859, entertained the visiting German company from Savannah in Charleston with an elaborate banquet.[97] Toledo had its Teutonia Fire Guards since 1856.[98] On one occasion, *The Toledo Blade* advertised the loss by the fire company of the brass cap to the plug of their engine, and pleaded that the finder return it, thereby conferring "a boon on the company and the public." [99] The publication of the American *Turnvereine* recommended German volunteer fire companies as a new field for physical training.[100]

German militia companies proved more popular than fire-fight-

[94] See an article by C. F. Huch, in *Mitteilungen des deutschen Pionier Vereins von Philadelphia* (1911), No. 22, pp. 13-23. See also *The New York Times,* July 30, 1863. In 1932, one of the New York clubs celebrated its 75th anniversary. See *ibid.,* July 24, 1932.

[95] See *New York World,* June 18 and 27, 1890. The first *Vogelschiessen* occurred in Washington, Missouri, in 1840, when the German pioneer farmers tried their marksmanship on a wooden bird and ended by crowning a *Schützenkönig,* or king of the sharpshooters. (See *Missouri Historical Review,* Vol. XVL, p. 354.)

[96] See *Der deutsche Pionier,* Vol. III, p. 334.

[97] See *Charleston Mercury,* February 12 and April 30, 1859.

[98] See *The Toledo Blade,* January 30, 1857.

[99] See *ibid.,* October 23, 1857.

[100] See M. D. Learned: "The German-American Turner Lyric," in *Reports of the Society for the History of the Germans in Maryland,* Vols. VIII-XIV, p. 123.

ing organizations. Like the Irish and other nineteenth-century groups, German immigrants seem to have thoroughly enjoyed the colorful uniforms, martial display, parades, and conviviality which these military organizations provided. German militia companies were formed in many cities, such as Cincinnati, Louisville, Columbus, New York, St. Louis, Milwaukee, and Chicago. They paraded in a variety of uniforms, sometimes accompanied by bands, and under various names—such as the German Huzzars; the Steuben Fusileers; or the Lafayette, Jefferson, Jackson, and Steuben Guards. In Philadelphia, in 1841, the Germans had a whole brigade, consisting of artillery, infantry, and rifle corps.[101] In Charleston, the German Palmetto Riflemen marched with a flag depicting Hermann, hero of the Battle of Teutoberg Forest, in martial pose and with the German revolutionary colors of red, black, and gold on one side, and The Star-Spangled Banner on the other.[102] During the Mexican War, a number of these companies enlisted for active service, and companies of Germans marched to the war from Columbus, Dayton, Cincinnati, St. Louis, Philadelphia, and Milwaukee.[103]

Of all the organizations introduced in the United States in the course of the last century by the German immigration, perhaps none represented a higher level of intellectual interest or broader cultural objectives than the *Turnverein*. As explained earlier, these gymnastic societies emphasized both physical and mental progress—"a chainless body and a fetterless mind." Although Follen, Beck, and Lieber made interesting beginnings in presenting the needs for a physical education program to Americans, the first turner societies were not organized in the United States until the fall of 1848. In that year, the first organization of its kind in this country was launched in Cincinnati, under the leadership of Friedrich Hecker, an insurrectionist in the unsuccessful rebellion in Baden and at that time an exile from Germany. Turner societies thereafter sprang up in many American cities. In Boston, the chief organizer was Karl Heinzen; in New York, it was Gustav Struve, a Frankfurt revolutionist, who took the initiative; in Milwaukee, August Willich was the center of the group. In 1850, the first

---

[101] See *The Baltimore Patriot and Commercial Gazette*, September 3, 1841.
[102] See *The Charleston Mercury*, November 30, 1859.
[103] See *Der deutsche Pionier*, Vol. III, pp. 379-380; *Mitteilungen des deutschen Pionier Vereins von Philadelphia* (1910), No. 15, p. 21; and No. 17, p. 16; and *Cincinnati Enquirer*, May 6, 17, and 19, and June 2, 1847.

turner hall in the United States was dedicated in Cincinnati. Thereafter a national publication, known as *Die Turnzeitung,* was established, and by 1853 the North American Turnerbund included 60 societies. The instructors in all these clubs were Germans who had received their physical education training in Germany. In 1875, a normal school for training teachers of physical education was opened in Milwaukee. The Father Jahn of American turner was George Brosius of Milwaukee, a veteran of the Civil War. He had thousands of pupils and, from 1875 to 1883, was superintendent of physical training for the public schools of Milwaukee. Camp Brosius, a turner summer camp, is maintained in Sheboygan County, Wisconsin, as a center of German cultural life.[104] Needless to add, the turner, as well as the German element as a whole, urged the introduction of organized work in light gymnastics in the public schools. They were successful in many American cities, where for years the directors of physical education were either Germans from abroad or graduates of the normal school maintained by the North American Turnerbund.

Turnfeste were held in the United States since the early 1850's. Besides gymnastics and group performances, they usually included parades, pageants, concerts, balls, public addresses, theatrical performances, and the presentation of tableaux and poses of Laocöon, the Discus Thrower, the Apollo Belvedere, and similar figures from antiquity. At the Chicago World's Fair, in 1893, 4,000 German turner gave an exhibition of drills and gymnastics, with nickel-plated wands.[105] Nearly every turner society had a singing and a dramatic section. For over 50 years, the Milwaukee Turnverein gave Sunday concerts for its members.

Of even greater significance was the interest of the turner organizations in cultural and intellectual matters. The members met in their halls for lectures and discussions on history, economic theory, government, and scientific subjects.[106] Reading rooms and libraries were founded. But the turner movement gained its greatest notoriety because of its interest in radical reform programs. It advocated the intiative, referendum and recall, direct popular election

[104] See Lizzie Rice Johnstone: "Camp Brosius," in *Wisconsin Magazine of History,* Vol. X, pp. 170-174; and Robert Wild: "Chapters in the History of the Turners," in *ibid.,* Vol. IX, pp. 123-139.
[105] See *Atlantische Studien,* Vol. IV, pp. 67-70; and Wild: *loc. cit.*
[106] See *Cincinnati Commercial,* October 9, 1881; and *The Toledo Blade,* February 11, 1873.

of all public officials, social welfare legislation, tax and tariff reform, and other measures considered socialistic at that time.

The early Socialist movement in the United States derived most of its support from the German element, and for years its conventions were conducted in English and German. Along with the interest in Socialism went a rationalist, anticlerical attitude toward the Church and organized religion. Social, political, and religious liberty and reform were the ideals of the turner movement, and a Socialist state was its goal. Turner literature was sharply anticlerical, and turner lyrics, written by leaders like Carl Heinrich Schnauffer and Johann Straubemüller, were fired with the spirit of equality and brotherhood. Before the Civil War, turner societies were centers of Free-Soilism and abolitionism, and militant opponents of nativism and the growing prohibition movement, which they regarded as invasions of personal liberty. Methodists, with their "fanatical" interest in temperance reform, were classified by the German turner as blood brothers of the nativists and Know-Nothings.[107] During the Civil War, the flower of the American Turnerbund went to the front, and over 60 per cent of its membership took up arms in defense of the Union.[108]

After the 1850's, the turner movement was less socialistic, but it remained inimical to all the foes of what it termed "progress." It fought the moneyed aristocracy and the Church in particular, and favored sweeping educational and social reforms. The revolutionary Communist and the sober, practical reformer were equally welcome in its membership. Since 1865, the word "Socialist" has no longer been used in the official name of the Nordamerikanischer Turnerbund. In 1909, the membership of the Turnerbund was nearly 40,000; by 1932, it had fallen to about 27,000. It is not difficult to understand, especially in view of the militant reforming spirit of the early years of the *Turnvereine* in America, why many native Americans were alarmed by their agnosticism and their socialism, and why some of the worst excesses of the nativist movement of the 1850's were directed against the "hair-lipped, red-Republican Germans." [109] "Frisch, frölich, frei, fromm" was the

[107] M. B. Learned: *loc. cit.*, Vol. VIII-XIV, pp. 79-134.
[108] See Carl Wittke: "The Ninth Ohio Volunteers," in *The Ohio Archaeological and Historical Quarterly* (April, 1926), pp. 1-18.
[109] See *Cleveland Plain Dealer*, June 25, 1856. For further material on the turner movement, see *Der deutsche Pionier*, Vol. XVII, pp. 270-271; Hermann Schlüter: *Die Anfänge der deutschen Arbeiterbewegung in Amerika* (Stuttgart,

old motto of the turner, with less and less emphasis on the fourth word. In 1880, the new official motto adopted was: "Frisch, frei, stark, treu." The enemies to be attacked were *das Pfaffentum, die Geld-Aristokratie,* and *das Muckertum.* The latter included prohibition, in particular, and bigoted nativism.[110]

The German immigrants of the nineteenth century may be roughly divided, with reference to their religious views, into three groups. There were the freethinkers, who included some of the most prominent Forty-Eighters, the German Lutherans, and the German Catholics. Other minor groups and other Protestant denominations were represented, but these were of much less significance.

Political, economic, and religious liberalism and radicalism generally went together. The rationalist movement in Germany, under the stimulus of Hegel and Feuerbach, had led to a wave of anticlericalism and to the establishment of many *freie Gemeinde,* independent congregations that broke away entirely from all organized religion, rejected the ritual and dogma of the churches, and tried to reconcile science and religion. The movement in Germany affected not only the Protestants but the Catholics as well; there were several *freie Gemeinde* among the German Catholics. As has been shown, many of the leaders of the German immigration of the 1830's and of 1848 were religious radicals. It was therefore not surprising that freethinking societies, rationalist clubs, and independent congregations should appear among the German element in the United States. At one time, there were nearly 75 German Protestant churches in the Ohio Valley alone that had broken all connection with synods or conferences of any kind.

The views of the freethinkers among the Germans varied all the way from atheism to what might today be called a liberal congregationalism, or the broad principles underlying a modern community

Germany, 1907), pp. 199-214; C. F. Huch: "Der sozialistische Turnerbund," in *Mitteilungen des deutschen Pionier Vereins von Philadelphia* (1912), No. 26, pp. 1-15; W. F. Kamman: *Socialism in German-American Literature* (Philadelphia, 1917); and Henry Metzner: *A Brief History of the American Turnerbund* (Pittsburgh, 1934).

[110] The comment of *The Boston Herald* for August 17, 1855, when the New England turner had staged a three-day program in Boston, is significant:

The day was warm, and the consumption of beer and wine was considerable. We did not, however, witness the slightest irregularity, and we should esteem it a fortunate circumstance if as large a number of Yankees were able to engage in a festival of the kind without committing more improprieties than were witnessed on this occasion.

church. The extremists among the Forty-Eighters held, with Feuerbach and other radicals, that all religion is a figment of the imagination. They made a new god of science and espoused a philosophy of materialism. Their societies and periodicals denounced the churches as temples of ignorance, where religion was dispensed as an opiate for the people.

In what corresponded roughly to a catechism for the freethinking congregation of New York in 1840, revelation, supernaturalism, creeds, and theological systems were summarily dismissed as unworthy of intelligent people. But the ethics of Christianity were extolled, along with what seemed wise, moral, and just in the principles of Confucius, Zoroaster, Moses, Plato, and Mohammed. Free will and cause and effect, instead of reward and punishment by a deity, and a "First Cause," were accepted as cardinal doctrines of the new rationalism. Ritual, sacraments, and a priesthood were of course rejected. Marriage was declared to be a civil function. Anyone might preach or lecture, and the prime object for living was ethical culture and the search for truth, virtue, and happiness. The catechism emphasized the nobility instead of the depravity of man, accepted reason as man's finest instrument, and defined religion as the rational search for happiness. A collection of hymns was prepared to stress these same themes.[111]

There were several freethinking German congregations in the 1840's in Philadelphia, New York, Milwaukee, St. Louis, and Boston; as well as congregations of free and independent Catholics in Richmond, New York, and Philadelphia, which were immediately attacked by Archbishop Hughes and the Catholic hierarchy.[112]

Some groups rejected the idea of a church or congregation altogether, calling themselves *Freimännervereine*. These groups generally considered themselves more radical than the rationalists. The movement was begun in 1850 by Friedrich Hassaurek, in Cincinnati, whence it spread rapidly to Indianapolis, Cleveland, Louisville, Milwaukee, Toledo, Detroit, Philadelphia, Trenton, New Ulm, Albany, Chicago, St. Louis, Hermann, Missouri, Buffalo, Galveston, and other German centers as far west as the Pacific coast. Some societies maintained schools, singing societies, and insurance projects in connection with their rationalist activities. By 1854,

---

[111] See Johann August Försch: *Die Gemeinde der Vernunftgläubigen zu New York. Ihre Grundsätze und Ansichten, Constitution, Katechismus, Gesangbuch* (New York, 1840).
[112] *The Boston Pilot*, October 6, 1860.

the movement was strong enough to enable the societies to hold state conventions, and, in 1876, a national convention of free-thinkers, including turner and German Socialists, was called to Philadelphia, in connection with the Centennial Exposition.

At gatherings of this kind, high-sounding resolutions were generally adopted denouncing the blue laws, which interfered with the Continental Sunday; opposing the observance of Thanksgiving Days, prayer, and *Bible* reading in the schools; and espousing a program of humanitarian and political reform which included revisions of the United States Constitution, progressive economic legislation, free schools, free trade, free land, and new political devices like the initiative, referendum, and recall.

As several prominent members of the rationalist group—such as Heinzen, Münch, and Eduard Mühl—were journalists, the movement supported a number of periodicals. Robert Reitzel (1849-1898), who had studied for the ministry and then became a free-thinker, was probably the greatest master of German prose in America, and the poet laureate of the proletariat and the German Socialists. His weekly, *Der arme Teufel,* founded in Detroit in 1884, was one of the last of the radical German journals in the United States. Most of these journals, like the freethinking groups they represented, led a precarious existence. The independent congregations had difficulty in raising money and could offer but little pay to their leaders (*Sprecher*); they had no support from affiliated groups, and occasionally were victimized by broken-down and unscrupulous ministers who had been expelled from one of the regular denominations.[113]

The Philadelphia *Gemeinde* celebrated its 50th anniversary in 1902 in its own hall, and as late as 1909 the Bund der freien Gemeinden und Freidenkervereine was still in existence, with 7 congregations and about 1,000 members. The movement reached its greatest strength in the decade before the Civil War. The views expounded by Reitzel and other leaders, it may be added, were not far different from those of Franklin, Jefferson, Washington, and Theodore Parker, or from the views of many modernist leaders of

[113] For further details on the German rationalists and freethinkers, see *Der deutsche Pionier,* Vol. VIII, pp. 503-505; and C. F. Huch: "Die freireligiöse Bewegung unter den Deutsch-Amerikanern," in *Mitteilungen des deutschen Pionier Vereins* (1909), No. 11, pp. 1-38; and "Die Konvention der Freigesinnten im Jahre 1876," in *ibid.* (1911), No. 23, pp. 1-18.

community churches or Ethical Culture Societies. In the 1850's, however, many a picnic party of German freethinkers was broken up by enraged nativists, who believed they were saving the nation from dangerous infidels.

Although the German radicals and freethinkers provided an intellectual fermentation among their fellow immigrants, it must be remembered that the more conservative Lutheran and Catholic Germans outnumbered the Forty-Eighters and their kind by at least two to one before the Civil War. A strong Lutheran element came from northern and eastern Germany. They represented religious conservatism, untouched by eighteenth-century rationalism and unaffected by German radicalism. They settled in America as farmers and as agricultural and city laborers, and became the backbone of a conservative American Lutheranism. These "Old Lutherans," as they were called, regarded the political refugees who had come from Germany in 1830 and 1848 as dangerous infidels. They were equally out of sympathy with the liberal features which had crept into the American Lutheran Church since the days of the patriarch Mühlenberg, and believed the time was ripe for a return to the confessional Lutheranism of the sixteenth century. The colonial Church had gradually yielded both to pietistic and liberal forces. It manifested a strong trend toward nationalism, laid less emphasis on the creed and ancient symbols, and, above all, had become Americanized to the extent of fraternizing with other denominations. It had even accepted certain "Methodistic" features, stressing the Puritan concept of good works rather than justification by faith alone. The break with the Lutheran Church of Germany had become practically complete; ministers and congregations of the Reformed and the Lutheran faiths frequently used the same churches, or actually united in one group, and English was rapidly displacing German as the language of the Lutheran service.

The reaction against this Americanized Lutheran Church of colonial days came in the nineteenth century with the immigration of thousands of so-called "Old Lutherans" from Germany. Their greatest leader was C. F. W. Walther, "Lutheran Pope of the West," who came to St. Louis in 1841, founded the first German Lutheran church there, established a church journal, *Der Lutheraner,* and later organized the Missouri Synod, which has been relentless to the present time in its warfare on the Puritan, "Methodistic," and more liberal tendencies that have appeared in the ranks of American Lutheranism. For several decades, a fierce ecclesiastical battle was fought between the two groups. From 1830 to 1870, the potential Lutheran population in the United States increased three times as rapidly as the total American population. Here were souls to be won for the true Lutheran gospel! The number of Lutheran pastors in the United States was small and help from aboard meager. Methodists, Presbyterians, and Baptists, with their superior technique for evangelizing the frontier, were dangerous rivals.

Fort Wayne and St. Louis became the great centers from which "Old Lutheranism" attacked the problem of winning the West. Concordia Seminary was founded in St. Louis and has remained the heart of the Missouri Synod, dedicated to fostering German art, learning, and religion in the New World. The preservation of the German language was recognized as an important duty, second only to the preservation of uncorrupted Lutheranism; for one was the support of the other. It is impossible to follow in detail the many battles over the sacraments and church doctrines and the use of the German language in which various groups, organized in rival synods, engaged for many decades.

Under the leadership of Walther and his coworkers, the Missouri Synod, founded in 1847, built up its power, and became more cohesive. It never interfered with politics and had no interest in the slavery controversy or the liberal movements in Germany. All revolutions were sinful and all governments of divine origin. Therefore, it taught the obedient acceptance of whatever government was in power. Its energies were confined to the religious battleground. It sent pastors to the seaport towns, erected immigrant homes, and tried in other ways to shepherd new arrivals from Germany into the fold of the true Church. It emphasized the importance of parochial schools and insisted that the young should be instructed in Lutheranism in the German language.

The Missouri Synod spread into all the states except two, although it was always strongest where the German element was largest. The pressure of this "Old Lutheranism", coming out of the West affected all the elder Lutheran bodies in the United States. Walther and his group insisted that the Lutheran Church was not merely one of the many Christian sects but "the ancient true Church of Christ on earth." Above all, Lutherans were warned to shun radical, socialistic, freethinking Germans as they would the Devil, for they were the sworn enemies of religion, property, and the family. In 1930, the Missouri Synod claimed a membership of 1,163,666, with over 3,000 pastors. There can be no question that "the leaven of historical Lutheranism from the West coupled with the Lutheran immigrant invasion from Europe left their indelible stamp upon the 'American Lutheran' church." [114] In spite of recent efforts to unite all forms of Lutheranism in America into one great organization, the German Lutherans, like the Scandinavians, are still divided among several synods and conferences.

Of all the non-Lutheran Protestant sects, the Methodists seem to have been more interested in the German immigrants than any other group. This interest dates back to the time of Bishop Asbury. In 1836, the Ohio Annual Conference of Methodists appointed Wilhelm Nast, who learned his Methodism in America, to a German mission on a central Ohio circuit. Nast became the founder and leader of German Methodism in the United States. In 1837, he translated the Methodist catechism and discipline into German. The Methodist Church voted financial support to German immigrants and, in 1838, founded a German Methodist paper in Cincinnati and sent out missionaries to meet German immigrants on their arrival in the United States. German Methodist missions were established in Cleveland, Pittsburgh, and elsewhere in the 1840's. Heinrich Böhm and Nast were the editors of *Der Christliche Apologete,* the great organ of Methodism in the Middle West. As early as 1849, the Methodist Missionary Society reported 6,350 church members in the German field, with nearly 100 churches and 83 regular mission circuits.[115] A separate German Methodist Conference was organized, and Nast remained the guiding spirit of German Methodism in the United States until his death in 1899.

The Roman Catholic Church in America received thousands of new communicants from the German immigrants from Bavaria and the south-German states. Indeed, so heavy was the influx of German Catholics and so rapid the establishment of German parishes that, as early as 1853, there were protests from German Catholic groups against the practice of sending Irish priests to minister to their religious needs, and the demand for bishops and priests of

---

[114] See Carl Mauelshagen: *American Lutheranism Surrenders to Forces of Conservatism* (Athens, Georgia, 1936), p. 191. I have followed this excellent study closely in my brief account of German Lutheranism.
[115] See *ibid.*, p. 62. See also *Ohio Annual Conference Minutes,* 1836-1840, 1845-1846, and 1849, in the manuscript collection at Ohio Wesleyan University.

their own nationality increased with the years.[116]   Some help for the development of German Catholic parishes in the United States came from Germany, from organizations like the Bavarian Ludwig-missionsverein, founded in 1838, and the Raphaelsverein, founded much later, both for the primary purpose of working among German immigrants.   Catholic religious orders sent scores of men and women to open schools, hospitals, and charitable institutions in the United States.   Scores of Catholic priests came to America during Bismarck's *Kulturkampf* with the Church.

The organization of German parishes followed rapidly on the heels of German immigration.   In 1834, for example, German Catholics at Minster and Glandorf, Ohio, had completed the organization of their churches.   Milwaukee was the seat of a bishopric and the home of a Catholic paper, *Der Seebote,* in the early 1850's.[117] In 1837, the German-Swiss Johann Martin Henni founded the first German Catholic Orphans Society in the United States in Cincinnati, and he later became the first German bishop in this country.[118] Germans or Austro-Germans, such as Dr. Salzmann, Franz Xaver Katzer, and the Bavarian Archbishop Heiss, were powerful figures in the development of Catholicism in Wisconsin.   Friedrich Rese came from Cincinnati to become the first bishop of Detroit, and Father Joseph Jessing of Westphalia published the *Ohio Waisenfreund* and established the Josephinum in Columbus, Ohio, to train students for the priesthood.   Bishop Joseph Schrembs of Cleveland was born in Bavaria.

To counteract the appeal of lodges and beneficent societies, such as the Freemasons, and to provide greater cohesion among German Catholics in the United States, the Deutsch-Römisch Katholischer Zentralverein was organized.   Some of its member societies were established as early as 1842, and by 1850 there were organizations of German Catholics for insurance and relief work in New York, Milwaukee, Alleghany, Pittsburgh, Baltimore, Buffalo, and Cincinnati.   The Zentralverein was formally organized in Baltimore in 1855 and has been continuously useful to the present time. Besides its interest in bringing about greater solidarity among German Catholics, it has supported relief work among needy Germans

[116] See *Ohio State Journal*, May 21, 1853; *Cleveland Plain Dealer*, September 5, 1887; and Peter Guilday: *The Life and Times of England* (New York, 1927), Vol. II, pp. 383-385.   So strong was the feeling against Irish control of the Church that, in 1887, 4,000 German Catholics staged a protest march in Chicago.

[117] See *Atlantische Studien*, Vol. IV, p. 487.

[118] See Körner: *Das deutsche Element in den Vereinigten Staaten von Nordamerika, 1818-1848*, pp. 290-292.

and newly arrived immigrants, provided insurance for widows and orphans, and been especially active in its demand for parochial schools—the only issue, except for prohibition and nativism, in which the organization has been politically active. A number of German Catholic papers were established in the United States in the last century. One of the best known, the daily St. Louis *Amerika,* was published from 1872 to 1925.[119] The Deutsch-Römisch Katholischer Zentralverein apparently reached its greatest membership in 1916, when it enrolled 150,000. By 1935, the number had dropped to about 57,000. An organization of German priests in America was founded in 1887 and, by 1892, had 900 members. In 1888, there were 30 German Catholic papers published in the United States.[120]

German-language newspapers in the United States have been more influential and numerous than the press maintained by any other foreign-language group in America. At the outbreak of the World War, there were more German-language newspapers in several states than all other immigrant publications combined. Even in 1930, after the World War had destroyed many long-established German newspapers because they could not withstand the hysteria against all things German which swept the United States at that time, the German press still exceeded all other foreign-language papers in output. The number of German papers still appearing in 1930 was 172, the nearest rival being the Italian press, with 126 papers.[121]

Many of the German newspapers were always edited with the liberal use of scissors and paste pot, and by translating material that had already appeared in English dailies. Others, in later years, carried little actual news, except accounts of the activities of German societies or personal items. Some were guilty of atrocious crimes against the German language, as their editors succumbed to the German-American German so characteristic of German communities in the United States.[122] On the other hand, some German-language papers were publications of high quality; their edi-

---

[119] For details on the German Catholics in America, see Engelbert Krebs: *Um die Erde* (Paderborn, Germany, 1929).

[120] See Kloss: *op. cit.,* pp. 137, 149, and 151-153.

[121] See N. W. Ayer and Son, *American Newspaper Annual and Directory,* 1930.

[122] Translating from English to German sometimes led to curious results, such as voting for "Herr Blank" and for "Herr Scattering," and to such atrocities as: Sie brachten der Königin Victoria drei Stühle (*chairs* for *cheers*), Committee für Wege und Meinungen, and "Dem Sieger gehört das Verdorbene." See also *Der deutsche Pionier,* Vol. I, p. 274.

torial work was done by men of intelligence and influence who, upon occasion, were able to play an important role in their communities.

By 1848, according to the Philadelphia *Demokrat*, there were 70 German newspapers in the United States: 35 in Pennsylvania, 9 in Ohio, 7 in New York, and 5 in Missouri. Of these journals, 41 were Democratic, 12 were Whig, 6 tried to be neutral, and 9 were religious papers.[123] By 1852, the total number of German newspapers in this country had nearly doubled.[124] In New York, the *New Yorker Staatszeitung* was established in 1834, and it remains to this day the largest and probably most influential of the German dailies. The paper reached its highest level under the editorship of Oswald Ottendörfer, who made it a tower of strength in the fight on the notorious "Tweed Ring" and who mobilized the New York Germans in support of the reformers. The *New Yorker Abendzeitung*, started somewhat later, was for a time under the distinguished editorship of Friedrich Kapp. In 1850, a German weekly, *Der Völkerbund*, was started by Karl Heinzen. By 1846, there were at least half a dozen German papers in New York, although some appeared only weekly or semiweekly.[125]

Johann Georg Wesselhöft's *Alte und Neue Welt*, published in Philadelphia in 1834, really began a new era in radical German-American journalism. Its circulation was prohibited in Germany in 1840 by the police. The paper was very critical of the new America, and sponsored German culture to such an extent that papers like the *New Yorker Staatszeitung* and the St. Louis *Anzeiger des Westens* took violent issue with its program. The latter, founded in 1835, was one of the most distinguished of all German dailies, and counted among its editors men like Wilhelm Weber and Carl Schurz. The *Illinois Staatszeitung*, established in 1848, had a long history, which extended beyond the World War. Its editors included such well-known leaders of the German element as George Schneider, Lorenz Brentano, Wilhelm Rapp, Hermann Raster, Anton Hesing, and Horace L. Brand. The *Chicago Abendpost*, which became a penny daily in 1889, was edited by Fritz Glogoener and Wilhelm Kaufmann. Chicago also supported a

[123] See *Mitteilungen des deutschen Pionier Vereins von Philadelphia* (1910), No. 16, pp. 39-40.
[124] See *New York Tribune*, March 5, 1852. This reports 133.
[125] See Körner: *Das deutsche Element in den Vereinigten Staaten von Nordamerika*, pp. 105-106.

number of German radical papers, such as the *Arbeiter-Zeitung*, whose editors included August Spies of Haymarket riot fame. By 1850, there were three German dailies in Cincinnati, of which the *Volksblatt* was undoubtedly the most influential. The *Freie Presse*, too, had a wide circulation and outlived its rival beyond the World War. For a time, Cincinnati Germans also supported a fortnightly comic paper called *Die Kratzbuerste*, as well as *Fliegende Blätter*, edited by Emil Klauprecht, which was probably the first German paper in the United States to be devoted to *belles lettres*.[126] Any discussion of Cincinnati publications must include mention of the work of Heinrich A. Rattermann and the annual volumes of *Der deutsche Pionier*, begun in 1869. These remain a storehouse of information on all phases of German life in the United States and reveal high standards of historical research and real literary merit, for which much of the credit must go to Rattermann himself.[127] Friedrich Kapp and Oswald Seidensticker were his able collaborators.[128]

In 1859, Pittsburgh had 5 German newspapers, a total exceeded only by St. Louis at that time. Baltimore has had many German papers, but the most important was *Der deutsche Correspondent*, established in 1841.[129] The number of German newspapers in the Southern states in 1876 was surprisingly large, and included the *Tennessee Post* (Nashville), the *Arkansas Freie Presse* (Little Rock), the *Richmond Anzeiger* and the *Virginia Staatszeitung* (Richmond), the *Deutsche Zeitung*, a New Orleans daily, the *Deutsche Zeitung* of Charleston, the Savannah *Abendzeitung*, the Alabama *Staatszeitung*, and a number of papers in Texas.[130] One of the leading German Catholic papers was the *Katolische Kirchenzeitung*, started in Baltimore and then moved to New York, and for many years edited by Maximilian Oertel.[131] Dr. Samuel Ludvigh, born in Austria and reared as a Catholic, became one of the great liberal editors among the Germans in the United States. He wrote a whole

[126] See *ibid.*, p. 192; *Cleveland Leader*, March 7, 1870; and *Cincinnati Commercial*, August 28, 1850.
[127] See also *History of Cincinnati and Hamilton County, Ohio—Past and Present* (Cincinnati, 1894), pp. 261 and 272.
[128] For a list of German newspapers in the United States in 1876-1877, with publishers, circulation, political affiliation, and so forth, see *Der deutsche Pionier*, Vol. VIII, pp. 289-320.
[129] See *ibid.*, Vol. III, pp. 106-109.
[130] See *ibid.*, Vol. VIII, pp. 289-320.
[131] See Körner: *Das deutsche Element in den Vereinigten Staaten von Nordamerika*, p. 133.

library of tracts and books, but probably his best-known publication was the quarterly *Die Fackel,* which he began in 1849.[132] Paul Carus ably edited, in English, the *Monist* and the *Open Court,* published in Chicago.[133]

Today the German-language press in the United States is declining rapidly. It suffered terribly from the hysteria and persecution of the World War years. In the larger cities—such as Chicago, Detroit, Milwaukee, St. Louis, Cleveland, Cincinnati, New York, and Philadelphia—German dailies apparently are still able to make money, and they probably will continue to do so for some years to come. In other cities, however, the German paper has become merely a weekly, which makes little effort to report news other than what emanates from the local German societies. These papers have ceased to be newspapers in the accepted sense and are today hardly more than German *Vereinszeitungen.* It should be remembered that, from the point of view of absorbing and Americanizing the immigrant, the steady decline of the foreign-language press is the best proof of its success.

The German element has always been interested in American education, partly because of a genuine interest in a sound school system, partly because of a sincere desire to maintain the German language in a new environment by having it taught to their children in the schools, and partly because some German-American leaders of the middle nineteenth century believed that American culture was at such a low ebb that a German scheme of education was essential to raise its level. "Am deutschen Wesen wird dereinst die Welt genesen."

In the period before the Civil War, many German private schools were established in the United States. Some were parochial schools connected primarily with Lutheran churches; some were supported by the freethinkers' societies already discussed. Germans often organized a *Schulverein* and then hired a teacher to instruct their children. Moreover, many Germans served as private tutors and especially as music teachers in American homes. German schools like Röseler von Oels' school in New York, the Zionsschule of

---

[132] See *Der deutsche Pionier,* Vol. I, pp. 354-360.
[133] For Indiana German papers, see W. A. Fritsch: *German Settlers and German Settlements in Indiana* (Evansville, Indiana, 1915), pp. 25-28. For German literary activity in the United States, including books, newspapers, theater, and so forth, see A. B. Faust, "Non-English Writings: I, German," in *The Cambridge History of American Literature* (New York, 1933), Vol. III, pp. 572-590.

Baltimore, the private school of Friedrich Schmidt in St. Louis, and those in Cincinnati and Milwaukee had considerable influence on the educational progress of these communities because of their good work and the pedagogical novelties they introduced.[134] The first German-English school west of the Mississippi was founded by Germans in St. Louis in 1836, and Friedrich Steines was called from his Missouri farm to become its teacher. Dr. George Engelmann, who came to Missouri in 1834, was a leader in education and science in the Middle West and one of the founders of the Western Academy of Science. Theodore Bernhard organized the school system of Watertown, Wisconsin, and introduced the first system of free textbooks in that state.[135] Georg Bunsen of Frankfurt introduced pedagogical innovations as superintendent of schools in Belleville, Illinois. The interest of the Germans, manifested in their conventions from 1837 to 1842, in establishing a German university in the United States and a normal school to train teachers of German has already been discussed.[136]

German-American private schools declined as the influence of the Forty-Eighters waned and with the rise of a second generation of German-Americans, who took advantage of the rapidly developing public-school system. The attack of those interested in preserving German *Kultur* in the United States therefore gradually shifted to a new front—namely, a demand that German be taught in the public schools. American educational leaders like Horace Mann in Massachusetts and Calvin E. Stowe in Ohio were greatly impressed with the superiority of the Prussian system of education— so much so that they helped to introduce it, with modifications, in their respective states. At a time when the Prussian schools were regarded as a model system of education and the German vote in many states was large enough to be a real factor in the elections, it was not difficult to secure the addition of German to the public-school curriculum.[137] German remained in the curriculum of the public schools of many states until the World War.

A Pennsylvania statute of 1837 and an Ohio law of the same

[134] See *Atlantische Studien*, Vol. II, p. 50.
[135] See W. F. Whyte: "Chronicles of Early Watertown," in *Wisconsin Magazine of History*, Vol. IV, p. 287.
[136] See also H. A. Rattermann: "Geschichte der deutschen Konventionen zu Pittsburg und Philippsburg, 1837-1842, und des ersten deutsch-amerikanischen Lehrerseminars," in *Deutsch-Amerikanisches Magazin*, Vol. I, pp. 87-104, 447-458, and 594-613.
[137] See Channing: *op. cit.*, Vol. IV, pp. 246 and 253.

decade permitted, not only the teaching of German in the public schools, but teaching *in* German as well, wherever there was sufficient demand for it. Later, teaching in German was prohibited in some states, but local school boards might retain the German language in the curriculum as before. During the World War, when Ohio and Nebraska passed laws denying the right to conduct schools in a foreign language, thus eliminating German as a subject of instruction in the elementary public schools, several test cases were carried to the United States Supreme Court. In *Robert Meyer versus the State of Nebraska* (1923), the Court finally declared all state laws prohibiting the teaching and use of German in private or parochial schools unconstitutional, being in violation of the Fourteenth Amendment, and held that the right to teach and of parents to have their children taught in a language other than English was within the liberty of the subject guaranteed by that amendment.[138]

In the 1840's, the Cincinnati schools recognized the absolute equality of German and English as languages of instruction, and for many years thereafter, teaching was conducted in German in some of the leading German centers in the United States. German teachers generally enjoyed a good reputation for scholarship and pedagogical competence, and even where teaching in the public schools was carried on in the German language, they prided themselves on the good English they taught their pupils.[139] Many German teachers came from abroad. As early as 1850, a German Teachers' Association was formed in New York City,[140] and German tutors seem to have been much in demand in well-to-do American families.[141] By 1870, a national organization of German teachers was launched in Louisville, Kentucky, with 117 German teachers present. By 1885, the number of teachers had risen to nearly 5,000, but already German-American leaders were complaining that the younger generation was rapidly forgetting the German tongue and that parents no longer insisted on having their children study German in the

[138] See Carl Wittke: *German-Americans and the World War* (Columbus, Ohio, 1936), pp. 179-182. For the whole history of German instruction in the schools, see L. Viereck, in *Report of the United States Commissioner of Education,* (Washington, D. C., 1900-1901), Vol. I, pp. 531-708.
[139] See *Der deutsche Pionier,* Vol. IV, pp. 100-106.
[140] See *New York Tribune,* October 14, 1850.
[141] See *Toledo Blade,* April 5, 1873; *Boston Transcript,* January 1, 1870; and *Cincinnati Enquirer,* January 22, 1847.

schools. German was introduced in the elementary public schools of New York in 1854; of Iowa in 1861; of St. Louis in 1864; of Chicago in 1865; of Minnesota and San Francisco in 1867; of Cleveland, Milwaukee, and Indiana in 1869; of Baltimore in 1874; and of Detroit in 1875.[142] In 1878, the National deutsch-amerikanische Lehrerseminar was opened in Milwaukee to train teachers of German for the public schools and to make them true pioneers of German culture. The school produced scores of competently trained teachers, and its director, Max Griebsch, enjoyed an enviable reputation among American pedagogical leaders.[143]

The German element in the United States has enthusiastically supported vocational training and has done pioneer work in the field of physical education. The German turner influence cannot be overemphasized in this field of the curriculum. Nevertheless, the kindergarten is the most unique and lasting of the German contributions to American education. Even the German name has been preserved. Friedrich Froebel established the first kindergarten in Blankenburg, Germany, in 1837. Before 1870, there were ten kindergarten in the United States, all but one founded and directed by Germans. The exception was that of Elizabeth Palmer Peabody of Boston. She, too, owed much to the influence of Mrs. Carl Schurz, who had studied with Froebel in 1849-1850. Miss Peabody did more than anyone else to spread the kindergarten idea in the United States. Perhaps the first exponent of the Froebel methods in the United States was Johannes Kraus, who lectured and wrote in the United States in 1851 and attracted the attention of Henry Barnard. Although there is still some controversy as to who established the first kindergarten in America, the credit is usually given to Mrs. Schurz, who organized a group of children in Watertown, Wisconsin, in 1856. The second kindergarten was begun in 1858, in Columbus, Ohio, by Caroline Louisa Frankenberg, who had taught under Froebel's direction in Dresden and Bautzen. In 1873, the St. Louis school board established a public kindergarten, as an integral part of the public-school system. Emma Marwedel established kindergarten on the Pacific coast, Alma

[142] See Kloss: *op. cit.,* p. 246.
[143] See *Der deutsche Kulturtraeger,* February 1913, pp. 66-71; and H. Schuricht: "Deutsches Schulwesen in den Vereinigten Staaten," in *Der deutsche Pionier,* Vol. XVII, pp. 138-147; and Vol. IV, p. 218; and *Cincinnati Commercial,* August 5, 1881. See also Kloss: *op. cit.,* pp. 243-246.

Kriege in Boston, and Maria Boelte in New York City. The German-Swiss Wilhelm Hailmann should also be mentioned in this connection.[144]

As late as the World War, German was taught, and usually well taught, in most of the public schools of the larger American cities. In 1915, for example, one year after the beginning of the World War, German was taught in 135 of the 275 public schools of Chicago, with an enrollment of over 20,000 students;[145] and in some cities, such as Erie, Pennsylvania, German was taught from the first grade on. In Columbus, Ohio, the school board had a violent altercation as late as 1873 over the continued use of German readers, all of which were still being printed in Saxony, but the teaching of German continued up to the World War.[146]

During the World War, patriots were successful in putting the "Hun" language out of the schools. Citizens' leagues and defense councils pleaded with parents not to let their children study the language of the Kaiser. The number of German students declined precipitously. German teachers were dismissed or transferred to other subjects, sometimes to teach "American citizenship." German textbooks were burned by high-school pupils eager for an excuse to get rid of a difficult subject in the curriculum, and their patriotic endeavors were lustily approved in many cases by parents and teachers. The burning was often performed to the accompaniment of martial strains from the town band, patriotic songs, and patriotic oratory.[147] With the return of sanity after the World War, German has been slowly reintroduced into high-school curricula, but it no longer enjoys its favored place among foreign languages and derives quite as much support from native American families as from parents of German blood.

The influence of the heavy German immigration of the nineteenth century upon American speech has been pointed out by Henry L. Mencken and other students of the American language.[148] Loan

[144] For the kindergarten movement in the United States, see John A. Walz: "Deutscher Einfluss im amerikanischen Erziehungswesen," in *Mitteilungen der Deutschen Akademie* (Munich, Germany, 1937), Vol. XII, pp. 198-210; and *German Influence in American Education and Culture* (Philadelphia, 1936). Also Elizabeth Jenkins: "How the Kindergarten Found Its Way to America," in *Wisconsin Magazine of History* (September, 1930); and "Froebel's Disciples in America" in *The American-German Review*, Vol. III, pp. 15-19.

[145] See *Jahrbuch der Deutschen in Chicago für das Jahr 1916*, p. 305.

[146] See *Ohio State Journal*, August 6 and September 1, 1873.

[147] See Wittke: *German-Americans and the World War*, pp. 179-190.

[148] See H. L. Mencken: *The American Language* (New York, 1921).

words—such as *pretzel, Hausfrau,* and *pumpernickel*—show the profound influence of the German element on American eating and drinking habits, and have been incorporated, with their original German spelling, into the American dictionaries. *Loafer* may come from the German *laufen* or it may be a mispronunciation of *lover.* *Dumb,* meaning stupid, suggests a direct borrowing of the German term *dumm.* The same is true of the colloquialism *dumbhead* (*Dummkopf*). *Hold on,* meaning to stop, seems to derive from the German *halt an.* Many other German terms—such as *Sängerfest, Stein, hoch, Männerchor,* and *Wanderlust*—are familiar to Americans who know no other German. *Swatfest* and *bush leaguer* are terms in common use in American baseball slang, and in each case one half of the word (*fest* and *bush*) is pure German both in spelling and meaning.

The role of the German element in American industry, science, and the fine arts will be discussed in a later chapter. There remains to be considered here, then, the part played by the German element in the political affairs of the United States. Although the German is generally regarded as less susceptible to the virus of American politics than the Irish, this generalization is true to only a very limited degree. The influence of the German vote has been decisive in many communities and, on occasion, extremely important in national politics.

First of all, it is important to appreciate the role of the German workingman and the intellectual radical in the development of the early labor movement in the United States. The discussion of the interest of Germans in the establishment of workers' utopias in the United States will be reserved for a later chapter. Most German immigrants did not carry their desire for social and economic reforms to such extremes, but thousands had a lively interest in advancing the cause of labor by more conventional means.

Prior to 1840, the early labor movement in the United States was generally led by English or Scotch immigrants. The German immigration at the middle of the century gave new life to the American labor movement, and new unions were speedily formed in the larger cities the majority of whose members were German workmen. This was especially true of the cabinetmakers, bakers, watchmakers, upholsterers, bookbinders, and piano makers—trades in which the highly skilled German artisan quickly assumed a position of commanding importance. By the spring of 1850, *The New York*

Tribune reported that the majority of the 2,000 cabinetmakers in New York were Germans. A plan was devised to raise $5,000 for the establishment of a coöperative shop to guarantee employment during the dull season. Thirty German button and fringe makers formed a union, and advertised in the newspapers asking others to join their organization. The iron and metal workers announced in the *Tribune* that "the Germans solicit the cooperation of their fellow workmen, without distinction of nation, at their future meetings." German upholsterers, cordwainers, confectioners, locksmiths, printers, and bakers followed the same policy in New York, Philadelphia, and elsewhere. In the movement which swept the country in the early 1850's to organize the mechanical trades, the skilled German artisans generally took the lead.[149]

The New York Herald ridiculed and burlesqued these German labor meetings in its news columns because of the inability of the participants to speak English, and denounced the movement as socialistic; but Greeley's *Tribune* deplored such tactics and supported the German artisans in their efforts to organize the various trades into labor unions.[150] By 1869, the German Workingman's Union of New York was strong enough to sponsor a course of lectures; and the United Cabinet Makers had a coöperative organization which built 12 houses, managed a loan association, and owned a park for its outings.[151]

It is evident that many of these early German labor unions were primarily interested in the coöperative movement and in social and insurance benefits rather than in the objectives of the later labor union movement. Before the Civil War, German workers' congresses were being held in New York and elsewhere. Often in conjunction with radical German intellectuals, they adopted comprehensive platforms for social, economic, and political reform.[152] German labor papers appeared in the larger cities, as far south as New Orleans. Most of them had a decided anticlerical and anti-

---

[149] See *New York Tribune*, April 15, 16, 18, 20, 22, 24, 26, and 30, 1850. The German tailors of New York planned a coöperative store, and several of the coöperatives opened in New York City were reported to be selling their goods at a saving of 12 per cent.

[150] See *ibid.*, April 23, 24, and 27, 1850.

[151] See *ibid.*, December 28, 1869; and June 17, 1870. See also *New York World*, September 20, 1868.

[152] See Louis P. Hemminghausen: "Reminiscences of the Political Life of the German-Americans in Baltimore During the Years 1850 to 1860," in *Annual Report of the Society for the History of the Germans in Maryland*, Vol. VIII-XIV, pp. 4-18.

capitalistic complexion, and some were revolutionary, Marxian, proletarian papers. The majority were short-lived. Some, in their unbounded enthusiasm for revolution, thought the United States should intervene in European countries in order to fulfill its historic mission to democratize the world.[153] Although alarmist papers like *The New York Herald* predicted a march of the discontented upon Wall Street, actually these radical German organizations had little influence on the English-speaking workers. For this the Germans themselves were largely to blame, because of their stubborn refusal to learn the English language. When Germans in Philadelphia and Cleveland proposed a labor paper in English, they got little support from their German colleagues.

The early German labor movement in the United States was led by many picturesque figures, such as Hermann Kriege of New York, Joseph Weydemeyer, and Heinrick Koch, a German watchmaker in St. Louis who published the *Vorwärts* and the *Antipfaff*. Undoubtedly the most influential and interesting character among them, however, was Wilhelm Weitling, who founded the *Arbeiterbund* of New York and published the *Republik der Arbeiter,* and who deserves a place in histories of American political and economic thought. Weitling was a tailor, born in Magdeburg. He was the illegitimate son of a French officer, and was raised in extreme poverty. In Paris, he became interested in the radical movement. In the United States, he invented a buttonhole machine; received seven patents; and, at the time of his death in 1871, was in litigation with the Singer Sewing Machine Company, charging that its experts had stolen his patents. Weitling was a pamphleteer in the cause of labor and, in the course of his propagandist efforts, was hounded out of Switzerland, Germany, and France by the police. He organized workmen's lodges in the United States to sponsor a program of State Socialism. In 1848, he returned to Germany to attend workers' congresses in connection with the revolutionary movement of that year. He met with little success and, in 1849, returned to the United States.

Weitling's program was essentially to arm the proletariat, physically and intellectually, for the coming social revolution. He had plans for a labor bank to provide for an issue of paper money based on all capital goods. All inheritances and all church and unused property were to be confiscated by the State. All wealth created

[153] See *Der deutsche Pionier,* Vol. VIII, pp. 90-97 and 155-159.

by work was to be stored in government magazines and used as a basis for currency to be issued by the government. The form of government somewhat approximated a workers' soviet. Workers, employers, and farmers were to turn their products over to the government in exchange for paper, thus eliminating—so Weitling thought—the capitalist profit system and the middleman. Guilds of workers and employers were to fix the value of all products and determine the amount of currency to be issued in exchange for them.

The plan, as outlined above, has not been presented in adequate detail. Moreover, it was full of inconsistencies, but Weitling was so optimistic over the rapid unionization of German workers in the 1850's that he believed his "Republic of the toilers" was imminent. He diligently promoted workers' congresses to endorse his plans, supported the coöperative movement, and made plans for a workers' utopia in the West. He had no sympathy with strikes for a few cents additional wages; he differed with Kark Marx in many respects; and, unlike many radical reformers of his time, he believed in Christianity. Weitling published scores of pamphlets on many subjects, including a proposal for a new language in which the dative case, "an aristocratic invention," would be eliminated. He was always in financial straits, but he had real gifts as a reformer and agitator. His followers espoused many reforms, such as homestead legislation, protection against mortgage foreclosures, the single tax, public libraries, adult education, and a program of public works that sounds strikingly modern.[154]

The transition from movements of this kind to formally organized Socialist parties was easily accomplished, and German radicals and German artisans played a significant role in the history of American Socialism. Indeed, it was not until 1900 that Eugene V. Debs and Victor L. Berger set out to "Americanize" the American Socialist party.

In the 1850's, many a German *Turnverein* took the name "Sozialdemokratischer Turnverein," and the early Socialist parties derived valuable support from the turner, as well as from German workers' organizations. The first Socialist party in America, which was

[154] See Hermann Schlüter: *op. cit.*; F. A. Sorge: "Die Arbeiterbewegung in den Vereinigten Staaten," in *Die Neue Zeit* (Stuttgart, Germany, 1890-1891), Vol. I, pp. 497-502 and 542-547; and Vol. II, pp. 193-202 and 232-240; and C. F. Huch: "Die Anfänge der Arbeiterbewegung unter den Deutsch-Amerikanern," in *Mitteilungen des deutschen Pionier Vereins von Philadelphia* (1910), No. 17, pp. 39-52.

founded in New York in 1867 and was very short-lived, developed from a German Communist club and the German Workers' Society of New York City. Most of the members of the Socialist Labor party of North America, founded in Newark in 1877, were Germans, and for the next 15 years German was used in its conventions. Exiled German Socialists, driven out by Bismarck's persecution, were welcomed with open arms in the United States and added new strength to the movement.[155] The *New Yorker Volkszeitung,* established in 1878 and edited by Dr. Adolph Douai, was the organ of the Socialist Labor party and was for years the leading Socialist paper in the United States.[156] In 1889, there were at least eight important German Socialist dailies in the United States.[157] The executive board of the First International in America consisted of three Germans, two Irish, two French, one Swede, and one Italian. In the 1870's and 1880's, many Germans became interested in the anarchist movement. August Spies, publisher of the Chicago *Arbeiterzeitung,* was one of those hanged in connection with the Haymarket riot, and the movement received a staggering blow from this unfortunate incident and the trial that followed it.[158] Of the ten indicted for murder, eight were Germans.

Needless to add, many Germans opposed the more radical tendencies of their fellow immigrants. The labor movement before the Civil War was overshadowed by the slavery issue, and not until the following generation was there a resurgence of a similar worker's philosophy. Many German radicals went to war in 1861. Gustav Struve, Josef Weydemeyer, F. Annecke, August Willich, Rudolf Rosa, and Fritz Jacobi were among this number, and some won commissions in the Union Army. The radical movement never represented more than a small minority of the German immigration, and it was as unpopular with the German majority as it was

---

[155] See *Cleveland Plain Dealer,* December 19, 1887; *Cincinnati Commercial,* February 21, May 2, and June 9, 1878; and *Cincinnati Gazette,* December 6, 1880.

[156] See Fred E. Haynes: *Social Politics in the United States* (New York, 1924), pp. 46-57.

[157] See also B. A. Uhlendorf: "German-American Poetry. A Contribution to Colonial Literature," in *Jahrbuch der Deutsch-Amerikanischen Historischen Gesellschaft von Illinois,* Vol. XXII-XXIII, pp. 109-295.

[158] See *Ohio State Journal,* November 8, 1889; and *Philadelphia Press,* September 20, 1887. See also A. J. Townsend: *loc. cit.* The *Illinois Staatszeitung* was violent in its attacks on the German anarchists. The German Socialist movement in Chicago reached its high tide in 1879, when Dr. Ernst Schmidt ran for mayor. For the latest information on the miscarriage of justice in the Haymarket trials, see Harry Barnard: *Eagle Forgotten, The Life of John Peter Altgeld* (Indianapolis, 1938).

with native Americans.[159]   The Whig press was particularly violent in its denunciations of German radicalism before the Civil War.[160] A Congressman from Alabama attacked the German reformers for their Continental views on the Sabbath, as well as for their political and economic radicalism, and he seemed particularly incensed that the reformers wanted to abolish "the Christian system of punishment" and introduce "the human amelioration system."   All of which proved to the honorable representative from Alabama that foreigners were incapable of appreciating liberty and that "Patriotism is natural with a native—but it must be cultivated in a foreigner." [161]   *The North American Review,* in 1879, tried to arouse its readers to an understanding of

> . . . how far this element of German Socialism has already fixed its fangs in the most susceptible portion of our people, and threatens . . . to diffuse its poison into all classes sufficiently indigent and sufficiently ignorant to join the great caravan of the discontented.[162]

Most German immigrants, prior to 1855, were Democrats.   As early as 1800, in Pennsylvania, the party had issued campaign literature in German urging Germans to vote for Jefferson.   In 1824, the German vote of Ohio was sufficiently significant to warrant a special campaign document addressed to the German voters of Ohio urging them to support Jackson for President.[163]   The affiliation of the immigrant with the Democratic party was natural, and Democratic leaders were quick to cater to new groups from which new votes came.   The very name of the party sounded well to immigrant ears, whereas "Whig" made so little appeal that Whig leaders actually discussed changing the name of the party on this account.[164]   The Democratic press eulogized the foreign-born voter, denounced his nativist Whig enemies, and generally supported proposals to print official documents in the German language.[165]   The *New York*

[159] See Hemminghausen: *loc. cit.,* p. 7.
[160] See *The New York Times,* August 12, 1861.
[161] *Congressional Globe,* 33C 2S, *Appendix,* p. 95.   For further comments on German-American radicalism, see also C. F. Huch: "Revolutionsvereine und Anleihen," in *Mitteilungen des deutschen Pionier Vereins von Philadelphia* (1910), No. 181 pp. 1-19; and Philipp Rappaport: "Ueber die Arbeiterbewegung in Amerika," in *Die neue Zeit,* Vol. VII, pp. 63-69.
[162] *The North American Review,* Vol. CXXVIII, pp. 371-387 and 481-492.
[163] See Eugene H. Roseboom: "Ohio in the Presidential Election of 1824," in *The Ohio Archaeological and Historical Quarterly,* Vol. XXVI, pp. 157-223.
[164] See *Ohio State Journal,* February 12, 1853.
[165] See *Life of Charles Reemelin* (Cincinnati, 1892); *Cincinnati Enquirer,* December 10 and 20, 1846; and *Ohio Statesman,* October 7, 1850.

Weekly eulogized the immigrants as "good citizens, ay! *better* citizens, vastly better, than those of 'Native' growth who revile them," and went into ecstasies over "every vessel that brings two or three hundred healthy families to settle upon the wasting portions of our Maker's footstool . . . ." [166]

Although the task of winning their votes seemed hopeless, the Whigs did not altogether abandon the newcomers to their Democratic opponents. As early as 1832, Henry Clay sang the praises of "the honest, patient and industrious German," and "the gay, the versatile, the philosophic Frenchman," and called Kentucky the Ireland of America.[167] Some of the early German arrivals who became merchants and professional men were Whigs, but they were overwhelmingly outvoted by the Democrats after the political refugees arrived from Germany and led their countrymen *en masse* into the party of Jefferson and Jackson.

Whig campaign papers in the German language were started in the 1830's and 1840's in New York, Philadelphia, Buffalo, and elsewhere, but many hardly outlived one election. In 1840, the Whigs of Pennsylvania supported Joseph Miller's *Der westliche Demokrat* in Westmoreland County, Pennsylvania.[168] Grund, a German who jumped from party to party, depending on political rewards, wrote for Harrison in 1840 and ridiculed Van Buren as a "Hollander," after having praised the latter as a German in 1836. Wilhelm L. J. Kinderlen was an active Whig in the 1840's and edited the Whig *Alte und neue Welt* and the *Stadt-Post*.[169] In 1849, the Whigs of New York were accused of trying to buy the immigrant vote by offering extra work on canals and public works.[170] Apparently the first successful German Whig paper was not established in New York City until 1850, in spite of the city's large German population.[171] But all these efforts were of little or no avail, for the majority of German immigrants continued to believe that the Democratic party

---

[166] See *New York Weekly*, July 18, 1846.
[167] See *Cleveland Herald*, October 12, 1844.
[168] See Summerfield Baldwin: "The Pennsylvania Argus: A Chapter in Westmoreland County Journalism," in *Western Pennsylvania Historical Magazine*, Vol. XVII, p. 89.
[169] See *Der deutsche Pionier*, Vol. IX, p. 224.
[170] See *Albany Argus*, November 6, 1849.
[171] See *New York Tribune*, April 11, 1850. For other instances of German Whig papers in Detroit, New York, and Milwaukee, see *New York Tribune*, October 25, 1851; *Sandusky Commercial Register*, July 3, 1851, and Ernest Bruncken: "The Germans in Wisconsin Politics," in *Parkman Club Papers* (Milwaukee, Wisconsin, 1896), pp. 225-238.

was the only genuine friend of the worker and the emigrant, and it was not until the slavery controversy affected all parties in the middle fifties that they were seriously shaken in their political allegiance.

In the decade preceding the Civil War, the slavery controversy became so acute that old party lines were shattered. German-Americans were deeply concerned with the revival of the slavery controversy by Douglas' Kansas-Nebraska Act of 1854; by the sectional battle that broke out over pending homestead legislation, an issue in which every immigrant was likely to be interested; and by the growing domination of the Democratic party by its Southern, slave-holding wing. In the shifting party alignments preceding the election of 1860, politicians of both major parties reckoned with the importance of the German vote and, to a lesser degree, with that of other foreign-born groups; and in some critical states in the Northwest, the immigrant vote was probably decisive in 1860. As early as 1852, some German-American leaders were beginning to manifest their displeasure with the Democratic party because of the latter's close identification with the slave interests.[172] "To those who would fain draw us into the ranks of the pro-slavery party by showing us a beer mug," wrote a disgruntled German two years later, "we will reply that we would rather submit to annoying measures than betray the grand principles of liberty." [173] The majority of German immigrants were not radical abolitionists. They were not inclined to attack slavery where it existed, but they did oppose the extension of the institution into the territories. Had not Douglas reopened this issue by his Kansas-Nebraska Act the political affiliations of the Germans might have continued with the Democratic party for years to come.

The Kansas-Nebraska Act of 1854 immediately aroused the hostility of the majority of German newspapers.[174] Mass meetings of Germans assembled in Buffalo, Chicago, Louisville, Galveston, Boston, Cincinnati, and other cities to protest against the repeal of the Missouri Compromise and the opening of the public domain to slavery.[175] In Chicago, Germans hung a picture of Douglas on the

[172] See *New York Tribune*, July 13, 1852.
[173] Quoted in Ernest Bruncken: "The Political Activity of Wisconsin Germans, 1854-1860," in *Proceedings of the Wisconsin State Historical Society* (1901), p. 200.
[174] See James Ford Rhodes: *History of the United States* (New York, 1920), Vol. I, p. 495; and *Western Pennsylvania Historical Magazine*, Vol. VI, p. 39.
[175] See *Cincinnati Gazette*, April 6, 1854; and *The Boston Pilot*, June 24, 1854.

wall of a market house labeled "The Benedict Arnold of 1854," and marched down Michigan Avenue to burn the "Little Giant" in effigy.[176] The Republican party was born out of this turmoil over the Kansas-Nebraska Act, and at once there began a spirited campaign to win the German vote. Democrats, of course, made every effort to prevent the defection. The importance of the German-American vote was almost immediately apparent in local campaigns in Iowa, Wisconsin, and Ohio.

In the campaign of 1856, many leaders of the German group supported Fremont, the first Republican candidate for President, although the bulk of German voters were still badly divided. The new Republican party contained a strong Puritan element from New England and many Know-Nothings, who were the sworn enemies of the immigrant. Well might the German leadership hesitate about leading its followers into a political party in which these elements were likely to be influential in shaping the party program. It was on this account that local Republican conventions, especially in the Northwest, passed high-sounding resolutions to flatter the foreign-born and to reassure them that neither nativism nor Puritanism was likely to control the new organization. Nevertheless, many German voters hesitated to make the change, and German Catholics especially remained true to their Democratic allegiance. German Buchanan clubs were organized by the Democrats in 1856, and the Democratic platform was particularly forceful in its denunciation of Know-Nothingism.[177] Many Catholics remained Democrats because they regarded the German Forty-Eighters as their bitter enemies, and the Catholic *Seebote* denounced the Republican party as a party composed of "temperance men, abolitionists, haters of foreigners, sacrilegious despoilers of churches, Catholic-killers." [178] In 1856, the *New Yorker Staatszeitung* still regarded slavery with equanimity, and Dr. Walther, patriarch of the German Lutherans, approved it on Biblical authority.[179]

Nevertheless, the desertion of the German vote to the Republicans was well under way in 1856. Leaders like Münch, Hecker,

[176] See F. I. Herriott: "The Germans of Chicago and Stephan A. Douglas in 1854," in *Jahrbuch der deutsch-amerikanischen historischen Gesellschaft von Illinois*, Vol. XII, p. 399.
[177] *Boston Transcript*, December 31, 1856.
[178] Quoted in Bruncken: "The Political Activity of Wisconsin Germans, 1854-1860," in *Proceedings of the Wisconsin State Historical Society* (1901), p. 197.
[179] See *ibid.*, p. 208; and Schlüter: *op. cit.*, p. 212.

Hassaurek, Körner, Froebel, Solger, and Schurz spoke in many cities for the Republican ticket. Campaign songs for Fremont were composed in the German language, and mass meetings of German turner endorsed Fremont and "free speech, free press, free soil, free work, and a free Kansas." [180] Lincoln, campaigning for Fremont in the German center of Belleville, is reported to have said: "God bless the Dutch . . . . [They are] more enthusiastic for the cause of Freedom than all other nationalities." [181]

The movement to make the Germans Republicans went on apace through 1857 and 1858.[182] In 1858, as a concession to the large German element in Iowa, the prohibition law was amended to permit the manufacture and sale of beer, cider, and light wines.[183] Although many Wisconsin Germans remained loyal to the Democracy, the Republicans carried Milwaukee in 1858, an event that created nation-wide comment. Suddenly, in 1859, an incident occurred in Massachusetts that threatened to drive the Germans back into the waiting arms of the Democrats. Massachusetts, still in the grip of the Know-Nothing craze that had captured the state government in 1855, attached a clause to its constitution depriving all naturalized citizens of the right to vote or hold office until two years after their naturalization had been completed. The incident became a national issue, and the Democratic party made full use of it to its own advantage. Many Germans blamed the Massachusetts "two-year amendment" on the Republicans and their Know-Nothing allies, and were convinced that the episode proved that the new party could not be trusted. Protests poured in from the Germans of the Middle West, and leading Republicans, including Lincoln, were forced to reply.[184] Germans called on their leaders to issue a manifesto of protest, and a portion of the radical German press advised its readers to vote Democratic in 1860. According to the enraged Germans, the Massachusetts amendment put the Negro

[180] See J. B. McMaster: *A History of the People of the United States* (New York, 1914), Vol. VIII, p. 272; *Mitteilungen des Deutschen Pionier Vereins von Philadelphia* (1906), No. 2, pp. 27-29; and *New York Tribune*, September 2, 1856.
[181] Quoted in Albert J. Beveridge: *Abraham Lincoln* (Boston, 1928), Vol. II, pp. 410 and 427.
[182] See *Toledo Blade*, April 27, September 21, and October 8, 1857.
[183] See *Iowa Journal of History and Politics*, Vol. VI, p. 87.
[184] See F. L. Herriott: "The Premises and Significance of Abraham Lincoln's Letter to Theodore Canisius," in *Jahrbuch der deutsch-amerikanischen historischen Gesellschaft von Illinois,* Vol. XV, pp. 181-254; and "The Germans in the Gubernatorial Campaign of Iowa in 1859," in *ibid.,* Vol. XIV, p. 451. For another article on the same problem, see *ibid.,* Vol. XIII, pp. 202-308.

above the naturalized white man and created an inferior rank of American citizenship.

Fortunately for the Republican party, German leaders like Schurz, Hecker, and Stallo refused to act. But the Republican leadership promptly began to make amends. Chase and Seward reassured the Germans of their opposition to all discriminations against the foreign-born;[185] and Republican state conventions in the North, beginning with Ohio, adopted resolutions denouncing and repudiating the "two-year amendment." Governor Grimes of Iowa, the chairman of the Minnesota Republican committee, and many others joined in these repudiations; and Lincoln wrote to the *Illinois Staatsanzeiger* explaining his position.[186] In several states, Germans were promptly nominated for state offices by the Republicans.[187] In 1859, Lincoln bought control of the *Staatsanzeiger* in his home town, and kept the paper for more than a year.

At the Republican convention in Chicago in 1860, every effort was made to prove to the numerous German delegates that the nativists and Puritans were not in control of the party. Beer flowed freely. Schurz was chairman of the Wisconsin delegation and a member of the Committee on Resolutions. As such, he wrote what became known as "the Dutch plank," which had the unanimous support of the German delegates and was included in the Republican platform of 1860. It read as follows:

> The Republican party is opposed to any change by which the rights of citizenship heretofore accorded to immigrants from foreign lands shall be abridged or impaired, and is in favor of giving a full and sufficient protection to all classes of citizens, whether native or naturalized, both at home and abroad.

Here was the answer to Massachusetts Know-Nothingism, and a battery of German speakers set out to win the German vote for Lincoln! [188]

It is evident that the slavery question was not the sole issue with German-Americans in 1860. There was another question on which

[185] See *Ohio State Journal*, May 6, 1859.
[186] Donnal V. Smith: "The Influence of the Foreign-Born of the Northwest in the Election of 1860," in *The Mississippi Valley Historical Review*, Vol. XIX, pp. 192-204.
[187] See also *Cincinnati Enquirer*, March 11, June 4, and April 28, 1859; and *Ohio State Journal*, May 17, 1859.
[188] See Körner: *Memoirs*.

the German vote could be mobilized, namely, the issue of free home-steads for actual settlers. The South had become more and more alarmed by the influx of European immigrants into the North and West, who were still further upsetting the political and economic balance between North and South. The *Charleston Mercury* for March 17, 1860, lamented:

> Whole towns and counties are settled by these people, in sufficient numbers to control the elections. The Home-stead bill is a grand scheme to settle the Northwest and create new States . . . it is the most dangerous abolition bill which has ever been directly pressed in Congress . . . . "

In another issue, the same paper defined as the three great ob-jectives of the abolitionists: *"Free land,* or squatter sovereignty in our Territories, *land for the landless,* or the Homestead bill, and Northern plunder through Protective Tariffs—all looking to the consummation of a sectional despotism of the North over the South." [189]

The same point of view was expressed in the debates in Congress on the homestead legislation. Southerners generally opposed the bill.[190] Senators Thompson and Crittenden of Kentucky, Senator Wigfall of Texas, and Senators Davis and Brown of Mississippi called it class legislation for foreigners,[191] an election bribe to the Dutch and Irish, and a scheme to destroy the South.[192] Northern and Western Republican Senators and Congressmen, however, gen-erally supported the Homestead Bill. In 1854, it was defeated by Southern votes; in 1860 it was killed by the veto of President Buchanan, a Democrat under Southern influence. Thus the immi-grants, and particularly the Germans, were convinced that the Democratic party had become the voice of the Southern slavocracy and the Republican party the champion of free soil and free farms. "Vote Yourself a Farm" was probably a more powerful slogan than "Bleeding Kansas" or the slavery issue with many immigrant voters in 1860.

It is a mistake, however, to assume that all German voters became Republicans in 1860. The number who did was large, but many remained Democrats in 1860 and throughout the war. In New

[189] *Charleston Mercury,* March 19, 1859.
[190] See *Congressional Globe,* 31C, 1 and 2S, pp. 482-484, 522-524, and 583-585.
[191] See *ibid.,* 33C, 1S, Part 2, p. 944.
[192] See *ibid.,* pp. 1536-1539, 1635-1636, 1652, and 1799.

York, the *National Zeitung,* edited by German Democrats,[193] denounced Lincoln the "dictator" and his "Asiatic despotism." Prominent Germans like Christian Kribben of St. Louis, George Engelmann, Dr. Franz Brunk, Reemelin of Cincinnati, Grund, August Belmont, Horn, Hübschmann, Schöffler, Dr. Brühl, Rothe, Eickhoff, Louis Fieser, Jacob Reinhard of the *Westbote,* and Judge Lang of Tiffin remained Democrats.[194] The *Buffalo Volksfreund* denounced the "black Republicans" and accused Fremont of being a Jew from Alsace whose real name was *Freiberger.*[195] The New York *Journal* was a Copperhead paper, and the *Staatszeitung* supported Governor Seymour.[196]

In the campaign of 1860 itself, Körner, Schurz, Francis Lieber, Hassaurek, and Münch and Krekel of Missouri made many speeches for Lincoln, although their first preference was probably Seward. Oswald Ottendörfer resigned from the Democratic National Committee. Schurz was a member of the Republican National Committee and in charge of its foreign department. He engaged German, Scandinavian, and Dutch campaign orators, and he himself traveled 21,000 miles to address his fellow countrymen in the leading German centers of Ohio, Illinois, Indiana, Pennsylvania, and Wisconsin. Two of his speeches—the one on Douglas' principles, the other an analysis of the slaveholder's philosophy—were given wide circulation. So were copies of the proposed Republican Homestead Bill, printed in several foreign languages.[197] Two careful students of the election of 1860 have concluded that the foreign-born vote in the Northwest was decisive for the Republicans and that a change of one vote in twenty would have given these states to Douglas. In the seven Northwestern states, with over 283,000 foreign-born voters, Lincoln's majority over Douglas was just under 150,000. In 1861, when the Republicans took charge of the government at Washington, the German element was remembered in the distribution of patronage as never before.[198]

According to the actuary of the United States Sanitary Commis-

[193] See *The New York Times,* September 3, 1861.
[194] See *Deutsch-Amerikanisches Magazin,* Vol. I, p. 28. See also Körner: *Das deutsche Element in den Vereinigten Staaten von Nordamerika,* pp. 287-289 and 347.
[195] See *Deutsch-Amerikanische Geschichtsblätter* (January 1904), p. 31.
[196] See *New York Tribune,* July 23, 1863.
[197] See Schafer: *loc. cit.* and *op. cit.*
[198] For the influence of the foreign-born vote in the election of Lincoln, see Smith: *loc. cit.;* and W. E. Dodd: "The Fight for the Northwest, 1860," in *The American Historical Review,* Vol. XVI, pp. 774-788.

sion, Benjamin A. Gould, the total number of persons born in Germany who served as volunteers in the Civil War was 176,817. These figures do not include Germans from the border states or those of German stock who came from Switzerland, Austria, and some of the other areas bordering on the German states, nor do they deal with second-generation German-Americans. Some estimates have placed the number of German-born in the Union Army as high as 216,000.[199] Either figure shows that German enlistment exceeded the proportion that might have been expected from this group.

Many recent immigrants had no family ties to keep them at home, and there was a decided preponderance of males of military age among the German immigration. Bounties made volunteering financially attractive. Immigrants were met upon their arrival by recruiting officers and induced to sign up for military service, and some were actually recruited abroad. Senator Wilson of Massachusetts boasted that nearly 1,000 Germans had been imported for service in four Massachusetts regiments, and the Irish immigration nearly doubled in the second year of the war.[200] By Federal act at the close of the war, all foreign soldiers, honorably discharged, were given full rights of American citizenship without the necessity of first papers and the usual delays. After all due allowance is made for artificial stimuli of this kind, the fact remains that the record of the foreign-born in the war was a striking manifestation of national unity and a gratifying reply to those nativists who had questioned the loyalty of "adopted citizens" in the decade before the war.[201] Many Germans had received military training abroad, and the United States became known as a kind of "overseas orphanage for cracked up German officers." Trained Germans were especially helpful in the artillery and engineering corps, and in making military maps.

It has been estimated that 6,000 Germans in New York, 4,000 in Pennsylvania, and similar proportions elsewhere responded to Lincoln's first call for volunteers. Turner regiments, such as the 9th Ohio Volunteers and the 20th New York, under Colonel Max

---

[199] See Wilhelm Kaufmann: *Die Deutschen im Amerikanischen Bürgerkriege* (Munich, Germany, 1911); and Faust: *op. cit.*, Vol. II, p. 523. The latter accepts the lower figure.

[200] Fred A. Shannon: *The Organization and Administration of the Union Army, 1861-1865* (Cleveland, Ohio, 1928), Vol. II, p. 78.

[201] See *The New York Times*, June 29, 1861.

Weber, were among the first to respond.[202]   Six months after the declaration of war, 6,000 Illinois Germans were in the Army, and as late as 1864, it was still possible to recruit a German regiment in and around Chicago.   The 32nd Indiana Infantry contained a large proportion of Germans.[203]   Two German companies were ready to leave Boston by May, 1861.[204]   The 107th Infantry, which served in the army of General Sigel, was made up of Germans many of whom could not speak English.[205]   In Wisconsin, the 9th regiment was German, the 15th Scandinavian, and the 17th Irish.   German ladies' aid societies presented flags to their departing volunteers, and German societies gave numerous concerts and entertainments to raise funds for the troops.[206]

In some of the rural counties of Wisconsin, the Germans volunteered very slowly, remaining antiwar Democrats.   There were anti-draft riots among the Germans of Ozaukee and Washington Counties, and Milwaukee County voted for McClellan in 1864.   As the war progressed, however, German farmers were gradually educated to an appreciation of its significance, primarily by the Forty-Eighters among them, who struggled vigorously against the inertia of the rank and file, which was not especially interested in either nationalism or abolitionism.[207]   German slackers in Milwaukee occasionally made trouble for the authorities.[208]   Among the German sectarians in the East, it was necessary to permit commutation of military service for financial payments or for service as teamsters and non-combatants.[209]

The number of Germans in the Confederacy has been estimated at approximately 70,000, of whom about 15,000 lived in New Orleans. One of the Louisiana Confederate regiments had six German companies and was commanded by Colonel Reichard. Georgia had a German artillery company commanded by Captain

[202] See *New York Tribune*, June 14, 1861; and Wittke: "The Ninth Ohio Volunteers," in *Ohio Archaeological and Historical Quarterly* (April, 1926), pp. 1-18.
[203] See Fritsch: *op. cit.*
[204] See *The Boston Pilot*, May 18, 1861.
[205] See Louis C. Aldrich: *History of Erie County, Ohio* (Syracuse, New York, 1889), p. 178.
[206] See *New York Tribune*, August 13, 1861.
[207] See Joseph Schafer: "Four Wisconsin Counties," in *Wisconsin Domesday Book, General Studies* (Madison, Wisconsin, 1927), pp. 158-168.
[208] See Shannon: *op. cit.*, Vol. II, p. 235.
[209] For the special problem raised for the Confederates by the Dunkards and Mennonites of the Valley of Virginia, see Edward N. Wright: *Conscientious Objectors in the Civil War* (Philadelphia, 1931), p. 167.

Steigen.[210]   The German militia company of Texas was dissolved
in 1861 because it would not give up its Union flag.   Some of the
Texas Germans escaped to Missouri and Mexico, while others joined
the Confederate Army.   Several companies of Germans were recruited for the Confederacy in Richmond, Virginia, and there was a
German battalion in Galveston.[211]   Wagener of Charleston became
a colonel of artillery in the Confederacy, and Fort Wagener, in
Charleston harbor, was named for him.   Karl Gustav Memminger,
who was brought to Charleston from Würtemberg at the age of
three, was Secretary of the Treasury under Jefferson Davis.

It is impossible to discuss in detail the service of the various
German regiments and companies or even the experiences of the
extraordinarily large number of Germans who were officers in the
Union Army.   But it is important to consider several of the major
campaigns in which they participated, if for no other reason than to
illustrate the controversies that arose over the value of these "foreign
legions."

General Ludwig Blenker's brigade, composed of New York and
Pennsylvania troops—largely Germans—saw service in the first
Battle of Bull Run, and came out intact in this battle of two
"armed mobs."   Blenker loved pomp and display, bands and showy
uniforms.   His division of 10,000 was attached to McClellan's army
and became the subject of a violent controversy which it is difficult
to resolve even now.   All the officers were German, and commands
were given in German.   Some of the officers were able; others were
mere adventurers or members of a bogus nobility.   Blenker's staff
loved champagne, and beer could be legally sold to his division.
Outsiders came in and were accused of clearing from $6,000 to $8,000
a month on the sale of beer to the soldiers.   There is no evidence
that Blenker was dishonest, and he died poor on the farm to
which he had retired, in 1863.   McClellan praised Blenker and his
two German adjutants, but like most West Pointers, thought poorly
of German officers in general.   The division was shot through with
jealousy, fed by an insatiate desire of some of the German career
officers for rapid promotion.[212]

[210] See Kaufmann: *op. cit.*, p. 140.
[211] See *Der deutsche Pionier*, Vol. XVII, pp. 45-46.
[212] At a mass meeting of Germans in New York after Bull Run, Kapp seriously
proposed a regiment armed with scythes, such as had been used in the Polish
Revolution.   (See *New York Tribune*, July 27, 1861.)   For more favorable views
of Blenker and Sigel, see *The New York Tribune*, July 23, 1861; *The New York*

THE GERMANS

The role of the Germans in saving Missouri for the Union, by tipping the balance in the struggle between Unionists and Secessionists which was going on in that state in 1861, is generally conceded to have been a decisive one. The St. Louis arsenal was held by pro-Southern troops, and the Governor was opposed to the Lincoln administration. The turner of St. Louis and others of the excellent group of Germans who inhabited the city and its neighboring counties quickly raised four German infantry regiments, an artillery regiment, and a German home guard of 3,000 under Colonel H. Almstedt. In May 1861, General Lyon, with 200 United States regulars and the German regiments, seized control of the Confederate Camp Jackson; and in the ten-month campaign in Missouri that followed, many Germans under General Franz Sigel distinguished themselves in the battle to hold Missouri in the Union, although many also went home after their three-month enlistment period had expired. The controversy over Sigel's tactics in Missouri need not concern us here.[213]

At Shiloh, the Germans under Colonel August Willich fought with courage and distinction. In the Penninsular campaign, Blenker cut rather a sorry figure, although most of the German troops made a good record. Schurz and Sigel fought well at the second Battle of Bull Run. Chancellorsville led to a heated controversy over the merits of the German troops, particularly concerning Schurz's qualifications as a general. The 11th Corps contained many German troops, and Schurz and Steinwehr commanded two of its three divisions. Sigel had been superseded by General Howard, who was very unpopular with the Germans. Schurz's division was defeated at Chancellorsville and driven back. It fought against

Herald, July 12, 1861; and Gustav Struve: *Diesseits und Jenseits des Ozeans, Zwanglose Hefte zur Vermittelung der Beziehungen zwischen Amerika und Deutschland* (Coburg, Germany, 1863-1864), pp. 50-56.

[213] See Kaufmann: *op. cit.,* pp. 213-236. West Pointers also criticized Sigel for his delays. *The New York Times* for February 21, 1863, gave full credit to the Germans for saving Missouri. See also W. E. and O. D. Smith (editors): *Colonel A. W. Gilbert, Citizen-Soldier of Cincinnati* (Cincinnati, 1934), pp. 53, 69, and 76; and Daniel Hertle: *Die Deutschen in Nordamerika und der Freiheitskampf in Missouri* (Chicago, 1865). A Confederate speaker told a crowd in 1861 that

> . . . Abraham Lincoln had given the State of Missouri to them [Germans] if they would send enough lop-eared Dutch to conquer the state, and that . . . he saw them, in the presence of the mothers, run bayonets through their infant children and hoist them up and carry them around on their bayonets.

(Raymond D. Thomas, "Study in Missouri Politics, 1840-1870," in *Missouri Historical Review,* Vol. XXI, p. 450.)

heavy odds, was left in an exposed and unsupported position, and was enveloped by a flanking movement carried out by that master strategist Stonewall Jackson. However, much of the blame for the loss of the battle was immediately put upon the "cowardice" of the Germans and the "foreign contingent." General Hooker said the Germans "ran like buffaloes"; Schurz demanded a court martial investigation; the nativist press exploited the controversy to the fullest; and Germans met in New York and elsewhere in indignation to protest against these attacks on their countrymen. Horace Greeley demanded that the German regiments be dissolved.[214]

Schurz was essentially a political general, of which there were many in the Union Army, and his military record was not entirely successful. He had difficulty in coöperating with his superiors. At Gettysburg, the 11th Corps fought well but again had to retreat, and once more "the Foreign Legion" came in for newspaper attacks as "cowardly Dutchmen" and "poltroons." [215] Schurz eventually was shelved by the War Department and put in charge of a training station for recruits, although his troops, after some reorganization, were attached to the army of Rosecrans and fought well in other engagements.[216]

German detachments served well in the many battles around Chattanooga, particularly the 9th Ohio and the 32nd Indiana divisions. Given another command in 1864, Sigel was surprised and defeated at the Battle of New Market in the Shenandoah Valley, although he later redeemed himself in holding up Early's advance on Washington. There were many Germans in Sherman's march through Georgia, although long before the end of the war, the old German formations had been dissolved and scattered, and it is therefore almost impossible to trace their later records.

Kaufmann lists about 500 German officers who served in the Civil War, which included only those born abroad and not German-Americans of the second generation.[217] Perhaps the most distinguished in this long list besides Schurz, Sigel, and Blenker are: Peter J. Osterhaus, a Forty-Eighter of Belleville, Illinois; Adolf V. Steinwehr, a professional soldier who had served in the Mexican

---

[214] See Kaufmann: *op. cit.*, p. 368.
[215] See *The New York Times*, May 5 and 11, and June 4, 1863; and *New York Tribune*, November 19, 1863.
[216] See Fuess: *op. cit.*, p. 108 *et seq.* It is perhaps significant that, after the war, Schurz seldom used the title "General."
[217] See Kaufmann: *op. cit.*, pp. 443-575.

War; August Willich, a radical Forty-Eighter and distinguished soldier; Gottfried Weitzel, a graduate of West Point; August B. Kautz of Baden, Germany, who served in the Mexican War at the age of 18; Gustav Struve; Friedrich Hecker, a leader of the insurrection in Baden; Alexander Schimmelpfennig, who was with Kossuth in Hungary; and Max Weber, Julius Stahl, Hubert Dilger, and August Moor of Leipzig. Dr. Abraham Jacobi, a distinguished physician, served as a staff doctor. The list of Germans who served as officers in the Confederate Army includes, besides General Wagener, W. K. Bachmann, Heros von Borcke, I. Buchholz, August Büchel, W. T. Eichholz, B. G. Eschelmann, and August Reichard. Most of these came from South Carolina, but Eichholz and Eschelmann represented the Texas Germans, and Reichard led the volunteers from New Orleans.[218]

In the years following the Civil War, German-Americans divided on public issues like every other group in the United States, and it is unnecessary to discuss their political alignments in detail, save on a few specific issues. Thus in 1863, many Germans were disgusted with Lincoln's conservative course in the war, and a national convention of radical Germans was held in Cleveland in which 14 states were represented. The convention advocated a radical and severe program of reconstruction for the South, and suggested Fremont for President.[219] By 1868, many Germans had returned to the Democratic fold (others had never left it), and supported Seymour for President in preference to Grant.[220] The *New Yorker Staatszeitung* supported the Democratic nominee, as did the Cincinnati *Volksfreund,* the Hamilton *National Zeitung,* and the Columbus *Westbote.* Seymour for President Clubs were formed by the Germans in New York, Philadelphia, Fort Wayne, Iowa, and elsewhere.[221] Schurz stumped among the Germans for Grant.

In 1872, Schurz and other German liberals, disgusted with radical reconstruction, the high protective tariff, and the scandals of Grant's first administration, played a prominent part in launching the Liberal Republican revolt of that year. Schurz presided at the Cincinnati convention, which ended in the unfortunate choice of Horace

[218] For Faust's account of the Germans in the Civil War, see *The German Element,* Vol. II, pp. 522-572.
[219] See *New York Tribune,* October 29, 1863.
[220] See *New York World,* September 3, October 6 and 30, and November 3, 1868.
[221] See *Cincinnati Enquirer,* July 22 and 25, September 5 and 21, and August 5, 13, and 15, 1868.

Greeley for President.   Later, the Democrats also endorsed Greeley
for want of any better alternative.   In some states, such as Wisconsin, the Germans resented Grant's alleged failure to appreciate
Schurz's qualities and were angered by the charges that arms from
United States arsenals had been sold secretly to France during the
Franco-German War of 1870-1871.[222]   Many Germans advocated
civil service reform and were eager to end radical reconstruction in
the South.   There was therefore abundant reason to hope that a
large proportion of German-Americans would vote the Democratic
ticket in 1872.

A great effort was made in 1872 to win the German vote for the
Liberal Republicans.   Schurz addressed large German meetings,
and the Republicans were so frightened that they called a special
German National Convention in October to endorse Grant.   But
German support of Greeley lagged decidedly.   Even Schurz expressed his disgust with the Liberal Republican nomination, and
leaders like Körner and Stallo did not endorse Greeley until late in
the campaign.   Greeley was a "Puritan" and a "teetotaller," and he
represented a certain Yankee type which was most unpopular with
the German element.   *The New York Times,* in an editorial on
the German vote, commented:

> . . . if any German chose to smoke a pipe or drink a glass
> of lager, he was denounced by Mr. Greeley as a swill-tub,
> a sot, a fool, etc.   He would close every 'garden' in the city,
> and make lager-beer drinking a penal offence.[223]

Besides being an unfair statement of Greeley's position, the comment, curiously enough, came from a paper which in the 1850's and
1860's had been militantly for temperance reform.   But Greeley
himself realized the situation and wrote to Schurz: "Of course the
most of the Germans dislike me, not so much that I am a Protection-
ist as that I am a Total Abstinence Man." [224]

The Republicans sent campaign material in German to all the
leading German-language papers; and Thomas Nast, the celebrated

[222] See Hermann J. Deutsch: "Disintegrating Forces in Wisconsin Politics of the
Early Seventies," in *Wisconsin Magazine of History,* Vol. XV, pp. 391-411.   See
also *ibid.,* pp. 168-181 and 282-296.

[223] *The New York Times,* July 14, 1872.

[224] Quoted in E. D. Ross: *The Liberal Republican Movement* (New York, 1919),
p. 166.   See also T. S. Barclay: "The Liberal Republican Movement in Missouri,"
in *Missouri Historical Review,* Vol. XX, pp. 3-78, 262-332, 406-437, and 515-564;
and Vol. XXI, pp. 59-108.

cartoonist of *Harper's Weekly,* himself of German birth, pictured Schurz sitting at a piano—a favorite way of cartooning Schurz, because of his musical talents—playing *Mein Herz ist am Rhein,* and Uncle Sam saying to him: "Look here, stranger, there is no law in this country to compel you to stay." [225] Although German Greeley for President Clubs were organized [226] and some German papers supported the editor of the *Tribune,* German leaders found it an almost superhuman task to try to stir up enthusiasm among their countrymen for a candidate whom Judge Stallo called a "brilliant chatterbox" and whose views were so "narrow" that they aroused the distrust of the German voters.[227] The *New Yorker Staatszeitung* called Greeley a fanatic.[228] Many leading German papers endorsed Grant, while others remained ominously noncommittal.[229] Some spoke of Schurz in most uncomplimentary terms,[230] and Hassaurek was described as "the mercenary Greeleyite." [231]

The leaders of civil service reform included many Germans; indeed, for a time Schurz was president of the National Civil Service Reform Association. In several campaigns, the German leadership was able to arouse German support for this reform. Schurz himself, the first German to be a member of the President's Cabinet, as Secretary of the Interior under Hayes, made his department "a demonstration station" for civil service. Blaine denounced him for introducing "Prussian methods" into American democracy, but historians are agreed that Schurz rendered his greatest service to the nation during this period of his career. In 1884, he supported Cleveland. He rejected Bryan in 1896 because of the silver issue, but supported him in 1900 on the issue of anti-imperialism. His independent voting was typical of many of his countrymen and contributed much to the success of the Independent movement in American politics after the Civil War.

On the sound money question, too, the Germans usually opposed the greenback and silver craze of the generation before 1900, although Reemelin and Hassaurek were prominent exceptions, favoring some kind of a devalued dollar after 1875. That year, in the

[225] Quoted in Fuess: *op. cit.,* p. 182.
[226] See *New York Tribune,* July 24 and August 8, 1872.
[227] See *New York Tribune,* September 18, 1872.
[228] See *ibid.,* July 13, 1872.
[229] See *ibid.,* July 25, 15, and 13, 1872. Practically every issue of the *Tribune* throughout the campaign was concerned with the German voter.
[230] See *The New York Times,* July 2 and 10, 1872.
[231] See *ibid.,* October 1, 1872.

critical gubernatorial contest in Ohio between Hayes and William Allen over "rag money," Schurz was brought back posthaste from Europe near the close of the campaign to address the Germans of the state on sound money, and no less critical an observer than Charles Francis Adams, Jr., gave Schurz the credit for the narrow majority by which Hayes won the contest.[232]

In later campaigns, the German vote was occasionally aroused to action when state legislation threatened German parochial schools, as in Wisconsin and Illinois in 1889 and 1890;[233] and as the prohibition and woman suffrage movement developed, the opposition of the vast majority of German-Americans to these reforms could regularly be counted upon. To German-Americans, both reforms smacked of Puritanism and feminism, and prohibition in particular was a piece of sumptuary legislation that violated every concept of personal liberty and tolerance. The National German-American Alliance, chartered in 1899 by act of Congress and dedicated to high cultural aims, became more and more absorbed in the battle against prohibition and blue laws, to the neglect of its other aims. Criticism of the Germans for making major issues of beer and wine was often the loudest from German leaders themselves. The intellectual leadership and idealism of the earlier German immigration was rapidly disintegrating. At many German festivals, infested with American politicians, who were treated in the most obsequious fashion, the bar was far more attractive than the program of speeches and music. George Sylvester Viereck, in his *American Monthly* for July, 1924, expressed a thought of which many German-Americans approved, when he wrote: "The German-American vote has floated too long on an ocean of beer." [234]

The process of amalgamation of various immigrant stocks into "the American citizen," whom Seward had so eloquently described in 1860,[235] went on rapidly among the German element in the years following the Civil War, especially in the Middle West. Leaders like Schurz urged the Germans to give up their clannishness and living in segregated city districts, and advised them against clinging too strongly to the customs of the fatherland.[236] Milwaukee, Schurz

---

[232] See F. W. Clonts: "The Political Campaign of 1875 in Ohio," in *The Ohio Archaeological and Historical Quarterly*, Vol. XXXI, pp. 38-95.
[233] See *Ohio State Journal*, August 29, September 3, and November 6, 1892.
[234] Quoted in Kloss: *op. cit.*, p. 302.
[235] See *Minnesota History Bulletin*, Vol. VIII, pp. 153-154.
[236] See Easum: *op. cit.*, pp. 113-114.

thought, suffered "from the presence of too many Germans." In noble words, he admonished his fellow Germans not to forget that

> . . . we as Germans are not called upon here to form a separate nationality but rather to contribute to the American nationality the strongest there is in us, and in place of our weakness to substitute the strength wherein our fellow-Americans excel us, and blend it with our wisdom. We should never forget that in the political life of this republic, we as Germans have no peculiar interests, but that the universal well-being is ours also.[237]

Resolutions of alarm drafted by some German groups with reference to the rapid assimilation of the German element in the United States were numerous before the World War and indicate how thoroughly the German was being Americanized.[238] As early as 1877, Otto Dresel had denounced "German nativism" as vigorously as American nativism, and had declared that complete absorption of the German element was "a logical, physical, psychological and historical necessity." [239]

The normal fusion process was rudely shaken by the outbreak of the World War. For the German element in the United States, this catastrophe initiated a period of emotional crisis, conflicts of loyalties, misunderstandings, persecutions, and tragedy which few of their fellow citizens appreciated. Everything German in the United States was presently regarded as part of an organized propaganda of the German government to make the United States an appendage of the Kaiser's empire. Hyphen hunting became a popular pastime among American superpatriots; and men and women whose integrity and fundamental decency had never before been questioned, and who had learned to think of no other home except the one they had found here, were now obliged to defend their good names before fellow citizens with whom they had hitherto lived in a spirit of good neighborliness.

That the German element was "pro-German" during the first three years of the war was to be expected, and during the period of American neutrality, it was as legal and reasonable to be "pro-

---

[237] See *ibid.*, p. 95.

[238] For resolutions of the Ohio Alliance urging the support of *Turnvereine,* German newspapers, and the German language, as a means of counteracting tendencies in the younger people to ignore these elements of German culture, see, for example, *Mitteilungen des deutsch-amerikanischen Nationalbundes* (Philadelphia), November, 1913, p. 29.

[239] *Der deutsche Pionier,* Vol. IX, pp. 132-140. See also *ibid.*, Vol. I, p. 247.

German" as it was to be "pro-Ally." That many German-Americans, in their ardor to defend their blood brothers against slander—especially in view of a widespread tendency to canonize the Allies in the United States—occasionally overstepped the bounds of discretion and common sense is also quite understandable. The German element carried on a lively campaign to raise relief funds for their suffering brethren abroad and to counteract what they considered the poisonous, pro-Ally propaganda of most of the American press. When the United States finally entered the war on the side of the Allies in 1917, the hour of trial for the German-Americans had struck. That they met the crisis with honor and devotion to their adopted country many in high places have abundantly testified.

Unfortunately, the war precipitated a violent, hysterical, and concerted movement to eradicate everything German from American civilization. It was led by a minority of extremists, but a large number of Americans approved of the "patriotic drive against Teutonism and the Huns." Mob rule broke out. German music, literature, church services, singing societies, and newspapers, as well as the teaching of German and everything that had even the faintest connection with Germany—including Bismarck herring and sauerkraut—came under the ban. The National German-American Alliance was voluntarily dissolved after a prolonged Congressional investigation which proved nothing except that the organization had been pro-German before 1917 and had spent most of its energy fighting the inroads of prohibition upon personal liberty. Many German-Americans had opposed it from the beginning, especially Catholic and Lutheran groups, some of the turner, and radicals and liberals of the Schurz variety. Suddenly the brewers were tainted with pro-Germanism; German newspapers had to beat a hasty editorial retreat, and scores were forced to suspend publication. German was expelled from the schools and German music from the concert programs. To many a German-American, it seemed as though the shining cultural monument of the Forty-Eighters had been destroyed forever.

Shortly after the close of the war, however, when the disillusionment of the American people over the results of the war became apparent, a reaction set in. The German element regained its self-respect and the respect of its fellow Americans in a comparatively short time. Unfortunately, the triumph of Hitler in more recent years again threatens the life of the German element in the

United States with disruption from within and with misunderstanding and suspicion from without. The German element is bitterly divided on the issue of Nazism. In a population as complex as that of the United States, any major event occurring abroad that affects one of the major groups in the American population acts like a cold draft of air suddenly blown across a molten mass. The fusion process is retarded, and crystallization begins again along the old lines of fracture.[240]

[240] For the story of the World War years, see Wittke: *German-Americans and the World War*. See also Clifton J. Child: "German-American Attempts to Prevent the Exportation of Munitions of War, 1914-1915," in *The Mississippi Valley Historical Review* (December, 1938), Vol. XXV, pp. 351-369.

10

The Scandinavians

THE TOTAL Scandinavian influx to the United States from 1820 to the outbreak of the World War has been estimated at over 2,000,000. By 1900, there were over 1,000,000 Scandinavians of foreign birth in the United States. Their children numbered nearly 2,000,000, thus making a total of over 3,000,000 of Scandinavian blood in America. The Scandinavian immigration did not really begin with any appreciable volume until the 1840's. By the close of the Civil War, it exceeded 10,000 a year for the first time. It dropped again in the 1870's because of the economic depression, but reached its highest point in the 1880's, with the climax in 1882, when 105,326 entered the country.[1] As there were only 18,000 of Scandinavian birth in the United States by 1850, the Scandinavian influx is therefore largely a feature of the post-Civil War period. The Danes were the last to come, and the Danish immigration did not reach 5,000 a year until 1880. The Swedes began coming in appreciable numbers after 1852, reaching the 5,000 mark in 1868. The Norwegians began coming in the 1840's, and Norwegian immigration reached 5,000 for the first time in 1866. The term *Scandinavian* is used to include Swedes, Norwegians, and Danes, but each group is proud of its individuality and eager to preserve it. Nevertheless, for practical purposes, these three groups may be considered as one in this discussion of several phases of Scandinavian immigration.

The Scandinavian immigrant to the United States has been the viking of the Western prairie country. As his forefathers in ancient days overran Britain and the plains of Normandy, so the modern Scandinavian-American has penetrated, peacefully but thoroughly, the prairies of the Mississippi Valley. The story of the coming of

---

[1] See G. T. Flom: "The Scandinavian Factor in the American Population," in *Iowa Journal of History and Politics*, Vol. III, pp. 57-91; and K. C. Babcock: *The Scandinavian Element in the United States* (Urbana, Illinois, 1914).

the Swedes, Norwegians, and Danes is largely the story of the conquest of the rolling prairie—a mounting procession of covered
wagons headed West, laden with human beings who broke the
prairie, lived in dugouts, sod shanties, and then log cabins, which
seemed palatial by comparison with their first abode. With the
help of oxen, they broke the prairie and prepared to build a permanent home. In spite of droughts and storms and grasshopper
plagues, they remained true to their purpose—namely, to carve a
homestead out of the undeveloped West. Theirs is the story of
hardy men and strong women, deeply religious, determined to succeed, not brilliant or spectacular, but the salt of the earth.

In time, little clusters of settlements arose. The pioneer Lutheran Church and preacher appeared in Scandinavian-American communities, until finally the railroad put an end to pioneer life. For
the most part, the Scandinavian-American saga is the tale of Scandinavian peasants wrestling with nature and battling with poverty.
They had little time to cultivate the arts or the intellectual life.
For many years, the only intellectual interest of the pioneer was to
listen to a good sermon by a pastor expounding the Gospel according
to Martin Luther. As the Reverend Gustaf Unonius wrote:

> I do not expect to "cut gold with jackknives." I am pre-
> pared to earn my daily bread by the sweat of my brow
> . . . . For this I am prepared, but I hope to be free and
> independent and to possess my own home, if ever so modest,
> and the happiness it confers.[2]

Most of the Scandinavian immigrants were recruited from the
lower classes, and their primary reason for coming to America was
to improve their holdings in the goods of this world. Religious
persecution and oppression had little to do with the Scandinavian
exodus, although in some cases religious controversies did contribute to the decision to emigrate. In the period from 1850 to the
1880's, Scandinavia experienced a succession of poor harvests and
hard times. The growing season was short; taxes were burdensome
and wages low, and there were numerous periods of unemployment.
Families were large and money was hard to get. The economic
crisis of 1864 and 1865 in Sweden was followed by three years of
crop failures, and "The Great Famine" remained a vivid memory in
Sweden for many years. It led to an exodus of thousands of bank-

---

[2] Quoted in Filip A. Forsbeck: "New Upsala: The First Swedish Settlement
in Wisconsin," in *Wisconsin Magazine of History*, Vol. XIX, pp. 3-31.

rupt landowners and agricultural laborers.[3] Many were dissatisfied, and fell an easy prey to the alluring advertisements of the
bounties of America which emigrant agents and steamship companies spread over the Scandinavian countryside. The "America
fever" became contagious, and was constantly fed by "America
letters" and the tales of immigrants who returned to their homes—
often at the expense of steamship companies eager for more passengers—to tell the story of their progress in the new land.

The Scandinavian countries were largely agricultural, but most of
the people had but small farms, which were often very unproductive
because of the stony soil. Only freeholders, who owned their farms,
were in fairly good circumstances. The cotter, who rented or leased
his land, found life hard; he was obliged to pay rent in kind or to
donate a certain number of days of labor to the owner for his farm.
There were changes in farming methods as the remnants of feudalism disappeared, and in a time of social and agricultural change,
the small farmer found it difficult to readjust himself to new conditions. Much of the land was poor. Nearly 60 per cent of Norway
is mountainous and over 40 per cent of Swedish soil was unproductive. In these respects, the Danes were in a more advantageous
position; consequently, Danish emigration was always relatively
smaller. The law of primogeniture still prevailed, forcing many a
younger son to seek his living elsewhere.

Political disturbances were not significant causes of emigration
from Scandinavia. There were no revolutions in 1830 and 1848 in
the Scandinavian nations. Government was fairly democratic and
illiteracy was practically nonexistent in Norway, Sweden, and Denmark. Military service was a burden that some wished to escape,
but this too was not significant. There were religious difficulties
with the State Lutheran Church, and in Sweden particularly, dissenting sects suffered from the intolerance and petty persecution of
the church hierarchy, so that many were eager to escape to a new
land where the congregational form of government and complete
religious toleration might supplant the burdens of a State Church.
In the 1880's, there was also friction among the workers as the industrial revolution progressed, and attempts by the government to
suppress the rising Social Democratic movement led many to emi-

---

[3] See Florence E. Janson: *The Background of Swedish Immigration, 1840-1930*
(Philadelphia, 1931), Ch. VII. For another contact between the United States
and Sweden, see also Adolph B. Benson: "Cultural Relations Between Sweden and
America to 1830," in *The Germanic Review*, Vol. XIII, pp. 83-101.

grate. But after all due allowance has been made for these contributing factors, the real explanation for the heavy Scandinavian exodus to America in the nineteenth century may be found simply by comparing the size of the cotter's plot with the 160-acre homestead that awaited the ambitious farmer in the American West. It was for this reason primarily that the Scandinavian conquest of the American Northwest was so rapidly accomplished. Steamship propaganda and the efforts of land and railroad agents did their part to insure the tide of immigration against drying up at the source.[4] All the leading steamship agencies advertised extensively in the Scandinavian press.

THE SWEDES

By the middle of the nineteenth century, American newspapers carried accounts of Swedish immigrant groups arriving in New York and marching in a body with their trunks, often in military formation and carrying Swedish and American flags, to the railroad depot of the line which was to carry them Westward into the promised land.[5] Swedish immigrants frequently came to the United States in ships carrying cargoes of iron to New York. These provided cheap passage for as little as from $12 to $15 per person, provided the immigrant was willing to furnish his own food. From seven to eight weeks was considered good time for the trip from Sweden to New York. At New York, the ship was likely to be met by the Reverend O. G. Hedström of the Bethel Ship Mission, who directed the new arrivals Westward.

The route followed usually proceeded by rail or by way of the Erie Canal to Buffalo and then by lake boat or overland into the prairie country of the Upper Mississippi Valley. The whole trip frequently required from four to five months, a long time for which to furnish provisions, so that the poorest of the Swedes either arrived destitute at the end of their journey or found it necessary to work en route as farmhands or with pick and shovel in railroad construction gangs. The Yellowstone division of the Northern Pacific, for example, was built largely by German and Scandinavian laborers,

---

[4] See G. M. Stephenson: *A History of American Immigration* (Boston, 1926), Ch. III.

[5] See *New York Tribune,* July 4, 1851; *Boston Transcript,* August 3 and 14, 1854; and January 31, 1870; and *The Boston Pilot,* September 4, 1852.

who then settled along the route. Wages were seldom more than $1.50 a day, and sometimes less.[6]

The experiences of Hans Mattson, who became a distinguished leader of the Swedish element in Minnesota, were more or less typical. He proceeded by rail to Buffalo, by lake boat to Toledo, and thence again by rail to Chicago. From there, he went by canal boat to LaSalle and then by farmers' wagons to Galesburg, Illinois. Here he worked in the neighborhood with pick and shovel for $.75 to $1 a day on a railroad gang. Here, too, he had his first experience with the ague or "shakes," which affected so many of the first prairie farmers. It was only after two years that Mattson was able to move on and settle in Minnesota. In later years, he wrote:

> Looking back to those days, I see the little cabin, often with a sod roof, single room used for domestic purposes, sometimes crowded almost to suffocation by hospitable entertainments to newcomers; or the poor immigrant on the levee at Red Wing, just landed from a steamer, in his short jacket and other outlandish costume, perhaps seated on a wooden box, with his wife and a large group of children around him, and wondering how he shall be able to raise enough means to get himself ten or twenty miles into the country, or to redeem the bedding and other household goods which he has perchance left in Milwaukee as a pledge for his railroad and steamboat ticket . . . . Poor, bewildered, ignorant and odd looking, he had been an object of pity and derision all the way from Gothenburg or Christiania to the little cabin of some country-man of his, where he found rest and shelter until he could build one of his own.[7]

[6] See *Cleveland Leader*, January 25 and 26, 1870.
[7] Hans Mattson: *Reminiscences, The Story of an Emigrant* (St. Paul, Minnesota, 1892), p. 48. A description of the departure from Sweden in 1850 also deserves to be quoted:

> We put our little emigrant trunk in father's old cart, and with many tears and the breaking of tender heart-strings we bade farewell to our brothers and sisters. Mother went with us as far as to the churchyard, so that she could say that she had followed us to the grave . . . . When we were a little past the farm called Bränslan, I turned to take a final look at our village, Norrbäck, and I felt as if my heart was being torn from my bosom. When we passed the dear old church, my soul was again stirred to its depths as I recalled that it was here I had been baptized and confirmed and had taken part in the worship, and now I would most likely never see it again . . . .

[Eric Norelius: *Early Life of Eric Norelius (1833-1862)*, translated by Emeroy Johnson (Rock Island, Illinois, 1934), p. 76.]

The young women in the party sometimes hired themselves out as maids in the towns and married women took in washing if they were near towns, in order to supplement the family income during the first two or three years, when the great overpowering ambition was to save enough to buy a farm.[8]

The Swedes were practical men of action and deep emotion, who seldom yielded to the jaded temperamentalism so characteristic of men of greater learning; but even they became discouraged on occasion and wrote home to say that all was not as rosy in America as depicted by immigration agents or by other immigrants eager to give the impression that they had been marvelously successful in their new venture. Thus a Swedish immigrant from Louisville in the 1850's wrote:

> We often find that he who relates that he owns a saw-mill only owns a saw and saw-buck, and he who describes the beautiful carriage he owns, is the owner of a wheelbarrow for which himself serves as the locomotive.[9]

Another disappointed traveler, who wrote in 1843 from the home of the Friman brothers, located about 45 miles southwest of Milwaukee, lamented:

> Their home was much poorer than any charcoal hut in Sweden, without floor, almost without roof, and with a few stones in a corner which were supposed to be a stove. Such was the magnificent house which they had written they were building to receive all the Swedes who would come . . . .[10]

Needless to add, reports of this kind were given wide circulation in the newspapers of the home country and were even read from the pulpit by preachers eager to stop the drainage of population from their parishes. Stories were circulated that immigrants would be sold into slavery either in Siberia or in the South. But all these efforts to stop immigration proved futile. They made little impression on the crofter who had toiled for decades on his stony patch in Sweden and perhaps had accumulated enough to sell his holdings for $500 on his departure to America, and who expected, within

[8] See Janson: *op. cit.*
[9] Quoted in Janson: *op. cit.*, p. 152.
[10] Quoted in George M. Stephenson (editor): "Letters Relating to Gustaf Unonius," in *Augustana Historical Society Publications,* Vol. VII, p. 114.

ten years, to be able to sell his Minnesota farm for $10,000.[11]   Rye
bread and skimmed milk was an Old World diet that could not
stand comparison with the higher standard of living in America.

Emigrant companies—such as the American Emigrant Company
of New York, the Columbia Emigration Company, and others—advertised in the Swedish press as semiphilanthropic enterprises to
protect immigrants from their unscrupulous countrymen; and some
of them, besides making a profit, actually did good work by having
their employees meet newcomers on arrival, providing them with
interpreters and clean boarding houses, and maintaining an employment department.   These companies bought and sold land in
many states and sometimes maintained a banking department for
the convenience of immigrant buyers.[12]   In addition, railroads—
such as the Illinois Central—maintained "Swedish-Norwegian Land
Agencies" and had their agents visit the Scandinavian villages, attend church in order to talk with the parishioners after the service
about America, arrange farmers' meetings, attend county fairs, pay
sextons to post their advertisements in the churches, and in other
ways seek to prove to prospective immigrants that the United
States flowed with milk and honey.

Life was not easy in the sod houses of the West.   Many a pioneer
home was nothing more than a board shanty, without floor or roof,
and only a quilt stretched over the bed for shelter from the rain.
Sanitary facilities were totally lacking, and malaria and cholera
ravaged the prairie country.   The "ague" recurred regularly to
plague the pioneer, probably because of the prevalence of swamps.
The "itch" and conjunctivitis, an eye disease, were common ailments
in Western communities.   Life in one-room cabins did not help to
raise health standards, and folk medicine, based largely on stupid
superstitions, could not take the place of proper medical care.[13]
The Scandinavian immigrant, like members of other immigrant
groups was frequently fleeced, in Gothenburg, New York, or
Chicago.   He was exploited by "runners" and others, who sold him
bogus tickets or land claims to which they had no title.[14]   The
United States government sent the reports of its Land Office to

[11] See Janson: op. cit., p. 307.
[12] See ibid., pp. 234-237.
[13] See Knut Gjerset and L. Hektoen: "Health Conditions and the Practice of
Medicine Among the Early Norwegian Settlers, 1825-1865," in Norwegian-American Historical Association Studies and Records, Vol. I, pp. 1-59.
[14] See G. M. Stephenson: "Isidor Kjellberg, Crusader," in Swedish-American
Historical Bulletin, Vol. II, No. 3, pp. 31-51.

American consuls in Sweden, to be made available there in Swedish translations, but many immigrants did not have the foresight to consult such official agencies. America was a land of toil and hazards, but the diligent, thrifty laborer and artisan could surely succeed.[15]

Space is not available to do more than briefly sketch the distribution of the Swedes in the United States. The first Swedish colony was begun in 1841 by a party led by Gustavus, or Gustaf, Unonius, at Pine Lake, Wisconsin. Although, by 1850, there were only half a dozen families left, their letters home had stirred many others to make the voyage to America. The Swedish settlement on Pine Lake, known as New Upsala, is of historic importance primarily because it was the pioneer of Swedish communities in the United States.[16] Peter Cassel was the founder of the first Swedish settlement in Iowa, where he arrived in 1842 to found New Sweden, in Jefferson County, the first permanent nineteenth-century settlement by the Swedes. By 1848, a Swedish Lutheran congregation was organized and, by 1854, the population had grown to 500, many of whom owned sizeable farms. In 1846, Swede Point, Iowa, was started. In 1849, nearly 150 Swedes, with their pastor, Esbjörn, settled in Andover, Illinois. By 1860, the Swedish settlements on the prairies of Illinois extended like a belt, west and southwest, from Lake Michigan to the Mississippi River, with special Swedish centers at Rockford, Rock Island, Moline, Swedona, Geneva, Galesburg, and in Henry and Kane Counties. By 1860, Chicago was the geographical center of Swedish-America, and Swedish was spoken on the streets until well past 1870.[17] From these Illinois settlements issued sons of the pioneers who established the first Swedish communities in Minnesota and other neighboring states. By 1855, Wisconsin, Iowa, and Michigan had small Swedish settlements, and there were about 500 Swedes near Lafayette, Indiana. In 1851, Daniel Larsen and about 60 skilled workmen settled in Brockton, Massachusetts, to become the nucleus for the Swedish element in the

[15] See G. M. Stephenson, "Documents Relating to Peter Cassel and the Settlement at New Sweden, Iowa," in *Swedish-American Historical Bulletin*, Vol. II, No. 1. See also *Year Book of the Swedish Historical Society of America* (Chicago, 1908-1915; and St. Paul, 1916 ——).
[16] See Mabel V. Hansen: "The Swedish Settlement on Pine Lake," in *Wisconsin Magazine of History*, Vol. VIII, pp. 38-51.
[17] See G. M. Stephenson: "The Stormy Years of the Swedish Colony in Chicago Before the Great Fire," in *Transactions of the Illinois State Historical Society* (1929), No. 36, pp. 166-184.

shoe industry, and by the next year there was a fairly large Swedish group in the mills and factories of Jamestown, New York. Worcester, Massachusetts, is another Eastern industrial center which still has a large number of Swedes in its population.[18] There was a New Sweden in Maine by 1870, attracted there by the Foreign Emigration Association of that state. The newspapers at Caribou, Maine, regularly printed one column in Swedish.[19] In 1860, the first Swedish church was organized in San Francisco, and in the 1870's, there were ten Swedish newspapers published in California, although most of them were short-lived.

It was after 1860 that the floodgates of Swedish immigration were opened and the rush of settlers proceeded into the Upper Mississippi Valley. In less than 25 years, Illinois, Wisconsin, Minnesota, and Iowa were studded with Swedish and other Scandinavian agricultural colonies.[20] In 1853, Frederika Bremer wrote of Minnesota as follows:

> What a glorious new Scandinavia might not Minnesota become! Here would the Swede find again his clear, romantic lakes, the plains of Scania rich in corn, and the vallies of Norrland; here would the Norwegian find his rapid rivers, his lofty mountains, for I include the Rocky Mountains and Oregon in the new kingdom; and both nations, their hunting fields and their fisheries. The Danes might here pasture their flocks and herds and lay out their farms on richer and less misty coasts than those of Denmark . . . .[21]

By the opening of the twentieth century, her prophecy was abundantly fulfilled. There are still 400 place names of Scandinavian origin on the map of Minnesota and whole townships peopled by the same nationality.[22] Sections of Iowa are still known as "the Scandinavian Northwest."[23] The Swedish element in Illinois has

[18] See E. V. Lawson: "Christina Nilsson's Visit to Brockton, Massachusetts, in November, 1870," in *Augustana Historical Society Publications*, No. 3, pp. 81-96.
[19] See *Cincinnati Gazette*, July 30, 1880.
[20] See Ernst W. Olson: *The Swedish Element in Illinois* (Chicago, 1917).
[21] Frederika Bremer: *The Homes of the New World* (London, 1853), Vol. II, pp. 314-315.
[22] See Roy W. Swanson: "Scandinavian Place-Names in the American Danelaw," in *Swedish-American Historical Bulletin*, Vol. II, No. 3, pp. 5-17; and "A Swedish Visitor of the Early Seventies," in *Minnesota History Bulletin*, Vol. VIII, pp. 386-421. See also W. W. Folwell: *A History of Minnesota*, 4 vols. (St. Paul, Minnesota, 1921).
[23] See G. T. Flom: "The Early Swedish Immigrants to Iowa," in *Iowa Journal of History and Politics*, Vol. III, p. 583 *et seq.*

achieved substantial prosperity, both on the farm and in industry.[24]

After 1868, the Swedes entered Kansas. Their settlements centered at Lindsborg and in the Smoky Hill Valley of Kansas. These settlements were started through the efforts of the First Swedish Agricultural Company of Chicago and the Galesburg Colonization Company, although some Swedes had come to Kansas as early as 1855. Many of the early settlers worked first on the Union Pacific and Santa Fé Railroads. The Galesburg Company bought its land from the Kansas Pacific Railroad and promptly resold it to individual settlers.[25] Missouri was opened by a Missouri Land Company which was a subsidiary of the Swedish Commercial Company. Nebraska received its Swedish stock for the most part after 1870, as a result of the advertisements of railroad companies and the work of the Nebraska immigration board. Many of the first Swedish settlers in Nebraska were attracted by the Union Pacific Railroad shops, built in 1865 in Omaha, which provided employment for blacksmiths, machinists, and carpenters. Stromsberg was founded by Illinois Swedes in 1872, and to the northwest there was a rural community known as Swedehome.[26] By 1906, there were 40,000 Swedes in Texas. At the other extreme of the valley, in the Dakotas, it is still possible to travel many miles cross-country without leaving land that belongs to a Swedish farmer.[27]

Today, the Swedish population in the United States is concentrated in the Upper Mississippi Valley, which contains over half of all the Swedes in this country, and in urban centers like St. Paul, Minneapolis, and Chicago. In general, the Swedes predominate over the other Scandinavian groups in Minnesota, Iowa, Illinois, Michigan, Nebraska, and Kansas. The Norwegians predominate in Wisconsin and the Dakotas.[28]

In the period from 1870 to 1890, one out of every four Scandinavians in the United States were engaged in farming, a percentage

[24] See Levin Faust: "The Rockford Swedes," in *Swedish-American Historical Bulletin*, Vol. III, No. 2, pp. 61-72.

[25] See Alfred Bergin: "The Swedish Settlements in Central Kansas," in *Kansas Historical Collections*, Vol. XI, pp. 19-46.

[26] See Joseph Alexis: "Swedes in Nebraska," in *Publications of the Nebraska State Historical Society*, Vol. XIX, pp. 78-85.

[27] See Myrtle Bemis: "History of the Settlement of the Swedes in North Dakota," in *State Historical Society of North Dakota Collections*, Vol. III, pp. 247-310.

[28] See also G. M. Stephenson: *The Religious Aspects of Swedish Immigration* (Minneapolis, 1932). This excellent volume is of much more general use for Swedish immigration than its title suggests.

higher than that for Americans or Germans and three times as high as for the Irish. It has been estimated that, by 1925, the Swedes alone had cleared or farmed over 12,000,000 acres. According to the Census of 1930, there were 1,562,703 people of Swedish stock in the United States, of whom 595,250 were born in Sweden. Four-fifths of the Swedish-Americans lived in rural communities.

The Swedes are generally described as even-tempered, serious-minded individualists. They have a strong sense of property own-ership and a deep religious sense, which often turns to the pietistic and puritanical, especially in contrast with their fellow Lutherans among the Germans. The Swedes are noted for their adaptibility to American conditions, for their ability and willingness to work hard, and for their marvelous physical stamina. They are essen-tially an industrious, law-abiding, simple-minded, honest folk. They come to the United States to stay, and no other immigrant group becomes so quickly Americanized. How many of the pioneers could truthfully say what a Swede wrote home in 1841?

> I have read the biographies of Washington, John Adams, Samuel Adams, John Quincy Adams, Webster, John Han-cock and others, and of Henry Clay, too, one of America's greatest speakers and at present a senator from Virginia [sic] . . . .[29]

Swedes are clean and neat, and save for a rainy day. The per-centage of home ownership is high among them. Families are large but, on the whole, well kept. Swedes also have an unsur-passed devotion to education, and send their children to school; the rate of illiteracy among them is extremely low. In more recent years, many Swedes have gone to the cities to become successful tradesmen and workmen, especially in the lumber and furniture business. Like other Scandinavians, the Swede has little difficulty in adjusting himself to the American democratic system of govern-ment, for he comes from a country in which he has already learned the technique of popular elections.

Somewhat like the German, the Swede believes strongly in physi-cal training, and at one time Swedish gymnastics were in consid-erable vogue in the United States. Swedish gymnastics originated with Per Henrik Ling, "father of Swedish Gymnastics," at the be-ginning of the nineteenth century, when Sweden, owing to heavy

[29] Quoted in Stephenson: *loc. cit.*, p. 57.

losses in war and serious depressions, needed a revival of its national spirit. In some respects, the Swedish gymnastic movement was like the German *Turnerbund*, arising from the same general feeling of national humiliation. How successfully young Swedish-Americans have taken to American sports may perhaps be illustrated by the comment of Grantland Rice, leading American sports' commentator, on their participation in football:

> The teams out West, especially the Minnesota teams are the most feared of our American teams, solely for the Norse power supplied to them by the huge muscular Swedes with which they are amply staffed.[30]

Also like the German, the Swede loves to sing, and Swedish singing societies have arisen in many Swedish communities.[31] The Freja Society, a male chorus of 60 voices, was organized in 1869 in Chicago as a singing society for Swedes and Norwegians. It developed from the Scandinavian National Quartette, which had been touring Wisconsin and Minnesota in native costume. In 1889, the Freja consolidated with the Swedish Singing Society of Chicago to form the Svenska Gleeklubben, an organization that won many prizes in competitive singing. In 1892, the American Union of Swedish Singers was formed in Chicago, which now includes 70 clubs. It presents quadrennial music festivals of genuine merit and is the successor of the United Scandinavian Singers of America, which was organized in 1886 but split on the rocks of Swedish, Norwegian, and Danish antagonism after having given three singing festivals. There are excellent Swedish male choruses in Chicago, Moline, Augustana, and elsewhere. In 1893, at the World's Fair in Chicago, the American Union of Swedish Singers gave concerts with a chorus of 500, assisted by artists from Sweden and the Theodore Thomas Orchestra. They sang Swedish compositions. A number of Swedish-American choruses have toured Sweden. Most Swedish colleges have active departments of music, and Bethany College at Lindsborg, Kansas, and Augustana College at Rock Island, Illinois, are famous for their annual renditions of Händel's *Messiah*. J. Victor Bergquist, who writes for organ and chorus, and Arne Oldberg, who writes piano and chamber music, are two Swedish-American composers of note. Howard Hanson, one of America's most dis-

---

[30] Quoted in *Swedes in America* (New Haven, Connecticut, 1938), p. 372.
[31] See A. O. Fonkalsrud: *Scandinavians as a Social Force in America* (Brooklyn, New York, 1913).

tinguished composers and conductors, was born in the little Swedish Lutheran community of Wahoo, Nebraska.

Besides musical societies and chorus singing, to which the Swedes are devoted, Swedish-Americans established many other societies for benevolent and cultural purposes as soon as the first stages of pioneering were past and time was available for things other than work. Among these organizations may be mentioned the Svea Society of Chicago, begun in 1857; lodges whose ritual is based on Norse mythology; and fraternal, beneficiary societies like the Independent Order of Vikings. The Swedish-American Historical Society, with its headquarters in St. Paul, has sponsored research and publication in the field of Swedish-American history—in itself convincing evidence that the group has now reached a stage of prosperity and stability enabling it to devote time and resources to the preservation of its history and achievements. Today, American Swedes have some 3,500 different organizations, including every possible form of activity, ranging from purely social clubs to the Swedish National Sanatorium for tuberculosis patients in Englewood, Colorado.

The Swedish Christmas season lasted 20 days in Sweden and was celebrated with music, feasting, and reading. Rooms were decorated with pictures, many of them derived from Biblical stories. All kinds of good things to eat were prepared by the Swedish housewife for weeks in advance of the Christmas season. After supper on Christmas Eve, clean rye straw was spread on the living room floor so that the children might play games and tussle with their elders. In America, the celebration has had to be greatly abbreviated, but the Christmas customs of the fatherland have not been forgotten. From pioneer cabin to stately Swedish Lutheran churches, Swedish-Americans everywhere inaugurate a festive week of Christmas celebration by singing Wallin's Christmas hymn, "All Hail to Thee, O blessed Morn." Decorations adorn even the humblest home and there is smörgosbord on every Swedish housewife's table.

A curious pioneer institution in early Scandinavian communities was the bathhouse. It was always used at Christmas and holiday times, and less regularly on other occasions. Perhaps it was a necessary institution in a cold climate. The bathhouse was built of logs and was about 16 feet square and 10 feet high. In the middle of the bare floor stood a large oven built of stone and brick. There was no chimney, and the smoke escaped through two holes in the gables. A fire was built in the stove and water was heated. Birch twigs, with leaves still on them, were laid in the water until they became extremely supple. The bather then took a steam bath and lashed himself with the birch twigs. He then ran out to roll in the snow and back again to repeat the whipping, sweating, and bathing —"as long as it would do any good." [32] Bathhouses were to be found on Swedish and Finnish farms throughout the Middle West, and generally served as indisputable evidence of the nationality of the owners.

As late as 1920, 97 per cent of all the population of Sweden was listed as Lutheran. Swedes were legally born into the State Church and could leave it only by formal action. Every one paid taxes for its support, although separatists paid less than members. By baptism and confirmation, Swedish children were officially enrolled in the State Church. It is unsafe to generalize about the difficulties which affected the State Church in Sweden during the nineteenth century, but there is no question about the fact that various dissenting groups arose. Some were indigenous to Sweden; others were the result of the proselyting efforts of Methodists, Baptists, Mormons, and other sects. There were fundamentalist revivals in protest against the alleged coldness, indifference, worldliness, and rationalism of the Lutheran Church. Drunkenness was a national curse. There were 170,000 distilleries in Sweden in 1830. The clergy was accused of too frequent tippling, and Sweden became a fertile field for the activity of temperance societies, many of which were adjuncts of the proselyting sects. Ministers of the State Church seemed to be losing some of their spiritual interests, and parishioners complained that their sermons were becoming merely literary performances on harmless subjects that had little in common with the austere, militant Lutheranism of other days. Some of the clergy of the State Church were *bon vivants,* who were more interested in the bottle and in dancing the first dance with every bride whom they married than in looking after the spiritual and moral health of their parishioners.

The result of this situation was that, when Swedish Lutheranism was introduced in the United States, it at once assumed a pietistic, puritanical, strait-laced form. Dancing, cards, drinking, secret societies, and the theater were denounced as inventions of the Devil. Lutheranism became more orthodox and rigid in Swedish-American

[32] See Norelius: *op. cit.,* pp. 83-84.

communities than it was at home, and took on very much of a revivalist flavor. Dissenters in America who had disapproved of the shortcomings of the State Church in turn became as intolerant of dissenters as the home Church had been. Many of their preachers were self-appointed men of great inspiration but little education. Swedish Lutheranism—in fact, Scandinavian Lutheranism—in America has been marked by an almost fanatical narrowness about what constitutes the true faith, with the result that the movement has been split into many factions and synods, which have engaged in almost constant bickering and theological warfare.[33]

Lars Paul Esbjörn is generally regarded as the father of the Swedish Lutheran Church in the United States. Gustaf Unonius had emigrated in 1841 and, after trying to farm in Wisconsin, had organized a congregation of Swedes in Chicago in 1849. He was regarded by other Lutheran pastors, however, as a proselyter and a traitor to Lutheranism, because he joined the Protestant Episcopal Church. Esbjörn started Lutheran congregations at Andover, Galesburg, Princeton, and Moline, Illinois, and thus laid the foundations for what was to become the Augustana Synod. He succeeded in getting substantial gifts from Jenny Lind, "the Swedish nightingale," for his plans to establish pioneer churches among the Swedes. Above all, he was instrumental in bringing Pastor T. N. Hasselquist to America in 1852. Hasselquist was so important in the development of Swedish Lutheranism in America that a brief summary of his activities will illuminate the whole religious life of the Swedes in the United States.

Hasselquist, a farmer's son, was a minister in the State Church of Sweden who became a pietist and a reformer. His first charge in the United States was the Swedish church in Galesburg, Illinois.[34] Hasselquist was a typical pioneer preacher who worked hard among the scattered Swedish settlements to counteract the inroads of the proselyting sects. In 1855, he established the *Hemlandet* and the *Rätta Hemlandet*, a religious paper, primarily to combat the proselyters in the war to preserve the true Lutheran faith. He founded Sunday schools and parochial schools, sometimes meeting with his

[33] See Stephenson: *The Religious Aspects of Swedish Immigration;* and "The Stormy Years of the Swedish Colony in Chicago Before the Great Fire," in *Transactions of the Illinois State Historical Society.* See also Janson: *op. cit.,* pp. 167-221.
[34] For this summary, see Oscar F. Ander: *The Career and Influence of T. N. Hasselquist, A Swedish-American Clergyman, Journalist and Educator* (Rock Island, Illinois, 1931).

flock in barns in the early years. By 1859, the Swedish Publication Society, also founded by Hasselquist, was transferred to Chicago and supplied the Lutheran churches with religious works, parochial school texts, and hymnals—such as the Swedish *Psalmbook* and the *Hemlandssänger,* which ran through a number of editions. The *Hemlandet,* also transferred to Chicago, carried on a religious war to the hilt with such anti-Lutheran Swedish sheets as *Den svenska republikanen i norra America* and the *Svenska Amerikanaren.* In 1870, when the famous Swedish singer Christina Nilsson visited Chicago, there was almost a battle royal among the Swedish element to determine which group should sponsor the reception given in her honor.

At the close of 1858, the Swedish Lutheran Church in America had 13 ministers and 28 congregations, and was strongest in Illinois and Minnesota. The total membership at that time probably did not exceed 3,000. By 1860, the number of congregations had risen to 39, the number of preachers to 17, and the number of communicants to nearly 5,000. It was in that year that the Scandinavian Evangelical Lutheran Augustana Synod was organized, with Hasselquist as president. A plea was made for money from the fatherland, and a seminary to train ministers was opened in the basement of a Norwegian Lutheran church in Chicago. The Synod dispatched a missionary to Montreal and Quebec to meet incoming immigrants and direct them to Illinois, and, in 1865, it began similar missionary work in New York.[35] In 1863, Hasselquist signed a contract with the Illinois Central Railroad to sell land on commission to settlers, in order to get Swedes out of the cities and bring them into the farming communities of Illinois. The seminary cleared $14,000 in five years from his activity as land agent for the railroad.[36]

The Augustana College and Theological Seminary, designed to convert "hired men" into ministers in three years under the most rigorous routine and discipline, was transferred to Rock Island, Illinois, in 1875, and has remained the center of Swedish Lutheran activities in the United States. Its primary mission has been "to follow the dispersed countrymen in America, who have come here to find earthly homes, with God's pure Word and Sacraments, and

[35] See Gustav Andreen: "The Early Missionary Work of the Augustana Synod in New York City, 1865-1866," in *Augustana Historical Society Publications*, No. 2, pp. 1-27.
[36] See also Paul W. Gates: *The Illinois Central Railroad and its Colonization Work* (Cambridge, Massachusetts, 1934), pp. 209-210.

to gather and retain them in regular Evangelical Lutheran congregations." [37] It did not long remain a joint project of all the Scandinavian peoples, for Norwegian and Swedish Lutherans soon became involved in many controversies over doctrinal matters—such as altar service, ministerial garb, and repentance—and these issues were greatly aggravated by the growing national consciousness of the two groups and the antagonisms that arose therefrom. Norwegians attacked the Augustana group for becoming too rapidly Americanized, and Hasselquist sorrowfully admitted that "Christianity does not seem powerful enough to overcome this nationalism." [38] In 1870, the Norwegians separated from the Augustana Synod and formed a Norwegian-Danish organization, which in turn split into two independent synods.

The Augustana Synod has remained the bulwark of Swedish-American Lutheranism. Hasselquist ruled with a strong hand and vigorously opposed secret societies, drinking, dances, and the theater. "Lutheran pulpits for Lutheran ministers" was a rule that was strictly observed, as well as "Lutheran altars for Lutheran communicants." The Synod remained under Hasselquist's domination from 1860 to 1890, and in that time grew from 17 pastors, 36 congregations, and 3,000 communicants to 325 pastors, 637 congregations, and 84,583 communicants. In 1925, its property was estimated at over $31,000,000, of which nearly $900,000 was invested in immigrant homes. Both Professors Ander and Stephenson have discussed in detail the almost endless theological bickering that has marked the history of this group. Nevertheless, the Swedish Lutherans have remained surprisingly united, in contrast with the numerous synodical splits that have occurred among German, Norwegian, Danish, and Finnish Lutheran groups. Moreover, the Augustana Synod, although often called the "daughter of the Church of Sweden" both here and abroad, got little support in its critical years from abroad. The Swedish-American Church has developed largely because it has manifested a strong spirit of self-reliance and assiduously cultivated its own resources.

The *Augustana* was the leading religious organ of the Augustana Synod. It devoted itself to combatting the "New Evangelism," the freethinkers, socialism, internationalism, the Knights of Labor, the Patrons of Husbandry, and all secret societies, as well as tobacco,

[37] Quoted in Ander: *op. cit.*, p. 106.
[38] Quoted in *ibid.*, p. 106.

dancing, drinking, and the theater. Hasselquist was a total abstainer, except for the use of wine at Communion, and he always
urged the Swedes to vote for prohibition. Politically, he was a
rock-ribbed Republican. The Augustana Book Concern of Rock
Island, Illinois, is the official publishing house of the Synod and the
principal concern of its kind owned and controlled by Swedes.[39]
Although contributions were received from the mother country to
help Swedish-American Lutheranism in its years of struggle, there
was no formal recognition of the Augustana Synod by the State
Church of Sweden until 1903. In 1923, a Swedish archbishop dedicated the new seminary buildings at Rock Island, and three years
later the college received a visit from the Swedish Crown Prince.
The tendency, however, has been to move farther away from the
Church of Sweden, and the Sunday schools and societies of the
Augustana Synod follow American models.[40] Hasselquist himself
always favored Americanization of the Church and spoke of the
efforts of German Lutherans to preserve the German language in
America as "the preaching of a language rather than a gospel."
English is today the official language of the Augustana Synod.[41]

Various Protestant groups have made heavy inroads upon the
Swedish Lutherans,[42] but their work cannot be discussed in detail
here. The Methodist activity among the Swedish-Americans may
serve as an illustration of this proselyting work. By 1850, there
were Swedish Methodist churches in Illinois, organized into four
circuits with six preachers. Jonas Hedstrom, the blacksmith-
preacher, pioneered in this work of winning the Swedes of Illinois
for Methodism. A missionary society, supported by the Methodist
Episcopal Church, was organized for the express purpose of working among Swedish and German immigrants. By 1877, the Swedish
Methodist churches in the Northwest, which had hitherto been
attached to several annual conferences, were combined as the Northwestern Swedish Annual Conference. Churches in Illinois, Michigan, Minnesota, Iowa, Kansas, and Nebraska became affiliated with
this new conference, although their membership at that time apparently did not exceed 4,000.[43] In 1907, the Mormon Church of Utah
had almost 70 missionaries in Sweden. From 1850 to 1909, the

[39] For an account of Swedish Lutheranism in Nebraska, see Alexis: *loc. cit.*
[40] See Ander: *op. cit.,* p. 223.
[41] See *ibid.,* pp. 229-230.
[42] See Stephenson: *The Religious Aspects of Swedish Immigration.*
[43] See *The New York Times,* September 23, 1877.

Mormons claimed over 17,000 converts in Sweden, of whom nearly 8,000—mostly young unmarried women and skilled artisans attracted by the high wages prevailing in Utah—came to the United States.

The Swedes have been perhaps more quickly Americanized than any other immigrant group. One reason for this has been their devotion to the American public schools. It is true that, on numerous occasions, the Swedes have denounced the "godless public schools." They also have on several occasions risen in political revolt against legislation that threatened their parochial schools or the preservation of their language. There were notable contests over these issues in Wisconsin, Illinois, and the Dakota territory at the close of the 1880's. Attempts were made to conduct "Swede school" in church basements, during vacations and on Saturdays, in order to teach the Lutheran *Bible* and Catechism and to keep the younger generation attached to the religion and language of their fathers. But these enterprises did not last long. The second generation was eager to shed all Swedish characteristics; names were changed to disguise their Swedish origin, and there was little literature available to preserve the Swedish nationality in a strange environment. As a matter of fact, most Swedish-Americans were workmen and farmers; they came from the humbler walks of life and were not particularly conscious of any national culture which should be preserved.

A number of Swedish colleges—such as Bethany College in Kansas, Augustana College in Illinois, Luther College in Wahoo, Nebraska, and Gustavus Adolphus College in Minnesota—survive to testify to the enthusiasm for colleges which swept the Swedish-American element in the generation before the World War. Professor Stephenson has called it the "college mania" and a "title sickness." The majority of these institutions had poor faculties, gave degrees with little discrimination among applicants, and were hardly more than academies. The weakest and poorest have long since dropped into oblivion. Classes in Swedish have dwindled, and at the University of Minnesota, where Scandinavian languages are taught, the Swedish classes are among the smallest in the whole institution.[44] The American public school has fixed an apparently impassable gulf between parents and children and, as with other

[44] For an account of present-day Swedish-American colleges, see *Swedes in America*, pp. 154-180.

immigrant groups, it has been the one natural and irresistible Americanizing influence among the Scandinavians. Some of the immigrant college libraries remain as priceless depositories of historical material for the study of immigrant groups,[45] and organizations like the Swedish Historical Society of America and the Society for the Advancement of Scandinavian Study have made outstanding contributions to immigrant literature.[46]

The Swedish-American press reflects both religious and secular interests. Politically, the Swedes have been rock-ribbed Republicans; religiously, the majority have been rock-ribbed Lutherans. Most Swedish-American papers are colored by these two affiliations. The *Hemlandet* was antislavery and helped to lead the Swedish immigrants into the newly established Republican party before the Civil War. It justified Know-Nothingism's attack on the "wild Irish," on Catholicism, and on the radical "irreligious Germans" who desecrated the Sabbath with their beer gardens. Swedish-Americans naturally favored the party which favored free homesteads. "Fria män, fritt land, fria hem och fritt arbete" was a slogan that won votes in 1860, and some Swedish Lutheran churches, in their enthusiasm for the Republicans, actually flew Swedish banners from their spires.[47] In 1860, the Swedish vote was still too small to contribute much to the Republican victory. After the Civil War, a Lincoln-worship was assiduously cultivated by the party among the Swedish voters. Campaign orators were employed by the Republican National Committee to spread the faith in the Swedish tongue, and Swedish-American newspapers were held in their staunch allegiance to the Republican party by a systematic apportionment of paid political advertisements at electiontime. To the average Swede, *Republikan* had always meant opposition to monarchy and special privilege. At least 16 attempts have been made to publish magazines in the United States in the Swedish language, but none survive.

It has been estimated that between 3,000 and 4,000 Swedes fought

[45] See Oscar F. Ander: *Guide to the Material on Swedish History in the Augustana College Library* (Rock Island, Illinois, 1934).

[46] For an account of Scandinavian colleges in the United States, see *American Scandinavian Review* (March, 1924). See also Albert F. Scherston: "The Historical and Cultural Background of Swedish Immigrants of Importance to Their Assimilation in America," in *Augustana Historical Society Publications*, No. 2, pp. 47-63.

[47] See Oscar F. Ander: "Swedish-American Newspapers and the Republican Party, 1855-1875," in *Augustana Historical Society Publications*, No. 2, pp. 64-78.

in the Union Army of the Civil War.[48] Charles John Stolbrand, who organized a Swedish battery in DeKalb, Illinois, rose to the rank of brigadier general. Company D of the 3rd Minnesota regiment was an exclusively Scandinavian outfit, commanded by Hans Mattson, and the 15th Wisconsin Infantry contained many Swedish and other Scandinavian volunteers.[49] There was a company of Swedes under Captain Arosenius in the 43rd Illinois and another under Captain Corneliuson in the 23rd Wisconsin regiment. The American consulate in Sweden was stormed by young Swedes eager to enlist in the hope of getting a bounty and having their traveling expenses to America paid. The pressure became so great that, in 1863, the American consul wrote: "Furnish me with ships, or free passages, and I could take a quarter of the working population of this country to the United States next spring." [50] Thirteen hundred Swedish volunteers came from Illinois, which had a total Swedish population of about 7,000 in 1861. Colonel Oscar Malmborg, who had served eight years in the Swedish Army and also in the Mexican War, commanded the 55th Illinois Volunteers. Other Swedish officers of note who served in the Civil War were Major Eric Forsse of the Bishop Hill Colony; Captains Axel Silfversparre, Frederick Sparrestrom, C. E. Landstrom, Andrew Stenbeck, and Andrew G. Warner; and Colonels Vegesack, Steelhammar, Elfving, and Brydolf.

After the close of the Civil War, the Swedish-Americans began to be politically recognized and rewarded. In 1869, Hans Mattson was elected secretary of state for Minnesota on the Republican ticket; in 1876, he stumped the Scandinavian settlements of the state; and, in 1881, Garfield appointed him consul general to India. From 1876 to 1881, he edited the *Minnesota Stats Tidning*, in Minneapolis. Lincoln appointed Charles J. Sundell of Chicago as American consul to Stettin, Germany, in 1861. In the 1870's, the Swedes began to hold office in Illinois, and there was a great increase in the number of Scandinavians sitting in the legislatures of the Northwestern states. In 1872, C. F. Peterson, editor of a Swedish-American paper, made speeches for Greeley in Chicago, though most Scandinavians supported Grant. The Republican organization distributed campaign literature in German and Swedish

[48] See Ander: *The Career and Influence of T. N. Hasselquist*, p. 88.
[49] See Mattson: *op. cit.*, pp. 62-70.
[50] Quoted in Janson: *op. cit.*, p. 156.

throughout the State of Minnesota.[51] Hasselquist and the *Hemlandet* supported Grant, largely because the Liberal Republican movement was supported by German liberals who favored "all kinds of liberty," including "Sabbath liberty."

As a rule, Swedish farmers were not enthusiastic over the Granger movement of the 1860's and 1870's. Swedish and Norwegian Lutherans alike looked upon the Patrons of Husbandry as another secret society, Masonic in origin and anti-Christian. The opposition of the Lutheran Church was so strong that it may have been a real factor in the decline of the Granger strength in states like Illinois and Iowa.[52] Nevertheless, agrarian discontent at various times has led to serious defections from the Republican party among the Scandinavians. In 1892, the Democratic party apparently made some inroads on the Swedish Republican vote; it advertised heavily in Swedish papers and financed several new publications. Perhaps a dozen Swedish journals deserted their old political allies, largely because of the unpopularity of the McKinley Tariff of 1890 and the alleged flirtation of the party leaders with the saloon interests.[53] In the campaign of 1896, the Swedish bureau of the Republican National Committee in Chicago left no stone unturned to hold the Swedish voters for McKinley. It sent out over 7,000 letters, nearly 800,000 books in Swedish, and 700,000 copies of Swedish newspapers.

There are always Swedish and Norwegian names on the ballots of states and cities in the Northwest, where these elements are strong, and the Scandinavian press is quick to demand political recognition and financial subsidy from the party that expects its continued support. Scandinavian bureaus and lecturers are still part of the equipment of the Republican party in national campaigns.[54] In 1921, 73 of the 86 counties of Minnesota had one or more Swedish officeholders. The names of Swedish-American leaders like Charles A. Lindbergh, Sr., the Lundeens and Lenroots, Charles A. Peterson, Floyd Olson, John Lind, and John A. Johnson, who have served as governors and congressmen, are nationally known. In 1930, there were still 43 Swedish newspapers published in the United States, according to *Ayer's Newspaper Annual and Directory*. Some are

[51] See *New York Tribune*, August 26, 1872.
[52] Oscar F. Ander: "The Immigrant Church and the Patrons of Husbandry," in *Agricultural History*, Vol. VIII, pp. 155-168.
[53] See Oscar F. Ander: "The Swedish-American Press and the Election of 1892," in *The Mississippi Valley Historical Review*, Vol. XXIII, pp. 533-554.
[54] See also G. M. Stephenson: "The Attitude of the Swedish-Americans Toward the World War," in *Mississippi Valley Historical Review* (July, 1920), pp. 77-95.

significant dailies published in Chicago, Duluth, and St. Paul.[55] Twenty years earlier, the number was 300; and Professor Stephenson has predicted that, by 1940, there will be few survivors. The amount of English printed matter appearing in Swedish papers in the United States is steadily increasing.

THE NORWEGIANS

Much that has been written about the Swedish-Americans could, of course, be duplicated for the history of Norwegian immigration to the United States. As the late Professor Babcock observed: "Nature is no spendthrift in any part of the Scandinavian peninsula," and Norwegians, like Swedes, have been forced to live very close to the margin of subsistence. The Norwegians came to America primarily for economic reasons. They brought with them a strong democratic tradition and a national consciousness much more developed than that of the Swedes. This may be one reason why the Norwegian-American has preserved a greater group solidarity in the United States than any of the other Scandinavian stock.

The Norwegians are a strong, resolute, stubborn people. Practically all are Lutherans, and combine a Lutheran piety and sense of duty with a strong desire for material advancement. They are thrifty and eager to acquire a homestead. They are strong and stubborn individualists, lovers of freedom, law-abiding, and vigorous defenders of their Church. The novels of Johan Bojer and more especially those of the late Ole Rölvaag are of more historical value in depicting the life and psychology of the Norwegian pioneers in America than reams of historical documents.

Rölvaag was born of fisherfolk, on the edge of the Arctic Circle. He left school at 14 to become a fisherman, like his Norwegian forbears. In 1896, he landed in New York with nothing more than a railroad ticket to South Dakota in his pocket. He worked on Western farms, entered college at 23, and became professor of Norwegian literature at St. Olaf's College in Minnesota. Out of his own rich experiences in the years when the Northwest was being transformed by Scandinavian immigrants, he wrote *Giants in the Earth, Peder Victorious,* and *Their Father's God*—a trilogy which will live, not only as great literature, but primarily as great historical documents.

[55] See also Robert E. Park: *The Immigrant Press and Its Control* (New York, 1922).

Per Hansa, Rölvaag's hero in *Giants in the Earth,* represents the primitive, conquering strength of the Norwegian pioneer in wresting his farm from the unbroken prairie. His wife, Beret, symbolizes the primitive fears of the pioneer woman, sighing out her soul in a sod hut in Dakota for the homeland, overwhelmed by the prairie's ominous silences, and sinking gradually from loneliness into insanity. It is the story of the heroism of the immigrant pioneer and of the heavy price exacted by the virgin prairie of those who would break up its vast stretches into farms. In his subsequent volumes, Rölvaag has told the story of the clash that occurs between the first and the second generations of all immigrant groups, the cleavage that arises over the language question, and the final tragic alienation of the immigrant mother from the child that has grown up in the new America.[56]

The Norwegian farmer, like his Swedish neighbor, experienced both joys and suffering during his first generation in the United States. His original dwelling was a sod hut, built up against a slope, with two or three steps to go down before reaching the dirt floor. The room was seldom more than 12 feet long, 14 feet wide, and 8 feet high. Daylight had to come in through the door and smoke go out through a hole in the dirt roof. The walls were bare, and the huge immigrant trunks brought from Norway served as chairs. Brooms were made from the tall prairie grass and pillows from the down of cattails. Prairie fires, snowstorms so heavy that farmers stretched wires to guide them from their houses to the barns, swarms of locusts, burning heat unrelieved for months by rain, the loneliness of the open country, and all the dread of nature's hidden forces were eventually overcome to build in the Northwest the "New Norway" of the United States of our time.[57] Little wonder that some were disillusioned and wrote home to their friends that, in America, it was 50 miles to the nearest mill and 25 miles to the nearest town, that there were neither schools nor churches in the wilderness, and that many died from exposure and malaria.

[56] See also Johan Bojer: *The Emigrants* (New York, 1925); and Willa Cather: *O Pioneers* (Boston, 1913). The latter, dealing with a Swedish peasant family, is concerned with this same struggle between the old and the new. Of great value is T. C. Blegen and M. B. Ruud: *Norwegian Emigrant Songs and Ballads* (Minneapolis, 1936).
[57] See, for example, Knut Gjerset: "A Norwegian-American Landnamsman: Ole S. Gjerset," in *Norwegian-American Historical Association Studies and Records,* Vol. III, pp. 82-100.

America was not paved with gold, and only the sturdiest of heart could survive.[58]

But the prizes were great in the American lottery of success. In two years, many a Norwegian who had been practically reduced to poverty by the expenses of the trip to Middle America could boast that he would not sell his little farm and his livestock for $1,000.[59] Thus a Norwegian wrote in the forties:

> What an impression it would make on a poor highlander's imagination to be told that some day he might eat wheat bread every day and pork at least three times a week! . . . Here even a tramp can enjoy a chicken dinner once in a while.[60]

To reach such prosperity cost from $25 to $38 for a ticket on a sailing vessel, the immigrant furnishing food and bedding, and perhaps the same amount to journey inland by canal or railroad. In the 1850's, it was possible to go by rail from Quebec to Chicago or Milwaukee for $8 or $10.[61]

Between 1836 and 1900, the emigration from Norway to the United States was over half a million, and by 1915 it totaled over three quarters of a million—a figure larger than four fifths of the entire population of Norway at the beginning of the nineteenth century. Norway lost a larger proportion of her total population by immigration to America than any other European nation except Ireland.[62] The great tide of Norwegian immigration came in the 1880's, with a decline in the next decade and another rise after 1900. By 1870, perhaps 90 per cent of the Norwegians in the United States were in Wisconsin, Minnesota, Iowa, and northern Illinois. By 1880, the "New Norway" extended from Lake Michigan westward into the Dakotas and on toward the Missouri River, and lay, roughly,

[58] For this note of disillusionment in immigrant letters, see, for example, T. C. Blegen: "The Norwegian Government and the Early Norwegian Emigration," in *Minnesota History Bulletin*, Vol. VI, pp. 115-140; and "Peter Testman's Account of His Experiences in North America," in *Minnesota History Bulletin*, Vol. VI, pp. 91-114. See also "Bishop Jacob Neumann's Word of Admonition to the Peasants," in *Norwegian-American Historical Association Studies and Records*, Vol. I, pp. 95-109; and another account in *ibid.*, Vol. III, pp. 1-12.

[59] See "Norwegian Immigrant Letters (1857)," in *Wisconsin Magazine of History*, Vol. XV, pp. 356-369.

[60] See Gunnar J. Malmin (editor and translator): *America in the Forties: The Letters of Ole Munch Raeder* (Minneapolis, 1929), pp. 64, 69, and 74.

[61] See G. T. Flom: *A History of Norwegian Immigration to the United States From the Earliest Beginning Down to the Year 1848* (Iowa City, 1909).

[62] See O. M. Norlie: *History of the Norwegian People in America* (Minneapolis, 1925).

north of a line from Chicago westward to Sioux City. This area includes half a dozen counties in northeastern Illinois, a dozen counties in central and north Iowa, the eastern third of the Dakotas, and almost all of the counties of Wisconsin and Minnesota. Today, there are between 1,250,000 and 1,500,000 of Norwegian blood in this area.[63] Utah and Washington, too, have attracted many Norwegians in the present century.[64]

The *Mayflower* of the Norwegian immigration was the sloop *Restauration,* a little boat somewhat over 50 feet long and with a capacity of about 38 tons, which arrived in New York in 1825 with about 50 Norwegian Quakers, who had been driven to emigrate for economic reasons and because of religious intolerance. Cleng Peerson, who had been in the United States from 1821 to 1824, met the shipload of immigrants on their arrival.[65] The majority settled about 35 miles northwest of Rochester, New York. The second Norwegian settlement was the Fox River Settlement in Illinois, a site selected by Cleng Peerson, who again was the trail blazer for this second contingent, composed of a group of six families, whom he induced to go out to the prairie in 1834. In the next years, hundreds of "America letters" were circulated in Norway. Ole Rynning came in 1837 and wrote his important *True Account of America for the Information and Help of Peasant and Commoner* in the winter of 1837-1838. It had a large circulation, passed through several editions, and described in detail the promise of America. Norwegians at home tried to counteract the effect of such "America Books" and letters by circulating the most incredible tales about the United States, but the Norwegian tide could not be stopped. Low wages, poor harvests, and potato rots made the hardships of America seem like a paradise to the poor Norwegian, and after the Civil War, the Norwegian immigration into the Northwest became a flood. Some political dissatisfaction and a strong reaction to the formalism of the State Church on the part of dissenting sects, such as the Quakers and pietistic followers of Hans Nilsen Hauge, were contributing factors of less importance.[66]

[63] See L. M. Larsen: "The Norwegian Element in the Northwest," in *American Historical Review,* Vol. XL, pp. 69-81.

[64] See Henry Sundby-Hansen: *Norwegian Immigrant Contributions to America's Making* (New York, 1921).

[65] For a partial list of descendants of the "Sloop" party, see Norlie: *op. cit.,* pp. 122-135 and 143-144.

[66] See T. C. Blegen: *Norwegian Migration to America, 1825-1860* (Northfield, Minnesota, 1931). This is by far the best book on Norwegian immigration. Un-

Detailed discussion of Norwegian settlements in all the states is precluded for want of space. The Norwegian colony in Potter County, Pennsylvania, established in the 1850's, was an early failure. It would probably have been entirely forgotten save for the fact that it was the particular creation of the famous Norwegian violinist, Ole Bull, who poured his concert earnings into what he hoped would develop into "a New Norway, consecrated to liberty, baptized with independence, and protected by the Union's mighty flag." [67] By 1860, there were over 10,000 Norwegians in Illinois, mainly in the region around Chicago; and, in 1853, a Norwegian paper was started in that city. As late as 1925, Chicago had nearly 50,000 inhabitants of Norwegian blood. Muskego was the parent colony for the Norwegians of Wisconsin, and as early as 1847, a Norwegian paper, the *Nordlyset,* was issued there.

Ole Munch Raeder described the Wisconsin prairie in words that must have found an echo in the hearts of many Norwegian pioneers. The houses on the prairie seemed "like ships on a sea of cornfields, wheatfields, and meadows gently rolling in the wind," and the woods like "a broken coast line with a promontory here and a deep recess there." The scene reminded him of the pleasant Danish landscape, although Wisconsin was "grander and more majestic," and "even its lonely and somber aspects give it an appearance of grandeur like that of such parts of Norway as are still untouched by the hand of man." [68] Probably the first Norwegian Lutheran church in the United States was built at Muskego in 1843, on land donated by Hans Christian Heg, patriarch of this first Norwegian settlement, who welcomed all newcomers to his huge hospitable barn.[69]

In Iowa, Norwegians settled in the northeastern part of the state, many of the first settlers coming from Wisconsin and Illinois. Decorah, Iowa, is the Norwegian capital of the state, the seat of Luther College and the home of the *Decorah Posten,* founded in 1874. As late as 1920, over 17,000 inhabitants of Iowa were born

fortunately, this first volume of a promised two-volume treatment stops before the high tide of Norwegian immigration was reached, but I have leaned on it heavily for my account.

[67] See *ibid.,* Ch. XIII, pp. 287-307.

[68] *Ibid.,* p. 138. See also Nils P. Haugen: "Pioneer and Political Reminiscences," in *Wisconsin Magazine of History,* Vol. XI, pp. 121-152, 269-300, and 395-436; and Rasmus B. Anderson: "Description of a Journey to North America," in *Wisconsin Magazine of History,* Vol. I, pp. 149-186.

[69] See T. C. Blegen: "Colonel Hans Christian Heg," in *Wisconsin Magazine of History,* Vol. IV, p. 140 *et seq.*

in Norway.[70]   In the same year, Minnesota had a population of over 90,000 who were born in Norway.   The greatest concentration of Norwegians in this state is in the southeastern portion.[71]

Paul Hjelm Hansen, a journalist and reformer who had come out to Wisconsin, was really the first to explore and advertise the possibilities of the Red River Valley for Scandinavian settlement.[72]   The full force of Norwegian immigration into North Dakota was felt by 1880 and continued into the twentieth century.   In general, the settlers followed the streams where wood and water were available, but the nearest market was often from 30 to 100 miles away.   This meant several days by oxcart over trackless prairies, and 20 miles a day with oxen was a good day's journey.[73]   Free homesteads, the propaganda of railroads like the Northern Pacific, which had land to sell, and the activity of the territorial commissioner of immigration brought thousands of Norwegian farmers to the Dakotas.   In 1880, the Norwegian *Grand Forks Tidende* was established, and apparently there were enough subscribers to make the paper a paying venture.[74]   By the 1890's, two Norwegian papers were started in Crookston, North Dakota.   The years from 1879 to 1886 were known as "the great Dakota Boom."   Many settlements in the northern counties were in advance of the railroads; in the southern part of the territory, they generally followed railroad expansion. By 1890, the Norwegians had pioneered the desirable agricultural areas in the eastern two thirds of North Dakota.   Of the total Scandinavian immigration to the state, the Norwegians made up half.

Most Norwegians were farmers or laborers, like other Scandina-

---

[70] See G. T. Flom: "The Coming of the Norwegians to Iowa," in *Iowa Journal of History and Politics*, Vol. III, pp. 347-383; and "The Growth of the Scandinavian Factor in the Population of Iowa," in *ibid.*, Vol. IV, pp. 267-285.

[71] See Carlton C. Qualey: "Pioneer Norwegian Settlement in Minnesota," in *Minnesota History Bulletin*, Vol. XII, pp. 247-280.

[72] See Alex Tollefson: "Historical Notes on the Norwegians in the Red River Valley," in *Collections of the State Historical Society of North Dakota*, Vol. VII, p. 131 *et seq.*

[73] See Omon B. Herigstad: "The First Norwegian Settlement in Griggs County, North Dakota," in *Collections of the State Historical Society of North Dakota*, Vol. I, pp. 131-153; and Vol. II, pp. 186-201.

[74] *The Fargo Daily Republican*, in 1883, wrote:

Come one, come all!   Why will ye delay,
The glorious opportunity to secure a homestead is fast slipping away!
In a few years at most, government land will be sold,
And you, yes you, will be left out in the cold!

(Quoted in Qualey: "Pioneer Norwegian Settlement in North Dakota," in *North Dakota Historical Quarterly*, Vol. V, p. 20.)

vian immigrants. A large number of the young women became servant girls and were rapidly Americanized. Some Norwegians worked
in the copper and iron mines near Lake Superior. The largest chair
factory in the United States was established by a Norwegian immigrant in Chicago. Within the past quarter-century, a large number
of Scandinavian engineers and mechanics have been attracted to
Michigan by the automobile industry. By 1930, there were 5,000
Norwegians in Wayne County, as many Danes, and about 13,500
Swedes, most of whom lived in Detroit and its immediate vicinity.[75]
Thousands of Norwegians, remaining true to the occupation they
followed in the homeland, found employment in the fisheries of
America. The majority of fishermen employed in the halibut fish-
eries are Norwegian immigrants, and Norwegians are also well rep-
resented in the whale and salmon fishing of the Pacific. By 1850,
Norwegian seamen were much in demand in America. They are
to be found in most of the lake ports, from Buffalo to Duluth.
Many are ship's captains and hundreds are employed in shipbuilding. A large part of the crews on American yachts, particularly
those that engage in cup racing, are recruited from experienced
Norwegian sailors. Andrew Furuseth, able leader of the International Seamen's Union of America, was of Norwegian stock.[76]

Norwegians are staunch Lutherans, like most of their fellow
Scandinavians. In Minnesota, Wisconsin, and the Dakotas, over
two thirds of the Protestant Church membership is still in the
Lutheran churches. The Norwegians were not so exposed or
susceptible to proselyting by other sects as the Swedes, but they
have had numerous schisms in their ranks because of internal friction. In the period before 1860, for example, no less than six
Norwegian synodical organizations were organized in the United
States. Unity has been hard to achieve and to maintain, and many
Norwegian Lutherans have remained closely affiliated with the
Missouri Synod of the German Lutheran group. The difficulties in
getting Scandinavian Lutherans to affiliate with one church body
have already been pointed out. The Norwegian Lutheran Synod
supported missionaries in New York to work among newly arrived

[75] See Carlton C. Qualey: *Norwegian Settlement in the United States* (Northfield, Minnesota, 1938), p. 182. This excellent volume complements and supple-
ments Blegen's study for the earlier period.
[76] See Knut Gjerset: *Norwegian Sailors on the Great Lakes* (Northfield, Minnesota, 1928); and *Norwegian Sailors in American Waters* (Northfield, Minnesota,
1933).

immigrants; and, in the Northwest, pious and devoted pastors rode long miles over roadless prairies and through blinding snowstorms to bring the consolations of Lutheranism to their widely scattered flocks.[77] The use of English in sermons and Sunday Schools progressed so steadily that a large majority of the churches in the Norwegian Lutheran synods have practically ceased to use the Norwegian language.[78] Peter Laurentius Lársen was the Nestor of Norwegian Lutherans. From 1857 to 1915, he served as pastor, and for all but two of those years as professor as well; from 1861 to 1902, he served as president of Luther College in Iowa.

Luther College was founded in 1861 by Norwegian Lutherans and was moved to Decorah, Iowa, in 1862. Its seminary is the oldest Norwegian seminary in the United States. Its college department emphasizes the classics and choral singing, and the college also supports a preparatory school and a normal department to train teachers, especially for Norwegian Lutheran church schools. In 1861, 80 per cent of the instruction was in Norwegian; 60 years later, only 8 per cent was in Norwegian. Dr. Larsen served as president of Luther College from its beginning. Trained as a university man and ordained as a preacher in Norway, he came to America in 1857 and preached first among the pioneers of Wisconsin. His family is one of the largest and most distinguished Norwegian families in the United States.[79]

In 1918, in the 12 states where most of the Norwegians live, there were 19 Lutheran colleges and professional schools, and numerous academies. Besides Luther College in Iowa, St. Olaf College in Northfield, Minnesota, which was founded in 1874 and is famous for its Lutheran choir, directed by F. Melius Christensen, is outstanding. It was the first coeducational school maintained by the Norwegian Lutheran Church. Norwegian colleges include Concordia, in Minnesota, and Augustana, in South Dakota. Clifton College was founded by Norwegians in Texas in 1896.[80] Luther College Museum is now being developed as a great depository for the records of the Norwegian element in the United States, and an effort is being made to make it a real museum of Norwegian pioneer

[77] See Anton Hillesland: "The Norwegian Lutheran Church in the Red River Valley," in *Collections of the State Historical Society of North Dakota*, Vol. VII, pp. 193-283.
[78] See Norlie: *op. cit.*, p. 357.
[79] See *Luther College Through Sixty Years, 1861-1921* (Minneapolis, 1922).
[80] See Norlie: *op. cit.*, p. 176.

life. The output of books by the Norwegian element has been large, especially in the field of religion and theology.[81]

Since 1847, the Norwegian element in the United States has never been without its own newspaper, and from 1850 to 1925 over 400 Norwegian papers were published in America.[82] The first of these was the *Nordlyset* of Muskego, Wisconsin, which, for a long time, was published in a log barn. The first Norwegian church paper appeared in 1851 and continued, with interruptions and under various names, up to the World War. Between 1850 and 1860, of the eight Norwegian papers that appeared in the United States, all but two were published in Wisconsin. None survived very long. The most important of the group was the *Emigranten*. Most Norwegian papers were Republican papers, but editors like Gabriel Bjornson and Jacob Seeman and papers like *Den Norske Amerikaner* and *Nordstjernen* remained Democratic in the 1850's. The first Norwegian papers in Minnesota were the *Nordiske Folksblad* of Rochester (1868) and the *Nordlyset* of Northfield (1870). North Dakota had two Norwegian papers by 1880, and in South Dakota the *Folkstidende* was established at Sioux Falls in 1879. Many of the early papers were hardly more than organs of warring factions engaged in church controversies. From 1860 to 1890, the Norwegians started 169 publications, of which 91 were ordinary newspapers, 35 Lutheran papers, 18 non-Lutheran religious papers, and the rest cultural.[83] The three largest Norwegian papers in the United States today are the *Decorah Posten,* founded in 1874 by B. Anundsen; the Chicago *Skandinaven,* founded by John Anderson in 1866; and the Minneapolis *Minnesota Tidende,* founded in 1887 by Thorwald Gulbrandson.

The Norwegians, like other immigrant groups, maintain many societies in America. In the Northwest especially, these are often organized in accordance with the districts in Norway from which the members came. These *Bygdelags* are primarily for social and cultural purposes, to perpetuate the traditions of the home com-

[81] See also Laurence M. Larsen: "The Norwegian Pioneer in the Field of American Scholarship," in *Norwegian-American Historical Association Studies and Records*, Vol. II, pp. 62-77; and G. T. Flom: "Norwegian Language and Literature in American Universities," in *Norwegian-American Historical Association Studies and Records*, Vol. II, pp. 78-103.

[82] See T. C. Blegen: "The Early Norwegian Press in America," in *Minnesota History Bulletin*, Vol. III, pp. 506-518.

[83] See Albert O. Barton: "The Beginnings of the Norwegian Press in America," *Proceedings of the State Historical Society of Wisconsin* (1916), pp. 186-212.

munity and to preserve historical records. The Sons of Norway, formed in Minneapolis in 1895, have a similar purpose—namely, to preserve the Norwegian cultural heritage—but combine with this certain benevolent and life-insurance features. The Norwegians like choral music and have many singing societies. Since 1904, there has been in existence a National Ski Association, which, by 1925, included some 20,000 members. National tournaments have been arranged annually since 1916.

Although most Norwegians came to the United States after the Civil War, the 15th Wisconsin regiment, already mentioned, contained many Norwegians. This regiment was presented by a Scandinavian club in Chicago, with a flag having the American colors on one side and a combination of Norwegian and American legends on the reverse side.[84] In general, the Norwegians have been Republicans, although there have been many exceptions. The large number of Congressmen of Norwegian descent—including Senators Asle J. Gronna, Knute Nelson, Hendrik Shipstead, and H. O. Bursum; and Congressmen Nils P. Haugen, A. J. Volstead, Herman B. Dahle, Halvor Steenerson, and O. J. Kvale—indicates that the Norwegian element in the United States has attained its full political maturity. Among Norwegian governors may be mentioned Peter Norbeck and Carl Gunderson of South Dakota, Arthur G. Sorlie of North Dakota, J. O. Davidson of Wisconsin, J. A. O. Preuss of Minnesota, and John E. Erickson of Montana. As the late Professor Larsen pointed out in a recent article: "The radio reports from Minnesota on election night sounded like a roll call in the steerage." In 1932, there were five Norwegian Congressmen and two Swedes elected from Minnesota.[85]

THE DANES

The Danes constitute the smallest part of the Scandinavian immigration to the United States. By 1920, there were approximately 190,000 people in the United States who were born in Denmark. In addition, there were 277,415 born in the United States of Danish parentage, thus making a total of about 467,000 of Danish stock.

[84] See Blegen: "Colonel Hans Christian Heg," in *Wisconsin Magazine of History*, Vol. IV, pp. 140-165.
[85] See Larsen: "The Norwegian Element," in *American Historical Review*, Vol. XL, p. 78. See also Jacob A. O. Preuss: "Knute Nelson," in *Minnesota History Bulletin*, Vol. V, pp. 329-347. See also L. M. Larsen: *The Changing West* (Northfield, Minnesota, 1938).

Of this number, Iowa has the largest and Minnesota the second largest group, but in neither state does the total reach 50,000.[86]

Danish immigration to America did not really begin until about the middle of the last century, when information concerning the economic opportunities available in the United States began to seep into the Danish peninsula from Norway and Germany. Immigrant letters and pamphlets began to reach prospective emigrants in the 1840's. Religious bodies in the United States sent missionaries to Denmark and encouraged their converts to migrate across the sea. By 1860, about 2,000 Danes had been attracted to Great Salt Lake by the Mormon missionaries.[87] Homestead legislation and the liberal attitude of Western states toward immigrants were important factors in starting the immigrant tide. Religious controversies in Denmark also played their part but, as in the case of other Scandinavians, the economic urge was dominant.

The Census of 1870 reported a Danish population in the United States of 30,000. The high-water mark of Danish immigration was reached in 1882, when 11,000 arrived in a single year. Not again until 1891 did the number exceed 10,000. In the 1880's, most of the immigrants from Denmark were small farmers and laborers; after 1890, more skilled artisans and professional men came. As the rate of illiteracy is very low in Denmark and the people are familiar with economic and political democracy, the Danes represented in every way a substantial and desirable addition to the American population.

There are small Danish communities in a number of Eastern cities, but most of the Danes went to the agricultural West—to Wisconsin and then to Illinois, Iowa, Kansas, Nebraska, the Dakotas, Minnesota, Oregon, and Texas. The first Wisconsin settlement was made in Waukesha County, in 1847. Racine acquired a large Danish group in later years. By 1875, Wisconsin was able to

---

[86] Not much has been done on the Danes in America except the thorough work of Thomas Peter Christensen. His *History of the Danes in Iowa* was a doctor's dissertation at the University of Iowa in 1924. I have drawn upon it heavily. As by-products of this investigation, Dr. Christensen has published "The Danish Settlements in Kansas," in *Collections of the Kansas State Historical Society*, Vol. XVII, pp. 300-305; "The Danes in South Dakota," in *South Dakota Historical Collections*, Vol. XIV, pp. 539-552; and "Danish Settlement in Minnesota," in *Minnesota History Bulletin*, Vol. VIII, pp. 363-385. See also G. T. Flom: "The Danish Contingent in the Population of Early Iowa," in *Iowa Journal of History and Politics*, Vol. IV, p. 220 *et seq.*; and W. C. Westergaard: "History of the Danish Settlement in Hill Township, Cass County, North Dakota," in *Collections of the State Historical Society of North Dakota*, Vol. I, pp. 153-180.

[87] Arthur C. Cole: *The Irrepressible Conflict* (New York, 1934), p. 130.

support a Danish paper, the *Stjernen,* which circulated in several Danish agricultural villages. Danish communities were established in Nebraska and Kansas, and on the California coast. Many of these settlements were on railroad lands or had the support of colonization companies. The Danish People's Society, for example, which was organized to preserve the religion and national customs of the Danes, established three Danish farming and dairying communities from 1894 to 1919.

Much proselyting was done by non-Lutheran Protestants in the early Danish settlements, and dissension broke out among the Danes themselves over theological questions, such as affiliating with other Scandinavian Lutheran synods. By 1892, the Danish Church in America had 56 ministers, many parochial schools, an immigrant mission in New York, a theological school at West Denmark, Wisconsin, and an orphanage in Chicago. In 1896, the United Danish Evangelical Lutheran Church of America was organized, and it has remained the largest Danish church body in the United States. Many Danes in the United States belong to no church.

By 1870, there were less than 3,000 Danes in Iowa, many of whom came from the German province of Schleswig-Holstein. All the important Danish settlements in Iowa were started after the Civil War. The bulk of the immigrants were farmers, agricultural laborers, and artisans who had few resources other then a determination to succeed. They were men of industry and perseverance who enjoyed an excellent reputation for honesty and integrity. Many worked at first for the railroads or for American farmers, and some bought out Yankee farmers as soon as they had saved enough to make the first payment. From the first, the Danes emphasized dairying and were interested in coöperative creameries.

The Danes of Iowa have supported a number of religious weeklies. A Danish-Norwegian woman's magazine, printed in Cedar Rapids and known as *Kvinden og Hjemmet,* had a circulation of over 26,000 in 1924. The most widely read Danish paper in the United States is *Den Danske Pioneer,* published in Omaha. Like other groups, the Danes support their own societies and lodges. The United Danish Societies of America were incorporated in 1913 to provide coöperative life insurance and certain social advantages. The Danish Brotherhood was a secret society that developed from an organization of Danish war veterans; it now has over 15,000 members. In 1922, the Danish Sisterhood had 8,000 members in

145 lodges. All of these societies make some effort to keep alive the memories of the mother country and to emphasize the Danish cultural heritage. In politics, the Danes have been divided, but generally have favored progressive movements. They opposed both prohibition and woman's suffrage. Laurence Gronlund was one of their best-known Socialist leaders in the last century. Jacob August Riis, well-known author, journalist, and reformer, was another distinguished Danish-American.

Danish customs still linger on in Danish-American communities, including the wearing of wooden shoes by some of the older generation. A rich twisted pretzel and a crisp cookie—known as *kringler* and *bekkenoedder*, respectively—sausages—especially *gryn poels*, in which barley has been mixed—and thick sour milk and cheese are favorite Danish-American foods. Christmas is celebrated in the Continental fashion. The season begins on Little Christmas Day, *Lillejuledag*, and lasts until Twelfth Night.

THE ICELANDERS AND THE FINNS

For the sake of convenience, two other groups may be included here. One is the Icelandic, the other the Finns. One of the oldest Icelandic settlements, and the largest in the United States, is in Pembina County, North Dakota. It was established in 1878.[88] The Icelandic immigration to America dates roughly from 1870. Minneota, an Icelandic settlement in Minnesota, was begun in 1875. There are other small colonies in Wisconsin and Michigan, in western Canada, and on the Pacific coast. The settlers were typical: poor pioneers who had to send their products by oxcart to distant markets. A favorite dish of the Icelandic farmer was *skir*, prepared from curdled milk and brown cheese, which was made of whey and boiled for many hours.

In 1884, the Icelandic Lutheran Synod of America was organized. By 1908, it included 43 congregations, many of which were in Canada, and over 7,000 communicants. An Icelandic Patriotic League was formed in 1917. The only paper in Icelandic in the United States is the monthly *Vinland*, published in Minnesota. Icelanders have sat in the state legislatures of Minnesota, and Sveinbjorn Johnson was an associate judge of the North Dakota Supreme Court.[89]

[88] See *North Dakota Historical Quarterly*, Vol. VI, No. 2, pp. 150-164.
[89] See Thorstina Jackson: "The Icelandic Communities in America: Cultural Backgrounds and Early Settlements," in *Norwegian-American Historical Associa-*

The Finns may also be included in this discussion of the Scandinavian element, although there are lively controversies among scholars concerning their exact racial origin. The Finnish population in the United States in 1920 constituted only about 1.1 per cent of the total foreign-born population. Including those of Finnish stock born in America, the total at that time did not exceed 273,000. In 1930, it had grown to 320,536.

The Finns began coming to the United States in small numbers in the decade preceding the Civil War. About 250 found jobs in the newly opened copper mines at Calumet, Michigan. After 1870, they began to enter New England, the first arrivals often being sailors who left their vessels in the New England ports to find employment in the granite quarries of Quincy, Massachusetts, and in the textile mills.

Most of those who have left Finland for the United States were the real Finns, and not the Swedish-Finns. The struggle for existence in Finland is a constant one, and nature's vicissitudes often interfere seriously with man's endeavors to eke out a living in this northern country. The relations of Finland with Russia and Sweden include many unpleasant chapters of her earlier history, when Russia's policies were arbitrary and oppressive and when the Swedes came in to occupy the best farming lands, leaving to the Finns only the poorer, back-country, upland areas. By the laws of inheritance, Finnish farms became smaller and smaller, and the task of making a living from these little parcels of land became ever harder. Generally speaking, the Finns have settled in those parts of the United States which are geographically most similar to their homeland—namely, in Michigan, Wisconsin, and Minnesota; in Massachusetts; and in the Pacific Northwest. Practically none are to be found in the South, and over half of the Finnish immigrant stock has settled in the rural sections of the United States.

The ultimate objective of almost every Finn has been to own a farm in America and to become an independent farmer. At first, many were forced to find jobs in copper and iron mines, in stone quarries and factories, or as lumberjacks, for which they had ample experience in the homeland. But savings from wages derived from

tion Studies and Records, Vol. III, pp. 101-122. See also Sveinbjorn Johnson: "The Icelandic Settlement of Pembina County," in *Collections of the State Historical Society of North Dakota*, Vol. I, pp. 89-131; and "The Icelandic Lutheran Synod of America," in *Collections of the State Historical Society of North Dakota*, Vol. II, pp. 144-146.

these occupations were ultimately destined to go into a piece of land. Little plots were acquired on the outskirts of communities in which Finns were employed, so that they would be easily accessible for week-end work during the period when the owners were still dependent on their wages to support a farm.

Finnish farms are distinguishable by the buildings on them. Besides the cow and horse barns, root cellar, tool house, and woodshed, they always contain the typical Finnish bathhouse and the odd-shaped hay barn. In the evolution of the family homestead, the Finns, like other pioneers, passed from tar-paper shacks to the log cabin and eventually to the frame farmhouse. The hay barn, so typical of Finnish farms, is a pentagonal structure, with its sides sloping inward toward the floor, which is several feet above the ground. Between the logs that make up the floor and sides, a space of several inches is left in order to keep the hay dry and to expedite the curing process. The roof is steep and sloping, and overhangs the sides.

The Finn has demonstrated many qualities that make a desirable pioneer. Like his Scandinavian neighbors in the West, he is persevering, tenacious, and thrifty. He has come to America to stay and is generally eager to complete the naturalization process as soon as possible. In his phlegmatic, stolid way, he becomes a devoted citizen of his adopted country. He appreciates public education and, in the Northwest, has been called "the backbone of the night school." Politically, the Finnish-American has been a progressive, and a large percentage of Finnish workers are ardent Laborites and Socialists. In religion, the Finn is Lutheran, and developed his own Finnish Lutheran Synod in America. A number of periodicals are supported by the Finns in America, who seem to be diligent readers. Finnish papers were published in Ashtabula, Ohio, since 1884. The *Amerikan Sanomet* still survives there, with a circulation of 800. In 1909, its circulation exceeded 11,000.[90] Perhaps the Finns' greatest handicap has been an addiction to strong drink.[91]

Much has been written in appreciation of the sterling qualities of the Scandinavians and their desirability as immigrants and permanent additions to the American stock. This brief survey of their

[90] See John I. Kolehmainen: "Finnish Newspapers in Ohio," in *The Ohio State Archaeological and Historical Quarterly*, Vol. XLVII, pp. 123-128.
[91] For an account of the Finns, see Eugene Van Cleef: "The Finn in America," in *The Geographical Review*, Vol. VI, pp. 185-214; and *Finland, the Republic Farthest North* (Columbus, Ohio, 1929).

history in the United States may well close with two such comments, which are typical. The one emanated from a student of American immigration who had no special interest in the Scandinavians, the second from an American who is an able and scholarly representative of the second generation of Swedes in the United States. Thus the late Professor Orth concluded his study of the Scandinavians with the comment:

> It is the consensus of opinion among competent observers that these northern peoples have been the most useful of the recent great additions to the American race. They were particularly fitted by nature for the conquest of the great area which they have brought under subjugation . . . . Above all, the Scandinavian has never looked upon himself as an exile. From the first, he has considered himself an American . . . . Without brilliance, producing few leaders, the Norseman represents the rugged commonplace of American life, avoiding the catastrophes of a soaring ambition on the one hand and the pitfalls of a jaded temperamentalism on the other. Bent on self-improvement, he scrupulously patronizes farmers' institutes, high schools, and extension courses, and listens with intelligent patience to lectures that would put an American audience to sleep. This son of the North has greatly buttressed every worthy American institution with the stern traditional virtues of the tiller of the soil. Strength he gives, if not grace, and that at a time when all social institutions are being shaken to their foundations.[92]

And Professor Stephenson, who bases his judgment on personal observation as well as long and thorough historical investigation, wrote:

> Coming almost entirely from the lower classes, the Scandinavian-Americans have produced comparatively few eminent leaders; but with their qualities of industry, thrift, honesty, love of home, respect for law and order, religious nature, interest in education, and physical stamina, they have played a respectable part in the development of American society.[93]

Perhaps both commentators have overestimated the conservatism of the Scandinavian-American stock and underestimated their capacity for leadership.

[92] S. P. Orth: *Our Foreigners* (New Haven, Connecticut, 1921), pp. 157 and 159.
[93] G. M. Stephenson: *A History of American Immigration* (Boston, 1926), p. 29.

11

The Swiss, Dutch, Russian-Germans, Welsh, French, and Jews

THE IMMIGRATION of Irish, Germans, and Scandinavians overshadowed all other immigration in the nineteenth century. Some of the smaller groups represented much the same culture as the Germans and Scandinavians. Others were of quite a different type. The distinctions between Swiss, Dutch, Germans, and Russian-Germans are not always easy to draw moreover, for all of them represented geographical and national divisions which were far more important than differences in their cultural patterns. Because of language similarities, they were frequently confused, and exact statistics concerning their immigration are difficult to get. However, each has been sufficiently important to deserve a brief discussion of their major settlements in the United States.

THE SWISS

Groups of Swiss emigrants settled in the Middle Western States of Michigan, Ohio, Wisconsin, Iowa, Indiana, Illinois, and Kentucky during the last half of the nineteenth century, and isolated settlements may be found in the Far West and Southwest as well. The Swiss, most of whom spoke a Swiss-German and represented an essentially Germanic culture, intermingled with the larger German communities to such an extent that it becomes difficult to establish their separate identity. In 1887, according to *Der deutsche Pionier*,[1] the most important separate Swiss colonies still in existence in the United States, with the dates of their establishment were: Highland, in Madison County, Illinois (1836); New Glarus, in Green County, Wisconsin (1845); Tell City, in Perry County, Indiana, (1856); Grütli, in Grundy County, Tennessee (1868); Helvetia, in Randolph County, West Virginia (1869); New Switzerland, in Haber-

---

[1] See *Der deutsche Pionier*, Vol. XVIII, p. 336.

[300]

shaw County, Georgia (1879); Rüttli, in Platte County, Nebraska (1880); and Bernstadt, in Laurel County, Kentucky (1881).

The Highland settlement in Illinois was at first called Helvetia. Its life was typically German, with a singing society and an amateur theater troupe; and its citizens were employed as farmers, in the vineyards, and in the local brewery.[2] Salomon Köpfli, son of Dr. Kaspar Köpfli, one of the original founders and a member of the Illinois Constitutional Convention, which assembled during the Civil War, was especially interested in the development of the state's educational system.[3]

New Glarus, Wisconsin, was settled by Swiss from Canton Glarus, in Switzerland. When an economic crisis struck this part of Switzerland in 1844, the Swiss government encouraged emigration. A colonization society was organized, and two agents were sent to the United States to select a site. Twelve hundred acres were bought, plus 80 acres of woodland, which were parceled out in 20-acre lots. In April, 1845, nearly 200 Swiss started for the United States, but only 108 went to Wisconsin. The first years were years of disappointment and controversy. Occasional contributions from Switzerland proved exceedingly welcome. New Glarus was located, as might have been expected, among the roughest hills of Green County. Its rocky slopes no doubt suggested the Alpine home. In 1846, cows were bought in an adjoining town, and the Swiss immediately began to engage in the dairy industry. The houses of the little settlement were built flush on the street, with no place for trees or sidewalks. A log church was erected in 1849. Its first preacher, Reverend Streissguth, was supported for two years from Switzerland. The community remained faithful to the Swiss Reformed Church until the advent of itinerant preachers led to the founding of an Evangelical Church. The Swiss settlements in and around New Glarus sent nearly 100 men into the Union Army, although most of the Swiss had been Democrats before the war and remained so. Swiss customs and institutions—such as a glee club, a rifle club, and annual *Kilbi* festivals—were observed in New Glarus for many years. In 1891, the community celebrated the 500th anniversary of the founding of the Swiss Republic with speeches, music, and patriotic tableaux. The leading industry of New Glarus is cheese making, and since 1870 the landscape in this vicinity has

[2] See *ibid.*, Vol. IV, p. 280.
[3] See *ibid.*, Vol. IV, pp. 272-274.

been dotted with cheese factories. A Cheese Manufacturers' Insurance Society was organized in 1887, and the next year a Cheese Exchange was established, along the lines of a stock market for the cheese industry.[4] Not only in Wisconsin, but in other parts of the United States as well—such as the Mohawk Valley of New York— the Swiss farmers have been prominent in the milk and cheese business.

Bern, Minnesota, a village in Dodge County, was laid out by Swiss families from the old Bern in 1856. Helvetia, in Carver County, was founded in the same year. Many Swiss settlers have intermingled with the Scandinavians and Germans in settlements like New Ulm and Winone, and in St. Paul and Minneapolis.[5] The Swiss settlements in South Dakota were begun by Mennonites who had originally moved to the Volga and who left Russia when their privileges were threatened. These Swiss-Germans and their descendants are found today in Turner and Hutchinson Counties, South Dakota, and are among the most prosperous farmers in the state.[6]

The leading Swiss communities in Indiana are Berne, Tell City, and Vevay.[7] The settlement of Vevay was primarily due to the efforts of the Dufour family, who came from a French canton of Switzerland and was interested in developing viniculture in the Ohio Valley. After failing in Kentucky, the promoters, in 1809, proceeded down the river some 70 miles from Cincinnati and settled in what became known as Vevay and in Switzerland County. Thirty-seven hundred acres were obtained on credit from the government, and the town was laid out in 1813. The county was organized the next year. In 1816, a classical school was established, as well as a short-lived library, which were to be supported by the Literary Society of Vevay. Although life was hard in the new

[4] See John Luchsinger: "The Planting of the Swiss Colony at New Glarus, Wisconsin," in *Wisconsin Historical Collections*, Vol. XII, pp. 335-382; and Vol. VIII, pp. 1-35. See also J. E. Emery: "The Swiss Cheese Industry in Wisconsin," in *Wisconsin Magazine of History*, Vol. X, pp. 42-52; and diaries and articles in *Wisconsin Historical Collections*, Vol. XV, pp. 292-337; Vol. VII, pp. 411-445; and Vol. XV, pp. 295-337. Consult also: "A Swiss Family in the New World; Letters of Jacob and Ulrich Bühler," in *Wisconsin Magazine of History*, Vol. VI, p. 317.
[5] See Bertha L. Heilbron: "Swiss Settlement in Minnesota," in *Minnesota History Bulletin*, Vol. VIII, pp. 174-175.
[6] See John J. Gering: "The Swiss Germans of Southeastern South Dakota," in *South Dakota Historical Collections*, Vol. VI, pp. 351-361.
[7] See *Der deutsche Pionier*, Vol. XVIII, pp. 140-143.

community, the settlement managed to survive. In 1825, its Swiss artillery company marched 70 miles to participate in the reception for Lafayette.[8] Tell City, Indiana, about 125 miles above Louisville on the Ohio River, was planned in 1856 by Swiss who advertised in the newspapers for volunteers to establish a Swiss colonizing society. Six thousand acres were bought and 400 shares of stock sold at $20 a share. Settlement was actually begun in 1858.

In the Osage Valley of Missouri, about 150 miles from St. Louis, the Swiss community of New Helvetia was established in 1844. It remained small and of little importance. In central Kansas are located the Swiss-German villages of Basel, Zurich, Unterwalden, and Luzern. Two Swiss colonies were started near Dallas, Texas, in 1868 and 1872, respectively. By 1880, the 200 Swiss in Dallas were sufficiently organized to support a singing society, a *Turnverein*, and an annual May festival (*Maifest*).[9] A small Swiss Socialist colony maintained itself for a short time in St. Tammany Parish, Louisiana.

In the early 1880's, about 100 Swiss left Bern to settle in West Virginia. Disappointed there, about half went to Laurel County, Kentucky, where the state authorities encouraged them to settle. Eventually, the Swiss were attracted to Lincoln County, where they developed a prosperous farming community. By the close of the 1880's, Bernstadt, Kentucky, had a population of nearly 1,000, with a Swiss singing society, a band, and a *Turnverein*.[10] In the neighboring state of Tennessee, the Swiss Captain E. H. Plumacher, in coöperation with the consul general of Switzerland in the United States, promoted a Swiss colonizing venture during the Reconstruction period after the Civil War, when several Southern states were trying to attract European immigrants. The site selected was in middle Tennessee, and the settlers were described as "men of means" who had come to plant vineyards and raise livestock.[11]

[8] See Perret Dufour: *The Swiss Settlement of Switzerland County, Indiana*, with an introduction by Harlow Lindley, Indiana Historical Commission (Indianapolis, 1925).

[9] See G. G. Benjamin: "The Germans in Texas," in *Americana Germanica*, (Philadelphia, 1909), p. 256. Reprinted from *German-American Annals*, Vols. VI and VII.

[10] See also Johann von Grüningen: *Eine kurze Beschreibung der Saaner-Kolonie nahe bei Stanford, in Lincoln County, Kentucky* (Frankfurt, Germany, 1882); and Otto Brunner: *Die Auswanderung nach den Vereinigten Staaten Nord-Amerikas* (Bern, Switzerland, 1881).

[11] See *Cincinnati Enquirer*, July 30, and September 1 and 18, 1868; and *Ohio State Journal*, November 22, 1869.

Apparently the Swiss who were induced to settle near Goldsboro, North Carolina, met with little success.[12]

Without following the details of Swiss settlement any further, it is evident that most of the Swiss were German in speech, habits, and customs. The life of Swiss-American communities therefore had much in common with, and was frequently a part of, the larger German-American group. New York City before the Civil War had a Schweizer Schützenklub (Swiss rifle club), a Grütli Verein, a Helvetia Männerchor, and a benevolent society. The Schützenklub held its first *Schützenfest* in West Hoboken, in 1853. In this case, however, the majority of the original membership seem to have been French-Swiss. The Philadelphia Schwing und Turnklub, founded in 1878, claims to be the oldest Swiss club of its kind in the United States. There was a Schweizer Schützenklub in San Francisco in the early 1860's, and the Schweizer Männerchor of St. Louis has been singing since 1880. Similar societies are to be found in Buffalo, Rochester, Cleveland, Cincinnati, and Columbus. Swiss singing societies and athletic and sharpshooting clubs bear such characteristic Swiss names as the Wilhelm Tell Männerchor and the Schweizer Alpenrösli. Perhaps four fifths of the total Swiss immigration is composed of German-Swiss. The weekly *Amerikanische Schweizerzeitung* has appeared in New York since 1868. The *Nord-Amerikanische Schweizerbund* has about 8,000 members. The only important Italian-Swiss paper is the San Francisco *Colonia Svizzera.*

Swiss artisans have found employment in the larger cities. The Swiss have been numerous in the hotel and restaurant business and in small business ventures. The famous "Oscar of the Waldorf" is Oscar Tschirky. Many a Swiss immigrant has spent his first days in the United States in a Hotel Rütli. Swiss watchmakers, famous for their skill, have for many years been employed in large numbers by companies like the Waltham Watch Company.[13]

THE DUTCH

The causes of the Dutch immigration to America in the nineteenth century did not differ greatly from those affecting other groups in the same period. Although these causes were primarily

---

[12] See *Cincinnati Enquirer*, December 24, 1868.
[13] See Adelrich Steinach: *Geschichte und Leben der Schweizer Kolonien in den Vereinigten Staaten von Nord-Amerika* (New York, 1889).

economic, owing to the density of population and pressure upon the means of livelihood, religious and social causes combined with economic factors in the Netherlands to stimulate thousands of the discouraged and dissatisfied to move to America. The Presbyterian form of church government in the Netherlands was virtually an oligarchy under royal patronage in the first half of the century. Orthodox Christians were dissatisfied with irregularities that crept into church doctrine and practice; and, in the 1830's, large groups, under the leadership of pietistic clergymen, began to secede from the State Church. The Separatists, in spite of the recognition they obtained in 1839 by royal decree, suffered from petty discriminations and persecutions, and their church schools were the cause of considerable friction. Taxes in Holland were heavy and the national debt was burdensome; wages were low and unemployment was frequent. Thousands of laborers led a mere hand-to-mouth existence. To the discontented, whatever the cause, emigration offered a chance for relief.

Small Dutch agricultural colonies arose during the last century in central and western Kansas and in Nebraska; in several counties in North Dakota, South Dakota, and Minnesota; and in western Canada. In 1847, the Reverend P. Zonne led his Dutch followers into Wisconsin, on Lake Michigan, about 20 miles south of the present Sheboygan, where he established the villages of Cedar Grove and Oostburg.[14] By 1850, there were Dutch settlements at Chicago, South Holland, and Roseland, in Illinois. By 1900, the number born in Holland and residing in the United States exceeded 105,000. Of these, over 30,000 were in Michigan, about 22,000 in Illinois, and nearly 10,000 in Iowa. In the next decade, all these settlements were greatly augmented by the arrival of another 30,000 Dutch immigrants. From 1820 to 1920, the total Dutch immigration reached nearly 340,000. The Census of 1930 reported 133,133 persons in the United States who were born in Holland. Of this number, 32,-128 were in the State of Michigan, mostly in Grand Rapids, Kalamazoo, and Holland. Large numbers of Dutch immigrants remained behind in the Eastern cities, as the activity of their societies and churches clearly shows.[15]

[14] See Sipko F. Rederus: "The Dutch Settlements of Sheboygan County," in *Wisconsin Magazine of History*, Vol. I, p. 256.
[15] See, for example, *The New York Sun*, January 18, 1894; *The New York Times*, October 19, 1877; and *The New York Tribune*, December 6, 1883.

A brief consideration of the Dutch communities of Michigan and Iowa must suffice for the purposes of this discussion of the Dutch element in the United States. These were the most important of the nineteenth-century Dutch settlements and, in both cases, reliable material is available to follow their development. The Dutch settlements in Michigan were founded primarily by religious dissenters who had broken with the State Church of the Netherlands and who migrated to the New World in congregations, under the guidance of their pastors. For these seceders, the State Church had become too liberal in doctrine and practice. Separatist pastors objected to alleged corruptions of the service and particularly to the *Evangelische Gezangen,* a collection of hymns used to supplement the psalms. The dissenters described these hymns as "one hundred ninety-two siren songs, designed to draw the members of the *Hervormde Kerk* (Reformed Church) from their Saviour and to carry them into the false doctrine of lies." [16] Differences of this kind, defended with typical Dutch stubbornness, led to conflicts and secessions, as well as to the breaking up of separatist meetings and the fining of their leaders. This persecution soon ended, however, but the economic depression of the 1840's made it difficult for a secessionist church to survive. Poverty and hard times in agriculture and industry led to an appeal to the Dutch Reformed Church in the United States for aid, and plans were presently made to move to America. "America Letters" also had their usual influence.[17]

In 1846, the Reverend Albertus van Raalte—after a prolonged fever, which may have inspired him to believe that he was a nineteenth-century Moses—left for the United States with his family and some 50 followers. After many hardships in steerage and on the journey inland, the party reached Detroit, where it began, with a rare combination of religious devotion and the practical-mindedness of the shrewd Dutch burgher, to clear the forests for a permanent home. After careful investigation, Van Raalte had selected for his New Holland in America the region around the Black River, in Ottawa County, western Michigan, near the modern Kalamazoo and Grand Rapids. In 1847, the group grew to 700 and was scat-

---

[16] Quoted in Aleida J. Pieters: *A Dutch Settlement in Michigan* (Grand Rapids, Michigan, 1923), p. 18. This is the best account, and I have borrowed from it heavily.
[17] See *ibid.*, pp. 37 and 38.

tered over three villages; by 1848, the total had reached 4,000. Other leaders who joined the group were the Reverend Cornelius Van Der Meulen, Martin Ypma, and Jannes Van De Luyster.[18]

The experiences of the Hollanders in Michigan were those of typical pioneers. Many hired themselves out to neighboring American farmers to raise cash for the completion of their first log cabins. The river and corduroy roads were their only means of communicating with the outside world. Malaria, smallpox, and dysentery depleted the settlements. Temporal matters were handled by a primary assembly of all the heads of families; spiritual affairs, which were considered of the utmost importance, were in the hands of a consistory of deacons and elders elected by the congregation. The latter enforced their edicts rigorously, even to the point of excommunication. Five trustees, with Van Raalte as president, administered the property of the colony. In a sense, the settlement was a theocracy, and, in the early days, some of the aspects of government and the administration of property and wages suggested a communistic society. By 1850, seven Dutch villages had been established in Michigan, with the typically Dutch names of Holland, Groningen, Zeeland, Drenthe, Vriesland, Overisel, and Graafschap. In 1856, a new church was dedicated. An academy had been projected and a paper, *De Hollander,* established.

The Dutch villages of Michigan rested on a stern Calvinistic foundation, and the Dutch Christian Reformed Church in these parts has remained ultraconservative to this day. Dancing, cards, and the theater were anathema to the early settlers; religion and the *Bible* were their major concern. The sale of intoxicating liquors was prohibited. Parochial schools were developed. Long church services were held two or three times on Sunday, as well as midweek prayer meetings. Music was frowned upon, except for the singing of psalms. For a time, the church authorities also assumed jurisdiction over civil disputes. The denial of the right to participate in the Holy Communion, celebrated four times a year, was regarded as one of the severest penalties that could be imposed. Recreations were few, including little more than the coffee hour (*kaffie kletz*), at which the women gathered, with their weekly mending, to talk.[19] The old Holland Academy, under the Reverend John Van Vleck, was

---

[18] See George F. Huizinga: *What the Dutch Have Done in the West of the United States* (Philadelphia, 1909).
[19] Arnold Mulder has written some modern tales about the Dutch of Michigan.

founded primarily as a preparatory school for those who planned to study for the ministry. In the 1860's, it developed into Hope College, the first Dutch college in the United States, located in Holland, Michigan. By 1920, its graduates totaled nearly 900, of whom about one third had become ministers. The leading school for the training of clergymen for the Dutch Christian Reformed Church is John Calvin College, in Grand Rapids.

Not until the third generation did the forces of Americanization really begin to make appreciable inroads on the Dutch communities and customs in western Michigan, and Dutch is still spoken to a great extent in the rural sections. Edam cheese, smoked beef, rusks, rye bread, and currant bread are as popular in America among the Dutch as in Holland.

During the 1850's, the Hollanders of Michigan, who had originally been Democrats, shifted slowly to the Republican party. In 1860, Douglas carried Holland township over Lincoln by a majority of 23. Van Raalte, however, urged his followers to vote Republican, largely because of the slavery issue; although the Hollanders, like the Germans in 1860, were not without their suspicions about the alleged affiliations between Republicans and Know-Nothings. The Holland Democratic Club of Grand Rapids declined so rapidly in membership that, in the spring of 1860, it "had to ride with the Irish" in a Democratic parade.[20] The G. A. R. post of Holland, Michigan, contained many Dutch veterans of the Civil War.

The Dutch in Michigan have been successful farmers for generations, concentrating on truck gardening and smaller agricultural products—such as beet sugar, celery, fruits, and dairying. The May tulip festival of Holland, Michigan, has become an annual occasion for the revival of Dutch customs. It attracts many visitors who come for miles to enjoy the display and the festivities. One of the largest branch factories of the H. J. Heinz Company is in Holland, Michigan, and at least one tenth of all the farmers who grow pickles for this company are to be found among the Dutch of western Michigan. Of all the cities in America, Grand Rapids is still the most Dutch, and it still supports Dutch newspapers and Dutch churches. The Dutch are primarily employed in the Grand Rapids furniture industry, although the Zeeland Brick Company and the

[20] See Henry S. Lucas: "The Political Activities of the Dutch Immigrants from 1847 to the Civil War," in *Iowa Journal of History and Politics*, Vol. XXVI, pp. 171-203.

Cappon and Bertsch Leather Company of Michigan are other successful Dutch concerns. The *Sheboygan Nieuwsbode* (1849) was the first Dutch newspaper to be published in the United States. Of the 21 Dutch newspapers printed in the United States 60 years later, 10 were located in Michigan.[21]

The Moses who led the Dutch to Iowa was Henry P. Scholte. Here, too, the Hollanders settled by religious groups in clannish farming communities. Orange City, Pella, and Muncie remain the centers of Dutch influence in that state. The Hollanders brought property with them and received a cordial welcome. It took them three weeks to reach St. Louis and two more days to reach Keokuk, by steamboat. Actually, they reached the site of their first Iowa settlement late in August, 1847. Scholte had secured title to 18,000 acres in the northeastern edge of Marion County, and here his 600 followers laid out the plans for the town of Pella. Frame buildings eventually superseded the original dugouts and sod houses, and Iowa cheese, made by Dutch farmers, quickly acquired a reputation for excellence in the St. Louis markets. Scholte advertised the colony in Holland, and others soon joined the Iowa Dutch communities, settling usually along the lakes and waterways. Few Dutch farmers occupied the Iowa corn and wheat belts. For the most part, as in Michigan, the Dutch of Iowa concentrated on truck gardening and smaller products—such as beet sugar, vegetables, and dairy products—for which neighboring towns furnished a steady market. The state government of Iowa looked with favor upon the newcomers and, by immigration propaganda, tried to attract more of them to Iowa. Pella became the distributing center from which later arrivals from Holland proceeded to Orange City, in Sioux County, where they were joined by Dutchmen from Wisconsin. In 1874, Henry Hospers began publishing *De Volksvriend* in Orange City.

The Dutch had come to stay; they acquired farms and held them, and they took steps immediately upon their arrival to become naturalized. Politically, the Dutch in Pella have been consistent Dem-

[21] For further information on the Dutch in Michigan, see Martin L. D'Ooge: "The Dutch Pioneers of Michigan," in *Michigan Pioneer and Historical Society Collections*, Vol. XXXVIII, pp. 204-212; G. Van Schelven: "Early Settlement of Holland," in *Michigan Pioneer and Historical Society Collections*, Vol. XXVI, pp. 569-579; H. Beets: "Dutch Journalism in Michigan," in *Michigan History Magazine*, Vol. VI, p. 435; and articles by Henry S. Lucas, Diekema, Vennema, and Van Schelven, in *Michigan History Magazine*, Vols. I, IV, and VI, *passim*.

ocrats, although Scholte was a delegate to the convention which nominated Lincoln in 1860. Sioux County has supported Dutch newspapers of both major parties. The *Weekblad* of Pella has been one of the largest Dutch newspapers in the United States. By 1910, Iowa had about 50 Dutch Reformed congregations, although in most towns, Dutch Reformed and Christian Reformed churches existed side by side. The former have been quicker to adopt the use of English in church services; both have helped to maintain Dutch clannishness. As Professor Van der Zee has suggested, culture, in the broad sense of the word, has come slowly into the lives of most Hollanders in Iowa. Books and periodicals are rare on Dutch farms. Wooden shoes are still manufactured for use in the home.[22]

THE RUSSIAN-GERMANS

In 1920, there were 116,535 persons living in the United States who were born in Russia but spoke German and 186,997 others born in the United States of this Russian-German stock. These immigrants are essentially Germans and not Russians, though long residence in Russia has left its mark on their language and customs. Most of them were not Mennonites driven out of Russia by persecution and military service, although perhaps somewhat over 10 per cent belonged to this religious group. The majority were Germans from the Volga and the Black Sea regions of Russia. They are scattered throughout the United States in hundreds of little communities, but particularly in agricultural states like Kansas, Nebraska, Minnesota, Iowa, and North Dakota.[23] The real home of this Russian-German stock in America is the prairie region between the Mississippi and the Rockies.

The first group from the Black Sea area came in 1847-1848 to grow grapes on Kelly's Island, Ohio, and to farm in Iowa. In 1873, several groups settled in Nebraska. Within the next 15 years, Rus-

---

[22] For this account, see Jacob Van Der Zee: *The Hollanders in Iowa* (Iowa City, 1912); "Diary of a Journey from the Netherlands to Pella, Iowa in 1849," in *Iowa Journal of History and Politics*, Vol. X, pp. 363-382; and "An Eminent Foreigner's Visit to the Dutch Colonies of Iowa in 1873," in *Iowa Journal of History and Politics*, Vol. XI, pp. 221-247. See also Henry S. Lucas: "The Beginnings of Dutch Immigration to Iowa, 1845-1847," in *Iowa Journal of History and Politics*, Vol. XXII, pp. 483-531; and "A Document Relating to Dutch Immigration to Iowa," in *Iowa Journal of History and Politics*, Vol. XXI, pp. 457-465.

[23] See *The New York Times*, January 2, 1879.

sian-Germans founded Kassel and New Danzig in South Dakota, and colonies like Leipzig in North Dakota. Later groups were attracted to the railroad lands of the Northern Pacific. Other colonies are to be found in almost all the Western states, and certain groups of Russian-Germans have moved on into Canada.[24] Some were Catholics; others, particularly those from the Volga region, Evangelical Protestants.

In Nebraska, Lincoln became the center of the Volga Germans, largely because the workshops of the Burlington Railroad offered immediate employment to hundreds of these immigrants. As late as 1924, the population of Lincoln comprised about 9,000 of this group. They live in the "Little Russia" on the west side, one of the worst sections of the city; but their houses and yards, many of which they own, are generally clean, in spite of overcrowding and neglect of sanitation. Infant mortality rates are high, and ventilation has never been the special forte of immigrants from eastern Europe.[25] In Kansas, settlements were similarly determined in many cases by the opportunity to find jobs in railroad construction gangs. In Colorado and other Western states, the rapidly developing beet sugar industry was the chief attraction.[26]

The immediate cause of the Russian-German immigration was the cancellation of their exemption from military service by the Russian government. But if this was the immediate cause, other factors—such as religious controversy and the propaganda of American railroad companies—were also effective in stimulating emigration. Advertisements in the German language issued by the Burlington and Quincy and the Union Pacific Railroads, and immigration agents of the Santa Fe Railroad, were well known in the German settlements along the Volga and in other Russian colonies. Economic discontent and the hunger for land brought most of this group to America. Here they settled in the early years of their residence in the United States in the typical sod houses and dugouts of pioneer days. Place names like Odessa in North and South Dakota and in Washington, Kulm in South Dakota, and Strassburg, Selz, and Karlsruhe in North Dakota testify to the desire of these

[24] See Richard Sallet: *Russlanddeutsche Siedlungen in den Vereinigten Staaten* (Chicago, 1931), pp. 1-49.
[25] See Hattie Plum Williams: "A Social Study of the Russian-German," in *University of Nebraska Studies*, Vol. XVI, No. 3, pp. 1-101.
[26] See also "The German Russians in North Dakota," in *Collections of the State Historical Society of North Dakota*, Vol. I, pp. 199-200.

immigrants to perpetuate in the New World the names of their ancestral homes.

Russian-German farmers were industrious, thrifty, and successful. In east European fashion, the farmhouse and barn were usually one and the same building. Families were large, and every member was expected to share in the farm tasks. Women wore head coverings as they did in Russia, and cooked menus that revealed both German and Russian influences.[27] The Russian-Germans in America are divided among several religious sects, and the churches remain their most important social organization. Their leading paper is the *Dakota Freie Presse* of Yankton, South Dakota, transferred in 1920 to New Ulm, Minnesota. The *Nord Dakota Staatspresse* appeared for a time in three languages—English, German, and Norwegian— and then suspended publication.[28]

Americanization is going on relentlessly, but several interesting customs showing strange mixtures of German and Russian influences still remain and are of interest to the student of the life of immigrant groups. Christmas, of course, is the most important holiday in the calendar. On Christmas Eve, instead of the traditional Santa Claus, a lady appears, dressed in white, with a blue girdle and veiled face. She rings a bell, knocks, and enters with the German greeting: "Gelobt sei Jesus Christus." The youngest child in the family is requested to say a prayer and is then rewarded with presents. The older children are sometimes treated with the rod. Nuts are then tossed into the air and, during the scramble, the figure disappears. On Christmas and Easter, every child is expected to call on his baptismal sponsors and is rewarded with sweets, which he is expected to carry away in a white cloth. At New Year, children call on their elders and receive coins. The young men usually greet the occasion with a generous discharge of firearms, and the young ladies pin ribbons on the young men's coats. During Holy Week, when all church bells are silent, boys go about the villages with wooden clappers to summon worshippers to the services.

Marriage customs also show a strange mixture of German and Russian practices. In earlier days, oral invitations from the fathers of the bridal couple were delivered by two men bearing canes decorated with ribbons. They were rewarded for their efforts with refreshments. Whoever accepted the invitation added a ribbon to

---

[27] See Sallet: *op. cit.*, p. 80.
[28] See *ibid.*, p. 90.

the canes. On the eve of the wedding, the guests and friends celebrated the *Polterabend* with music, dancing, and ribald hilarity. On the morning of the wedding day, the couple knelt on a cloth, facing each other, to receive the blessings of parents and relatives. On the way to church, the bride preceded the groom; on the way from church, the order was reversed. Along the way, young men saluted the couple with incessant shooting. Marriages were celebrated for days, in the best Continental fashion. At the wedding feast, which the couple attended but of which they did not partake, the bride was robbed of her shoe. It was generally auctioned off, and the best man was expected to redeem it for money. Dancing followed, during which gifts—such as money and dry goods—were pinned on the bridal gown. At these festivities, dances and folksongs of Germany blended with those from Russia. *Kranzkuchen,* huge plaited cakes with holes in the center big enough to hold a man's arm, were special delicacies on these occasions.[29]

THE WELSH

The Welsh who came to the United States in the early nineteenth century either engaged in farming or practiced their old occupation as miners. Before the Irish came, Welsh coal miners furnished much of the labor supply in the anthracite regions of Pennsylvania. Pittsburgh has one of the most important Welsh communities in the United States today. Many of the workers in the slate quarries of the United States are of Welsh extraction, especially in the quarries of New York and Pennsylvania. There has also been an influx of Welsh tinworkers.[30] From 1830 to 1850, the men of Cornwall went into the lead-mining region of southwestern Wisconsin. By 1850, there were about 7,000 in this area, and today the language used by the older inhabitants in this district gives evidence of a persistent Welsh influence.[31] Many of the Welsh in the Wisconsin lead-mining region soon abandoned their original occupation to become farmers and successful stockbreeders. There is still a village

[29] For a description of these customs, see the Reverend Francis S. Laing: "German-Russian Settlements in Ellis County, Kansas," in *Kansas Historical Collections*, Vol. XI, pp. 489-528, especially 518-528.
[30] See Ebenezer Edwards: *Welshmen as Factors* (Utica, New York, 1899), p. 328. This book is a veritable hodgepodge of names and without scientific merit or organization.
[31] See Louis A. Copeland: "The Cornish in Southwest Wisconsin," in *Wisconsin Historical Collections*, Vol. XIV, pp. 301-334.

of Wales in Waukesha County and a Cambria in Columbia County, Wisconsin.[32]

The Welsh Baptist church in Utica, New York, was organized in 1801. At the beginning of the nineteenth century, the only appreciable immigration into Oneida County was Welsh. In 1802, a Welsh Congregational church was established in Utica, and 12 years later, the Ancient Britons Benevolent Society was founded there.[33] Remsen is an old Welsh settlement in up-State New York. In 1843, a Welsh Society was formed in New York City for social and benevolent purposes, to preserve the purity of the Welsh language, to celebrate Welsh national holidays, and to protect Welsh immigrants from fraud and exploitation.[34] Three Welsh magazines were published in New York State in the early 1840's.[35] In 1857, the Welsh community in Oneida County imported Humphrey R. Jones, famous Welsh preacher of Wisconsin, to conduct revival services.[36] In 1861, the Association of Welsh Congregational Churches of New York included 22 churches.[37] There was enough of a Welsh community in Boston in 1870 to warrant special observance of Saint David's Day.[38]

The Welsh scattered Westward as the farming frontier advanced. In Pittsburgh, a number of Welsh citizens organized a colonization society to aid their countrymen in emigrating from the crowded Eastern industrial sections to the West.[39] The leading Welsh communities in Ohio are in Jackson County; at Radnor, in Delaware County; and in the "Welsh Hills" of Licking County, near Newark.[40] In 1892, there were about 700 Welsh in Osage County, Kansas, and over 1,000 in the neighborhood of Emporia, with six churches holding services in Welsh in the former and three in the latter.[41] Welshmen participated in the gold rush to California, and a Welsh

[32] See Joseph Schafer: "Four Wisconsin Counties," in *Wisconsin Domesday Book, General Studies* (Madison, Wisconsin, 1927), Vol. II, p. 105.
[33] See M. M. Bagg: *The Pioneers of Utica* (Utica, New York, 1877), pp. 101-147, 365, and 472.
[34] See *New York Old Countrymen*, January 18 and March 1, 1843.
[35] See *ibid.*, February 15, 1843.
[36] See *Christian Advocate and Journal*, February 18, 1858.
[37] See *New York Tribune*, September 26, 1861.
[38] See *Boston Transcript*, February 21, 1870.
[39] See *The New York Times*, August 12, 1877.
[40] See W. H. Jones: "Welsh Settlements in Ohio," in *Ohio Archaeological and Historical Quarterly*, Vol. XVI, pp. 194-227. For a description of Paddy's Run, Ohio, see *Cincinnati Commercial*, November 18, 1881.
[41] See W. H. Carruth: "Foreign Settlements in Kansas," in *The Kansas University Quarterly*, Vol. I, No. 2, pp. 77-79.

Presbyterian church was organized in San Francisco in 1873. A Cambrian Mutual Aid Society had been started there three years earlier.[42]

The Welsh have been rapidly assimilated. Politically, they have generally been Republican, and the *Y Drych,* the oldest Welsh newspaper in the United States, supported the party even during the schism of 1872.[43] Without question, the one institution for which the Welsh in America are best known is the *Eisteddfod,* an institution imported from Wales and dedicated to competitive singing and literary activities. As early as 1860, the first *Eisteddfod* west of the Rockies was held by Welsh gold miners in North San Juan, California.[44] In 1865, the Welsh Musical Union was organized among the Welsh farmers and miners of Wisconsin for the purpose of holding annual musical conventions and offering prizes for musical compositions.[45] In 1887, the Welsh of Pittsburgh won first prize in a national *Eisteddfod,* and Scranton took second place.[46] Welsh choral societies gave frequent concerts in the Welsh churches and in concert halls.[47] In 1897, a Cymradorion Society was organized in California among the Welsh to encourage music, literature, and good fellowship.[48] In recent years, the annual *Eisteddfod* at Jackson, Ohio, has attracted nation-wide attention; although the *Eisteddfod* at Utica, usually held on New Year's Day, remains the best known of these literary and musical competitions. Church singing and community singing remain perhaps the greatest recreation of the Welsh in the United States. In 1930, there were 60,205 foreign-born Welsh in the United States. Pennsylvania had the largest number, with New York, Ohio, Illinois, and Michigan following next in order.

The French

The legacy of the French to the Mississippi Valley region is well known to American historians and has already been touched upon in an earlier chapter. Detroit, St. Louis, and New Orleans, the

[42] See David Hughes: *Welsh People of California, 1849-1906* (San Francisco, 1923), pp. 16 and 40.
[43] See *The New York Times,* August 17, 1872. See also *Cincinnati Enquirer,* August 19, 1868; and *Cincinnati Commercial,* September 20 and October 7, 1881.
[44] See Hughes: *op. cit.,* pp. 31-33.
[45] See *Wisconsin Magazine of History,* Vol. V, pp. 414.
[46] See *Cleveland Plain Dealer,* December 27, 1887.
[47] See *Cincinnati Commercial,* August 10, December 3, and December 27, 1881.
[48] See Hughes: *op. cit.,* p. 54.

largest cities of the valley, bear their old French names, and New Orleans has preserved its French architecture and much of the French language and culture to this day.[49] Offspring of the old French element have been leaders in the social and business life of Detroit and St. Louis until recent times. In some of the states of the old Northwest—such as Illinois, Wisconsin and Michigan— there are still groups of descendants of the early French settlers of colonial times, and the map of the Mississippi Valley abounds in place names of rivers and towns that suggest their French origin. In Wisconsin, 14 counties have French names.[50] Charles Dickens, visiting St. Louis in 1842, described the old French portion of the town, with its narrow and crooked streets, its quaint and picturesque houses "built of wood with tumble down galleries between the windows," the queer little barber shops and drinking palaces, and "the old tenements with blinking casements," as follows:

> Some of these ancient habitations, with high gable gar-
> ret windows perking into the roofs, have a kind of French
> shrug about them; and being lopsided with age, appear to
> hold their heads askew besides, as if they were grimacing in
> astonishment at the American improvements.[51]

The influence of New France in the valley of the Mississippi is well known, and is part of the romance of the early West. What is perhaps not so generally appreciated is the fact that, from 1820 to 1920, nearly 353,000 French immigrants entered the United States. The Census of 1930 lists 135,592 persons in the United States who were born in France. The French have not lost many of their people to other countries by the great *Völkerwanderung* of the last century, but enough came to the United States to establish significant centers of French life and culture in nineteenth century America. It would perhaps be expected that New York and other port towns would acquire an appreciable French element, but it is interesting to find at least some distribution of French immigrants into the interior as well.

In 1851, 20,000 French immigrants entered the United States. Some were revolutionary refugees in these middle years, such as the

---

[49] See, for example, *New Orleans City Guide* (Federal Writer's Project, Boston, 1938).

[50] See Louise P. Kellogg: "France and the Mississippi Valley: A Résumé," in *Mississippi Valley Historical Review*, Vol. XVIII, pp. 3-22.

[51] See also Edward De Laureal: "Emigration from the French West Indies to St. Louis in 1848," in *Missouri Historical Society Collections*, Vol. II, pp. 13-25.

Germans; many came for purely economic reasons. There were enough in the booming Midwestern town of Chicago in 1850 to introduce French social habits which were in sharp contrast with the manners of the frontier.[52] The majority of the French immigrants after 1820 represented the working class and professional men, who settled in the cities. In 1824, when Lafayette visited the United States, there were enough French in New York to send a welcoming delegation of several hundred to the pier to greet their illustrious countryman.

The kaleidoscopic changes of the French Revolution and the Napoleonic era led to considerable immigration of French refugees to England, the West Indies, and the United States. For years, fantastic tales were in circulation in the United States to the effect that Napoleon himself had fled to America and had somehow been aided in his escape by Stephen Girard, the eccentric, wealthy merchant from Bordeaux, who became one of the greatest shippers, bankers, and businessmen in the Philadelphia of the early nineteenth century. All these tales were, of course, only idle gossip, and Napoleon ended his stormy career quite unromantically on the Island of St. Helena. His brother Joseph, however, came to America and lived the life of a gentleman farmer in New Jersey for 16 years. His home became a refuge for other French exiles.[53]

Marshal Grouchy and his sons arrived in Baltimore in 1816 and were guests of the Duponts of Delaware the next year. Lakanal, a learned member of the French Institute, became a farmer in Kentucky, opposite the French-Swiss settlement of Vevay, Indiana. Near the close of 1816, a company was organized at Philadelphia to secure a land grant from Congress and to promote the cultivation of the vine and olive in America. The French Agricultural and Manufacturing Society, as this enterprise was pretentiously designated, had as its president General Charles Francis Antoine Lallemand, who had settled in Philadelphia with Henri Dominique Lallemand. Nicholas S. Parmentier acted as secretary. Congressional lands were secured in Alabama, and a party of 140 left Philadelphia with an assortment of vines and olive plants to inaugurate the new project. On their arrival at Mobile, a public dinner was given in their honor. Proceeding up the Tombigbee

[52] Arthur C. Cole: *The Irrepressible Conflict* (New York, 1934), pp. 128-129.
[53] See J. S. Reeves: "The Napoleonic Exiles in America, 1815-1819," in *The Johns Hopkins University Studies in History and Political Science*, Vol. XXIII, pp. 523-656.

River, they laid out two towns, Demopolis and Aigleville. It turned out that both were located outside their grant. To this American frontier, the French brought their books, guitars, silks, parasols, and ribbons; and at night, the village was said to resemble "a miniature French town." [54]

Unlike typical American pioneers, the French immediately began building a town. Demopolis still exists, although the famous figures of French military history who were its founders have long since been forgotten. The venture was a failure; most of the settlers abandoned their claims and the colony dispersed to Mobile and elsewhere. Another colony, Champ d'Asile, on the Trinity River, in Texas, was equally short-lived. For a time, it was under military discipline and was an interesting place to visit because the campaigns of the Great Emperor were refought here almost daily. But as a colonizing effort, the scheme was a failure, and many of its promoters drifted away to New Orleans and eventually to France. The Spanish had opposed the French Texas venture and the United States, too, eyed it with suspicion and distrust.[55]

In Pennsylvania, on the right bank of the Susquehanna, in Luzerne County, a party of French royalist exiles had established a French colony known as Azyl, or Asylum, in 1794. The colony was planned by de Noailles, brother-in-law of Lafayette, who bought the land from Robert Morris. The Old French Road still exists to mark the site of this French speculation in American public lands. The town itself existed for about ten years, and while it lasted, was unique for its French shops on the public square, its little theater, chapel, and bakery. It was reported that one house was always kept in readiness to receive the King and Queen, whenever they might seek refuge in America.[56] In this section of Pennsylvania, French names are still to be found among the present-day population. French exiles tried to raise vines and mulberries in New York. There was a sizable colony of French refugees in Philadelphia and others scattered through the American states. New Orleans, incidentally, had an active Napoleonic cult for years; and

[54] See Howard Mumford Jones: *America and French Culture, 1750-1848* (Chapel Hill, North Carolina, 1927), pp. 155-156.

[55] See Reeves: *op. cit.* See also J. B. McMaster: *The Life and Times of Stephen Girard*, 2 vols. (Philadelphia, 1918), Vol. II, Ch. XII; and Gaius Whitfield: "The French Grant in Alabama; a History of the Founding of Demopolis," in *Alabama Historical Society Transactions* (1904), reprint No. 16.

[56] See J. G. Rosengarten: *French Colonists and Exiles in the United States* (Philadelphia, 1907).

Charleston, South Carolina, had its Jacobin Club of French *émigrés*.

The French element, like other immigrant groups, continued to take a lively interest in the affairs of Old France. In 1848, when news of the French Revolution reached America, the French in New York City staged public meetings, fraternized with the German and Irish residents, and planned a grand illumination of the city and a mammoth festival to celebrate the triumph of liberalism, with speeches in three or four languages. There was so much excitement over the European news in this eventful year that, every time a boat came in sight, the streets of New York were filled with people, eager for the latest dispatches.[57] In 1850, the French Democratic Republicans of New York celebrated the anniversary of the proclamation of the French Republic with a banquet at the Coliseum. The editor of the *Courrier des Etats Unis* presided; there were numerous toasts, and the Lafayette Guards were present in full-dress uniform to lend color to the occasion.[58] In 1870-1871, the excitement of the French, as well as of the Germans, again rose to fever pitch by the news that reached America from the battlefields of the Franco-Prussian War. When the war ended and Alsace-Lorraine was torn from France, refugees from these provinces arrived in New York, and arrangements were made to settle them in the city or to help them move Westward. When France was eventually evacuated by the Germans, French residents of New York marked the happy event by a celebration.[59] Bastile Day was observed annually in French-American communities. The 100th anniversary of the fall of the Bastille was celebrated as far west as San Francisco, where a three-day festival—consisting of a concert, a parade, and dramatic performances—marked the occasion.[60] Bastile Day is still celebrated annually in New Orleans.

The French colony of New York displayed great vigor even before the Civil War. The *Courrier des Etats Unis* had been established in 1825 by Charles Lassalle. In 1846, a French paper, *Le Franco-Americain,* was started in New York City.[61] In 1853, another French paper, *Le Républican,* was added to the list.[62] In 1847,

[57] For a description of the event, see G. J. Malmin (editor and translator): *America in the Forties; the Letters of Ole Munch Raeder* (Minneapolis, 1929), p. 165.
[58] See *New York Tribune,* April 19, 1850.
[59] See *Toledo Blade,* April 15, 1873.
[60] See *Ohio State Journal,* July 15, 1889. See also *Cleveland Plain Dealer,* July 15, 1889.
[61] See *New York Weekly News,* May 16, 1846.
[62] See *Boston Transcript,* July 2, 1853.

on the occasion of Lafayette's birthday, the French Benevolent Society sponsored a concert [63] and the French military company of the city paraded through the streets in honor of the event.[64]   In the early 1850's, a radical French labor group, known as the Société de la Montagne, worked in close coöperation with the German Arbeiterbund in New York;[65] and, in 1863, the French Liberals of the city established a national club, after the German example.[66]   Advertisements in New York dailies list the activities of various French societies—such as the Cercle Français; the Société Française de L'Amitie, which seemed to be especially devoted to masquerade balls; and the Société Française de Bienfaisance, which held its annual meeting at Delmonico's.[67]

Although the French obviously preferred city life and were essentially city dwellers, a few French colonies were scattered through the Middle West.   There was a French group near the French-Swiss settlements in Switzerland County, Indiana.   Kentucky has a Bourbon County, a Paris, and a Versailles.   In the decade before the Civil War, there was some French immigration to Illinois, and Chicago began to have French confectioneries and a French church and hotel.   In 1857, the *Journal de L'Illinois* was begun at Kankakee, with 1,200 subscribers.   A new settlement had been started at St. Anne in 1852.   Cincinnati, in 1851, had a French military battalion of over 300 and a French Protestant church, where regular weekly services were conducted in French.[68]   In 1873, it was reported that a colony of French silk weavers and ribbon makers had gone to Kansas; [69] and Olmsted, traveling through Texas in 1856, stumbled upon the village of Castroville, a place of about six hundred population, with others scattered over neighboring farms. Castroville was founded in 1844 by Alsatians who spoke French, maintained two churches, and read French newspapers.[70]

[63] See *Anglo-American* (New York), September 25, 1847.
[64] See *Cincinnati Enquirer*, September 28, 1847. See also *ibid.*, March 18, 1847.
[65] See Sorge, in *Die neue Zeit*, Vol. II, p. 238.
[66] See *New York Tribune*, October 28, 1863.
[67] See *The New York Times*, October 31, 1868; and October 28 and December 23, 1877; and *New York Tribune*, September 12, 1863. For activities in other cities, see, for example, *Baltimore Patriot and Commercial Gazette*, April 20, 1841; and *Boston Transcript*, July 23, 1856.
[68] See *Cincinnati Commercial*, April 3 and August 7, 1851.
[69] See *Ohio State Journal*, November 12, 1873.
[70] See Frederick L. Olmsted: *A Journey in the Seaboard Slave States* (New York, 1856), pp. 276-278. For the French settlement of Louisville, in Stark County, Ohio, see *Cleveland Plain Dealer*, May 2, 1885. For an attempt to settle refugees from Alsace-Lorraine in New Strasburg, see *Toledo Blade*, February 11, 1873.

New Orleans, of course, has been the most distinctly French city in the United States and has retained enough of these characteristics to make it perhaps the most picturesque Old World city in North America. New Orleans never capitulated to the Puritannical Sunday, as did New York, Boston, and Philadelphia in the first half of the nineteenth century. The stores of New Orleans were open on Sunday; people sang and played guitars on the streets, and the French theater had its gala performances on the Sabbath.[71] Frederika Bremer, in 1853, discoursed on the French opera in New Orleans, the levity of the people, the old French burial ground, and the famous French market, which she found to be "one of the most lively and picturesque scenes of New Orleans." She wrote:

> One feels as if transported at once to a great Paris marché, with this difference, that one here meets with various races of people, hears many different languages spoken, and sees the productions of various zones . . . . People breakfasted and talked and laughed, just as in the markets at Paris.[72]

New Orleans was the most important operatic center in the United States until after the Civil War. It boasted of being "a little Paris," with its appropriate vices and virtues. From 1806 to 1811, 70 operas were given in the New Orleans Théâtre St. Pierre. Between 1820 and 1860, a notable French literature was produced in the city—including novels, history, and poetry—in which names like Plaçide Canonge, Charles Testut, Dominique Roúquette, and Charles Etienne Arthur Gayarré are outstanding. More recently, the French literature of Louisiana has been collected in the volumes of *Comptes Rendus* of *L'Atheneé Louisianais*.[73]

Even the New Orleans Christmas celebration was different. There was no Santa Claus, but a Papa Noël. The family assembled around the fireplace to wait for the midnight Mass. The elders drank wine, sang, and played games until the midnight bell of the cathedral summoned them to the Mass which commemorated the birth of Christ. The presents distributed by Papa Noël were trifling; the real gifts from parents to children were presented on

[71] For a description of New Orleans in 1826, see *Reise des Herzogs Bernhard zu Sachsen-Weimar*, Vol. II. p. 73.

[72] Frederika Bremer: *The Homes of the New World* (London, 1853), Vol. III, pp. 13, 15, 16, and 42.

[73] See Edward J. Fertier: "French," in *The Cambridge History of American Literature* (New York, 1933), Vol. III, pp. 590-598.

New Year's Day, when there was great feasting, kissing, and exchanging of presents.[74]

At the outbreak of the Civil War, the French of New York met at the Steuben House to organize a regiment of French volunteers and to pledge their support to the Union. Petitions were signed asking for the suppression of the *Courrier des Etats Unis,* which was accused of "Copperhead" sympathies.[75] The Lafayette Guards, an entirely French militia company, went promptly into the Civil War. Their colonel was M. Le Baron Regis de Trobriand, described by *The New York Herald* as "a gentleman well known in French literary circles as an able and accomplished writer." [76] Their uniforms consisted of heavy duck pantaloons and blue overcoats. "Madame Susand—a blooming young lady—accompanies the regiment as vivanderie; and an important fact to be mentioned is that M. Soyer is cook." [77] Many French served in the Garibaldi regiment of New York and in Colonel Abram Duryee's Zouaves.[78] The 55th New York Volunteers was largely composed of relatively wealthy Frenchmen. The Count of Paris was on General McClellan's staff.[79] In 1868, a French Grant and Colfax Campaign Club conducted its meetings in French and invited Swiss, Belgians, and Canadians to attend.[80] As late as 1915, the late Senator Henry Cabot Lodge ended an address to the Club Républicaine Franco-Americaine du Massachusetts with a ringing peroration in French.[81]

It is in the fields of manners, fashions, and cooking that the French have exercised their greatest influence on American culture. This influence was apparent as early as 1800, as a result of the great interest on the part of American Republicans in the progress of the French Revolution. French dancing, language and fencing schools, dishes, customs, dress, books, and music immediately became fashionable. Inns and taverns were renamed *hotels,* and ordinary American cooks and bakers became *restaurateurs* who ran French

[74] For an account of the special French Creole literature and *bayoux* songs of Louisiana, see Dorothy A. Dondore: *The Prairie and the Making of Middle America* (Cedar Rapids, Iowa, 1926), pp. 285-287.
[75] See *New York Times,* May 2, 1861; and *New York Tribune,* May 18, August 31, 1861, and September 2, 1861.
[76] *The New York Herald,* July 23, 1861.
[77] *Ibid.,* September 1, 1861.
[78] See *ibid.,* July 4, 1861; and Cole: *op. cit.,* p. 310.
[79] See F. A. Shannon: *The Organization and Administration of the Union Army* (Cleveland, 1928), Vol. I, p. 42.
[80] See *The New York Times,* July 26 and August 17, 1868.
[81] See Walter Millis: *Road to War* (New York, 1935), p. 218.

ads in American newspapers. Philadelphia had a circulating library of 1,250 volumes in French, and French newspapers appeared in leading cities—such as the New York *Gazette Française;* the Philadelphia *Le Courrier Politique de l'Univers, Le Courrier de l'Amérique,* and *La Chronique des Mois ou les Cahiers Patriotique;* and the Charleston, South Carolina, *Le Moniteur Français.*[82] Before 1800, Madame Mentelle and Pierre Guerin were advertising French schools for ladies and gentlemen of central Kentucky, to give them training in French, manners, and "decorative" dancing. In the period from 1830 to 1850, French dancing masters and chefs even were popular in the Middle West.[83]

In the period after the Civil War, the advertisements in the New York dailies not only deal with the quest of American housewives for French cooks and butlers, gardeners, waiters, and dressmakers,[84] but are even more concerned with "French lessons by a Parisian lady with pure pronunciation," French boarding and day schools for young ladies, and French teachers of language and music. Occasionally, such advertisements were printed in French.[85] Among cultivated Americans from colonial times to the present, it has always seemed socially preferable to know French rather than German. The American social *salon* aped that of Paris, and French toilet articles, wearing apparel, and dancing steps added a certain elegance to the American social *milieu* in "the fabulous forties." The French milliner and dressmaker dictated the fashions of the *élite,* while French tightrope walkers, jugglers, and dancers exploited the prevailing fads on the stage and in the museums.

French cooking has always held high rank with American gourmets, and deservedly so. Perhaps the French influence on American cooking and eating habits began with the Huguenots, at New Rochelle. At least, there are early comments on the culinary arts that flourished in this old New York settlement. Breads made with yeast instead of leaven, soups, omelettes, entreés, and the artichoke —all were introduced by French immigrants—not to mention the taste for French wines. Jefferson brought a French cook to the White House, and thus probably deserved the denunciation of

[82] See J. B. McMaster: *The History of the People of the United States* (New York, 1914), Vol. V, p. 280.
[83] See *Kentucky Gazette,* July 25, 1798. As a girl, Mary Todd Lincoln attended one of Mentelle's schools.
[84] See *The New York Times,* July 2 and December 12, 1877.
[85] See *ibid.,* July 2 and 11, August 22, and October 16, 1877; and *New York Tribune,* September 9, 1863.

Patrick Henry, who attacked the great Democrat for "abjuring his native victuals." [86] As early as 1806, a traveler who encountered Frenchmen in pioneer Cincinnati commented that "their publicity consists in their introduction of the dance, music, billiards, and the fabric of liquors, sweetmeats and savory patties." [87] French cookbooks and cafés have remained popular in the United States, and to this day, if a cartoonist is called upon to draw a Frenchman, he is likely to put him in a chef's uniform.

According to the Census of 1930, there are 64,194 foreign-born Belgians in the United States. They have been employed principally in the factories and apparently make good workmen, with a genuine and intelligent interest in American labor standards. The two Belgian newspapers printed in the United States are *De Gazette van Moline*, of Illinois, and *De Gazette van Detroit*.

Brief mention must be made of another French addition to the American population, namely, the immigration of French-Canadians from Quebec. Most French-Canadians have come into the United States since 1870. They represent a French influence quite different from that discussed hitherto, for they are the descendants of the French of colonial days who have preserved in Canada a civilization which is a strange mixture of the language and customs of the days of Louis XIV and the slow but persistent infiltrations from long residence in North America, but with practically no cultural or spiritual ties with the France of today.

When New France was surrendered to the British in 1763, her total population did not exceed 70,000 people. From this little nucleus has sprung the present-day French-Canadian stock of over 3,000,000. So great has been the virility of this French stock that, without further immigration from France and cut off from all national ties with the land of their origin, the French-Canadians have developed an intense and enduring national spirit, which has not only permeated the province of Quebec but has accompanied the sons and daughters of French Canada in their migrations to the Canadian West and to many parts of the United States. The French-Canadians, more than almost any other group in North America, have made a part of the continent their permanent legacy. They are eager to preserve their institutions and customs, in which they have succeeded to a remarkable degree, as the language, law,

[86] See Jones: *op. cit.*, p. 303.
[87] Quoted in *ibid.*, p. 161.

customs, and church of present-day Canada clearly show. The French-Canadian is first and foremost a *Canadien*. This means that he is the descendant of a seventeenth-century French stock, proud of his ancient culture and insistent that the present Dominion of Canada is really a bilingual federation, composed of two distinct nationalities.[88]

There are French-Canadian settlements in the Middle West. For example, the communities of Bourbonnais, south of Chicago, and Kankakee, St. Anne, and Assumption, in Illinois, have a large French-Canadian population, which was attracted in part by the land policy of the Illinois Central Railroad.[89] After the Civil War, there was a group of French-Canadians near Columbus, Ohio, who came from Montreal to engage in the brickmaking industry.[90] In recent years, with the phenomenal rise of the automobile industry in Detroit and its vicinity, French-Canadian workmen have come to this region. But the mecca of the French-Canadian immigrant has been and remains the New England section. Here the immigrants from Quebec have swarmed into industry and agriculture in such numbers that they have been called "the Chinese of the Eastern states." Their arrival in the 1880's and 1890's raised a storm of criticism comparable in its nature to the opposition to the Oriental invasion of the West coast.[91] One reason was the apparent indifference of the French-Canadian laborer to American labor unions.

The movement into New England began with the economic revolution in that section. Young unmarried French-Canadians crossed into the New England states to work in the summer months in the brickyards and mill towns. In general, these itinerant workmen came down the Lake Champlain route, the historic route between Canada and the Eastern United States. Prior to the Civil War, most of them returned to Quebec with their savings. This was true even of the French-Canadian habitant, who had left his run-down farm to work a year or two in Boston, so that he might rehabilitate himself with his American earnings on the ancestral homestead.

[88] See Carl Wittke: *History of Canada* (New York, 1933), Ch. III; and Elizabeth H. Armstrong: *The Crisis of Quebec, 1914-1918* (New York, 1937), Ch. I.
[89] See Paul W. Gates: *The Illinois Central Railroad and Its Colonization Work* (Cambridge, Massachusetts, 1934), pp. 234-238.
[90] See *Ohio State Journal*, November 20, 1892.
[91] See *ibid.*, August 9, 1889.

After the Civil War, the floodgates in Quebec began to open. In the period from 1870 to the late 1890's, the immigration fever, described as "le mal des Etats-Unis," found thousands of victims in French Canada. The French habitant was regarded as a desirable worker; he did not immediately join labor unions. New England mill owners sent recruiting agents into the villages of Quebec. By 1900, there were 134,000 French-Canadians in Massachusetts, or 16 per cent of the state's foreign population. Rhode Island had 31,000 French-Canadians, a total exceeded only by the Irish, fellow religionists with whom the French seldom lived in harmony. The percentages for Maine, New Hampshire, and Vermont were equally large; and, by 1900, the French-Canadians were firmly entrenched in all of New England, except Connecticut. The depopulation of the rural areas of Quebec had gone on so rapidly that both the Church and the State began to make plans to stop this heavy loss of population.

The Catholic hierarchy soon decided that, instead of trying to stop a movement which seemed to be more or less permanent, it would send its priests along with the French-Canadians, thus extending the faith into New England. There has been much proselyting in the French-Canadian sections of New England and endless friction with the Irish Catholics, who hitherto dominated the Church and furnished most of the priests. The first French-Canadian parish church in New England was established in 1850 in Burlington, Vermont, but not until after a lively controversy with the Irish, who opposed the creation of a separate French parish.[92] The fight against Irish priests was actually carried to Rome. By 1891, there were 86 French-Canadian parishes and 53 parochial schools in New England, and 70 Catholic parishes that shared their services with the French. At the present time, there are many Catholic congregations in New England, with names like Notre-Dame des Canadiens, Sacré-Coeur de Marie, Preçieux Sang, Saint Jean Baptiste, and L'Étoile de la Mer. In the end, the Church probably favored French parishes because of a keen realization that language is usually the strongest bond to hold an immigrant church group together and that "qui perd sa langue perd sa foi." [93] At

[92] See D. M. A. Magnan: *Histoire de la Race Française aux Etats-Unis* (Paris, 1912), p. 249 *et seq.;* especially pp. 265-267.
[93] Magnan: *op. cit.,* pp. 310-333.

any rate, French Catholic churches now dot much of the landscape in the ancient stronghold of the Puritans.

At first, French-Canadians worked long hours for low wages, did not join unions, remained docile employees, permitted their children to work, and often violated the compulsory school attendance laws. In 1885, the French-Canadians of Massachusetts were 40 per cent illiterate. In more recent years, however, the French-Canadian workman has become more susceptible to the arguments of the labor organizer and more loyal to trade unionism, although in some sections he still enjoys a bad reputation among workers for "scabbing." After 1900, when the total of the French-Canadian element in New England had reached 275,000, the stream of immigration began to dry up somewhat, owing to Quebec's industrial expansion and the plans of Church and State to develop a little Quebec in the Canadian West, so as not to lose population to the United States.

The New England French-Canadians have become politically American, but many are still French in language and culture. Most of them vote consistently Republican, probably because the Irish, who are their bitter economic and social rivals, vote the Democratic ticket. Their political influence, however, has been largely a development of the present century. By 1890, 13 French-Canadians had seats in the lower houses of New England legislatures. Aram J. Pothier became Governor of Rhode Island. The French-Canadian representation in the legislatures of Maine, New Hampshire, Rhode Island, and Massachusetts has increased; and, in many localities, the French-Canadian vote has become important in bitter contests with Irish-controlled local organizations. Cities like Fall River, Massachusetts, and Manchester, New Hampshire, are almost bilingual; and other New England cities like Nashua, Woonsocket, and New Bedford have large French populations. In many of these cities, the French-Canadians have pushed the Irish out of the mills, only to be in turn crowded out by the incoming Slavs, Italians, and Greeks of the newer immigration.

There are a number of French-Canadian societies in the United States, most of them strongly under the influence of the priesthood, which dominates the life of French-Canadian communities to a remarkable degree. Among the better-known organizations may be mentioned l'Union Saint Jean Baptiste, les Artisans Canadiens-

[327]

Français, les Francs-Tireurs, and l'Ordre des Chevaliers de Jacques Cartier.[94] In 1900, 11 French-Canadian journals were published in New England.[95]

THE JEWS

The Jewish immigration in colonial times was small and consisted largely of Portuguese and Spanish Jews. In the nineteenth century, two great waves of Jewish immigration may be noted: first, the German Jews and those who came from the old Austro-Hungarian Empire, between whom it is often hard to distinguish; and second, the influx of Russian Jews, who came in such huge numbers that they quickly outnumbered all other Jewish groups. It is difficult to be precise about some of these groups, notably the German Jews, because no matter what the champions or foes of the Jews may say about a Jewish "race," anthropologists and biologists are unaware of any such phenomenon. The Jews have lived in many countries for many centuries, and in Germany especially they became an integral part of the population—so much so that it becomes difficult to separate the Jewish strain from the large non-Jewish German immigration of the nineteenth century.

The bulk of the German Jews came to the United States about the middle of the last century. Many came with the German Forty-Eighters. They represented the rank and file of the German population—poor or middle-class workmen and small merchants, with very few professional men among them. The causes for their departure for America were essentially the same as those which prompted the great German immigration already discussed. The Jewish population of the United States rose from 15,000 in 1840 to nearly a quarter of a million in 1880, most of this increase being due to the arrival of German Jews.

The German Jews scattered throughout the country into scores of villages and cities, where their enterprise and business ability

---

[94] See Magnan: *op. cit.*, pp. 289-295.

[95] For further information on the French-Canadians in the United States, see A. R. M. Lower: "New France in New England," in *New England Quarterly*, Vol. II, pp. 278-295; Alexandre Belisle: *Histoire de la Presse Franco-Americaine* (Worcester, Massachusetts, 1911); Felix Gatineau: *Histoire des Franco-Américains de Southbridge, Massachusetts* (Framingham, Massachusetts, 1919); Marie Louise Bonier: *Debuts de la Colonie Franco-Américaine de Woonsocket, Rhode Island* (Framingham, Massachusetts, 1920); and E. Hamon: *Les Canadiens-Français de la Nouvelle-Angleterre* (Quebec, 1891). For an account of French Catholics in the United States, see *The Catholic Encyclopedia* (1909), Vol. VI, pp. 271-277.

brought remarkable success to a surprisingly large number. A large number began life in the United States as peddlers, many with packs on their shoulders. They were the itinerant peddlers who wandered through the country and whom one encounters in the literature of the New West or as the peddlers of "Yankee notions" on Southern plantations. It was this type which inspired so many American "Jew stories" and the stage characters of the vaudeville houses. But peddling with a pack quickly provided enough profit to secure a horse and wagon, and after that came the shop and the store.

In New York and elsewhere, the evolution of many a prominent Jewish family of today can be described in terms of the peddler who became a second-hand clothing merchant and then the owner of a large store, and whose descendants became the merchant princes of the department-store era. Furthermore, although many Jews brought little learning with them from Germany, they had a high respect and a desire for learning, and their greatest ambition was to secure an *entré* for themselves and their children into the learned professions. To this group of immigrants belong many of the most distinguished present-day American Jewish families. The list would include the Seligmans, Solomon Loeb and Jacob H. Schiff of Kuhn, Loeb and Company, Benjamin Altman of the Altman department store, the Lazarus family of Columbus, Ohio, Julius Rosenwald, the Warburg family, the Guggenheims, Gimbel Brothers, Otto H. Kahn, and Adolph S. Ochs of *The New York Times*. The father of the famous Straus brothers —Oscar, Nathan, and Isidor—came from Germany in 1852, peddled with horse and wagon through the South, and opened a store in Georgia. From such humble beginnings came Macy's, in New York, and Abraham and Straus, in Brooklyn. The sons Isidor and Oscar had notable careers as public servants and philanthropists. Among the intellectual leaders of this group of German Jews coming either from Germany or Austria may be mentioned the Goldmarks, the Dembitz, Brandeis, and Adler families, Isaac M. Wise, the Flexners, the Untermeyers, the Frankfurters, and many others.

The first German Jewish congregation in Boston was organized in 1843.[96] In the 1850's, Charleston, South Carolina, had a flourishing Hebrew Benevolent Society,[97] and there were prosperous

[96] See *The Jewish Advocate,* October 10, 1930.
[97] See *Charleston Mercury,* January 11, 1859.

Jewish communities in Cincinnati, Memphis, Nashville, Tennessee, Cleveland, and scores of other cities in the Middle West and South. Cincinnati had four synagogues in 1855. In Cleveland, the sons of Manuel Halle founded the Halle Brothers' Company, and two of the city's leading bosses—"Czar" Louis Bernstein and Maurice Mashke—were the descendants of German Jewish immigrants. San Francisco and Portland have important Jewish communities, and many of the great department stores in these and other cities developed from the German Jew's peddler's pack. After the financial foundations had been securely laid by the parents, the children found leisure to devote to public affairs and the professions. They went to college, and the public careers of men like the Lehman brothers, the Morgenthaus, and other prominent leaders of Jewry today are ample evidence of their capacity to profit abundantly by the educational and social opportunities the United States had to offer.

From 1848 to 1880, the German Jew reigned supreme in American Jewish life, owing to his superiority in numbers, his intellectual powers, his wealth, and his public spirit. To the present time, his descendants remain the most distinguished leaders of American Jewry, outnumbered by later Jewish arrivals but still the most influential. The American Jewish reform movement begins with the German Jews after 1848, and the American Jewish fraternal order, charitable institutions, and organized philanthropy are largely the creation of this same immigrant group.

The first Jewish reform society was organized in Baltimore in 1842, the second in New York in 1845, and the third in Albany, under Rabbi Isaac M. Wise, three years later. By 1855, two reform congregations were established in Cincinnati, and before the end of the decade, two others had come into existence in Philadelphia and Chicago. These were little struggling societies promoted by German Jews who wished to modernize orthodox Jewry and bring it more in conformity with modern science and progress. From these humble beginnings arose the American Jewish Reformed movement of later years, and the battle within the ranks of American Judaism between modernists and fundamentalists.

Most of the leaders of the reform movement were rabbis who were born and educated in Germany. Many were inspired by the same flaming liberalism that marked the Forty-Eighters. The list includes such distinguished leaders as David Einhorn, Max Lilienthal, Samuel Adler, Bernard Felsenthal, Samuel Hirsch, and Isaac M. Wise. Of this number, Wise was undoubtedly the most influential. Born in Bohemia, he early came under the influence of German liberalism and, in 1846, set out for the United States. In 1854, he became rabbi of the congregation Ben Yeshurun of Cincinnati. Here he founded an English paper, *The Israelite,* which still exists; instituted the Friday-night reformed service; and brought about the establishment of Hebrew Union College for the training of rabbis who would be as familiar with modern science, philosophy, and social problems as with the ancient Hebrew lore. The college was opened in the basement of the Temple in 1875 and is today perhaps the best of its kind in the United States. In 1889, Wise organized the Central Conference of American Rabbis. Wise was a scholar and a progressive thinker, and he made a lasting imprint upon the movement to modernize and intellectualize American Jewry. His successor as president of Hebrew Union College, Dr. Kaufmann Kohler, represented the same group of liberal, highly trained rabbis who came from Germany. He broke with orthodoxy to the extent of introducing Sunday services. The work of Felix Adler and the Ethical Culture movement, especially in its educational and social service aspects, is regarded today as one of the most important contributions to recent American social progress.

Jewish charities have always been unstintingly supported by Jewish Americans. The first Jewish lodge in America, the Independent Order B'nai B'rith (Sons of the Covenant) was started in New York in 1843. Its original name was German, Bundes Brüder, and its ritual was originally in German. It remains the most influential of all the Jewish organizations of its kind in the United States and has expanded its lodge work and charitable program to include a broad interest in social service, orphanages, schools, hospitals, and educational work.[98]

From 1877 to 1927, the Jewish population of the United States increased from less than 250,000 to over 4,000,000. Practically all of this later immigration came from Russia and the countries in eastern Europe near Russia. The entire group has therefore been

[98] See Lee J. Levinger: *A History of the Jews in the United States* (Cincinnati, 1930), pp. 175-260; H. Graetz: *Popular History of the Jews* (Philadelphia, 1891-1898), Vol. VI; Israel Goldstein: *A Century of Judaism in New York* (New York, 1930); Henry S. Morais: *The Jews of Philadelphia* (Philadelphia, 1894); *Publications of the American Jewish Historical Society* (Baltimore, Maryland, 1892—); and *The American Jewish Yearbook* (Philadelphia, 1899—).

labeled as Russian Jews. From 1880 to 1920, owing to this immigration, the Jewish population of the United States increased more rapidly than the population as a whole. Of the total number of Jewish stock in the United States today, the vast majority have been in the United States less than 50 years and represent the immigration from eastern Europe. In view of these numbers, it is not surprising that native Americans became alarmed and that an anti-Jewish agitation was launched in some quarters, even to the extent of reviving the old forgeries of the so-called *Protocols of the Elders of Zion,* which were reported to envisage the erection of a universal Jewish state on the ruins of modern civilization. The anti-Semitic agitation, in its early stages at least, had many of the characteristics of earlier demonstrations against other immigrant groups, notably the Irish.

In Russia, about 95 per cent of all the Jews had been forced to live in certain portions of the country known as the Pale of Settlement, comprising roughly the area of ancient Poland. Nearly three fourths of these Jews were engaged in petty commerce and industry. Practically all the tailors and shoemakers in the Pale were Jews, and the middleman for the Russian agricultural population was also a Jew—the peddler, petty retailer, and moneylender who dealt in grain, cattle, fur, and hides.[99] Some of the Jews acquired cash by their transactions and became moneylenders to both peasants and those of higher social caste. That they frequently drove hard bargains and oppressed the peasants is generally admitted, even by Jewish historians.

The Jews in Russia were restricted in their freedom to move about; special taxes were imposed on them, efforts were made to keep them from owning or renting land, and their economic activity was rigidly restricted to certain occupations. Their condition became increasingly unbearable after a Nihilist plot on the life of Czar Alexander II led to pogroms in 1881 and to further restrictions in 1882. In a sense it is true that "the Crazy Nihilist who hurled a bomb at Czar Alexander II was the ultimate creator of the New York Ghetto and the man who added 3,000,000 Jews to the American population."[100] The laws of 1882 were rigorously ap-

---

[99] See Samuel Joseph: *Jewish Immigration to the United States from 1881 to 1910* (New York, 1914). This is the best treatment available.

[100] Burton J. Hendrick: *The Jews in America* (New York, 1923), p. 39.

plied; Jews were expelled from the agricultural villages into the towns and driven back into the Pale, and the pogrom of 1881 was followed by other massacres in 1882, 1903, and 1906. The Russian burocracy did little to prevent these outrages, on the ground that "the Western borders are open to the Jews." In a sense, the Jew in Russia, Roumania, and other eastern areas was really the victim of an economic transformation that was changing an old, backward, and medieval system to a more modern, commercial, and industrial order. The Jews had served backward agricultural areas, and an agricultural crisis meant ruin for them. Undoubtedly some of the opposition to the Jews was justified because of their exploitation of the people, especially through their monopoly in rum and liquor peddling. Economic anti-Semitism led to violent racial and religious persecution. Since the Jews generally were on the liberal side of political controversies, they could expect little sympathy from the government of the Czar.

Figures for the total of the Jewish immigration are unreliable until after 1899, but Joseph estimates the total from 1881 to 1910 at over 1,562,800. Of this number, 71.6 per cent came from Russia, nearly 18 per cent from Austria-Hungary, and 4.3 per cent from Roumania. The Russian immigration increased in a geometric progression during these three decades.[101] It was largely a family immigration, and the immigrants came to stay. Nearly half of them had no trade, while nearly 37 per cent were skilled artisans, and the rate of illiteracy among them was about 26 per cent. The great majority of the new arrivals settled in the commercial and industrial cities of the North Atlantic states. "Social solidarity and communal responsibility" has marked their group settlements to an unusual degree.[102]

The flood of Jewish immigration after 1880 put a heavy strain upon the charitable institutions of American Jews—such as the United Hebrew Charities of New York, the Philadelphia Association for the Protection of Jewish Immigrants, and the Baltimore Hebrew Benevolent Society—and, for a time, the major part of their energy and resources went into emigrant aid. It is not surprising therefore that some attempt was made to get the Jewish immigrant out of the congested ghettos and on the farms. Most of these enter-

[101] See Joseph: *op. cit.*, pp. 93 and 113.
[102] See *ibid.*, p. 157.

prises were failures. The Jew has remained a city dweller. Nevertheless, several of these attempts to establish Jewish agricultural communities deserve brief mention.

In 1882, 17 families settled on farms in Colorado, and 67 families established the Alliance Colony at Vineland, New Jersey. Some 60 families of Russian Jews were assisted by the Alliance Israelite Universelle to settle on Sicily Island, Louisiana. Some went to Davison County, in South Dakota; others to Burleigh and Ramsey Counties, in North Dakota. New Odessa, in Oregon, was a shortlived Socialist colony of Jews from Russia who called themselves "Sons of the Free." The Kansas settlement of Beersheba was sponsored by Cincinnati Jews, and other settlements in that state were promoted by Jews from New York, especially at Hebron, Gilead, and Touro. The only survivals of this period of Jewish colonizing effort in the 1880's were Alliance, Rosenhayn, and Carmel, in New Jersey, and all were near enough to Philadelphia to secure financial support and a ready market for their goods. Moreover, the land was good and the East was not cursed by the droughts, hailstorms, and swarms of insects that attacked the Western settlements.

Since 1900, the Jewish Agricultural and Industrial Aid Society has been greatly interested in getting more Jews out of the congested cities. It has made loans to Jewish farmers and prospective farmers. It publishes a weekly, the *Jewish Farmer,* in Yiddish, and sponsors instruction in better farming methods. Similar organizations have worked in Chicago to promote Jewish settlements in the West. By the outbreak of the World War, the number of Jews engaged in farming in the United States was estimated at somewhat over 18,000, involving over 3,400 farms and 437,000 acres of land. The largest Jewish farming communities in New York are near Syracuse and Albany. The New Jersey colonies maintain a compact social organization and produce mostly grapes, berries, and garden truck for near-by city markets. Groups of Jewish families have gone into other Eastern states. Huron County, Michigan, had a Palestine for a few years, and there were enough Jewish farm families in North Dakota to warrant the employment of a rabbi to visit the scattered settlements. A Federation of Jewish Farmers of America has been in existence since 1909. There are two Jewish schools on the secondary-school level where agricultural courses are taught, generally to boys who cannot attend agricultural colleges.[103] As part of the "New Deal" experiment in resettlement, 200 Jewish families have been removed from the congested clothing centers of the East and a half million dollars appropriated to establish them on subsistence farms in Monmouth County, New Jersey.

The Russian Jewish immigration, however alarming it has seemed to some Americans, constitutes one of the most interesting groups among all those who came to the United States while the doors to America remained open. The New York ghetto, housing a million Jews, is largely a product of this immigration. Being essentially small traders, peddlers, tailors, and shoemakers, the Russian Jews became pushcart peddlers and small storekeepers, or drifted by the thousands into the needle trades and the tobacco factories. The New York sweatshops were peculiarly Jewish institutions, and the whole system of subcontracting and homework led to that trinity of evils in modern industry: long hours, low pay, and female and child labor. The Garment Workers' Unions, through which the exploited found relief from these intolerable conditions, have recruited both their membership and their leaders largely from the Russian Jewish group, and are today among the most successful and intelligently led organizations in the labor movement.

In spite of the lack of opportunities abroad, many of the new arrivals were greatly interested in intellectual things, perhaps because during centuries of oppression only their minds could be free. Political and economic radicalism has marked the Russian Jewish sections of New York. Abraham Cahan, editor of the Yiddish *Forward,* the largest Yiddish daily in the world, Morris Hillquit, distinguished Socialist leader, and Meyer London, Socialist Congressman, were products of this Russian Jewish immigrant environment. Marxism and the trade union gospel are thoroughly understood among Jewish garment workers. They are eager to learn and to progress, and the second generation has invaded American colleges and universities in numbers sufficient to alarm some college administrators.

Paradoxical as it may seem, the Russian Jew has brought about a revival of orthodoxy in religion. The New York ghetto houses many a peddler or needleworker who is a Hebrew scholar and an

[103] See Leonard G. Robinson: *The Agricultural Activities of the Jews in America* (New York, 1912); and *Philadelphia Press,* November 19, 1887.

authority on the rabbinical works—a *Ben Torah,* or man of learning. The Russian Jewish immigration brought in a host of Talmudists and Hebraists, who sponsored a kind of counterreformation in American Jewry. They were quickly at odds with the German reformers, and emphasized the necessity of returning to a more conservative, orthodox Judaism. The Hebrew school flourished in the ghetto tenements as it had in Russia, generally after regular public-school hours.

The attempt to revive Hebrew as a literary language in the United States failed, but the Russian Jewish immigration led to a remarkable revival of Yiddish, not only as a newspaper language, but as a vehicle for better literature and the stage. Yiddish is basically a German dialect which the Jews carried with them from Germany into eastern Europe and which, on its extended migrations, including the United States, has been greatly modified by Slavic and English additions to its vocabulary. The first successful Yiddish newspaper in the United States was the *Jewish Daily News,* started in New York in 1885 by Kasriel R. Sarasohn. In 1930, there were three Yiddish dailies in New York, with the Yiddish *Forward,* which was founded in 1897 as a radical Socialist paper, far in the lead. Its editor, Abraham Cahan, previously edited the Socialist *Arbeiter-Zeitung.*

The translation, in 1899, of Morris Rosenfeld's *Liederbuch* as *Songs of the Ghetto,* by Leo Wiener of Boston, brought Rosenfeld, a Russian Jewish sweatshop worker, to the public attention as a poet of social justice. Another ghetto poet, the Russian Morris Winchevsky, was known as the "grandfather of Yiddish Socialism." S. Blumengarten and Michael Kaplan's *Ghetto Klangen* deserve notice in this connection also. One of the best of the Yiddish prose writers is Z. Libin (Israel Hurowits), who has said of himself: "My muse was born in the dark sweat shop, her first painful cry resounded near the Singer machine, she was brought up in the tenement tombs." [104] Leon Kobrin won distinction as a realist; his first novel was *A Moerder aus Liebe.* Abraham Cahan's *The Rise of David Lavinsky* gives an excellent picture of ghetto life in English.[105]

The Yiddish theater has been distinctly an American enterprise.

[104] See Nathaniel Buchwald, in *The Cambridge History of American Literature* (New York, 1933), Vol. III, pp. 589-609; especially, p. 605.
[105] See also Mary Antin: *The Promised Land* (Boston, 1917); Anzia Yezierska: *Hungry Hearts* (Boston, 1920); and *Bread Winners* (New York, 1925); and Sholom Asch, *America* (New York, 1918).

Its founder was Abraham Goldfaden, although Jacob Gordin was the first to put it on a higher aesthetic and dramatic level. In 1918, Maurice Schwartz founded the Yiddish Art Theatre, which led to a genuine revival for the Yiddish stage. Sholom Asch's *God of Vengeance* and Jacob Gordin's *God, Man and the Devil* attracted attention far beyond Yiddish circles, and such distinguished American actors and actresses as Jacob P. Adler and Bertha Kalisch made their debut in the Yiddish theater. The Russian Jews, in spite of their poverty, have been noted for their interest in music and drama. From their ranks have come Mischa Elman, Levitzky, Alma Gluck, the Schildkrauts, Solom Asch, the Warfields, and Irving Berlin, the greatest tunesmith of Tin Pan Alley, as well as several modern theater and moving-picture magnates. These immigrants from Eastern Europe have abundantly repaid America for what she did for them. The more recent Jewish refugees from Hitler's Germany will no doubt do the same.

The life of a typical Russian Jewish community in a city like New York represents almost all possible contrasts and cannot possibly be fairly described in any short summary. It is the story of Jewish street hawkers and pushcart men, of shops with Hebrew signs, of tenement sweatshops for garment workers and cigar makers, of political and economic radicalism in East Side coffee shops converted into workingmen's clubs, and of the Old World devotion to Jewish ritual and age-old customs. It is the story of ghetto hospitality, of family parties to celebrate engagements and weddings, at some of which a glass was broken by ardent Zionists to remind their guests that Zion still lay in ruins, of dances at which the profits came largely from the checkroom and the barroom—a ghetto teeming with life and strange conflicts between the old and the new, between the old generation of Russia and the second generation born in the United States, which is aggressively at work lopping off as fast as possible all the earmarks of Judaism and becoming "Allrightnicks," the name applied in derision by East Side Jews to the Jew who has established himself too quickly in the American community. It is the story of a people who support orthodox synagogues and radical labor movements and political parties at one and the same time. It is the story of the "Cheder" school to teach the children Hebrew after school hours. It is also the story of a constant moving "uptown" into better surroundings, as soon as a measure of business success had produced a certain bourgeois social snobbery in the second

[337]

generation. Finally, it is the story of dropping telltale Russian Jewish names for nondescript American ones, as families leave Hester Street for the Bronx.

It is absurd, of course, to suppose that the ghetto swarms with nothing but geniuses. It is equally absurd to assume that all Jews are the shouting, crude, gesticulating, unkempt, and aggressive pushcart men and pawnbrokers of the East Side. There are as many class distinctions drawn between Jews—German and Russian, rich and poor, intellectual and stupid, honest and dishonest, attractive and unattractive—as prevail among any other group in the American population.[106] Only the sporadic outbursts of anti-Semitism serve to close these gaps, to retard Americanization, and to restore a united front against the aggressor.[107]

[106] For an interesting article on this subject, see Konrad Bercovici: "The Greatest Jewish City in the World," in *The Nation* (September 12, 1923), pp. 259-261.

[107] See Lee J. Levinger: *The Causes of Anti-Semitism in the United States* (Philadelphia, 1925); Charles S. Bernheimer: *The Russian Jew in the United States* (Philadelphia, 1905); and Beatrice C. Baskerville: *The Polish Jew* (New York, 1906).

12

Immigrant Utopias

MANY YEARS AGO, in *The Blithedale Romance,* Nathaniel Hawthorne wrote:

> In my own behalf I rejoice that I could once think better of the world probably than it deserved. It is a mistake into which men seldom fall twice in a lifetime, or, if so, the rarer and higher the nature that can thus magnanimously press onward . . . . Whatever else I may repent of, therefore, let it be reckoned neither among my sins nor follies that I once had faith and force enough to form generous hopes of the world's destiny.

In all ages, men have toyed with ambitious plans for social regeneration. Although most of their efforts have ended in failure, they have usually left a residue of ideas that has had some effect on the world's thinking and has contributed to some small degree to this vague thing we call "social progress." It was to be expected that, among the men and women who came to a New World to try their fortunes, there should have been some who dreamed of an entirely new social order. In colonial and nineteenth-century America, there was ample room for almost any kind of a political, economic, or social experiment, without infringing on the equal rights of one's neighbors. America was hospitable to such schemes of regeneration or at least could afford to be tolerant of them. The Mississippi Valley, with its great open spaces, seemed especially fitted for the experiments of social reformers, and scores of little communities, inspired by some particular Utopian vision, dotted the map of the valley in the middle of the last century.

These experiments ran the whole gamut of social experimentation. All of them had something socialistic or communistic about them, if we use these terms with their later meanings. The line could not be sharply drawn then, as it cannot now, between what

[339]

was socialistic and what was communistic. Some communities were held together by a strong religious bond; for these, the communistic features of their experiments were merely necessary consequences of their desire to hold the group together in order to achieve the more important end of religious salvation. Some communities had no religious basis but were the creation of political and social philosophers who often eschewed religion altogether, as a mark of superstition. In general, those Utopian colonies lasted longest which had a religious bond to hold their members together in a homogeneous whole. Religious communities, moreover, usually benefited from having a single leader, a chosen one of God, who could act as an inspired and despotic patriarch. If he were able and gifted, and if he combined spiritual leadership and business genius, he might succeed in preserving the community at least during his lifetime. Some of these Utopias—such as the Brook Farm settlement, to which so many New England intellectuals belonged—were the work of native Americans, but scores were the work of immigrants. Practically every immigrant group had among its numbers some who were interested in founding communities in America which should be entirely different from the prevailing political, social, or religious order.

Communistic or socialistic societies existed in all periods of American history, from colonial times to the present. As late as 1868, there were 78 communistic societies in the United States, a number considerably smaller than 25 years earlier, when social experimentation seems to have reached a peak.[1] The actual number of such experiments cannot be determined. Many were so small and short-lived that their history remains unrecorded; some of the most important colonies still await historical treatment. In the great American laboratory, these experiments arose in nearly every state, from the Atlantic to the Pacific. The motive power that inspired them was akin to the spirit that prompts great religious revivals. Like revivals, too, they were likely to lose momentum quickly after the first excitement was past.

Schemes for the regeneration of mankind, either by a new religion or a new social order, have not been limited to any one period of our history. In 1684, a group of so-called Labadists settled on the Bohemia River, in Delaware, in order to found a community which might observe the Sabbath more strictly and discard the doctrine

[1] See *New York World*, October 15, 1868.

of original sin. After 15 years, only a handful were left, who eventually disappeared among the general population. In 1693, Johann Jacob Zimmermann, famed astronomer and mathematician, set out for America to await the millennium, which, according to his refined calculations, was due in 1694. Zimmermann died at Rotterdam before he could prove himself wrong, but his followers went on to Pennsylvania and, under Johann Kelpius, established themselves as a community which became especially well known among the Pennsylvania Germans for the ability of its members to cast horoscopes and perform astrological feats.[2] During its early years, the Moravian community of Bethlehem, on the Lehigh River, was a communistic colony.[3] The most important of the colonial experiments in communal organization, however, was the Ephrata community, established by Conrad Beisel.

Beisel must have been a man of great ability. Besides his qualifications as a religious leader, he had great and unique talents as a musician and composer, in addition to being a good business manager. Beisel was a member of the Dunkards, a German sect that began coming to Pennsylvania in 1719. Presently, Beisel concluded that the seventh day of the week was the proper one on which to observe the Sabbath and, in 1728, with three men and two women, he seceded from his earlier religious affiliations to go off into the open country and found the cloister of Ephrata. The experiment was essentially one in religious communism and lasted until the present century. In its prime, the community had 300 members. By 1900, however, the number had dwindled to 17; and in 1934, the court appointed a receiver for the property, for which there was but one claimant left. Steps are now being taken to preserve the old buildings which still stand as an historical monument and park, under the protection of the State of Pennsylvania.

In Beisel's time, the community had a paper mill, an oil mill, a printing press, a schoolhouse—which attracted children from outside the group—and dwellings for the members—dormitories for the men and the women who were expected to live as celibates and homes for such as were married. The meeting house was built

[2] For an account of Zimmermann, see Howard Robinson: *The Great Comet of 1680, a Study in the History of Rationalism* (Northfield, Minnesota, 1916), pp. 31-33. For an account of Kelpius, see Heinz Kloss: *Um die Einigung des Deutschamerikanertums* (Berlin, 1937), pp. 93-98.

[3] See Hellmuth Erbe: *Bethlehem, Pennsylvania, eine kommunistische Herrnhuter Kolonie des 18. Jahrhunderts* (Stuttgart, Germany, 1929).

according to the description of the building of King Solomon's Temple in the *Book of Kings,* without metal and by using wooden pegs for nails, "so that there was neither hammer nor ax nor any tool of iron heard in the house while it was building." Beisel enforced the utmost frugality and simplicity upon his cloistered community. The only deviation from the rigid routine resulted from Beisel's great emphasis upon music. The founder wrote many hymns and printed collections of his compositions, which to this day interest the student of composition and harmony because of their curious musical inventions. Beisel's chorals were sung far beyond the borders of Ephrata. Members of the community followed a strict routine of piety and labor for the common good. As long as Beisel lived, his colony prospered. After his death, in 1786, the community was finally incorporated under state law and was managed by a board of trustees. Celibacy and the cloistered life were abandoned. Today, the buildings of old Ephrata remain one of the most interesting monuments of the time when the Pennsylvania German sects looked for the Garden of Eden in America.

In the early nineteenth century, some 300 pious, simple-minded German peasants from Würtemberg, in South Germany came to Tuscarawas County, Ohio, to establish the communistic settlement of Zoar. By 1817, these Würtembergers had built a blockhouse. On April 15, 1819, over 150 signed an agreement establishing communism. This agreement was reinforced in 1824, when another group signed the covenant; and, in 1832, the colony was incorporated as "The Separatist Society of Zoar."

The leader in Zoar was Joseph Bäumler, or Bimeler, as his name was generally spelled in America. He combined good managerial ability with religious leadership, and until his death, in 1853, guided the community with great success. Zoar was a typical German peasant village, with broad, fertile acres, and the small industries—such as flour, woolen, and planing mills, foundry, machine shop, pottery, and tileworks—which are essential to a small self-sufficing agricultural community. For many years, Zoar was also famous for its excellent beer, and Clevelanders like Marc Hanna occasionally found solace from their worldly cares by spending short vacations at the hotel in Zoar.

Under the original communal agreement, every member was provided, from the common fund, with all the daily necessities of life and two suits of clothes a year. Each member was assigned to his tasks, which he was expected to perform for the common weal. Little time was left in this routine of piety and labor for reading or amusement. Singing was practically the only diversion, and this, too, was limited to religious music. At first, the plan included celibacy, but after Bimeler married his housekeeper, this rule was abandoned. Toward the close of the nineteenth century, the community gradually lost its isolation. It came into competition with the outside world; it had to import laborers at harvest time; and, above all, it had to accommodate a stream of visitors. There were secessions from the communist ranks, and a growing restlessness appeared among the younger people. In 1884, Zoar was incorporated as an Ohio village, with a mayor and village council. This was a significant step toward breaking down the isolation of the community.

In the third generation, secessions were especially heavy. Children of Zoar parents found employment outside the community, and it became necessary to hire more and more workers from the outside. Under these conditions, the devotion of the older members was not sufficient to hold the group together. In 1898, communism was officially abandoned because of the insistent demand of the younger generation. Each of the 136 members received a cash dividend, a home in the village, and some land—perhaps a small return for three generations of labor, if calculated on a purely business basis. On the favorable side of the ledger, however, must be recorded the peace and contentment and economic security that had endured for nearly three generations. Today, the village of Zoar still retains some of the characteristics that mark the typical peasant village in South Germany. Several of the buildings will be preserved under the care of a local historical society and the Ohio State Archaeological and Historical Society.[4]

Similar to the Zoar experiment and in rather close relation with it were the settlements of the Harmony Society, another group of German pietists who sought salvation in the United States. The founder of this group was Johann Georg Rapp, a weaver and vine gardener of Würtemberg, who had been persecuted for his religious views. Almost all of his followers were peasants, who accepted Rapp's program of religious communism without question. In

[4] See E. O. Randall: *History of the Zoar Society* (Columbus, Ohio, 1904). There is an excellent unpublished doctor's dissertation on Zoar by Dr. Edgar B. Nixon in the Library of the Ohio State University, in Columbus. This is based on a careful and exhaustive study of Zoar manuscripts.

1803, some 5,000 acres of good land were acquired in Butler County, Pennsylvania, and on this the first 600 members built the town of Harmonie, or Harmony, as it was known to its American neighbors. An agreement was signed merging all private possessions in the Harmony Society. Hereafter, no one was to work for wages and all were to be supported from the common treasury.

It is unnecessary to describe the religious vagaries that held this group together. They included curious notions about the Creation, the fall of man, and the second coming of Christ to Palestine. The *Bible* was accepted as the sole guide of life. Religious services were somewhat like the Lutheran service, and the confessional was encouraged as a necessary part of religious discipline. Two services were always held on Sundays and one on Wednesday evenings. The three great festivals of the year, which were celebrated with music and feasting, were the *Harmoniefest,* which marked the anniversary of the founding of the society; *Danksagungstag,* Thanksgiving Day; and the *Liebesmahl,* or Lord's Supper. Celibacy was imposed in 1807, although married couples were not separated but expected thereafter to regard each other "as brothers and sisters in Christ."

From 1805 to 1815, the group lived in Pennsylvania. Then, probably because the Upper Ohio Valley was regarded as a poor grape country, the whole community moved to Indiana. The sale of the old property for $100,000 involved a heavy loss, but within a year, the group had built a New Harmony, about 50 miles from the mouth of the Wabash River. Here the community thrived under the leadership of Frederick Rapp, an adopted son of the founder. Frederick Rapp was something of a poet, musician, and artist; a member of the Indiana Constitutional Convention; and, above all, a good businessman. He painted pictures, composed hymns, and collected Indian relics, and had enough time left to bring the colony to a high degree of prosperity. Government was in the hands of an ecclesiastical aristocracy dominated by Rapp, until his untimely death, in 1834. Thereafter, a council of nine elders was chosen to guide the spiritual life of the community, and two trustees, removable by the elders, were to handle its business. Rapp, the original founder, died in 1847, at the age of 90.

Many of the buildings of the New Harmony still stand. Its property in 1820 was valued at over $1,000,000. After ten years in Indiana, the community suddenly resolved to move back to Pennsylvania. The prevalence of malaria in Indiana and trouble with meddlesome neighbors may have been partly responsible for this decision. Moreover, having become skilled in manufacturing, the community wanted to expand into an Eastern market and thereby escape the "wildcat" banking and currency of the Western states. Perhaps another reason was the fact that Robert Owen, father of English Socialism, was ready to buy out the community and make it the scene of his own experiment with a "Community of Equality."

Owen's New Harmony was without doubt the most widely advertised and best known of all the communistic experiments in America. To discuss it here would require too great digression from the present theme of non-English immigrant Utopias. Suffice it to say that, despite its early failure, New Harmony had notable members who deserve to be remembered for their pioneering work in such reforms as public education, manual training, preschool education for children, trade schools, coeducation, temperance reform, and the founding of workingmen's institutes. Moreover, from this parent colony sprang dozens of little offshoots—such as Macluria, Nevillsville, Yellow Springs, and Kendall, in Ohio; Blue Springs and Forestville, in Indiana; and Coxsackie, Franklin, and Haverstraw, in New York.[5]

In 1825, the Harmony Society, under Frederick Rapp, returned to Economy, Pennsylvania, which it was able to buy in large part from the cash balance acquired from the sale of hats, saddles, and other products manufactured in Indiana at an annual value of $50,000. Economy was situated on the Ohio River, about 20 miles from the community's first settlement and about 18 miles from Pittsburgh. The membership of the community at this time was over 500. At the time of Frederick Rapp's death, in 1834, it numbered over 400 members. By the end of the Civil War, this number had shrunk to 170, and from then on the decline was uninterrupted. In 1903, there were only four members left.

At Economy, an estate of some 3,000 acres, it was resolved to concentrate on manufactures rather than agriculture, and the community advertised its products extensively to the outside world. The attempt to raise silkworms, though a failure, attracted wide attention. In 1831, the value of manufactured woolen goods ex-

[5] See J. B. McMaster: *A History of the People of the United States* (New York, 1914), Vol. V, p. 94; and Heinrich Semler: *Geschichte des Socialismus und Communismus in Nord Amerika* (Leipzig, Germany, 1880). For a history of American communities, see also John Humphrey Noyes: *History of American Socialisms* (Philadelphia, 1870).

ceeded $84,000, and that of cotton was nearly $17,000. Labor had to be hired from the outside. Men were paid $3.50 a week for a 12-hour day, and women less than half that amount. The community also produced silk, wine, whiskey, beer, flour, and hats. In spite of this attention to business, Rapp built beautiful buildings and lovely gardens and vineyards, which attracted visitors from many miles around.

Economy was an ecclesiastical aristocracy, German in customs and language, and held together as a communistic society by the bond of religion. The community probably reached the high-water mark of its prosperity in 1866. The value of its real estate went steadily up, owing to the oil boom in Pennsylvania. Oil was struck on the colony, its timber acreage was valuable, and the community owned coal lands as well. In 1877, it invested $650,000 in the stock of the Pittsburgh and Lake Erie Railroad. One of its trustees was an executive of the road for a time, and eventually the stock was sold at a large profit to the Vanderbilts. The trustees of the community speculated repeatedly in real estate and stocks, sold off land as the community membership became smaller in order to induce business enterprises to locate on their land, and then frequently bought stock in these companies. The discovery of oil and gas led to a heavy influx of strangers, who were employed at the wells, and more and more of the houses and stores belonging to the community were rented to nonmembers. On several occasions when the old communistic methods proved inadequate to support the community, because of a steadily declining membership, revenues from outside investments saved the day. To the end of its legal existence, the society was solvent and indeed had a surplus, but this was not of its own making, in the sense that it was produced by its own community effort. Property was sold on several occasions in the early 1890's to meet the debts of the community.

A reporter of *The New York World* has left us a good description of the Economy of the early 1890's. He alighted at the Economy station on the Pittsburgh, Fort Wayne and Chicago Railroad, at the base of the hill on which the town proper was located. In the town, he found the streets laid out with remarkable regularity and very clean, and communism "reigning supreme." On the hill were a silk and woolen factory. "No person is seen strolling along the streets during working hours. The corner lounger is absent." The buildings were uniform in appearance and had rear entrances. In the center of the town stood a large brick temple of Grecian style and, directly opposite, the modest brick house of the chief executive of the colony. The reporter quickly learned that Acts 4:32-35 was the basis for the communism of the members, but that many who lived in the village had not taken the vows. The farms covered over 3,000 acres. Each member could get anything he needed, for any article he required was his. Father Henrici, leader of the community in 1890, was a former official of the Pittsburgh and Lake Erie Railroad, a director of the Lake Shore and Michigan Southern Railroad, and an official in several banks and business enterprises in Beaver Falls. The reporter found that it was against the principles of the community to compute the size of their holdings. The society maintained a brass band and two choirs, and Henrici, in spite of his 87 years, still directed the choir and played the organ. Living in peace with the world and devoting their lives to hard labor and almsgiving were the major concerns of the community.

Few people joined the community in these later years, and the rule of celibacy made native reproduction impossible. The membership had dropped off till there were but three women and one man left. In 1903, a syndicate of Pittsburgh capitalists bought all but eight acres of the communal property for $2,500,000. It was agreed, as part of the terms of sale, that the music hall and the Great House and garden of Frederick Rapp should be preserved, and that the right to use the church and several dwellings should be guaranteed to the remaining members during their lifetime.[6]

Brief reference to two other German communities established on a religious basis must suffice. Neither was as important as those already discussed, and both were on a smaller scale. In St. Nazianz, Wisconsin, Father Oschwald of Baden established a Catholic communistic society composed of 113 colonists from Baden, Germany. Part of the membership lived in cloisters; some married and acquired private property; and, in time, strangers came in to disturb the original settlers. Oschwald's mind was occupied with many curious plans. He had studied medicine in Munich and had established the Spiritual-Magnetic Association of the Holy St. Gregor of Nazianz. Because of friction with the Catholic hierarchy, he led his followers in 1854 to the forests of Wisconsin. There he bought

[6] For an account of this group of settlements, see John A. Bole: *The Harmony Society* (Philadelphia, 1904); George B. Lockwood: *The New Harmony Movement* (New York, 1905), pp. 7-42; *The New York World*, February 13, 1890; and W. A. Hinds: *American Communities* (Oneida, New York, 1878), pp. 7-22.

3,000 acres, and the community was administered by himself and 12 elders. A huge cross was erected in the clearing, where the entire community met to pray in unison. Membership was restricted to German Catholics. The founder died in 1873, and thereafter conflicts arose over the administration of the colony. After some litigation, the name of the community was changed to the Roman Catholic Society of St. Nazianz. The old constitution remained in force until 1896, when the Archbishop of Milwaukee assumed jurisdiction and assigned the administration of the colony to one of the religious orders of the Church. In 1902, there were still 100 members of the commune living in cloisters and led by five elders. Everyone was assigned specific tasks, and all the products of the community were stored in common warehouses.[7]

In Missouri, a German group under the leadership of Dr. Wilhelm Keil of Prussia founded the community of Bethel, in Shelby County, in 1844. The experiment continued until 1879. Keil was a poorly educated German who came to Pittsburgh in 1836. IIe seems to have started to practice medicine and to have learned most of his technique from the powwowing old women of the Pennsylvania countryside. He was supposed to have written a book in blood to cure certain ailments and to be an expert in the Black Art. During these early years of his career in the United States, he was known as *der Hexendoktor*.

In 1838, Keil was converted to Methodism by Wilhelm Nast, the leader of German Methodism in the United States. For a time, he preached in Ohio and Pennsylvania, and then was expelled from the Church. His own version of this crisis was that he had objected to the practice of paying preachers a salary. As an independent, he enlisted a large following and soon developed a mystic, supernatural system of religion in which he was the Central Sun and his subordinates his *Lichtfürsten*. In an age when all of America seemed to be excited about social reform and religious extremes, it was not difficult for Keil to assemble a colony of his followers and lead them into Missouri.

The transfer of his followers to Missouri began in 1844. Excellent farming country was selected for the new venture and, in 1845, some 500 German farmers were settled at Bethel. All property was to be held in common, and Keil promised his people nothing except work, bread, and water. Some of his membership were seceders

---

[7] See Engelbert Krebs: *Um die Erde* (Padeborn, Germany, 1929), pp. 207-210.

from the Harmony Society; some were skilled artisans. When members withdrew, they were paid off with individual tracts of land and were permitted to continue to work for the society. Keil preached vigorously to his followers and instituted the confessional, probably as a means of maintaining his authority over them. No other church ritual was permitted. Mills, a distillery, and a tannery to manufacture deerskin gloves were established. Practically no one kept accounts; products were stored in common barns; and, as time went on, the land was really held by a few in trust for the whole group. In spite of a rigorous routine of labor and religion, life seems to have been fairly gay, and band concerts were weekly features.

In 1855, Keil left for Oregon to found another colony, which he called Aurora. Here he died in 1877. By wagon train, Keil and his followers reached the Willamette Valley and settled in Marion County. Bethel, Missouri, sent supplies to support the new colony, which was also conducted on a communistic basis, and Keil tried to govern both settlements. When the colony was dissolved at the time of his death, Aurora had 236 members. Its property was valued at over $45,000, and the holdings at Bethel at $65,000. When the final liquidation occurred, in 1879, Bethel was allowed $47,214.25 and Aurora $62,592.10. These amounts were divided among the members, according to their length of service. In 1883, Bethel was incorporated as a town. Aurora had a population of 122 in 1900. Both communities, in spite of the eccentricities of their leader, had lived in extraordinary harmony. Their history was not disturbed by the endless litigation and controversies over constitutions and agreements which marked so many of these social experiments.[8]

The best-known religious community among Scandinavian immigrants was undoubtedly the Swedish colony of Bishop Hill, in Illinois. It was established by the followers of Eric Janson, a peasant and prophet of a devotionalist religion, who attacked the practices of the State Church and wished to restore the simplicity and sincerity of the early Lutheran faith. Eric Janson's character was

[8] See W. G. Bek: "The Community at Bethel, Missouri, and Its Offspring at Aurora, Oregon," in German-American Annals, new series, Vol. VII, pp. 257-276 and 306-328; and Vol. VIII, pp. 15-44 and 76-81; and "A German Communistic Society in Missouri," in Missouri Historical Review, Vol. III, pp. 51-74 and 99-125; and Dailey Harold: "The Old Communistic Colony at Bethel," in Pennsylvania Magazine of History and Biography, Vol. LII, pp. 162-167.

many-sided and not above reproach. He was later charged with fraud, demagogism, and other sins, but there can be no doubt about his original sincerity. He became overconfident and too ambitious; he was ignorant and emotional and, under the pressure of constant irritation and persecution, was driven to extreme measures. It is not necessary to go into the details of his religious faith.

In 1846, he and some of his followers departed for the United States. Within the next three years, 1,500 of his disciples came to America. The story of their transatlantic voyage and of the hardships encountered during the first winter in the United States is so tragic that it stands out even in a period when immigration was always beset with hardships, suffering, and death.

In 1846, about 400 Swedes arrived in Illinois who, under the directing genius of the Prophet, undertook to build the New Jerusalem. Communism was established, not so much as a matter of doctrine or faith, but as a matter of necessity to hold the group together. The first winter brought terrible hardships to the little group huddled together in dugouts and caves, suffering from fevers and cold and famine, and having only the crudest implements with which to cultivate the prairie. But devotional services were held twice each day and three times on Sundays, and the community managed to survive. All farmland was acquired and held in common, and all were to work only for the common good. The thrift and devotion of these Swedish pietists eventually brought prosperity to the colony. More land was bought and, in 1848, a brick dormitory, dining hall, and church were built, a sawmill and flour mill were erected, textile mills were set up, schools were established, and better farm equipment was purchased. In 1850, a delegation from the colony was sent to California to seek gold in the name of the Lord! In 1849, the colony suffered the loss of 143 of its members through an epidemic of cholera, evidently brought into the community by a party of Norwegian canal workers.

Many charges have been made against the private and public morals of Eric Janson. These need not concern us here. The colony was eventually disrupted by a domestic tangle and love affair subsequent to the arrival of John Root, a Stockholm adventurer, who fell in love with Janson's cousin and whose marriage the prophet stubbornly opposed. At last Root was permitted to marry, but only on the agreement that, if he ever left the community, his wife might remain. Root refused to work, absented himself for long periods from the colony, and finally kidnaped his wife and carried her off to Chicago. Mob demonstrations and threats of lynching by frontiersmen of the neighborhood were followed by extended legal proceedings, and, in 1850, Root shot Janson in the courthouse where the trial was in progress.

Jonas Olson, en route to California at the time to prospect for gold, at once turned homeward to assume leadership of the leaderless colony. It was discovered that Janson had been a poor manager and that the community was in debt. In 1853, the Bishop Hill Colony was incorporated under the law of Illinois and its management vested in seven trustees. Under this religious and business oligarchy, the colony experienced a new era of material progress. But Olson became more arbitrary, and expounded the law to his followers in sermons more belligerent than those of the Prophet himself. Dissensions and controversies multiplied, outsiders came in, and the trustees indulged in unwise speculations. Another little town, Galva, was started on the Chicago, Burlington and Quincy Railroad, and a Swedish weekly was published there for a time.

In 1855, the colony owned 8,028 acres of land, 50 town lots in Galva, 10 shares of railroad stock, 586 head of cattle, 109 horses and mules, and 1,000 hogs. Nevertheless, by the close of the 1850's, the colony had suffered such business reverses that it was forced to borrow money. Internal factional strife ended in a peasants' revolt, and the leadership was deposed in 1860. In 1861, the communal property was divided among the membership. Suits and countersuits, assessments, and forced auction sales followed, until finally, in 1879, the Swedish farms were sold at the courthouse in Cambridge in settlement of debts and claims. The debt of the colony was about $400,000, or somewhat over $1,000 a share. Some of the members tried to salvage their religious organization, and Jonas Olson continued to preach to a small band of the faithful. He died in 1898, in his 96th year. Methodists and Seventh Day Adventists made many converts among the erstwhile Jansonists.[9] Today, a

9 For further details on the Bishop Hill Colony, see G. M. Stephenson: *The Religious Aspects of Swedish Immigration* (Minneapolis, 1932), Ch. IV and footnote references; and "Astrology and Theology," in *Swedish-American Historical Bulletin*, Vol. II, No. 3, pp. 60-69; M. A. Mikkelsen: "The Bishop Hill Colony," in *The Johns Hopkins University Studies in History and Political Science* (1892); and Silvert Erdahl: "Eric Janson and the Bishop Hill Colony," in *Journal of the Illinois State Historical Society*, Vol. XVIII, pp. 503-575.

village of nearly 300 people marks the site of the Prophet's New Jerusalem, and some of the old buildings are left as mute witnesses of its former prosperity.

The last of these religious communities to be discussed here is also the most famous and the one that has endured the longest. Amana, or the Community of the True Inspiration, was a settlement of German pietists in Iowa, which did not abandon its communistic life until 1930, when it, too, succumbed to the Great Depression.

Amana consists of seven old-fashioned villages along the Iowa River, embracing a tract of over 26,000 acres of the most fertile farming country in the State of Iowa. Its builders were German mystics who believed in the possibility of divine inspiration in modern times as well as of old and who traced their religious ancestry back to the pietists of the sixteenth and seventeenth centuries. They defied Lutheran formalism, refused to take legal oaths or to render military service, and would not send their children to schools controlled by the Lutheran clergy. In 1817, under the leadership of Michael Krausert, a Strasbourg tailor, Barbara Heinemann, a simple, illiterate German peasant girl, and Christian Metz, a carpenter, the sect experienced a spiritual renaissance. Barbara Heinemann and Metz were the group's last instruments for divine inspiration, and both lie buried in the common burying ground in Iowa.

Communism was begun in Germany, and the first divine suggestion to move to the United States came in 1826. It was not until 1842, however, that several members were sent to the United States to explore its possibilities. Metz, G. A. Weber, Wilhelm Noe, and G. Ackermann constituted the advance guard, which bought 5,000 acres of the old Seneca Indian reservation near Buffalo, at $10 an acre. Six villages were built by the 800 immigrants who then came over; stores and mills were erected, and complete communism was adopted. According to the constitution "approved by the Lord" in 1843, everything except clothing and household goods was to be held in common. A select council of elders governed the settlements, and a board of 16 trustees held title to the property for the community. Communism was adopted, not as a matter of economic theory, but as a necessity to hold the group together and to provide for the old and feeble and the poor.

By 1854, the community needed more land. Buffalo, with its contaminating city influences was only a few miles away; real-estate values were going up, and the time seemed opportune for moving

West. Committees explored the West and decided to buy land in the garden spot of Iowa. After ten years, during which not a dollar was lost in liquidating the old holdings, the community of Amana was established in Iowa. By 1862, six villages lay within a radius of six miles in the Iowa River Valley, and the village of Homestead was bought outright to make the seventh, in order to give the community access to a railroad for its products. In 1859, the community was legally incorporated. It lived under a simple constitution of ten articles until 1930.

At its highest point of success, Amana had a membership of 1,800. By 1921, the membership had dropped to 1,500, and it has dropped somewhat more in recent years. In 1920, the real and personal property of the community was listed at over $2,100,000. The community has prospered and is still in good financial condition. Its people are honest, plain, quiet, peaceful German peasants and artisans, with little interest in intellectual pursuits or the outside world and with an unusually tender concern for the aged and infirm.

Each village has from 40 to 100 houses, ranged for the most part along one long street, after the fashion of a German *Dorf*. Each home is separate, thus providing families with a certain opportunity for individualism. All homes are owned in common, but household equipment is individually owned. With the exception of the home of the doctor, who obviously cannot conform to a community routine, the houses have no kitchens or dining rooms. Each village has its "kitchen houses," where the cooking is done, dining rooms, common bakeries, dairies, and a school, all of which are kept immaculately clean. The church is not a pretentious, special building, but a room with benches and a table, where the men sit on one side of the aisle and the women on the other. An elder leads in the devotional service, which is based in part on the inspirational books of the community. To take care of visitors, hotels have been erected, where simple but ample meals are served.

The affairs of each village are governed by a body of elders. Formerly chosen by inspiration, the elders are now men of special piety and altruism, appointed by the Great Council. The number of elders in each village varies. In each village there is also a council of the brethren, the *Bruderrath,* composed of resident trustees, elders, and foremen of industries; and it is this body which assigns the tasks, revises the allotment of communal property, appoints foremen, and keeps the accounts. Government was thus lodged in

[353]

the hands of a spiritual aristocracy, and mass meetings of the people were seldom held.

Ruling over the village organizations is the Great Council of the Brethren, *der grosse Bruderrath,* composed of a board of trustees of thirteen members, who are the supreme spiritual and temporal leaders of Amana. They are elected annually by popular vote from the whole number of elders. They in turn elect their own officers, direct all the internal and external affairs of the community, and make an annual accounting to the membership. They also serve as the high court of appeals for the settlement of any questions which the village elders cannot handle satisfactorily.

The community has been kept homogeneous, and dozens of offers to remove the colony to other regions where real-estate speculators offered fancy inducements have been wisely declined. The community has been fortunate in its choice of leaders, who, for the most part, have been men of intelligence, business ability, and genuine spirituality. On joining the group, the novice formerly surrendered all his earthly goods and received a receipt for his property. On withdrawal, he was given his original deposit plus interest. Every member received a small allowance in the form of credit at the village general store. Of this, he might dispose as he saw fit. In the past, scores of applications for membership were received and declined each year, and every effort was made to preserve the society's homogeneity by limiting membership to immigrants from Germany or to members of similar societies. Many of the young people left the community but, for a time, over half returned. Since there have been practically no accessions in recent years from Germany and since growth must come entirely from within, it is obvious that the days of Amana are numbered.

Besides farming, which is conducted on a large and scientific scale, the community is famous for its print goods and woolen products. Amana blankets are sold in some of the country's leading department stores. The aim of the community has been to be self-sufficient. It supports a supervised library, a nursery, and a kindergarten. Its schools are public, in the sense that they receive a share of the state school levy, but this is because Amana constitutes a whole township. Doctors, dentists, and teachers are trained at the expense of the community at the University of Iowa and at the teachers' college in Cedar Falls. The people dress simply and plainly, though not in uniform costume, and dancing, cards, and other worldly amusements are prohibited. During the Civil War and the World War, the community remained true to its conscientious opposition to war and suffered some persecution from irate neighbors who failed to understand their religious views.

In 1930, owing largely to the economic depression and in part to the demands of a younger, dissatisfied group, Amana formally abandoned communism and was reorganized as a stock company, under the usual rules applicable to corporations in a capitalistic society. Nevertheless, the community's obligations to the old and the unfortunate in this time of transition were not forgotten, and special provisions were drawn up temporarily to carry over certain communistic features into the new capitalistic system. Thus ended the last of the immigrant pietistic experiments with social regeneration. In the words of Amana's historian:

> Eloquently the simple, silent, clover-scented Amana cemetery with its incense-breathing hedge of cedar speaks of the many sacrifices of personal ambition, of material prosperity, and of individual pleasures dear to the human heart, made and suffered by those who have endeavored to "remain true," to "believe faithfully," and to live together in unity.[10]

Very different from the experiments of religious mystics, revivalists, and reformers described hitherto were the many Utopias established by political and economic theorists who were enamored with the new doctrines of Marxism, Fourierism, and other varieties of Socialism, Communism, and coöperative enterprise. Most of these communities had no religious bond to weld the opponents of the private profit system into a homogeneous group, and few lasted very long.

The number of economic and political Utopias launched by enthusiastic immigrants in the United States during the first three quarters of the nineteenth century is large. Some were the schemes of radical German workingmen carried away by the doctrines of that working class Messiah, the philosopher-tailor, Wilhelm Weitling.[11] In the 1850's, there was a short-lived Norwegian communist settle-

[10] Bertha M. H. Shambaugh: "Amana," in *The Palimpsest*, Vol. III, pp. 193-228. Mrs. Shambaugh's larger study is *Amana That Was and Amana That Is* (Iowa City, 1932). See also Charles Fred Noe: "A Brief History of the Amana Society, 1714-1900," in *The Iowa Journal of History and Politics*, Vol. II, pp. 162-187. Dr. Noe was the physician of Amana.
[11] See Wolfgang Joho: *Wilhelm Weitling* (Heidelberg, Germany, 1931).

ment at Green Bay, Wisconsin, led by Nils Otto Tank. Danish Socialists, led by Louis Albert François Pio, Paul Geleff, and W. A. Hansen established a socialist colony near Hays City, Kansas, in 1877, which lasted only six weeks. In the 1880's, a Jewish socialist colony was developed by immigrants from Southwestern Russia who called themselves "Sons of the Free" and who managed to maintain their settlement at New Odessa, in Douglas County, Oregon, for several years, by selling ties and working on the railroad.[12] Thomas Hughes, celebrated author of *Tom Brown at Rugby,* tried to found a New Rugby in the mountains near Knoxville, Tennessee, to which he hoped to bring England's "robust and superfluous husbandmen."[13] Although the variety of Utopian settlements is great, a discussion of several colonies established under the influence of German and French theorists must suffice as illustrations of the desire for social reform which permeated the ranks of immigrants during part of the last century. It was the same spirit that captured the imagination of Americans like Emerson, Hawthorne, Margaret Fuller, Horace Greeley, John A. Collins, and Adin Ballou.[14]

In the middle forties, a number of German workers' communities were projected by the radical element among the German immigration. Heinrich Adam Ginal, for example, a Lutheran preacher in Pennsylvania who had founded a free, rationalist congregation in Philadelphia in 1841, published a scheme for the establishment of a *Beglückungsverein,* in order to increase human happiness. Based on his proposal, a workers' organization of 300 members was created. Each member deposited his savings, and a capital stock of $20,000 was accumulated. With this amount, 30,000 acres were bought in McKean County, Pennsylvania, and the settlements of Teutonia and Ginalsburg established. In this colony of German workers, no one was to use cash. Every member worked for the good of the whole body and received labor certificates in exchange for the work he had contributed. With these certificates, he could buy the products of the labor of others. At its peak, the colony numbered 400 members. After two years of initial prosperity, it failed with a loss of $40,000, owing to internal friction and the failure to provide all

[12] See Leonard G. Robinson: *The Agricultural Activities of the Jews in America* (New York, 1912), p. 43.

[13] See *Cincinnati Commercial,* July 1, October 1, and November 26, 1881.

[14] For an account of other colonies, see Charles Nordhoff: *The Communistic Societies of the United States* (New York, 1875); and Frederick A. Bushee: "Communistic Societies in the United States," in *Political Science Quarterly,* Vol. XX, No. 4.

that was needed for the support of the community.[15] Similar attempts were made at Germania, Wisconsin, and Helvetia, Missouri, the latter settlement being under the leadership of an Alsatian, Andreas Dietsch.

In 1846, 40 young men of Darmstadt went to Texas to establish a German socialist colony, which was to be devoted to stock raising and agriculture and was to be subject to a minimum of the restraints that arise from government. The colony failed almost immediately. It had been named Bettina, in honor of Bettina von Arnim, the literary friend of Goethe.[16] The settlement at New Ulm, Minnesota, was supported by the socialistic Turnerbund of North America, and had certain socialistic features.[17] Hans Balatka of Munich, who later became famous in Milwaukee and Chicago as a director and composer of merit, was a member of a group of Forty-Eighters who tried a coöperative experiment in Wisconsin in the 1850's.[18]

The first national convention of German workingmen held in Philadelphia was greatly interested in the founding of workers' colonies, on the Weitling pattern of a "republic of the toilers," but the only attempt actually made to put these theories into practice was the colony of Communia, in Clayton County, Iowa. Among its founders were survivors of Dietsch's Helvetia colony and Heinrick Koch, the radical German watchmaker of St. Louis, who edited the *Anti-Pfaff*. Koch had led a group of communist volunteers in the Mexican War and had received a land grant for his services. After a quarrel, Koch's title was bought in 1849 for $600, and the radical watchmaker moved on to Dubuque to become a politician and to deal in government contracts.[19]

In 1851, Weitling visited his old friends at Communia, and the colony became definitely a part of his Arbeiterbund. By putting in all the money that had been raised to start a workers' bank, Weitling managed to buy over 1,200 acres. Houses were erected, one for each five families, and a common kitchen and dining room were built. In his enthusiasm, Weitling called his settlement "the holy ground of brotherly coöperation," although there were hardly

[15] *Mitteilungen des deutschen Pionier Vereins von Philadelphia* (1907), No. 3, pp. 23-28.
[16] G. G. Benjamin: "The Germans in Texas," in *Americana Germanica* (Philadelphia, 1909), pp. 255-256.
[17] See T. S. Baker: "America as the Political Utopia of Young Germany," in *Americana Germanica*, Vol. I, pp. 62-102.
[18] See C. V. Easum: *The Americanization of Carl Schurz* (Chicago, 1929), p. 110.
[19] See Schlüter: *op. cit.*, p. 111.

more than 15 members in 1851. At one time or another, the Arbeiterbund contributed nearly $10,000 to this "republic of the toilers."

The first secession occurred in 1852. The next year, Weitling had himself elected administrator of the colony and insisted on getting guarantees for the money that had been advanced by the Arbeiterbund. Bitter quarrels and lawsuits followed. In 1855, Communia, which two years earlier had consisted of 36 men, 13 women, and 21 children, failed, and carried Weitling's Arbeiterbund and other schemes to the wall with it. Bitterly disillusioned, Weitling returned to New York, where he got a job as registrar of German immigrants at Castle Garden, because of his standing with the Democratic party, which he held up to the Civil War.

In the 1840's, great interest developed in the United States in Fourierism and Icarianism. François Charles Marie Fourier wrote his *Theorie des Quatre Mouvements* in 1808. He believed in coöperative production and buying, in order to avoid waste, and he had an elaborate scheme to end the drudgery of labor. He advocated the setting up of communistic groups, to be divided into phalanxes of about 1,600 persons each. Each group was to inhabit a *phalanstère*, or common building, and be assigned land for coöperative, communistic production.

It has been estimated that, in the first half of the 1840's, more than 30 communities were established in the United States on Fourier's plan. In 1844, Warren Chase started the community of Ceresco where now Ripon, Wisconsin, stands. He obtained a charter from the legislature and built a *phalanstère* 32 by 108 feet to accommodate 20 families. Another Fourierite community was begun near Kalamazoo, Michigan. Albert Brisbane and Horace Greeley contributed financially to the support of Fourierism and, for a time, participated in a New Jersey phalanx. Dozens of phalanxes, most of them promoted by native Americans, of varying success and duration, sprang up throughout the United States. Even the Brook Farm group was converted to Fourierism, and became the Brook Farm phalanx. In Pennsylvania, an Austrian professor of Biblical studies gathered a group of Germans to found a phalanx which was to be known as the Peace Union settlement. In 1854, Victor Considérant founded a Fourieristic phalanx in Texas, and another attempt was made by French immigrants at Silkville, Kansas. The net result of these experiments was hardly more than to suggest the possibilities of the coöperative movement. Of longer duration were the Icarian settlements established by French immigrants, in accordance with the doctrines of Etienne Cabet. Cabet, an editor and politician who was exiled from France from 1834 to 1839 for his opposition to Louis Philippe, was distressed by the calamities and disorders he encountered in his reading of the history of mankind. He began to look for a cause and a remedy. In 1840, he wrote his *Voyage au Icarie,* an exposition of communism, and followed it with his *True Christianity,* in which he tried to show that communism and Christianity were in essence identical. He further elaborated his views in his paper *Le Populaire,* and won many converts in France and elsewhere.[20]

In 1848, during the French Revolution, the "advance guard" of 69 Icarians set out for Texas. Discouraged by malaria, they returned to New Orleans, where they met Cabet and nearly 300 others in 1849. Cabet led his followers to Nauvoo, Illinois, the deserted city of the Mormons, where land and houses were cheap. An administrative body elected by the whole community on the basis of equal suffrage and consisting of a president, secretary, treasurer, and seven directors began to govern the colony. In addition, there was an elective General Assembly, which convened every Saturday evening. *Père* Cabet served as president for a number of years, and by 1855, the settlement housed 500 Icarians.[21]

To join the Icaria at Nauvoo, Illinois, each applicant had to be elected by the community, spend three months there on probation, and have at least 300 francs. The community buildings included a school, dining hall, kitchen, infirmary, laundry, library, bakery, mills and distilleries, and workshops for various trades. A foreman was appointed each month for each line of work, and jobs were rotated so as to break the monotony. There were no religious services on Sunday, and a majority of the members were so-called freethinkers. The school had a liberal curriculum and used some novel pedagogical devices. Music classes, concerts, a 50-piece orchestra, and a theater were developed. French wine and the French joy of life pervaded the community, the majority of whose members

[20] For a translation of Cabet's own account, see Thomas Teakle: "History and Constitution of the Icarian Community," in *The Iowa Journal of History and Politics,* Vol. XV, pp. 214-286.
[21] See Mrs. I. G. Miller: "The Icarian Community of Nauvoo, Illinois," in *Transactions of the Illinois State Historical Society* (1906), pp. 103-107; and Ruth A. Gallaher: "Icaria and the Icarians," in *The Palimpsest,* Vol. II, pp. 97-112.

were French. A constitution of 183 articles defined the aims and duties of the community, and the colony was formally incorporated under Illinois law. One of the incorporators, A. Piquenard, was the architect of the capitol buildings in Des Moines and Springfield, Illinois.

Their constitution defined the Icarians as true Christians. Mutual help was the basis of their communal life. Lawyers and lawsuits were prohibited, and all the features of the capitalist profit system were forbidden. Work, not money, was to be the keystone of the Icarian system. Man was defined as by nature sociable, and consequently sympathetic, affectionate, and good. Man was unhappy only because the right social organization had not been found to give him that happiness which nature intended him to have. All kinds of work were to be equally esteemed, and labor-saving machinery was to be introduced as rapidly as possible, until man would at last be free and have nothing more to do than direct the machines.

Unfortunately, these noble principles could not maintain harmony. Factional quarrels disrupted the community, and Cabet moved to Iowa, where a new Icaria of log houses was built in Adams County. It would be futile to follow other secessions in detail. Cabet was eventually forced out of his own Icaria and, with 200 followers, established a new community near St. Louis, where he died. This Missouri community failed in 1864. The Iowa Icaria was dissolved by court order in 1878, and two factions divided the property. The more radical group incorporated another Icaria near the old Iowa settlement. Eventually, they joined some Icarians already living in California to build a new "Icaria-Speranza," with a constitution that was a curious compromise between communism and individualism. The old remnant in Iowa struggled on a few years longer. In 1895, these Icarians formally dissolved partnership. One member was appointed receiver, and the assets were divided according to years of service, with each orphan minor receiving $850.[22]

It is not difficult to become ironical or cynical about these Amer-

[22] For interesting sidelights on the Icarians, see A. J. F. Ziegelschmid: "Gerhart Hauptmann's Ikarier," in *The Germanic Review*, Vol. XIII, No. 1, pp. 32-39; and Frederick W. J. Heuser: "Gerhart Hauptmann's Trip to America in 1894," in *The Germanic Review*, Vol. XIII, pp. 3-31. In Hauptmann's *Atlantis*, he refers to Karl Bitter and Willy Kimbel, whom he met in the United States. The former appears here as Bonifazius.

ican experiments with Utopia. Nevertheless, they constitute an important chapter in the story of the immigrants' hopes for a promised land. They were conceived at a time when Americans dreamed generous dreams about the future of mankind and when, on the whole, they were remarkably tolerant of those who sought to revolutionize the social order. Emerson, like other intellectuals of his day, had first-hand knowledge of some of these Utopias. With gentle humor, he referred to philosophers who, in their theories, had "skipped no fact but one, namely, life." But even he concluded that,

> . . . in a day of small, sour and fierce schemes, one is admonished and cheered by a project of such friendly aims and of such bold and generous proportions.

13

Culture in Immigrant Chests

IMMIGRANTS, from whatever land they may have come, brought with them memories and experiences of an older social order and a cultural pattern which represented a civilization different from that of the United States in its early years. Centuries of art and culture find expression in the embroidered bodice of a Jugoslavian peasant or in the *Bauerntracht* of a Bavarian maid. Civilizations much older than our own are mirrored in the folksongs, traditions, customs, and folklore of any immigrant group. It is not a question, for the moment, of relative values. Rather, it is a matter of appreciating what there may be of Old World culture in the soul of even the poorest and most ignorant immigrant who has found his way to the United States.

It is to be regretted that many immigrants conform so quickly and completely in all respects to "American standards" and become genuinely ashamed of their heritage. The man with two cultural homes is much less to be feared than the man who has none at all. In the pages that follow, some effort will be made to present, at least in a general way, a picture of some of the values European immigrants brought with them to enrich our American civilization. I do not mean to overstress their contributions, as the necessity of listing so many names may seem to convey. Unfortunately, there appears to be no other way of dealing with the subject. A mere recital of names becomes extremely dull; it may also give the impression that the list is complete and that none but immigrants have represented anything of value in the development of American life, which, of course, is far from the truth. Because science and invention and the humbler talents of the skilled artisan are also vital parts of an evolving civilization, I have not limited myself in this chapter to the fine arts alone but have included other contributions that have been important in the industrial progress of the United States.

[362]

PAINTING

In the field of painting, the United States has but lately come into its own. In colonial times, and during much of the nineteenth century, when life provided little leisure or economic surplus for the cultivation of the fine arts and American energies went largely into the expansion of the continent, the number of outstanding painters was not large. Gerret Van Randst of New York and Christopher Witt of Philadelphia were Dutchmen who attained some distinction as painters of portraits in the colonial period. In 1711, Gustavus Hesselius, a Swede, began his career as an artist in Delaware and Maryland.[1] By the middle of the nineteenth century, American tastes ran to Currier and Ives lithographs, and whatever taste for painting was developed in America before the Civil War was due largely to the influence of French and German portrait painters. But in order to make a living, these immigrant artists painted everything from portraits of local celebrities to cabins of river boats and signs on business houses.

Emmanuel Leutze, a German, painted "Washington Crossing the Delaware" (1851) and "Westward Ho" for the national capitol. Another German artist and expatriate, Albert Bierstadt, painted Western scenes in the most bizarre fashion and on a huge scale.[2] Constant Mayer, who died in 1911, was a French portrait painter of some note. Gustav Kruell (1843-1907) was a German wood engraver. James Smilie (1807-1885), a Scotchman who came to the United States in 1828 from Edinburgh, found employment as an engraver of bank notes. From this occupation, he progressed to an engraver of landscapes. William John Hennessy (1839-1917) was an Irish painter and illustrator; and Charles Cromwell Ingham, another Irish immigrant from Dublin, who died before the close of the Civil War, specialized in painting women's portraits. Constantina Brumidi, an Italian political prisoner who found refuge in the United States, was a well-known painter of frescos and murals. The Cincinnati Museum has some 100 paintings, besides etchings and sculpture, by Frank Duveneck. Though born in Kentucky, he taught in Munich and Florence and then settled in Cincinnati in 1888. As the leader of the Cincinnati Academy, he exercised great influence on the development of American art. Foreign-born

[1] See J. T. Adams: *Provincial Society* (New York, 1927), pp. 148-149.
[2] See Arthur C. Cole: *The Irrepressible Conflict* (New York, 1934), pp. 240 and 382.

painters of distinction include the Norwegian Jonas Lie, the Danes
Emil Carlsen and Rehling Quistgaard, the Swede John F. Carlson,
the Icelander Emile Walters, the Italian Albert Operti, the Dutch-
man Leonard Ochtman, the Armenian Hovsep Pushman, and the
Germans William Ritschel, Carl Rungius, F. Winold Reiss, Joseph
Lauber, William Wendt, Gustav Wiegand, Karl Buehr, and Joseph
and Frank Leyendecker. The great theater painter, Joseph Urban,
came to the United States from Austria.[3]

SCULPTURE

Among American sculptors, foreign-born artists have taken high
rank. Karl Bitter was born in Vienna and came to the United
States at the age of 21. At the time of his death, in 1915, he was
recognized as one of the most outstanding artists in America. Con-
fining himself in his art to a close interpretation of Americanism, he
produced such masterpieces as the Dewey Arch (1899), the Eques-
trian Statue of General Sigel, and the Carl Schurz Memorial in New
York, and the statue of Thomas Jefferson at the University of Virginia, which he completed shortly before his death. His public
service in the profession included his appointment as director of
sculpture for the Pan-American Exposition, the St. Louis World's
Fair, and the Panama-Pacific Exposition, and as a member of the
art commission for New York City.[4] Augustus Saint-Gaudens was
born in Ireland of a French father and an Irish mother. The
father was a shoemaker, the mother the daughter of a plaster-mill
worker. Saint-Gaudens was brought to New York as an infant of
six months, and grew up in the Bowery. Elisabet Ney, perhaps the
greatest woman sculptor of the last generation, came to the United
States in 1870 with her Scotch husband, Dr. Edmund Duncan Montgomery. She had already attained distinction in Europe. Settling
in Texas, where her husband was finishing his work *The Vitality
and Organization of Protoplasm,* she made statues and busts of Sam
Houston and Stephen F. Austin for the Chicago World's Fair of
1893, and the recumbent statue of Albert Sidney Johnson for the
state cemetery at Austin. Her Lady Macbeth is in the Washington
National Gallery, and her former home in Austin now houses the
Elisabet Ney Museum.[5]

[3] See Allen H. Eaton: *Immigrant Gifts to American Life* (New York, 1932), pp. 129-137.
[4] For further details, see Ferdinand Schevill: *Karl Bitter* (Chicago, 1917).
[5] See Preston A. Barba: "Elisabet Ney, The Singular Destiny of a German

Perhaps of somewhat lesser artistic merit, but nevertheless among the distinguished artists who have figured prominently in the development of sculpture in the United States, must be included the two Frenchmen Philip Martiny and Louis Amateis, both of whom did excellent work in architectural sculpture and in works of art for expositions and public buildings. George Julian Zolnay, a Roumanian, did many Confederate memorials in the South. The six Piccirillis brothers, who were all sculptors, came from Italy. Perhaps their best-known memorial is the one in Central Park, New York, to commemorate the loss of the Battleship Maine.[6] Laeurt Thompson (1833-1894) was an Irish sculptor of distinction. Charles J. Mulligan, another Irishman, began work as a stonecutter in the United States. He was discovered and trained by Lorado Taft, and did several well-known statues, including his George Rogers Clark and Lincoln as rail splitter. Adolph Weinman, a German engraver, designed the American dime and half-dollar. The silver dollar, designed in 1915, was the work of Anthony de Francisci, a native of Italy; and the Lincoln penny was the creation of Victor Brenner, who had come to the United States as a boy from Russia.[7] Carl Milles is a Swedish-American sculptor of note.

Music

The musical tastes of the United States of George Washington's time were not on a high artistic level, to state the situation in moderate terms. The New England Puritan tradition was not favorable to the development of a high standard of musical excellence, and the Quaker influence in the Middle Atlantic section was no better. Colonial New England was primarily interested in psalm singing, and used five tunes for all the psalms. Skill in singing aroused distrust; some believed that only the elect should sing, and instrumental accompaniments were discouraged lest attention to the instrument should "divert the heart from the attention of the matter of song." The introduction of an organ in King's Chapel, in Boston, gave the Puritans many unhappy hours. The Quakers, in their rigid, simple service, were as opposed to music as their New England brethren.

Woman," in *The American German Review*, Vol. III, pp. 16-21. For the two biographies of Elisabet Ney, see Bride Neil Taylor: *Elisabet Ney, Sculptor* (New York, 1916); and Eugen Müller, *Elisabet Ney* (Leipzig, Germany, 1931).

[6] See Eaton: *op. cit.*, pp. 128-129.
[7] See *ibid.*, pp. 124-125.

The music of the frontier consisted mostly of playing dance tunes on several fiddles, which were often out of tune. The ambition of the fiddler was to play fast rather than well. The old-time fiddlers had no notion of harmony and played mostly "by ear." Clarinet and fiddle was also a favorite combination. When two fiddlers played together, number one often tried to outdistance number two, and whoever finished the tune first was regarded as the better man.[8] As late as the 1830's, a Virginia physician, who heard a little orchestra of Germans play in Washington, Missouri, naïvely commented:

> You Germans are a queer people. You don't make music as we Americans do. If several of us play simultaneously, we at least play the same melody, but the five of you have each played a different piece.[9]

Dances and anticlassical tunes were the only melodies that seemed to please the untrained American ear. At the beginning of the nineteenth century, a band trying to play part of a Haydn symphony was showered with eggs and vegetables by a New York crowd, who called for *Yankee Doodle* and the *President's March*. As late as the 1850's, European travelers commented upon the low musical taste of the Americans, who seemed to like only waltzes, quadrilles, and polkas. In 1854, the New York Philharmonic Orchestra was bitterly attacked for playing only the music of the German masters. The musicians were warned not to bite the hand that fed them![10]

In the colonial period, Swedes and Germans brought along their fiddles and flutes and their folksongs, and the Scotch-Irish their bagpipes and "David's harp," which they carried with them to the frontiers of Kentucky and Tennessee. The Tennessee and Kentucky Mountains still preserve many Scotch airs, ballads, and folk dances, and many an Irish reel and jig has been blended with the Negro breakdown.[11] The Huguenots loved the dulcimer, and Charleston—rather than Boston or New York—usually attracted European artists first on their arrival in the United States. But the fact remains that the musical taste of Americans as contrasted with Europeans of the same period was decidedly inferior. To Euro-

[8] See Gert Göbel: *Länger als ein Menschenleben in Missouri* (St. Louis, 1877), pp. 81-83.
[9] Quoted in *Missouri Historical Review*, Vol. XVI, p. 352.
[10] See F. L. Ritter: *Music in America* (New York, 1883), p. 315.
[11] See Henry W. Shoemaker: *The Music and Musical Instruments of the Pennsylvania Mountains* (Altoona, Pennsylvania, 1923).

pean immigration, and primarily to the musicians included in that migration, must go much of the credit of the phenomenal progress from *Yankee Doodle* to *Parsifal* and Beethoven in 75 years. Indeed, the influence of foreigners on American music is now so universally recognized that, until very recently, American-born artists found it to their advantage to Europeanize their names.

The Moravians used instrumental music in their church services from early colonial times, and during the first half of the eighteenth century, many organs were installed in the German churches of Philadelphia and its vicinity.[12] The first pretentious concert, involving a large number of both vocal and instrumental performers, seems to have been given in 1786 in the Reformed German Church of Philadelphia. As early as 1800, there was a German music dealer in Lancaster, Pennsylvania, who imported music from a publisher in Leipzig.[13] Moreover, at the end of the eighteenth century, there were a number of prominent French musicians—such as Victor Pelissier and Henry Capron—in the larger seaboard towns, some of whom were exiles of the French Revolution.[14] The majority of the early teachers of music in America were English. The early musical life of Eastern cities was an offspring of English conditions, and English teachers first brought the music of German masters to the American public.[15] English singers and English operettas were popular with many Americans before the close of the eighteenth century, and it was only after the turn of the century that Italian opera became known in New York. Filippo Trajetta published *Rudiments of the Art of Singing*, and his pupil, Lorenzo Da Ponte, established a conservatory in Philadelphia.[16]

"The seeds that produced our singing societies were brought to New York, not from the older settlements of New England, but from Europe," wrote H. E. Krehbiel, one of America's most distinguished music critics and historians of American music. Although many other groups—such as the Scandinavians, Hungarians, Bohemians, Welsh, and Slavs—have been devoted to choral music and have maintained successful singing societies for many years in the United States, it was the German immigrant more than any other who made

[12] See Robert R. Drummond: *Early German Music in Philadelphia* (New York, 1910).
[13] See O. G. Sonneck: *Early Concert Life in America* (Leipzig, Germany, 1907).
[14] See Ritter: *op. cit.,* p. 146; and J. T. Howard: *Our American Music, Three Hundred Years of It* (New York, 1931), pp. 97 and 107.
[15] See Drummond: *op. cit.,* p. 50; and Sonneck: *op. cit.,* p. 157.
[16] See Ritter: *op. cit.,* pp. 181-183.

the largest contribution in developing chorus singing of a high order in nineteenth-century America. Although many German immigrants were trained musicians and skilled performers, the important thing is that, wherever a German immigrant community was established, a *Männerchor* or *Liederkranz* was organized. Here sang the German butcher, carpenter, shoemaker, and small businessman, who plied their trade all week long but made Sunday, and usually one evening a week, available for rehearsals, in which they learned to sing the four-part songs of the fatherland and its great composers under a competent, paid director.

German immigrants writing home from the Missouri frontier in the 1830's begged for German song books and musical compositions. In Watertown, as late as 1860, people came in oxcarts to hear the Milwaukee Musikverein present opera with only piano accompaniment or to listen to a German orchestra whose kettledrums were made out of brewer's kettles.[17]   Many a German immigrant family, especially among the leading Forty-Eighters, embarked at Hamburg or some other port with books and chests full of music or, like the Wehle family of Prague, included two grand pianos among their impedimenta for the trip to America.[18]   When Johann Heinrich Weber of Koblenz arrived in St. Louis in 1834, his musical library included, among other things, Bach, Beethoven, Handel, Haydn, and Mozart. Some of these compositions were scored for full orchestra.[19]

There are numerous German singing societies in the United States today who have reached, or soon will reach, the century mark in their existence. The Philadelphia Männerchor was founded in 1835, the Baltimore Liederkranz the year following. The New York Liederkranz was organized in 1847. At the time, there was another German singing society in New York known as Der Gesangverein der Sozial Reformer. The New York Liederkranz has given excellent concerts each year since its founding, and included in its membership some of the most distinguished of the New York Germans. In the Civil War, it sent over 100 of its members to the

---

[17] See C. V. Easum: *The Americanization of Carl Schurz* (Chicago, 1929), p. 109; and W. F. Whyte: "Chronicles of Early Watertown," in *Wisconsin Magazine of History*, Vol. IV, p. 287. See also *Missouri Historical Review*, Vol. XIV, p. 232.
[18] See Josephine Goldmark: *Pilgrims of '48* (New Haven, Connecticut, 1930), p. 211.
[19] See E. C. Krohn: "Century of Missouri Music," in *Missouri Historical Review*, Vol. XVII, pp. 130-158, 285-320, and 440-463.

front.[20] By 1846, there were three German singing societies in Cincinnati, enough to give a small *Sängerfest*. In 1838, the first male chorus of Cincinnati Germans met in an inn "over the Rhine." Eleven years later, the first German Sängerbund of North America was launched in Cincinnati. The Columbus (Ohio) Männerchor was established in 1848 and still maintains a vigorous organization. The St. Louis Oratorio Society was founded in 1846 by a German organist from Mühlhausen. The Milwaukee Musikverein was organized in 1849 and gave its first concert the next year. The Chicago Liederkranz, founded in 1871, was for years directed by Hans Balatka, who had earlier directed the Milwaukee society. Even before 1850, German singing societies were exchanging visits and entertaining each other with concerts, and from this practice developed the *Sängerfeste*, which remain a characteristic cultural interest of all German-American communities today.

As already indicated, the first German federation of singing societies was the Sängerbund, launched in Cincinnati in 1849 and representing the Middle West. The next year, the Nordöstlicher Sängerbund was organized in Philadelphia for the Eastern section of the United States. Another organization represented the federated singers of the turner societies. Even in far-off Texas, the German singing societies had celebrated nine *Sängerfeste* before 1875. Many smaller organizations existed to further musical competition among localities or special districts. For many German immigrants in the United States, the cultivation of German music has been the most important cultural link with the fatherland.[21]

The *Sängerfeste* staged by German singers in the latter half of the last century were gigantic festivals, both musically and socially. The visiting singers arrived from all directions, and there were grand receptions, parades, torchlight processions, and, needless to add, plenty of good food and beer. The program provided for instrumental music, solos, and choral singing. Excellent orchestras were engaged. Occasionally, outstanding soloists sang with the ensemble or contributed selections to the concert programs. Great mass choruses, composed of all the visiting singers, sang under the

---

[20] See H. Mosenthal: *Geschichte des Vereins deutscher Liederkranz in New York* (New York, 1882).

[21] It was Konrad Krez, who was sentenced to death in 1848 and escaped to the United States, who wrote:

Das deutsche Lied, in diesem fremden Land,
Ist gleich der Palme, die im dürren Sand der Wüste wächst . . . .

direction of distinguished conductors like Karl Bergmann, Franz van der Stucken, and Arthur Claassen. Occasionally, too, the ensemble faltered and broke down (*umgeschmissen*), owing perhaps to the lack of rehearsals or too much conviviality. Prizes consisted of banners and loving cups, and, in true German fashion, there was keen competition and much dispute over the results. At the banquets, which were a necessary part of these musical competitions, there were always long addresses (*Festreden*) and greetings by the mayor and governor.

In time, these *Sängerfeste* became huge affairs, and involved the construction of special concert halls and a huge budget. In 1883, for example, Buffalo built a special hall to seat 5,500, at a cost of $160,000. Seventy-eight societies attended, and a mass chorus of 1,000 voices performed.[22] In 1870, Cincinnati issued a special appeal to its citizens to contribute $25,000 to entertain the visiting German singers.[23] The Cleveland *Sängerfest,* in 1873, was incorporated with a capital stock of $90,000, to be sold in shares of $15 each.[24] In 1893, the building constructed for the *Sängerfest* in Cleveland had a seating capacity of 8,000.[25] In Milwaukee, a crowd of over 15,000 attended the huge picnic which closed the celebrations of the *Sängerfest* in 1879.[26]

The programs at these great musical conventions usually represented music of real merit. In 1853, for example, the evening concert by the mass chorus included Mendelssohn's *Festgesang an die Künstler* and Fischer's *Meeresstille.* In Cleveland, in 1855, the Detroit club sang *Sängergruss* and the Akron society *Wanderers Lied,* and Hans Balatka directed the orchestra.[27] In 1881, Balatka directed a male chorus of 2,200, a mixed chorus of 1,600, and an orchestra of 150 pieces. Besides classical choral compositions by the great German masters, the programs generally included German folksongs and occasionally some of the songs of Stephen C. Foster, which have always been popular with German-American singers.[28]

[22] See *Cincinnati Enquirer,* July 8, 1883.
[23] See *ibid.,* January 26 and March 3, 1870.
[24] See *Toledo Blade,* April 30, 1873.
[25] See *Cleveland Plain Dealer,* June 16, 1893.
[26] See *The New York Times,* June 30, 1879.
[27] See *Cleveland Plain Dealer,* June 6, 1855.
[28] For further details on German *Sängerfeste,* see *Ohio State Journal,* June 18, 1859; *Boston Transcript,* March 28, 1856; C. F. Huch: "Die ersten deutschen Sängerfeste in Amerika," in *Mitteilungen des deutschen Pionier Vereins von*

Carl Zerrahn of Mecklenburg-Schwerin, one of the Forty-Eighters who played flute in the famous Germania Orchestra in New York, directed the Boston Händel and Haydn Choral Society from 1854 to 1895. Its concerts included, besides the better-known oratorios, some of the leading cantatas and compositions of Bach, Mendelssohn, and Gounod.[29] In 1873, the New York Oratorio Society, directed by Dr. Leopold Damrosch, gave its first concert in Knabe Hall. Its members, according to the *New York Tribune,* were recruited largely

> . . . from German families of the highest quality—a section of the community which manifests a better taste and warmer enthusiasm for music, and much more perseverance in the drudgery that vocal societies must undergo, than any other nationality.[30]

The famous Cincinnati May Festivals, begun in 1873 under the direction of Theodore Thomas, owe much to the German element of that city for both their origin and continued success.[31]

In the period from 1860 to 1890, many Italian teachers of voice settled in New York City. They gave a real stimulus to singing, particularly to operatic music. Irish melodies sold widely in the 1860's.[32] The French population of New York supported a Cercle d'Harmonie, which corresponded to the German singing societies.[33] In later years, other immigrant groups—such as the Scandinavians, Hungarians, and Czechs—organized singing societies, but none has carried its country's songs to America with anything like the enthusiasm of the German immigrant for his *Männergesang.*

Gottlieb Graupner, a native of Hanover, who made his way to Boston by way of Charleston, South Carolina, is generally regarded as the father of orchestral music in America. Coming to Boston in 1798, he organized, with the aid of the Russian consul, a little band of musicians who gave a number of concerts as amateurs. It

Philadelphia (1911), No. 19, pp. 1-15; and another article by the same author in *Mitteilungen des deutschen Pionier Vereins von Philadelphia* (1906), No. 1. See also (1912), No. 24, pp. 1-25; and No. 25, pp. 1-24; and *Atlantische Studien,* Vol. III, p. 45.
[29] See *Boston Transcript,* March 30 and May 12, 1866; and *Cincinnati Enquirer,* July 29, 1883.
[30] Quoted in H. E. Krehbiel: *Notes on the Cultivation of Choral Music and the Oratorio Society of New York* (New York, 1884), pp. 63-64.
[31] See *Cincinnati Enquirer,* October 2, 1883.
[32] See *Boston Transcript,* July 3, 1862.
[33] See Ritter: *op. cit.,* pp. 357-358.

is doubtful whether Graupner's claim to fame can be fully sustained, for there were instrumental performers among the Moravian settlements at an early date and, in 1783, a band of musicians from Hamburg had played in Philadelphia. The fact remains undisputed, however, that, without foreign musicians, the development of American orchestras—especially for symphonic music—is unthinkable. As late as 1930, the New York Philharmonic Orchestra, with 114 men, included 72 naturalized citizens, who were distributed by nationalities as follows: 2 Austrians, 1 Englishman, 10 Germans, 6 Dutch, 4 Hungarians, 13 Italians, 1 Lithuanian, 1 Palestinian, 1 Scotchman, 1 Roumanian, 1 Spaniard, and 29 Russians. Of the 12 alien members of the orchestra, 2 came from Belgium, 5 from France, 3 from Holland, and 1 each from Hungary and Italy. The personnel of the Philharmonic is not greatly different from that of other American symphony orchestras.[34]

One of the most important organizations in the development of American orchestral music was the Germania Orchestra, organized in New York by 23 Forty-Eighter *émigrés*. In 1848 and later, the Germania Orchestra gave concerts in New York, Philadelphia, Baltimore, and Boston. In Philadelphia, the receipts for one concert did not reach $10. The orchestra experienced its first financial triumphs in Boston. The nucleus of this famous orchestra was Joseph Gungl's Berlin orchestra. Its membership included Carl Zerrahn, who played first flute; Carl Bergmann, who later conducted the New York Philharmonic; Wilhelm Schultze, who later played first violin in the famous Mendelssohn Quintette of Boston; and Carl Sentz, who became a conductor in Philadelphia. H. F. Albrecht, viola and clarinet player, eventually joined the Icarians at Nauvoo.

During the six years of its existence, the Germania gave over 800 concerts, and played for many cantatas and oratorios as well. Its performances were of high quality, though they included everything from the lighter dance tunes and popular potpourris to Beethoven symphonies. One of its most popular numbers was a potpourri called *Up Broadway,* which brought in everything from Castle Garden, Barnum's Museum, a volunteer fireman's parade, and dance and church music to the *Star Spangled Banner.* The Germania was the first orchestra to play the Tannhäuser *Overture* in the United States, and it introduced Bostonians to Beethoven's

[34] See Eaton: *op. cit.,* p. 16.

Ninth Symphony. As a result of its extended traveling, the orchestra did significant pioneer work. Because its performances were good, American tastes and understanding of music were raised to a higher level.[35]

The beginnings of a better technique for ensemble playing and correct music reading date largely from the efforts of Theodore Thomas, who came to the United States from Hanover in 1845, as a lad of ten. First in Cincinnati and then in Chicago, up to 1905, he exerted tremendous influence on the musical education of the American people, especially in the Middle West. His successor, Frederick Stock has continued the uphill work of educating Western tastes to good music. The New York Symphony was directed first by Dr. Leopold Damrosch and then by his son Walter. Both were born in Silesia. The Boston Symphony has had among its conductors such distinguished musicians as George Henschel of Breslau, Wilhelm Gericke, Arthur Nikisch, Emil Paur, Dr. Karl Muck, and its present director, a Russian, Sergei Alexandrovitch Koussevitzky. The Cincinnati Symphony has played under the batons of Van der Stucken, Leopold Stokowski, a Pole who lived in England, Dr. Ernst Kunwald of Vienna, Ysaye the Belgian, and Fritz Reiner, an Austrian. It is unnecessary to continue the list. Wherever symphony orchestras have been developed, their roster shows a large percentage of foreign-born musicians. They have introduced American concertgoers to Schumann, Brahms, Wagner, and the other great foreign composers, and have constantly emphasized the importance of fine ensemble performance.[36]

In later years, Czechs, Italians, and Russians have filled the places in orchestras and bands once monopolized by Germans. There is hardly a brass band or symphony orchestra of note that does not have its quota of musicians from these groups. During the Civil War, the Czechs furnished more musicians than soldiers for the army. Some of the best bandmasters have been Czechs—such as Joseph Buchar of West Point, W. E. Boleska of the Brooklyn Navy Yard, and Frank Karasek and others in United States Army posts.

[35] See Ritter: *op. cit.*, pp. 317-326; *Boston Transcript*, November 21, 1853; Howard: *op. cit.*, Ch. VII; W. S. B. Mathews: *Hundred Years of Music in America* (Chicago, 1889), p. 65; and J. Bunting: "The Old Germania Orchestra," in *Scribner's Monthly*, Vol. XI, pp. 98-107.

[36] See also Adolf Brune: "Einfluss deutscher Musiker auf die Entwickelung deutscher Musik in Chicago," in *Jahrbuch der Deutschamerikaner für das Jahr 1918*, edited by Dr. Michael Singer (Chicago), pp. 131-143.

One local of the Cleveland Federation of Musicians at the beginning of the century contained 179 Czechs on its roster of members, 12 from one family. Dvorák's *New World Symphony*, it is interesting to point out, was completed at Spillville, Iowa, the birthplace of Joseph J. Kovarik, a Czech who played in the New York Philharmonic.

Captain W. H. Santelmann, leader of the United States Marine Band for nearly 30 years, was a native of Offensen, Germany, who studied music in Leipzig before coming to the United States.[37] During the last half of the nineteenth century, Patrick Gilmore, a native of Dublin, was probably the greatest American bandmaster. Gilmore's band gave monster concerts, and played in the Civil War. In 1869, Gilmore directed the Great National Peace Jubilee in Boston, a musical deluge which lasted for a week. The program opened with a tremendous rendition of *Ein' feste Burg* by organ, orchestra, and chorus; and probably reached its climax when 100 red-shirted Boston firemen pounded out the *Anvil Chorus* on 100 anvils, in conjunction with 100 cornets, 200 violins, and all the other instruments of the orchestra playing, a chorus of 10,000 voices raised in song, and cannon booming their contribution to the uproar. Gilmore was a great showman and advertiser, but he was also an accomplished cornetist and an excellent musician. In contrast with his musical debauch of 1869, it may be added that he was also the composer of the simple melody *Seeing Nellie Home*.[38]

No doubt the greatest Irish-American musician of them all was Victor Herbert, who was born in Dublin and reared in England by a grandfather who was a well-known Irish painter and writer. Having received his musical education in Germany, he came to the United States in 1886, at the age of 27. Here he directed the Pittsburgh Symphony Orchestra and other orchestras, performed as a 'cello soloist, and wrote several operas, over 40 operettas, and hundreds of other compositions that have endeared him forever to the hearts of all American music lovers. In spite of his tremendous activity in the world of music, Herbert never forgot the sorrows of the land of his birth. In 1916, he was elected first national president of the Friends of Irish Freedom.

Finally, it may be added that the "little German band" was once

[37] See *The New York Times*, December 19, 1932.
[38] For an excellent article on Gilmore, see *The Boston Transcript*, April 28, 1934. This is based on George R. Leighton's article in *The American Mercury*.

an institution in the United States. Composed usually of a half dozen or more tolerable musicians, of whom one was always a seasoned immigrant who knew his way about, while the rest were "greenhorns," the little German band, dressed in blue German caps, came into many American cities as regularly as the flowers of spring. These musical immigrants came in droves, via steerage, of course. Eventually, American musicians' unions began to protest against this undesirable competition, and in the end, a number of cities passed ordinances prohibiting the playing of bands, organs, or other musical instruments on the streets, thus ending another typically immigrant institution.[39]

New Orleans was the first city in the United States to introduce and firmly establish grand opera before the Civil War. Until after the war, French and Italian opera predominated wherever this type of music received recognition. New Orleans had regular seasons of French opera as early as the 1790's. In 1809, the Théâtre d'Orleans was begun. It was several times rebuilt up to 1859, when it was superseded by the French Opera House of New Orleans. Regular seasons of opera were given annually. In the 1840's, the French opera troupe of the Crescent City came occasionally to New York City to give such operas as *La Fille du Regiment, Norma,* and *Lucia di Lammermoor.* Italian opera was introduced in New York in 1825, with a presentation of Rossini's *Barbière* by a first-rate troupe. The performance was given at the Park Theatre, and the audience included Joseph Bonaparte.[40]

German opera was presented in 1855 in Niblo's Garden, in New York, though it was generally followed by more popular vocal and instrumental concerts, which seemed more palatable to the listeners' tastes.[41] Weber's *Freischütz,* Flotow's *Martha,* and Albert Lortzing's *Zar und Zimmermann* seem to have been the most popular operas of this period. In 1859, Carl Bergmann opened the opera season in New York with *Tannhäuser,* but it was Dr. Leopold Damrosch who staged the first season of German opera at the Metropolitan in 1884, when he gave 57 performances in the course of the winter.[42] With-

[39] See, for example, *Ohio State Journal,* November 1, 1889; and *Philadelphia Press,* April 4, 1889.
[40] See Mathews: *op. cit.,* p. 60. See also Joseph L. Russo: *Lorenzo Da Ponte, Poet and Adventurer* (Columbia University Press, New York, 1922), especially pp. 124-128 and 131-133.
[41] See *The New York Tribune,* May 1, 1855.
[42] See Irving Kolodin: "The German Influence on the Metropolitan Opera," in *The American-German Review* (March 1936), p. 4.

out question, Damrosch and Anton Seidl exercised more influence than any other conductors on the introduction of German operas, and both were distinguished Wagner enthusiasts. Among great German soloists who helped to make opera popular in the United States were Albert Niemann, who was the first to sing Tristan in America, in 1887, Lilli Lehmann, Emil Fischer, Emma Juch, Rosa Sucher, Johanna Gadski, Konrad Behrens, Marcelle Sembrich, Andreas Dippel, Otto Goritz, Walter Kirchhof, and Ernestine Schumann-Heinck.

The introduction of grand opera was not an easy task. When the *Freischütz* and *Faust* were sung in Boston in 1866, the audience was pitifully small.[43]   Three years earlier, when Beethoven's *Fidelio* was sung at the New York Academy of Music, the *New York Tribune* chided even the German element of the city for its poor support.   The editor's comment was:

> What is the use of giving Beethoven's music to Germans. They talk of him and when his opera is played hardly a corporal's guard comes to see it—and that in a city of which it is said there are as many Germans as in any city in Europe with the exception of two.[44]

Lohengrin, in German, was performed in New Orleans for the first time by Fryer's German opera troupe in 1877.[45]   The Cincinnati festival of grand opera originated in 1881 in Music Hall, a large auditorium built by a German Jew, Samuel Pike, whose real name was Hecht.   Italian opera flourished in New York by the time of the Civil War, and received new popularity in later years because of Adelina Patti and Enrico Caruso.

Chamber music, one of the highest types of musical performance, really dates, on a professional and artistic level, from the days of the Mendelssohn Quintette of Boston.   Founded in 1849, this group consisted originally of August Fries, Francis Rziha, Edward Lehman, Wulf Fries, and Thomas Ryan.   Ryan was born in Ireland, three members were Germans, and the fifth a Czech.   The Mendelssohn Quintette traveled in concert for nearly 50 years and was not disbanded until 1895.   In 1855, Theodore Thomas founded the Mason-Thomas Quintette, which also included three German musicians.   Franz Kneisel, who for so many years was first violinist

[43] See *Boston Transcript,* February 2, 1866.
[44] See *New York Tribune,* December 8, 1863.
[45] See *The New York Times,* December 4, 1877.

of the Kneisel string quartette, was born in Roumania of German parents. Theodore Eisfeld, born in Wolfenbüttel in 1816, did yeoman work in developing chamber music in New York. His quartette gave its first concert in 1851, and was composed at that time of Eisfeld, Noll, Reyer, and Eichhorn. Otto Dresel played the piano.[46] In more recent times, the Flonzaley Quartette was one of the most successful exponents of chamber music.

The number of immigrants who became great teachers and founders of music conservatories in the United States is so large that only a few can be mentioned here. August Waldauer came to St. Louis in 1844, where, for 20 years, he directed the Beethoven Conservatory and various musical societies. In 1851, he had traveled as a violinist with Jenny Lind, the Swedish nightingale, who was so popular in America that, for years, all Swedes were called "Jenny Lind men." Daniel Schlesinger of Hamburg gave piano lessons at $3 a lesson in New York in 1836. At his death, "a grand musical solemnity" was given for his family by a 60-piece orchestra, which played selections from Weber and Beethoven. German teachers did so much in the nineteenth century to develop American interest in music that much of our musical terminology today is German rather than English or Italian.

The Boston Conservatory of Music owes its existence largely to Julius Eichberg of Düsseldorf. Robert Goldbeck was the guiding genius of the New England Conservatory. The New York Grand Conservatory of Music was founded by Ernst Eberhard of Hanover.[47] Dr. Florence Ziegfeld of Oldenburg, father of the "Flo" of Follies fame, developed the Chicago Musical College. Hans Balatka was director of the Balatka Academy of Musical Art in Chicago. Joseph H. Chapek of Prague was concertmaster of the Boston Symphony Orchestra and first violinist of the Chicago Symphony Orchestra, and, in 1885, he founded the Chapek Music School in Chicago. Bernhard Listermann (1841-1917) headed the violin department of Ziegfeld's college for many years. Karl Merz (1836-1890) was a distinguished teacher of organ and piano. Among other piano virtuosi of the nineteenth century who appeared on the American concert stage and taught a large number of distinguished pupils were the Germans Dr. Louis Maas of Boston, Emil Liebling of Chicago, Carl Wolfsohn of Philadelphia, and Carl

[46] See Ritter: *op. cit.*, p. 275.
[47] See Mathews: *op. cit.*, pp. 465-496.

Faelten of the New England Conservatory. August Hyllested of Chicago was born in Stockholm and Fannie Bloomfield Zeisler in Austria. Charles Wels came to New York from Prague and Otto Bendix to Boston from Copenhagen. Constantin Sternberg of St. Petersburg taught for many years in Atlanta.[48] Dirk Hendrik Ezerman, a Dutch cellist, was head of the Philadelphia Conservatory of Music. Among the composers of music of a lighter type, Irving Berlin of Moscow should be mentioned, as well as Rudolf Friml, a Czech, and Sigmund Romberg, who was born in Hungary and came to the United States in the present century. Vladimir Sasko, a Slovak-American composer of Slovak rhapsodies, has in late years received increasing recognition for his compositions.

Finally, the number of makers of musical instruments in the United States who were Germans is remarkable. The story of the development of the house of Steinway and Sons is the tale of the arrival in New York of a German mechanic and his three sons, who worked for two years with three different American piano manufacturers in order to learn American methods and then began to make Steinway pianos. In 1855, they won three prizes at the Crystal Palace Exhibition. Heinrich Steinweg, founder of the firm, was born in Braunschweig and learned his trade in Goslar as a piano maker and organ builder. He came to the United States in 1850. The names of other well-known American piano manufacturers testify to their German origin, particularly Knabe, Weber, Lindemann, Stultz and Bauer, Kranich and Bach, and Wurlitzer. Georg Gemünder of Ingelfingen, Würtemberg, became one of the best violin makers in the United States, and the Gemünder violin has perpetuated his name. Mathias Schwab started his organ factory in Cincinnati as early as 1831.

DRAMA

For an entire generation, the Irish immigration had a profound effect upon the development of the American theater. On the vaudeville stage and in the regular theaters, the stage Irishman had, by 1850, become such a full-grown giant that he threatened to dwarf all other stage types, including the Yankee. He was represented as a bizarre individual, preposterously dressed in a red-flannel fireman's shirt, effecting a swagger, and with a shillelah in hand to knock out all others in the cast at the proper moment; and

[48] See *ibid.*, pp. 112-167.

he spoke with a brogue that seems to have been especially appealing to the risibilities of the audiences of Civil War days. The Irishman was so celebrated in farce, vaudeville, concert halls, and burlesque that Henry James wrote with some disgust in the March 11, 1875, issue of *The Nation:*

> Our drama seems fated, when it repairs to foreign parts for its types, to seek them first of all in the land of brogue and "bulls". . . .

Barney Williams (Bernard Flaherty) was probably one of the best of these portrayers of the sons of Erin, and he was enthusiastically described in 1854 as without an equal on the American stage

> . . . in the presentation of the genuine Paddy, the true Irish peasant, the broad unmistakable wideawake "broth of a boy," alike ready to fight or shake hands, equally at home with the girls or the boys, and nothing lothe to drink with these and flirt with those . . . .[49]

Williams was born in Cork but grew up in the Bowery. He knew the Irish volunteer fire companies from first-hand observation, and loved to portray the character of the noble fireman on the stage. John Drew, father of America's most famous stage family, was born in Dublin in 1827, and played roles like "Handy Andy" and "The Irish Emigrant." Irish airs, jigs, and reels, the Irish brogue, and Irish liquor were featured on the American stage for 40 years and were even incongruously introduced in blackface minstrelsy, when that form of entertainment almost monopolized the American theater.

Irish plays on the American stage either were farce comedies, with an Irish scene and much Irish singing and dancing, or plays that were based on Irish history and glorified the Irish nationality. Special skits were written to contrast the Irish with the Yankee or more phlegmatic German types. The evolution of Irish humor runs straight along from these early skits to Gallagher and Shean, Edward Harrigan's hilarious comedies about the relations of the belligerent Mulligans with their foes, the Lochmüllers,[50] to Mr. Dooley's witty dialogues with Hennessey.[51]

---

[49] *Spirit of the Times,* January 14, 1854.
[50] See A. M. Schlesinger: *The Rise of the City* (New York, 1933), p. 295.
[51] See Constance Rourke: *American Humor, A Study of the National Character* (New York, 1931), pp. 138-139, 78, 92, and 289-290.

Between 1850 and 1855, the following list of plays produced in Philadelphia will indicate the vogue of the Irish drama in ante-bellum days: *Ireland and America, Ireland as It Is, Irish Blunders of Handy Andy, Irish Assurance and Yankee Modesty, The Irish Emigrant and the Philadelphia Carman, Andy Blake, or the Irish Diamond, The Irish Attorney, The Irish Farmer, The Irish Broom-Maker, The Irish M. D., The Irish Secretary, The Irish Know Nothing,* and *The Irish Thrush and the Swedish Nightingale.*[52] *The Irish Emigrant's Lament* had been popular in the 1840's.[53] By 1860, John Brougham and Dion Boucicault reigned supreme as dramatists on the American stage. Brougham came to the United States in 1843 and wrote many of the popular burlesques of the time, as well as *The Irish Yankee* and *The Irish Emigrant.* Boucicault came to New York in 1853. Both were born in Dublin. Samuel Lover, who came to the United States in 1846, wrote *Rory O'More* and *Handy Andy.* He won great popularity because of his thorough familiarity with the national peculiarities of his eccentric country-men.[54]

A better appreciation of the standards of the Irish drama in the middle decades of the last century may be obtained by noting briefly the characters and plots of several plays. Scores of plays followed much the same pattern, and the Irish drama became a stereotyped form of entertainment showing little variation. *Ireland and America, or Scenes in Both* related the story of an Irish "rolickin blade" who was kidnapped into the British Army because a red-coated captain desired his Peggy. The hero escaped to the United States, "to breathe the free air of that glorious land of liberty" which is "the home of the stranger." The scene of the second act was located in the United States, where the villainous kidnaper-captain, driven in disgrace from Her Majesty's service, had become an immigrant "runner" in New York. Peggy arrived in due time and was victimized promptly by the captain, only to be saved by her Irish lover, who had become prosperous in the promised land and had returned to the old immigrant boarding house dressed in the clothes he wore upon his arrival in order to extricate innocent immigrants

[52] For a list of these plays, see Arthur H. Wilson: *A History of the Philadelphia Theatre, 1835-1855* (Philadelphia, 1935), pp. 545-672.

[53] See E. D. Branch: *The Sentimental Years, 1836-1860* (New York, 1934), p. 180.

[54] See Allan Nevins (editor): *The Diary of Philip Hone, 1828-1851* (New York, 1927), Vol. II, p. 775.

from the clutches of their exploiters.[55] In *Irish Assurance and Yankee Modesty,* a farce in two acts in which the part of Pat was written expressly for the famous Barney Williams, the story dealt with the experiences of a lovable, impish, roguish Irishman, whose blarney was irresistible to ladies and who served as a "fixer" in love matches.[56] Another popular play in the 1850's was entitled *Temptation, or The Irish Emigrant.* The hero was O'Bryan, a poor hungry, and ragged, but honest and industrious emigrant. The action of the play seemed to have little purpose except to prove that "a ragged waistcoat is seldom suspected of covering an honest heart." [57] As illustrative of another popular type, *The Irish Yankee, or The Birthday of Freedom* may be cited. Here the hero was an American, born of Irish parents, who still spoke with a rich brogue. The play rehearsed the opening episodes of the American Revolution, the Battle of Bunker Hill, and the Tea Party, except that here it was the Irish Yankee who carried the news which brought Washington to Boston to accept his commission as commander in chief of the Continental Army. The play ended with Washington reading the *Declaration of Independence* to his officers, but the final lines were reserved for the Irish hero, who shouted, as the curtain slowly descended:

Now, boys, for a shout that will be heard across the water. Liberty all over the world, and where it is not given with a good will, may it be taken by a strong hand.[58]

Accompanying this vogue for Irish plays was the first great epidemic of Irish songs that swept the United States. Many Americans are still moved by tales of the little green isle across the sea and of Irish hearts and Irish eyes, provided the music has been made sufficiently sentimental by the craftsmen of Tin Pan Alley.

The Jewish comic literature type of Abe and Mawruss, and Mrs. Feitelbaum and her kind seems to have disappeared, and the Jew is much less caricatured today than he was a generation ago. Nevertheless, a play like *Abie's Irish Rose* could hardly have had its

[55] See Samuel French (editor): *American Drama,* acting edition (New York), No. 73.
[56] See *ibid.,* No. 64.
[57] See *ibid.,* No. 65.
[58] See *ibid.,* No. 88. Other plays in the same collection are: *The Irish Broom-Maker, or A Cure for Dumbness,* No. 75; *The Irish Post,* No. 82; *The Irish Tiger,* No. 84; and *O'Flannigan and the Fairies,* No. 81. The last-mentioned deals with a drunken Irishman who sees fairies and has so many other wild experiences that he reforms and gives up drinking altogether.

smashing success in any other country except the United States. German comic types such as those found in *Philip Sauerampfer, Schan Schorsch Zintfade, Grocery and Saloonkeeper,* and *Hansjörg* have almost disappeared, and live on only in a few German newspapers today as serials.

In the first half of the nineteenth century, French theater companies visited some of the larger Eastern cities, and many French plays were reworked into English presentations. In New Orleans, Corneille, Racine, and the French classics were popular in the French playhouses.[59] In 1863, Manager Juignèt began his third season of French theatricals at the French theatre in New York. The performances combined comic opera, one-act vaudeville, and musical numbers.[60] In the late 1870's, the Théâtre Français on 23rd Street, in New York, presented a whole season of French plays.[61]

German theaters were developed as early as the 1840's, and in some of the larger cities, the German element was able to support German stock companies, with few interruptions, up to the time of the World War. The German theater then succumbed to the hysteria of the war years. In New York, the first German plays were presented at the Franklin Theatre, on Chatham Street, in the early 1840's. Few of the productions before 1848 had much literary merit, and the cast was not outstanding. Kotzebue's comedies were popular, and there was an occasional play of Schiller, Grillparzer, or Kleist. The scenery and stage mechanics were crude, the illumination and the music poor, and the acting quite mediocre. Often audiences could be attracted into the theater only if they were promised a dance following the performance.

After 1850, and largely because of the influence of the Forty-Eighters, there was a renaissance in German drama in the United States. In 1854, the Stadttheater was opened in New York, under competent direction, and Schiller and Shakespeare were presented, though the productions were frequently disappointing. In the beer and wine rooms, small companies presented lighter plays, depending very often on the sale of beer and wine to raise their expenses. These were known as *Liebhabertheater.* Under the guidance of the German actor Otto Hoym and the benevolence of Edward Hamann, the Stadttheater was steadily raised to a higher cultural level.

[59] See Howard M. Jones: *American and French Culture, 1750-1848* (Chapel Hill, North Carolina, 1927), p. 347.
[60] See *The New York Tribune,* October 30 and November 24, 1863.
[61] See *The New York Times,* October 3, 1877.

Kotzebue's comedies disappeared from the repertoire, and Lessing, Körner, and Goethe were added.[62]   In 1872, the Germania Theatre was opened in New York; seven years later the Thalia opened its doors; and, after 1888, the Irving Place Theatre became the home of German drama.   In the season of 1878-1879, 233 performances of 52 different plays were given at the Germania Theatre.   The leading producers in New York were Adolf Neuendorff, Heinrich Conried, Gustav Amberg, and Maurice Baumfeld.[63]

The first attempt to create a German theater in Cincinnati, other than *Liebhaberbühnen* connected with singing societies and *Turnvereine,* was made in 1846 by Herr and Frau Christian Thielmann. In 1851, Hassaurek and his associates in the Freie Männer Verein created Das Deutsche Institut, where plays were given four times a week until 1861.   The repertoire included Schiller and Shakespeare.   Visiting stars of the German drama—such as Heinrich Börnstein of St. Louis, Fanny Janauschek, and Marie Seebach— visited Cincinnati occasionally in the 1860's and 1870's.   The turner of Cincinnati sponsored a Stadttheater, which reached its highest level of artistry in the years from 1871 to 1875.   After 1876, Das Deutsche Theater managed to eke out a rather precarious existence in Robinson's Opera House until 1881, when a law was passed in Cincinnati forbidding Sunday performances.   Among the more competent directors of German plays in Cincinnati were Alexander Wurster, Filip Szwirschina, and Otto Ernst Schmid.   The lastnamed was in charge of Cincinnati's German theater when the World War broke out.   He managed to present plays through the season of 1917-1918, but then three of his players were interned as alien enemies and the German Theatre of Cincinnati closed its doors.[64]

[62] See F. A. H. Leucks: *Early German Theatre in New York, 1840-1872* (New York, 1928).

[63] See Edwin H. Zeydel: "The German Theatre in New York City," in *Jahrbuch der deutsch-amerikanischen historischen Gesellschaft von Illinois,* Vol. XV, pp. 255-309. See also Michael Singer: "Deutsches Bühnenleben in Amerika," in *Jahrbuch der Deutsch-Amerikaner für das Jahr 1918* (Chicago, 1918), pp. 273-312; and C. F. Huch: "Das deutsche Theater in Philadelphia vor dem Bürgerkriege," in *Mitteilungen des deutschen Pionier Vereins von Philadelphia* (1907), No. 6, pp. 13-31; "Das deutsche Theater in New York bis zum Jahre 1860," in *Mitteilungen des deutschen Pionier Vereins von Philadelphia* (1908) No. 7, pp. 10-20; and No. 8, pp. 14-29.

[64] See Ralph Wood: "Geschichte des Deutschen Theaters von Cincinnati," in *Jahrbuch der deutsch-amerikanischen historischen Gesellschaft von Illinois,* Vol. XXXII, pp. 411-522; *Cincinnati Commercial,* October 15, 1881; and *Cincinnati Enquirer,* January 21, 1847.   For an account of the German theater in Toledo, see *Toledo Blade,* January 26, May 16, and November 2, 1857.

The first German theater performance given in St. Louis in 1842 was Schiller's *Räuber*. Not until 1859 was a permanent theater established. The greatest promoter of a German theater in St. Louis was Dr. Heinrich Börnstein, himself an actor and owner of the St. Louis *Anzeiger des Westens*. He wrote plays, acted parts, and sponsored a society for the encouragement of German drama. In spite of his efforts as director of the St. Louis Opernhaus, it was some years before the German element transferred its allegiance from variety bills in beer gardens, where the admission was ten cents, including a free glass of beer, to a theater of higher quality. In 1861, St. Louis broke up the German theater by arresting performers for acting on Sunday, thus forecasting the later experiences of German troupes in Cincinnati and elsewhere. In 1862, a Deutsches Stadttheater was opened in St. Louis. In the next five years, nearly 1,000 performances were given. From 1871 to 1880, Louis Pelosi raised the standards of the St. Louis German theater considerably, but the real renaissance dates from 1892, when the Germania Theater was established. This enterprise was supported by a Germania Theater Verein, whose members subscribed for a certain number of performances each year and provided a guarantee fund. When the Germania failed, the Victoria Theatre was opened in 1913, with Goethe's *Faust,* under the direction of Hans Loebel. The leading lady of the Pabst German Theater of Milwaukee appeared as Gretchen, and a leading player of the New York German theater played Mephistopheles. The season of 1913-1914 ended as an artistic success but with a deficit of $12,000. The deficits in New York and Milwaukee, however, were even larger.[65]

In Chicago, Jacob Rittig produced *Kabale und Liebe* in 1856. By the late 1870's, the German theater was well established, with such outstanding actors as Christian and Louise Thielmann and Ferdinand Welb. Frequently, German theater companies divided their forces between Chicago and Milwaukee, and the latter troupe usually gave Sunday performances in Chicago. The Germania Theater in Chicago was managed and supported by a Verein deutscher Theaterfreunde and gave daily performances until the World War. In Milwaukee, an excellent plan of coöperation was worked out between the high schools and the German stock company by which students of German were expected to attend German theater

[65] See Alfred H. Nolle: "The German Drama on the St. Louis Stage," in *German-American Annals,* new series, Vol. XV, pp. 28-65 and 73-112.

performances regularly.[66]   The German theater continued in Chicago, New York, Philadelphia, St. Louis, Cincinnati, Milwaukee, and San Francisco until the World War.[67]

To a surprising degree, immigrants and those directly descended from immigrant parents have risen to places of distinction in the moving-picture industry of modern times.   Luise Rainer, and the directors Eric von Stroheim and Joseph von Sternberg are Austrians. Marcus Loew, Warner Brothers, and the Zukor, Goldwyn, and Lasky studios represent Jewish leaders of importance in Hollywood. Al Jolson, Eddie Cantor, Ed Wynn, and Fannie Brice have become famous entertainers on the stage, in the movies, and on the radio. Edna Ferber and Fannis Hurst, of Jewish blood, have produced novels that have been utilized for screen scenarios.   Among the great American theater producers should be mentioned other distinguished leaders of Jewish stock, such as David Belasco, the Frohmans, and the Schuberts.   Anna Q. Nilsson, Greta Garbo (Greta Lovisa Gustafsson), and the late Warner Oland (Johan Verner Ölund), creator of the "Charlie Chan" roles, are Sweden's best-known contributions to Hollywood.   Edgar Bergen, of "Charlie McCarthy" fame, was born in Chicago of parents who came from Hässleholm and whose real name was Berggren.

THE PROFESSIONS

After completing the monumental task of editing the *Dictionary of American Biography*, Dr. Dumas Malone, in an article prepared for *The American Scholar* in 1935, appraised the contributions of the immigrant groups to the intellectual life of America.   Since the living were not included in the *Dictionary*, his conclusions cannot be expected to do justice to the newer immigrants who have come from eastern and southern Europe.   Nevertheless, the conclusion is irresistible that the foreign-born have done their full proportionate part in the development of American intellectual and scientific interests.   Indeed, it is in these fields, rather than in

[66] See Michael Singer: "Deutsches Bühnenleben und das Deutsche Theater in Chicago," in *Jahrbuch der Deutschen in Chicago für das Jahr 1916*, pp. 103-121.

[67] Adolf Philipp probably should be cited for his success as a German-American playwright.   It was he who wrote the popular musical comedy *Alma, wo wohnst du?*, a hit in both English and German from 1909 to 1912.   (See *The New York Times*, July 31, 1936.)   It is also interesting to point out that Ringling Brothers, of circus fame, were the sons of August Rüngeling, a saddle and harness maker of Hanover, who came with his Alsatian wife first to Milwaukee and then to Iowa.   See Earl Chapin May: *The Circus from Rome to Ringling* (New York, 1932), p. 130.

politics or war, that immigrants have attained their greatest distinction. In the preceding pages, the names of many for whom the United States is only an adopted fatherland have appeared because of the important role they played in this nation's development. The list could easily be extended beyond all reasonable limits and become a mere recital of family names. In what follows, some additional names have been selected from hundreds of others who have made important contributions to science, invention, business, and industrial progress in the United States. The list is intended to be merely representative; no doubt, some of equal importance have been omitted. Other names, such as those of Andrew Carnegie and Sir William Osler, are still so much in the public mind because of their distinguished work that they need hardly be included.

Medicine. Shortly after the Revolution, Dr. James Gardette and Dr. Joseph Le Maire introduced dentistry to the United States, and remained here to practice their profession. Both had come to Providence with the French Army during the war.[68] Dr. Chovet lectured on anatomy in Philadelphia and had a fine wax collection of the human body. La Mageur, who arrived in Philadelphia in 1784, advertised that he could "transplant teeth," and offered to buy from anyone who had front teeth to sell.[69]

With the German immigration, many physicians came to the United States to practice their profession. Dr. Georg Engelmann, for example, who came to St. Louis in 1833, was a chemist, botanist, and geologist, in addition to being a practicing physician, who helped found the Western Academy of Science in St. Louis.[70] Joseph Goldmark, a German Jew of Vienna, who had participated in the Revolution of 1848, hung out his shingle as a doctor in the United States. He was shocked at the low standards of American medical education. In 1857, he patented a new mercury compound and, during the Civil War, put his scientific knowledge at the disposal of the government for the manufacture of explosives, safety caps, and cartridges. Dr. Abraham Jacobi, another outstanding Forty-Eighter, was a distinguished pediatrist. He opened the first free clinic for children's diseases in the United States and was a pioneer in infant feeding. He also published eight volumes

[68] See D. R. Fox: *Ideas in Motion* (New York, 1935), p. 67.
[69] See J. B. McMaster: *A History of the People of the United States* (New York, 1914), Vol. I, pp. 65-66.
[70] See Gustav Körner: *Das deutsche Element im der Vereinigten Staaten von Nordamerika, 1818-1848* (Cincinnati, 1880), pp. 327-331.

of medical works, some of which were translated into Italian and Russian. The Society of German Physicians of New York included, beside Dr. Jacobi, Dr. Ernst Krackowizer, Dr. Hans Zinsser, and Dr. Hans Kudlich—all well known in their profession. Simon Baruch made important contributions to hydrotherapy and surgery for appendicitis. The Scotchman Arthur Cushing made important experiments with the use of digitalis. Gustav Brühl, also a Forty-Eighter, was one of the first throat specialists in Cincinnati. Carl Beck was a skilled New York surgeon and an early user of the X ray. Dr. Christian Detjen of Baltimore was another pioneer in X-ray work. Dr. Carl Barck, trained at Freiburg, was for many years head of the department of opthalmalogy at St. Louis University. Dr. Alexis Carrel, a Frenchman who won the Nobel Prize in 1912 for his surgical work, is a more recent example of the talent that has come to the United States from abroad.

Germans were especially important in the spread of homeopathy in the United States. Dr. Wilhelm Wesselhöft and Dr. Konstantin Hering were among the founders of The North American Academy of the Homeopathic Healing Art, established in Allentown, Pennsylvania, in 1835. The enterprise collapsed in the panic of 1837, whereupon Wesselhöft went to Boston to practice and Hering to Philadelphia. Dr. Fritz Husmann of the latter city and Dr. Jacob Schmidt of Baltimore were also active in early homeopathy in the United States. Dr. Josef H. Pulte carried the movement into the West, and Dr. Hoffendahl followed Wesselhöft into New England. Dr. Hering published the *Rise and Progress of Homeopathy* (1843) and *Materia Medica*. Johann Helfrich, in 1849, published the first book in America which tried to apply homeopathic methods to the field of veterinary medicine. The Swiss Dr. Henry Detwiller also was a prominent pioneer in American homeopathy. It is interesting to add that, because of the great popularity of homeopathy among the Germans, German Methodist circuit riders carried homeopathic medicines in their saddlebags as they made the rounds of their frontier charges.[71]

Germans also made significant contributions to the development of pharmacy in the United States. In the 1850's, the *deutsche Apotheke* was in evidence everywhere, and German pharmacists had no difficulty in finding employment in the United States. In New

[71] See *ibid.*, pp. 69 and 424-425; and *Mitteilungen des deutschen Pionier Vereins von Philadelphia* (1907), No. 4.

York City, in the decade before the Civil War, there was a German pharmacy for every 50 families. German immigration brought the trained prescription druggist to the United States, thereby exercising a wholesome effect on American pharmacists. At that time, only the German druggist had a fundamental training in chemistry. The result was that many Germans founded manufacturing pharmaceutical houses, some of which have prospered for nearly 100 years. Other German pharmacists became teachers in the early schools for training druggists. Johann Michael Maisch, for example, who was born in Germany in 1831, became professor of pharmacy in the New York College of Pharmacy and, in 1863, was supervisor of the Army Medical Laboratory, where medicines were produced for the Civil War armies. Maisch was a most active contributor to the American pharmaceutical field and published extensively. Drs. Louis and Charles E. Dohme, in 1860, founded one of the largest pharmaceutical companies in the United States in Baltimore.[72]

Architecture, Engineering, and Construction. In the fields of architecture, engineering, and construction the foreign-born have produced some outstanding leaders. Major L'Enfant will always be remembered for his plans for the development of the national capital. L'Enfant came to America in 1777; he was wounded at Savannah, while serving as engineer in the Continental Army. In 1789, he supervised the remodeling of the New York City Hall, as the first meeting place for Congress. The Park Theatre in New York was planned in 1798 by Brunel, another French engineer. Picquenard, who was a member of the French colony of Icarians, designed the capitol building at Des Moines, Iowa.

Many civil engineers who supervised the railroad construction of the last century were Germans trained in the technical schools of Germany. Heinrich Kayser served as city engineer of St. Louis for 16 years. He helped to build dykes and levees for the Mississippi and to plan the city's waterworks and sewage system. His successors as city engineers were all Germans—namely: Franz Hassendeubel, Frederick Bischoff, and Charles Pfeiffer. The Cincinnati waterworks were started in 1817 by a company in which the leading figure was a German engineer, Albert Stein, and the chief financial supporter was an Englishman, Colonel Samuel W. Davis. Pumps and

[72] See *Mitteilungen des deutschen Pionier Vereins von Philadelphia* (1911), No. 19, p. 25.

wooden pipes were used in Cincinnati's first waterworks system. Later, Stein constructed similar plants in Richmond, Lynchburg, Nashville, and other Southern cities.[73] Before the close of the Revolution, an Irishman, Christopher Colles, lectured in Philadelphia on pneumatics and hydraulics; after the war, he advocated a system of canals between the Hudson and the Great Lakes.[74] The Irishman Michael M. O'Shaughnessy, who came to the United States in 1885, built the waterworks which bring the water from the Sierra Nevadas to San Francisco.

Charles Conrad Schneider of Saxony constructed the famous cantilever bridge across the Niagara River in 1883. He was not the first, however, to achieve distinction in this difficult field of engineering. The Roebling family is much better known. John A. Roebling, founder of the great engineering company which still bears his name, was born in Thuringia in 1806. He studied at the University of Berlin, became sufficiently influenced by Hegel to write *Roebling's Theory of the Universe,* and began his career in the United States as a pioneer farmer. He found America most attractive, particularly because of its genuine spirit of democracy. Roebling laid out Saxonburg, Pennsylvania, and worked on Pennsylvania canals and railroads.   In 1841, he made his first wire rope, and the Roebling steel wire cable has remained an indispensible invention for all kinds of construction work. In 1845, Roebling built his first suspension bridge over the Monongahela River, at Pittsburgh. He was chief engineer for the Niagara Suspension Bridge in 1850 and for the Cincinnati-Covington Bridge in 1863. Roebling was not the first to construct a wire cable suspension bridge, but no one before his time had constructed one capable of carrying the weight of a railroad train. In 1869, while engaged in his most important task—namely, the building of Brooklyn Bridge —he died of lockjaw, as the result of an accident which occurred while he was supervising its construction. The bridge was completed in 1883 by his son, Washington A. Roebling.[75] Another son supervised the difficult engineering feat of moving Cleopatra's Needle from Egypt to Central Park, New York. He also built the industrial town of Roebling, New Jersey, where for many years most of the workmen were Germans. In 1931, the Roebling Company

[73] See *Der deutsche Pionier,* Vol. IX, pp. 6-17.
[74] See McMaster: *op. cit.,* Vol. II, p. 76.
[75] See Hamilton Schuyler: *The Roeblings, A Century of Engineers, Bridge-Builders and Industrialists* (Princeton, New Jersey, 1931).

furnished all the cable work for the George Washington Bridge over the Hudson, the greatest engineering feat in the long history of the company.

Gustav Lindenthal, another of the leading bridge builders in the United States, was an Austrian trained in Vienna, who came to America in 1874. Perhaps his best-known project was the building of Hell Gate Bridge, connecting the Pennsylvania and the New York, New Haven and Hartford Railroads, over the East River. The bridge was finished in 1917.[76] John F. O'Rourke, born in Tipperary in 1854, was the Irish engineer who built several of the tubes under the East and Hudson Rivers and six tunnels for New York subways. He also invented the O'Rourke air lock for caissons. Ambrose Light and Ambrose Channel are named after John Wolfe Ambrose, an Irish Presbyterian engineer who first urged the building of an adequate channel from New York Harbor to the sea. Duncan Phyfe, a Scotchman who built tables, chairs, and secretaries has become one of the patron saints of antique dealers.[77] Niels Poulson (1843-1911), a Dane who came to the United States at the age of 21, became a wealthy builder and ironmaster. With part of his earnings, he endowed the American-Scandinavian Foundation to foster closer relations between the United States and the Scandinavian countries. Peter Larson, another Dane, was construction engineer for Western railroads. Swedes who contributed to the field of engineering and construction were John B. Collin, construction engineer for the Pennsylvania Railroad, and John W. Nyström, who had great influence on naval construction and mechanical engineering through the publication of his *Pocket-Book of Mechanics and Engineering*.[78]

Miscellaneous fields. It may also be pointed out that Thorstein Veblen, one of the few original thinkers in economics America has had, was the sixth child, in a family of twelve children, born to a Norwegian farm family in Wisconsin. He taught for a year in a Norwegian community school before beginning his university career at Chicago, Stanford, Missouri, and the School for Social Research.[79] Maximilian Scheele De Vere, who came to the United States from Sweden in 1843, was one of the founders of the American Philo-

[76] See *The New York Times*, August 2, 1935.
[77] See Eaton: *op. cit.*, pp. 143-152.
[78] See G. A. Akerlind: "The Status of the Swedish Engineer in the United States," in *Year Book of the Swedish Historical Society, 1909-1910*, pp. 34-36.
[79] See Joseph Dorfman: *Thorstein Veblen and His America* (New York, 1934).

logical Society.   Anton J. Carlson, the noted physiologist, emigrated at the age of 16.   Henry Johnson, born in Sweden in 1867, has done outstanding work in training teachers at Columbia, especially in the field of history.   Carl Emil Seashore, the noted psychologist, was born in Sweden in 1866 as Sjöstrand.   Carl Sandburg's father was August Johnson, a Swedish immigrant who settled in Illinois in the 1870's and changed his name because Illinois had so many other Johnsons in that period of heavy Scandinavian immigration.   Peter F. Collier, an Irish lad who worked in the Dayton, Ohio, carshops and peddled the *Bible* from door to door in New York, was the founder of *Collier's Weekly*.

In the field of science and research, several Swiss achieved distinction in the United States.   Louis Agassiz won a permanent place in the history of geology and zoölogy.   In 1863, during the darkest days of the Civil War, he was laying the foundations for a National Academy of Sciences.   He has been called "the most influential immigrant since Hamilton and Gallatin." [80]   The geographer and geologist Arnold Henry Guyot was a professor at Princeton.   Leo Lesquereux (1806-1889), a well-known paleobotanist, settled in Columbus, Ohio, and became an authority on the coal fields of the Appalachian region.   Louis Francis Pourtales, also a Swiss, was division chief of the United States Coastal Survey.   Ferdinand Rudolph Hassler, who came to Philadelphia from Switzerland in 1805 and was employed as teacher at West Point, introduced analytical geometry in the United States.   Claude Crozet, a Parisian who had served as an engineer under Napoleon, introduced descriptive geometry here in 1816.[81]

The Reverend Louis D. von Schweinitz, a Moravian, was the first important mycologist in the United States.   He made a collection of mushrooms.[82]   Johann David Schoepf, a Hessian surgeon with the troops in the American Revolution, had been trained in medicine and natural science at Erlangen.   He published the first systematic work on American geology, marked the "fall line," wrote papers on American ichthyology, and made the first attempt to prepare a complete American materia medica.[83]   Frederick Adam Julius, Baron von Wangenheim, a Hessian captain, made a systematic study

[80] C. R. Fish: *The Rise of the Common Man* (New York, 1927), pp. 240-241.
[81] See Fox: *op. cit.*, p. 12.
[82] See D. R. Fox: "The Vanished Naturalist," in *Proceedings of the Association of History Teachers of the Middle States and Maryland*, Vol. XXVIII, p. 4.
[83] See Fox: *Ideas in Motion*, pp. 73-74.

of American trees. When he returned to Prussia as a forester, he called the estate on which he nursed the cutlings he had brought from this country in 1784 "America." The Reverend Frederick V. Melsheimer, a Brunswick chaplain who was wounded at Bennington, remained in the United States as a Lutheran pastor, published the first study of American insects, and has sometimes been called the "father of American entomology." [84] The work of J. J. Audubon in ornithology is well known. This Frenchman, who was not only an ornithologist but also a merchant, dancing master, and painter, came to the United States for extended periods in 1803, 1806, 1831, 1836, and 1839, and died here in 1851. In the field of agricultural chemistry, one of the sons of Theodore Erasmus Hilgard, a "Latin Farmer" of Belleville, Illinois, did distinguished work in California. Charles A. Goessmann, of Naumburg, Germany, did outstanding work at Massachusetts Agricultural College; and Professor Heinrich Weber, in the same field, taught for many years at Ohio State University.

MANUFACTURING AND BUSINESS

In the field of manufacturing and business, which have generally been regarded as the special province for the enterprise and genius of the Yankee, it is surprising to find many foreign-born leaders. In early Baltimore, Germans were pioneers in sugar refining, glass manufacture, and in the brewing and canning industries. One of the best-known shipbuilders in Baltimore was Jacob Brusstar. In Cincinnati, as early as 1836, Frederick Rammelsberg of Hanover introduced machine methods in the manufacture of furniture. The Welshman David Thomas, who came to the United States in 1840, contributed so much to the development of hot blast furnaces that he is known as the "father of the American iron business." In Wisconsin, the zinc smelting business was largely due to the stimulus provided by two German graduates of the school for mines in Freiburg, E. C. Hegeler and F. W. Matthiesen, who came to Mineral Point in 1858. Joseph Koenig and Conrad Werra gave Wisconsin its early lead in the manufacture of aluminum products. Mathhiesen also started the Western Clock Company, which manufactures the Big Ben alarm clock. Mathias Schwalbach, a clockmaker of Milwaukee, helped to complete the first workable model for a type-

[84] See *ibid.*, pp. 74-75.

writer, in 1867. Frederick Weyerhaeuser became the lumber king of Wisconsin and America.[85]

A Scotch immigrant, Andrew S. Hallidie, developed the cable car to solve the transit problem on hilly streets like those of San Francisco. Christian Daniel, a German machinist, made the Goodyear welt system a practical success by his inventions of shoe machinery. Herman Frasch, who came to America in steerage, invented methods to refine oil and to extract sulphur from its deposits. Karl Friedrich Hereshoff established a marine engineering firm that built excellent yachts. Otto Mergenthaler, a German Jew of Würtemberg who came to Baltimore at the age of 18, revolutionized the printing business by his invention of the linotype. Louis Prang of Silesia, a refugee of 1848, made significant contributions to lithography and color printing. Many of the largest firms in this field are still directed by Germans or the descendants of German immigrants.

Jacob Rausch, a German who came to Cleveland, established a well-known carriage manufacturing business; Wilhelm Neracher invented and manufactured an automatic fire-sprinkling system; and Leonard Yeckel, who once worked for Rockefeller at $.90 a day, founded the first large concern in Cleveland for the manufacture of ice cream.[86] Michael Cudahy, an Irish boy who was brought to Milwaukee in 1849, introduced the summer curing of meats under refrigeration. Alexander McDougal, a Scotch immigrant, had 40 patents on ship construction. John McTammany invented the perforated music roll for player pianos; Robert Dunbar was an expert builder of grain elevators; and George A. Audsley was a well-known architect and also an organ builder. All three were Scotch. German metallurgists like Albert Arent and Frederick Anton Eilers were especially important in the metallurgical development of the Rocky Mountain area. Perhaps the three greatest "electrical wizards" in this age of electricity were Charles P. Steinmetz, a young German Socialist from Breslau; Michael Pupin, who came to the United States as an illiterate Serbian boy; and Guiseppe Faccioli, a native of Rome whose father had fought under Garibaldi and who performed remarkable experiments in artificial lighting for the

[85] See Frederick Merk: *Economic History of Wisconsin During the Civil War Decade* (Madison, Wisconsin, 1916), pp. 75, 115, and 156.
[86] See W. G. Fordyce: "Immigrant Institutions in Cleveland," in *The Ohio State Archaeological and Historical Quarterly* (October, 1936).

General Electric laboratories at Pittsfield. A cripple, like Stein-metz, he worked in a wheel chair.[87]

Guiseppe Tagliabue, (1812-1878), who came to the United States with a bellows, glass tubes, a pan of tallow, and less than $5, became a leading manufacturer of thermometers and made instruments for the Geodetic Survey. Emile Berliner, who came from Germany at the age of 19, did remarkable work in developing the telephone and gramophone. Dr. Leo Baekeland, a Flemish Belgian, discovered bakelite and invented the paper used in photography known as Velox. William S. Knudsen, of Danish stock, is vice president of General Motors. Stromberg-Carlson radio sets are manufactured by a company both of whose founders were Swedes. The Swedish-American George Berkander has pioneered in the manufacture of plastic jewelry, and Bror G. Dahlberg, born in Sweden in 1881, is president of the Celotex Corporation. A Swedish sailor, Wilhelm Mattson, organized the Matson Navigation Company. John Erics-son, born in Stockholm, achieved immortality in American history by his invention of the *Monitor* during the Civil War. It is not so well known that Ericsson also perfected the screw propeller and won a prize awarded by the American Mechanics Institute for a steam fire engine. John Adolph Dahlgren, son of the Swedish consul in Philadelphia, became an officer in the United States Navy and made notable inventions in naval gunnery. Ole Evinrude, a Norwegian, invented the outboard boat motor in 1909, and became president of a $4,000,000 corporation which manufactured half of the nation's outboard motors in 1929, under the name of the Evin-rude Motor Company.[88] Victor Bendix, born in Moline, Illinois, of Swedish parents, invented the Bendix spring, and thus made possible the self-starter for automobiles. The Stromberg carburetor was the work of John S. Gullborg, born in Västergötland. Ernst Frederik Verner Alexanderson, born in Upsala, came to the United States in 1902. He became chief engineer for the Radio Corpora-tion of America, and worked out the modern selective receiver for radios. A Swedish-American, Carl Oscar Hedstrom, built the first "Indian" motorcycle in a shop in Springfield, Massachusetts; and Gideon Sundbäck, born in Sweden and educated in Germany, pro-vided the present generation with the zipper fastener, which he perfected in 1913.

[87] See *The New York Times,* January 14, 1934; and J. W. Hammond: *Charles Proteus Steinmetz* (New York, 1924).
[88] See *The New York Times,* July 14, 1934.

Joseph Bulova, president of the well-known Bulova Watch Company, so thoroughly advertised over the radio in the last decade, was born in Czechoslovakia and came to this country at the age of 18, after having worked at watchmaking in Bohemia.[89]   Frank A. Assmann, who came to the United States from Germany at the age of 19 and first worked in a tin shop in New York, rose to be president of the American Can Company and was an organizer of the Continental Can Company.[90]   Max Henius, a Dane and a noted chemist, probably trained more brewmasters in the United States than any other person, through the influence of the Wahl-Henius Chemical Laboratory and Brewing Institute of Chicago, of which he was president and to which he contributed as an internationally known expert on the chemistry of fermentation.[91]

Foreign-born Americans also made great contributions to the manufacture of scientific apparatus in the United States. This is especially true in the field of optical instruments. The Bausch and Lomb Optical Company of Rochester, New York, is nationally and internationally known. Its founders were John J. Bausch of Würtemberg, who learned to be an optician abroad before coming to the United States in 1849, and Henry Lomb of Hesse-Kassel, a young cabinetmaker who came to New York in the same year. They found the optical business in America on a low plane and discovered that microscopes were regarded as mere playthings. In 1853, Bausch entered the optical business, and Lomb gave him financial support. In 1855, the two became partners. The firm made the first spectacle lenses in America, and later manufactured microscopes and vulcanite frames for glasses. In 1890, a connection was established with the Zeiss Optical Works of Jena, Germany. Wherever lens products are needed in the United States today—particularly in the scientific laboratories, where telescopes, cameras and microscopes are used—the firm of Bausch and Lomb is known.[92] Another well-known firm in the same field is Gall and Lembke of New York City, founded by Professor Charles F. Lembke, a German astronomer from Heidelberg.[93]

[89] See *The New York Times*, November 19, 1935.
[90] See *ibid.*, February 20, 1936.
[91] See *ibid.*, November 16, 1935.
[92] See Everett W. Melson: "The Bausch and Lomb Optical Company," in *The American-German Review* (June, 1937), pp. 44-47; and L. B. Elliott: *Souvenir Commemorating the Semi-Centennial of the Founding of the Bausch and Lomb Optical Company* (Rochester, New York, 1903).
[93] See *The New York Times*, May 29, 1933.

Eberhard Faber, of Nuremberg, came to New York in 1849, and developed the pencil business which has perpetuated his name. Charles L. Fleischman, a Jew from Budapest, made Cincinnati the center of the yeast business. Peter A. Juley, a German who came to the United States in 1884 and was employed as staff photographer for *Harper's Weekly,* was a pioneer in the development of color photography. German, Dutch, and French silversmiths and iron-workers have been prominent in these trades since colonial times. Pierre Samuel Du Pont de Nemours, philosopher friend of Jefferson, started the powder business and became the founder of the Du Pont dynasty of Delaware.[94]

Even in the development of that typically American institution, the chain grocery, the names of two foreign-born Americans must be recalled. James Butler, founder of the James Butler Grocery Company, which at one time operated 1,350 chain grocery stores and was the first chain of this type in the United States, was an Irish Catholic who came to the United States at the age of 20 with nothing but a steamship ticket and a robust constitution. His first jobs were on farms and in hotels, until he entered the grocery business in New York with his savings of $2,000.[95] H. C. Bohack, who opened his first grocery three years after his arrival from Germany as a youth of 17, became president of the Bohack chain of 740 stores in Brook-lyn and Long Island. His first job as a German immigrant was at $7 a week and board. In 1885, after three years in the United States, he opened his first store, together with a partner, in Manhattan.

In the brewing business, the Germans not only were the pioneers but had a virtual monopoly of the manufacture of beer in the United States for many years. Lager beer first came into general popularity at the time of the Civil War, partly because of the heavy German immigration and partly because of the war taxes imposed on liquor. In the 1850's, lager beer houses had appeared upon the American scene. As an editor, in 1853, commented:

> The commencement of one of these establishments ap-
> pears to be very simple. A German obtains a cellar, a cask
> of beer, a cheese, a loaf of bread, and some pretzels—puts
> out a sign and the business is started.[96]

[94] See Gilbert Chinard: *The Correspondence of Jefferson and Du Pont De Nemours* (London, 1931).
[95] See *The New York Times,* December 9, 1934.
[96] *Ohio State Journal,* September 6, 1853.

By 1880, a city like Cincinnati was famous for three things: beer, pork, and music. The city had 25 breweries.[97]

The first breweries in Cincinnati had been started by Scotch and English brewers of ale. A demand arose in the 1830's for the better and less potent German beer, which could be enjoyed in daily consumption. Better chemical processes were introduced from Germany, and the tendency soon was decidedly away from the powerful ale and toward a mild beer. Germans like Noll, Jüngling, Herancourt, Glossner, and Müntzenberger were among the first reformers in the production of a better German beer.[98] The Moerlein Brewing Company of Cincinnati was founded by Christian Moerlein, a Bavarian who dug cellars in Cincinnati upon his arrival in the United States at $.50 a day. He saved enough to start a brewery in 1841. In 1865, Milwaukee, the home of Schlitz and Pabst beers, produced 55,000 barrels of beer. Beer brewing entered Wisconsin with the German immigration. Prior to the Civil War, brewing was a widely dispersed local industry; by 1872, Milwaukee was the leading beer exporting center in the United States, largely as a result of the brewing and business skill of German immigrants like Philip Best, Frederick Pabst, Charles Melms, Valentin Blatz, Joseph Schlitz, Franz Falk, Frederick Miller, and Jacob Obermann.[99] These were the beers "that made Milwaukee famous." St. Louis acquired the Annheuser-Busch Company. In many cities, the German names of breweries still indicate the monopoly of the German brewmaster in this field of manufacturing.

Closely allied to the manufacture and sale of beer was the hotel business. In the days before the modern hotel with its 1,000 rooms, the German hotelkeeper enjoyed an excellent reputation, from the Waldorf-Astoria of olden times to the little German inns scattered about the country, where the traveler could always be sure of cleanliness and a good table.

It is also important to note the prevalence of Germans in the canning business. H. J. Heinz and Company and the Lutz and Schramm Company lead in this field of manufacturing. William Ziegler, a Pennsylvania German, developed the Royal Baking Powder Company, and William G. Numsen was a pioneer canner and packer in Baltimore.

[97] See *Cincinnati Gazette,* July 2, 1880.
[98] See *Der deutsche Pionier,* Vol. IV, pp. 24-31.
[99] See Merk: *op. cit.,* pp. 151-155.

The culture of the vine was an old occupation of many German immigrants and, in the 1850's, vineyards were developed on the hills around Cincinnati and around Hermann, Missouri. Nicholas Longworth owned the wine cellars of Cincinnati, and Hermann, Missouri, shared with Cincinnati the distinction of being "the cradle of grape culture" in America. In Toledo and Sandusky, Germans developed and controlled the wine business. The technique introduced by German vine growers was that learned from generations of their ancestors along the Rhine, with its graduated hillsides and large trellises and stakes to which the vines were attached.[100]

Nurseries, gardening, forestry, and horticulture were other fields in which immigrants found ready employment. John Rock, a German who fled to the United States and served in the Civil War, became the leading nurseryman in California, where he introduced new varieties of grapes and figs. Patrick Barry (1816-1890), an Irishman, was a well-known horticulturist and edited a magazine in this field. William Saunders, a Scotchman, introduced various foreign plants in the United States, and Scotch gardeners have been much in demand, both on private estates and as growers for florists. Along with Germans, they were eagerly sought in the United States, as may be seen from the advertisements in the daily press. The first director of the first school of forestry in the United States, at Cornell, was Bernhard Edward Fernow, who, in 1886, became chief of the division of forestry of the United States Department of Agriculture. German botanists and landscape architects figured prominently in the development of New York Central Park.[101] H. A. Siebrech, who emigrated from Germany in 1866, opened the first florist shop on Fifth Avenue, New York, and became a well-known landscape architect. Gottlieb M. Kern was a landscape gardener of note in St. Louis, and Johann Notmann worked at this profession in Philadelphia. Adolph Strauch of Cincinnati made his reputation largely by laying out Spring Grove Cemetery.

German, Swiss, and Danish immigrants have been prominent in developing the dairy industry. By 1870, Green County, Wisconsin, led that state in the manufacture of cheese, with special preëminence in Swiss and Limburger cheese, the industry being concentrated in

[100] See *Atlantische Studien*, Vol. IV, p. 125; Göbel: *op. cit.*, pp. 141-146; and Frederich L. Olmsted: *A Journey Through Texas*, p. 6.
[101] See *Toledo Blade*, October 12, 1857; and *Der deutsche Pionier*, Vol. X, pp. 86, 93.

the private dairies of Swiss farmers.[102]   In the development of dairying in Wisconsin, now the greatest dairy state of the Union, the leaders of the industry and the experts of the University of Wisconsin's College of Agriculture have had to look to Swiss, German, Scandinavian, and other immigrant groups for the practical execution of their plans, rather than to the native element, who refused to be "tied to a cow" day in and day out.   Foreigners proved much more susceptible to new methods and more willing to apply themselves to the exacting routine of dairying, which permits no vacations and little visiting.   Hans Buschbauer of Jefferson County, Wisconsin, has become one of the leading writers on dairying and scientific agriculture, and his work has been published in English and German.[103]   The Danes in Iowa and other parts of the West have been leaders in the organization of coöperative dairies.

In the important field of cookery, Lorenzo Delmonico, a Swiss who came to New York in 1832 is known as America's "teacher of gastronomy."   In a city like New York and in other large metropolitan centers, the national foods of many lands have enriched the menus of the American population.   Italian spaghetti and ravioli, French frogs' legs and snails and crêpes suzette, foreign cheeses, and seeds and condiments from the Far East make their irresistible appeal to the American gourmet and can best be found in the immigrant sections of the larger American cities.   The menu of a typical Chinese restaurant is long and bewildering, ending with golden brown kumquats, lichee nuts, almond cakes, and Canton ginger.   The Russian has introduced *borsch*, the national Russian soup.   Swedish restaurants specialize in *smörgåsbord*, the Swedish *hors d'oeuvres*.   German pigs knuckles, beer, and sauerkraut remain a standard dish in German rathskellers, while Bavarian kitchens offer cold plates of sausages, herring, Westphalian hams, pumpernickel, *Sauerbraten*, potato salad, and delicious homemade *Kuchen*.   Hungarian restaurants are popular for their spicy foods and wines, and for the ever-present paprika and goulash.   Italian eating houses specialize in *antipasto*, minestrone, spaghetti, ravioli, scallopini, and sharp salads.   Pork and dumplings are Czech favorites, as well as roast duck and fancy pastries.   Dumplings and soups are popular in Polish eating houses, along with *Golombki*, a cabbage stuffed with

[102] See Merk: *op. cit.*, pp. 24-25.
[103] Joseph Schafer: "A History of Agriculture in Wisconsin," in *Wisconsin Domesday Book, General Studies* (Madison, Wisconsin, 1922), Vol. I, p. 154.

meat, rice, and butter, and featherlight sugared crullers for dessert. All these delicacies introduced to American palates by immigrant cooks from many lands suggest the heavy debt which American dietetics owe to European peoples. It is literally true that one may make a gastronomical tour of the world without ever leaving the bounds of an American city like Cleveland or New York.[104]

Advertisements in the daily newspapers of a generation or two ago frequently specified the nationality preferred for positions like cooks, gardeners, coachmen, housemaids, druggists, and artisans of many kinds, and it is significant to see how often the advertisements ended with the phrase "German (French, Scandinavian, and so forth) preferred." The role of the skilled European workman in the development of American enterprise is one that cannot be easily portrayed, however, merely by listing names, for the story of these immigrant contributions is largely a record of the work of countless thousands whose names were never recorded in the annals of American industry and business.

Bakers were usually Germans and, in the 1870's and 1880's, many bakers' unions were almost solidly German in membership.[105] Butchers, especially those that specialized in sausage making, were also likely to be Germans, as their many stalls in the city markets of today still testify. For a time, Italians disputed with Germans for supremacy in barbering and shoe cobbling. Russians, in later years, worked in large numbers as stone masons. The pearl-button industry in the United States has been developed largely by Czecho-Slovaks. The sponge industry along the Gulf is a virtual monopoly of Greeks. The Welsh were pioneers in the American slate industry. Watchmakers were French, Swiss, and German, and, in 1850, it was necessary to have a French-speaking vice president in the New York union of watchmakers.[106] The Italians have been among the best jewelry workers at Tiffany's and excellent as designers for the garment trade. The Chinese laundry, as an institution, came in with the Oriental immigrants. As bookbinders, printers, and lithographers, and as workers in metal and glass foundries, chemical, leather, wagon, furniture, and piano factories, and breweries the

[104] See Catherine Mackenzie: "Alien Dishes in New York," in *New York Times Magazine* (January 27, 1935), p. 19; and Beatrice Franks: "Making a Gastronomic World Tour of Cleveland," in *Cleveland Plain Dealer Magazine* (May 6, 1934), p. 6.
[105] See *Cleveland Plain Dealer*, August 4, 1887.
[106] See *New York Tribune*, April 19 and 30, 1850.

German artisan has found ready and steady employment. In many of these trades, German, Scandinavian, and Czech immigrants quickly displaced native competitors because of their superior Old World skill and training.

Foreigners may have been less inventive and daring than the Yankees, but they were often superior to their American countrymen in those qualities that make for high-grade, dependable, and thorough craftsmanship. Moreover, thousands of American apprentices have been trained by these foreign-born master craftsmen.[107] They were thorough workers, determined to succeed in a new land, and American employers eagerly sought their services. With the plain, homely virtues of perseverance, industry, patience, and thrift, many an immigrant workman combined a rich measure of the idealism of the true pioneer. The record of countless thousands remains unrecorded and may soon be forgotten, but these people were among the builders of a greater America.

[107] In recent years, exhibitions of art and crafts of immigrant groups have been held in New York, Buffalo, Cleveland, *etc.* See Eaton: *op. cit.*, pp. 32-56 and 143-152. See also Carl Wittke: "The German Element in Industry and Science," in *The German Club of Chicago World's Fair Souvenir Year Book* (Chicago, 1933), pp. 31-36.

PART III

THE NEW IMMIGRATION AND NATIVISM

|14|

The Czechs and Slovaks

THE NEW IMMIGRATION

FOR SEVERAL decades, ever since the immigrant tide to America shifted from the countries of western and northern Europe to those of the southern and eastern parts of the Continent, it has been customary to speak and write about the "new immigration," as contrasted with the old. Moreover, comparisons between these two groups have resulted almost universally to the disadvantage of the more recent arrivals.

From 1820 to 1930, some fourteen million from southern and eastern Europe entered the United States, although it is only since 1880 that the "new" immigrant tide reached the proportions of a great inundation. That there were significant and striking differences between the new arrivals and the older German, Irish, Scandinavian, and Anglo-Saxon stock is apparent to even the most casual observer. The newcomers from southern and eastern Europe represented peoples who were strikingly different in language, customs, political experiences and ideologies, and personal standards of living. Italian, Greek, and Slavic tongues sounded strange to Americans whose ears had gradually become attuned to German or Scandinavian.

The newer immigrants arrived in great masculine hordes. A large proportion were merely "birds of passage," a new phenomenon in the history of American immigration; for they came, not to stay and to acquire citizenship, but to save enough money to return as speedily as possible to the fatherland. As a result, they were less concerned with the American standard of living than earlier immigrants, who looked upon the United States as their permanent home; they were slower to join the labor movement; they were content for the time being to live in the worst quarters of industrial towns; and

[405]

they took little interest at the outset in the political and economic questions which exercised their fellow workmen who had a more permanent stake in American society.

If the bird of passage eventually returned to the United States, he was likely to return with a wife or the beginnings of a large family of children. The alarming fecundity of the newer immigrants quickly overpopulated the foreign quarters that sprang into existence in many American industrial, urban centers. The life of some of these immigrants was hardly more than the constant procession of the pushcart and the baby carriage. Students of population statistics were greatly alarmed and had little difficulty in showing what disastrous results awaited a country in which 50 Roumanian or Italian peasants would have a perfect army of offspring in several generations, whereas the stock of 50 Harvard or Yale men would probably be extinct within the same length of time.

When the immigrant tide ceased to flow as strongly from northern and western Europe as it once did, steamship companies turned their propaganda to the ports of the Mediterranean and into areas in southern and eastern Europe. It must never be forgotten that the immigrant provides a very profitable cargo for steamship companies, for he loads and unloads himself. By the close of the nineteenth century, northern Europeans were less attracted to the United States. There was no longer the same opportunity for agricultural expansion, and the era of free lands and a steadily moving frontier line in the United States was coming to an end. Certainly the differential between opportunities offered in recent decades by the United States and those available in the home country was appreciably greater for southeastern than for northwestern Europeans.

The transit of European civilization to America continued, but now it moved in a somewhat different way. Most of the newcomers became city dwellers and city builders. Indeed, four fifths of the immigrants settled in that part of the United States which lies between an east and west line drawn from Washington, D.C., to St. Louis and a north and south line extending from St. Louis northward. This is but another way of saying that the newcomers went into the industrial, urban centers of the nation. Cheap foreign labor was available in such quantities that immigration became a factor in the rapid industrialization of the nation after the Civil War, although it may also have delayed the development and use of labor-saving machinery. Indeed, it has been argued that the restrictions on immigration after the war may, in turn, have helped to stimulate the planless, technological development of the last decade, which is one of the causes of our present discontent.

In the modern period, the horde of immigrants arriving in New York in one single year was greater than the whole barbarian invasion that conquered Rome. Our larger cities became a modern Babel of tongues. Steamship companies wanted profits; industry wanted cheap labor; and the immigrant wanted a chance to rise from his low station in life to the American middle class. These forces proved irresistible. Up to the World War, America remained true to her historic mission of providing a haven for the poor and the oppressed. By 1930, the number of residents of the United States born abroad or with one or both parents foreign-born was approaching forty million. Three and a half millions of these had come from Poland, four and a half from Italy, and two and three quarters from the old Russia. The Slavic group alone included Poles, Bohemians, Ruthenians, Slovaks, Russians, Bulgarians, Serbs, Croatians, Montenegrins, Slovenians, as well as some minor groups. America, in a very real sense, became a boiling melting pot, for here the old European process of dividing peoples into nations was reversed for an unconscious process of eventually welding them into a new, composite American type.

It is impossible to discuss in detail the history of each of the many immigrant groups that comprised this new immigration. Space is not available, and the data is still lacking for any final appraisal of these immigrant stocks. Only the major groups can be treated in some detail. It is much too soon to appraise intelligently and scientifically the consequences of mixing these new ingredients in the American melting pot. There are vigorous exponents of a point of view which holds that the whole immigration from southern and eastern Europe was undesirable, because it represented an ignorant, unassimilable, strange mass of human beings whom few of us could understand. Many believed they endangered the American standard of civilization as well as American democracy. For years, the new arrivals were blamed for the increase in crime in the United States, although every competent statistical investigation has shown that the crime rate among the first generation immigrant is proportionally lower than for the rest of the country and that the increase occurs only in the second generation. With the rise of labor disputes and radical programs of political and economic reform, it became customary in some quarters to blame all existing discontents on the newly arrived immigrant. All mobs were described as "foreign mobs," made up of "foreign scum, beer-smelling Germans, ignorant Bohemians, uncouth Poles, wild-eyed Russians." [1] Journalists wrote of "the socialistic, atheistic, alcoholic European classes," and the Chicago *Tribune* explained:

> The enemy forces are not American [but] Hussite desperadoes with such names as Wazinski, Hitt, and other Cossack and Teutonic appelations . . . rag-tag and bobtail cutthroats of Beelzebub from the Rhine, the Danube, the Vistula and the Elbe. [2]

It is well to compare these comments with similar attacks on "wild Irishmen" and "red, hair-lipped Germans" in earlier decades. The building of an American civilization does not seem to have been essentially different in the various periods of United States history. It is also helpful to recall a sentence from Mr. Dooley's famous essay on immigration, in which he says:

> As a pilgrim father that missed th' first boats, I must raise me Claryon voice again' th' invasion iv this fair land be th' paupers an' arnychists iv effete Europe. Ye bet I must—because I'm here first . . . .

The creator of this popular column proposed a meeting of the Plymouth Rock Assocyation "to discuss th' immygration question," which was to be attended by "Schwartzmeister an' Mulcahey an' Ignacio Sbarbaro an' Nels Larsen an' Petrus Gooldvink" and was to gather "at Fanneilnoviski Hall at th' corner iv Sheridan and Sigel sthreets." But when his old friend Hinnisy asked what was to be done with "th' offscourin' iv Europe," Mr. Dooley's only reply was: "I'd scour thim some more."

The majority of the Slavs, who constitute so large a proportion of the new immigration, did not go on farms in America. Their money was generally exhausted immediately upon arrival. Thus, it became impossible for them to travel on to the frontier of cheap agricultural lands. Moreover, in the late nineteenth century, farm laborers received lower wages than factory workers. The isolation of the American pioneer farm did not intrigue the European peas-

---

[1] See Harry Barnard: *Eagle Forgotten, The Life of John Peter Altgeld* (New York, 1938), p. 83.
[2] Quoted in *ibid.*, pp. 132-133.

ant, who had grown to manhood in a compact village community. So the Slavs drifted into the mining and industrial sections of the country or worked on the construction gangs that "laid the steel . . . from ocean to ocean" and whose graves were "marked by the telegraph poles." [3]

The Slavic immigrant, like many who came before him, was the victim of sharks, immigrant runners, boarding-house keepers and shady employment agencies. When he found a job, he was likely to be victimized again by the straw boss in the mines or the mill and to be forced to live in the most undesirable tenement districts. "My people do not live in America," commented one Slavic leader; "they live underneath America. America goes on over their heads." [4] Training for "good citizenship" was generally left to the political boss, the ward heeler, the "fixer," the shyster lawyer, the owner of the slum, the labor racketeer, and the local saloonkeeper. Overcrowded homes were the rule, with the usual results as far as health and morality were concerned. Slavic women were at a premium in the United States, and to have a wife was a decided asset for the "boarding boss." Women went into the factories—especially as cigar and garment workers—even when married, in which case they frequently employed someone at a cheap rate to look after the house and family. Weddings and christenings too frequently depended for their success on the number of empty beer kegs rolled out after the festivities, and priests did not always succeed in preaching the gospel of temperance. Nevertheless, Slavs, like other people, eventually acquired homes and gardens; women's hats superseded the Old World kerchief, as an early symbol of the Americanization process; and the innate love for music and dancing to the tune of violin, accordion, or guitar helped to provide some relief from American industrial peonage and to preserve the ties of an ancient and picturesque culture.

THE CZECHS

Accurate statistical data on the immigration of most Slavic groups is difficult, if not impossible, to obtain because of the confusing overlapping of cultural and language frontiers with national boundaries. The situation was further complicated by the disruption

---

[3] See Archibald MacLeish: "Burying Ground by the Ties," in *Frescoes for Mr. Rockerfeller's City* (New York), pp. 12-14.

[4] Quoted in Emily G. Balch: *Our Slavic Fellow Citizens* (New York, 1910), p. 419.

of old empires after the World War and by the emergence of several new political units. Czechoslovakia is a case in point. The old Bohemia, which became the nucleus of the new state, had an ancient culture and, as part of the old Habsburg Empire, had many German characteristics as well as those more typically Slavic. Czechoslovakia has been a stable, progressive, liberal democracy among the postwar succession states. The immigrants from this area, especially from the old Bohemia, represented probably the most intelligent and highly civilized of the Slavic groups to come to the United States.

There were a few Bohemian religious refugees in seventeenth-century colonial America, and Augustina Hermann of Bohemia Manor, Maryland, has been claimed by Czech writers as the first Czech immigrant to the New World. Previous to 1840, however, Bohemia was fairly prosperous, and there was little thought of a migration across the Atlantic. The first great impetus to emigration came after the failure of the Revolution of 1848, when a number of Bohemian liberals, fighting for the rights of their suppressed nationality, fled to America. The gold rush of 1849 probably furnished another incentive; indeed, the economic motive was probably more important than the political, even after 1848. At any rate, from this time to the end of the American Civil War, over 40,000 Bohemians, mostly from the backward, southern districts of their homeland, arrived in the United States. Like other immigrants of the period, they came over in crowded immigrant ships, some of which actually had stalls built on the decks to transport their cattle. From New York, the newcomers proceeded in the usual way to Albany, usually by water and for a fare of $.50. Then they scattered inland from Buffalo to Chicago, Wisconsin, Iowa, and other parts of the Northwest. Racine, Wisconsin, and Cedar Rapids, Iowa, became centers for the distribution of Bohemian immigrants into the agricultural sections of the United States. There was a "little Bohemia" in Minnesota and, after 1863, the tide turned into Nebraska, Kansas, and Texas.[5] Urban communities of Bohemians also began to develop on the Lower East Side of New York and in St. Louis.[6]

In 1867, Austria permitted free immigration from Bohemia. The greatest influx came, however, after 1870, primarily for economic

[5] See Thomas Capek: *The Cĕchs in America* (Boston, 1920).
[6] See Thomas Capek: *The Cĕchs Community of New York* (Boston, 1921).

[410]

reasons. A large percentage of the newcomers were skilled artisans. The rate of illiteracy among the Bohemians was very low as compared with all other groups represented in the new immigration. They had come to stay, and the Bohemian city colonies of Chicago, New York, St. Louis, Cleveland, and elsewhere grew steadily in importance. By 1920, Chicago had a Czech colony of 100,000 and Cleveland one of nearly 50,000. In both cities, the Czechs had become important in public affairs and in the political life of their communities. Anton J. Cermak became the first Slavic mayor of Chicago. Although they clung to their language and customs and took great pride in their racial history, for the most part, the Bohemians became successful artisans and city dwellers, who acquired their own homes in the United States and carried on a community life distinguished, not only by its preservation of the folk culture of Bohemia, but also by its generally high level of intelligence. By 1930, the total Czechoslovak stock in the United States was nearly 1,400,000.

There are many Bohemian communities in the agricultural sections of the present-day United States. In the 1850's, the Bohemians came to Wisconsin, where to this day they have been among the state's most successful and dependable farmers. In 1860, the first Bohemian newspaper in the United States was started at Racine, Wisconsin. Its editor was Carl Jonas, who became a leader of the Wisconsin Bohemians and wielded sufficient political influence to become lieutenant governor of the state. His paper was printed in German type. Jonas, like most Bohemians, voted the Republican ticket, but in Grant's second administration, he turned Democrat.

Bohemians were among the early homesteaders in the Upper Mississippi Valley. They represented a wholesome, neat, industrious, and intelligent peasant class, who settled in colonies and tried to preserve their language and customs. There is a Prague in Nebraska as well as in Czechoslovakia. Settlements like Wilbar, the county seat of Saline County, remained a Czech community for many years. Little English was spoken on the streets; farmers came in to eat their lunches in a saloon that was more like the Continental beer garden; and for a time, a little theater was maintained to present Czech drama in the Czech language. In many a small Nebraska Bohemian settlement, little pastry shops dispensed pastries unknown to the typical American community and suggestive of some of the best shops of Prague and Vienna. Nebraska place

[411]

names—such as Prague, Shestak, Jelen, and Tabor—are lasting testimony of Bohemian settlement in that state. Omaha has a large Bohemian element. The founder of the *Omaha Bee* was Rosewater, born Rozwaril. In 1869, the first Bohemian play and concert in Nebraska was produced in a log schoolhouse in Saline County, and a society was organized in the same year for the reading and discussion of books. Among this music-loving people, even the smallest agricultural villages had Bohemian orchestras. After the World War, there were still eight Bohemian papers published in Nebraska,[7] and, in 1919, there were Bohemian churches in 44 towns and villages of the state.[8]

Many of the Bohemians of Nebraska and Kansas came into these states by way of Iowa, which early acquired a large Bohemian population. Besides Cedar Rapids, which became a kind of distributing center, there are today notable Bohemian settlements in Iowa, such as Spillville and Protivin. Bohemians were among the first farmers to brave the grasshopper and other plagues of Kansas, and to become permanent homesteaders in that state after the Civil War.[9] Bohemian farming communities arose in Minnesota,[10] and the first Bohemian pioneers reached North Dakota in 1871, by way of Wisconsin.[11] In the Southwest, Texas attracted a large number of Bohemians, and the state still had six Czech newspapers in 1910. There is also a Prague in Texas. The first Bohemian settlement in Texas was at Cat Springs, from which point other communities, such as La Grange and Dubina, were established. Bohemians and the early German settlers in Texas intermarried freely as both groups spread their agricultural communities over the state. The descendants of many of these early families—such as the Sebesta, Siller, Donbrava, Haidusek, and Maresh families—are still prominent in the affairs of Texas. In 1915, Slavic was introduced in the curriculum of the University of Texas, and, in 1930, Czech was being taught in the public schools of a number of Texas towns.[12]

[7] See Sarka B. Hrbkova: "Bohemians in Nebraska," in *Publications of the Nebraska State Historical Society*, Vol. XIX, pp. 140-158.

[8] See *ibid.*, p. 146. See also Ferdinand F. Doubrava: "Experiences of a Bohemian Emigrant Family," in *Wisconsin Magazine of History*, Vol. VIII, pp. 393-406.

[9] See F. J. Swehla: "Bohemians in Central Kansas," in *Kansas Historical Collections*, Vol. XIII, pp. 469-512. This is a personal memoir.

[10] See Esther Jerabek: "The Transition of a New World Bohemia," in *Minnesota History* (March, 1934).

[11] See William H. Ebznic: "Bohemians in Richland County," in *Collections of the State Historical Society of North Dakota*, Vol. IV, pp. 62-80.

[12] See Estelle Hudson: *Czech Pioneers of the Southwest* (Dallas, Texas, 1934).

In spite of the interest which attaches to these agricultural communities, the great bulk of the Czech immigration are city dwellers. Their city colonies have been the most important, and it is from these that Czech leadership has generally come. The Bohemians constitute a substantial, intelligent citizenry, who have risen rapidly to positions of economic security and importance in the crafts, in business, and in industrial and professional lines.

Perhaps no other newer immigrant group is so well organized into social and fraternal and protective societies. The oldest of their lodges is the C. S. P. S. (Bohemian Slavonian Protective Association), started in St. Louis in 1854. Other organizations—such as the Western Bohemian Fraternal Order and the Federation of Bohemian Women—have large memberships organized in many lodges throughout the United States. The *Sokol* of the Bohemians, represents an organization like the German *Turnvereine,* and its members gather at stated intervals for huge gymnastic exhibitions. In 1906, a Komensky Club was organized at the State University of Nebraska for the cultural development of Bohemian communities; within a dozen years, it had 26 clubs in 6 states. Although many of these lodges and societies are primarily for protective insurance, they and scores of other clubs serve also as centers for the preservation of Czech culture in America. They celebrate the anniversary of their great national hero, John Hus,[13] and, like the Germans, organize great outings for Bohemian sharpshooters and turner[14] or stage great conventions of gymnasts.[15] Amateur theatricals and the activities of singing societies bulk large in the life of every Bohemian community. The larger cities have their full quota of singing societies, and Bohemians never tire of giving Smetana's *The Bartered Bride.* New York and Chicago are the national headquarters for many Bohemian organizations.

In New York City, although the Czechs have now scattered over many parts of the metropolis, their loyalty is still to the "little Bohemia" that grew up on Second Avenue in the neighborhood of 75th Street. On stated occasions, they still appear here in native costume to attend some folk festival. The largest colony of Czechs today is on the Upper East Side of Manhattan, extending north from 65th to 80th Streets and from Second Avenue to the East River. Once this area housed some 50,000 Czechs, but today, owing

[13] See *Cleveland Leader,* June 24, 1870.
[14] See *The New York Times,* July 16, 1877.
[15] See *Cleveland Plain Dealer,* August 14, 1900.

to their scattering into other neighborhoods of Greater New York, the number probably does not exceed 30,000. Nevertheless, Bohemian life still centers in this Upper East Side settlement. Here are most of the lodge halls, little cigar factories and other industries, newspapers, and churches. Here, too, are the Czech eating places, famous for such native dishes as roast goose with dumpling and sauerkraut, and cakes with almonds and poppy seeds. First Avenue from 65th to 75th Streets is popularly known as "Bohemian Broadway." In this neighborhood, two daily papers are published: Karel Leitner's *New Yorkske Listy,* which is nearly 60 years old, and Michael Kovacik's *New Yorkske Demick.* What is true of life in the Czech colony of New York might easily be duplicated for Cleveland, Chicago, and other cities.[16]

For most groups, the immigrants' church has been probably the strongest single force in preserving their racial solidarity. This is much less true of the Czechs. For decades, their religious life has been split into two militant camps. Under the Austrian regime, all sects except Roman Catholicism had been suppressed. The result was that political opposition to Austria and rationalism and freethinking in matters of religion frequently went hand in hand. Immigrants from rural sections were generally loyal Catholics, and dissent was usually more prevalent among those who came from industrial and urban areas. Among many of the so-called Czech intelligentsia, religious dissent became the rule, and many who were merely anticlerical in their positions were labeled freethinkers and atheists.

The religious life of the Bohemians in America reflects this same sharp division. The St. Jan Nepomuk church parish of St. Louis was organized as early as 1854. In Chicago, the proportion of Catholics and non-Catholic dissenters of various types is fairly equal. In agricultural states—such as Texas, Wisconsin, Minnesota, Nebraska, and Iowa—the Catholic Church predominates, although even these states have active dissenting rationalist groups. In Cleveland, for example, a split occurred as early as 1870 over the organization of a fraternal insurance society which the priest opposed, and about half the Czechs left the Church to become followers of Tom Paine

[16] See, for example, Wellington G. Fordyce: "Immigrant Institutions in Cleveland," in *The Ohio State Archaeological and Historical Quarterly,* October, 1936, April 1937, and April 1938. These three articles give an excellent picture of the life of practically all the immigrant groups of our largest and most interesting cities.

and Robert Ingersoll. In 1915, there were eight Catholic and eight Protestant churches with mixed parishes of Czechs and Slovaks in Cleveland. Many Czechs, on moving away from their communities, have simply ceased attending any church.

Among the most interesting organizations to be found among the Czechs are the freethinker's societies, which are closely akin to the *Freimännervereine* of the German radicals and rationalists described earlier. These organizations, of which there are still many in the larger cities and some in the agricultural sections, rejected all religious orthodoxy and church forms of any kind, and were simply gatherings of rationalists and freethinkers intent upon intellectual and ethical improvement. In 1920, there were still five Liberal Thinker's Societies in Nebraska, four of them in Omaha. In Chicago, the Czech freethinkers have their own cemetery, and, in 1907, they founded the League of Freethinkers.

It is perhaps needless to add that religious radicalism was often accompanied by political and economic radicalism, so that Bohemians were prominent in the early Socialist movement in the United States as well as in the brief history of the anarchist movement in the years before the Haymarket riot in Chicago. L. J. Palda has been called the father of Czech socialism in the United States. The bulk of Bohemians seem to vote Democratic, however, and the city councils of Cleveland, Chicago, and elsewhere, as well as the state legislatures of Nebraska, Iowa, and Wisconsin, have had their regular quotas of Bohemian-American members.

The Bohemian-American press still maintains enough influence to enlist the support of politicians, and shows a greater vigor than that of many foreign-language publications of the older immigrant groups. *Orgán Bratrstva,* the official organ of the Bohemian-Slavonic Benevolent Societies of the United States and Canada, is published monthly at Oak Park, Illinois. In 1933, there were 50 Czech papers published in the United States, most of them in the Middle West. Between 1860 and 1911, 326 Czech journals were established in the United States, of which 85 survived.[17] At the present time, 6 Czech dailies are still in existence.

In 1907, a Department of Bohemian was established at the University of Nebraska, and Professor Jeffrey D. Hrbek was called from Iowa City to occupy the first chair of Bohemian in any state university in the United States. Among distinguished leaders of Bohe-

[17] See Thomas Capek: *Fifty Years of Czech Letters in America* (New York, 1911).

mian stock in the United States may be mentioned Dr. Ales Hrdlicka of the Smithsonian Institute; Thomas L. Sidlo, a law partner of Newton D. Baker; the Mandas of New Jersey, well known among horticulturists; Rudolph Ruzicka, the wood engraver; the musicians Victor Kolar, Joseph J. Kovarik, and Rudolf Friml; and an imposing array of university professors in many fields, such as Bohumil Shimek, Robert J. Kerner, Anthony, John, and Charles Zeleny, Frederick G. Novy, Alois F. Kovarik, and Frank E. and Claude Horack.[18]

THE SLOVAKS

The home of the Slovaks is the southern slopes of the Carpathians, along the northern boundary of the old Hungary, from the section which, before the World War, was the northeastern corner of Hungary. The Slovaks are close to the Czechs in language and blood; indeed, early Slovak writers frequently used Czech as their literary language.

Slovak immigration to the United States began about 1873, although there are no separate statistics available for the Slovaks because for years they were included in the immigration from Hungary. From 1899, when separate figures became available, to 1909, 345,111 Slovaks came to the United States. Many were birds of passage, although a large number came to escape military service, to improve their economic status, or to escape the policy of Magyarization imposed by Hungary upon this suppressed national group. By 1920, there were 400,000 of Slovak blood in the United States.

The Slovaks have often been described as sluggish and unprogressive. Many represented a decidedly lower standard of living than that of the Czechs. The rate of illiteracy was high, being between 25 and 30 per cent. Intemperance was almost a Slovak national sin, although by no means limited to this group of newcomers. Many of the new arrivals were of peasant stock or wandering journeymen. In the United States, they went into the mining and industrial centers to become the marginal workers of American big industry. The birth rate in these Slovak communities was very high and the standard of living very low. The church, the saloon, and the lodge were the centers of social life. But the remittances sent home through American banks and postal money orders show

[18] See also *World's Fair Memorial of the Czechoslovak Group* (Chicago, 1933).

that the Slovak immigrant was by no means improvident. His folk music and the gay-colored embroidery of his national costume suggested an old, colorful civilization, which could not be entirely suppressed by the smoke and dirt of American coal and steel towns. The suppressed nationalism of the Slovaks flowered in the sun of American freedom, and organizations like the American Slovak League began making substantial financial contributions to the nationalist movement in the fatherland. With the total absence of censorship in the United States, Slovak papers sprang into existence, devoted largely to a discussion of the aspirations of the Slovak nation.

The National Slovak Society of the United States, organized in 1890, required all its members to acquire American citizenship. The organizations of the Slovaks in the United States now include a membership of nearly 300,000. In 1931, the Czech Sokol Union and the Slovak Gymnastic Union combined to form the Sokol Gymnastic Federation of America.

Slovaks are scattered through nearly 700 settlements in 37 states. The largest community is that of Pittsburgh, which numbers about 35,000. Other large Slovak communities are Youngstown and Bridgeport, Connecticut. There are more Slovaks in Pennsylvania than in any other state, owing to their employment in the heavy industries. Next in order come the settlements in Ohio, New York, and New Jersey. Although the overwhelming majority of Slovaks are to be found in the industrial areas, in the steel, coal, and coke industries, some have gone on farms in New England, Pennsylvania, and Virginia, and there is even a Slovaktown in Arkansas and a Masaryktown in Florida. Four Slovak dailies are being published in the United States at the present time, of which the oldest is the New York daily, *Slovak v. America.* The first Slovak paper in the United States was the *Amerikansko Slovenske Noviny* of Pittsburgh.

In a very real sense, Czechoslovakia was "made in America." The Czechs and Slovaks in this country provided much of the agitation and a large portion of the funds at the time of the World War to disrupt the old Austro-Hungarian Empire and to create a Czechoslovak national state. In September, 1918, a large assembly of the oppressed peoples of Austria-Hungary living in the United States met at Carnegie Hall, New York, with Paderewski representing the Poles, Stoica the Roumanians, and Hinkovitch the South Slavs. Out of gatherings of this kind eventually came The Mid-European

Democratic Union. Each group presented its program of liberation, and resolutions were signed with great ceremony in Independence Hall, Philadelphia.

The Czechs took a leading part in these proceedings, for their propaganda had been effectively carried on in the United States since 1914. In June, 1918, a convention was signed in Pittsburgh between the Slovaks and Czechs giving Slovakia an autonomous administration in the proposed Czechoslavak state. The Czech National Alliance and the Slovak League addressed frequent appeals and manifestos to the American people, and during the World War years, the Czechs in the United States raised nearly $675,000 for their cause. Czechoslovakia entered the family of nations after the World War as one of the succession states which followed the disruption of the old Central Europe after 1918. To a large measure, the success of this propaganda was due to the brilliant leadership of the late Dr. Thomas G. Masaryk, who had many connections in the United States, and to the aid which came from Czech and Slovak immigrants who had become prosperous in the United States.[19]

As a result of the recent forceful occupation of Czechoslovakia by Nazi Germany, and the arrival of President Benes and other Czech patriot leaders in the United States, it is reasonable to expect a renewed agitation for Czechoslovak self-determination and independence, similar to the prewar activities of the Czechs in the United States.

[19] For a brief account of these activities, see Thomas G. Masaryk: *The Making of a State* (New York, 1927), especially pp. 207-263 *passim*.

15 The Poles, Jugoslavs, Russians, Hungarians, and Other Minor Groups

THE POLES

ALTHOUGH THE Polish immigration to the United States is largely a phenomenon of the period between 1870 and the World War, there were Poles in significant numbers in the United States before the Civil War. A few Poles lived in colonial Virginia, and the *Journal of the Virginia House of Burgesses* contains a reference to "some Polanders to make pitch, tar and potash." A small colony settled along the Passaic and Raritan Rivers in colonial New Jersey, and some were indentured servants in the Southern colonies. In the Revolutionary War, Thaddeus Kosciuszko and Casimir Pulaski became national heroes for future generations of Polish-Americans. The former came to Philadelphia in 1776 as a young military engineer and fought with Greene in his Southern campaign. In 1784, he led an unsuccessful Polish revolt, and

> Hope for a season bade the world farewell
> And freedom shrieked as Kosciuszko fell.

Pulaski came to America on Franklin's endorsement. He raised Pulaski's Legion, mostly among the Germans, and accepted a banner for his legion from the Moravian nuns of Bethlehem, Pennsylvania. He fell mortally wounded at Savannah in 1779.[1]

[1] See Miecislaus Haiman: *Poland and the American Revolutionary War* (Chicago, 1932). Kosciuszko's account for services rendered to the United States amounted to $12,280.54, which Congress recognized. (See *American State Papers, Claims*, p. 207; and *3 Laws of the United States*, p. 25.) Under the warrants issued to Revolutionary soldiers, he selected five 100-acre lots in the nineteenth range in the United States Military Survey, for which President Adams issued him a patent in April 1800. [See *Franklin County Deed Book* (Ohio), Vol. XXI, p. 447.] Those lots constituted a tract on the eastern side of the Scioto River, in Franklin County, near the Delaware, Ohio, county line. [See William E. Peters: *Ohio Lands and Their History*, third edition (Athens, Ohio, 1930), pp. 364-365.] For an account of the Poles in the colonial period, see also Miecislaus Haiman: *Polish Pioneers of Virginia and Kentucky* (Chicago, 1937).

After the unsuccessful Polish rising of 1830, some 350 Polish exiles came to the United States, and Congress granted them land in Illinois. Again, after similar fruitless rebellions in 1848 and 1863, Polish political refugees fled to America. Polish settlements had been begun in Texas and Wisconsin before the Civil War. The first Polish church was established in the Panna Marya settlement in Texas in 1855,[2] and Polonia, in Portage County, Wisconsin, was founded in the 1850's. In 1853, the 23rd anniversary of the Polish rebellion of 1830 was celebrated in New York with Polish, German, and Italian speeches.[3] Eight years earlier, a similar celebration was described in the *New York Weekly News*,[4] with representatives of all the important immigrant groups appearing on the program. In 1859, Polish exiles in Cincinnati arranged a banquet to commemorate the Warsaw uprising of 1830 at which two actual participants were present as honor guests.[5] During the Civil War, Polish volunteers were quartered at the Park Barracks in New York City,[6] and plans were made to raise an entire Polish regiment.[7]

The heavy influx of Poles did not begin until 1870. From 1870 to 1880, 35,000 entered the country, and the figure jumped to 236,000 in the next decade. From 1900 to 1910, the total immigration was nearly 875,000. The tide continued to rise until the World War, reaching its highest point in 1912-1913, when 174,365 entered in one year.[8] By 1920, there were 3,000,000 of Polish parentage in the United States, although here again it must be remembered that the Poles were not always sharply distinguished for statistical purposes from the Ruthenians and similar groups. By 1920, Chicago had a Polish colony of 350,000; New York, one of 250,000; Buffalo, one of 80,000; Milwaukee, one of 75,000; and Pittsburgh, one of 200,000. In Detroit, the group grew steadily with the development of the automobile industry, reaching 300,000 in 1930. The 1930 Census listed 1,268,583 foreign-born Poles in the United States and

[2] See Miecislaus Haiman: *The Poles in the Early History of Texas* (Chicago, 1936).
[3] See *Boston Transcript*, December 1, 1853.
[4] See *New York Weekly News*, December 6, 1845.
[5] See *Cincinnati Enquirer*, November 30, 1859. For a description of a later meeting of the exiles, see also, *Cleveland Leader*, January 28, 1870; and *New York Tribune*, December 1, 1863.
[6] See *The New York Times*, May 13, 1861.
[7] See *ibid.*, April 18, 1861.
[8] See Paul Fox: *The Poles in America* (New York, 1922). For a standard work, written from the sociological point of view mainly, see William I. Thomas and Florian Znaniecki: *The Polish Peasant in Europe and America*, 5 vols. (Boston, 1920).

fixed the total Polish stock, with one or both parents Poles, at 3,342,198.

This huge immigration to the United States was due largely to economic reasons. Polish villages suffered acutely from overpopulation because of the primitive agricultural methods that still prevailed. Low slum conditions existed on many Polish farms, and mud roads and manure piles were outstanding characteristics of Polish agricultural areas. The industrial development of Poland had hardly begun; wages were low and taxes high. Land for the peasant had been subdivided into extremely small lots, especially in regions like Galicia. Thousands of Poles migrated into Germany as seasonal laborers at harvesttime. Poland as a nation, of course, did not exist until after the World War. Her people were mostly peasants; the rate of illiteracy among them was nearly one in four and intemperance was one of their conspicuous vices. Steamship agencies found among the Poles a fertile recruiting ground for steerage passengers to America.

In the Polish immigration to America, the men outnumbered the women by about two to one. They represented, for the most part, a rather stolid, patient, peasant type, but capable of hard work and thrift under more promising conditions. They found employment either in the mines and metal centers of the East or in farming communities. Many were birds of passage, and there was always a large Jewish mixture in the Polish immigration. The majority were unskilled workers, only about one in 16 having a trade. But they were willing to work hard and to save, and managed, on a meager diet of stale bread and sausage, to accumulate savings even as the lowest paid industrial workers.

About three quarters of a million Poles went on farms, and Polish farming communities arose in Massachusetts, in the Connecticut Valley—where they succeeded in areas abandoned by the New England stock—in New York, Ohio, Indiana, Wisconsin, Illinois, Texas, and elsewhere in the West. The advance of Polish settlement can usually be traced by the establishment of Roman Catholic parishes, for more than three fourths of the Poles were devout members of that Church. Polish place names—such as Pulaski, Sobieski, Krakow, Opole, Wilno, Tarnow, Chojnice, Kosciuszko, Poznan, Polishville, and Gniezno—are scattered over the United States map in profusion.

The Polish immigration to Wisconsin went on steadily after 1856.

The first settlement, at Polonia, in Portage County, was located among earlier German, Irish, and French communities. In 1863, a separate Polish Roman Catholic Church was established in Polonia. In the next decade, Poles settled at Miel Creek, Junction City, and at other points, especially in Portage County. By 1865, the first Polish church was opened in Milwaukee, and the Poles have ever since been important in the life and industry of that city. Certain wards of Milwaukee are overwhelmingly Polish, and that city is the fifth largest Polish center in America today. As early as 1886, there was a separate Polish company of the National Guard in Milwaukee. Poles have sat in the Wisconsin legislatures since the 1880's, where they have been politically recognized, especially by the Democrats, in the distribution of local and state offices. Beginning with 1891, the state laws of Wisconsin and the Milwaukee city ordinances had to be printed in Polish, and the *Kuryer Polski,* established in Milwaukee in 1888, became a quasiofficial organ for the Polish group. The first Polish paper in Wisconsin, the *Przysci Ludn,* appeared in 1878.[9] The leading Milwaukee Polish dailies today are *Kuryer Polski* and the *Nowiny Polskie* (Polish News).

Texas has a farming community of Silesian Poles, which was established in 1856 and is described in Olmsted's *A Journey Through Texas* (p. 270). By 1906, Texas had a Polish population of 17,000. Radom, Illinois, is a Polish farming community started by Poles who worked in Chicago factories. Edna Ferber's *American Beauty* (1931) tells the story of the reclaiming of abandoned farms by Poles in the Connecticut Valley. At Old Hadley, Massachusetts, Polish farmers raise onions and tobacco in great quantities.

The majority of the Poles, however, are city dwellers, common laborers in factories, mines, and streets. In the Pennsylvania anthracite fields and mill towns, employers used agents to recruit Poles and Slovaks to replace the Irish pick-and-shovel workers. Poles are employed in great numbers in textile mills, stockyards, packing houses, and sugar refineries. Nearly one half the Poles in the United States today are to be found in the industrial states of New York, New Jersey, and Pennsylvania. Their largest settlement, however, is in Chicago, where the total Polish stock now exceeds 500,000. The old Polish colonies of Pittsburgh, Buffalo, Cleveland,

⁹ See Frank H. Miller: "The Polanders in Wisconsin," in *Parkman Club Papers, 1896* (Milwaukee), pp. 239-246; and F. Niklewicz: *Poles in the State of Wisconsin* (Green Bay, Wisconsin).

and Milwaukee have continued to grow, and literally scores of Polish communities have developed in the northeastern part of the United States since 1900.

Like other elements in the newer immigration, the Poles began life in America as marginal workers under conditions that alarmed the older members of the communities in which they settled. They lived very clannishly and on a low standard. Their customs seemed peculiar and their life seemed to center around their societies and parish churches. Their wedding and funeral ceremonies were regarded as curious manifestations of Old World superstition. Intemperance was all too prevalent, and occasional disorders marked Polish social occasions. Withal, the Polish worker slaved at his job, saved his money, and developed a perfect mania to acquire a little house and a little plot of land. Polish building and loan associations were established; Polish business houses sprang up in Polish districts; and cities like Cleveland developed Polish Chambers of Commerce. Gradually, the Polish element became interested in American politics and took out naturalization papers. In the second and third generations, a small group of professional men began to appear.

The Poles are well organized in America into hundreds of societies and some large national federations. The largest and oldest of these is the Polish National Alliance, with headquarters in Chicago and with a program for the moral and material development of Polish immigrants, as well as for the preservation of their national traditions. At present, it has about 275,000 members, publishes a daily and weekly paper, and maintains an immigrant home in New York City. Cleveland has a Polish Library Home and a Polish Language Continuation School.

A cursory examination of the files of a publication like the *Polonian Review* furnishes abundant evidence of the process of Americanization as it is at work in Polish-American communities. A Polish Arts Club, headed by Max Drezmal, has given Polish music at Ravinia.[10] "Polish Day" has been celebrated annually in Chicago since 1925, with Polish folk music and the dancing of the mazurka;[11] and radio stations in Chicago, Cleveland, and other cities broadcast "Polish hours." Chicago has a large Polish theater and a Chopin Movie Palace, which runs Polish pictures. Chicago has

[10] See *Polonia–Review,* August 1930.
[11] See *ibid.,* July 1929, and July 1930.

ten Polish judges and claims to be the second largest Polish city in the world. Polish journalists point with pride to musical celebrities like Leopold Stokowski and Ganna Walska, and athletes like Al Grabowski, Stan Coveleskie, Urbanski, Ryba, Bronko Nagurski, Al Simmons, and the sprinter Stella Walsh (Stanislawa Walasiewicz).[12] Cleveland has a Kosciuszko Singing Society, a Frederick Chopin Harmonia, and a Polonia Theatre Stock Company. Pola Negri, Gilda Gray, and Paul Muni are Polish movie stars. Helena Modjeska achieved fame on the legitimate stage, and her son is a successful bridge engineer. The *Polonian Review* of April, 1930, pleaded for Polish plays and a Polish theater in Chicago, and strenuously objected to the use of the word "Polacks" in American stage comedies.[13] At the same time, it pointed out with pride the Polish contributions to the diet of the nation, such as stewed tripe à la Warsaw, chopped cabbage with sour cream dressing, stuffed cabbage, cheese dumplings, and beef roulade polonaise.[14]

In 1918, the first national convention of Poles in the United States assembled at Detroit. A Polish Central Relief Committee, with Paderewski as honorary president, has carried on propaganda for an independent Poland since 1915, and Polish-Americans contributed hundreds of thousands of dollars to the cause of liberation. In 1935, the Polish Roman Catholic Union Archive and Museum was organized in Chicago; and the Archives of the Polish National Committee of Chicago, containing about 30,000 letters, documents, pictures, and pamphlets dealing with the work of the Polish-Americans during the World War in enlisting volunteers for the Polish army in France and in working for an independent Poland, were turned over to this depository for safekeeping and cataloguing. In 1929, Pulaski Sesqui-Centennial celebrations were arranged in a number of American cities. Four years earlier, the Kosciuszko Foundation was established in the United States, to carry on an educational program. The University of Michigan has also a chair in Polish.[15] In 1930, there were 15 dailies and 64 Polish weeklies published in the United States. The largest Polish daily is *The Zgoda* of Cleveland, with a circulation of 32,435 in 1931.

The Roman Catholic Church continues to play a leading role in the life of every Polish-American community, not only as a religious

[12] See *ibid.*, September 1930.
[13] See *ibid.*, May 1930.
[14] See *ibid.*, July 1930.
[15] See *ibid.*, December 1930, p. 7.

force, but as an important social agency as well. Only about seven per cent of the Poles are Protestants. Most Poles are deeply religious. They contribute liberally, in consideration of their limited means, to the support of their churches and they are deeply attached to its ritual and symbolism. The religious affiliations of the Poles seem to have disintegrated more slowly in America than those of any other immigrant group. Nevertheless, there has been some friction within the Church itself. This has been especially acute wherever Poles were served by Irish priests. As some Irish have been contemptuous of "foreigners" of the newer immigration, so some of the Poles have objected strenuously to what they call an "Irish Catholic Church." In some cases, this feeling developed to the point where Poles demanded control over their local church properties and actually seceded to form a Polish National Independent Catholic Church. This organization, centering largely in Pennsylvania, now represents about 90 churches, with a membership of over 60,000. It has its own seminary to train young men for the priesthood in Scranton, Pennsylvania, and it supports its own weekly, *Straz*. This independent church is essentially Catholic in all its major dogmas, but substitutes Polish for Latin in the service of the Mass, minimizes auricular confession, and has been developing a tendency to permit marriage of the clergy. A number of benefit "unions" have been developed as part of a program that places considerable emphasis upon economic security and the social gospel.

The Poles have supported parochial schools, for the most part taught by convent sisters, and the clergy has generally insisted on the use of such schools. Nevertheless, the majority of Polish children today attend public schools.

THE JUGOSLAVS

Jugoslavia, another product of the World War, has absorbed the population once known as Serbs, Montenegrins, Slovenes, Croats, and Dalmatians.

The Jugoslavs are to be found mostly in the industrial areas of Pennsylvania, Ohio, Illinois, Michigan, New York, and New England, and in Minnesota, Wisconsin, Indiana, and California. Like other Slavic groups, the majority are employed in the mines and in industrial centers. Relatively few are engaged in agriculture. Immigrants from prewar Serbia and Montenegro went either into

[425]

New England mill towns or the mines or worked on construction gangs. The Slovenes have a large colony at Joliet, Illinois, founded as early as 1873, and some agricultural settlements of importance in Iowa and Minnesota. The Croats, of whom there were only 72,138 listed in the United States Census of 1930, use the Latin alphabet, although their language is similar to that of the Serbs. The Croats and Slovenes are Roman Catholics; the Serbs belong to the Greek Catholic Church. The headquarters of the Serbian Orthodox Church in the United States is at Libertyville, Illinois. The Croats are to be found mainly in the mines and coke furnaces of Pennsylvania and West Virginia or in the silver and copper mines of the Far West, especially in Montana. Many are employed in lumber camps. In Michigan, there is one town known in Croatia as New Lipa.

Many Jugoslavs are birds of passage, rather impassive and patient marginal laborers, unskilled and poor. Their standards of living are relatively low; intemperance is one of their serious problems; and the rate of illiteracy among them is high. Crowded by necessity into immigrant colonies, they preserve their old costumes, songs, language, and folk festivals in an isolation often fostered by their ecclesiastical leaders. The Dalmatians, true to habits formed in their native environment, have found employment in the United States as fishermen, sailors, and longshoremen, or have gone into the oyster fisheries in New Orleans or into the vineyards of Missouri and California. Despite an extraordinarily high rate of illiteracy among them, many have progressed because of an innate shrewdness, and some have opened small businesses, especially restaurants.

The heavy migration of Jugoslavs began in the late years of the last century and came mostly from the old Austro-Hungarian Empire. Large American cities—such as New York, Buffalo, Chicago, Cleveland, Detroit, and Milwaukee—have sizeable colonies of Jugoslavs. In the Chicago area, there are some 50,000 Slovenes, and Cleveland has about the same number. Many are employed in the garment trades of the East and in the textile districts. Others settled in the anthracite coal regions of Pennsylvania and New York or in the steel and coal areas around Pittsburgh, Wheeling, and Youngstown. Pittsburgh has a large Serb colony. In West Virginia, many are employed in lumber camps or coal mines. In northern Michigan, they settled in the copper-mining region. Fully three fourths of the total Jugoslav immigrant group depend for their livelihood on the coal and metal industries.

The Jugoslavs are highly organized into singing and dramatic clubs, *sokols* for gymnastics and physical training, and benevolent insurance and protective societies. Among Slovenian fraternal organizations the more important are: the Carniolian Slovenian Catholic Union, started in Joliet, Illinois, in 1894; the Slovenian National Benefit Society, founded in Chicago in 1904; and the Slovenian Workingmen's Benefit Association, established in Johnstown, Pennsylvania, in 1908. There is also a National Croatian Society. The lodge is the center of social life, although these various organizations represent a great variety of objectives. Some are mutual benefit associations and almost all are interested in sponsoring certain national aims, although many serve as mere pleasure clubs or associations to stage Sunday dramatic performances or concerts and dances. When the National Slavonik Society held its convention in Cleveland as long ago as 1893, it had representation from 116 lodges.[16]

The Church membership of the Jugoslavs is divided between the Roman Catholic and the Greek Orthodox Churches, depending largely on where the immigrant came from. Both Churches emphasize the need for parochial schools, most of which are taught by nuns of various religious orders. From 40 to 50 publications are issued in the United States in the language of the Jugoslavs, of which 8 are daily papers. Probably the three most distinguished individual representatives of the South Slavs in the United States are Nikola Tesla, who perfected many electrical inventions for the Westinghouse Company, Dr. Michael Pupin,[17] whose work on telephone and telegraph circuits brought him fame, and the publicist Louis Adamic.

THE RUSSIANS

There are special difficulties involved in dealing with Russian immigration, because for many years statistical records did not differentiate between real Russians and the Jews, Poles, Lithuanians, Latvians, and even Finns who emigrated from the old Czarist Empire. For the present purposes, all other groups are excluded and

[16] See *Cleveland Plain Dealer*, May 30, 1896.
[17] See Michael Pupin: *From Immigrant to Inventor* (New York, 1925).

the discussion is confined to the real Russians, including the Ruthenians or Ukrainians (Little Russians), who are to be found also in parts of the old Galicia, Northern Hungary, and Bukowina. By 1920, some 350,000 of these "Little Russians," many of them birds of passage, found their way into the steel mills and mines of the United States.

The first Russian contact with North America came, of course, by way of Bering Sea and Alaska. As early as 1747, Russian fur traders crossed into Alaska. In 1795, the first Russian Orthodox Church was founded there because of the activity of missionaries sent out by the Russian Holy Synod to minister to the needs of settlers and traders in Alaska. Russian influence was slowly extended down the Pacific Coast. Sitka was founded by the Russian-American Company in 1804. When Alaska was finally sold to the United States after the Civil War, many Russians returned home. The headquarters of the Russian Church were moved to San Francisco in 1872.

The events of these early years are, however, no longer of primary interest, except to the historian of the Pacific Coast area. The Russian immigration with which this chapter is concerned was the product of the industrialization of the United States. The Russians who came during the last generation went into industry, into the coal and steel areas, into lumber and fishing farther west, or into the fruit-growing regions of California and Florida. Up to 1899, the immigration of Russian Slavs was relatively unimportant. Thereafter, the figures rose steadily until the World War. The 1920 Census listed 392,049 foreign-born Russians, and if those born in the United States of Russian parentage be added, the figure exceeds 730,000. By 1930, the Russian Orthodox Church claimed to have 200 congregations in the United States, with nearly 120,000 members.

Russian immigrants were among the most unskilled and economically insecure of all the newer arrivals. Many had hardly enough to meet the financial requirement for admission into the country, and most of them landed at New York with practically nothing in the way of reserves. Over half found jobs in New York and Pennsylvania, where they usually had to do the lowest, most unskilled kind of labor in mill and mine. Forced to work long hours for low pay, Americanization became almost "arithmetically impossible." [18] As their jobs were hazardous and they themselves were viewed with suspicion by their fellow workers, they saw American industry at its worst. Barred by lack of skill from joining a craft union, they either remained unorganized, or joined the I. W. W. or other radical groups. When they were permitted to join unions, as in the case of the United Mine Workers, they seem to have proved entirely dependable. Russians have been important as stone masons also and, in New York, they constituted the bulk of the membership of the Window Washers' Union and the House-wrecker's Union, Local 95.

The Russian marginal worker had to live in the overcrowded and cheapest worker's tenements. Here his isolation was almost complete and he had little opportunity for favorable contacts with American conditions, save through the "straw boss" for whom he worked, the rent collector, the policeman, the saloonkeeper, and the ward heeler. The overwhelming majority of Russian immigrants were unmarried, a condition which contributed to neither their health nor their moral standards. The Russians were less organized than other groups, although they too soon set up sick benefit and insurance societies. Their Church was extremely orthodox; priests tried to rule with a rod of iron and, until the Bolshevik Revolution, received contributions from the Czar. Many Ukrainians are Roman Catholics. Their priests marry, have beards, and use the Julian calendar. The saloon, the movies, cards, dancing, and playing the balalaika constituted the chief diversions for a life filled with hard and long working hours. That the Russians were particularly susceptible to socialism and later to communism is not altogether surprising under these conditions, nor is the fact that they were under suspicion during the "Red hunt" of 1919-1920, after the Bolsheviks had overturned the old Russia by revolution. Long before these exciting events, however, Serge Shevick had been one of the founders of the Socialist Labor Party in America. [19]

The Ukrainians settled in large numbers in the soft coal region around Pittsburgh and in the hard coal centers of Scranton and Wilkesbarre. Chicago had a colony of 25,000; Detroit, one of over

[18] See, for example, some of the case studies in the *Interchurch World Movement of North America Report on the Steel Strike of 1919* (New York, 1920); and *Public Opinion and the Steel Strike* (New York, 1921).

[19] For an excellent sociological treatment, see Jerome Davis: *The Russian Immigrant* (New York, 1922).

15,000. Although 90 per cent are employed in industry and the mines, the Ukrainians nevertheless have created some farming communities in the United States. In the New England mill sections, they frequently work in the mills all day and then toil on a small plot of farmland in the evenings. On Long Island, they have engaged in fruit and truck gardening; and there are Ukrainian farming settlements near Great Meadows, Millville, and Plainfield, in New Jersey, and others in Wisconsin, Michigan, and North Dakota.[20] At present, there are six Russian dailies in the United States. Perhaps the most important Ukrainian paper is the *Svoboda,* published in Jersey City, New Jersey. The second generation is being slowly Americanized, especially through the public schools.

Quite different from this type of Russian immigrant is the Russian intellectual, of whom many have come to the United States in the last decades partly because of the tremendous upheavals in Russian society brought about by the Russian Revolution. Distinguished musicians like Ossip Gabrilowitch, Mischa Elman, Jascha Heifetz, and Nikolas Sokolov, and scholars like Michael Rostovtsev, Vladimir G. Simkhovich, I. M. Rubinow, P. S. Galtzev, and Vladimir N. Karapatoff have been adornments to the cultural life of modern America. Perhaps of even greater popular acclaim, however, are such Ukrainian-American "stars" as George Kojac of the Olympics and Anna Sten of the movies.

THE HUNGARIANS

Under this caption are included, not all the people who came from the old Hungary, but only those of Magyar stock. In 1910, for example, although the number of Hungarians was listed as 338,151, only 227,742 claimed to be Magyars. By 1930, the Hungarian Magyar stock in the United States, including those born here of Magyar parentage, totaled a little over 590,000.

The Hungarian migration was, strictly speaking, a part of the new immigration, although Americans probably first became "Hungarian-conscious" after the Hungarian revolt of 1848, when Louis Kossuth became an international hero and was hailed with special acclaim when he visited the United States, as a symbol of all the oppressed of Europe who were yearning for freedom. The New York papers, especially for the year 1851, were full of accounts of

[20] See Wasyl Halich: "Ukrainian Farmers in the United States," in *Agricultural History,* Vol. X, pp. 25-39.

the cordial receptions given Kossuth[21] and the welcome extended to Hungarian refugees who came to the United States to establish new homes. At Dr. Beecher's church in New York, for example, tickets were sold for a Hungarian refugee fund and a large sum was quickly raised.[22] Mass meetings, to express sympathy for the Hungarian revolutionists, were held in New York and other cities in 1849. At one New York meeting, attended by 30,000, three speaker's stands were erected: one for Americans, one for the Germans, and one for the French and Italians. The *Albany Argus* reported that

> . . . the Irish too, were in great glee, and none . . . in that dense multitude of humanity felt a deeper sympathy than they for the cause of Hungary . . . .[23]

A band of Hungarian patriot exiles came to America soon after the failure of the Hungarian revolt of 1848 and eventually settled the community of New Buda, in Decatur County, Iowa. They were led by Count Ladislaus Ujhazy and were welcomed to the United States by a personal letter from President Taylor. The United States government presently established a post office at New Buda, Iowa, and Ujhazy was appointed postmaster. The group, which contained a number of Magyar aristocrats, built a large log "castle." Implements and funds were secured in St. Louis; and, in 1858, Congress permitted the members of the community to buy the land on which they had squatted at $1.25 an acre, without interest from the time of their arrival.

But long before this, in 1853, Count Ujhazy had moved on with some of his followers to San Antonio, Texas, in search of a better climate and a better grape country. Among other picturesque members of the New Buda community were Francis Varga, who later held public office in Iowa; Ignace Hainer, who became professor of modern languages at the University of Missouri; and George Pomutz, who became a typical promoter and advertised the

[21] The manufacturers of Lyon's Magnetic Powder and Pills seized upon this strategic moment to advertise in *The New York Tribune* for October 6, 1851:

> Kossuth's coming, so they say;
> He's a lion in his way,
> And made tyranny his prey;
> But for bugs and such as they
> Our own Lyon is O.K.
> Rats and mice, too, he can slay . . . .

[22] See *ibid.*, December 29, 1851.
[23] *Albany Argus*, August 29, 1849.

"City of New Buda" by preparing a plaque showing Kossuth Platz, Boehm University, and a fine system of public parks that never existed. He sold lots as far east as Hoboken and even induced some Germans to come to the settlement. Later, Pomutz served in the Civil War and became consul general to Russia.

The community has only an historic interest. Most of its members were impractical farmers, whose ignorance of farming methods greatly amused their frontier neighbors. The population of New Buda never exceeded 75, but for years the little group of exiles kept up a steady correspondence with Kossuth and leaders in American public life.[24] When Kossuth died, in 1894, at the ripe age of 96, the Hungarian colony of New York City and other communities staged huge parades, especially on the day of the funeral in Budapest, and observed a period of mourning.[25]

Although there are small Hungarian agricultural communities in the United States—for example, there is a Budapest, California, and a Kossuthville, Florida—the major contribution of the Hungarians has been made as city dwellers, as laborers in industry and coal mines or as skilled craftsmen, notably tailors, or as small storekeepers and restaurant proprietors. The Magyar stock is well represented, especially in the states of New York, Ohio, Pennsylvania, New Jersey, Illinois, and Michigan; and there are Hungarian colonies of importance in cities like New York, Cleveland, Chicago, Detroit, Akron, and other industrial centers. The majority of Magyars, especially in the two decades before 1920, were birds of passage, and a steady stream of Hungarians returned to the motherland after the close of the World War. There has also been considerable migration from one city to another within the United States, owing to fluctuating conditions of employment.

It is generally conceded that the Magyar group represents an intelligent, neat, and thrifty immigrant stock. They learn English quickly and, as businessmen, have prospered in their new environment. Hungarian cafés have a patronage that far transcends the boundaries of the Hungarian colonies in which they are established.

The Hungarians are intensely patriotic and devote themselves to keeping alive the national traditions, folk dances, and folk music

[24] See Lillian M. Wilson: "Some Hungarian Patriots in Iowa," in *The Iowa Journal of History and Politics*, Vol. XI, pp. 479-516. See also *New York Tribune*, April 29 and June 19, 1850; *Mammoth Weekly Steubenville Herald*, January 22, 1851; and *The New York Times*, May 3, 1861.
[25] See *The New York Sun*, March 22 and 28, and April 1 and 5, 1894.

of their homeland. They are especially gifted musically. Before the war, only a small percentage became naturalized American citizens. Scores of Magyar organizations and benevolent societies have been created in the United States, and a vigorous and large Magyar press serves as a bond to hold the group together. The *Szabadsag* of Cleveland, founded by Tihamer Kohanyi as one of the earliest Hungarian dailies in this country, has become one of the largest in the United States. The largest Hungarian daily paper in the United States today is the *Amerikai Magyar Nepszava,* published by Geza Barko, in New York.

The majority of the Hungarians are Roman Catholics, although Protestantism has made considerable progress among them. There is also a strong Jewish mixture in the Hungarian population. In Cleveland, for example, the Black family, an able family of Hungarian Jews, founded the Bailey Company, one of Cleveland's largest department stores, financed the *Szabadsag,* and helped establish the Cleveland textile industry. Joseph Pulitzer, probably the greatest immigrant, journalist, and philanthropist of recent years, was born in Hungary of a Magyar-Jewish father and an Austro-German mother. Others with a similar Hungarian background are: Samuel Rothafel, the famous "Roxy" of the Roxy Theatre; Harry Houdini, the magician; and Erno Rapee, the conductor. Franklin Marshall College is the only college in the United States to have a department of Hungarian language, literature, and history.[26]

OTHER MINOR GROUPS[27]

The Bulgarians. Small groups of Bulgarians have settled in Granite City, Illinois, near St. Louis in Madison, Illinois, and in Chicago, Butte, Indianapolis, Seattle, and Portland, Oregon. Most of these immigrants came after the revolution in Macedonia, in 1904, closed the doors to Bulgarian expansion in that direction. Many returned to their homes after several years in the United States. The only Bulgarian paper of importance in the United States is the *Naroden Glas,* started in Granite City in 1907. The Bulgarians

[26] See *The New York Times,* February 25, 1934. For a valuable account, see: D. A. Souders: *The Magyars in America* (New York, 1922).
[27] For convenient summaries of these smaller groups and other immigrant groups, see Francis J. Brown and Joseph Slabey Roucek (editors): *Our Racial and National Minorities* (New York, 1937). For popular sketches of Polish and Russian, as well as Scandinavian, German, and Italian groups, "in a non-statistical, human-interest" fashion, see William Seabrook: *These Foreigners* (New York, 1938).

have more than a score of small social and mutual benefit societies in the United States by which they cultivate their songs and customs.

The Lithuanians. Thousands of Lithuanians, once a submerged Baltic nationality, have come to the United States since 1880. The great majority live in the big cities or work in the coal fields of Pennsylvania, West Virginia, and Illinois. Some are farmers in New England, New Jersey, and Wisconsin, although in general the Lithuanians have shunned agriculture and sought out the mines and factories. By 1920, there were about 200,000 Lithuanians in the United States. The Census of 1930 reported 193,606 foreign-born Lithuanians and 439,195 of Lithuanian parentage. Chicago has a colony of 100,000 Lithuanians. Many have gone into the tailoring business or operate the disproportionately large number of saloons to be found in Lithuanian areas. The Lithuanians are Roman Catholics, although there has developed a small Lithuanian National Catholic Church in the United States, which uses the native tongue in its services. Like other groups, the Lithuanians have their quota of societies. They support three daily papers in the United States. Dances and dramatics are favorite pastimes, and these have received a new impetus from the nationalist revival that followed the World War. The American Lithuanian press developed a lively and successful propaganda during the war years for an independent Lithuania. Jack Sharkey, whose real name is said to be Juozas Zukanskas, is a Lithuanian who for a time achieved fame in the American heavyweight prize ring.

The Latvians. In 1930, there were 20,673 foreign-born Latvians and 17,418 additional of Latvian stock in the United States. Half of these live in four large cities—namely, New York, Boston, Philadelphia, and Baltimore. The majority are Protestants, and naturalization and Americanization have been going on rather rapidly among them. The only important paper of the Latvian group is the *Boston Strahdneekn Zihna,* a radical workers' weekly.

The Italians

POPULAR WRITERS have loved to point out that America was "discovered by a 'wop' and named after another." Much more important, however, is what the millions of swarthy, picturesquely dressed peasants from sunny Italy who poured into the United States after 1880 did to build American railways, subways, roads, and sewers as gang laborers, and what they and their children have been able to accomplish in America as they rise in the social and economic scale, because of opportunities which few would have enjoyed at home. Today, New York City has more people of Italian stock than Rome—1,070,355 persons of Italian birth or parentage, according to the Census of 1930, out of a total of 4,651,195 of Italian stock living in the entire United States. In one year, 1907, more Italians were admitted than the present-day population of Venice.[1] From 1820 to 1930, over 4,628,000 Italian immigrants arrived, and of this number over 3,500,000 came in the present century.

Although Italian immigration up to 1880 was hardly more than a trickle, as compared with the later inundation, and although more Italians went into South America than into North America throughout the nineteenth century, there is abundant evidence of the presence of an appreciable group in the American population before 1880. Before 1860, Italian immigration consisted largely of vendors of plaster statuary, organ grinders with their monkeys, and political refugees. As early as 1836, there seem to have been some Italian castmongers who sold casts of Napoleon, Diana, and the Graces in American city streets, as "missionaries of art" in an undeveloped country.[2] There are well-authenticated records of Italian

[1] See Joseph H. Senner: "Immigration from Italy," in *The North American Review* (June, 1896), pp. 649-657; and the excellent WPA Federal Writers' Project: *The Italians of New York* (Random House, New York, 1938).
[2] See E. D. Branch: *The Sentimental Years* (New York, 1934), p. 168.

street musicians in the late eighteenth century. Filippo Mazzei, who came to Virginia to raise vines, olives, and silk, became an influential friend of Thomas Jefferson; and teachers of Italian, such as Lorenzo da Ponte, gave language instruction in New York in the early nineteenth century.[3]

Several hundred political exiles of the *Risorgimento* fled to the United States before 1860,[4] and Garibaldi worked for a time in Antonio Meucci's candle factory on Staten Island. In July, 1850, the *L'Eco d' Italia* had already completed six months of its existence as a New York paper.[5] An Italian church was dedicated in Philadelphia in 1852[6] and another in New York in 1866.[7] A Boston paper, in 1857, suggested that Italian organ grinders be put to work with shovels to fill in the Back Bay region.[8] Italians in New York, Cincinnati, and elsewhere followed events in the homeland with keen interest and, in 1859, sponsored meetings to celebrate the victories of French and Sardinian armies in the struggle for Italian liberation and unification.[9] During the American Civil War, Count Luigi Palma di Cesnola, a Piedmontese, became colonel of a New York cavalry regiment; and the Garibaldi Volunteers of New York, under Colonel Utassy, enrolled 600 men within less than three weeks after the firing on Fort Sumter.[10] Italian schools were in operation in the 1860's and Italian benevolent societies met in convention in Philadelphia in 1868.[11] In the late 1870's, New York had a "Circolo Italiano," and Italian outings and entertainments were frequently described in the New York papers.[12]

New York's first Little Italy was located on Mulberry Street. In the 1880's, it was "a little world in itself," with its Italian stores, restaurants, boarding houses, banks, butcher shops, and bakeries, its Italian steamship agencies and printing offices, and its Italian physi-

[3] See Giovanni Schiavo: *The Italians in America Before the Civil War* (New York, 1934).
[4] See *New York Tribune*, April 15, 1853.
[5] See *ibid.*, July 27, 1850. See also *Boston Transcript*, October 18, 1853.
[6] See *The Boston Pilot*, October 30, 1852.
[7] See Schiavo: *op. cit.*, p. 293.
[8] See *Boston Traveller*, April 3, 1857.
[9] See *Cincinnati Enquirer*, March 27 and July 15, 1859. See also Arthur C. Cole: *The Irrepressible Conflict* (New York, 1934), p. 126.
[10] See *The New York Times*, May 3 and 24, 1861.
[11] See *Cincinnati Enquirer*, August 7, 1868. See also *New York Tribune*, October 24 and December 10, 1863; and *Ohio State Journal*, August 28, 1873.
[12] See *The New York Times*, September 10 and November 1, 1877. For other evidences of Italian activity before 1885, see, *Cincinnati Commercial*, February 3, 1878, and July 17 and September 14, 1881; and *Cincinnati Enquirer*, October 7, 1883.

cians and lawyers.[13]   Other Little Italies followed in Harlem, around 108th Street between First and Second Avenues, and in the streets adjacent to Washington Square.   So strong was the cohesion between various groups coming from the same locality or province of Italy that they settled in well-defined neighborhoods in New York's Italian colonies.[14]

The causes of the rapid increase in Italian immigration after 1870 are the familiar ones of pressure of population on the means of subsistence, industrial stagnation, primitive agricultural methods, heavy taxes, government monopolies, and a semifeudal, oppressive aristocracy of large landholders.   Italy was exploited by a privileged minority.   Soil conditions, malaria, insect pests, corruption in local government, and overpopulation were other factors.[15]   The Italian immigrant, however, was among the first to introduce that new phenonemon of American immigration history, the bird of passage. From 1908 to 1916, 1,215,998 Italians left the United States.

By 1880, New York had an Italian colony of 80,000, and the floodgates of Italian immigration were being forced open.   The earlier immigration had been small and came largely from northern Italy, but it now shifted so that fully four fifths came from southern Italy, a more backward section.   Most of the newer immigrants were men; they came from unprogressive rural communities, where the rate of illiteracy was high, and they constituted the unskilled workers who could find employment only at very low wages.   From 1890 to 1900, 655,888 arrived, and 2,104,309 more came in the next decade, about two thirds of whom were men.   Of the total number, about 800,000 had returned home by 1910.   At the time of the World War, there were large Italian colonies in New York, Philadelphia, Chicago, Baltimore, Detroit, Omaha, and in the New England textile centers, and large agricultural colonies scattered from the Atlantic Coast to California.[16]

The newcomers were transplanted from their sunny Italian hill farms to the railroad and mining camps and to the construction gangs of American cities.   They performed the lowliest tasks for meager wages and lived in clannish isolation, with standards of

[13] See *The New York Tribune*, December 6, 1888.
[14] See R. E. Park and H. A. Miller: *Old World Traits Transplanted* (New York, 1921), p. 146.
[15] See Robert F. Foerster: *The Italian Emigration of Our Times* (Cambridge, Massachusetts, 1919); and Antonio Mangano: *Sons of Italy* (New York, 1917), pp. 41-68.
[16] See Philip M. Rose: *The Italians in America* (New York, 1922).

sanitation that were shocking, to say the least, to their more fortunate neighbors. The second generation, born and reared in such
environments and under great economic stress, broke with many of
the old traditions, and their names began to appear on the lists of
criminals and delinquents. Crimes of violence ranked especially
high among them. The United States Army Intelligence Tests
gave them a very low rating. In Italy, the rate of illiteracy decreased from 68.87 per cent in 1872 to 23 per cent in 1920. The
American public schools solved this problem for the American-born
Italians. Hard work, low wages, large families, tenement houses,
poor food, and saloons tell the story of the maladjustment of the
first and second generations.[17] To call these people South Italian
"scum" in the face of their remarkable progress in recent decades is,
however, to do them a rank injustice as a class. Their problems in
a new environment were complex social problems, but hardly bio-
logical. The Italians represented a stout-hearted, physically fit
peasantry, whose thrift and industry brought thousands unexpected
success.[18]

The Italian immigrant to the cities became a common laborer,
employed on construction gangs. In New York, he crowded out the
Irish and Poles in the building of subways and streets. In Philadelphia, he joined the street-cleaning force. In Chicago and Kansas City, he went into the stockyards. In New Jersey, he went into
the silk mills; in New England, into the textile towns; and in
Pennsylvania, into the mines and steel mills. Kansas City and St.
Louis have their "Little Italies"; in St. Louis, "Dago Hill" is near
the clay pits and brickyards where the Italians work.[19] Utica,
Schenectady, and Reading have large Italian colonies, and there is
a large community of Italian cigarmakers in Tampa, Florida.[20]
Large numbers entered the garment trades or became stone- and
cementworkers. Many an Italian laborer who returned to Italy
took his American shovel along to hand down as an heirloom to
his children.

[17] See Enrico C. Sartorio: *Social and Religious Life of Italians in America*
(Boston, 1918).
[18] See Antonio Stella: *Some Aspects of Italian Immigration to the United States*
(New York, 1924), p. 38.
[19] See Giovanni Schiavo: *The Italians in Missouri* (New York, 1929), pp. 56-59
and 151-159.
[20] See *United America*, August 15, 1925. See also Giovanni Schiavo: *The
Italians in Chicago* (Chicago, 1928); James Geddes, Jr.: *Italian Contributions to
America* (Boston, 1929); and G. La Piana: *The Italians in Milwaukee, Wisconsin* (1915).

To a surprising degree, the Italian has repeated the experience of the Irish. He has risen rapidly from pick-and-shovel work to more skilled trades, and from bootblacking and peddling and barbering to more pretentious business enterprises. The Italian element has now displaced the Jews in New York as the largest single group in the needle industries. Thousands have joined the building trades' unions as masons, carpenters, plumbers, and electricians. Many Italians have become officials in labor unions. Luigi Antonini is head of the American Labor Party of New York. Others are interior decorators, textile designers, and builders of furniture. Italians constitute a large percentage of the membership in the musicians' union. Some Italian bootblacks have prospered to become "shoe-shine kings," and now control scores of establishments. Fruit, vegetable, and candy peddlers prospered and opened confectioneries, restaurants, hotels, and groceries. A few became importers of olive oil, macaroni, and ravioli, or manufacturers of spaghetti and cheese. San Francisco, Chicago, New York, and other cities have Italian Chambers of Commerce. Hundreds of the second and third generations entered the professions and made a notable record, which will be commented on later.

While this gradual evolution to a higher American standard of living was going on, there was, of course, abundant reason to look with alarm upon conditions prevailing in the Italian quarters of our larger cities. In New York, Italians lived for a time at a density of 1,100 to the acre, and, as Professor Foerster pointed out, life in the streets was the "pressure of baby cart on push-cart." Twenty-five years ago, there were sections of New York City, in the Sicilian district, where 1,231 people lived in 120 rooms,[21] and only Greeks and Syrians surpassed the Italians in the use of all rooms for sleeping purposes. The disease and death rate from tuberculosis was especially high. Local gangs terrorized the community. The South Italians were surpassed only by the Turks and Portuguese in illiteracy. Social life centered around the saloon, the cheap movie, and the dance hall, and the immigrant's most frequent contacts with Americans were through the saloonkeeper, the ward heeler, and the party boss seeking votes. Great religious festivals not only involved the expenditure of money and time that might well have been used for other purposes but impressed many American observers as mani-

[21] See John H. Mariano: *The Second Generation of Italians in New York City* (Boston, 1921), pp. 16-17.

festations of medieval superstition. Church holidays and saints' days were observed with meticulous care. The padrone system, by which boys were imported illegally to work for their employers under conditions suggesting feudal serfdom, aroused great antagonism, and immigration officials found it difficult to break up the practice.

Newspapers carried lurid stories of the kidnaping of thousands of Italian children who were being held in virtual slavery in American cities.[22] Over four fifths of the Italian immigrants were between the ages of 18 and 45, and many were unmarried. It was difficult to pass through the Italian quarters of any city, especially on a warm day, for men, women, and children swarmed out on the fire escapes and into the streets.[23] Laborers protested bitterly against the cheap competition of the Italian worker, and riots were not infrequent in which workmen descended upon gangs of Italians and drove them from their jobs.[24] Occasionally, the Italian was denounced as a radical Socialist,[25] and newspapers featured cutting and stabbing episodes by intoxicated Italian workmen on pay day[26] or fantastic stories about the activities of the Camorra and Black Hand Societies, organizations which Italians themselves were eager to suppress because of their brutal exploitation of their own people. The riots in New Orleans in 1891, which led to the murder of a police chief, seemed to give support to the charges of Italian lawlessness.[27] Gambling prevailed in some quarters, and the Church seemed to be powerless to deal with the situation. As one New York paper commented:

> The flood gates are open. The bars are down. The sally-ports are unguarded. The dam is washed away. The sewer is choked . . . the scum of immigration is viscerating upon our shores. The horde of $9.60 steerage slime is being siphoned upon us from Continental mud tanks.[28]

In the meantime, while the Italians clustered in the cities and industrial areas were experiencing their most severe test in making the necessary adjustments to American conditions, a considerable

[22] See *Toledo Blade*, June 17 and 27, 1873.
[23] See *New York Tribune*, July 29, 1932.
[24] See, for example, the *New York Sun*, March 21 and May 11, 1894.
[25] See *ibid.*, June 18, 1894.
[26] *Ohio State Journal*, December 30, 1889.
[27] See David S. Muzzey: *James G. Blaine* (New York, 1934), pp. 411-413.
[28] Quoted in Foerster: *op. cit.*

proportion of Italian immigrants made its way to the land.[29] In the New Jersey barrens, Italians developed berry farms, pepper fields, and vineyards. In western New York, they reclaimed the swampy soil and extended their farms into the Hudson River Valley. In Arkansas, they grew apples and peaches. In California, as in the Hudson River Valley and Finger Lakes region of New York, the Italians became successful winegrowers. Antonio Moramarco is known as the Italian vineyard king of California. Over 46,000 Italians are scattered through the California fruit belt. In the South, Italians were employed in raising cotton, sugar cane, and rice. Around larger metropolitan centers, Italian farmers developed truck gardens to supply the city populations.

Wherever Italians have settled, they have developed an active social life through scores of organizations of all kinds and through the religious activities centering in the Roman Catholic parishes, to which the great majority are loyal. There is no better indication of the social and civic progress of the group than the ever-widening activity of these societies. Mutual benefit societies participate in the religious and secular festivals of this pleasure-loving people. Electric-light festoons are stretched across the streets of Italian quarters to celebrate the day sacred to some patron saint. Bands play for these fiestas, and processions, led by the priest, and followed by Italians in quaint native costume, bear holy images through the streets. In 1927, there were over 200 Italian mutual benefit societies in Chicago alone. Social clubs, under many names, sponsor dances, sports, and entertainments. Chicago has several Italian dramatic companies, and the Dante Theatre, in the heart of little Italy, is devoted to Italian films and vaudeville. The 80,000 Italians of Greater Boston have some 70 organizations, mostly mutual benefit societies. At their parades and festivities, as on Columbus Day, they turn out in full regalia, usually ending the day with sumptuous banquets. Milwaukee has more than a dozen Italian beneficial societies. In New York City, there are Italian medical and legal societies, an Italian teachers' association, and an Italian Educational League to encourage American-born children of Italians to spend more years in the public schools.

Among the Italian newspapers, the New York *Il Progresso Italo-*

[29] See H. M. Claghorn: "Agricultural Distribution of Immigrants," in *Reports of the United States Industrial Commission* (Washington, D. C., 1901), Vol. XV, Ch. 10.

Americano easily occupies first place. It was founded in 1880 and is at present owned by Generoso Pope. The *Corriere d'America* is a daily tabloid issued by the same publisher. *La Stampa Libera* is the leading Italian Socialist paper in New York, and the *Il Grido della Stirpe* is an outspokenly Fascist weekly. Needless to add, Italian communities have been badly divided over Mussolini and Fascism in recent years—so much so that it has been necessary for the Italian press to use its influence to stop the disgraceful riots that have broken out between Fascists and anti-Fascists.[30] The oldest Italian paper in New England is the *Gazzetta,* edited for many years by James V. Donnaruma. Philadelphia has its *L'Opinione* and New Haven its *Il Corriere.* *La Voce del Popolo Italiano* has a large circulation in Cleveland. In Chicago, the oldest Italian paper was the daily *L'Italia,* founded in 1886. The Chicago Italian Socialist paper is *La Parola del Popolo.* In 1898, *La Tribuna Transatlantica* was established in that city. It is printed in a curious vernacular showing the influence of American words upon the Italian-American vocabulary.

Wealthy Italians have supported many philanthropies. Celestino Piva, a New York silk manufacturer, and Dr. Carlo Savini support hospitals in New York. One Italian savings bank in New York had deposits of nearly $8,000,000 in 1921. Real-estate holdings of Italians have risen to the hundreds of millions. New York City, in 1920, had 400 Italian doctors and 600 Italian lawyers. The Society for Italian Immigrants in New York and the Society of St. Raphael for the Protection of Italian Immigrants in Boston help new arrivals with their problems.[31] The Sons of Italy is probably the most important of all the Italian-American societies. When the grand lodge of Massachusetts met recently in Lawrence, Massachusetts, representatives were present from 114 lodges from that one state alone.[32] In 1921, this society had 125,000 members in 887 lodges; today its membership is estimated at 350,000. There is at least one national fraternity for Italian college and university students.

Politically, the initial preference of the Italians seems to have been for the Republican party, although they were slow to become naturalized. By this time, however, the country has become quite accustomed to Irish politicians addressing Italian meetings in prepared

[30] See *United America,* May 28, 1927.
[31] See *Annual Report* (Boston, 1902-1903).
[32] See *Boston Transcript,* August 16, 1934.

speeches in the Italian tongue and on behalf of the Democrats. Italian voters, led by Irish politicians, have been among the interesting phenomena of American politics. The relationship has not always been harmonious, and Italian church parishes have bitterly protested the Irish monopoly of the ecclesiastical hierarchy. As early as 1892, Chicago had an Italian alderman, and, in 1894, Italians sat in the Illinois legislature. By the 1920's, there were a score of Italian political clubs of both parties in that city. In 1937, the Italian Federation of Democratic Clubs in New York claimed 150,000 members. The first Italian was elected to public office in New York in 1897.[33]

The weekly *United America,* published in New York City in English for the Italian group, and many Italian language papers have often chided the Italian element for its failure to take a greater interest in American political campaigns. Italian journalists have eagerly accepted political advertisements and have urged Italian voters to vote for Italian candidates wherever possible.[34] *United America* insisted that Italians should "no longer be used as pawns by the political bosses" and, while admitting that "racial blocks are inconsistent with the democratic ideal of amalgamation," contended that only by such blocks could political recognition be obtained.[35]

A *Who's Who* of prominent Italian-Americans would contain hundreds of names. Indeed, the first edition of such a volume was issued in 1935 by the Vigo Press, in New York. It contained 620 names, explaining that 25,000 professional men of Italian antecedents in the United States would be eligible for inclusion in later issues.[36] A number of names, necessarily selected at random, will

---

[33] See *United America,* November 14, 1925.
[34] See *ibid.,* November 5, 1927.
[35] See *ibid.,* November 12, 1927. See also, for example, a political advertisement printed in *ibid.* for October 20, 1926, in behalf of Al Smith and Senator Wagner, which read in part as follows:

> Votate per tutti i candidati democratici . . . .
> Per Governatore dello Stato di New York
> Alfred E. Smith . . . .
> Per Senatore degli stati uniti
> Robert F. Wagner . . . .
> Per giudice delle general sessions
> Max S. Levine . . . .

The comment on Wagner read:
Il giudice Wagner emigro negli Stati Uniti, dalla Germania insieme a suo padre, quando aveva otto anni.
[36] See *The New York Times,* December 23, 1935.

illustrate the rapid progress of the Italian element in practically every phase of American life.

Among the best-known political figures are Mayors Fiorella H. La Guardia of New York and Angelo Rossi of San Francisco; Judges Ferdinand Pecora, Salvatore A. Cotillo, John J. Freschi, and Charles Poletti of New York State; and Edward Corsi, New York Commissioner of Public Welfare and author of *In the Shadow of Liberty* (1934). Congressman Vito Marcantonio of New York and Palmisano of Maryland also deserve mention. Among the leading architects of Chicago are the Italians Louis Pirola and Scipio Del Campo. Guiseppe Bellanca won fame in aeronautics, and Guiseppe Faccioli is chief engineer of the General Electric Company. Gene Pope (Generoso Pope) started in New York as water boy on a road gang and now owns both leading Italian dailies in that city. Angelo Patri and Anthony J. Pugliese and Michael Anagnoss are well-known leaders in American education. Courses of instruction in Italian are now standard features of the public-school curriculum in cities where there are large Italian neighborhoods. New York City has an Italian Educational Broadcasting Corporation, and Station WOV is the only station in the United States which broadcasts all its programs in one foreign language.[37] The number of Italian musicians is legion. Giovanni Martinelli, Caruso's successor at the Metropolitan Opera, appears in benefit concerts for poor and aged Italian countrymen and is one of the founders of the Dante Alighieri Society of Jersey City.[38]

In the field of business, it may be pointed out that there are 10,000 Italian groceries, 673 drugstores, 757 restaurants, and 875 butcher shops owned and operated by Italians in Greater New York alone.[39] The La Rosa Macaroni Company was established in 1914 by one who had arrived as a penniless immigrant from Sicily. The Atlantic Macaroni Company has been in existence since 1897. The largest Italian candy factory in New York, the Margarella Candy Corporation, was started by an Italian immigrant who came to the United States in 1898.[40] Italian wine companies do an annual business running into the millions of gallons. In the field of sports, an unfailing sign of the successful operation of the Americanization process is the emergence of stars like Joe Di Maggio, Frank

[37] See *United America,* October 22, 1927.
[38] See *ibid.,* April 14, 1928.
[39] See *The Italians of New York,* p. 171.
[40] See *ibid.,* pp. 182-183.

Crosetti, and Tony Lazerri in baseball; Jimmy Smith, born Joe Falcaro, as bowling champion; Johnny Wilson, who changed his name from Giovanni Panici, as middleweight boxing champion; and Gene Sarazen, claimed by the Italians under the name of Eugenio Saraceni, as open golf champion. Unfortunately, there has also been an occasional Al Capone of Alcatraz.

Better evidence of the progress of Americanization is the appeal to Italian-Americans, in Italian papers, to stress their achievements in America. *United America,* for example, in its issue of July 4, 1925, called on the Italian element, which built railroads, conduits, streets, bridges, and factories in America and which worked in the orange plantations and in the vineyards of California, to contribute also to its adopted fatherland "the artistic temperament and idealistic inclinations of the Italian race." Similar appeals urged Italians to become naturalized, to send their children to college, and to end the "Little Italies." An editorial of May 7, 1927, severely attacked the Irish because a Boston paper had referred disparagingly to the Italians in the north end of Boston, commenting sarcastically:

> Half a generation after their progenitors dug peat out of the bogs of the "Auld Sod," with the indigenous smell of the soil still clinging to them, they plunge into an orgy of adjective slinging.

In contrast with Italian devotion to America, the editorial referred to

> . . . certain Irish in South Boston and in Charleston who wave Sinn Fein flags and purchase bonds in a mythical Irish Liberty Loan, and who parade for St. Patrick on a day disguised as Evacuation Day . . . who have allied themselves with the most corrupting gang of grafters that ever held political office . . . who send ex-convicts to office and place on a sacred pedestal a vulgarian with the ideals of a bartender and the mentality of a ferrygate tender, [and whose] souls are so inexorably bound up with the traditions of Rome.

In a similar vein, *United America* attacked the Germans and their Steuben Society, contrasting them with nationalities like the Italians which had helped free the world from "Hundom." [41]

The Italian Benevolent Society has inaugurated a nation-wide campaign against the costly religious festivals conducted by Italian societies, with fireworks, bands, and parades, on the ground that, by

[41] See *United America,* January 29, 1927.

such demonstrations, the Italian element is losing prestige among the Americans, who laugh at them "while so much money is spent and while the Feast Directors are busy for this or that Saint . . . ."[42] In 1925, when a New York mayor stopped an Italian religious procession, many Italians applauded.[43] Rupert Hughes' biography of George Washington was criticized as part of an organized British propaganda in the United States to make Americans ashamed of 1776 and to bring them back "into the smug Anglo-Saxon fold."[44]

Simultaneously with such discussions, efforts were made to have streets in New York named after prominent Italians, and parents were urged to teach their children Italian.[45] But Americanization moved irresistibly onward. Giovannina becomes Jenny; Domenica, Minnie; Giovanni, John; and Guiseppe, Joe. Family names like Aquinas and D'Adamos become Quinn and Adams respectively. Cappucio is translated by Hood, Passarella by Pass, La Rocca by Stone, and Scimeca by Shoemaker. An editorial in *United America*, "Time for Epitaphs," in 1927, was devoted to the "old guard" who once controlled the Italian colonies and now deplore the rise of a new generation:

> The clouds of oblivion are gathering rapidly around the "Old Guard." All those "prominenti," the so-called leaders of the colony, may as well become resigned to their fate; a fate inexorably decreed by nature. Their feeble bleatings against Americanism are but the last gasps of expiring persons . . . .[46]

[42] See *ibid.*, July 23, 1927.
[43] *Ibid.*, September 19, 1925.
[44] See *ibid.*, January 23, 1926.
[45] See *ibid.*, January 30, July 10, and September 11, 1926.
[46] *Ibid.*, November 19, 1927.

17 Greeks, Armenians, Portuguese, Spanish, and Mexicans

THE GREEKS

GREEK immigration is largely an event of the present century. Its causes were purely economic and not political, for Greece has been —at least until after the war—a fairly democratic country, without oppressed religious sects or other dissenting groups and with military service not sufficiently burdensome to cause much dissatisfaction. But Greece has been a backward agricultural country, with little manufacturing, low wages, high prices, and a low standard of living. Emigration agents of Mediterranean steamship lines did their work effectively, and "America letters" from Greeks in the United States helped to induce others to come.[1]

The majority of the 300,000 Greek immigrants who came to the United States in the decade before 1917 were young men and boys, unskilled laborers, without family ties, and with a rate of illiteracy exceeded among the major groups only by the South Italians. The Greeks became city dwellers, catering to the minor wants of the American people and finding employment in bootblacking establishments, confectioneries, candy kitchens, flower and fruit stores, restaurants, and later movie theaters. The padrone system flourished and solved the labor problem. Greek colonies settled in centers like New York and Chicago and in textile towns like Lowell, Massachusetts. A "Little Greece" developed in these settlements with typical Greek coffee shops and Greek Orthodox communities, which promptly appealed to the New York bishop of the Church to provide them with a priest. Greek churches, with their Byzantine towers and cupolas, arose as new features on the city's sky line.

[1] For one of the best studies on Greek immigration, see Henry Pratt Fairchild: *Greek Immigration to the United States* (New Haven, Connecticut, 1911). It is this which I am following here. For another excellent account, see J. P. Xenides: *The Greeks in America* (New York, 1922).

In the textile towns, the Greek immigrant began life amidst the filth, poverty, and overcrowding of the tenement-house districts. Ignorant of the English language, he took advantage of night schools to improve his status. In New York, Greek communities developed around 30th Street, on Sixth Avenue and between Second and Third Avenues. In Chicago, the Greek colony grew up around the Hull House district, quickly displacing the earlier Italian settlement in that neighborhood. Some of the larger cities had virtually self-sufficing Greek communities, with Greek business houses, street signs, and coffee houses dispensing Greek pastry, and where the children—what few there were in those early years—played Greek games in the streets. By 1910, four Greek newspapers were published in New York and Chicago, and the former already had a Greek political club.

Greek communities had few paupers, and their inhabitants, through great thrift and industry, rose rapidly in the economic scale. Many were birds of passage, and family life was at first almost totally absent, with some unhappy results. Gambling—not intoxication—was the major vice, and although Greeks committed few major crimes, they acquired a bad reputation in some communities for trying to evade the law in such minor matters as the sanitary regulations and various other requirements fixed by codes and licensing boards for small businesses and restaurants. Naturalization was slow and political interest at first slight, except for the constant agitation for a Greater Greece. Sunday was a pleasure day, and Greek societies sponsored dances, theatricals, and folk festivals on these free days. Greek societies multiplied rapidly in the United States, ranging all the way from local pleasure clubs to mutual benefit societies and propaganda agencies for a greater fatherland. Church schools taught the children religion and national traditions and the Greek language after public-school hours. In the Greek Orthodox churches, the old religious festivals and customs were carefully observed; services were in Greek, and the Christmas season was celebrated in accordance with the Julian calendar. Many Greek homes had family altars and an icon, facing toward the east, with candles burning before it. Factional political quarrels arising over the controversies that divided the homeland sometimes had serious repercussions in Greek-American organizations, including the Church.

In 1930, there were 303,751 of Greek stock in the United States.

Chicago had a Greek population of 50,000; New York, one of about 35,000. Other cities with sizable Greek communities were Detroit, Boston, St. Louis, Akron, and a number of the New England textile centers. In Tarpon Springs, Florida, there were about 2,000 Greek sponge fishers. By 1920, it was estimated that the Greeks in the United States had remitted $120,000,000 to their families at home.

The Hellenic Association of Boston, founded in 1905 primarily to provide for a Greek church, has sponsored annual festivals and maintains a school in Boston. Thousands of Greeks went home to fight for the fatherland in the Balkan Wars, and the Pan-Hellenic Union of New York raised large funds to equip Greek-American regiments for service abroad. For a time, there was a National Pan-Epirotic Union of America, created to disseminate propaganda to win northern Epirus for Greece.[2]

The first Greek newspaper in the United States was the *Atlantis,* started in New York in 1894, and it remains one of the largest Greek papers in the world. Greek businessmen have risen to prominence and affluence, especially in the wholesale grocery business, in the restaurant and hotel business, and in the moving-picture industry. Anargros Melachrinos' cigarettes have become a favorite American product. Greeks participated in the American Expeditionary Forces during the World War, and the American Legion has a few "Hellenic Posts" in cities like Chicago and San Francisco. A publication like the *Greek Review,* an illustrated periodical issued monthly by the Greek Review Publishing Company of Chicago, proves the rapid Americanization of the Greeks in America, chronicles their enterprise and business success, and tries to preserve an interest in modern and ancient Greek culture, at the same time encouraging adjustment to conditions in the United States.

THE ARMENIANS

Over 100,000 immigrants from the Levant had come to the United States by 1920: Armenians, Arabs, Turks, and Syrians—all birds of passage who peddled rugs and laces and linens in the streets of American cities or opened shops to display their wares. By 1930, the Syrian stock numbered 131,942 and the Turkish 80,959.

Of these groups, the Armenians have aroused the greatest interest. They came from the historic kingdom of Armenia, lying south of the

[2] See W. I. Cole: *Immigrant Races in Massachusetts—The Greeks,* (Massachusetts Bureau of Immigration, Boston).

Black Sea and extending west from the Gulf of Alexandretta on the Mediterranean to the Caspian Sea, and south to Mesopotamia. The history of this ancient kingdom is one of the most tragic in all human experience. It fell victim to the ambitions and brutalities of Persians, Russians, and Turks. "Armenian massacres" are well understood in America, and American missionaries have brought home blood-curdling tales that have appealed deeply to the sympathy of Americans for a downtrodden and mistreated people.

By 1894, there were perhaps 3,000 Armenians in the United States, largely as a result of the efforts of American missionaries. The real flood of Armenian immigration did not come until after the massacres of 1894 and 1896. From 1894 to 1917, over 70,000 came to the United States. The newcomers were recruited almost entirely from the peasants and poorer artisan classes. The males outnumbered the females by five or six to one. From 1920 to 1931, 26,146 more came to the United States.

Massachusetts today has approximately 22,000 Armenians. They are to be found in Worcester, where they began as unskilled laborers in the wire mills, in Watertown, in Boston, and in a small rural colony in Methuen. Others have gone into foundries at Whitinsville, Milford, and Millbury, into the textile mills in Lawrence, and into the Lynn, Brockton, and Haverhill shoe factories. In Fresno County, California, there is an Armenian farming colony of 4,000 which raises grapes and fruit. In New York City, the Armenians work as waiters, railroad porters, and oriental rug repairers; in Pennsylvania, as in Massachusetts, they have gone into the mills and factories or into the mines. Some are to be found in the shirt-and-collar factories of Troy, New York, and in the silk mills of New Jersey. Many are small tradesmen, especially importers of Oriental rugs. Like other groups, the Armenian unskilled workers were herded into small, overcrowded workers' apartments.

The first of the Oriental rug merchants in Boston was Hagop Boghigian, who settled there in 1885. Armenians have been especially successful in Boston as photoengravers. At Norfolk Downs, the Ziljians family makes the best cymbals in this country, from an alloy based on a secret formula which has been in the family for generations, ever since the business was started in Constantinople in 1603. Dr. Varazted Kazanjian, a professor at the Harvard Dental School and a world-famous plastic surgeon, started his career in America in 1895, by working in the wire mill in Worcester at $.90 a day.

The most important philanthropic society among the Armenians is the Armenian General Benevolent Union. There are also several Armenian women's organizations and the Armenian National Union, which is a patriotic organization interested in caring for Armenian refugees and in carrying on propaganda for the liberation of Armenia. During the World War, the Armenians of Massachusetts alone gave over $1,000,000 to the cause of Armenian liberation. In 1909, an Armenian association was established in New York City to help immigrants and in 1906 the Armenian Educational Society was created to make student loans. The Armenian National Church is losing ground in America rapidly. Boston still has an Armenian daily paper, the *Hairenik*, established in New York in 1899 and later moved to Boston, where it became a daily in 1916. The first Armenian paper in this country, the *Arekag*, was started in Jersey City, New Jersey, in 1888, and the first in Massachusetts appeared in Lynn in 1895.

Armenian customs have rapidly lost ground in the new American environment. This is particularly true of some of the old wedding and baptismal customs. The two principal religious holidays are Christmas and Easter. Easter is of far greater importance. Christmas is celebrated on January 6. Armenian food has survived longer in the United States than other Armenian institutions and customs. The peculiarly shaped Armenian bread, the free use of spices and oils and fats in cooking, the cereal *bulghur*, which is basic to perhaps 90 per cent of all Armenian dishes, remain indispensible elements in the Armenian-American housewife's cuisine.[3] Armenian restaurants and cafés feature Armenian foods and also provide an opportunity for playing of cards, billiards, and backgammon, games in which Armenians seem to be especially skilful.

THE PORTUGUESE

The Portuguese, first attracted to America when a group of sailors from the Azores came to New Bedford, Massachusetts, are today to be found mostly in the New England factories and in the gardens and orchards of central California. By 1920, the Portuguese stock in the United States numbered approximately 106,000, of whom two thirds were in New England centers, such as Boston,

[3] See *The Armenians in Massachusetts* (W.P.A. Federal Writers' Project, Boston, 1937); and M. Vartan Malcom: *The Armenians in America* (Boston, 1919).

Cambridge, Providence, Fall River, Lowell, and New Bedford. Fishing and working in the cotton mills are their chief forms of employment. Some have settled in the Connecticut Valley to engage in tobacco farming and do market gardening. The largest Portuguese colonies in America are New Bedford, Massachusetts, and Oakland, California, where station KROW regularly broadcasts a "Portuguese hour."

As early as the 1850's, there were two Portuguese settlements in Illinois, one north of Springfield and the other near Jacksonville. Each numbered about 500 settlers and was composed almost exclusively of Protestant Portuguese exiles from Madeira, who came to the United States by way of the West Indies. Their coming to America aroused much comment in the American press.[4] About 1846, some 1,200 refugees, who had been converted in Madeira by a Scotch missionary to Protestantism, left for Trinidad and other West Indian islands to escape persecution for their religious views. The climate and other conditions in Trinidad not proving suitable, the American Protestant Society, which sent an investigator to their West Indian colony, had little trouble inducing the settlers to come to Illinois, where the American Hemp Company promised them land and employment. When the Portuguese reached New York, they found that these promises had not materialized. Left stranded, they were helped by contributions from New York and from residents of Springfield, Illinois, to proceed Westward. En route from New York to Illinois, public meetings were held in Albany, Buffalo, and Chicago to raise money to meet their expenses, and when finally they settled in Illinois, the people of Sangamon County were asked to contribute food, clothes, and furniture. In 1850, the Madeiran Church was reorganized in Illinois, and it remained under the jurisdiction of the Free Church of Scotland until 1856.[5]

The great influx of Portuguese to the United States began in 1890. Commercial intercourse between New Bedford and the Azores

---

[4] See, for example, *The New York Tribune*, October 19, 1850.

[5] See George R. Poage: "The Coming of the Portuguese," in *Illinois State Historical Reports*, Vol. XVIII, pp. 101-135. See also *Geschichtsblätter der Deutsch-Amerikanischen Gesellschaft von Illinois* (January, 1904), p. 32. On February 13, 1859, the *Cincinnati Enquirer* reported that the Portuguese of New York had organized their first military company in the United States, with a comment from the *Journal of Commerce*:

> The martial rage has not yet extended to our Chinese population, but we expect soon to see them marching down Broadway, in national costume, pig-tail and all, preceded by their favorite musical instrument, the gong!

began about 1830, and by 1867 a priest was sent to minister to the Portuguese in this old New England whaling center. By 1899, the Portuguese and the French-Canadians were the dominant labor groups in the cotton mills of New Bedford.

The Portuguese are composed of several distinctive groups. In the Portuguese of the mainland, there is probably some Moorish or Negro admixture. In the Azores, there is a Flemish admixture and perhaps also a Negroid element. Economic conditions were the primary causes of the Portuguese migration to the United States. Agricultural methods were almost as primitive in some sections of Portugal as in Roman days. The Azores were exploited by absentee owners. High taxes, high prices, the evils of tenant farming, the absence of industry, oppressive military service, and the attractions of America, as reported by steamship agents and "America letters," provided the stimulus for Portuguese emigration. The rate of illiteracy in Portugal, in 1911, was reported as being nearly 70 per cent. The money wages of a Portuguese immigrant could be multiplied from seven to ten times by coming to New England. From 1899 to 1919, the total Portuguese immigration to the United States was 143,653, but of this number many returned to their homes. The literacy test of 1917 struck the Portuguese as especially hard; it was this and the World War which brought Portuguese immigration almost to an end.

Perhaps the lowest cultural group among the Portuguese immigrants are the Bravas, from the Cape Verde Islands. They are very dark-skinned and are to be found mostly in New Bedford and in the cranberry bogs of Cape Cod. Next in the cultural scale are the Azoreans and then those who come from the mainland. Nine tenths of the Portuguese immigrants were unskilled. They began life in squalid tenements, and the mortality rate, especially among infants, has been high. In towns like Fall River, Massachusetts, women and children supplement the family income, which is usually decidedly below a proper American standard of living. In farming communities, the "Ports" have been able to supplement their earnings by cultivating little plots of land or by beginning as hired laborers and then renting a farm. As farmers, they work hard, cultivate intensively, and are extremely frugal. Portuguese ownership of farm property has been steadily increasing.

Welcomed at first as cheap labor in the mill towns of New England, the Portuguese soon provoked much criticism, in part because

they succumbed to the propaganda of labor organizers and participated actively in recent strikes. The Portuguese constitute a low-
income group. Their habits are thrifty and they have slowly risen,
but they began on an extremely low level. Families have been large
and sanitary improvements have only gradually been introduced.
Portuguese parents were slow to take advantage of the public schools
for their children, and few children were permitted to remain in
school long enough to reach the upper grades. A few Portuguese
have been able to open little business places in towns like Fall River
and New Bedford.

At first, the Portuguese showed little interest in becoming naturalized or participating in American political life. The labor organizer working among them has probably done more than any
other force gradually to change this attitude. Like other immigrant
groups, the "Ports" have numerous societies and social and athletic
clubs. Their societies pay sick and death benefits and operate
under various names, such as the Azoreana, St. Michael's Portuguese
Benefit Society, and the St. Pedro Portuguese Society. Loyal to the
Roman Catholic Church, the Portuguese find church ceremonies,
pageants, and pilgrimages an interesting and important part of their
religious duty. Religious processions and *fiestas*—such as the one
of Espirito Santo, in June—have been as common among the Portuguese as among the Italians, although with both groups this particular form of religious observance is rapidly waning. Superstitions of various kinds have a strong hold on the Portuguese. Thousands still live on a low standard of comfort and decency, but poor
as it is, what they have in the United States is still better than what
they left behind in Portugal. New Englanders continue to complain of the shortcomings of this group, but at the same time admit
their usefulness in the mills and factories and wonder at their success
in farming abandoned New England homesteads.[6]

THE SPANISH

Immigration from Spain has been negligibly small. Nevertheless, a word may be said of the Spanish heritage of America, dating
from early colonial times. State names like Florida, Colorado,
Nevada, and California are Spanish in origin. The map of the

[6] For the best study of the Portuguese, see Donald R. Taft: *Two Portuguese
Communities in New England* (Columbia University Studies, New York, 1923)
This is the text I have followed here.

Southwest is dotted with Spanish place names for rivers, lakes, mountains, and towns. Much of Western mining law and the law dealing with water rights goes back to a Spanish, not an English, source. The early laws of Louisiana dealing with business transactions were founded on the *Siete Partidas*. Although there were only about 1,200 of Spanish stock in California when that area became a possession of the United States, Spanish influences there are apparent to the present time. Towns have Spanish names—such as Santa Barbara, Santa Cruz, Monterey, San Jose, Jolla, and Los Angeles.

The Southwest is distinguished to a large measure from the rest of the country by the quaint architecture of Spanish colonial times, military posts, presidios, mission stations, mission plays, and Spanish decorative and culinary arts. Spanish colonial architecture was distinctive because of its peculiar arches, arcades, cloisters, tiled floors, and grilled windows. Southwestern Indians speak Spanish, and parts of New Mexico and Arizona are today bilingual. Much of the folklore of the Southwest, the legends and ballads, and the historical romance that clings to California is Spanish in origin.

The American language has absorbed terms like *cargo, commodore, flotilla, armada,* and *embargo,* dating back to Spanish nautical terms, and military terms like *guerilla* and *grenade.* Other words of Spanish origin in our everyday vocabulary are *alfalfa, cigar, desperado, Eldorado, gala, grandee, merino, sierra, siesta, sombrero, tornado, barbecue,* and dozens more.[7] In 1920, the Spanish press still held third place in the number of foreign-language publications issued in the United States, partly as the result of post-war Mexican immigration. The Spanish edition of *The Pictorial Review* once had a circulation of 125,000.[8] The leading Spanish paper in the United States today is the New York *La Prensa.* The largest fraternal society is *La Union Benefico Espanola.*

THE MEXICANS

The *New York Tribune* of October 28, 1883, reported a large masquerade ball, preceded by a torchlight procession of Mexican military companies in picturesque uniforms and sponsored by the

[7] See W. R. Shepherd: *The Spanish Heritage in America* (New York, 1925), reprinted from an article in the *Modern Language Journal* for November, 1925.
[8] See Robert E. Park: *The Immigrant Press and Its Control* (New York, 1922), pp. 13, 135, 436, and 313-319.

Mexicans of New York, for the benefit of fever sufferers in their homeland. The item is interesting historically, but Mexican immigration has been essentially a post-war phenomenon, stimulated greatly by passage of the American quota laws, which closed the doors to Europeans who had once supplied the cheap labor required by American agriculture and industry. It has been estimated that, from 1910 to 1928, over 1,000,000 Mexicans entered the United States. The Mexican embassy, in 1926, estimated the number of old and new Mexicans in the United States at nearly 900,000. Many enter illegally on a long and poorly guarded border; many return to Mexico for the winter when their seasonal employment is ended. Probably 100,000 pass back and forth across the international border each year. The greatest number, of course, enter Texas, California, and Arizona; but in later years, others have gone into the more Northern and Eastern agricultural states or have moved about the country as laborers on construction gangs. Toledo, Ohio, has a Sociedad Mutualista Mexicana.

Most Mexican immigrants are extremely poor and move about, following the seasonal crops. Many look like Indians and live in a kind of fatalistic surrender to their lowly lot. They constitute a highly transient population. They live in unsanitary hovels; their children seldom attend school; and Americanization among them is a slow process. In the eight years before 1927, it has been estimated that $5,000,000 a year were sent back to Mexico by postal money orders. The vast majority of Mexicans are unskilled pick-and-shovel workers. Some are share croppers. A small portion in the Southwest are artisans and small shopkeepers, live in Mexican quarters in the towns, and send their children to American schools. In some areas, they are discriminated against much as is the Negro in the Southern states. The League of United Latin-American Citizens, formed in Harligen, Texas, in 1929, is trying to deal with this problem and to speed the Americanization process.

Birthdays, weddings, and christenings are celebrated in Mexican settlements, no matter how poor, with music and dancing, American songs sometimes blending with Mexican ballads to the accompaniment of the guitar. Superstitions of every kind are a vital part of the rich body of Mexican folklore and folk ballads. There are a number of Mexican societies in the United States, and a Spanish-American Alliance was founded by Mexicans in Tucson. The latter is an organization with lodges and secret ritual which provides its members with insurance. A number of Mexican papers are published in the United States. Octaviano Larrazolo, who came into the United States as a child, has been Governor of the State of New Mexico.[9]

Mexican art, basket weaving, and pottery are attracting increasing attention in the United States, and Mexican scenes have been used frequently in recent years by movie directors and producers of musical comedies. Mexican immigration has had practically nothing to do with these developments, but they may contribute a little to a more intelligent understanding of some of the problems of our Latin-American neighbor and to an appreciation of its ancient Spanish and Indian culture.

[9] See Manual Gamio: *Mexican Immigration to the United States* (Chicago, 1930), especially pp. 84-107. See also Manuel Gamio: *The Mexican Immigrant: His Life Story* (Chicago, 1931). This is a collection of statements by Mexicans living in the United States.

18

Oriental Immigration

THE STORY of Oriental immigration is a brief and strange interlude in the general account of the great migrations to America. Although of relatively small proportions and localized mostly on the West coast, the problem of Chinese and Japanese immigration aroused an excited public opinion from coast to coast and produced an agitation that had serious international repercussions. The Chinese were the first to raise the problem of an apparently unassimilable Oriental group, but hardly had the controversy over Chinese immigration been brought to an end, when the Oriental "menace" appeared in a new and more acute form through the arrival of thousands of Japanese.

THE CHINESE

A small number of Chinese merchants came to California as part of the gold rush of 1849. By 1852, some 14,000 Chinese had become a part of the population of the new State of California. By 1855, the number approached 37,000, and in the 30 years from 1850 to 1880, some 300,000 Chinese entered the United States.

Apparently the early arrivals from the ancient Oriental Empire received a cordial welcome, and if their appearance and mode of living seemed queer, they were nevertheless accepted without much discussion on the West coast, where all sorts and conditions of men had assembled to build a new Pacific frontier. Chinese participated in the events celebrating the admission of California to the Union. In 1859, it was reported that some 2,000 Chinese marched in a Fourth of July celebration in Placerville, California, "accompanied by musicians of their own country." [1] In San Francisco, the Chinese built a temple at an estimated cost of $20,000 and brought in an idol from China valued at $30,000. Apparently very few, except

[1] See *The Cincinnati Enquirer*, August 12, 1859.

the Methodists, were inclined to interfere with the Chinese in their mode of worship.[2]

The Chinese immigrant usually came without his family. He came as a workman and as an adventurer seeking his fortune, but not as a prospective citizen. He was eager to preserve his Chinese customs. He continued to wear his queue and pajamas and to eat with chopsticks, and he probably hoped, in accordance with ancient Chinese custom, that his bones might eventually rest in the land of his fathers. The Chinese "Celestial" acquired a reputation for docility and patience. He was welcomed as cook, butler, laundry-man, gardener, and laborer in the mines; and, in the first two decades of his residence in America, employers paid tribute to his neatness and patience. He was a workman who minded his own business and was not likely to be led astray by the vagaries of labor organizers.

Thousands of Chinese coolie laborers were imported under contract to work in the mines and to build the great transcontinental railroads. Leland Stanford and other railroad builders insisted that it would have been impossible to build the transcontinental roads without the Chinese, and testified that they were "nearly as efficient as Irish laborers" and much more tractable and trustworthy. Prominent citizens of San Francisco gave dinners to the representatives of the Chinese "Six Companies," which controlled Chinese emigration, and hailed with joy the Burlingame Treaty of 1868, which permitted unrestricted Chinese immigration. In 1869, the Central Pacific Railroad employed 10,000 men, of whom nine tenths were Chinese laborers. They were paid from $30 to $35 a month and managed to save a large part of that. Later, as railroad building declined, Chinese workmen found jobs manufacturing cigars and shoes or sewing shirts by machine, or as domestics, laundrymen, or workers in the orchards and vineyards of California. Few ever questioned the assertion that the Chinaman was a hard worker. Long after he had ceased to be a docile laborer on the railroads, he worked on reclamation projects in California, digging ditches and building dikes, standing waist-deep in water. The peak of Chinese immigration was reached in 1882, with nearly 40,000 arrivals. In 1860, there were 34,933 Chinese immigrants in the United States. Two decades later there were 105,465 and, in 1890, the total had reached 107,488. By 1920, the number had declined to 61,639. Over half continued to live on the Pacific Coast.

[2] See *ibid.*, August 14, 1859.

In spite of the early welcome accorded Chinese immigrants, especially by employers, an agitation to restrict their admission to the United States began soon after California's admission to statehood. Governor Bigler referred to the problem in a special message in 1852,[3] and some of the early mining regulations were drawn so as to discriminate against the Chinese. Rumors multiplied about the filth and immorality of the "Chinatown" areas, and of the blackmail and violence of Chinese secret societies like the Six Companies and the Hatchet Men. But the main reason for opposing the Chinese was a growing conviction, which became almost an obsession with American workingmen, that Chinese labor was undermining the American standard of living and was indeed being deliberately exploited to keep down wages.

Local and state laws began to appear on the statute books imposing irritating restrictions on the Chinese. Unprincipled whites persecuted the Chinese, and the California courts frequently abetted them in their activities, although the Federal judiciary eventually overthrew discriminatory legislation as unconstitutional and in violation of the Burlingame Treaty of 1868, which had guaranteed the Chinese free immigration and most-favored-nation treatment.

From 1862 to 1868, Chinese immigration declined, owing to economic conditions, hostile legislation, and the activity of "anticoolie" clubs organized by workingmen on the West coast. The Burlingame Treaty had been welcomed even in California, but the reaction to its provisions quickly changed when Chinese immigration statistics again began to mount. Moreover, by 1870, some of the great railroad building projects had been completed, and thousands of Chinese filtered back into California to seek other employment. As the economic depression in California deepened, reaching a climax in the crash of 1873, labor difficulties increased, and many workmen blamed the Chinese for a major part of their difficulties.

There is evidence that a concerted effort was being made by some employers to use the Chinese to depress the American scale of wages and to break strikes. In 1870, for example, Chinese laborers were shipped from California to North Adams, Massachusetts, to break a strike among shoemakers.[4] An anticoolie meeting was held in Tremont Temple, Boston, to protest against reducing American

---

[3] See Rodman W. Paul: "The Origin of the Chinese Issue in California," in *The Mississippi Valley Historical Review*, Vol. XXV, pp. 181-196.
[4] See *Boston Transcript*, June 13, 1870.

labor to the standard of "rice and rats." [5]   In 1877, Chinese were sent across the country to replace striking workmen in a cutlery plant in Beaver Falls, Pennsylvania.   The *Cincinnati Enquirer* referred to "John Chinaman" as the "coming man" among the cigarmakers, and protested vigorously against the importation of "rat-eaters" to take work from the hands of white Americans.[6] Scores of Chinese had also been sent into the South to work on plantations, to develop rice culture, and to replace Negro labor on the railroad projects of Alabama and Texas.[7]

The agitation against the Chinese reached major proportions in the early 1870's, when an Irishman, Dennis Kearney, began to influence the workmen of San Francisco and other California towns by his agitation for "$4 a day and roast beef" and "the Chinese must go."   Led by the Knights of St. Crispin, shoemakers who were especially bitter about Chinese competition, parades were arranged, petitions were addressed to the state legislature and to Congress, and mass meetings resolved that the time had come to drop all partisan politics and to unite on a program of Chinese exclusion. The Irish on the Pacific Coast were especially aroused against their Chinese competitors in the labor market, and Irish yells like "Immeriky fur Immerikans, bejabers" resounded through the streets of several Pacific Coast cities.[8]   An anti-Chinese convention was called to consolidate the movement, and labor throughout the country was urged to rally against the Oriental menace.   Local authorities responded by issuing new irritating regulations, singling out the Chinese by means of occupational taxes and new regulations for hand laundries and by interfering with their customs and traditions. By the time the courts caught up with these cases and declared most of the regulations void, their purposes had been accomplished.

Unfortunately, the agitation soon passed all legal bounds.   Violence broke out in several places.   Chinese houses were destroyed by gangs of San Francisco hoodlums, and riots ended in the burning of 25 Chinese laundries in San Francisco in the summer of 1877.[9]

[5] See *ibid.*, June 30, 1870.
[6] See *Cincinnati Enquirer*, April 11, 1870. See also *The Cleveland Leader,* June 6, 1870.
[7] See *Cincinnati Enquirer*, January 8 and June 24, 1870; *The Cleveland Leader,* January 19, June 17, 20, and 23, and July 27, 1867; and *Ohio State Journal,* November 3, 1873.
[8] E. P. Oberholtzer: *A History of the United States Since the Civil War* (New York, 1931), Vol. IV, p. 257.
[9] See *The New York Times,* August 1, 1877.

Chinese workers were threatened by unemployed American work-men, and Chinese immigrants were attacked in the streets as they. were released from quarantine.[10] In Rock Springs, Wyoming, 28 Chinese were killed and 15 were injured, and property to the extent of nearly $150,000 was destroyed by a riot which had serious inter-national reverberations. President Cleveland sent two messages to Congress urging the payment of indemnities to the stricken Chinese families. Violence also occurred in Seattle, Tacoma, and in other Pacific Coast towns. There was special concern lest Chinese filter in from the Canadian border. In 1871, 15 were hung and 6 shot in the first serious riot in Los Angeles, as Kearney's "Pick-Handlers' Brigades" declared war on the Chinese.

Chinese exclusion quickly became an issue in California politics. In the 1850's, prominent Know-Nothings had called attention to the dangers of a Chinese invasion of the United States,[11] and on the Pacific Coast, Irish Catholics and others of European stock who were the victims of nativism in the East, combined to save the republic from the Chinese. By 1867, the state platforms of both major parties in California contained anti-Chinese planks, and California Senators began to air the question on the floor of Con-gress. There is some evidence to show that the anti-Chinese senti-ment of the California Republicans was not altogether sincere, for although they kept up the agitation during election campaigns, many of their supporters represented large interests that welcomed the Burlingame Treaty and desired a cheap and abundant labor supply. In 1869, the Democratic platform of California, eager to conciliate the Irish Democrats who had risen to leadership in the labor unions, opposed the adoption of the 15th Amendment to the Federal Constitution because it would help to bring in "hordes of pagan slaves" and "build up an aristocratic class of oligarchs . . . created and maintained by Chinese votes . . . ."[12]

In 1870, a California anti-Chinese convention opposed all candi-dates who employed Chinese labor or favored its admission to the United States. Anti-Chinese societies arose, with slates of candi-dates for office. A People's Protective Alliance was formed in 1873. This was followed by a "League of Deliverance," which spread into

[10] *The Boston Transcript*, June 1 and 6, 1870.
[11] See the speech by N. P. Banks, at Worcester, Massachusetts, in *The Boston Daily Advertiser*, September 9, 1857.
[12] Quoted in Mary Coolidge: *Chinese Immigration* (New York, 1909).

several Pacific Coast states and was designed to initiate a boycott of Chinese goods and services.

As the economic depression following the panic of 1873 deepened, a Workingman's party rose to political power in California, and Kearney's denunciation of the Chinese, as he addressed huge meetings of unemployed on the sand lots, referred more and more frequently to a liberal use of hemp and fire, not only against the Chinese, but against the capitalist class as a whole. A committee of public safety had to be organized to keep order. The Workingman's party grew rapidly, enlisting white immigrants of every nationality, including an influential group of German Socialists, in the fight against their yellow-skinned competitors. Successes of the party in local elections led to the choice of one third of the delegates to the California State Constitutional Convention. The work of this body reflected the presence of a powerful anti-Chinese labor bloc by favoring provisions to exclude the Chinese from voting and from employment on public works. Referendum votes held in 1879 in California and Nevada on the Chinese question showed an overwhelming public sentiment against the Oriental. The Workingman's party, however, died out rapidly with the return of better times and with the passage of restrictive legislation.

Even under the favorable Burlingame Treaty, naturalization had been denied to the Chinese. In 1875, Congress struck at contract labor. Early in his administration, President Hayes vetoed a bill which would have limited the number of Chinese passengers on any incoming ship to 15, not so much because he was opposed to the measure, but because he believed the question should be handled by treaty. Republicans and Democrats alike began to angle for California's electoral votes and, in 1880, both major parties favored the restriction of Chinese immigration in their national platforms.

In 1880, a new treaty was concluded with the Chinese government abrogating the Burlingame Treaty and permitting the mutual exclusion of immigrants, except such as were teachers, students, merchants, and travelers. In 1882, Congress passed a law to exclude Chinese laborers. For years the discussion raged on as to the extent to which this law was successful and the amount of illegal immigration that came in from Mexico and British Columbia by means of a sort of Chinese Underground Railway. In 1892, the Geary Act strengthened and continued the policy of exclusion for another ten

[463]

years. A new treaty was made in 1894 to clarify the situation still further. In 1904, Congress continued all laws concerning Chinese exclusion "without modification, limitation or condition," and the final quota law passed after the World War excluded all Orientals as immigrants.

For years after 1882, and occasionally even now, the newspapers discuss the evasion of the law by the smuggling of Chinese into the United States, but the Chinese question has ceased to agitate the American body politic, even in California.[13] Occasionally, Chinese have protested against invasions of their civil rights, and a few have protested against the exclusion policy.[14] But in general, both parties to the controversy have accepted exclusion as the final chapter in the story of Chinese immigration.[15]

According to the Census of 1920, the total number of Chinese stock in the United States was 61,639. Of this number, 18,079 were born in the United States of Chinese parents, 19,564 lived in California, and 4,559 in New York. The total had decreased 10,000 since 1910. Thousands of Chinese living in the United States today are American citizens by virtue of having been born here, and thousands of residents of American "Chinatowns" have never seen the land of their fathers.

San Francisco had two Chinese theaters as early as 1870, and there are similar institutions in New York City.[16] Chinese New Year festivals and Chinese foods and customs have long since been accepted as interesting curiosities of the American melting pot.[17] The old San Francisco Chinatown disappeared with the fire of 1906. New York's Chinatown is on the East Side, near Italian, Jewish, and other immigrant sections. In San Francisco, the Chinese have their own banks, theaters, shops, and a telephone exchange, which is operated by Chinese girls. One bank in California, organized in 1907 and with its stock exclusively held by Chinese the majority of whom were born in the United States, has deposits of nearly $5,000,-000. A Chinese steamship company owned by San Francisco Chinese operates several steamers across the Pacific.

[13] For a typical newspaper comment, see *The New York Tribune*, October 26, 1883; and *The Cincinnati Enquirer*, October 16, 1883.
[14] See, for example, *The New York Sun*, September 23, 1892.
[15] See also Lucile Eaves: *A History of California Labor Legislation*, in *University of California Studies* (Berkeley, California, 1910).
[16] See *The Cleveland Leader*, March 19, 1870; and *The Philadelphia Press*, June 26, 1889.
[17] See *The New York Sun*, February 5, 1894.

Chinese restaurants are known to be clean, and it has become fashionable to patronize them and to eat many other foods there besides chop suey. Scores of Chinese societies provide for the social and benevolent interests of their people, and there are Chinese Chambers of Commerce in San Francisco and New York. In 1923, there were five daily and three weekly Chinese newspapers in the United States. The leading Chinese publications in San Francisco were *The Chinese World, The Young China,* and *The Chinese Republic Journal.* Chicago's *Kung Shong Yat Po* is also well-known. The Chinese American Citizens' Alliance has local "parlors" in several cities.[18]

Chinese responded wholeheartedly to the cry for help from the motherland when Japan began her recent rape of China, and by the end of August, 1937, the 17,000 Chinese in San Francisco had spontaneously contributed $1,250,000 to the Chinese government's defense fund. Apparently most of the donations came in amounts of $1,000, $5,000, and $10,000. It was reported that, in the same period, the Chinese colony in Seattle had raised $30,000, and similar "drives" for relief funds were launched in New England by the All-New England Chinese Patriotic Society, which includes the Chinese Merchants' Association and the Chinese Women's League of Greater Boston. "Bowl-of-rice parties" and fireworks marked the relief drives in New York and Chicago. Chinese schoolboys and schoolgirls in Boston sold memorial poppies and buttons with the flag of the Chinese Republic, and Chinese-Americans have been crowding around their newspaper offices to read, in Chinese characters, the news from the battle front, which many of them recognize only through the tales their fathers and grandfathers have told them about the land of their origin.[19]

THE JAPANESE

With the satisfactory solution of the Chinese problem, the controversy over Oriental immigration developed to a new crisis because of the increase of arrivals from Japan at the turn of the present century.

[18] See J. S. Tow: *The Real Chinese in America* (New York, 1923).
[19] See *The New York Times,* August 22, 1937. For other data on Chinese Immigration, see Eliot G. Mears: *Resident Orientals on the American Pacific Coast* (New York, 1927), emphasizing their legal and economic status; O. Gibson: *The Chinese in America* (Cincinnati 1877); and George F. Seward: *Chinese Immigration in Its Social and Economic Aspects* (New York, 1881).

The island empire of Japan has an area less than that of California. Much of it is rocky and mountainous, and only a small part of it fit for cultivation. For centuries agriculture was the main occupation of the Japanese people. With the rapid increase in population—the Japanese population nearly doubled in the last 50 years—agriculture became more and more intensive, and the law of diminishing returns began to operate with increasing effectiveness. When modern Japan turned to industry, she found herself handicapped by a dearth of certain important raw materials and by a labor policy that hampered efficient production. In accordance with the doctrines of imperialist expansion, which Japan learned from the Western World, her rulers embarked upon a policy of militarism and navalism, and vigorously opposed any schemes to reduce the pressure of population upon resources by limiting the size of families. The result was a pressure to emigrate, and Japanese began to try their fortunes in Australia, Canada, Brazil, and the United States, only to meet with growing opposition and restrictive legislation in each of the new areas in which they tried to settle.

From 1868 to 1924, 198,070 passports were issued by the Japanese government for immigration to the United States. By 1930, there were 138,834 Japanese in this country, many of whom were born in the United States and are therefore citizens. Before 1891, Japanese immigration to the United States never exceeded 1,000 a year, so that, in 1890, the total number of Japanese in the United States was given as 2,637. In the following decade, over 27,000 came to the United States, and over 58,000 more came from 1901 to 1910. According to the Census of 1910, there were at that time 72,157 Japanese in the United States, of which number 4,500 had been born here.

In 1907, the United States took steps to prevent the Japanese from coming in from Mexico, Canada, and especially Hawaii, stepping stone to the American mainland. In 1908, owing to the anti-Japanese agitation, to be discussed presently, a "gentleman's agreement" went into effect with Japan by which the Japanese government stopped granting passports for all laborers, except "former residents," "parents, wives, or children of residents," and "settled agriculturists." According to the testimony of the American Secretary of State, Japan enforced this gentleman's agreement honestly and with reasonable efficiency until its end, in 1924.

From 1911 to 1920, over 70,000 Japanese returned to Japan; from

1921 to 1924, there was actually a net loss in the Japanese stock in the United States totaling 1,210; and from 1925 to 1928, there was another net reduction of 12,938. The Census of 1900 listed only 985 Japanese women in the United States; by 1920, the number had risen to 38,303, of whom nearly two thirds were married, showing the growth of normal family life among the Japanese immigrant group. By 1932, there were about 72,000 American-born Japanese in the United States.

Besides the conditions in Japan already referred to, there were other incentives to Japanese immigration. Immigration agents and emigration companies, before 1907, imported contract labor from Japan for the sugar plantations of Hawaii, whence many made their way to the American mainland, especially as the source of cheap labor supply from China dried up after the passage of the Chinese exclusion acts. At first, the Japanese found ready employment and even a welcome in the mines, canneries, and lumber camps, on the railroads and farms, and as domestics. The concentration of young agricultural workers from Japan on the Pacific Coast was quite natural. By 1930, there were 97,456 Japanese in California, or 1.7 per cent of the total population; 17,837 in Washington, or 1.1 per cent of the population; and 4,958 in Oregon, or .5 per cent of the total population.

Unlike many Chinese immigrants, young Japanese were eager to become Americans and to establish themselves permanently in the economic life of their new country. By 1909, Japanese peasants owned 16,000 and leased 137,000 acres in California. By 1920, these figures had mounted to 74,769 and 383,287 acres, respectively. This meant that the Japanese element, which constituted about 2 per cent of the population of California, cultivated, by lease or ownership, about 1.67 per cent of the developed farmland of California. Moreover, although the total population of California has been steadily increasing, the rate of increase of the Japanese group has been declining and their birth rate has been falling, in accordance with the experience of other second-generation immigrant groups.

The Japanese were employed in domestic and personal services, as gardeners, butlers, cooks, waiters, and chauffeurs. At the turn of the century, some entered the city trades to become barbers, restaurant and boarding-house keepers, or operators of little stores selling flowers or small art objects. Thousands worked in railroad and logging camps, in mines, in the fishing and canning industries—

especially those dealing with tuna and salmon—or on section gangs. In later years, the Japanese have had to meet the competition of Mexicans in these occupations.

By 1920, there were at least 15,000 Japanese laborers who hired themselves out as seasonal farm workers through Japanese employment agencies, which used the "boss system" and shipped their men around to harvest the perishable crops as they ripened for the market. In these Japanese clubs of migratory workers, the men lived together, paid dues to their organization, employed a secretary to watch the labor market for them, got their pay through the boss or agent, and lived in "bunk-house" gangs. By experience and physical traits, the Japanese were especially well fitted for the cultivation of the smaller crops—such as sugar beets, grapes, berries, garden truck, and citrus fruits—which require intensive cultivation.

By rigid industry and thrift, enterprising Japanese were able to lease or even acquire ownership of farms, or to work on some sort of share-cropping or cash tenancy basis. By 1910, Ushijima, known as the "Potato King," operated nearly 9,000 acres, of which he himself owned 420. Japanese farming activities reached their highest point on the Pacific Coast in 1920, after which they declined. The Japanese flower markets in San Francisco and Los Angeles give abundant evidence of the success of this group in floriculture. The estimated crop value of Japanese farm owners increased nearly a dozenfold from 1909 to 1919.

The anti-Japanese agitation began with the present century, although there were signs of friction as early as the 1890's. In 1906, the San Francisco Board of Education, strongly supported by the *San Francisco Chronicle,* excluded Japanese from the public schools and proposed a separate school for Japanese pupils, for reasons that were not simply racial but, in part at least, arose from the presence of a few young Japanese men in the lower elementary grades. It was claimed that there were only 93 Japanese in 23 San Francisco schools at the time, of whom 25 were born in the United States, and only 12 of the total number were above 17 years of age. Similar laws were passed in other Far Western states. The Japanese government protested at once, whereupon the United States government instituted two suits to test the constitutionality of the measure. However, the whole issue was temporarily solved by the gentleman's agreement with Japan already described. In 1921, the Japanese government also agreed, by an arrangement facetiously called "the ladies agreement," to refuse passports to so-called "picture-brides" who were coming over to marry Japanese immigrants.

The agitation against the Japanese enlisted much support among American labor groups, and candidates were occasionally pledged to support anti-Japanese policies. In 1913, the California state legislature passed its first crop of alien land bills, so drawn as to single out the Japanese without actually mentioning them by name. These measures provided that aliens ineligible for citizenship could not acquire real property in the state unless specifically permitted to do so by treaty, and that such aliens could not lease land for more than three years. In spite of the vigorous opposition of the American State Department and no less than five protests from Japan, the laws were passed practically unchanged.

It was true that other states had laws prohibiting aliens to hold land, but the Japanese protested vigorously that they were being singled out in this legislation for special discrimination. The Tokyo government regarded the legislation as an affront to national pride, refused to test the legislation in American courts, and virtually contended for an acknowledgement of racial equality. There were anti-American demonstrations in Tokyo and anti-Japanese demonstrations in Washington. Efforts to negotiate a new United States-Japanese treaty were unsuccessful, and the controversy might have led to serious trouble if it had not been for the outbreak of the World War, which gave Japan a chance to satisfy some of her imperialistic ambitions in the Far East at the expense of Germany and eventually made her, at least for a time, one of the powers associated with the United States in the war to make the world safe for democracy.

Meanwhile, aided by American legal talent, Japanese ingenuity found ways to evade the laws of 1913 by forming corporations to own or lease land in which American citizens owned a majority of the stock or by buying land in the name of minor, American-born Japanese children. In 1920, after a spirited election campaign, the California legislature undertook to plug the loopholes in the laws by making it illegal for aliens ineligible for citizenship to become members of corporations or guardians for minors, in order to lease or purchase land which the alien could not acquire in his own right. This law forbade the three-year leasehold permitted in the earlier measure.

Since 1923, strictly speaking, Japanese-born immigrants could not engage in agriculture in California, except as laborers, unless they already owned land before the enactment of these restrictive measures. There was no law to prevent the American-born Japanese from going into farming. Moreover, although the laws are still on the books and, in fact, have been theoretically stiffened by subsequent legislation, Californians today seem to have forgotten about their existence. Actions under the laws apparently must be taken by county district attorneys, and there seems to have been no desire on the latters' part to act in an inquisitorial fashion. Land is being operated by Japanese farmers, and it is not probable that in all cases they are either American-born or merely hired hands.

In 1922, in the Ozawa case, the United States Supreme Court specifically ruled that Japanese could not be naturalized in the United States. By the immigration law of 1924, Japanese were excluded from the United States entirely, except in a few minor cases—such as tourists, students over 15, teachers, and wives and children of those already here. In the Congressional debate leading to the enactment of this drastic legislation, it was stressed that the Japanese were a dangerous, proud, and unassimilable race, who were racially and economically undesirable. In spite of protests from President Coolidge and Secretary Hughes, the measure was passed with overwhelming majorities. Among the California organizations who enthusiastically supported total exclusion may be mentioned the American Legion, the State Federation of Labor, the State Grange, and the Native Sons of the Golden West.

By 1930, about one half of the Japanese population in the United States was American-born. Even their most unfriendly critics admit that the Japanese are eager for an education, sending their children to public schools and often to private schools so that they may learn Japanese. There is a Young Men's and a Young Women's Buddhist Association in the United States, and various Japanese societies are federated into the Japanese Association of America, with headquarters in San Francisco. The Japanese make ample provision for the more unfortunate among their people. They do not apply to American organizations for charity, and the Jikei-Kwai, organized in 1906 after the San Francisco fire and earthquake, is their leading charitable organization in California.

The Japanese section of Los Angeles, known as Little Tokyo, is famous for its chrysanthemum festivals and its gay Japanese customs, such as "Doll Day" in March and "Boy's Day" in May. Electric signs in Japanese characters advertise the wares of Japanese merchants. Japanese dailies in the United States today carry English sections, and some Japanese periodicals are printed entirely in English. The antagonism of generations is apparent among the Japanese as with other groups, and there are churches in which services must be held in English for the younger Japanese children. The American-born Japanese now have a slight majority in the Los Angeles area. Buddhism is losing ground among the younger generation under the impact of American ideas and customs. In 1929, there were 1,303 Japanese in American colleges and universities; of this number, about two thirds were American-born. The tragedy of the American-born generation of Japanese is often greater than that of the first arrivals, for they find themselves neither totally Japanese nor quite American, but encounter all the prejudices of both groups.[20]

OTHER MINOR GROUPS

It may be added that the Census of 1930 revealed 45,208 Filipinos in the United States and 63,052 in Hawaii, and that Filipino communities are developing in Chicago, New York, and Washington, D. C. For the most part, the Filipino immigration is one of young, unmarried men, who find jobs as cooks, elevator boys, bellhops, and the like. Moreover, there are Hindus working in gangs in the rice and cotton fields of California, some of them peculiar individuals with beards and long hair, who are dubbed "rag heads." Whether a new agitation against the Oriental in the form of the Hindu and Filipino will develop remains to be seen.

[20] For an account of Japanese immigration, see Yamato Ichihashi: *Japanese in the United States,* (Stanford, California, 1932); Raymond L. Buell: *Japanese Immigration* (Boston, 1924); S. L. Gulick: *The American Japanese Problem* (New York, 1924); and H. A. Millis: *The Japanese Problem in the United States* (New York, 1915).

19

Closing the Gates

FROM COLONIAL TIMES until after the World War, the doors to the United States stood open to practically every immigrant who wished to come from Europe to America. The American people as a whole extended a generous welcome to the newcomers and were proud of a tradition that made the United States the asylum for mankind, a haven of refuge from the hardships and persecutions that existed in other lands. By this policy of an unqualified welcome to the immigrant, the American people attested, not only to their generous spirit, but to their confidence in the soundness and stability of American institutions as well. Nevertheless, there has not been a period in the years since the United States have been a nation in which there were not some manifestations of a nativist spirit that found reason for alarm in the unrestricted admission of unassimilated foreigners and feared for the future of American institutions. Even in the colonial period, this attitude was apparent on the part of a small minority, and in the nineteenth century it led to violent outbursts that, for a time, threatened the normal political life of the nation. Finally, after the World War, the United States reversed its century-old policy of an open door for immigrants and, by the enactment of the quota laws, so materially reduced the number of immigrants who might enter that an epoch in American history came to a close. To the various movements restricting immigration attention must now be directed.

NATIVISM BEFORE 1850

In the colonial period, there were occasional voices raised in protest against some of the non-English elements that entered the seaboard colonies. To the Quaker government of Pennsylvania, Scotch-Irish frontiersmen were frequently a source of trouble and disturbance. Quaker proprietors found them to be restless, aggressive, and lawless squatters; and English officials regarded them as rebels against constituted authority and one of the main causes of the appeal to arms in 1775. Irish redemptioners were described as "the most audacious rascals existing." [1] Moreover, the colonies were a dumping ground for undesirables from the British Isles whom the government sent across the Atlantic. As *Niles Register* put it many years later: "John Bull has squeezed the orange, but insolently casts the skins in our faces."

As early as 1729, a Pennsylvania statute sought to protect the colony against such as were likely to become public charges and to penalize persons who brought them in. An import duty was imposed on foreigners and Irish servants brought into Pennsylvania, in order "to discourage the great importation and coming in of numbers of foreigners and lewd, idle, and ill-affected persons" who endangered the "quiet and safety of the peaceable people" and were likely to become public charges. Persons over 16 years of age were required to take an oath of allegiance within 48 hours of their landing and to pay 12-pence. Immigrants in general were taxed 40 shillings, and the master of a ship bringing in Irish servants was required to pay 20 shillings. The tax on convicts was 5 pounds, and those who brought them were required to furnish a 50-pound bond for their good behavior.[2] Most of the colonies had special discriminatory legislation against "Papists" and Jews. Rhode Island was the only genuine exception. Most colonial leaders would probably have agreed with John Cotton that "it was toleration that made the world anti-Christian."

Opinions about the Pennsylvania Germans were not always favorable. Penn's secretary and Governor Gordon denounced their ignorance and clannishness and feared that they would remain "a distinct people from his Majesty's subjects." Franklin feared for the English language and for English institutions because of the heavy influx of unassimilated Germans; and William Smith, first provost of the University of Pennsylvania, envisaged the possibilities of an alliance between Germans and French to eject the British from North America. Smith advised sending preachers and teachers among the Germans to teach them, not only a sound Protestant

---

[1] See Michael J. O'Brien: *A Hidden Phase of American History* (New York, 1919), p. 108.
[2] See *Statutes at Large of Pennsylvania, from 1682 to 1801* (Harrisburg, Pennsylvania, 1908), Vol. IV, pp. 135, 139, and 164.

faith, but sound government as well. He advised Parliament to deny political rights to immigrants for at least 20 years. The motive behind the "charitable scheme to educate the poor Germans" was not only religious but distinctly political. The attack on the French Huguenot settlement in Massachusetts at the close of the seventeenth century was probably due also, in part, to nativist opposition to a people who spoke a different language and "walked another way."

The first organized political attack on the foreign-born in the national period of United States history was marked by the enactment of the Alien and Sedition Laws in the administration of John Adams. Historians have generally considered these repressive measures only in the light of the crisis that existed at the close of the eighteenth century in the relations between the young republic and France. To be sure, this was an important cause for the legislation against foreigners, as a means of protecting the nation against sedition, but it was not the only cause. There was a political motive in the minds of many Federalists who wished to deprive the party of Jefferson of its immigrant support.

The Naturalization and Sedition Acts were designed primarily, not as a defense against France or any other foreign power, but as a weapon of offense against the Jeffersonians. The Federalist and Jeffersonian philosophy of government were sharply different. Many immigrants who entered the United States since 1789 were political refugees driven out by the kaleidoscopic changes of the French Revolution and the forces it had loosed in other countries. French, English, Scotch, and Irish revolutionists escaped to the "land of the free" across the water, where they immediately began to espouse their radical views. Their natural political affiliation was with Jefferson's group, for they found little sympathy among the anti-French, pro-British, aristocratic Federalists. As journalists and prospective American voters and officeholders, the newcomers joined in the attack on President Adams and the Federalists. Jefferson himself believed the Constitution was "fast galloping toward monarchy," and his followers, infected with an utterly uncritical gallomania, launched a scurrilous attack on the party in power.

It was natural for many Federalists to want to strike back and to break the alliance between Jefferson's party and the immigrants, who, after a brief period of five years, could be naturalized and become full-fledged American voters and politicians. Some wanted to give immigrants all except political rights. Harrison Gray Otis of Massachusetts would have favored closing the doors to America altogether; he publicly advocated depriving the naturalized citizen of the right to hold office. Many wished to deprive the immigrant of the right to vote also. Otis believed that "the indiscriminate admission of wild Irishmen and others to the right of suffrage" would endanger liberty and property in America. He proposed a $20 tax on certificates of naturalization, frankly admitting that his purpose was to destroy the foreign vote. His attacks on the French Revolution indicated that he believed the American government was fighting for its life against the insidious propaganda of a leveling democracy. He wanted to keep out "the mass of vicious and disorganizing characters" who were fomenting world revolution, including in this group, in addition to the French radicals, "the hordes of wild Irishmen" who came to disturb American tranquillity. The reference was undoubtedly to the Scotch-Irish, for another New England Federalist, Uriah Tracy of Connecticut, in a description of his journey into Pennsylvania in 1800, described his alarm at finding so many "United Irishmen, Free Masons," who are "the most God-provoking Democrats on this side of Hell." [3] Rufus King, minister to England, worked hard to prevent Irish political exiles from reaching the United States, because in America they arranged themselves "upon the side of the malcontents." The legislature of Massachusetts proposed an amendment to the United States Constitution excluding all foreign-born citizens from Congress.

It was from motives such as these that the Naturalization Act was passed raising the residence requirement for citizenship in the United States from 5 to 14 years. Similar motives prompted the Sedition Act, whose major purpose was to treat political opposition as a crime. Both laws were speedily repealed when Jefferson became President, and neither had any great effect, except to give Jeffersonians the opportunity to plead the cause of the "poor aliens" and to defend the American Bill of Rights. In the campaign of 1800, which drove the Federalists from power forever in the national government, the Jeffersonians shrewdly stressed the nativist sentiments of the Federalists, especially among the foreign-born voters of states like Pennsylvania.[4] For years, the Democratic party re-

[3] See Samuel E. Morison: *The Life and Letters of Harrison Gray Otis* (Boston, 1913), Vol. I, p. 107. See also the whole discussion of the Alien and Sedition Laws.
[4] See *The Pennsylvania German*, Vol. X, p. 6.

mained the special friend of the immigrant, and the opposition was always more or less tarred with the charge of being unfriendly to the "adopted citizen." As late as 1814, it was suggested in the Hartford Convention that an amendment be added to the United States Constitution to the effect that no one hereafter naturalized should be eligible to any elective or appointive office under the national government. Albert Gallatin, the noted Swiss coworker of Jefferson, was especially in disfavor with the Federalists, but, in addition, New England extremists who composed the Hartford Convention thought such an amendment would break the power of the Democratic party over the foreign vote.[5]

The opposition to the foreign-born was not limited to New England. In New York, Irish names were common in public affairs by the end of the eighteenth century. Thomas Addis Emmett and William James MacNevin, men of the highest culture and ability, had come to the United States after the unsuccessful Irish rebellion of 1798. They and their followers became Democrats, supporting DeWitt Clinton, who was also of Irish blood, always posed as the friend of Ireland, and denounced the "Anglomen and monocrats" of the Federalist party. The antagonism to the Irish, who were denounced as uncouth, dirty, ignorant, stupid, and immoral, reached riot proportions between New York nativists and Irishmen on Christmas, 1806. Alexander Hamilton, however, advocated courting instead of fighting the immigrant vote and, in 1802, proposed a Christian Constitutional Society to instill true patriotism and do relief work among the immigrants. In 1810, the Federalists, in a desperate effort to regain power during the temporary unpopularity of the Jeffersonians, as a result of their embargo policy, produced a campaign song for the gubernatorial election in New York which contained the following stanza:

Come Dutch and Yankees, Irish, Scot
With intermixed relation;
From whence we came, it matters not;
We all make, now, one nation.[6]

[5] See also J. B. McMaster: *A History of the People of the United States* (New York, 1914), Vol. II, pp. 332-333; and F. M. Anderson: "The Enforcement of the Alien and Sedition Laws," in *American Historical Association Reports* (1912), pp. 15-126; and Edward Channing, *History of the United States* Vol. IV, pp. 219-225. English refugees like Joseph Priestly were equally feared, who, by "joining chemic with religious hate, try'd to decompose the church and state."
[6] See D. R. Fox: *The Decline of Aristocracy in the Politics of New York* (New York, 1919), p. 115. See also, *ibid.*, pp. 75-78 and 88.

By the 1830's, conditions were ripe in America for the first organized outbreak of nativists against the foreigner. By 1826, it was estimated that there were 150,000 Irish Catholics in the New York diocese, and parishes were rapidly being established inland as the Irish immigrant followed the advancing trail of internal improvements. Before 1830, some ten Irish newspapers had been established in the United States. Some, such as *The Jesuit* of Boston—later renamed *The Boston Pilot*—the St. Louis *Shepherd of the Valley,* and the New York *Truth Teller* were essentially ecclesiastical papers. The Catholics themselves became involved in a long struggle over lay trusteeism involving local parish control, which led to a shower of pamphlets and did the Church little good. Aggressive Catholic leaders like Bishop Hughes of New York demanded a share in the school levy for Catholic parochial schools and, when nativists attacked the Catholics, urged their followers to defend their churches against attack by force, if necessary. A flood of vile books was released upon the country by anti-Catholic writers who used the Church and the school issue as an excuse for obscenity. The Catholics retaliated, until there was a veritable war of newspapers and books on the fundamental question of whether Roman Catholicism and good American citizenship could be compatible.[7]

The number of publications produced by the rising battle over Catholicism seems almost incredible. Since Irish immigrants were really the first to bring the issue of church allegiance and American republicanism to the fore, the spearhead of the nativist attack was always directed against them. Samuel F. B. Morse was one of the most active producers of this new type of literature. To distinguish honest argument from obscenity and pornography in these publications is not always easy. In 1837, Morse published *Confessions of a French Catholic Priest, to which are added Warnings to the people of the United States.* This was followed, in 1841, by *Our Liberties defended; the Question discussed; is the Protestant or Papal System most favorable to Civil and Religious Liberty,* and later by *Imminent Dangers to the Free Institutions of the United States through Foreign Immigration, and the Present State of the Naturalization Laws.* In 1835, there appeared Rebecca Theresa Reed's *Six Months in a Convent,* which sold 10,000 copies in a week and turned out to be by quite a different author, who had never

[7] See Henry A. Brann: *John Hughes* (New York, 1892); and Louis D. Scisco: *Political Nativism in New York State* (New York, 1901), pp. 17-23.

[477]

been in the Charleston nunnery from which Rebecca Reed was supposed to have escaped. Dowling's *History of Romanism,* 671 pages of spicy gossip, appeared in 1846 and went through a dozen editions. Morse denounced the missionary work of the Leopoldine Foundation among the Catholics in the United States as a foreign conspiracy to win America for the Pope and called on all true Americans to shut "the open portals of naturalization," through which the enemies were pouring to destroy American liberties.[8] In Cincinnati, Alexander Campbell, founder of the Campbellite Church, debated with Bishop Purcell for four hours on each of eight days, in 1836, on the issues arising between the Churches from the use of the *Bible* in the public schools. Protestant divines lectured on the incompatibility of the Papacy with free institutions and American liberty. Lyman Beecher toured the East in the 1830's and 1840's, exhorting his countrymen to oppose the dark designs of foreign potentates to wreck the American experiment in republicanism, thundering:

> In the beginning, this eruption of revolutionary Europe was not anticipated, and we opened our doors wide to the influx and naturalization of foreigners. But it is becoming a terrific inundation . . . What is to be done to educate the millions which in twenty years Europe will pour out upon us.[9]

In 1836, Philip Hone confided to his *Diary*:

> All Europe is coming across the ocean, all that part at least who cannot make a living at home; and what shall we do with them? They increase our taxes, eat our bread, and encumber our streets, and not one in twenty is competent to keep himself.[10]

"Can one throw mud into pure water and not disturb its clearness?" was the simple question with which "an American" attacked the problem of immigration in 1835. Resolutions of the Louisiana Native American Association, in 1839, denounced the immigrants as "the outcast and offal of society, the pauper, the vagrant, and the

[8] See Peter Guilday: *The Life and Times of John England* (New York, 1927), Vol. II, p. 205.
[9] Quoted in G. M. Stephenson: "Nativism in the Forties and Fifties, with Special Reference to the Mississippi Valley," in *Mississippi Valley Historical Review*, Vol. IX, pp. 191-192.
[10] Allen Nevins (editor): *The Diary of Philip Hone* (New York, 1927), Vol. I, p. 209.

convict . . . ." The American Protestant Society was formed to do missionary work among French, German, Irish, and other Catholics, in order "to secure the permanency of our free institutions" and to rescue America from the errors of Romanism. "Millions of ignorant men are left to live and die upon our shores, ignorant of the principles of civil and religious liberty," lamented the Society in its *Sixth Annual Report* in 1849. Nevertheless, the report magnanimously concluded that

> . . . they are immortal beings, [and] all the motives of self-preservation with reference to our precious institutions, all the feelings of compassion and benevolence for perishing men that ever glow in the heart of Christians, cluster around these gathering multitudes . . . .

Missions were founded among the Irish, and preachers and missionaries were sent to the Germans of Rochester and Buffalo and out into far-off Wisconsin, and to the Portuguese exiles from Trinidad, in Illinois. A Presbyterian paper, in 1848, saw God's wisdom at work in the immigrant tide; it was now possible to begin evangelizing without incurring the expense of going abroad to attack the seats of Romanism.[11]

That violence should follow this battle of books and pamphlets was perhaps inevitable. Without in the least condoning the attacks of American vigilantes in the war of nativism, it must be admitted that immigration laws and the administration of the naturalization act were lax beyond all reason. Political machines were being built up by the exploitation of as yet unassimilated immigrants in the larger cities, and hundreds who landed in the morning from an Atlantic vessel frequently voted before nightfall at the behest of the local boss. Poverty and disease added to the taxpayer's burden. The percentage of foreign paupers in institutions was high, and tax rates were going up. Both criminals and paupers were being sent to the United States. The Irish were unusually turbulent, especially when fired with spirituous enthusiasm on Election Day. Catholics opposed the activities of Protestant *Bible* societies and occasionally petitioned to have Protestant singing and *Bible* reading stopped in the public schools. Their protests against prejudiced textbooks were frequently justified. It must also be admitted that

[11] See *Annual Reports of the American Protestant Society* (New York, 1848 and 1849). See also Harmon Kingsbury: *The Immigrant's Good Samaritan* (New York, 1848).

some of the leaders of the Catholic hierarchy were hardly diplomatic in their aggressive attack on the school question and that Catholic papers were often as narrow and abusive toward the Protestants as the latter were in their bigoted eloquence about the "scarlet woman" of Rome. Bishop England, in 1840, addressed two essays to the Catholic voters in which he urged them to merge with the general population until abused, and then to "prefer a capable friend to a capable enemy." [12]

The first nativist Protestant associations were formed in the early 1830's. In 1834, the Ursuline Convent in Charleston, Massachusetts, was desecrated and burned, as a result of the excitement arising over the alleged treatment of an escaped inmate. A mass meeting of distinguished citizens of Boston and the immediate intervention of Bishop Fenwick to dissuade the Irish from marching on Boston to take revenge prevented more serious trouble. Similar outbreaks occurred elsewhere. In 1835, for example, a Protestant assembly in New York was broken up by Irish Catholics, who were promptly disavowed by the clergy.[13] In 1837, an engine company returning from a fire collided with an Irish funeral procession in Boston, with the result that a general riot involving thousands broke out in the city. Incidents like these were always followed by a new crop of attacks and counterattacks in print, many of which achieved notoriety only as contributions to pornography. They centered on convent life and "popish brothels," and the alleged abuses connected with the confessional. No tale was too fantastic for the credulity of excited minds convinced that the flower of Christianity had been in the dead grasp of the Pope until "God's gardener, Luther, transplanted it."

In the 1830's, local nativist political parties appeared in New York and elsewhere on the Eastern seaboard, usually in close alliance with the Whigs. In New Orleans, strangely enough, Judah P. Benjamin was one of the leaders in forming the Louisiana American party.[14] In 1840, the fight over the use of public funds for Catholic schools was started in New York, with Governor Seward supporting the Catholic claim for a prorata distribution against the protests of the New York City school system, which was decidedly Protestant

[12] See Guilday: op. cit., Vol. II, pp. 498-499.
[13] See Scisco: op. cit., p. 23.
[14] See W. D. Overdyke: "History of the American Party in Louisiana," in Louisiana Historical Quarterly, Vol. XV, pp. 581-88; and Vol. XVI, pp. 84-91, 256-277, 409-426, 586, and 608-627.

in composition and viewpoint.[15]   In 1841, Bishop Hughes, at a mass meeting, advocated a separate Catholic ticket, since candidates of both regular parties were unfavorable to sectarian schools.   In 1844, a nativist mayor was elected in New York, with strong Whig support. Several members of Congress were claimed by the nativists, and, in 1845 and 1847, national native-American conventions were held to advocate a 21-year residence requirement for naturalization, the limitation of officeholding to native Americans, the restriction of immigration, and educational reforms.   Members of the Pennsylvania Constitutional Convention tried in vain to get an amendment prohibiting all immigrants who arrived after 1841 from holding public office in the state.[16]   Since the Whigs flirted rather openly with nativism, it was to the political advantage of Democrats to denounce the nativists and to curry favor with the foreign-born voters.   Giles of Maryland eulogized the immigrant in the halls of Congress, and even Yancey of Alabama, in 1845, favored "throwing wide the door to this our fair temple of freedom, and giving to all the freest access to worship at her altars."   The latter opposed all restrictions on immigration in vigorous language, ending with a burst of eloquence in commemoration of Lafayette and Washington.[17]

The 1840's maintained the tradition of rioting over immigration and religion so well established in the 1830's.   In 1842, there were riots in a New York election between Orangemen and Irish.[18]   The worst disturbances, however, occurred in Philadelphia—the "City of Brotherly Love" had a reputation for rioting—in 1844, when civil war raged for several days and parts of the city had the appearance of a battlefield.   The trouble started over a Catholic bishop's protest against the reading of the Protestant *Bible* in the schools and the forcing of Catholic children to join in Protestant exercises. When the Board of Education excused the children, Protestants were immediately called upon by excited nativists to stop the Catholic attempt "to kick the *Bible* from the schools."   Nativist meetings were held in the Methodist church at Kensington.   The excitement spread; Irish laborers broke up one of the meetings, and a nativist crowd was fired upon from the Hibernia hose house.

[15] See Scisco: *op. cit.*, p. 32.
[16] See McMaster: *op. cit.*, Vol. VII, pp. 370-372.
[17] See *Congressional Globe*, 29C. 1S.   December 17, 1845.
[18] See Nevins: *op. cit.*, Vol. II, p. 596.

Nativist political meetings were attacked with clubs and stones. On May 6, nativists fired on Irish residents with fatal results and drove out the nuns and orphans from a nunnery. Two Catholic churches were burned, and for days the city was in the hands of a mob. The police authorities seemed to be unusually ineffective in dealing with the rioters. New riots broke out early in July, and the mob became so large that it seriously threatened the militia. The troops were finally withdrawn to prevent a still more bloody encounter. Catholic families left by the hundreds to escape the enraged mob. In New York, Bishop Hughes' threat to meet force with force and his stationing of armed men in the churches probably prevented similar bloodshed there.[19]

A nativist Congressman from Pennsylvania attributed the Philadelphia riots of 1844 to "drilled bands of foreign robbers," who attacked American freemen "armed only with moral power," but to most moderates in America, nativism now bore the stigma of mob violence. Although nativism won local victories in several cities, it declined rapidly after these riotous incidents. The Mexican War, moreover, with the consequent reopening of the slavery controversy, provided a national issue that pushed other questions into the background. But nativism was not dead; this was merely a lull before the next storm. In the 1850's, nativism broke out again, with a fury never equaled, before or since, in the history of American politics.[20]

KNOW-NOTHINGISM

The revival of nativism in the decade before the Civil War and its climax in the Know-Nothing party were due, to a considerable degree, to the heavy immigration from Ireland and Germany after 1848 and to the abuses that came to light in the elections of the late forties and early fifties in metropolitan centers, where the melting pot was temporarily boiling over. In part, too, they were due to the disintegration of the older political parties over the slavery issue and the desire on the part of many confused voters to find a new issue and a new political allegiance in these years of bitter party controversy.

[19] See McMaster: *op. cit.*, Vol. VII, pp. 370-385. For an account of other riots, see *Albany Argus*, October 12 and 13, 1849.
[20] For the best discussion of nativism up to 1860, see Ray A. Billington: *The Protestant Crusade, 1800-1860* (New York, 1938).

Life in the slums of New York, inhabited by low-class immigrants in the 1850's, can hardly be described in too vivid terms. The Five Points District, in the old sixth ward in New York, and the Old Brewery were notorious even in New York, where the population were rather calloused to the condition of the poor. Negroes and poor Irish housed together in indescribably overcrowded, unsanitary tenements. Saloons, "blind tigers," dance halls, and houses of prostitution were numerous and generously patronized. The police were afraid to enter the worst areas. Missionaries who had more courage or more faith than officers of the law were often driven out. Gangs like the "Roach Guards," "Shirt Tails," "Dead Rabbits," and "Plug Uglies" dominated these districts and, although not invariably led by Irishmen, recruited a large percentage of their membership from this and other immigrant groups. The Tammany boss made a political alliance with the voters and utilized the gangsters for political purposes. The Bowery Boys, though not a part of these notorious gangs, were known the nation over as pillars of Tammany Hall. Crime was prevalent in the immigrant sections, in tenements and slums, and the police were virtually powerless. Gangsters were hired by all parties, and even the Native American party, in the 1830's, used them in its fight against Tammany. The politician and the saloonkeeper continued their close alliance.[21] In other cities, such as Baltimore and Philadelphia, conditions were not essentially different.

The buying of votes in local elections was easy where large groups of immigrants could be mobilized by their leaders to march to the polls, and native American and foreign-born politicians were quick to realize the value of this new voting strength. Voters were bought in blocks and voted in blocks; they were imported on Election Day from the outside or shifted about from one voting place to another as "repeaters." Ballots were printed and distributed by the party organizations, so that vote buying and selling could be easily controlled. Registration of voters was so lax as to make it difficult to check these abuses, and naturalization papers could be obtained before Election, free of charge and without too many questions asked, from friendly judges. In the 1840's, it was the general practice to advertise in the German papers of New York just before Election Day that all Germans wishing to be naturalized should

[21] See Herbert Asbury: *The Gangs of New York: An Informal History of the Underworld* (New York, 1928).

apply to the German committee of Tammany Hall, where they would receive their citizenship papers gratis. Irish immigrants landing in the morning might be voters by nightfall. As late as 1868, when the Scotchman William M. Tweed was mobilizing the Irish-American vote for Tammany, between 20,000 and 30,000 were naturalized in New York City courts in the six weeks before election. Both Democrats and Republicans paid the necessary fees. One judge naturalized over 10,000 in two weeks.[22]

That American democracy had not yet learned the processes of orderly elections is abundantly clear from scores of descriptions of conditions in the two decades before the Civil War. The immigrants were not alone to blame, for city politics before their arrival had not been pure and undefiled. But after all due allowance for partisanship and exaggeration has been made, there is much truth left in the description of a New York election of 1840 by Philip Hone, in which he pointed out that,

> . . . in the heterogeneous mass of vile humanity in our population of 310,000 souls, the men who decide the elections are unknown; they have no local habitation or name; they left their own country for ours to better their condition by opposing everything good, honest, lawful and of good report, and to effect this they have banded themselves into associations to put down at all hazards the party in favor of order and good government. A mighty array of these banditti paraded the streets last night under the orders of the masters who, no doubt, secretly directed their movements, attacking every place where the Whigs met. National Hall in Canal Street, the Conservative headquarters, was besieged by this army of Jack Cades, and its appearance this morning is a melancholy sample of the effects of unrestrained power in the hands of a mob of political desperadoes. All the windows of this large building are broken; bushels of brickbats cover the floors, and the doors show where the ruffians tried to get admission by setting fire to the house . . . .[23]

The Irish weekly *Citizen*, published in New York, although condemning the Know-Nothings, added:

> We fear that some of [the Irish] have been a noisy, turbulent and intolerant class, who did no credit to the charac-

[22] M. R. Werner: *Tammany Hall* (Garden City, New York, 1928), p. 135.
[23] Nevins: *op. cit.*, Vol. I, pp. 508-509.

ter of their native country, and were of little benefit to the land of their adoption. We fear, too, that some of the ultra Catholic journals went far beyond the bounds of prudence in writing on religious subjects.

The editor advised the Irish to give up "their intemperate habits, their rows, their faction fights." [24]

While conservative-minded and substantial propertyholders were protesting against immigration because it raised taxes, brought in paupers who had to be supported, polluted elections, and endangered the institutions of property, American laborers were protesting against the competition that came from abroad. Labor has opposed unrestricted immigration ever since such secret orders as the United American Mechanics made their appearance in the 1840's, and nativism has sometimes been an avowed objective of these organizations. American workmen demanded preference over the imported "pauper labor" of Europe, which was dragging down the standards of the American workingman. Manufacturers, miners and railway and canal builders were accused of deliberately seeking cheap labor abroad. As one indignant commentator in 1854 wrote:

> It is no secret that foreign workers have become an article of importation, professedly to provide for deficiency in the labor market but in reality to obtain efficient workers at low wages . . . . The protective tariff and unrestricted immigration is the invariable policy of master coal miners, master iron workers, master machinists, master woolen and cotton manufacturers.

Apparently what labor wanted in these years was free trade in goods and a prohibitive tariff on "pauper labor." [25] A nativist paper, in 1851, frankly announced in its prospectus:

> The interests of mechanics and working men and women, who have been sorely pressed by the unfair competition and combinations of pauper Europeans, will receive attention at our hands.[26]

[24] Quoted in Edith Abbott: *Historical Aspects of the Immigration Problem* (Chicago, 1926), p. 818.
[25] See Frank J. Warne: *The Tide of Immigration* (New York, 1916), pp. 193-194.
[26] Quoted in E. D. Branch: *The Sentimental Years, 1830-1860* (New York, 1934), pp. 389-390.

In addition to these political and economic causes, there was a revival of genuine nativist sentiment in the 1850's, with a strong Protestant tinge, as evidenced by many new publications on the old theme of protecting the purity of American institutions against European contamination emanating especially from Rome. Although the Irish bore the brunt of this attack, as in former years, the German element came in for its share of denunciation, and several of the most violent disturbances involved conflicts between Germans and nativists. The charge against the Germans was mainly that so many were freethinkers, rationalists, atheists, and desecrators of the Puritan Sabbath. In the decades just before and after the Civil War, Puritanism fought its losing battle with the Continental Sunday, not only in the East, but in the Middle West as well. The Reverend James W. Alexander wrote disconsolately in 1857:

> Protestantism has lost its glory in the land of Luther . . . . Ever since the outbreak of 1848, the convulsed masses have been heaving with equal violence against the altar and the throne. Many of the ringleaders in these connections have reappeared in our land.[27]

Evangelical American Protestants seemed to be equally troubled by Irish papists and German radicals, and much proselyting was undertaken among both groups. The American Tract Society hired men who could speak the language of various immigrant groups to distribute literature among those speaking foreign tongues who rejected the *Bible* and advocated "infidelity, Socialism and other soul-destroying errors."[28] The Presbyterian General Assembly opposed the efforts of the foreign-born "to bring in upon us the wretched immoralities of European Society," by which apparently was meant the improper observance of the Lord's Day.[29] As late as 1867, a stern Calvinist bitterly attacked the introduction of Christmas customs by the foreign population. He regarded such customs as "Popish idolatries," manifesting a "spirit of infidelity to the lust of pleasure."[30]

That the Germans were often aggressive in forcing their customs

---

[27] James W. Alexander: *A Collection of Fugitive Papers* (Oberlin College Archives). For this item, I am indebted to my colleague, Dr. Robert S. Fletcher.
[28] See *The New York Times*, May 12, 1853.
[29] See *Minutes of Presbyterian General Assembly* (1859), p. 534.
[30] See "Diary of George Duffield," in *Mississippi Valley Historical Review*, Vol. XXIV, pp. 64-65.

upon an unwilling community and in expressing their contempt for the uneducated "barbarians" and "Methodists" who defended the Calvinist Sabbath cannot be questioned. Their indiscretions were no doubt responsible for some of their troubles. On one occasion in the 1850's, while Wisconsin was in the midst of a political fight over a temperance law, Milwaukee Germans went to the polls with enormous, arm-long ox horns slung over their shoulders, filled with beer, and when these were emptied, they filled them again from beer wagons standing in the street. Little wonder that the temperance paper commented:

> It does not lessen the desire for a Maine law to live near a *Bier Halle* and band of music every Sabbath. Let the Germans respect our customs if they want us to respect theirs.[31]

Meetings of Germans were held to protest or defy the enactment of liquor laws or Sunday closing laws.[32] In Newark, New Jersey, 10,000 Germans petitioned the City Council for a repeal of the Sunday laws and provoked *The New York Times* to an editorial on "Sunday-keeping," in which the editor protested vigorously against converting the Sabbath "into a Saturnia" and against sacrificing to pleasure-seeking Germans "our most sacred institutions." [33] The *Cleveland Plain Dealer* protested against the noisy observance of New Year's Day by "a lot of German rowdies" and asked:

> Must the Sabbath be desecrated, the City Ordinances violated, and the peace of the whole city disturbed to give lager beer loafers the liberty of perpetuating a custom which is forbidden by our laws, dangerous to life, and corrupting to public morals? [34]

In political campaigns, the German element at times was very aggressive, and when their candidate lost, it blamed the "nativists" in violent language at protest meetings.[35] Occasionally German laborers were used as strikebreakers,[36] and New York in the 1850's

---

[31] See Joseph Schafer: "Prohibition in Early Wisconsin," in *Wisconsin Magazine of History*, Vol. VIII, pp. 281-299.
[32] See *The Boston Pilot*, June 23, 1855.
[33] See *The New York Times*, June 11, 1853.
[34] *The Cleveland Plain Dealer*, January 3, 1855.
[35] See *Der deutsche Pionier*, Vol. I, p. 339.
[36] See *New York Weekly News*, April 25, 1846.

was infested with professional German beggars who committed petty thefts.[37]

When Know-Nothings attacked "red Republicans," they meant especially the radical Forty-Eighters and German freethinkers, who attacked the churches, denominationalism, and Puritanism. The turners were especially unpopular, because they were supposed to combine infidelity with political and economic radicalism. On a number of occasions, turner picnics, balls, and parades were attacked by nativists, and bloody riots followed. In 1855, during a riot in Columbus, Ohio, the turners fired revolvers into the crowd.[38] Bloody encounters occurred in Louisville, Boston, Cincinnati, and elsewhere in the 1850's, when Know-Nothingism was at its height, and it is impossible in some instances to determine which group precipitated the fighting.[39]

It is significant to point out that, at the height of the Know-Nothing disturbances, the Irish found it difficult to coöperate with their fellow sufferers, the Germans, and some of the Catholic clergy denounced the German "infidels" with as much fire as the nativist leaders. To *The Boston Pilot*, all turners were atheists, Sabbath-breakers, freethinkers, red Republicans, and advocates of free love. German organizations were denounced as "barbarous clubs," whose members were "in a state of semi-barbarism." "Americans are beginning to see," the editor concluded, "that these foreign anarchists are deadly enemies to our government." [40] "Universal Republicans from Central Europe" and "bigoted nativists at home" seemed to be enemies of the same foul stripe, and on one occasion *The Boston Pilot* seemed to prefer Know-Nothings to German infidels, commenting:

> To keep them [the Germans] from getting power will be the effect of the know-nothing crusade if successful, and if the know-nothings perform this one good action, posterity will look charitably over the multitude of political crimes committed by that organization of ignorance and bigotry.[41]

[37] See Arthur C. Cole: *The Irrepressible Conflict* (New York, 1934), pp. 155, 254-255.
[38] See *Boston Herald*, July 6, 1855.
[39] See *Der deutsche Pionier*, Vol. I, pp. 250-253; and Vol. IV, pp. 186-187; *New York Tribune*, September 27, 1850; *Boston Transcript*, September 6, 1854; *Toledo Blade*, March 7, 1857; *Boston Traveller*, January 13, 1857; *Cincinnati Enquirer*, October 21, 1859; *The Boston Pilot*, August 5, 1854; and Nevins: *op. cit.*, Vol. I, pp. 344 and 451.
[40] *The Boston Pilot*, January 14, 1854.
[41] *Ibid.*, July 29, 1854. See also *ibid.*, August 2, 1852; and January 7, 14, and 21, and April 1, 1854.

Know-Nothingism was essentially anti-Catholic in all parts of the United States except the South, where little was said of the religious issue and discussions were confined to the evils of immigration. Revelations of expriests and the rantings of antipopery preachers like the "Angel Gabriel" again whipped excited Protestants to the point of mob action. Charles Pascal Telesphore Chiniquy, twice suspended from the Catholic priesthood for grave moral delinquencies, represents a type of antipopery preacher who reflected little credit upon his Protestant confrères. Incidentally, it was he who later posed as the confidant of Lincoln and circulated the stories of Lincoln's assassination as part of a Jesuit plot, a pure fabrication that will not down in spite of the many times it has been exposed. Alessandro Gavazzi, an Italian priest, was another who came to America "to destroy the Pope"[42] under American police protection. He advised Protestants against employing Catholic servant girls, lest they turn out to be Jesuit spies.[43] Gavazzi, in 1858, published *My Recollections of the Last Four Popes.* The "Angel Gabriel" (John S. Orr) mounted the steps of the New York City Hall each Sunday, blew loud blasts on his trumpet, asked his companion to play several tunes on the accordion, and then launched his attacks on the Catholics.[44] Know-Nothing literature insisted that Washington had had the Pope in mind when he counseled against foreign entanglements and that the Mississippi Valley was not only "the Pope's heritage" but already mapped and surveyed by the Jesuits.[45] Orangemen were especially enthusiastic about distributing anti-Catholic literature of this type. Occasionally, German liberals like Henry Boernstein, who edited the St. Louis *Anzeiger des Westens,* joined in the enterprise. Even the homestead law was described as a "scheme of the Jesuits to extend the Catholic religion in our country, and to cripple or put down the Protestant faith."[46]

The *Uncle Tom's Cabin* of Know-Nothingism was *Maria Monk's Awful Disclosures of the Hotel Dieu Convent of Montreal, or the*

[42] See McMaster: *op. cit.,* Vol. VIII, pp. 76-83.
[43] See *The New York Times,* June 16 and March 25, 1853.
[44] See McMaster: *op. cit.,* Vol. VIII, pp. 86-87.
[45] See Branch: *op. cit.,* p. 390; and Ray A. Billington: "Anti-Catholic Propaganda and the Home Missionary Movement, 1800-1860," in *Mississippi Valley Historical Review,* Vol. XXII, pp. 361-384. See also Thomas O'Gorman: *A History of the Roman Catholic Church in the United States* (New York, 1895), p. 454.
[46] See also speeches in *Congressional Globe,* 30C., 1S., especially by Representative Levin of Pennsylvania.

Secrets of Black Nunnery Revealed, first published by Harpers in 1836 and followed by *Further Disclosures by Maria Monk* in 1837, which were published in large editions to feed the nativist excitement of the 1850's. These books reeked with stories of immorality and obscenity, and developed in lurid detail all the orthodox stories of illegitimate births and priestly cunning that still make the rounds in anti-Catholic literature. Maria Monk happened to have several babies out of wedlock, but by the time the second child arrived, she blamed neither Protestant nor Catholic clergy for her indiscretions.

The popularity of Know-Nothingism in the South was due to other factors than the anti-Catholic agitation, for, in many parts of the South, the religious issue was not stressed. In 1855, the Know-Nothings won notable victories in Kentucky, Tennessee, and Louisiana, and, in 1856, 480,000 of the 874,000 votes polled by Fillmore, the American candidate for President, came from below Mason and Dixon's line. The South opposed immigration, as has already been pointed out in an earlier connection, because immigrants helped to destroy the political balance between North and South and added to the antislavery vote. Southerners had steadily opposed the Homestead Bill on the ground that it was an abolitionist, free-soil measure designed to fill the West with immigrants and thus to tip the balance still further in favor of the free-state section. Southerners had come to believe that they had made a great mistake in not insisting that it be a felony to bring in an Irishman or a German when it was considered piracy to bring in an African. Senator Thompson of Kentucky wanted to keep the "socialism of France" and "Kossuthism from Hungary and Italy" out of the United States, and Senators Brown of Mississippi and Dawson of Georgia gladly joined forces with him in opposition to the Homestead Bill.[47] Furthermore, old political alignments were breaking up, and Southern Whigs could no longer support their old party because of its division over the slavery question. It was perhaps asking too much to expect them immediately to join the Democratic party. Instead, the Know-Nothing party in 1856 became their political refuge and turned out to be a halfway station for many Southern Whigs on their way to the Democratic camp.

[47] For Know-Nothing opposition to the Texas Germans, see also John P. Sanderson: *Republican Landmarks* (Philadelphia, 1856); and Olmsted: *Journey Through Texas,* 436-437 and 500-502.

In 1850, various nativist lodges were combined into the Supreme Order of the Star Spangled Banner, or the Sons of the Sires, "whose daily horror and nightly specter was the Pope." Organized eventually into three degrees—much after the Masonic pattern—the initiate swore mighty oaths in the presence of "Sam" to have no traffic with Catholics, to eject Catholics from public office, and to vote only for native Americans. Equipped with all the paraphernalia of grips, ritual, passwords, and signs, the movement grew rapidly and presently began to strike terror into the hearts of old-line politicians by the mysterious influence it exercised in elections. In 1854, it exerted real influence in local campaigns in Massachusetts, Pennsylvania, and Maryland, and, without making any public appeal, came within 35,000 votes of polling as many votes for the governorship of New York as their major party opponents. Know-Nothings appeared in Congress, and a candidate considered a joke in Massachusetts was elected to the governorship by 33,000, carrying a Know-Nothing legislature in with him. He was reëlected in 1855 and again in 1856. In 1855, there were governors and legislatures of Know-Nothing persuasion in seven states, and Horace Greeley, who hated the movement, believed that from 75 to 100 members of Congress were either openly or secretly attached to the Know-Nothing Order. The *New York Herald* seriously discussed the possibility of a Know-Nothing President in 1856. The Democrats denounced the movement vigorously in order to hold the immigrant vote; the Republicans flirted with the new movement so openly that the new political liaison later became quite embarrassing.

In the meantime, the country was experiencing another epidemic of rioting. Stones were thrown through the windows of Catholic churches in Boston,[48] the turner hall in Cincinnati was attacked,[49] and large numbers of Germans and Irish were injured in election riots.[50] A Catholic church was blown up in Dorchester, Massachusetts, although the *Methodist Christian Advocate* attributed the force of the explosion to the guns and powder supposed to have been stored in the church.[51] "Guards of Liberty" organized in Rhode Island to fight the Catholics;[52] the papal nuncio was burned

---

[48] See *The Boston Transcript*, July 9, 1855.
[49] See *Der deutsche Pionier*, Vol. XVIII, pp. 368-373.
[50] See *The Boston Pilot*, March 18, 1854.
[51] See *ibid.*, July 29, 1854.
[52] See *ibid.*, August 5, 1854.

in effigy in Cincinnati and other towns,[53] and Catholic church services were stopped by rowdies in Bath, Maine.[54] Catholic sisters were showered with rotten eggs in Chillicothe, Ohio,[55] and there were other outrages against churches and priests.[56] Foreign militia companies were disbanded; the Irish were dismissed from hotels and fire departments; and advertisements for male and female help began to read: "Irish need not apply." [57] Ruffians in Baltimore, during local elections, delighted in striking Irish and German residents with large shoemakers' awls, the symbol of their nativism. German picnics were annoyed by the firing of sling shots and revolvers, and the turner formed military companies in self-defense.[58] In view of these disturbances, immigration declined in 1855 to less than half of what it had been in the preceding year.

In New York, a secret society was organized for boys too young to join the Know-Nothings. The emblem of this "Order of the American Star" was a star with a 67 on it, the age at which Washington died. The chief duty of these young enthusiasts seemed to be to escort street preachers into Roman Catholic neighborhoods and to stand guard while they abused the Irish and the Pope.[59]

The strategy of the persecuted foreigners in meeting these assaults varied. The Germans tried to show scientifically and logically how valuable immigration had been to the United States in dollars and cents.[60] Others organized to strike back, either politically— through the *sag nichts* organizations sponsored by the Democratic party—or, if necessery, by force.[61] Other Germans opposed the idea of a union of foreigners against nativism because "it would drive us into a union with Irishmen, those American Croats . . . ." [62] The

---

[53] See *The Cleveland Plain Dealer*, January 25 and February 8, 1854.
[54] See *The Boston Herald*, November 13, 1855.
[55] See McMaster: *op. cit.*, Vol. VIII, pp. 76-78.
[56] See *The Boston Herald*, August 25, 1855; and *The Boston Pilot*, September 16, 1854.
[57] See *The Boston Pilot*, September 30 and October 21, 1854; *Boston Herald*, August 8 and December 3, 1855; and *Cleveland Plain Dealer* June 7, 1854.
[58] See L. P. Heminghausen: *"Reminiscences of the Political Life of the German-Americans in Baltimore,"* in *Annual Report of the Society for the History of the Germans in Maryland*, Vol. VIII-XIV. See also Joseph Schafer: "Knownothingism in Wisconsin," in *Wisconsin Magazine of History*, Vol. VIII, pp. 3-21.
[59] See McMaster: *op. cit.*, Vol. VIII, p. 86.
[60] See Louis Schade: *The Immigration Into the United States of America from a Statistical and National Economical Point of View* (Washington, D. C., 1856).
[61] See *Steubenville Herald*, January 16, 1856; *Cleveland Plain Dealer*, March 27, 1855; and *Der Westbote*, October 6, 1854.
[62] See *Wisconsin Demokrat* for August 17, 1854, quoted in Ernest Bruncken: "The Political Activity of Wisconsin Germans, 1854-1860," in *Proceedings of the State Historical Society of Wisconsin* (1901), pp. 196-197.

strategy of the Irish was to expose the Know-Nothing ritual [63] and to caution patience, prudence, and common sense. Irish immigrants were urged to become citizens and to acquire farms in the West if possible.[64] When their militia companies were disbanded, they were urged to form new ones. *The Boston Pilot* actually favored a plan to make naturalization more difficult [65] and welcomed a decline in immigration because this would mean fewer radicals and infidels. Irishmen were advised to ignore the insults of street preachers, to stay at home, and to keep cool.[66] At elections, the Irish were urged to go quietly and singly to the voting booths and to return to their homes as quickly as possible, and to attend no political meetings or caucuses.[67]

In view of all the excitement, the accomplishments of Know-Nothing governors and legislators were not impressive. In Massachusetts, where the order was in control of the state government for a time, the foreign militia companies were disbanded and some fire departments were reorganized. Playing at war by organizations "officered by foreigners in strange dress and mustering under strange flags" came to an end.[68] To strike at the foreign organ grinder, the Massachusetts legislature proposed to make his playing a workhouse offense.[69] Studies were made of the almshouses and houses of correction, and it was claimed that a large majority of the inmates were foreigners.[70] Finally, a "smelling committee" was appointed to investigate the Massachusetts nunneries and convents. It reported that enough had been uncovered to warrant legislation, but the smelling committee had meantime fallen into such disrepute, because of its junketing trip through the convents, that it in turn had to be investigated, and several members were expelled from their seats in the legislature. For example, it was reported that, at Roxbury, the committee "frightened the women, and scared all the girls, fingered their rosaries, pulled at their curls." [71] Governor Gardner, in his message to the legislature, opposed the use of any language in Massachusetts but English and is said to have appeared

[63] See *The Boston Pilot*, September 2, 1854.
[64] See *ibid.*, December 1, 1855.
[65] See *ibid.*, March 18, 1854.
[66] See *ibid.*, May 13, June 3, and July 8, 1854.
[67] See *ibid.*, October 14, 1854.
[68] See John P. Sanderson: *op. cit.*, pp. 232-233.
[69] See *The Boston Transcript*, April 19, 1855.
[70] See *ibid.*, July 19, 1854; and January 9, February 16, and April 25, 1855.
[71] *The Boston Pilot*, June 30, 1855.

in homespun.[72]   The *Boston Herald* denounced the Know-Nothing legislature as a body with the "minimum amount of brains . . . compatible with the existence of a legislator." [73]   Although Gardner was reëlected to the governorship in 1855, the new legislature had quite a different complexion.[74]   In Maryland, petitions were circulated, without results, to suppress the convents of the state.[75] In New York, the Know-Nothings became politically powerful in 1855 and won in the state elections of that year.[76]   Curiously enough, the candidate for governor was said to have been born of German-Jewish parents in India.   The colored voters of Albany voted Know-Nothing to show their hatred for the Irish, and a German ran for state treasurer on the Know-Nothing ticket.[77]

In national politics, the Know-Nothing movement reached its climax in 1856, when it nominated Millard Fillmore, who had joined the order, as its Presidential candidate.   True to the old tradition of coöperation between Whigs and nativists, Fillmore was also the candidate of what was left of the Whig party.   The Know-Nothings demanded an end to pauper and criminal immigration, the repeal of state laws which permitted foreigners to vote before they had completed the naturalization process, and the repeal of Congressional land grants to unnaturalized foreigners.   They opposed the "aggressive policy and corrupting tendencies"of the Roman Catholic Church, favored filling public offices with Americans by "birth, education, and training," opposed exclusion of the *Bible* from the public schools, and advocated a 21-year residence requirement for naturalization.   The platform was a curious hodgepodge, which, in addition to the planks noted above, demanded the enforcement of the fugitive slave law to please the South and condemned Pierce and the Kansas-Nebraska Act with the obvious purpose of pleasing the North.   As a matter of fact, the movement was already

[72] See *ibid.*, January 20, 1855.
[73] See *The Boston Herald*, November 1, 1855.
[74] See *ibid.*, November 7, 1855.
[75] See *The Boston Transcript*, February 16, 1856.
[76] See Scisco: *op. cit.*, p. 167.
[77] See *ibid.*, pp. 123, 125, 217, and 236.   For additional data on the Know-Nothings, see J. B. McMaster: *With the Fathers* (New York, 1902), pp. 87-106; George H. Haynes: "The Causes of Knownothing Success in Massachusetts," in *American Historical Review*, Vol. III, p. 67 *et seq.*; Samuel C. Busey: *Immigration: Its Evils and Consequences* (New York, 1856); and John P. Senning: "The Knownothing Movement in Illinois from 1854 to 1856," in *Journal of the Illinois State Historical Society*, Vol. VII, pp. 7-33; and Fred H. Harrington: "Fremont and the North Americans," in *The American Historical Review*, Vol. XLIV, pp. 842-848.

on the decline, torn to shreds by the growing slavery controversy. In 1856, the Democrats denounced Know-Nothingism, whereas the Republicans found it advantageous to cater to all elements.

In the meantime, nativism had been thoroughly aired on the floor of Congress. Nathaniel Banks of Massachusetts [78] and William S. Barry of Mississippi denounced Know-Nothingism in the House. The gentleman from Mississippi apparently believed that Know-Nothingism was "a combination of all the 'isms' . . . Abolitionism, Free-soilism, Whigism, Women-Rightism, Socialism, Anti-Rentism" . . . mingling their currents in one common channel." [79] L. M. Keith of South Carolina denounced the movement as an ally of abolitionism,[80] but at the same time argued that the North had used immigration to acquire political dominion over the South. Samuel A. Smith, a Tennessee Democrat, opposed Know-Nothingism because it was a refuge for the Whigs,[81] and J. S. Millson of Virginia opposed the order as another attempt to grab the spoils of office from the two old parties,[82] who apparently should have a monopoly in this field of government. Thomas Ruffin of North Carolina compared the secrecy of Know-Nothingism with the Jesuitism it denounced. He praised the Irish militia companies in Boston, who had made possible the return of fugitive slaves, and sang the praises of the Germans in the West. He reminded his hearers that politicians who, before election, court the foreigner by praising his "rich Irish brogue" or "sweet German accent" after election describe the same people as "splay-footed Irish bog trotters" and "damned lop-eared Dutchmen." Ruffin warned the South to stay with the Democratic party.[83] O. R. Singleton of Mississippi denounced secret organizations as totally un-American and likely to lead to a reign of terror, and informed the South that there was a colored Know-Nothing lodge in Elmira, New York.[84] J. R. Chandler of Pennsylvania spoke as a Catholic to deny all intention on the part of the Pope to intervene in American politics.[85]

Among the staunch defenders of Know-Nothingism in the House of Representatives were L. M. Cox of Kentucky and A. R. Sollers

[78] See *Congressional Globe*, 33C., 2S., Appendix, pp. 48-53.
[79] See *ibid.*, p. 59.
[80] See *ibid.*, pp. 66-70.
[81] See *ibid.*, pp. 151-155.
[82] See *ibid.*, pp. 246-248.
[83] See *ibid.*, pp. 349-353.
[84] See *ibid.*, pp. 266-271.
[85] See *ibid.*, pp. 111-116.

of Maryland. Both defended its secrecy, and the latter denied that the order waged war on Catholics, insisting that its sole purpose was to keep religion out of politics and to prevent the union of Church and State.[86] Samuel D. Evans of Texas deplored the clannishness of the immigrant and regretted that even the "tender and beautiful attraction of sexual sympathy" will not break down the barriers between Irish and German.[87] William S. Barry of Mississippi, in spite of his disapproval of the secret Know-Nothing Order, saw in German infidelity and Sabbath desecration one of the most legitimate causes for its existence.[88] Thomas P. Akers of Missouri labored to prove that the American party was not proscriptive but merely wished to prolong the probationary period for naturalization because "the machinery of our government is delicate and complex in its structure" and "its motion is regulated by the great balance-wheel of free suffrage," wherefore it must not be touched by a foreigner until he can do so with safety for American institutions.[89] W. R. Smith of Alabama was probably the most eloquent defender of nativism. He described in frightful language the dangers of Oriental immigration and wanted to impose oaths of allegiance before letting any European get off his ship. He feared plotters of revolution and believed that "the sooner our children are taught that the Jesuits and priests have been raised from their cradles to seduce us, the better for us." [90] So much for Congressional eloquence!

Fillmore carried but one state, Maryland, in 1856, though he polled over half his vote in the South. The returns indicated that, in many parts of the South, the Know-Nothings had temporarily absorbed the Whigs. Within another year, the movement was stone-dead. The last meeting of its National Council was held in June, 1857, and the order lingered on for only a little while longer in local and state politics. The abandonment of secrecy was one reason for its decline, for this removed the mystery which had been its strength with friends and foes alike. Splits occurred as a result of contests for personal power. The South repudiated anti-Catholicism and turned to the Democratic party. But above all, Know-

[86] See *ibid.*, 70-72.
[87] See *ibid.*, 34 C. 3 S., p. 573.
[88] See *ibid.*, 33 C., 2 S. *Appendix*, 53-60.
[89] See *ibid.*, 34 C. 3 S., *Appendix*, January 14, 1857.
[90] See *ibid.*, 33 C., 2 S., *Appendix*, pp. 94-103.

Nothingism could not avoid the controversy over slavery and, like other groups, went to pieces on that issue.

In an attempt to avoid the dangerous sectional contest, the order had added a third, or Union, degree to its ritual requiring members to take an oath to maintain the Union. It was all to no avail. By the summer of 1855, the Know-Nothings of Ohio and Massachusetts were clearly committed to abolitionism, and the Pennsylvania group was split in its state convention by the secession of the free-soilers and abolitionists. In Illinois, the state council adopted anti-slavery resolutions after a hard fight.[91] The platform of 1856 pleased very few by its crude attempt to straddle all the issues; and delegates from Ohio, Pennsylvania, Iowa, Illinois, Connecticut, Rhode Island, and Massachusetts seceded from the Convention, denouncing the platform. They called another convention, endorsed Fremont, the Republican candidate, and soon joined the ranks of the new party—much to the discomfort and alarm of foreign-born Republicans, whom the party leaders would now have to try to drive in double harness with their erstwhile nativist enemies. In 1846, an enthusiastic Pennsylvania Congressman had said that nativism was "as natural to our soil as the mountains that rise in the clouds, or the rivers that water our plains,"[92] but Know-Nothingism disappeared as fast as it had come, lost sight of in the slavery controversy that was rapidly approaching the appeal to arms.

Know-Nothingism had accomplished little of practical significance, and, in the course of the Civil War, the doors were thrown open wider than ever before to all immigrants who wished to come. Much of its program was based on intolerance and bigotry, nursed by the clannishness, aloofness, and aggressiveness of the Roman Catholic Church and the German radical group. Its desire to stop fraud in elections and to regulate immigration, naturalization, and registration more effectively was based on sound reasons and was entirely justifiable. Paupers and criminals and other undesirables had not been excluded hitherto, and there were many such who passed within our gates. There were legitimate reasons to protest against the turbulence and irregularities of the "foreign vote." Most of the members of the Know-Nothing order probably were sincere, patriotic, middle-class Americans.

[91] *The Boston Herald*, July 3, 6, and 14, 1855.
[92] See *Congressional Globe*, 29 C. 1 S., *Appendix*, p. 46.

THE A. P. A. AND K. K. K.

Nativism is a hardy perennial, and the storms of the Civil War and Reconstruction did no more than sear its leaves. The roots remained sound. With the flood of "new immigrants" who entered the United States after the Civil War and submerged the older strains, which had now become "desirable" and "respectable," there was adequate new nourishment to feed the new growth of nativism. It came to full bloom again in the A. P. A. agitation of the early 1890's and in the Ku Klux Klan of the War and post-war years.

Various lodges survived the debacle of Know-Nothingism in the 1850's. Although they were essentially social and fraternal and benevolent societies, nativism remained a part of their middle-class 100 per cent American psychology. The Junior Order of United American Mechanics may serve as a typical example. It consistently opposed the entrance of pauper immigrants, demanded a head tax on immigrants, and advocated 21 years' residence for naturalized Americans before they might hold public office.[93] At special ceremonies of the order in Philadelphia, Bishop Potter of New York deplored the constant dilution of the quality of American manhood by unrestricted immigration. "Who shall respect a people who do not respect their own blood?" he asked. "Pan, who was the son of everybody, was the ugliest of the gods."[94] Lodges of the Patriotic Order of the Sons of America frequently made their picnics the occasion to expound their fears of immigration.[95] "Unrestricted immigration," wrote another commentator on the quality of the newer arrivals, "acts slowly upon a people, like the oozing leak of a sewer pipe into the crystal water of a well."[96] The desire to stop the competition of cheap foreign labor usually received a patriotic coloring by stressing the danger of admitting anarchists and dynamiters who sought "to exalt the red flag of the commune above the stars and stripes."[97]

It is significant that many moderates advocated a drastic change in American immigration regulations. John A. Roebling, descendant of an immigrant, favored a reduction in immigration by 75

[93] See *The Cleveland Plain Dealer,* July 21 and September 19, 1887.
[94] See *The Philadelphia Press,* May 1, 1889.
[95] See *ibid.,* May 14, 1889; and *The Ohio State Journal,* July 5 and December 7, 1889.
[96] Julia H. Twells: "The Burden of Indiscriminate Immigration," in *American Journal of Politics,* Vol. V, pp. 608-616.
[97] See *The Ohio State Journal,* September 11, 1892.

per cent, a literacy test in the rudiments of English, and temporary restrictions "until that day when, our own national problem solved, we are able to offer all the world, not a tenement house and four dollars a week, but true American prosperity." [98] The Reverend B. W. Williams, although opposing wholesale and indiscriminate debarment, favored a more stringent policy, because of the difference between the character of the old and the new immigration. He accused the newer arrivals, as some of their predecessors had been accused earlier, of ignorance and viciousness, of holding "licentious and demoralizing social theories," and of atheism, agnosticism, and Sabbath desecration.[99] Chauncey M. Depew, eloquent spokesman for Americanism and the New York Central Railroad, apparently believed that foreigners came to the United States "to destroy our government, cut our throats, and divide our property." Immigrants were still being naturalized in platoons before Election Day in the 1890's, with expenses paid by campaign managers, as they had been in the 1850's. In 1895, John Fiske was president of an Immigration Restriction League, and on his staff of vice presidents were men like George F. Edmunds, Richard Mayo-Smith, Robert Treat Paine, Nathaniel S. Shaler, Leverett Saltonstall, and Samuel B. Capen.

The policy of "separatism" followed by the Catholic Church after the close of the Civil War played its part in fanning the embers of nativism into flame again. Leaders of the Church sponsored, not only separate schools, but separate fraternal orders and other Catholic institutions as well. Some of its members had views on social questions that clashed with Protestant puritanism, and the old battles over Sunday observance were fought all over again by two groups between whom there was not only a religious cleavage but sometimes also economic and social barriers. Catholic attacks on the public schools were often indiscreet, in spite of irritating provocations, and the two points of view seemed irreconcilable. When clerical pressure was used to keep Catholic children out of the public schools, because of their alleged Protestant bias, there almost immediately followed the cry against "double taxation" by Catholic parents who paid taxes for public education and had to support their parochial schools as well.

[98] John A. Roebling: "Economic Aspects of Immigration," in *The American Magazine of Civics*, Vol. IX, pp. 235-245.
[99] See B. W. Williams: "Our Attitude Toward Foreigners," in *The American Magazine of Civics*, Vol. VIII, pp. 64-68.

The quarrels over the school question regarding public support, standards, curriculum, and other details have been live issues in some state legislatures until very recently. In the 1870's, there was much discussion of the "Poughkeepsie Plan" and the "Faribault Plan," by which boards of education leased parochial schools, paid the operating expenses, employed Catholic teachers approved by the Church and properly qualified, and tacked special religious instruction on to the regular curriculum. The plan was put into operation in some cities, although the clergy itself was divided on the question. Needless to add, it immediately became a political issue and helped to feed the membership of a new crop of Anti-Catholic societies.

The technique and organization of these societies need not delay us long. In almost every respect, they followed the example of their predecessors. The Democrats were usually accused of an alliance with the Catholics, whereas the Republicans flirted with the nativists and made an issue of the school question; and a number of local and state elections in the 1870's and 1880's began to reflect these controversies. Large Eastern cities were beginning to have their first Catholic mayors, and Tammany was more and more becoming the citadel of the Irish. Massachusetts was described as a "Roman Conquest," and the Irish question became an issue in national politics—especially in 1884, 1888, and 1892, as already noted. The opposition of some of the Catholic hierarchy to organized labor and other reforms provided another excellent opportunity to mobilize American workingmen against a "foreign" Church. Enlightened clerics like Cardinal Gibbons and Archbishop Ireland, on the other hand, worked hard to "Americanize" the Church on these issues, but their labors were generally overlooked in the excitement over alleged Papal control of American institutions.

The A. P. A. The American Protective Association was born in Clinton, Iowa, in 1887, through the efforts of Henry F. Bowers. By 1893, it claimed a huge membership in 20 states, although exact figures were never made available. It was surprisingly strong in the Middle Western *"Bible* belt," where the rapid growth of the Catholic Church had become as alarming to nativists as it was elsewhere. As a matter of fact, the Church practically doubled its membership in the United States in the last quarter of the nineteenth century, largely as a result of heavy immigration. Catholics began to compete in the professions as well as in the trades with their Protestant neighbors, thereby adding to the religious issue an economic motive for forming a new anti-Catholic group.

The A. P. A. admitted foreign-born citizens, provided they believed in God and would have no traffic with Roman Catholics. W. J. H. Traynor, who made the A. P. A. a national enterprise, came from Canada and was Grand Master of the Orange Lodge of Michigan. It is significant that the movement was especially strong among the Scotch-Irish. In Missouri, Nebraska, Ohio, Wisconsin, and Illinois, and in New England cities, the school question was immediately brought to the fore. In Wisconsin and Illinois, laws that made school attendance compulsory caused a storm of protest from all defenders of separate schools, Protestant and Catholic alike, because this legislation also provided that teaching in the elementary grades be in the English language. In the bitter political campaigns fought over these issues, the A. P. A. planted the seed of its new anti-Catholic and antiforeign crusade.[100] Whatever the merits of the issue, these campaigns frequently resulted in the raising of standards in the separate schools.[101]

The rising labor issue in the late 1880's led to bitter opposition between American workmen and Slavic, Italian, and other competitors from southern and eastern Europe. Because the Catholic priesthood opposed secret societies and included labor groups— such as the Knights of Labor—in this category, the Church gained a reputation in some quarters of being unfriendly to organized labor. Presently the "Jesuit plot" to capture the American school system was broadened to include an assault upon American labor standards and trade unions as well. The monopoly of public offices by the Irish in Boston and New York, for example, added fuel to the flames. In New York, Tammany's slogan was said to be: "Put no American on Guard"; in Boston, it was: "No American Need Apply" (for the spoils of office).

Against this background of political and economic dissension, and the hard times and unrest of the early 1890's, it was fairly easy to build up the A. P. A. to its peak, in 1893-1894. The anti-Catho-

[100] See W. F. Whyte: "The Bennett Law Campaign in Wisconsin," in *Wisconsin Magazine of History*, Vol. X, pp. 363-390; and Louise P. Kellogg: "The Bennett Law in Wisconsin," in *Wisconsin Magazine of History*, Vol. II, pp. 3-25.
[101] See also William C. Doane, Bishop of Albany: "The Roman Catholic Church and the School Fund," in *The North American Review* (January, 1894), pp. 30-40.

lic issue provided the emotional stimulus. Unfortunately, Monseigneur Satolli arrived in Washington as a Papal delegate in 1892, thus giving an apparent basis to the charge of Catholic dictation in America. In 1893, certain spurious documents, alleged to be Papal encyclicals, were widely circulated. They purported to be Papal decrees absolving Catholics from their allegiance to the United States and setting the date when the Catholics should rise in one holy massacre to slay their Protestant neighbors. Protestant ministers and the usual quota of expriests and nuns were employed to tell again the old story of Papal intrigue. On occasion, even Germans were hired to address their listeners in the German tongue, for anti-Catholicism overshadowed all other issues. The most frightful tales of priestcraft were circulated in magazines like the *A. P. A. Magazine* and the *Patriotic American* of Detroit. There were tales of priests who refused to bury war veterans until the Stars and Stripes had been removed from their coffins, of the drilling and arming of Catholic societies, and of the impending massacre, when the Papal flag would fly on every flagstaff and the Stars and Stripes be thrown "a bloodsoaked rag in the sewer." It was charged that President Cleveland had a private wire connecting the White House with Cardinal Gibbons,[102] and the panic of 1893 was blamed on the Jesuits.

In retaliation against the alleged designs of an alien priestcraft, the Toledo A. P. A.'s bought Winchester rifles. Catholic picnics were stoned and Catholic businessmen boycotted; campaigns were waged to have Catholic teachers and board members dismissed from the school system; and, on July 4, 1895, there was a street riot in Boston during a parade.[103] Eugene V. Debs, a former Catholic, was described as a disguised Jesuit and unfairly attacked for his handling of the Pullman strike in Chicago. There were the usual crop of convent stories and threats to liberate inmates of convents and monasteries by force, if necessary.

Some Catholics wanted to organize to fight the A. P. A. with its own weapons, and, in 1896, the American Catholic League was formed. Cardinal Gibbons, however, denounced the organization, opposing all secret societies and arguing that it was the duty of all

[102] See W. J. H. Traynor: "The Aims and Methods of the A. P. A.," in *The North American Review* (July, 1894), pp. 67-76; and Allen S. Will: *Life of Cardinal Gibbons* (New York, 1922), Vol. I, p. 539.
[103] See William Byrne: *The Catholic Church in the New England States* (Boston, 1899), Vol. I, pp. 97-100.

voters to select the best man for office, regardless of his religious affiliations. Some of the bishops openly deplored the quality of the recent immigration, and prominent members of the Catholic laity believed it very unwise to create a Papal legation in Washington. "The Papal delegate," wrote one protester, "has been and is a source of strength to the Apaists." [104] Bishop Spalding charged, with much truth, that employers were using the religious frenzy of the A. P. A.'s to sow dissension among their workers and to break up the labor unions. Spalding endorsed universal, compulsory public education. The agitation for a division of the school fund was disapproved by many Catholics who believed that it merely added to A. P. A. membership. Catholic patriots—such as Philip Sheridan, Charles Carroll, and Roger B. Taney—were revived by Catholics in these A. P. A. days to remind their Protestant neighbors that no one Church had a monopoly of patriotism.[105]

The Protestant ministry as a whole maintained strict silence while these attacks on their Catholic brethren were going on, and some ministers profited by the movement and accepted lucrative speaking engagements in its behalf. A noble exception was Dr. Washington Gladden, distinguished liberal minister of the First Congregational Church of Columbus, Ohio, and something of a national figure as one of the first exponents of the new social gospel. In magazines like the *Century* and the *Arena*, he courageously exposed the anti-Catholic forgeries and denounced the bigotry and intolerance of his Protestant brethren.[106] His championship of religious toleration and fair play cost him the presidency of Ohio State University, because of the influence of an A. P. A.-controlled Ohio legislature.

The connection between the A. P. A.'s and the Republican party was close. In 1894, the organization claimed 1,000,000 members, and affiliations with another 250,000 who belonged to similar so-

[104] See George P. Lathrop: "Catholic Loyalty," in *The North American Review* (August, 1894), pp. 218-224. See also, J. L. Spalding, Bishop of Peoria: "Catholicism and Apaism," in *The North American Review* (September, 1894), pp. 278-287.
[105] See also "Bishop Keane's Defense of the Church Against the Attack of the A. P. A. and Anti-Catholic Movements in General," in *Catholic Oratory, a Compilation of Sacred and Sublime Orations* (New York, 1895), pp. 1-6; George P. Lathrop and William C. Doane, Bishop of Albany: "Hostility to Roman Catholics," in *The North American Review* (May, 1894), pp. 563-582; and Charles Robinson: "The Threatened Revival of Knownothingism," in *The American Journal of Politics*, Vol. V, pp. 504-525.
[106] See *The Ohio State Journal*, October 3, 1892.

cieties. The order won local triumphs in Ohio, Colorado, Wisconsin, Michigan, Iowa, Indiana, Missouri, and elsewhere, and claimed 100 members in the 54th Congress. In the Northwest, it enrolled Germans and Scandinavians in the battle against Catholicism, and counted many Canadians in its membership in Michigan. A press of some 70 weeklies kept up the defamatory attacks on the Papacy and the Catholic Church. The Democrats opposed the movement, and the South generally regarded it as a mere camouflage for the Republican party.

In spite of constant assertions by its leaders that the A. P. A. had nothing in its ritual against the "religious dogmas of any ecclesiastical corporation" and was not opposed to the foreign-born as such, it nevertheless stressed the dangers of immigration to American institutions and denounced the "immigrant vote" as such. The organization favored naturalization requirements ranging from 7 to 21 years' residence and selected immigration, as well as drastic restriction. No employment was to be given to unnaturalized foreigners and no language but the "American language" was to be taught in the public schools.[107]

The A. P. A. boom that set in after 1893, when "the ambitious politician suddenly awoke to the realization that baptism in A. P. A. water was attended with pleasant and profitable political consequences," [108] proved to be short-lived. President Traynor believed the A. P. A. had become too aggressive for its own good. Many politicians welcomed its support before election, and then proved to be weak and unreliable after the campaign was over. There was internal dissension in the order; its promises could not be carried out and its membership could not be held to the high emotional pitch to which it had been keyed. Some of its leaders proved to be spoils politicians as bad as the Irish and other foreign bosses whom they denounced. There were charges of corruption, such as those that broke up the Ku Klux Klan in more recent times. Other organizations split off from the main stem, some for purely financial reasons. In spite of the close affiliation with the Republicans, the A. P. A. leadership refused to support McKinley for President in 1896, which was probably a serious mistake. Most important, however, in explaining the collapse of the A. P. A. is the populist and

[107] See *Public Opinion*, Vol. XVI, p. 45.
[108] See W. J. H. Traynor: "Policy and Power of the A. P. A.," in *The North American Review* (June, 1896), pp. 658-666.

free-silver crusade of the 1890's. As Know-Nothingism was smashed on the rocks of the antislavery contest in 1856, so A. P. A.-ism went to pieces before the larger issues of free silver and "Bryanism" in 1896. Officially, the A. P. A. died in 1911, when its last president died, although virtually, it expired in 1900. It had accomplished nothing of its legislative program, although in 1892, the Prohibition and Populist party platforms contained planks directed against the immigrant.[109]

After the collapse of the American Protective Association, small lodges and societies continued its nativist and anti-Catholic tradition. Up to the World War, the immigration from Catholic countries remained heavy, thus providing one of the factors necessary for a possible revival of nativism. "The Guardians of Liberty" were organized in 1911, and made special headway among Masons and anti-Catholic Protestants. *The Menace*, an anti-Catholic weekly, was said to have had a circulation of nearly 1,500,000 at the time the World War broke out.

The K. K. K. The war brought on an intense wave of nationalism in all countries, and the United States was no exception. With it came the "Nordic cult" and a dramatic revival of nativism, which blossomed out in the Ku Klux Klan. This organization was formed in Atlanta, Georgia, by W. J. Simmons, a former circuit rider of the Methodist Church and professor of history at Lanier University, who seems to have had a special weakness for display and secret societies but who revealed none of the venal qualities of those who eventually took the leadership of the Klan out of his hands.

On the battlefields of the World War, the "wop," the "dago," the "hunky," and the "nigger" seem to have fought as loyally to make the world safe for democracy as any blue-blooded Yankee, but their patriotism was quickly forgotten under the economic stresses and strains of the post-war years, when they again entered the com-

[109] For further data on the A. P. A. movement, see Humphrey J. Desmond: *The A. P. A. Movement* (Washington, D. C., 1912); W. J. H. Traynor: "The Menace of Romanism," in *The North American Review* (August, 1895), pp. 129-140; *Ohio State Journal*, July 1 and November 6, 1892; *A. P. A.—An Inquiry Into the Objects and Purposes of the So-called "American Protective Association,"* by "An American"; W. G. Puddefoot: "Is the Foreigner a Menace to the Nation?" in *The American Magazine of Civics*, Vol. IX, pp. 1-11; Elbert Hubbard: "The New Disease," in *The Arena* (June, 1894); Washington Gladden: "The Anti-Catholic Crusade," in *The Century* (March, 1894); and *Recollections* (Boston, 1909). For a most valuable study, see A. P. Stauffer: *Anti-Catholicism in American Politics, 1865-1900* (unpublished Doctor's dissertation, Harvard University Library).

petition for jobs. Above all, the fear of bolshevism spread like a blight over liberal America. Attorney General A. Mitchell Palmer staged an orgy of "red-baiting," and almost everything of foreign origin was likely to be regarded with suspicion. The United States quickly wearied of its European debauch and sobered up to demand that, hereafter, America should be maintained strictly for Americans. We wanted nothing more to do with Europe or any of its problems. War debts were not paid; the allies began to dispute over who won the war; and Uncle Sam, once hailed as a saviour of civilization, now was branded as a mere money-grabber, who had conserved his powers until the end, when he could safely come in for a share of the glory.

Many high-minded but somewhat hysterical American patriots suddenly awoke to a realization of the need for Americanization. Every immigrant group felt the impact of this new movement, immediately becoming sensitive to its own peculiarities and therefore likely to resist any forcible methods to change them. In the meantime, the literacy test had finally been passed in 1917 over a Presidential veto, and the United States was fast moving toward a quota law to restrict further immigration or, rather, to prevent its revival after the war years. It is against this political, economic, and psychological background that the Ku Klux Klan must be considered.

In 1915, Colonel Simmons launched the New Klan, with all its wizards, kleagles, dragons, cyclops, klonklaves, and klaverns, and all the other paraphernalia which have a special affinity for the letter *k*. In 1920, Simmons hired the "Southern Publicity Association," consisting of Edward Y. Clarke and Mrs. Elizabeth Tyler, to do the necessary promotion work and to manage the finances of his invisible empire. To become a "citizen" of this empire, one paid $10, which was to be variously divided among local and state kleagles, district goblins, and national headquarters in Atlanta. In 1922, Hiram Wesley Evans, a Texas dentist, forced himself into the organization as Imperial Wizard, and by 1925 the hooded order was said to have between four and five million members. Little effort was made by the organizers to keep out undesirables; the enthusiasm for the cause and the lure of profits were too great to suggest such caution. The Klan invaded the North, and had its greatest memberships in Ohio and Indiana. In Pennsylvania,

[506]

where the number at one time exceeded 260,000, the Pennsylvania Dutch—strange to say—became the most loyal Klansmen.

The program of the Klan included the "Christian religion," white supremacy, the protection of pure womanhood, "pure Americanism," the Constitution, states' rights, liberty and justice, better relations between capital and labor, the destruction of lawless elements and foreign agitators, the limitation of foreign immigration, and other equally lofty principles. The Klan stood for native, white, Protestant supremacy, and therefore opposed the Catholic, the Jew, the Negro, and the foreign-born, although by no means with impartial vigor in every part of the country. The Klan fought the bootlegger and the pacifist, probably regarding them both as lawbreakers of equal degree. It wanted bigger and better patriotism, and set out to control Church and school to that end. It concerned itself with the contents of textbooks; [110] in a number of states, it entered politics; and it undertook the censorship of private and public morals by floggings and startling displays of fiery crosses to bring the wrongdoer back to the paths of virtue. "White supremacy," "Nordic superiority," and "pure Americanism" became synonymous terms, and any liberal who questioned these vague concepts was denounced as worse than a "communist" or a "foreign agitator." "In a nation toleration becomes a vice when fundamentals are in danger." [111]

The arguments of the Klan are strangely suggestive of recent emanations from the dictatorships of Europe. Klansmen were told not to believe what they read in the papers, for the American press was controlled by Catholics, Jews, and immigrants. Tradesmen, small businessmen, and many typical middle-class Americans, whose education had not gone beyond the elementary schools, believed earnestly and honestly that a real menace to American institutions emanated from foreigners and Catholics. Said Imperial Wizard Evans:

> We believe that the American stock, which was bred under highly selective surroundings . . . and should not

[110] See Bessie L. Pierce: *Citizens' Organizations and the Civic Training of Youth* (New York, 1933), pp. 112-125.
[111] Quoted in Emerson H. Loucks: *The Ku Klux Klan in Pennsylvania* (Harrisburg, Pennsylvania, 1936), p. 36. This, in my opinion, is the best analysis of the Klan available, and although it is limited by title to Pennsylvania, is of great general value.

be mongrelized . . . automatically and instinctively developed the kind of civilization which is best suited to its own healthy life and growth; and that this cannot be safely changed except by ourselves and along the lines of our own character.[112]

Obviously, people born abroad could not understand the American spirit or American ideals like a native!

The American public school, "the little red schoolhouse," was once more brought into battle against the parochial school. The Klan sponsored a Federal Department of Education with wide powers and demanded *Bible* reading in the schools, prominent display of the United States flag, and the expulsion of all Catholic influences from the public schools. In their ruthless scrutiny of everything, in order to detect hidden symbols of the Roman hierarchy, Klansmen claimed to find a cross on American paper money tucked away in one corner of the bill. Catholics were to be expelled from public offices and no more elected. Under Woodrow Wilson, it was said that Secretary Tumulty, "a Catholic of the Catholics, commanded the entrance to the White House," and when Al Smith, a Catholic, actually ran for President in 1928, perfect paroxysms of fear swept the hooded ranks of the Klansmen and furnished the issue which prevented an earlier demise of their invisible empire.[113] It was maintained that Jews and Catholics controlled the moving-picture industry and thus had found another channel for poisoning the American nation.

Religion and patriotism are easily mixed in times of national strain. The Klan made visitations to many Protestant churches, leaving behind them copies of the *Bible* and flags or even a money gift for the minister. Under Klan stimulus, an old familiar hymn, became:

> Let the fiery cross be burning,
> Spread its beams o'er land and sea;
> Satan's wiles forever spurning,
> Bringing Christ to you and me.[114]

Church visitations proved to be good advertising.

The Klan satisfied the craving of many Americans for excitement and it catered to their pet hatreds—namely, Pope, foreigner, Jew,

---

[112] Quoted in *ibid.*, p. 98.
[113] See Michael Williams: *The Shadow of the Pope* (New York, 1932).
[114] Quoted in Loucks: *op. cit.*, p. 121.

"nigger," and Catholic. For thousands, its pageantry of robes and fiery crosses broke the monotony of rural and small-town life, giving them a sense of dignity and importance. But the decline of the order was as rapid as its rise. The Roman and the Russian scare failed to materialize, and even pillowcases and night riding become monotonous and lose their glamor. Times improved, and Herbert Hoover was safe in the White House, instead of Al Smith. Even auxiliary orders like the Imps (I Maintain Protestant Supremacy) and the Yellow Dogs could not revive the original thrill over Klan mysteries. Above all, the Klan had entered politics and became hardly more than just another bloc fighting for jobs. The public wearied of mob tactics, and the leaders of the Klan began to fight among themselves for the political and financial boodle. D. C. Stephenson, who captured the Klan and the Republican machine in Indiana, ended his career in jail with a life sentence for misconduct with a girl. Suits and countersuits were filed, as officials sought to grab the financial profits. It is a sorry story of racketeering, grafting, and terrorism by which the leaders exploited the credulity and ignorance of the rank and file, and no tactics were too low for this battle for political and financial power. The decent elements revolted, and the Klan eventually broke down primarily from attacks from within rather than from without.[115]

By 1928, the membership of the Klan in Pennsylvania had declined to 10,500, from a total of over 250,000 at one time. By 1930, the membership was less than 5,000. The decline was proportionate in other areas, and the invisible empire of 4,000,000 or 5,000,000 Klansmen collapsed, as had so many of its predecessors in earlier years, to live on only in small, local social clubs.[116]

IMMIGRATION LEGISLATION

The story of the actual legislation concerning immigration, culminating in the Quota and National-Origins Laws after the World War, can be quickly told.

Up to 1835, there was but one Federal enactment, the Law of 1819, which regulated the carriage of steerage passengers at sea and, for the first time, provided for the compilation and collection of statistics on immigration. It was many years, however, before

[115] For details, see *ibid.*, especially Chs. XI and XII.
[116] See also Preston W. Slosson: *The Great Crusade and After, 1914-1928* (New York, 1931), pp. 287-319, on "The Cult of Nationalism."

these statistics were adequate or accurate. State governments dealt with immigration to their ports in their own way, but for many years the Federal Congress did little but debate the question.

Before 1850, the question of the constitutionality of state regulation was carried to the Supreme Court on two occasions. The first of these cases involved an act of the New York legislature and is known as the *Mayor of the City of New York v. Miln*. It reached the United States Supreme Court in 1837. Alarmed by some of the features of the immigration movement in the 1830's, when figures began to rise sharply, several states of the North Atlantic section seriously considered ways and means to deal with the undesirables. A large number of the immigrants were women and children and infirm, who landed penniless and quickly became public charges. Shipmasters seeking cargoes and profits did little to exclude persons of this kind from the immigrant traffic. Indeed, they offered inducements in the form of low rates to any who desired to come to the United States and had no concern for the welfare or the future of their passengers once they were landed in an American port. Public opinion demanded that the shipmasters be held responsible either for the deportation of such undesirables or for the cost of caring for those who became public charges. Several state legislatures memorialized Congress for regulatory legislation, but without effect. The New York legislature thereupon passed a law requiring the master of every vessel carrying immigrants to New York to report within 24 hours the name, nativity, age, and occupation of every passenger to the mayor of New York City. Failure to do so involved a penalty of $75 for each person not reported or falsely reported.

The case that went to the Supreme Court arose from the refusal of a shipmaster to obey this law. The defendant argued that the regulation involved interstate and foreign commerce and could therefore not be passed by a state. New York contended that only the police power of a state was involved. The issues for the court to decide were whether the act in question was an exercise of the police power of a state or a regulation of commerce by a state, and, if the latter, whether the state had the power to legislate in the absence of a Federal law on the subject. The majority of the Court held that the act was a police measure and therefore entirely within the power of the state. Justices Taney, Barbour, Wayne, McLean, Thompson, and Baldwin concurred in this decision.

Justice Story dissented, on the ground that the act in question was a regulation of commerce, and devoted most of his opinion to the argument that the Federal government has exclusive jurisdiction in interstate and foreign commerce.

Twelve years later, in 1849, the United States Supreme Court was again asked to pass upon the constitutionality of immigration legislation by a state. The evils incident to the congestion of immigrants in Eastern port towns had not abated. Paupers and petty criminals continued to find their way into the United States, and Congress had done nothing to deal with undesirable immigrants. Several legislatures had enacted laws placing a tax on alien passengers, to be collected at the port of arrival, and bonds were required from the masters of vessels who brought them in. A Massachusetts statute provided that the fees collected be used to maintain a marine hospital. New York used its fee for the maintenance of pauper immigrants who became public charges. The two laws were passed on simultaneously, and the litigation is known as *The Passenger Cases*.

In the earlier case of 1837, the penalty for not registering alien passengers had been imposed upon the shipmaster. Now the fee was collected from the immigrant. Daniel Webster, who was counsel in both cases, maintained that both devices were unconstitutional. The personnel of the Court had changed in the meantime, and only three of the judges who had ruled in 1837—Taney, McLean and Wayne—were still on the bench. A majority of five judges now held that the New York and Massachusetts statutes were unconstitutional interferences with foreign commerce. Each judge wrote his own decision, and it would require too much space to analyze each opinion. Suffice it to say that, by 1850, the Supreme Court held that the alien passenger was foreign commerce and that the Court itself assumed jurisdiction over such cases. It was also established that regulations designed to protect the health and morals of a state and which did not levy fees or duties on the immigrant were within the power of the state, as long as they were reasonable and not in conflict with Congressional legislation.

From the middle thirties to the Civil War, nativism was rampant in the United States, and Congress contained members of Native American parties, or of the Know-Nothing order. Immigration was repeatedly discussed on the floor of Congress, although it is notable that the outstanding leaders of the two houses seldom had much to say on the issue. Moreover, very little was accomplished in the way of legislation. In 1836, a Senate resolution directed the State Department to study the question of the immigration of paupers and criminals. Two years later, a resolution of the House instructed a committee to investigate frauds in connection with naturalization and to study the desirability of raising the residence requirement for citizenship. Another question to be considered was the kind of legislation that might be passed to keep out vagabonds and paupers deported by other countries. A select committee reported the urgent need for immigration legislation, and some Native Americans suggested the scheme of consular inspection of immigrants at ports of departure, which has since been adopted. A bill proposing a fine of $1,000 on shipping companies bringing in undesirables was not even considered on the floor of Congress. Bills introduced by Know-Nothings in the 1850's died without action. The only legislation passed involved amendments to the Law of 1819. In 1847 and 1848, changes were enacted to provide better conditions for steerage passengers, but of these the nativists heartily disapproved. Meanwhile, New York set up its own immigration commission and established Castle Garden, in response to conditions already described.

During the Civil War, when immigration naturally declined somewhat and men were being drafted for war industries or the Army, the whole emphasis was placed on attracting more man power to the United States rather than on limiting admissions. Reference was made in earlier chapters to the recruiting of immigrants, here and abroad, for war service. In 1863, President Lincoln urged a law to stimulate immigration, in order to fill the vacuum created by the enlistment of over 1,000,000 workers for the war. On July 4, 1864, he signed a bill authorizing the President to create a Commissioner of Immigration, under the State Department, and permitting the importation of laborers from Europe under contract. The act permitted contracts for twelve months' labor to pay off the immigrant's passage to the United States, and such contracts were not to be construed by the courts as slavery or involuntary servitude. An immigration office was to be opened in New York to provide for the distribution of immigrants and to protect them against exploitation. Several companies were at once organized to deal in immigrant contract labor, but the protests against their business mounted rapidly. It was charged that the

United States would be made a "dumping ground," and labor protested vigorously. The law was repealed in 1868.

President Grant repeatedly urged the need for Federal legislation to control immigration, and the courts held definitely that immigration legislation was a regulation of commerce and that Congress should assume control. The alarm over the change from the old to the new immigration was spreading, and an increasing number of Americans began to concern themselves about "the unguarded gates." In 1875, a Federal law was passed to exclude prostitutes, but the period of national control did not really begin until 1882.

In his message of 1881, President Arthur strongly recommended Congressional action, as a result of which the first general Federal immigration law was passed in 1882. The law provided for a head tax of $.50 on all immigrants, to be collected on arrival, and it excluded lunatics, idiots, those likely to become public charges, and convicts. It is important, however, to note that criminals did not include political offenders or those who had been in trouble because of their religious convictions.

Without following the details, suffice it to say that the head tax was gradually increased until it reached $8. In 1885, a law prohibiting the importation of contract labor was passed, but it proved to be defective and was amended two years later. Deportation of those gaining admittance in violation of the immigration statutes was left to the Secretary of the Treasury. Later, in 1903, when the Department of Commerce and Labor was established, the commissioner general of immigration was transferred to this department and also vested with the responsibility for administering immigration regulations. Still later, when the department was divided, the responsibility for enforcing immigration laws and deportations was vested in the Secretary of Labor, where it has remained.

In the meantime, both houses of Congress studied the whole immigration question. A number of investigations revealed a lack of enforcement machinery, evasions, frauds, and inadequacies in the law. In 1889, a standing committee on immigration was created in the Senate, and a select committee on immigration and naturalization in the House. In 1890, a joint investigation was made. Political parties began to demand restrictions of immigration and, in 1891, another immigration law was passed. This added to the classes to be excluded polygamists (as a result of the excitement over the Mormons in Utah) and sufferers from dangerous and loath-some diseases. It forbade advertising for labor by companies in foreign countries and prohibited transportation companies from soliciting or encouraging immigration. More important, however, was a provision for the necessary quota of Federal officials to enforce the law, so that, for the first time, Federal control became a reality. Medical inspection was provided for as part of the Marine Hospital Service, and transportation companies were obligated to return at their expense within one year any alien whom they had brought in contrary to law. It should be added that organized labor in the United States lobbied for this restrictive legislation, while the Atlantic steamship companies and their allies lobbied against it.[117] As the result of further Congressional study, a provision was put into the Quarantine Act, in 1892, to give the President the right temporarily to stop all immigration if he thought there was danger of an epidemic.

In 1897, Congress passed its first literacy test bill for immigrants. One purpose of the new device was, without question, to discrimi-nate against the new immigration and to favor the old. The law provided that all who were physically able and over 16 years of age must pass a test to show their ability to read and write English or some other language. The law was generous in its exceptions, however. Parents, grandparents, wives, and minor children of ad-missible immigrants could be exempted from the literacy test. President Cleveland vetoed the bill on March 2, 1897, two days before he left the White House. Essentially, his argument was that, if immigration were to be restricted, some other more equitable and practical plan must be found, and he had little difficulty in prov-ing that the literacy test was merely a test of opportunity and not a test of innate ability, character, or general usefulness to the United States. It tested whether the immigrant had had a chance to learn to read and write but not whether he would be a desirable or undesirable addition to the American stock. Presidents Taft and Wilson vetoed similar measures, on substantially similar grounds, in their respective administrations. The literacy test finally became a part of the American system of immigration regu-lations when, in 1917, during the excitement and hysteria of the war years, it was passed over President Wilson's veto.

[117] See, for example, Fritz Josephy: *Die deutsche überseeische Auswanderung seit 1871* (Berlin, 1912), pp. 46-47.

The year 1902 brought further investigations and an excellent report by the Industrial Commission. In 1903, it was made unlawful to assist in the illegal admission or naturalization of an alien anarchist, an exclusion prompted by the assassination of President McKinley by a Polish anarchist at the Pan-American Exposition in Buffalo. In 1907, the Immigration Commission was created, and the President was authorized to take up the whole question of the migration of population in international conferences with foreign nations. Other provisions dealt with the abusive use of passports to gain entrance into the United States from our insular possessions. In 1910, a law was enacted to strike at the white slave traffic. Meanwhile—in 1882, 1884, 1888, 1892, 1902, and 1904—laws had been passed to exclude the Chinese. These have been referred to in the chapter on Oriental immigration.

The World War virtually stopped immigration for a time. This probably provided the necessary pause for a review of the traditional American policy of keeping the door open for immigrants. Undesirables had been debarred with increasing effectiveness by the authorities at Ellis Island and at other ports of entry, but numerically, there was no limit on those who might enter. The era of free lands was coming to an end in the United States, and the evils of industrialism were descending rapidly on the New Canaan. In the larger cities, the competition between alien and native-born laborers was becoming keener, and organized labor viewed unrestricted immigration as a device by which capitalist employers used docile laborers from abroad to keep wages down and to break up unions. Eastern and southern Europeans seemed harder to assimilate than the older immigrants, and they were swarming to the United States by the thousands. Men like Lothrop Stoddard and Madison Grant raised a cry of alarm against the barbarians storming the gates of America and preached the gospel of Nordic superiority. Nativists combined with more moderate students of immigration to argue that, whatever else might be said, the United States could no longer absorb 1,000,000 aliens a year without disaster to all classes concerned.[118]

The World War accentuated nationalism and 100 per cent Americanism, which added the necessary psychological factor to the economic, social, and political arguments favoring a restriction of immigration. In 1917, the literacy test was at last established, over

[118] See Madison Grant: *The Conquest of a Continent* (New York, 1933).

the veto of three Presidents. In the same year, besides raising the head tax, an additional exclusion was provided including anarchists and all who favored the overthrow of law and government by force and violence, thus leaving the door wide open to many confusing and different interpretations. Deportation could now be enforced within five years of the time of arrival, and before long a "Red Ark" departed from the United States carrying out undesirable aliens, whose political and economic views were considered unsound and dangerous.

Congress might have stopped with these enactments had it not been for the reactions that followed the close of the World War. The United States was through with Europe and had no interest in the radical experiments that broke out in Russia and elsewhere. A popular song entitled "Don't Bite the Hand That's Feeding You" made it perfectly clear that, whoever did not wish to preserve the *status quo* in the United States, should "go back to where he came from." Moreover, it was assumed that millions of Europeans would flock to the United States after the war to escape the burdens of war debts, reconstruction, and defeat, and that thus the whole American standard of living would once more be jeopardized by a flood of pauper labor from abroad. An analysis of the debates in Congress will show that there was a general feeling of dissatisfaction with the newer immigrants as contrasted with the old, a belief that immigration would increase unemployment in the United States and depress labor standards, and a growing feeling that American social and political institutions must be protected against "reds," "hyphenates," and others who were likely to criticize the established order. It was agreed, moreover, contrary to the traditional policy of the United States since its beginning as a nation, that political and religious refugees should no longer receive special exemptions from immigration restrictions.

In 1921, Congress passed an emergency law limiting annual immigration from European countries to 3 per cent of the number of foreign-born of each nationality present in the United States in 1910. In 1924, the quota basis was changed to 2 per cent, and hereafter this percentage was to be computed on the Census of 1890 instead of that of 1910. Obviously, this change was intended to favor immigration from the British Isles and northern and western Europe and to strike with special discriminatory force against the Greeks, Italians, and Slavs from southern and eastern Europe. Finally, after July 1, 1927, the total number of immigrants who might come into the United States in any one year was arbitrarily fixed at 150,000, and this number was only slightly raised in 1929. This was the so-called "National-Origins Law." The number of immigrants to be admitted from each country was to be apportioned in accordance with the contribution of that stock to the national population in 1920.

The national-origins plan is theoretically appealing, but it proved utterly impossible to compute a quota on this basis accurately or scientifically. A commission, of which Herbert Hoover was a member, reported that it was impossible to discover where the 100,-000,000 Americans in the United States in 1920 had really come from. The Census of 1790 was very inaccurate, and not until 1850 were immigrants listed by the countries of their origin. President Hoover asked Congress to repeal this feature of the law. Congress remained adamant, however, and national-origins quotas have been in effect since 1930, although no one suggests that they can be scientifically computed. Canadians and Latin-Americans are not affected by this law, and there are other exemptions intended to apply common sense and to prevent the breaking up of homes and families. American consuls abroad must issue certificates to prospective immigrants before they depart for the United States. The law clearly discriminates against South and East Europeans, so that the floods from Italy, Greece, and elsewhere have almost dried up. Mexicans have filled the vacuum in the American labor market by crossing the border to supply the cheap labor which used to come from Europe.[119]

The question of computing the exact quotas of immigration has become an academic one, for, since 1930, the exodus from the United States has exceeded the number of arrivals and quotas for some nationalities have not been filled for years. Even a return of good times will hardly change the situation. The quota for Great Britain and Ireland, for example, is 83,754; but in 1938, only 4,351—just over 5 per cent—came. The total number of immigrants arriving in the seven years ending June, 1938, was 277,538— a little over a quarter of the number that could have come. Not even the German quota was filled until that year, although Hitler

[119] For a convenient summary of immigration legislation through 1917, see Philip Davis: *Immigration and Americanization* (Boston, 1920), pp. 326-359 and 376-419.

came to power in 1933. Moreover, from 1931 to 1938, 249,744 foreigners left the United States for good.

The story of American immigration has been told. According to the Census of 1930, in several states, the number of foreign-born is less than in 1920, and this decline will be steady and uninterrupted hereafter. The Census of 1940 will probably be very interesting in this respect.

The fusion of immigrant strains will of course continue for many years, but the immigrant traffic is ended. The shipping industry must henceforth look for profits to Americans going to Europe on pleasure jaunts in "tourist third" or cabins de-luxe. Their forbears probably came to the United States in steerage.

INDEX

Index

INDEX

INDEX

Corpus Christi procession, 150
Correspondent, Der Deutsche (Baltimore), 231
Corriere d'America (New York), 442
Corriere, Le (New Haven), 442
Corsi, Edward, 444
Côte des Allemands (Louisiana), 206
Cotillo, Salvatore A., 444
Cotton, John, 473
Courier, Der Deutsche, 206
Courrier de l'Amérique, Le (Philadelphia), 323
Courrier des Etats-Unis (New York), 319, 322
Courrier Politique de L'Universe, Le (Philadelphia), 323
Craighead, Thomas, 60
Creoles, 32
Cretin, Joseph, 151
Crevecoeur, Hector St. John de, 4, 97
Croatians, 407, 425, 426
Crosetti, Frank, 445
Crozet, Claude, 391
Cudahy, Michael, 393
Curwen, Samuel, 58
Cushing, Arthur, 387
"Customs House Catholics," 166
Czechs, 371, 373, 374, 376, 377, 378, 395, 400, 410-416, 417-418 *(See also* Bohemians)
Czech National Alliance, 418

D

"Dago Hill" (St. Louis), 438
"Dagos," 138, 505
Dahlberg, Bror G. 394
Dahle, Hermann B., 293
Dahlgren, John Adolph, 394
Daillé, Pierre, 24
Dairying, 203, 210, 295, 301, 398, 399
Dakota Freie Presse (Yankton, South Dakota), 312
Dalmatians, 425, 426
Damrosch, Leopold, 371, 373, 375, 376
Damrosch, Walter, 373
Danes, 3, 15, 36, 110, 203, 262, 264, 273, 278, 293-296, 356, 364, 378, 390, 394, 395, 398, 399; and religion, 294-295; as farmers, 294; causes of immigration of, 294; in politics, 296

Daniel, Christian, 393
Danish Brotherhood, 295
Danish customs, 296
Danish People's Society, 295
Danish press, 295
Danish Sisterhood, 295, 296
Danish societies, 295
Danske Pioneer, Den (Omaha, Nebraska), 295
Dante Alighieri Society, 444
Dante Theatre (Chicago), 441
Da Ponte, Lorenzo, 367, 436
Darusmont, Wright, 21
Davidson, J. O., 293
"Dead Rabbits," 483
Debs, Eugene V., 240, 502
Decorah Posten (Iowa), 288, 292
Del Campo, Scipio, 444
Delmonico, Lorenzo, 320, 399
Demagogenverfolgung, 191
Democratic party, and the immigrant, 158, 162, 166, 167, 173, 179, 180, 181, 192, 242, 243, 245, 246, 249, 255, 292, 308, 310, 415, 443, 462, 475, 476, 484, 490, 491, 495, 496, 500, 504
Demokrat (Philadelphia), 230
Demopolis (Alabama), 318
Denization, acts of, 5
Dentistry, 386
Depew, Chauncey, 499
Detjen, Christian, 387
Detwiller, Henry, 387
Deutsche Ansiedlungsgesellschaft, 202
Deutsche Gesellschaft, 69
Deutscher Pionier, Der, 231, 300
Deutscher Westlich Ansiedlungsverein, 203
Deutsche Zeitung (Charleston, South Carolina), 231
Deutsche Zeitung (New Orleans), 206, 231
Deutsch-Römisch Katholischer Zentralverein, 228, 229
Deveaux, Andrew, 30
DeVere, Maximilian Scheele, 390
Devoy, John, 181
DeWitt, Thomas, 17
Dickinson, Jonathan, 60, 62
Dietz, Johan Jost, 20
Dilger, Hubert, 255
Di Maggio, Joe, 444
Dippel, Andreas, 376

INDEX

INDEX

"German Day," 214
"German Flats" (New York), 69, 95
German folk art, 92-93
German folklore, 81, 82, 89
German food, 214, 215, 237
German Friendly Society, 74
German handicrafts, 85-86
Germania Orchestra, 371, 372, 373
German Methodist Conference, 227
German military companies, 195, 204, 205, 214, 217
German music, 91-92, 198, 199, 201, 202, 203, 204, 206
German press, 87-88, 194, 199, 200-207, 210, 211, 229-232
German Reformed Church, 66, 75, 76, 79, 89, 204, 225, 367
German societies, 204, 205, 206, 207, 216-225
German Society of Maryland, 71-72, 125
German Society of New York, 125
German Society of Pennsylvania, 8
Germantauner Zeitung (Pennsylvania), 88
German theater, 195, 204, 212, 382-385
Germantown (Pennsylvania), 70, 76, 86, 88, 89, 214
German Workingman's Union, 238
Gerstäcker, Friedrich, 196
Gettysburg, Battle of, 254
Ghetto, xiii, 332, 335, 336, 337
Ghetto Klangen, 336
Giants in the Earth, 284
Gibbons, Cardinal, 500, 502
Giessener Auswanderungs Gesellschaft, 197
Gilmore, Patrick S., 157, 183, 374
Gimbel Brothers, 329
Ginal, Heinrich Adam, 356
Ginalsburg (Pennsylvania), 356
Girard, Stephen, 317
Gladden, Washington, 503
Glogoener, Fritz, 230
Gloria Dei Church, 37
Gluck, Alma, 337
Gnadenhütten (Ohio), 78
God, Man and the Devil, 337
God of Vengeance, 337
Goessmann, Charles A., 392
Goldfaden, Abraham, 337
Goldmark, Joseph, 194, 329, 386
Goodyear welt, 393

Gordin, Jacob, 337
Gordon, Lord Adam, 52, 87, 473
Goritz, Otto, 376
Graffenried, Christopher de, 73
Grand Forks Tidende (North Dakota), 289
Grant, Madison, 515
Grant, Ulysses S., 179, 255, 256, 257, 282, 322, 513
Gräter, Franz W., 191
Graupner, Gottlieb, 371
Gray, Gilda, 424
"Great Awakening, The," 60
Greek Catholic Church, 426, 427, 429, 447, 448
Greek Review (Chicago), 449
Greeks, 327, 400, 405, 439, 447-449
Greeley, Horace, 65, 116, 120, 125, 166, 175, 178, 180, 205, 214, 238, 254, 256, 257, 282, 356, 358, 491
Greensville College, 62
Griebsch, Max, 235
Gronlund, Laurence, 296
Gronna, Asle J., 293
Grund, Francis J., 105, 191, 243, 249
"Guardians of Liberty," 491, 505
Guerrard, Peter J., 29
Gulbrandson, Thorwald, 292
Gullborg, John S., 394
Gunderson, Carl, 293
Gustavus Adolphus College, 280
Guyot, Arnold Henry, 391
Gwynnyd (Pennsylvania), 34

H

Hagar, Jonathan, 72
Hagerstown, 72
Hailmann, Wilhelm, 236
Hainer, Ignace, 431
Hairenik (Boston), 451
Halle, Manuel, 330
Hallidie, Andrew S., 393
Hancock, John, 25, 272
Händel and Haydn Choral Society, 371
Hanna, C. A., 58, 63
Hanna, Marc, 65, 342
Hansen, Paul Hjelm, 289
Hansen, W. A., 356
Hanson, Howard, 273
Harmony Society, 343-345, 349
Harper's Weekly, 257

[530]

INDEX

INDEX